CORPORATE COMPLIANCE

ANSWER BOOK

2022 Edition

PLI PRESS is Practising Law Institute's highly regarded publishing division. Our team of dedicated publishing and information professionals is committed to providing you the highest-quality analysis and practice guidance while keeping you updated on current legal developments.

Each year, **PLI PRESS** publishes more than 100 treatises, practice guides, books on lawyering skills, yearbooks, answer books, and journals—written and updated by leading practitioners in their respective practice areas, and edited and managed by our in-house legal editors. We also produce more than 200 Course Handbook titles annually, each corresponding to one of PLI's award-winning CLE programs.

QUESTIONS ABOUT THIS PUBLICATION?

If you have questions about updates to this publication, billing, or shipments, or would like information about our other products, please contact **PLI customer service** at info@pli.edu or at (800) 260-4PLI.

For any other questions or suggestions about this book, please contact the PLI Press **editorial department** at plipress@pli.edu.

For general information about Practising Law Institute, please visit **www.pli.edu**.

To view a full list of PLI Press publications,
visit **www.pli.edu/plipress**.

Save 20% on your next PLI Press book by visiting **pli.edu/savings**
(discount offer applies to U.S. and Canadian orders only)

Practising Law Institute • 1177 Avenue of the Americas • New York, NY 10036

CORPORATE COMPLIANCE

ANSWER BOOK

2022 Edition

VOLUME 2

HOLLAND & KNIGHT LLP

Edited by
William F. Gould
&
Megan Mocho Jeschke

Practising Law Institute
New York City

#319481

Legal Editor: Jacob Metric

LCCN: 2010924112
ISBN: 978-1-4024-3911-7

Table of Chapters

Table of Contents

Chapter 2   Implementation of an Effective Compliance and Ethics Program

Steven D. Gordon

Chapter 3   Assessing and Managing an Ethical Culture
David Gebler

Chapter 4   Risk Assessment and Gap Analysis
Kwamina Thomas Williford

Chapter 5   Records Management

Ieuan G. Mahony

Chapter 6   Internal Investigations
Wifredo A. Ferrer & Michael E. Hantman

Chapter 7 Electronic Discovery
Sonya Strnad

Chapter 8   Voluntary Disclosure of Wrongdoing
Michael Manthei

Chapter 9   Witness Preparation
Daniel I. Small

Chapter 10   Settling with the Government

Steven D. Gordon

Chapter 11   Corporate Compliance Monitors

Jose P. Sierra, Lynne M. Halbrooks & Sonya Strnad

Chapter 12   The False Claims Act

Michael Manthei & William F. Pezzolo

Chapter 13   Privacy and Security of Personal Information
*Maximillian J. Bodoin, Hwi Harold Lee &
Ieuan G. Mahony*

Chapter 14 Procuring Computing Resources: IP Licensing, Outsourcing, and Cloud Computing

*Elizabeth R. Burkhard, Nicholas M. Hasenfus &
Ieuan G. Mahony*

Chapter 15 Government Contractors

Eric S. Crusius & Christian B. Nagel

Table of Contents

Chapter 16 Suspension and Debarment from Federal Contracting and Programs

Steven D. Gordon

Chapter 17   International Investigations
Michael E. Hantman & David C. Kully

Chapter 18   Foreign Corrupt Practices Act

*Wifredo A. Ferrer, Michael E. Hantman &
Marcelo Ovejero*

PART I
FCPA's Anti-Bribery Provisions

I

PART II
FCPA's ACCOUNTING PROVISIONS

Chapter 19   Export Controls

*Antonia I. Tzinova, Ronald A. Oleynik, Jonathan M. Epstein,
Andrew McAllister & Libby Bloxom*

Chapter 20 Corporate Political Activity

*Christopher DeLacy, Charles E. Borden,
Samuel C. Brown & Rachel T. Provencher*

Chapter 21 Environmental Law

Stacy Watson May

Chapter 22   Consumer Product Safety Act
Colin P. Smith & Robert E. Tonn

Chapter 23 Healthcare Organizations and Providers

Jeremy Sternberg & William Pezzolo

Chapter 24 Medicare Part D

Jeffrey W. Mittleman, Ilenna J. Stein & Andrew Namkung

Chapter 25 Managed Care Organizations

Jeffrey W. Mittleman

VOLUME 2

Chapter 26 Pharmaceutical and Medical Device Manufacturers
*Michael Manthei, William F. Gould, Sara M. Klock,
Jennifer C. Lee & William F. Pezzolo*

Chapter 27   HIPAA Security and Privacy
Shannon B. Hartsfield

Chapter 28   The Affordable Care Act: Employer Obligations
Kenneth A. Jenero

Chapter 29   Anti-Money Laundering
Gabriel Caballero, Jr.

Chapter 30 Sarbanes-Oxley Act of 2002

Jerome W. Hoffman & John A. Canale

Chapter 31   SEC Investigations of Public Companies
Stephen P. Warren & Allison Kernisky

Table of Contents

Chapter 32 Directors and Officers Liability Insurance
Thomas H. Bentz, Jr.

Chapter 33   Cyber Liability Insurance
Thomas H. Bentz, Jr.

Chapter 34   Executive Compensation

*Robert J. Friedman, Victoria H. Zerjav, Louis L. Joseph,
Ariadna Alvarez, Nicole F. Martini, Kerry L. Halpern &
Cory A. Thomas*

Chapter 35   Institutions of Higher Education

Paul G. Lannon, Jr. & Nathan A. Adams IV

Chapter 36 Labor and Employment Law

Kenneth A. Jenero

Table of Contents

Chapter 37   Anti–Human Trafficking

*William N. Shepherd, Barbara A. Martinez &
Jeff Schacknow*

26

Pharmaceutical and Medical Device Manufacturers

Michael Manthei, William F. Gould, Sara M. Klock,
Jennifer C. Lee & William F. Pezzolo*

This chapter assesses the major risk areas associated with the development and marketing of pharmaceuticals and medical devices—highly regulated industries whose regulatory structures present many compliance challenges. This chapter gives a high-level overview of the major risk areas; it does not attempt to catalogue every possible risk. Nor does it address in detail the FDA approval process itself. As a detailed discussion of the approval process is beyond the scope of this treatise, it is assumed that the reader has a basic understanding of the process.

This chapter focuses on labeling and advertising, sales, marketing and pricing, and biomedical research/clinical trials.

*   The authors wish to acknowledge Christopher A. Myers for his contributions to this chapter.

Acronyms, initialisms, and abbreviations used in this chapter:

AHRQ	Agency for Healthcare Research and Quality
AKS	anti-kickback statute
AMA	American Medical Association
ANDA	abbreviated new drug application
ASP	average sales price
AWP	average wholesale price
BLA	biologics license application
CDC	Centers for Disease Control
CMS	Centers for Medicare and Medicaid Services
DOD	Department of Defense
FDA	Food and Drug Administration
FDCA	Food, Drug, and Cosmetic Act
GCP	good clinical practice
HHS	U.S. Department of Health and Human Services
ICH	International Conference on Harmonisation of Technical Requirements for Registration of Pharmaceuticals for Human Use

IND	investigational new drug
IRB	Institutional Review Board
NDA	new drug application
NIH	National Institutes of Health
NSF	National Science Foundation
OHRP	Office of Human Research Protection
OIG	Office of Inspector General
PDMA	Prescription Drug Marketing Act
PhRMA	Pharmaceutical Research and Manufacturers of America
PHS	Public Health Service
PHSA	Public Health Service Act
PMA	Premarket Approval
SBIR	Small Business Innovation Research
VA	Department of Veterans Affairs
WHO	World Health Organization
WMA	World Medical Association

Overview

Q 26.1   What are the major risk areas in the pharmaceutical and medical device industry?

The areas that present the most significant financial, operational, and reputational exposure include:

- biomedical research/clinical trials[1]
- FDA approval;
- labeling and advertising;
- marketing and sales; and
- pricing and price reporting.

Biomedical Research/Clinical Trials

Q 26.2   What are the major compliance risks arising from the conduct of biomedical research?

- Conflicts of interest;
- Protection of human subjects;
- Charging for investigational drugs; and
- Medicare coverage.

Conflicts of Interest

Q 26.3   What rules and regulations govern conflicts of interest in clinical trials?

There are four sets of federal standards that address conflicts of interest in clinical research. Generally the conflicts rules and regulations require disclosure when an investigator has a financial interest in the sponsor or in the outcome of the investigation. They also impose requirements to limit conflicts of interest and preserve academic freedom. Finally, they set time frames for preservation of relevant documents.

A number of non-government professional and institutional associations publish their own guidelines. These industry guidance documents expand, augment, and interpret the official government regulations and guidance discussed below. The three non-government sets of guidelines discussed later in this chapter are the most well-known and widely recognized.

Failure to follow the conflict-of-interest rules and regulations may result in delayed approval of products, rescission of federal grants, initiation of federal investigations, imposition of fines, debarment from future participation in federal grant and other programs, and ancillary litigation.

TABLE 26-1

Rules, Regulations, and Guidelines Governing Biomedical Research/Clinical Trials

Government Rules and Regulations

1. Public Health Service Rules
2. National Science Foundation Requirements
3. National Institutes of Health Guidelines
4. FDA Financial Disclosure Requirements

Association Guidelines

1. *Conflicts of Interest in Academic Health Centers, Policy Paper No. 1,* The Association of Academic Health Centers (1990)

2. *Conflicts of Interest in Institutional Decision Making,* The Association of Academic Health Centers Task Force on Science Policy (1994)

3. *Principles on Conduct of Clinical Trials: Communications of Clinical Trial Results,*[2] Pharmaceutical Research and Manufacturers of America (PhRMA) (rev. June 2015)

Q 26.4   What are the Public Health Service Rules?

These are standards established by the Public Health Service (PHS) (a division of the Department of Health and Human Services) aimed at avoiding conflicts of financial interest and at promoting objectivity in research funded by PHS grants.[3]

Q 26.4.1   To whom do the PHS Rules apply?

The rules apply to each institution that applies for PHS research grants, except for Phase 1 Small Business Innovation Research applications.[4] Through the institution, the PHS Rules also apply to each investigator.[5] As used in the rules, a qualified "institution" is any domestic or foreign, private, or public entity or organization.[6] Individual applicants, as opposed to institutional applicants, will be assessed on a case-by-case determination.[7]

Q 26.4.2   What do the PHS Rules require?

The PHS Rules require that each institutional applicant maintain *and enforce* written conflict-of-interest policies (and inform each investigator of the policies) that, at a minimum, do the following:

(1) Designate an institutional official to solicit and review financial disclosure statements from each investigator who is planning to participate in PHS-funded research.

(2) Require and provide a mechanism for the training of and disclosure by investigators pursuant to the institution's policy on financial conflicts of interest to investigators. Initial disclosure by investigators of "significant financial interests" must be made no later than the time of application for PHS-funded research.

(3) Provide a mechanism to update financial disclosures either annually or as new significant financial interests are obtained.

(4) Include guidelines for the "designated institutional official" to identify and determine if a "significant financial interest" is a "conflict of interest" and manage such conflict of interest. Management of an identified conflict of interest requires development and implementation of a management plan and, if necessary, a retrospective review and mitigation report.

(5) Provide initial and ongoing "financial conflicts of interests" reports to PHS and maintain records of actions under the institution's policy on financial conflicts of interest for at least three years from submission of the final expenditure report to PHS or, where applicable, from other dates specified in 45 C.F.R. § 75.361.

(6) Establish adequate enforcement mechanisms and provide for sanctions or other administrative actions where appropriate.

(7) Certify to PHS that there are procedures in place to identify and to manage conflicts of interest, that such procedures are promoted and enforced, that the institution will submit

financial conflicts of interest reports to the PHS and make such information available promptly upon request.

(8) If the institution carries out the PHS-funded research through a subrecipient, clarify in writing with the subrecipient whether the institution's conflicts of interest policy will apply to the subrecipient's investigators. If the institution's conflicts of interest policy will apply to the subrecipient's investigators, then the subrecipient must make certain certifications to ensure compliance with the institution's financial conflicts of interest policy and enact a mechanism to submit disclosures of significant financial conflicts of interest to the institution and financial conflicts of interests reports to PHS.[8]

Q 26.4.3   What is a "significant financial interest" under the PHS Rules?

"Significant financial interest" means an investigator's interest (and those of the investigator's spouse and dependent children) in one of the following that reasonably appears to be related to the investigator's institutional responsibilities:

- a financial interest that exceeds $5,000 in a twelve-month period in a publicly traded entity through salary, consulting fees, honoraria, paid authorship, equity or other ownership interest;

- a financial interest that exceeds $5,000 in a twelve-month period in a non-publicly traded entity through any equity interest; or

- intellectual property rights, upon receipt of income related to such rights.

"Significant financial interest" shall not include:

- salary, royalties, or other remuneration paid or provided by the institution to the investigator so long as the investigator is currently employed or otherwise appointed by the institution;

- ownership interest in the institution held by the investigator, if the institution is a commercial or for-profit organization;

- income from investment vehicles, so long as investigator does not have direct control of such investment vehicles;

- income from seminars, lectures, teaching engagements, service on advisory committees or review panels sponsored by or for a federal, state, local government agency, institution of higher education, academic teaching hospital medical center, or research institute affiliated with an institution of higher education;

- a financial interest in a non-public entity that exceeds $5,000 in a twelve-month period;

- salary or other payments for services (e.g., consulting fees or honoraria);

- equity interests (e.g., stocks, stock options, or other ownership interests); and

- intellectual property rights (e.g., patents, copyrights, and royalties from such rights).[9]

Q 26.4.4   What types of remuneration do not constitute a significant financial interest?

(1) Salary, royalties, or other remuneration paid by the institution to the investigator if the investigator is employed by the institution, including intellectual property rights assigned to the institution and agreements to share royalties related to such rights;

(2) Any ownership interests in the institution held by the investigator, if the institution is a commercial or for-profit organization;

(3) Income from seminars, lectures, or teaching engagements sponsored by federal, state, or local government agency, an institution of higher education, an academic teaching hospital, a medical center, or a research institute that is affiliated with an institution of higher education;

(4) Income from service on advisory committees or review panels for a federal, state, or local government agency, an institution of higher education, an academic teaching hospital, a medical

center, or a research institute that is affiliated with an institution of higher education; and

(5) Income from investment vehicles, such as mutual funds and retirement accounts, as long as the investigator does not directly control the investment decisions made in these vehicles.[10]

Q 26.4.5   Who is considered an "investigator" to whom the significant financial interest disclosure and other requirements apply under the PHS Rules?

"Investigator" means the project director or principal investigator and any other person, regardless of title or position, who is responsible for the design, conduct, or reporting of research funded by the PHS, or proposed for such funding, which may include, for example, collaborators or consultants.[11]

Q 26.4.6   What are the responsibilities of the designated institutional official?

The designated official must:

(1) review all investigator disclosures of significant financial interests;

(2) determine whether any significant financial interests relate to PHS-funded research;

(3) determine whether a financial conflict of interest exists; and, if so,

(4) develop and implement a management plan that shall specify the actions that have been, and shall be, taken to manage such financial conflict of interest.[12]

Q 26.4.7   What is a "financial conflict of interest" for purposes of the PHS Rules?

The PHS Rules state that a financial conflict of interest means a significant financial interest that could directly and significantly affect the design, conduct, or reporting of the PHS-funded research.[13]

Q 26.4.8   What mechanisms are available to "manage" financial conflicts of interest as required by the PHS Rules?

There are no specific requirements. The PHS Rules, however, give the following examples of conditions or restrictions that might be imposed to manage conflicts of interest:

(1)   Public disclosure of significant financial conflicts interests (e.g., when presenting or publishing the research);

(2)   For research projects involving human subjects research, disclosure of financial conflicts of interest directly to participants;

(3)   Modification of the research plan;

(4)   Appointment of an independent monitor capable of taking measures to protect the design, conduct, and reporting of the research against bias resulting from the financial conflict of interest;

(5)   Change of personnel or personnel responsibilities, or disqualification of personnel from participation in all or a portion of the research;

(6)   Reduction or elimination of the financial interest (e.g., sale of an equity interest); or

(7)   Severance of relationships that create financial conflicts.[14]

Q 26.4.9   What are the consequences for failing to comply with the PHS Rules?

Investigators: If the failure of an investigator to comply with the institution's financial conflicts-of-interest policy or a financial conflict-of-interest management plan appears to have influenced the design, conduct, or reporting of the PHS-funded research, the institution shall promptly notify the PHS awarding component of the corrective action taken or to be taken.[15]

The PHS awarding component will consider the situation and, as necessary, take appropriate action, or refer the matter to the institution for further action, which may include directions to the institution on how to maintain appropriate objectivity in the PHS-funded research project.[16]

If HHS determines that a PHS-funded project of clinical research whose purpose is to evaluate the safety or effectiveness of a drug, medical device, or treatment, has been designed, conducted, or reported by an investigator with a financial conflict of interest that was not managed or reported by the institution as required by the PHS Rules, the institution shall require the investigator(s) involved to disclose the financial conflict of interest in each public presentation of the results of the research and to request an addendum to previously published presentations.[17]

Institutions: If an institution fails to comply with the PHS Rules, HHS or the PHS awarding component may at any time inquire into any investigator disclosure of financial interests and the institution's review of, and response to, such disclosure, regardless of whether the disclosure resulted in the institution's determination of a financial conflict of interest. HHS may require that further corrective action be taken or that funding be suspended pursuant to 45 C.F.R. Part 74 until the matter is resolved.[18]

Q 26.4.10   Beyond suspension of funding or imposition of additional corrective action, what other consequences might there be for a failure to comply with the PHS Rules?

Civil Monetary Penalties: The PHS Rules specifically state that the provisions of 45 C.F.R. Part 79 imposing civil penalties for fraud apply to violations of the PHS Rules. Thus, if a claim for original or ongoing grant funding is supported by a statement that is knowingly or recklessly false, fictitious, or fraudulent, or that omits material information or that is supported by a written statement that includes any knowingly or recklessly false, fictitious, or fraudulent statement, HHS can institute proceedings to impose civil monetary penalties.[19]

Suspension and Debarment: A civil judgment for fraud can be the basis for a government-wide debarment or suspension of the investigator or of the institution from all non-procurement government programs.[20] The investigator or institution thus can be not only suspended or debarred from PHS, but also prohibited from participating in federal healthcare programs like Medicare and Medicaid, because the suspension or debarment is "government-wide." It is thus a potential "death penalty" for institutions that also are participating Medicare or Medicaid providers or whose products otherwise are reimbursed by federal healthcare programs.

The Federal False Claims Act: If compliance with the PHS Rules is material to the grant award, then false statements or misleading omissions about compliance potentially can violate the FCA.

Q 26.5 What are the National Science Foundation requirements?

The National Science Foundation (NSF) requirements are conditions of grant awards, rather than regulations. They appear in the NSF *Grant Policy Manual.*[21] Amendments in 1995 to the NSF requirements conformed them to the PHS Rules. With two exceptions, the NSF requirements are essentially identical to the PHS Rules. First, the NSF requirements apply only to grantees having in excess of fifty employees. The second difference is that conflicts are reported to the NSF Office of General Counsel.

The "National Science Foundation Rules of Practice and Statutory Conflict-of-Interest Exemptions" are codified at 45 C.F.R. § 94.1 *et seq.* and 45 C.F.R. § 680.10 *et seq.*

Though the NSF requirements properly are "conditions," and not "rules" or "regulations," they have an equivalent force. Failure to comply with the NSF requirements can result in suspension of ongoing funding or disqualification from future grant funding.

Q 26.5.1 To whom do the NSF requirements apply?

The NSF requirements apply to grant and cooperative agreement recipients.

Q 26.6 What are the National Institutes of Health Guidelines?

The National Institutes of Health (NIH) Guidelines, like the NSF requirements, are not formal regulations. They are guidelines for the development of sponsored research agreements. The formal title is

"Developing Sponsored Research Agreements: Considerations for Recipients of NIH Grants and Contracts."[22] The NIH Guidelines provide NIH grantees with points for consideration when negotiating sponsored research agreements with commercial entities. "The intent is to assist Grantees in ensuring that those agreements comply with the requirements of the [Bayh-Dole Act] and NIH funding agreements while upholding basic principles of academic freedom."[23]

Q 26.6.1   What are the main "considerations" for sponsored research agreements?

The following are general considerations that apply to all agreements:

(1) Agreements should ensure preservation of academic freedom.

(2) Agreements should allow for timely dissemination of research findings.

(3) Grantees should encourage development and commercialization of technology resulting from NIH-funded research.

(4) Grantees must comply with the Bayh-Dole Act's U.S. manufacturing requirement and the requirement that, in the marketing of NIH-funded inventions, preference be given to small business firms (fewer than 500 employees).

(5) Grantees must timely notify NIH of inventions, patents, and licenses.

In addition, there are special considerations for nonprofit grant recipients (*see* Q 26.7.1). Finally, there are conditions that require "heightened scrutiny" (*see* Q 26.7.2).

Q 26.7   What is the Bayh-Dole Act?

The Patent and Trademark Act Amendments of 1980, commonly known as the Bayh-Dole Act,[24] provide the legal framework for the transfer of university-generated, federally funded inventions to the commercial marketplace. The policy and objectives of the Bayh-Dole Act are to:

(1) promote collaboration between commercial concerns and non-profit organizations, including universities;

(2) promote the utilization of inventions arising from federally supported research or development;

(3) encourage maximum participation of small business firms in federally sponsored research-and-development efforts;

(4) ensure that inventions made by nonprofit organizations and small business firms are used to promote free competition and enterprise;

(5) promote the commercialization and public availability of inventions made in the United States by U.S. industry and labor;

(6) ensure that the government obtains sufficient rights in federally sponsored inventions to meet the needs of the government and protect the public against non-use or unreasonable use of inventions; and

(7) minimize the costs of administering policies in this area.[25]

Bayh-Dole's provisions have been implemented through regulations issued by the Department of Commerce and adopted by HHS.[26]

Q 26.7.1   What are the considerations for nonprofit grantees?

The following considerations are designed to aid nonprofit grantees in administering the Bayh-Dole Act and in complying with the requirements of NIH funding agreements:

(1) Grantees must ensure that the rights to inventions resulting from federal funding are not assigned without NIH approval. An exception to this is when the assignment is made to an organization that has as one of its primary functions the management of inventions, in which case, the assignee will be subject to the same provisions as the grantee.

(2) Grantees must share royalties collected on NIH-supported inventions with the inventors; and the balance of any royalties or income earned, after payment of expenses, including

payment to inventors and incidental expenses to the administration of subject inventions, must be used to support scientific research or education.

(3)   Grantees must employ reasonable efforts to attract small business firms as licensees of the subject invention. Additionally,
grantees must prefer small business firms as licensees if their
plans or proposals to bring the invention to practical application are just as likely to succeed as plans or proposals from
other businesses. However, grantees must be satisfied that
the small business firms have the capability and resources
to carry out plans or proposals. The decision to give a preference in any specific case is at the discretion of the grantee.[27]

Q 26.7.2   What considerations require "heightened scrutiny"?

Grantees should subject their sponsored research agreements to
heightened scrutiny when any of the following apply:

(1)   the amount of financial support from the sponsor meets or
exceeds $5 million in any one year or $50 million total over
the total period of funding under the agreement;

(2)   the proportion of funding by the sponsor exceeds 20% of the
grantee's total research funding;

(3)   the sponsor's prospective licensing rights cover all technologies developed by a major group or component of the
grantee organization—such as a large laboratory, department
or center—or the technologies in question represent a substantial proportion of the anticipated intellectual output of
the grantee's research staff; or

(4)   the duration of the agreement is for five or more years.[28]

If any of these criteria apply, the Department of Commerce considers it to be more likely that the proposed sponsored research agreement will adversely affect open commercial access, especially for
small businesses, to a grantee's federally funded research activities
and may delay or impede the rapid development and commercialization of technology.

Recipients should also use special care if:

(1) The scope of the sponsored research agreement is so broad that the subsequent exclusive licensing of technology under the agreement provides a single sponsor with access to a wide array of grantee research findings and technologies that effectively exclude other organizations from reasonable access to a grantee's technology.

(2) The rights granted to the sponsor to review and license resulting technology or inventions are disproportionate to the amount of money the sponsor contributed.

(3) The sponsorship involves an unusual practice or stipulation that might generate public concern or undermine rather than serve the public interest.[29]

Q 26.8   What are the FDA financial disclosure requirements?

The FDA issued its financial disclosure regulations in response to concerns about the integrity of clinical data in support of marketing applications that could be biased by financial conflicts of interest.[30] The FDA may consider clinical studies and the resulting data inadequate if, among other things, appropriate steps have not been taken in the design, conduct, reporting, and analysis of the studies to minimize bias.

Anyone who submits a marketing application to the FDA for any drug, biological product, or device is required (1) to certify the absence of "disclosable" financial interests of, or arrangements with, clinical investigators; or (2) to disclose those financial interests.[31] This requirement applies to any clinical study submitted in a marketing application that the applicant or FDA relies on to establish that the product is effective, and any study in which a single investigator makes a significant contribution to the demonstration of safety.[32]

Q 26.8.1 What is a "disclosable" financial arrangement?

There are four categories of "disclosable" financial arrangements:

(1) *Compensation affected by the outcome of clinical studies* means compensation that could be higher for a favorable outcome than for an unfavorable outcome, such as compensation that is explicitly greater for a favorable result or compensation to the investigator in the form of an equity interest in the sponsor of a covered study or in the form of compensation tied to sales of the product, such as a royalty interest.[33]

(2) *Significant equity interest in the sponsor of a covered study* means any ownership interest, stock options, or other financial interest whose value cannot be readily determined through reference to public prices (generally, interests in a non–publicly traded corporation), or any equity interest in a publicly traded corporation that exceeds $50,000 during the time the clinical investigator is carrying out the study and for one year following completion of the study.[34]

(3) *Proprietary interest in the tested product* means property or other financial interest in the product including, but not limited to, a patent, trademark, copyright, or licensing agreement.[35]

(4) *Significant payments of other sorts* means payments made by the sponsor of a covered study to the investigator or to the institution to support activities of the investigator that have a monetary value of more than $25,000, exclusive of the costs of conducting the clinical study or other clinical studies (e.g., a grant to fund ongoing research, compensation in the form of equipment, or retainers for ongoing consultation or honoraria) during the time the clinical investigator is carrying out the study and for one year following the completion of the study.[36]

Q 26.8.2 What are the obligations of the investigator?

The investigator must provide information to the sponsor sufficient to allow it to file the certification or disclosure statement, as appropriate. The investigator also must update the sponsor promptly of any changes in the information provided.[37]

Q 26.8.3   What factors will the FDA consider in assessing a disclosable financial interest's potential to bias a study?

The FDA will evaluate the information in each disclosure to determine the impact of the financial interest on the reliability of the study results. In assessing the potential of an investigator's financial interests to bias a study, the FDA will take into account the design and purpose of the study. Study designs that include safeguards against bias, such as multiple investigators (most of whom do not have a disclosable interest), blinding, objective endpoints, or measurement of endpoints by someone other than the investigator, may be deemed adequate to protect against any bias created by a disclosable financial interest.[38]

Q 26.8.4   What actions may the FDA take if it believes that an investigator's financial interest may have compromised the integrity of the research data?

First, the FDA likely will reject any marketing application that omits the required financial disclosure information or certification.[39] If the FDA determines that the financial interest of any investigator raises a serious question about the integrity of the data, the FDA will take whatever action it deems necessary to determine the reliability of the data, including:

(1)   initiating agency audits of the data derived from the clinical investigator in question;

(2)   requesting that the applicant submit further analyses of data (e.g., to evaluate the effect of the clinical investigator's data on overall study outcome);

(3)   requesting that the applicant conduct additional independent studies to confirm the results of the questioned study; and

(4)   refusing to treat the covered clinical study as providing data that can be the basis for an agency action.[40]

Protection of Human Subjects

Q 26.9   What rules govern the protection of human subjects?

Research involving human subjects is governed by national legislation, agency regulation, and international declarations:

- The Common Rule;
- FDA Regulations;
- HHS Regulations;
- ICH Guidance; and
- World Medical Association Declaration of Helsinki.

Q 26.9.1   What is the Common Rule?

The Common Rule governs most federally funded research involving human subjects.[41] Fifteen federal agencies beyond HHS have adopted the Common Rule. By executive order, the CIA also must comply with the Common Rule.[42] Its three basic requirements are aimed at protecting human research subjects:

(1) informed consent of research subjects;

(2) review of proposed research by an Institutional Review Board (IRB); and

(3) assurance of compliance with the regulations filed with the Office of Human Research Protection (OHRP).

Q 26.9.2   What are the FDA regulations concerning human-subject research?

The FDA regulates human-subject research that generates data to support a company's application for drug, device, or biologics marketing approval. Its regulations govern the form and scope of informed consent and also the structure of IRBs.[43] (See Q 26.10.4 for more about IRBs.)

While the FDA regulations are drafted to be consistent with the Common Rule, there are some major differences:[44]

(1) *Scope.* The Common Rule covers all research using federal funds, while the FDA regulations govern only research that supports marketing applications. Both sets of regulations will apply to much research, but it is possible that some research will not be covered by either set of regulations and, therefore, that there would be no federal protection of human subjects.

(2) *Definitions.* The Common Rule specifically applies only to living human subjects; the FDA regulations do not. Only the FDA regulations define the concepts of "investigator" and "sponsor." In contrast, the Common Rule defines "institutions" and "research" that is subject to regulation.

(3) *Emergency use.* The FDA allows investigators to use test articles without consent in emergency situations.[45] HHS has adopted different emergency-use provisions that are incorporated into its version of the Common Rule.[46] But, the Common Rule as adopted by the other signatory agencies has no emergency-use provisions.

(4) *Financial conflicts of interest.* Both the Common Rule and FDA regulations provide that no IRB member may participate in initial or ongoing oversight of a study with respect to which the member has a financial conflict of interest.[47] However, only the FDA requires certification and disclosure of financial conflicts for *investigators*.[48]

(5) *International research.* The Common Rule allows a department or agency head to approve the substitution of foreign procedures if she determines that the substituted foreign procedures afford protections at least equivalent to the Common Rule.[49] FDA regulations may not be waived in the conduct of foreign clinical trials used to support an investigational new drug (IND) application. (See Q 26.11.1 for more about INDs.) However, a non-IND study may be incorporated into "an application for marketing approval" (e.g., an IND, a new drug application (NDA) or a biologics license application (BLA)) if the study was conducted in accordance with "good clinical practice" (GCP).[50]

(6) *Parental consent.* The Common Rule does not address parental consent. HHS-specific additions to its version of the Common Rule and FDA regulations generally require the consent of a parent or guardian and the assent of the child for the child to participate in a clinical trial.[51] Additional HHS regulations, but not the FDA regulations, state that the IRB may waive the requirement for parental consent if such consent is not reasonable to protect the subject (e.g., abused or neglected children). If parental consent is waived, these additional HHS regulations provide an alternative mechanism to protect the child.[52]

Q 26.9.3   What are the HHS regulations concerning human-subject research?

The HHS version of the Common Rule is codified at 45 C.F.R. Part 46, subpart A. In addition to adopting the basic Common Rule, HHS has adopted protections for specific populations as follows:

- *Subpart B.* Additional Protections for Pregnant Women, Human Fetuses, and Neonates Involved in Research.

- *Subpart C.* Additional Protections Pertaining to Biomedical and Behavioral Research Involving Prisoners as Subjects.

- *Subpart D.* Additional Protections for Children Involved as Subjects in Research.

These additional requirements are set forth clearly in the above-cited regulation, so they are not reported here.

Q 26.9.4   What is the ICH guidance?

The International Council for Harmonisation of Technical Requirements for Pharmaceuticals for Human Use (ICH)[53] includes regulators and pharmaceutical industry representatives from the United States, the European Union, and Japan. There also are three "observers": The World Health Organization (WHO), the European Free Trade Association, and the International Federation of Pharmaceutical Manufacturers and Associations.

The purpose of the ICH is to make recommendations on ways to achieve greater harmonization in the interpretation and application of technical guidelines and requirements for product registration in order to reduce or obviate the need to duplicate the testing carried out during the research and development of new medicines.[54] Among its recommendations is the *E6 Good Clinical Practice: Consolidated Guidance* (E6).[55]

E6 sets guidelines for the activities of both clinical trial sponsors and investigators. These guidelines address the composition, function, operation, and responsibilities of IRBs and so-called independent ethics committees (non-U.S. equivalents of IRBs).[56] In much the same terms as the Common Rule, E6 sets standards for the informed consent of human subjects.[57]

Additionally, E6 addresses a variety of other aspects of clinical trials that are not covered by the Common Rule. For instance, it recommends guidelines for development of clinical trial protocols. It also establishes a list of "Essential Documents."

> These are documents that individually and collectively permit evaluation of the conduct of a trial and of the quality of the data produced. These documents serve to demonstrate the compliance of the investigator, sponsor, and monitor with the standards of GCP and with all applicable regulatory requirements.[58]

Q 26.9.5   What is the World Medical Association Declaration of Helsinki?

The World Medical Association (WMA) is an international association of medical professionals. In 1964, it first adopted its *Declaration of Helsinki: Recommendations Guiding Medical Doctors on Biomedical Research Involving Human Subjects*. Most recently amended in 2013, the "Declaration of Helsinki" is a set of broad principles intended to guide physicians' professional judgment in the conduct of experiments involving human subjects. Its principles are not as detailed as the Common Rule or E6 but still contain useful guidance on the importance of obtaining consent from the subject or, if that subject cannot give informed consent, obtaining informed consent from others interested in the subject's welfare.[59]

Informed Consent

Q 26.10   What are the general requirements for informed consent?

Generally, for consent to be considered "informed," the request for consent must be in writing and must be provided in a manner that minimizes the risk of coercion. It must be given in language that the subject can understand. It also may not include any exculpatory language that would release the institution, investigator, or sponsor from liability for negligence.

Beyond these basic requirements, a request for consent must contain all of the following elements:

(1)   a statement that the study involves research and an explanation of the purpose of the research, the expected duration of the research, a description of the procedures to be followed, and an explanation of the procedures that are experimental;

(2)   a description of the reasonably foreseeable risks or discomforts that the subject might endure;

(3)   a description of any benefits to the subject or to others from the research;

(4)   a disclosure of alternative procedures or treatments, if any, that might be beneficial to the subject;

(5)   a statement of the extent to which records identifying the subject will be held confidential;

(6)   if the study involves more than minimal risk, an explanation of any compensation being offered, an explanation of any medical treatment that will be offered if an injury occurs, and a statement of where the subject may obtain further information;

(7)   identification of a contact person to whom the subject may address questions about the study, and the subject's rights and identification of a person to whom the subject may report study-related injuries; and

(8)   a statement that participation is voluntary, that there is no penalty for refusing to participate, and that the subject may withdraw from the study at any time without penalty or loss of benefits.[60]

Q 26.10.1   Are there exceptions to the informed consent requirements?

Yes. As noted, both the FDA regulations and the Common Rule contain exceptions for emergencies. Additionally, the Common Rule contains exceptions for certain studies that involve no more than a minimal risk.

Q 26.10.2   What are the "emergency exceptions" to the FDA's informed consent regulations?

The FDA regulations have two emergency exceptions. One sets standards for IRB approval of a protocol that does not require informed consent from all subjects. The other states the circumstances under which the investigator otherwise may proceed to administer the study agent without informed consent in life-threatening situations.

The IRB Exception. Under the first exception, the IRB may allow a study to proceed without requiring informed consent from all subjects upon finding that:

(1)   the human subjects are in a life-threatening situation;

(2)   available treatments are unproven or unsatisfactory;

(3)   the collection of valid scientific evidence, which may include evidence obtained through randomized placebo-controlled investigations, is necessary to determine the safety and effectiveness of particular interventions; and

(4)   the investigation could not be practicably carried out without the exception.[61]

Additionally, the IRB must determine that:

(1)   obtaining informed consent is not feasible—for instance, because the subjects will be incapacitated, the likely subjects cannot be identified in advance (e.g., in the study of emergency

interventions or agents applied in cases of severe trauma), or the intervention must be administered before informed consent could be obtained; and

(2)   there is the prospect of direct benefit to the subject.[62]

Even if obtaining informed consent is deemed infeasible, the protocol must include an informed consent document and procedure, and it must establish a therapeutic window based on scientific evidence during which the investigator will try to obtain informed consent. Further, the informed consent procedure must be followed in individual instances where it is in fact feasible to do so.[63]

Finally, the protocol must include at least the following additional protections:

(1)   consultation (including, where appropriate, consultation carried out by the IRB) with representatives of the communities in which the clinical investigation will be conducted and from which the subjects will be drawn;

(2)   public disclosure to the communities in which the clinical investigation will be conducted and from which the subjects will be drawn, prior to initiation of the clinical investigation, of plans for the investigation and its risks and expected benefits;

(3)   public disclosure of sufficient information following completion of the clinical investigation to apprise the community and researchers of the study, including the demographic characteristics of the research population, and the study's results;

(4)   establishment of an independent data monitoring committee to exercise oversight of the clinical investigation; and

(5)   if obtaining informed consent is not feasible and a legally authorized representative is not reasonably available, then the investigator must commit that she will try (if feasible during the therapeutic window) to contact a family member of the subject to see if he objects to the subject's participation in the clinical investigation. The investigator will summarize efforts made to contact family members and will make this information available to the IRB at the time of continuing review.[64]

The Investigator Exception. An investigator may administer the study agent without obtaining informed consent if, before the use of the study agent, both the investigator and a physician who is not otherwise participating in the clinical investigation certify in writing all of the following:

(1)   the human subject is confronted by a life-threatening situation necessitating the use of the test article;

(2)   informed consent cannot be obtained from the subject because of an inability to communicate with, or obtain legally effective consent from, the subject;

(3)   time is not sufficient to obtain consent from the subject's legal representative; and

(4)   no alternative method of approved or generally recognized therapy is available that provides an equal or greater likelihood of saving the life of the subject.[65]

If the investigator determines that the immediate use of the study agent is necessary to preserve the subject's life and that there is not enough time to obtain the independent evaluation described above, the investigator may administer the study agent. Then, within five working days after the use of the agent, the investigator's decisions must be reviewed and evaluated in writing by a physician who is not participating in the clinical investigation.[66]

Q 26.10.3   What are the exceptions to the Common Rule's informed consent regulations?

Emergency Exception. Under the Common Rule, assuming that the clinical trial is not also governed by the FDA regulations, the head of the agency that has incorporated the Common Rule may waive application of some or all of the provisions of the Common Rule to specific research activities or classes of research activities provided that the alternative procedures to be followed are consistent with the principles of the Belmont Report. Thus, the applicable agency head could waive the informed consent requirements in emergency situations.[67]

Other Exceptions. An IRB may approve a consent procedure that does not include, or that alters, some or all of the elements of informed consent set forth above, or waive the requirement to obtain informed consent provided the IRB finds and documents that:

- The research or demonstration project is to be conducted by or subject to the approval of state or local government officials and is designed to study, evaluate, or otherwise examine:

  (a) public benefit of service programs;

  (b) procedures for obtaining benefits or services under those programs;

  (c) possible changes in or alternatives to those programs or procedures; or

  (d) possible changes in methods or levels of payment for benefits or services under those programs; and

- The research could not practicably be carried out without the waiver or alteration.[68]

The same exception holds true, furthermore, if the IRB finds that:

- the research involves no more than minimal risk to the subjects;

- the waiver or alteration will not adversely affect the rights and welfare of the subjects;

- if the research involves using identifiable private information or identifiable biospecimens, the research could not practicable be carried out without using such information or biospecimens in an identifiable format;

- the research could not practicably be carried out without the waiver or alteration; and

- whenever appropriate, the subjects will be provided with additional pertinent information after participation.[69]

Q 26.10.4   What are the membership requirements for IRBs?

IRBs are generally composed of volunteers who examine proposed and ongoing scientific research to ensure that human subjects are properly protected. The Common Rule requires that each IRB have the following:

- at least five members;

- members with varying backgrounds to promote complete and adequate review of research activities commonly conducted by the institution;

- members that are not entirely of one profession;

- at least one member whose primary concerns are in scientific areas and at least one member whose primary concerns are in non-scientific areas;

- at least one member who is not affiliated with the institution and who is not part of the immediate family of a person who is affiliated with the institution; and

- a membership diverse in race, gender, and cultural backgrounds that is sensitive to community attitudes.

Furthermore, if an IRB regularly reviews research that involves a vulnerable category of subjects, such as children, prisoners, pregnant women, individuals with impaired decision-making capacity or economically or educationally disadvantaged, consideration shall be given to the inclusion of one or more individuals who are knowledgeable about and experienced in working with these categories of subjects.

Finally, members who have a conflict of interest may not participate except to provide requested information to the IRB.[70]

Q 26.10.5   What are the operational requirements for IRBs?

IRBs meet as necessary. Reviews must be conducted at convened meetings with a majority of the members present and with at least one member whose primary concerns are in non-scientific areas present.[71]

The IRB must have written procedures:

(1) for conducting its initial and continuing review of research and for reporting its findings and actions to the investigator and the institution;

(2) for determining which projects require review more often than annually and which projects need verification from sources other than the investigator that no material changes have occurred since previous IRB review;

(3) for ensuring prompt reporting to the IRB of changes in research activity; and

(4) for ensuring that changes in approved research, during the period for which IRB approval has already been given, may not be initiated without IRB review and approval except where necessary to eliminate apparent immediate hazards to the human subjects.[72]

The IRB also must have written procedures for ensuring prompt reporting to the IRB, appropriate institutional officials, and the FDA of:

• any unanticipated problems involving risks to human subjects or others;

• any instance of serious or continuing noncompliance with these regulations or the requirements or determinations of the IRB; or

• any suspension or termination of IRB approval.[73]

Q 26.10.6   What are the criteria for IRB approval of research?

The IRB has the authority to approve, require modifications in (to secure approval), or disapprove all research activities under its jurisdiction. To approve research, the IRB must determine that all of the following criteria are satisfied:

(1) informed consent is sought from each subject according to the informed consent requirements;

(2) risks to subjects are minimized;

(3) risks to subjects are reasonable in relation to anticipated benefits, if any, to subjects, and the importance of the knowledge that may reasonably be expected to result;

(4) the selection of subjects is equitable;

(5) when appropriate, the research plan makes adequate provision for monitoring the data collected to ensure the safety of subjects;

(6) when appropriate, there are adequate provisions to protect the privacy of subjects and to maintain the confidentiality of data; and

(7) if some or all of the subjects are likely to be vulnerable to coercion or undue influence, such as children, prisoners, pregnant women, mentally disabled persons, or economically or educationally disadvantaged persons, that the study has additional safeguards to protect the rights and welfare of these subjects.[74]

Q 26.10.7   What is "expedited review"?

The IRB need not approve every research project through the formal process described above. The IRB may use "expedited review" procedures if it determines that the research presents no more than a *minimal risk* or that the research involves minor changes in previously approved research during the period for which the original approval was authorized.[75] An expedited review may be carried out by the IRB chairperson or by one or more experienced reviewers designated by the chairperson from among the members of the IRB. In reviewing the research, the reviewers may exercise all of the authorities of the IRB *except* that the reviewers may not disapprove the research. A research activity may be disapproved only after review in accordance with the non-expedited procedure.[76]

Q 26.10.8   What is "minimal risk"?

"Minimal risk" means that the probability and magnitude of harm or discomfort anticipated in the research are not greater in and of themselves than those ordinarily encountered in daily life or during the performance of routine physical or psychological tests.[77]

Q 26.10.9   What is an "assurance of compliance" with the Common Rule?

Each institution engaged in research governed by the Common Rule, with the exception of research eligible for exemption under the C.F.R.—that is, research supported by funds from a federal agency or department that has adopted the Common Rule—must provide written assurances satisfactory to the department or agency head that it will comply with the Common Rule.[78]

Charging for Investigational Drugs

Q 26.11   Is it appropriate to charge for investigational drugs?

Charging for an investigational drug in a clinical trial under an IND application is not permitted without the prior written approval of the FDA. In requesting such approval, the sponsor must:

(1) provide evidence that the drug has a potential clinical benefit that, if demonstrated in the clinical investigations, would provide a significant advantage over available products in the diagnosis, treatment, mitigation, or prevention of a disease or condition;

(2) demonstrate that the data to be obtained from the clinical trial would be essential to establishing that the drug is effective or safe for the purpose of obtaining initial approval of a drug, or would support a significant change in the labeling of an approved drug (e.g., new indication, inclusion of comparative safety information); and

(3) demonstrate that the clinical trial could not be conducted without charging because the cost of the drug is extraordinary to the sponsor. The cost may be extraordinary due to manufacturing complexity, scarcity of a natural resource, the large quantity of drug needed (e.g., due to the size or duration of the trial), or some combination of these or other extraordinary circumstances (e.g., resources available to a sponsor).[79]

Q 26.11.1   What is a "treatment IND"?

A "treatment IND" is the process under which an investigational drug is made available to patients with serious diseases or conditions when there is no comparable or satisfactory alternative therapy to diagnose, monitor, or treat the patient's disease or condition.[80]

Q 26.11.2   Is it appropriate to charge for the study drug under a treatment IND?

A sponsor or investigator may charge for an investigational drug for a treatment use under a treatment protocol or treatment IND provided that there is:

(1) reasonable assurance that charging will not interfere with developing the study drug for marketing approval;

(2) evidence of sufficient enrollment in any ongoing clinical trial(s) needed for marketing approval to reasonably assure FDA that the trial(s) will be successfully completed as planned; and

(3) evidence of adequate progress in the development of the drug for marketing approval.[81]

Additionally, the sponsor must provide satisfactory evidence of the following criteria:

(1) the drug is being investigated in a controlled clinical trial under an IND designed to support a marketing application for the expanded access use or all clinical trials of the drug have been completed;

(2) the sponsor is actively pursuing marketing approval of the drug for the expanded access use with due diligence; and

(3) when the use is for a serious disease or condition, there is sufficient clinical evidence of safety and effectiveness to support the expanded access use or when the use is for an immediately life-threatening disease or condition, the available scientific evidence, taken as a whole, provides a reasonable basis to conclude that the investigational drug may be effective for the use and would not expose patients to an unreasonable and significant risk of illness or injury.[82]

The FDA must be notified in writing in advance of commencing any such charges. Authorization for charging goes into effect automatically thirty days after receipt by FDA of the information amendment unless the sponsor is notified to the contrary.[83]

Medicare Coverage in Clinical Trials

Q 26.12   Will Medicare pay for the healthcare services given to Medicare beneficiaries participating in clinical trials?

Yes. Since mid-2007, Medicare has covered the *routine costs* of qualifying clinical trials as well as reasonable and necessary items and services used to diagnose and treat complications arising from participation in all clinical trials. All other Medicare rules apply.[84]

Q 26.12.1   What does Medicare consider "routine costs"?

Routine costs of a clinical trial include all items and services that are otherwise generally available to Medicare beneficiaries (i.e., there exists a benefit category, it is not statutorily excluded, and there is not a national non-coverage decision) that are provided in either the experimental or in the control arms of a clinical trial.

Routine costs do *not* include:

(1) the investigational item or service itself, unless otherwise covered outside of the clinical trial;

(2) items and services provided solely to satisfy data collection and analysis needs, and that are not used in the direct clinical management of the patient (e.g., monthly CT scans for a condition usually requiring only a single scan); and

(3) items and services customarily provided by the research sponsors free of charge for any enrollee in the trial.[85]

Routine costs in clinical trials *do* include:

(1) items or services that are typically provided absent a clinical trial (e.g., conventional care);

(2) items or services required solely for the provision of the investigational item or service (e.g., administration of a non-covered chemotherapeutic agent), the clinically appropriate monitoring of the effects of the item or service, or the prevention of complications; and

(3) items or services needed for reasonable and necessary care arising from the provision of an investigational item or service—in particular, for the diagnosis or treatment of complications.[86]

Q 26.12.2   What is a "qualifying" clinical trial?

To qualify for coverage of routine costs, a clinical trial must meet the following three requirements and also have the additional "desirable characteristics" described below:

(1) The subject or purpose of the trial must be the evaluation of an item or service that falls within a Medicare benefit category (e.g., physicians' service, durable medical equipment, diagnostic test) and is not statutorily excluded from coverage (e.g., cosmetic surgery, hearing aids).

(2) The trial must not be designed exclusively to test toxicity or disease pathophysiology; it must have therapeutic intent.

(3) Trials of therapeutic interventions must enroll patients with diagnosed disease rather than healthy volunteers. Trials of diagnostic interventions may enroll healthy patients in order to have a proper control group.[87]

The three requirements above are insufficient by themselves to qualify a clinical trial for Medicare coverage of routine costs. Clinical trials also should have the following desirable characteristics (some trials are presumed to have these characteristics and automatically qualify):

(1) the principal purpose of the trial is to test whether the intervention potentially improves the participants' health outcomes;

(2) the trial is well-supported by available scientific and medical information or it is intended to clarify or establish the health outcomes of interventions already in common clinical use;

(3) the trial does not unjustifiably duplicate existing studies;

(4) the trial design is appropriate to answer the research question being asked in the trial;

(5) the trial is sponsored by a credible organization or individual capable of executing the proposed trial successfully;

(6) the trial complies with federal regulations relating to the protection of human subjects; and

(7) all aspects of the trial are conducted according to the appropriate standards of scientific integrity.[88]

Q 26.12.3   What types of clinical trials are deemed to automatically qualify for reimbursement of routine costs?

(1) Trials funded by NIH, CDC, AHRQ, CMS, DOD, and VA;

(2) Trials supported by centers or cooperative groups that are funded by the NIH, CDC, AHRQ, CMS, DOD, and VA;

(3) Trials conducted under an IND application reviewed by the FDA; and

(4) Drug trials that are exempt from having an IND under 21 C.F.R. § 312.2(b)(1) will be deemed automatically qualified until CMS develops specific qualifying criteria for these types of studies. At the time CMS promulgates such criteria, the principal investigator will need to certify that the trial meets such qualifying criteria. This certification process will affect only the future status of the trial and will not be used to retroactively change the earlier deemed status.[89]

Q 26.12.4   Does Medicare cover the costs of treating complications arising from the study?

Medicare will cover the costs of treating complications arising from clinical trials, assuming the services required in the treatment of the complication are otherwise covered.[90]

FDA Approval

The Basics

Q 26.13   What products does FDA approve?

FDA generally approves drugs, biologics, and medical device products. Drug products include new drugs, generic drugs, and over-the-counter drugs.

Drug Approval

Q 26.14   What is a new drug?

The FDCA defines a new drug to include drugs that are not generally recognized among qualified experts as safe and effective for use under the conditions prescribed, recommended, or suggested in its labeling, as well as any drugs that is recognized as safe and effective under certain conditions, but has not been used to a material extent or for a material time under such conditions. Under this definition, drugs that: (1) contain an active chemical formula that has not yet been approved by the FDA, or (2) have been approved by the FDA for purposes other than its new intended purpose, are considered to be new drugs.[91]

Q 26.15   What does FDA require to approve a new drug product?

All drugs must be demonstrated to be safe and effective before they can be approved to be marketed in the United States. To ensure their safety and effectiveness, the FDA utilizes a risk-based framework for the approval of drugs products. Under this framework, the FDA has established distinct pathways.

Q 26.16   How does FDA approve a new drug?

Before a new drug can be introduced into the market, it must be approved by the FDA through the NDA process. An NDA must include clinical information about the drug, the collection of which generally requires shipping samples of unapproved drugs to investigators in multiple states. To resolve this dilemma, the FDA permits drug developers to transport otherwise-unapproved new drugs through interstate commerce for investigational purposes, subject to the IND application process.[92]

Q 26.17   What does an IND require?

An IND application[93] will generally contain the following parts:

- Cover sheet;
- Introductory statement and general investigational plan;
- Investigator's brochure;
- Protocols for each planned study;
- Chemistry, manufacturing, and control information;
- Pharmacology and toxicology information;
- Previous human experience with the investigational drug;
- Additional information; and
- Other relevant information.

Q 26.18   How does FDA approve a new drug?

Once the drug developer has obtained sufficient clinical information pursuant to an IND, it can apply for approval to market the drug through the NDA process. In general, an NDA[94] for a new chemical entity must contain the following parts:

- Application form;
- Index;
- Summary;
- Technical sections;
- Samples and labeling;
- Case report forms and tabulations;
- Patient information;
- Claimed exclusivity; and
- Financial certification or disclosures statements.

Q 26.19   What is a generic drug?

Generic drugs are chemically equivalent to drugs that have already been approved through the NDA process.[95]

Q 26.20   How are generic drugs approved?

Generic drugs are approved through an ANDA, which focuses on the generic drug's bioequivalence, or whether it is effectively the same as an already-approved new drug with respect to active ingredients, dosages form, strength, route of administration, and conditions of use that are not subject to an exclusivity provision or existing patent.[96]

Q 26.21   What are the benefits of bringing a generic drug to market?

Generic drug developers are provided a number of protections including: (1) procedures to challenge the patent exclusivity of equivalent new drugs, (2) a first-to-file 180-day exclusivity period among manufacturers seeking an ANDA for equivalent generic drugs, and (3) safe harbors that allow generic drug manufacturers to conduct certain premarket activities without the risk of patent infringement litigation from new drug manufacturers.[97]

Q 26.22   What does an ANDA require?

An ANDA[98] must generally contain the following parts:

- Application form;
- Basis for ANDA submission;
- Conditions of use;
- Active ingredients;
- Route of administration;
- Bioequivalence;
- Labeling;
- Chemistry, manufacturing, and controls;
- Samples;
- Patent certification; and
- Financial certification.

Q 26.23   What is FDA's review process of NDAs and ANDAs?

In general, the FDA has 180 days in which to complete its initial review of an NDA or an ANDA. The FDA will either approve the application or provide a complete response letter to the applicant.[99]

Q 26.24   What is an over-the-counter drug?

Over-the-counter (OTC) drugs are drug products that may be marketed for use by the consumer without a prescription by a healthcare professional.[100]

Q 26.25   How are OTC drugs approved?

An OTC drug that meets the definition of a new drug can be approved through the NDA process. Alternatively, an OTC drug that meets the definition of a generic drug and can be shown to be bioequivalent to a reference listed drug can be approved through the ANDA process. Additionally, certain OTC drugs can obtain approval through the FDA's OTC Drug Monograph Process, which was established to evaluate the safety and effectiveness of OTC drugs that fall within certain identified drug categories.[101]

Q 26.26   What happens once FDA approves a drug?

Upon approval, all drug products are subject to additional premarket regulations, regardless of the specific pathway by which the drug was approved. In particular, the FDA requires all drug establishments to register and to list their drug products. The FDA also imposes extensive regulation pertaining to labeling, advertising, and marketing; current good manufacturing practices, and adverse event reporting.[102]

Biologics Approval

Q 26.27   What is a biologic?

In the simplest terms, a biological product (also called a "biologic") is a preparation, such as a therapeutic drug or a vaccine, made from living organisms, either human, animal, yeast, or microorganisms. This is in contrast to a drug, which a chemical preparation. The statutory definition of a biologic is a "virus, therapeutic serum, toxin, antitoxin, vaccine, blood, blood component or derivative, allergenic product, or analogous product...applicable to the prevention, treatment or cure of a disease or condition of human beings."[103]

Q 26.28   How does FDA approve biologics?

Most biological products are regulated under authority granted in the Public Health Service Act (PHSA).[104] The majority of biological products subject to the PHSA also meet the definition of drugs under the FDCA.[105] While the FDA *approves* NDAs for new drugs, it *licenses* biologics for marketing via a biologics license application (BLA)—pursuant to the PHSA.[106] A BLA must be submitted along with data derived from nonclinical laboratory and clinical studies which demonstrate that the manufactured product meets prescribed requirements of safety, purity, and potency.[107]

In order to conduct clinical trials to derive this data, a biologics manufacturer needs to submit, and FDA must grant, an IND. As mentioned above, an IND is a request for authorization from FDA to administer an investigational drug or biological product to humans. This authorization must be secured prior to interstate shipment and administration of any biological product that does not hold a BLA.

Q 26.29   After the biologics manufacturer obtains an IND, what is required in a BLA?

The contents of a BLA application are generally very similar to those of an NDA, and include:[108]

- Application form;
- Index;
- Summary;
- Technical sections;
- Samples and labeling;
- Case report forms and tabulations; and
- Establishment summary.

Q 26.30   What happens once FDA approves a biologic?

Similar to drug products, biologic products are subject to additional premarket regulations, including labeling, advertising, and marketing; current good manufacturing practices, and adverse event reporting requirements.[109]

Q 26.31   Are there generics of biologics?

Biologics have no generic equivalents. The molecules of a biologic typically are so complex that manufacturing a generic, i.e., an exact copy, is not possible. Biosimilars, sometimes called follow-on biologics, are similar to the reference product and exhibit the same therapeutic characteristics. As part of the Patient Protection and Affordable Care Act, Congress passed the Biologics Price Competition and Innovation Act (BPCIA), which established an abbreviated licensure pathway for biosimilars.

Medical Devices

Q 26.32   How does FDA approve medical devices?

The FDA utilizes a risk-based approval framework to ensure the safety and effectiveness of medical devices. Under this framework, the FDA has established three classes of devices. Under FDA regulations, a device's safety and effectiveness is determined based on multiple factors, including: (1) the persons for whose use the device is represented or intended; (2) the conditions for use as recommended or suggested in the labeling; (3) the probable benefit to health from the use of the device, weighted against any probable injury or illness; and (4) the reliability of the device.[110]

- Class I: A device may be categorized in Class I if either: (1) general controls are sufficient to reasonably assure its safety and effectiveness, or (2) there is insufficient information to determine whether general controls are sufficient, but the device is "not life-supporting or life-sustaining or for a use which is of substantial importance in preventing impairment of human health, and which does not present a potential unreasonable risk of illness or injury."[111]

- Class II: A device may be categorized in Class II if general controls are insufficient to reasonably assure its safety and effectiveness, and additional special controls are necessary to provide such assurance.[112]

- Class III: A device will be categorized in Class III if both general and special controls would be insufficient to reasonably assure its safety and effectiveness and the device is "life-supporting or life-sustaining, for a use which is of substantial importance in preventing impairment of human health, or if the device presents a potential unreasonable risk of illness or injury."[113]

Q 26.33   What class of devices does FDA approve?

Generally, FDA only approves Class III medical devices through a premarket approval (PMA) application.

Q 26.34   What is required under a premarket approval application?

The PMA application is intended to provide the FDA with all scientific data and other technical information necessary for the agency to determine the device's safety and effectiveness. PMA applications generally contain the following information:[114]

- Name and contact information of the applicant;

- Detailed summary of the data and information in the application;

- A complete description of the device. Pictorial representations, where appropriate, are acceptable;

- Reference to any performance standards either in effect or proposed at the time of submission that is relevant to the device's safety and effectiveness;

- Technical sections containing data and other information about the device;

- For PMAs supported by data from a single investigation, a justification showing that such data are sufficient to demonstrate the device's safety and effectiveness;

- A bibliography of all published reports not otherwise submitted, whether adverse or supportive of the application, that are or should be known to the applicant and that concern the device's safety and effectiveness;

- One or more samples of the device, if requested by the FDA and if practicable. If it is impracticable to provide such samples. Then the application should indicate where the FDA can examine and test a sample device;

- Copies of all labeling proposed for the device;

- An environmental assessment, if applicable;

- A financial certification; and

- Any other information requested by the FDA.

Q 26.35   What happens once the PMA is submitted?

Within forty-five days of submission, FDA will make a threshold determination of whether the application is sufficiently complete so as to permit a substantive review.[115] If the application is complete, then it will be formally filed with the FDA. Upon filing, the FDA will conduct a substantive review of the application, which will likely include additional review by a relevant advisory committee.[116]

Within 180 days of the filing, the FDA will either approve or deny the application. Under the FDCA, an application can be denied if: (1) there is an inadequate showing of reasonable assurance that the device is safe and effective under the conditions of use proscribed, recommended, or suggested in the labeling; (2) the methods used in, or facilities or controls used for the manufacture, processing, packing, or installation of the device do not comply with the applicable good manufacturing practices; (3) the proposed labeling is false or misleading in any way; or (4) the device does not comply with applicable performance standards and the applications lacks any justification for such deviation.[117]

Additionally, under FDA regulations, the application can be denied if: (1) the applicant does not permit the FDA to reasonably inspect the facilities, controls, and records related to the device; (2) a nonclinical study referenced in the application was not conducted in compliance with good laboratory practice; or (3) a clinical study involving human subjects referenced in the application was not conducted in compliance with applicable regulations pertaining to IRB review or informed consent. If there is no such basis for denial, then the FDA will approve the application.[118]

Q 26.36   How does FDA regulate digital health products?

FDA regulates digital health products that meet the definition of a medical device under the FDCA as medical devices. FDA has established three general categories for digital health products: (1) the product is a medical device subject to FDA's rules and regulations; (2) the product is a medical device but falls under FDA's enforcement discretion; (3) the product is not a medical device.

Product is a medical device subject to FDA's rules and regulations. FDA regulates a number of software functions as medical devices if those functions are intended to cure, mitigate, treat, or prevent disease or if those functions are intended to affect the structure or any function of the body. These types of products are software functions that are an extension of one or more medical devices by connecting to such device(s) for purposes of controlling the device(s) or analyzing medical device data; software, such as mobile applications, which can transform a mobile platform into a regulated medical device by using attachments, display screens, or sensors or by including functionalities similar to those of currently regulated medical devices; and lastly, software performing patient-specific analysis and providing patient-specific diagnosis, or treatment recommendations, e.g., software functions that are used in active patient monitoring to analyze patient-specific medical device data are medical devices

The product is a medical device but falls under FDA's enforcement discretion. FDA's application of the definition of a medical device is highly fact-specific. While a product may technically meet the definition of a medical device, because the product poses a lower risk to the public, FDA intends to exercise enforcement discretion over these devices, meaning it will not enforce requirements under the FDCA.[119] These types of products tend to help the user self-manage their disease or condition, without providing specific treatment. For example, a software product that provides supplemental clinical care, by coaching or prompting the user.[120]

The product is not a medical device. There are two general categories of products that are not medical devices because they do not meet the definition of the FDCA.[121] The first is those products that are statutorily excluded from the definition of medical device under the 21st Century Cures Act, such as clinical decision support software.[122] The second are those products that could be used in a healthcare environment, in clinical care, or patient management, but which FDA has deemed not to be medical devices.[123] Because these software functions are not considered medical devices, FDA does not regulate them.[124] For example, FDA does not regulate products that record the clinical conversation a clinician has with a patient and send it to the patient to access after the visit; or products that allow a user to record data, such as blood glucose or blood pressure from a device to eventually share with a healthcare provider.[125]

Labeling and Advertising

Labeling: The Basics

Q 26.37   What is labeling?

The FDCA defines labeling to include all labels and other written, printed, or graphic materials upon a regulated article (like a drug or medical device) or "accompanying such article" in interstate commerce.[126] The Supreme Court interpreted the phrase "accompanying such article" broadly in *United States v. Kordel*, to mean that the labeling need not physically accompany the drug or medical device. Instead, material "accompanies" the regulated product "when it supplements or explains it, in the manner that a committee report of the Congress accompanies a bill."[127] *Kordel*'s companion case explained that the written material must still be part of an integrated transaction in selling the drug or device.[128] *Kordel* notwithstanding, FDCA regulation defines labeling very broadly:[129]

> [b]rochures, booklets, mailing pieces, detailing pieces, file cards, bulletins, calendars, price lists, catalogs, house organs, letters, motion picture films, film strips, lantern slides, sound recordings, exhibits, literature, and reprints and similar pieces of printed, audio, or visual matter descriptive of a drug and references published (for example, the "Physicians Desk Reference") for use by

medical practitioners, pharmacists, or nurses, containing drug information supplied by the manufacturer, packer, or distributor of the drug and which are disseminated by or on behalf of its manufacturer, packer, or distributor are hereby determined to be labeling. . . .[130]

Most recently, the FDA has begun to assert that websites referenced on a product's packaging constitute labeling.[131]

Labeling: Requirements

Q 26.37.1   What must a prescription drug label include?

The label and labeling for an approved prescription drug product must be identical to that approved by the FDA during the application process. The FDA will approve labeling for a drug found to be safe and effective where the applicant satisfies the general drug labeling requirements found at 21 C.F.R. § 202.1 *et seq.* as well as the specific prescription drug labeling requirements found at 21 C.F.R. §§ 202.60 *et seq.* and 202.100.

Q 26.37.2   What must an over-the-counter drug label include?

The label and labeling for an over-the-counter drug must include information as approved by the FDA or as permitted under several final or draft product category monographs. Additionally, the label must include the general drug labeling requirements found at 21 C.F.R. §§ 202.1 *et seq.* and 201.60 *et seq.* with certain aspects of that required information placed in a "Drug Facts" box.[132]

Q 26.37.3   What must a medical device label include?

The label and labeling for all medical devices must comply with the general labeling requirements found at 21 C.F.R. § 801.1 *et seq.* Specific labeling requirements for OTC devices can be found at 21 C.F.R. § 801.60 *et seq.*, for prescription medical devices at 21 C.F.R. § 801.109, and for in vitro diagnostic medical devices at 21 C.F.R. § 119.

Q 26.37.4   What happens if labeling does not comply with FDA requirements?

A drug or device is "misbranded" if its labeling does not contain all required contents, the label contents are not displayed as required (type size, location on label, etc.) or the label contents are otherwise "false or misleading."[133] In particular, a drug or device is misbranded if the label does not contain adequate instructions for its intended use and required warnings.[134] (This requirement is complex and is important in "off-label" marketing, discussed below in this chapter.)

Q 26.37.5   What are the potential consequences of noncompliance with label requirements?

Introducing a misbranded drug or device into interstate commerce is a crime.[135] Penalties include imprisonment for up to a year for a first offense or up to three years for a subsequent offense or for any offense committed with the intent to defraud or to mislead.[136] Criminal fines of up to $10,000 per violation also may be imposed.[137]

The government also has at its disposal an array of civil sanctions. It may impose civil monetary penalties for certain violations.[138] It may seek an injunction restraining further violations of the FDCA labeling and advertising requirements.[139] Under certain circumstances, the FDA may seize the misbranded drugs or medical devices.[140]

Advertising: The Basics

Q 26.38   Generally speaking, how important is advertising/labeling compliance?

Advertising and labeling are fraught with compliance risk. The stakes are extremely high. Drug and device advertising and labeling expose the manufacturer *and* its officers and directors not only to simple regulatory risk, but also to potential criminal and civil liability under a variety of legal theories. For instance, if an advertisement fails to satisfy the requirements of the applicable statutory and regulatory provisions, the drug or device may be considered misbranded under the FDCA.[141]

In recent years, manufacturers have paid billions of dollars in civil and criminal fines to state and federal authorities to settle claims arising from alleged advertising and labeling violations. Moreover, manufacturers may be held liable under the federal False Claims Act for causing the submission of false claims for payment to federal healthcare programs, such as Medicare, if they fail to appropriately advertise and market their products.[142] In connection with these settlements, manufacturers (and in some instances, their officers) have been forced to plead guilty to criminal violations. Beyond mere fines, the finding of criminal liability can result in the so-called death penalty; that is, the manufacturer may be debarred, or excluded, from participation in all federal programs, including Medicare and Medicaid.

In an apparent effort to encourage corporate compliance, the government has recently been making a concerted effort to hold corporate executives, including corporate counsel, personally accountable. Specifically, the government has recently excluded corporate executives from participating in federally funded reimbursement programs after those executives, including a company lawyer, pled guilty to criminal misdemeanor misbranding.[143] Additionally, the government has prosecuted, unsuccessfully, a corporate lawyer for obstruction of justice and for making false statements to the government after she oversaw an internal investigation concerning misbranding allegations. Notably, the court in that case acquitted the in-house lawyer observing that the case "should never have been prosecuted" by the government prosecutors.[144]

Q 26.39   What is "advertising"?

"Advertising" under the FDCA includes both traditional and online advertising. It includes ads in journals, magazines, other periodicals, and newspapers, or on the radio, television, or through telephone systems. Similarly, "advertising" can be conducted through fax machines, on computer programs, blogs, social networking sites such as Facebook or Twitter, and other web postings.[145]

Advertising: Requirements

Q 26.39.1   What must prescription drug advertisements include?

Advertisements must include:

- the established ("generic") name;

- the proprietary ("brand") name (if any);

- the formula showing quantitatively each ingredient;

- information in "brief summary" that discusses side effects, contraindications, and effectiveness;[146]

- for broadcast advertisements, the "brief summary" or an adequate alternative for disseminating the product's label in conjunction with the advertisement;

- for broadcast advertisements, a "major statement" of the product's most important risk-related information in the broadcast's audio or in the audio and visual parts of the broadcast;

- for all published direct-to-consumer advertisements, conspicuous inclusion of the statement "You are encouraged to report negative side effects of prescription drugs to the FDA. Visit MedWatch or call 1-800-FDA-1088."

And advertising must be true, fairly balanced, and not misleading.

Q 26.39.2   What is the "brief summary" of side effects, contraindications, and effectiveness?

The "brief summary" required by the FDA regulations is familiar to all and often lampooned. In television and radio advertisements it is the list of side effects, contraindications, warnings, precautions, special considerations, important notes, effectiveness, etc., included at the end of the advertisement.[147]

The FDA has issued draft guidance concerning an appropriate method for formulating the "brief summary" in consumer-directed print advertising. That draft guidance encourages companies advertising drugs with approved labeling to present the drug's most significant side effects and contraindications in either (1) a box similar to the warning label on the package itself, or (2) a Q&A format. In either case, the writing must be direct, clear, and consumer-friendly.[148] The draft guidance summarizes social science research showing these two formats were best for helping consumers understand and remember warning information. A decision to follow such guidance (as opposed to simply including all risks contained in the approved labeling) should be made with consideration of product liability implications.

Q 26.39.3 Must a broadcast advertisement contain the "brief summary" of side effects, contraindications, and effectiveness?

Advertisements broadcast through media such as radio, television, or telephone communications systems must include the "brief summary" in the audio or visual parts of the presentation unless adequate provision is made for dissemination of the approved or permitted package labeling in connection with the broadcast presentation.[149] The FDA has published a guidance document explaining a method to comply with the "adequate provision" requirement. That method involves providing for access to the approved package labeling through multiple opportunities such as web, print periodicals, and toll-free telephone numbers.[150] It should be noted that regulations and the FDA guidance for broadcast advertising require that major risks be disclosed in the broadcast advertisement itself. The FDA guidance terms this disclosure the "major statement."

Q 26.39.4 What does the FDA consider true, balanced, and not-misleading advertising?

Applicable regulations define these in the negative; that is, rather than describing the characteristics of ads that are true, fairly balanced, and not misleading, the regulations spell out a long list of characteristics of advertisements that are false, lacking in fair balance, or otherwise misleading (*see* Table 26-2).[151] The regulations also include a long list of characteristics of advertisements that *may be* false, lacking in fair balance, or otherwise misleading (*see* Table 26-3).[152]

Q 26.39.5   Are there exceptions to these advertising requirements?

Yes, there are a few exceptions, but only to the requirement to provide a "brief summary" (as described above). The following are examples of exempt advertisements:

1.   *Reminder advertisements*—advertisements intended to call attention to the name of the drug, but that do not contain indication statements or dosage recommendations.[153] Reminder advertisements must contain the proprietary (brand) name and established (generic) name of the drug and/or each active ingredient, and may contain quantitative ingredient statements, dosage forms, quantity of packages contents as sold, price, and the name and address of the manufacturer, packer, or distributor. While the advertisements can contain other information, there can be no other representations or suggestions relating to the drug being advertised. Reminder advertisements need not carry balancing information, prescribing information, or a brief summary. However, the agency broadly construes the prohibition on "other representations or suggestions about the drug" to include anything that is remotely related to the drug. The reminder advertisement exception does not apply to drugs carrying a boxed warning.[154]

2.   *Advertisements of bulk-sale drugs*—sales of the drug in bulk packages to be processed, manufactured, labeled, or repackaged and that contain no claims for the therapeutic safety or effectiveness of the drug.

3.   *Advertisements of prescription-compounding drugs*—ads that promote sale of a drug for use as a prescription chemical or other compound for use by registered pharmacists.[155]

TABLE 26-2

Advertisements That Are False, Lacking in Fair Balance, or Otherwise Misleading

A prescription drug advertisement is false, lacking in fair balance, or otherwise misleading if it:

(1) contains a representation/suggestion, not approved or permitted for use in the labeling, that a drug is better, more effective, useful in a broader range of conditions or patients (humans or, in the case of veterinary drugs, other animals), safer, has fewer, or less incidence of, or less-serious side effects or contraindications than substantial evidence/clinical experience has shown whether or not such representations are made by comparison with other drugs or treatments, and whether or not such a representation/suggestion is made directly or by using published or unpublished literature, quotations, or other references.

(2) represents/suggests that a drug is safer or more effective than another drug in some particular when substantial evidence/ clinical experience has not demonstrated that.

(3) contains favorable information/opinions about a drug previously regarded as valid but that have been rendered invalid by contrary and more credible recent information, or contains references/quotations significantly more favorable to the drug than substantial evidence/clinical experience has shown.

(4) selectively presents information from published articles or other references that report no side effects or minimal side effects or otherwise make a drug appear to be safer than has been demonstrated.

(5) presents information from a study so as to imply that the study represents larger or more general experience with the drug than it actually does.

(6)   refers to literature/studies that misrepresent the drug's effectiveness by not disclosing that claimed results may be due to concomitant therapy, or (in the case of ads promoting a drug for use by man) by not disclosing credible information available concerning the placebo effect on results.

(7)   contains favorable data/conclusions from nonclinical drug studies (e.g., in lab animals or in vitro), suggesting they have clinical significance when in fact no such significance has been demonstrated.

(8)   uses an apparently favorable statement by a recognized authority but fails to refer to concurrent or more recent unfavorable data or statements from the same authority on the same subject(s).

(9)   uses a quote or paraphrase out of context to convey a false or misleading idea.

(10) uses literature, quotations, or references that purport to support a claim but in fact do not support/have relevance to the claim.

(11) uses literature, quotations, or references for the purpose of recommending or suggesting conditions of drug use that are not approved or permitted in the drug package labeling.

(12) offers a combination of drugs for the treatment of patients suffering from a condition amenable to treatment by any of the components rather than limiting the indications for use to patients for whom concomitant therapy as provided by the fixed combination drug is indicated (unless such condition is included in the uses permitted by the regulations).

(13) uses a study on normal individuals without disclosing that they were normal, unless the drug is intended for use on normal individuals.

(14) uses "statistics" on numbers of patients, or counts of favorable results or side effects, derived from pooling data from various insignificant or dissimilar studies so as to suggest that such "statistics" are valid if they are not or that they are derived from large or significant studies supporting favorable conclusions when such is not the case.

(15) uses erroneously a statistical finding of "no significant difference" to claim clinical equivalence or to deny or conceal the potential existence of a real clinical difference.

(16) uses statements/representations that a drug differs from or does not contain a named drug/category of drugs, or that it has a greater potency per unit of weight, in a way that suggests falsely or misleadingly or without substantial evidence/clinical experience that the advertised drug is safer or more effective.

(17) uses data favorable to a drug derived from patients treated with dosages different from those recommended in approved or permitted labeling if the drug advertised is subject to section 505 of the act, or, in the case of other drugs, if the dosages employed were different from those recommended in the labeling and generally recognized as safe and effective.

(18) uses headline, sub-headline, or pictorial or other graphic matter in a misleading way.

(19) represents/suggests that properly recommended drug dosages for certain classes of patients or disease conditions are safe and effective for other classes of patients or disease conditions when they are not.

(20) presents required side-effect or contraindication information using a general term for a group in place of disclosing each specific side effect and contraindication (employs the term "blood dyscrasias" instead of "leukopenia," "agranulocytosis," "neutropenia," etc.) (except as otherwise permitted).

TABLE 26-3

Advertisements That May Be False, Lacking in Fair Balance, or Otherwise Misleading

An advertisement may be false, lacking in fair balance, or otherwise misleading if it:

(1) contains favorable information/conclusions from a study that is inadequate in design, scope, or conduct to furnish significant support for such information/conclusions.

(2) uses "statistical significance" to support a claim that has not been demonstrated to have clinical significance or validity, or fails to reveal the range of variations around the quoted average results.

(3) uses statistical analyses and techniques on a retrospective basis to discover and cite findings not soundly supported by the study, or to suggest scientific validity and rigor for data from studies the design or protocol of which is not amenable to formal statistical evaluations.

(4) uses tables/graphs to distort or misrepresent the relationships, trends, differences, or changes among the variables or products studied; e.g., by failing to label the abscissa (X axis) and ordinate (Y axis), thus creating a misleading impression.

(5) uses reports/statements represented to be statistical analyses, interpretations, or evaluations that are inconsistent with or violate the established principles of statistical theory, methodology, applied practice, and inference, or that are derived from clinical studies the design, data, or conduct of which substantially invalidates the application of statistical analyses, interpretations, or evaluations.

(6) contains claims concerning the mechanism or site of drug action that are not generally regarded as established by scientific evidence by experts qualified by scientific training and experience without disclosing that the claims are not established and the limitations of the supporting evidence.

(7) fails to provide sufficient emphasis for side-effect and contra-indication information, when such information is contained in a distinct part of an advertisement, because of repetition or other emphasis in that part of the advertisement of claims for effectiveness or safety of the drug.

(8) fails to present side-effect and contraindication information with a prominence and readability reasonably comparable with that of information relating to the drug's effectiveness, taking into account typography, layout, contrast, headlines, paragraphing, white space, and any other techniques apt to achieve emphasis.

(9) fails to provide adequate emphasis (e.g., by the use of color scheme, borders, headlines, or copy that extends across the gutter) for the fact that two facing pages are part of the same advertisement when one page contains side-effect and con-traindication information.

(10) in an advertisement promoting use of the drug in a selected class of patients (e.g., geriatric patients or depressed patients), fails to present with adequate emphasis the significant side effects and contraindications or the significant dosage con-siderations, when dosage recommendations are included in an advertisement, especially applicable to that selected class of patients.

(11) fails to present on a page facing another page (or on another full page) of an advertisement on more than one page side-effect and contraindication information when such informa-tion is in a distinct part of the advertisement.

(12) fails to include on each page or spread of an advertisement the side-effect and contraindication information or a prom-inent reference to its presence and location when it is pre-sented as a distinct part of an advertisement.

(13) contains information from published or unpublished reports or opinions falsely or misleadingly represented or suggested to be authentic or authoritative.

Q 26.39.6   Does the FDA pre-approve advertising?

Any advertisement may be submitted to the FDA for comment prior to publication. FDA comments must be in writing. If the manufacturer is notified that the submitted advertisement is not in violation and, at some subsequent time, the FDA changes its opinion, the manufacturer is notified and will be given a reasonable time to correct the advertisement before any regulatory action is taken.[156]

Q 26.39.7   Is pre-approval of advertising ever mandatory?

If the FDA receives reliable information that has not been widely publicized that a drug may cause death or serious damage and it has notified the manufacturer of such information, then the manufacturer *might* need to get prior FDA approval for future advertisements. In this circumstance, the FDA will notify the manufacturer of the information and request that it submit a program for ensuring that such information will be publicized promptly and adequately to the medical profession in subsequent advertisements. If the manufacturer fails to submit a program, or if the FDA deems a proposed program to be inadequate, then the manufacturer *must* submit advertisements for the drug to the FDA for prior approval.[157] Once the information has been widely publicized to the medical profession, the FDA will notify the manufacturer that prior approval of advertising no longer is required.[158] The manufacturer also will have an opportunity for a regulatory hearing before the FDA with respect to any determination that prior approval is required for advertisements concerning a particular prescription drug, or that a particular advertisement is not approvable.[159]

Drugs approved under the accelerated approval process (drugs approved to treat serious or life-threatening illnesses where the approval is usually based upon surrogate endpoints) are approved on condition that promotional materials be submitted to the FDA thirty days before use.[160] While these provisions do not require FDA approval, they do permit the FDA to object to the promotional materials before first use.

The FDCA has been amended to require prior submission of certain direct-to-consumer television advertisements for prescription drugs.[161] Implementation of these new provisions has been delayed in part due to statutory funding provisions of the legislation. In the meantime, FDA has issued draft guidance on the issue, stating that it expects that the following six categories of advertisements will require preclearance:

(1) the initial TV ad for any drug or for a new or expanded indication for a drug;

(2) all TV ads for drugs subject to a risk evaluation and mitigation strategy;

(3) all TV ads for Schedule II controlled substances;

(4) the first TV ad for a drug following a safety labeling update that affects its boxed warning, contraindications, or warnings and precautions;

(5) the first TV ad for a drug, when the previous TV ad for that drug was the subject of an FDA enforcement letter;

(6) any other TV ad the FDA believes needs to be precleared.[162]

In some instances, prior submission is required by operation of federal and state consent decrees resulting from enforcement action.

In the past, the FDA has stated in its drug approval letters that sponsors must submit copies of proposed launch materials to the FDA, in advance, for review. While the formal FDA position now appears to recognize that the agency generally cannot require such submissions (and in fact, the agency appears unwilling to even overtly encourage such submissions), the agency places a high priority on reviewing such draft launch material in an effort to enhance the probability of compliance. Many companies find such pre-launch submissions to be useful.

Q 26.39.8   Must advertisements be filed with the FDA?

Prescription drug sponsors must submit specimens of all labeling or advertising devised for promotion of the drug. Such materials must be submitted at the time of initial dissemination (for labeling material) and publication (for advertising material) under cover of FDA Form 2253.[163]

Q 26.39.9   How should firms file online promotion and advertising?

The FDA has issued draft guidance that recognizes the unique challenges of advertising and promotion through the use of online communication, including websites, blogs, and social media. Static promotional materials, such as emails and websites with fixed content, should be submitted to the FDA when initially disseminated. However, for online content that allows interactive or real-time communications, such as a Twitter feed, the FDA additionally requires the submission of a Form FDA 2253 or 2301 once each month, listing, among other things, the dates of the most recent content updates. For online content that is not publicly accessible, the firm must submit the actual content using screenshots or other similar methods.[164]

Q 26.39.10   What about advertising on social media, particularly those platforms with character space limitations?

The FDA's oversight of advertising also applies to manufacturers' advertising on social media platforms, even those with character limitations such as Twitter. The FDA issued a draft guidance on issue, emphasizing that "if a firm chooses to make product benefit claims, the firm should also incorporate risk information within the same character-space limited communication."[165] Generally, the FDA recommends that each transmission of communication (e.g., individual tweets) regarding the benefits of a product should include the appropriate risk information such that each single transmission of communication is accurate and non-misleading.

Misbranding

Q 26.39.11   What happens if drug/device advertising does not comply with FDA requirements?

A drug or medical device that does not comply with FDA advertising requirements will generally be deemed to be misbranded. There are many ways a drug or medical device can become misbranded. In general, these consist of false or misleading statements on product labels or in product labeling, inadequate prominence or placement of required information in product labels or product labeling, inadequate or dangerous instructions for use, and omission of required labeling information from the product labeling or labels.[166] Additionally, false or misleading statements in prescription advertising or restricted medical device advertising may misbrand those products.[167] In recent years, a common allegation in misbranding cases is that a drug or medical device promoted for off-label use is misbranded because its approved labeling lacks adequate directions for the intended (off-label) use.

Q 26.39.12   What are the possible consequences of a misbranding violation?

Penalties include imprisonment for up to a year for a first offense or up to three years for a subsequent offense or for any offense committed with the intent to defraud or to mislead.[168] Criminal fines of up to $10,000 per violation also may be imposed.[169]

The government also has at its disposal an array of civil sanctions. It may impose significant civil monetary penalties of up to $500,000 for certain violations.[170] It may seek an injunction restraining further violations of the FDCA advertising requirements.[171] Finally, under certain circumstances, the FDA may seize the misbranded drugs.[172]

Typically, the FDA will send the manufacturer a warning letter or an "untitled letter" before taking more serious action such as seeking an injunction or seizing the drug. The letter will recite the alleged violations and will identify the language or other aspects of the ad or labeling that the FDA deems to be lacking fair balance, misleading, or otherwise inappropriate. The letter will demand specific action and a written response.

If the FDA considers the response to be adequate, then the matter may end there. However, it is important that the manufacturer respond. The failure to respond may result in the FDA seeking more severe sanctions.

Whether a manufacturer responds appropriately to a letter from the FDA or not, it may face liability from DOJ, OIG, individual states, or consumer groups. DOJ may enforce the FDCA misbranding provisions directly. OIG and the states may effectively do so by creative application of other laws such as the False Claims Act and various state consumer laws. The manufacturer's response letter should be carefully crafted to minimize the likelihood it will be used against the manufacturer in any subsequent proceedings.

"Off-Label" Use

Q 26.40   What is meant by "off-label"?

All drugs and medical devices are approved, cleared, or permitted for distribution containing adequate directions (or a similar requirement) in their labeling for their intended use. Uses other than those approved, cleared, or permitted intended uses are considered "off-label."

Q 26.40.1   Is it illegal for a physician to prescribe a drug "off-label"?

With the exception of the prescription and distribution of human growth hormone, it is not illegal for a physician to prescribe a drug or medical device "off-label." However, many payors will not reimburse the cost of drugs used off-label, or they might limit off-label reimbursement only to those off-label uses that have come to be generally accepted over time in the medical community.

Q 26.40.2   Is advertising or promotion of off-label uses permitted?

While there is no statute or regulation that specifically prohibits off-label promotion, the position of enforcement authorities tends to be that promotion of off-label uses is prohibited. When pressed on the interplay between the government's frequent assertion that "off-label promotion" and "off-label marketing" are illegal and the First Amendment requirements attendant to such speech restrictions, the government makes absolutely clear that off-label promotion is not a crime, but is instead evidence of intended use that can cause a drug or medical device to become misbranded.[173]

The FDA and others argue that off-label promotion violates the FDCA in two ways: first, that it constitutes the introduction into interstate commerce of an "unapproved new drug"; second, that it constitutes the illegal introduction into interstate commerce of a misbranded drug or device.[174]

The FDCA prohibits the introduction of an unapproved drug, and the FDA contends a drug becomes a "new drug" if it is introduced into interstate commerce for a use different from the one for which the drug was approved (the "intended use"). Likewise, a drug is misbranded, the government contends, if its labeling does not include adequate directions for its intended use.

The government's assertion that "off-label" promotion is unlawful is particularly nettlesome, because the line between permitted activities and "promotion" is extremely unclear. For instance, FDA regulations state that the regulatory scheme is "not intended to restrict the full exchange of information concerning [a drug or medical device], including dissemination of scientific findings in scientific and lay media," but is intended to "restrict promotional claims of safety and effectiveness."[175] Additionally, notwithstanding the government's assertion that a drug or medical device must be introduced into interstate commerce with labeling sufficient to guide its intended use, the agency has issued a guidance permitting the distribution, including distribution by sales representatives, of scientific or medical journal articles, scientific or medical reference texts, and clinical practice guidelines concerning certain unapproved uses of approved or cleared drugs and medical devices.[176]

While manufacturers and others disagree to a point, what can be said with certainty is that off-label promotion is a high priority for enforcement authorities, whose enforcement efforts have resulted in the government imposing fines totaling in the billions of dollars.

Q 26.40.3   How might off-label promotion constitute misbranding?

The FDA approves drugs and devices only after the manufacturer shows that the drug is safe and effective for the specific use described in the manufacturer's application for approval or clearance.[177] Once approved or cleared, the FDA requires that the product labeling, among other things, include adequate directions for all intended uses, absent which the product is deemed to be misbranded.[178] While the government's argument is more complex than presented here, it essentially maintains that a product's approved labeling cannot contain "adequate directions" for an off-label use because the manufacturer cannot write "adequate directions" for uses that were not approved by the FDA and that were not thereby proven to be safe and effective or that otherwise meet regulations for approval or clearance.[179]

Q 26.40.4 How might off-label promotion constitute the introduction of an unapproved new drug?

A "new drug" is defined as one that is not recognized as safe and effective for its intended use.[180] The intended use is demonstrated by the "objective intent of the persons legally responsible for the labeling of drugs."[181] The FDA ascertains a manufacturer's objective intent by looking at how the manufacturer distributes the drug, including the manufacturer's labeling claims, advertising materials, oral and written statements, and other circumstances surrounding the distribution of the drug.[182]

It is the FDA's position, therefore, that the manufacturer's promotion of a drug or device for an unapproved use creates a new "intended use." This new intended use has not been proven through the FDA approval process to be safe and effective. The FDA reasons that, consequently, promotion of the off-label use is the equivalent of introducing an unapproved "new drug" into interstate commerce in violation of the FDCA.[183]

Q 26.40.5 How does the FDA determine the "intended use" of a regulated product?

The FDA has published regulations explaining how it determines "intended use" for drugs[184] and for medical devices.[185] Both of these regulations make clear that in determining the intended use of a product the FDA will look not only to the labeling and advertising of the regulated product, but also to the circumstances around the sale of the product, including the statements of the marketer's employees and even evidence that the seller knows the use to which a purchaser intends to put the product. The agency has stated that it intends to exercise enforcement discretion in its interpretation, but it has declined to make clear those circumstances in which knowledge of the intention of a customer to use a product off-label will not misbrand the product on the argument that the product fails to contain adequate directions for that off-label use. Moreover, as explained elsewhere in this chapter, the agency permits the dissemination of off-label-use information by sales representatives under the agency's draft guidance for distributing scientific and medical publications. Additionally, the agency has long made clear that drug and medical device manufacturers may answer unsolicited questions from customers and potential customers about off-label uses so long as the responses to those questions are concise, directed to the specific question asked, and accurate.

The ambiguity created by the government's discretionary approach to defining "intended use" is probably inconsistent with constitutional due process requirements for criminal prosecutions.[186] Nonetheless, drug and medical device companies typically prefer to settle criminal matters rather than litigate them. Moreover, such due process constraints likely do not apply to civil enforcement actions, such cases being brought under the False Claims Act (a favorite among government attorneys for enforcing the FCA's misbranding rules).

Sales, Marketing, and Pricing

State and Federal Regulation

Q 26.41   What laws and other guidance apply to the sale and marketing of pharmaceuticals and medical devices?

Other than the labeling and advertising rules discussed above, there are no federal statutes or regulations that exclusively regulate the sales and marketing practices of pharmaceutical and medical device manufacturers. Instead, there is a maze of federal and state laws, both criminal and civil, and much non-statutory guidance that serve to limit the sale and marketing activities of pharmaceutical and device manufacturers. These provisions particularly impact the relationship between manufacturers on the one hand and prescribers, purchasers, and managed care organizations on the other. The main laws, other than the FDCA, used to restrict sales and marketing activities are the federal Anti-Kickback Statute and the federal False Claims Act. (They are discussed in greater detail below. The False Claims Act is also discussed at length in chapter 12.)

It is the enforcement of these laws, usually brought alongside criminal FDCA allegations, that has led to the many recent high-profile and high-dollar settlements between the federal and state governments and manufacturers. In addition to the advertising and labeling requirements discussed above, the laws and non-statutory guidance impacting the sales and marketing of pharmaceuticals and medical devices include those listed in Table 26-4, below.

Q 26.41.1   How do the states regulate sales and marketing practices?

Encouraged by budgetary constraints and federal incentives, states are passing their own versions of the False Claims Act and Anti-Kickback Statute. States are also using their consumer protection laws to address what they allege to be sales and marketing abuses. Finally, many states have passed, or are considering, statutes that require manufacturers to report the value of cash or items provided to physicians in a position to prescribe or order the manufacturer's product.

Anti-Kickback Statute

Q 26.42   What is the federal Anti-Kickback Statute?

The federal Anti-Kickback Statute (AKS) is a federal criminal statute that prohibits the knowing or willful payment or receipt of any remuneration to induce or to recommend the referral of items or services that may be reimbursed in whole or in part by federal healthcare programs.[187] Violations of the AKS are punishable as felonies with fines of up to $25,000 per violation and imprisonment for up to five years.[188]

Remuneration broadly includes any benefit, either cash or "in-kind," and regardless of whether the benefit is provided directly or indirectly.[189] The AKS consequently implicates any payment or gift from a manufacturer to any person in a position to influence the prescription or purchase of the manufacturer's products.

TABLE 26-4

Statutory and Non-Statutory Guidance Affecting Sales and Marketing of Pharmaceuticals and Medical Devices

Laws affecting sales and marketing of drugs and devices

1. Federal Anti-Kickback Statute (42 U.S.C. § 1320a-7b(b))

2. Public Contracts Anti-Kickback Statute (41 U.S.C. § 52)

3. Federal False Claims Act (31 U.S.C. § 3729)

4. Civil Monetary Penalty Statute (42 U.S.C. § 1320a-7)

5. Robinson-Patman Act (15 U.S.C. § 13(c))

6. False Statements to a Federal Agent (18 U.S.C. § 1001)

7. Health Care Fraud (18 U.S.C. § 1035)

8. Prescription Drug Marketing Act (42 U.S.C. § 1320a-7h)

9. Physician Payments Sunshine Act (42 C.F.R. § 403.900)

10. Patient Protection and Affordable Care Act (Pub. L. No. 111-148)

11. State anti-kickback statutes and false claims acts

12. State consumer protection laws

13. State reporting statutes

Non-statutory guidance

1. PhRMA Code[190]

2. AdvaMed Code[191]

3. AMA Ethics Opinion E-8.061

4. OIG Compliance Program Guidance for Pharmaceutical Manufacturers

5. OIG Advisory Opinions, Special Fraud Alerts, Bulletins, and Other Guidance

Q 26.42.1   What are some of the key risk areas implicating the AKS?

There are several areas that the OIG has identified as being inherently risky for pharmaceutical and medical device companies, especially when marketing and promoting their products. This is not an exclusive list of problematic activities, nor does it mean that the described practices necessarily violate the AKS.

- Discounts and rebates
- Switching arrangements
- Product support services
- Educational grants
- Research or other charitable donations
- Equipment and storage lease arrangements
- Formularies
- Pricing spreads
- Capital equipment pricing arrangements
- Product trainings, education, and sales meetings
- Consulting arrangements
- Gifts

The key factor is the party's intent. The AKS prohibits only those activities undertaken for the purpose (or at least *a* purpose) of inducing or rewarding referrals that result in federal healthcare program payments.[192] To more clearly define the scope of the AKS, the OIG has created a number of "safe harbors" that identify financial relationships that will not be prosecuted as kickbacks.[193]

Q 26.42.2   What are the primary AKS considerations with regard to discounts and rebates?

Product discounts are permitted but only if properly documented and reported, and only if they constitute a reduction in the product's price. There is a specific safe harbor relating to discounts. The essential requirements are that the discount or rebate be stated on the face of the invoice or, in the case of a rebate, the formula to be determined in advance in writing. The discount cannot take into account the volume or value of referrals between the parties, and the records of the discount or rebate must be made available to HHS or reported on the entity's Medicare cost reports, if it is required to file one. Moreover, the government has taken the position that reductions in price, if conditioned on recipients performing promotional or conversion activities, are suspect and do not qualify as "discounts" within the meaning of the discount exception or safe harbor to the AKS.[194]

Q 26.42.3   ... "switching arrangements"?

"Switching arrangements" refers to a pharmaceutical or medical device company providing remuneration to a clinician each time a patient's prescription is switched to one of the company's products. OIG views these arrangements as highly suspect under the AKS, so they usually should be avoided.[195]

Q 26.42.4   ... product support services?

Product support services are "value-added" services offered in connection with the purchase of products. They may include billing, reimbursement, or other support. Provisions of these types of services can become problematic where the services eliminate a normal business cost or risk (e.g., non-payment by insurance companies) or an expense to the customer.[196]

Q 26.42.5   ... educational grants?

Companies often sponsor educational conferences or otherwise support education. This may include donating to third-party educational, professional, charity groups for the advancement of medical or public health education. It might also mean providing grants to allow individuals to attend educational conferences.

Educational grants should adhere to the following guidelines:

- Educational grants should only be provided to organizations with bona fide educational purposes.[197]

- The grant should be made to the conference organizers and not to any individual.

- If the company is sponsoring a conference, the conference organizers and not the sponsoring company should be responsible for planning the content of the presentations selecting speakers and selecting invitees. Companies may buy space or booths to advertise their products at the event.[198]

- The non-drug or device company organizers must determine how to use the grant money, for example, to defray overall costs, to sponsor speakers, to pay for hospitality, or to provide items permissible under the AdvaMed Code.[199]

- Grant-making functions within a company should be separated from marketing functions. Decisions on how to award grants should never be based on the actual or potential volume or value of products purchased by the grantee.[200]

- If the company is sponsoring students, fellows, or other healthcare workers to attend a conference, the donation should be made directly to an educational institution. The institution and not the pharmaceutical or medical device company should decide which individuals receive these funds.[201]

Q 26.42.6   ... research or other charitable organizations?

Companies making donations to various organizations with bona fide charitable purposes should ensure that the donations are well documented and are not connected to a request or promise for business.[202]

Pharmaceutical and medical device companies frequently fund independent investigators' research into the effectiveness of their products. This practice is fine if carried out appropriately, even when the researching party is or could be a purchaser of the studied product.[203] The research should be funded at fair market value and should be only for genuine significant scientific and medical purposes—never as a pretext to generate sales or prescriptions. Research agreements should be in writing. Again, the research grant decisions should be kept separate from sales and marketing departments to reduce any possible implications of inducing business through the guise of donations.[204]

Studies conducted in support of an FDA application for marketing approval of a drug or device generally present fewer fraud and abuse risks, but relationships with investigators and institutions still should be scrutinized. All studies—especially "investigator initiated studies" conducted post-approval—should be carefully scrutinized, including by the company's compliance and legal departments.

Q 26.42.7   ... equipment lease and storage agreements?

Equipment lease and storage agreements should be closely scrutinized to ensure that the terms offered are at fair market value. Determinations of fair market value should be documented.[205]

Q 26.42.8   ... consultant training, education, and sales meetings?

A vital element of any pharmaceutical and medical device company's business is educating its current customers on how to use its products properly. Manufacturers also often hire healthcare practitioners as consultants to provide this education to their peers. These education and sales functions are permitted if properly conducted.

Gatherings to train consultants or to provide product education and training should take place in environments conducive to learning or to effective product presentations or scientific discussions, such as a conference room or quiet restaurant, so that the educational or business function can be the focus of the meeting. Meetings should be held at business hotels and not at resorts.[206]

The company may provide attendees with modest, occasional meals or other hospitality in connection with meetings so long as they are reasonable in value for the setting and region and are otherwise consistent with trade codes. A company representative should remain at the meeting; the representative may not simply purchase a meal for a group if the meal is not tied to a business or educational purpose.[207] Attendees should have a legitimate need to attend.[208] Moreover, guests and spouses should not attend such meetings.[209]

Q 26.42.9   ... consulting arrangements?

Healthcare providers consult with companies in a variety of different ways. Providers speak on behalf of the company at promotional events; they provide scientific knowledge; they conduct clinical trials; they advise on matters related to marketing. Enforcement authorities, while recognizing the legitimate value of these relationships, also view them as ripe for abuse. Therefore, arrangements for bona fide business services with customers should be carefully crafted to minimize anti-kickback risk:

- Clinicians should not be paid to passively attend meetings or for ghostwritten papers or speeches.[210]

- Agreements should be in writing and should detail what services the clinician will provide.[211]

- Any compensation should be set in advance, not relate to the amount of prescriptions or referrals, and reflect fair-market value for similar services.[212]

- Any expenses to be reimbursed should be documented, reasonable, and necessary.[213]

Consultants must be selected based on their qualifications, and not on their expected quantity of prescriptions or referrals.[214] Consultants must be selected by those with the necessary skill and knowledge to assess the consultant's medical and scientific credentials. Thus, sales and marketing personnel frequently will be unqualified to select consultants.

Consultants giving informational presentations on behalf of the company must disclose clearly that they are being paid by the manufacturer. All materials used for such presentations also should be marked clearly to indicate the manufacturer's sponsorship. The company also must educate consultants giving informational presentations about the prohibitions on off-label marketing and take steps to ensure that the presentation does not include off-label information except in response to unsolicited questions from program attendees.

Q 26.42.10   ... gifts?

Gifts can never be given for the purpose of inducing or rewarding customers for product purchases or referrals. Yet it may be acceptable, on infrequent occasions, to give items of minimal value having a genuine educational value or patient benefit.[215] Gifts should never be in the form of cash.[216] The PhRMA Code gives guidance to pharmaceutical companies as to the types of gifts that are appropriate. Likewise, the AdvaMed Code provides guidance to medical device companies as to the types of gifts that are appropriate. In addition, providing gifts or payment reductions to patients potentially can implicate the Civil Monetary Penalties statute.[217]

False Claims Act

Q 26.43   What is the federal False Claims Act?

The False Claims Act (FCA) establishes civil liability for anyone who knowingly presents or causes to be presented a false or fraudulent claim for payment by the federal government.[218] Treble damages are available plus a fine per false claim. Fines for false claims submitted before November 2, 2015, range from $5500 to $11,000.[219] Fines for false claims after that time are roughly double that and increase with inflation each year.[220] The current range (for false claims submitted after March 1, 2019) is $11,181 to $22,927.[221] Violation of the False Claims Act also raises the risk of exclusion from federal healthcare programs.[222]

Q 26.43.1   How does the marketing of drugs and devices implicate the False Claims Act?

Drug and device companies usually do not submit claims to government payors for their products. Nonetheless, the government has successfully argued that marketing materials or practices that are false or misleading can cause the submission of false claims and trigger liability under the FCA. Moreover, under recent revisions to the FCA, any claim for reimbursement of a drug or device that results from an illegal kickback is "false or fraudulent" and is subject to a claim under the FCA.[223] (For a more complete treatment of the issues under the FCA, see chapter 12.)

Prescription Drug Marketing Act

Q 26.44   What is the Prescription Drug Marketing Act of 1987?

In 1987, Congress passed the Prescription Drug Marketing Act (PDMA) to regulate how prescription drugs are marketed and sold by many of the stakeholders in the drug supply chain. The PDMA amended the FDCA by:

1. banning the sale, purchase, or trade of (or the offer to sell, purchase, or trade) drug samples and drug coupons;

2.   restricting re-importation of prescription drugs to the manufacturer of the drug product or for emergency medical care;

3.   establishing requirements for drug sample distribution and the storage and handling of drug samples;

4.   requiring wholesale distributors of prescription drugs to be state-licensed and requiring the FDA to establish minimum standards for state licensing;

5.   establishing requirements for wholesale distribution of prescription drugs by unauthorized distributors;

6.   prohibiting, with certain exceptions, the sale, purchase, or trade of (or the offer to sell, purchase, or trade) prescription drugs that were purchased by hospitals or other healthcare entities, or donated or supplied at a reduced price to charities; and

7.   establishing criminal and civil penalties for PDMA violations.[224]

Q 26.44.1   Is it still permissible to provide free samples?

Yes, although manufacturers should be sure that samples are not later sold or billed to patients or to third-party payors. Pharmaceutical and device companies should train their sales associates to inform recipients that the samples are not to be sold. Further, all individual sample units and accompanying documentation should be clearly labeled stating that the units are samples and are not to be sold.[225]

Open Payments (Physician Payments Sunshine Act)

Q 26.45   What is the Physician Payments Sunshine Act?

The Physician Payments Sunshine Act (Sunshine Act) was enacted in 2010. The Sunshine Act requires certain group purchasing organizations and manufacturers that participate in federal healthcare programs to track payments or other transfers of value provided to physicians and teaching hospitals and report this information to CMS each year.[226] Group purchasing organizations and manufacturers also are required to report any ownership or investment interest held in the respective entity by a physician or a physician's immediate family member annually.[227] Failure to report the required information can carry hefty penalties from $1,000 to $100,000 for each payment, transfer of value, ownership, or investment interest not reported in accordance with the law.[228]

Q 26.45.1   Who is required to track and report information?

The Sunshine Act applies to manufacturers of a covered product that operate within the United States.[229] Entities under common ownership of such manufacturer, and wholesalers or distributors who hold title to a covered product, also may be subject to the Sunshine Act.[230] A group purchasing organization operating within the United States that purchases, arranges for, or negotiates the purchase of a covered product for entities or a group of individuals must also track and report information.[231]

Generally, a covered product is a drug, device, biological, or medical supply for which payment is available under Medicare or Medicaid programs.[232] Covered products include prescription drugs and biologics, as well as medical devices requiring premarket approval by or notification to the FDA.[233]

Q 26.45.2   Who is considered to be a physician?

Under the Sunshine Act, physicians include the following professionals: Doctor of Chiropractic Medicine, Doctor of Dentistry, Doctor of Medicine, Doctor of Osteopathy, and Doctor of Optometry.[234] However, medical residents are not included within the definition of physician.[235]

Q 26.45.3   What must be reported?

Generally, payments, other transfers of value, and any ownership or investment interest must be reported. Examples of reportable payments or other transfers include, but are not limited to the following: compensation for speaker or consulting services, gifts, food and beverage, entertainment, traveling and lodging, grants, royalties, and space rental or facility fees.[236]

In addition to payments and other transfers of value, group purchasing organizations and manufacturers also are required to report additional information, such as the full name of the physician or the teaching hospital, business address of the physician or teaching hospital, National Provider Identifier (if applicable), any professional license numbers, date of the transfer, and the nature of the payment or transfer.[237]

Q 26.45.4 What are considered reportable ownership and investment interests?

The Sunshine Act defines ownership or investment interests to include stocks and stock options, partnership shares, memberships in limited liability companies, loans, and bonds.[238] However, interest in a publicly traded security or mutual fund is not considered reportable ownership or investment interest.[239]

Q 26.45.5 Are there any exclusions to what must be reported?

CMS publishes a de minimis threshold for reporting each year on its website. Payments and other transfers of value under this threshold are excluded from the reporting requirement.[240] For the 2019 data collection period, the threshold for an individual payment or other transfer of value is $10.79 and the total aggregate annual threshold is $107.91.[241] This means that each payment or transfer of value under $10.79 is excluded from the reporting requirements. However, if the total amount of payments or value transferred to a physician or teaching hospital within a year exceeds the total annual threshold, then all payments or transfers made during the year must be reported.[242]

Further, the statute provides specific exclusions for the following items: product samples intended for patient use, educational materials that benefit patients, discounts, rebates, and any payment or transfers of value made to a physician within a personal relationship.[243]

Q 26.45.6   Must companies report information under both federal and state law?

Some states have their own reporting requirements that may be applicable to manufacturers. To the extent that state reporting requirements overlap with federal requirements, state law will be preempted unless certain exceptions apply.[244] This means that absent any exceptions, manufacturers would only need to report information under state law if the information is not already covered under federal law. For example, some states require reporting for payments or other transfers of value provided to other types of healthcare practitioners, which is broader than the current scope of the Sunshine Act.[245]

Pharmaceutical Pricing and Price Reporting

Introduction to the Pharmaceutical Distribution and Payment System

Q 26.46   What is the pharmaceutical supply chain?

The pharmaceutical supply chain refers to the series of transactions through which prescription medicines are delivered to patients. Generally, medications are: made by manufacturers; transferred to wholesale distributors; stocked at retail, mail order, and other types of pharmacies; and dispensed by the pharmacies to patients. In addition to manufacturers, wholesalers and pharmacies, the supply chain includes a number of entities that, while never taking physical possession of a prescription medication, still exert substantial influence over the distribution of, and payment for, medications. These entities are usually involved in the provision of prescription drug insurance coverage and include health plans, pharmacy benefit managers (PBMs), and the federal government.

Q 26.46.1   How does money flow through the pharmaceutical supply chain?

Underlying the physical distribution of branded prescription medications from manufacturers to pharmacies are three distinct payments directly based off a drug's wholesale acquisition cost or WAC.[246]

WAC, otherwise known as the drug's "list price," is the price at which a manufacturer lists its drugs for sale to wholesalers or other direct purchasers.[247] By statute, WAC does not include any prompt pay or other discounts, rebates or other price concessions that would reduce the cost of the medication.[248]

In the first transaction, manufacturers sell their drugs to wholesalers at negotiated discounted rates off of WAC.[249] Second, wholesalers contract with retail and mail-order pharmacies, who agree to purchase medications at WAC plus some negotiated percentage, netting wholesalers a small margin.[250] Third, pharmacies contract with health plans or PBMs (on behalf of their health plan clients) to establish reimbursement rates for the drugs they dispense to insured consumers.[251] The reimbursement rates PBMs negotiate with pharmacies are generally derived from a drug's list price.[252]

On the insurance or reimbursement side of the supply chain, patients pay premiums to health plans in exchange for a drug coverage benefit.[253] Health plans usually contract with PBMs to manage the plan's drug benefit. In this role, PBMs provide a number of services to their health plans' clients including: establishing a network of pharmacies to ensure beneficiary access to medications, handling claims adjudication and pharmacy payment, administering clinical programs to improve medication adherence, and most importantly, creating preferred drug lists or formularies that determine which medications in a particular therapeutic class the plan will cover and in what amount.[254]

PBMs manage their formularies according to a multi-step process designed to ensure that their clients' insureds have access to clinically appropriate products at competitive prices. Typically, formulary placement decisions are based on the stepwise consideration of the following factors: safety, efficacy, uniqueness, and net drug cost.[255] In an effort to lower a drug's net cost, and thereby secure placement on a PBM's formulary, manufacturers offer PBMs price concessions, in the form of rebates, off of their product's "list price." PBMs then pass all or a portion of this rebate on to their plan client.

Q 26.46.2   To what entities do manufacturers offer price concessions?

Manufacturers offer discounts, rebates and other price concessions to nearly every entity involved in both the physical distribution and reimbursement sides of the supply chain. Price concessions on the distribution side of the chain generally involve volume or prompt pay discounts offered by manufacturers to wholesalers or pharmacies. On the reimbursement side, manufacturers typically pay rebates to PBMs or directly to insurers (if the insurer does not contract with a PBM and manages its own drug benefits) to secure their product's placement on a formulary. Additionally, as discussed in more detail below, manufacturers are statutorily required to offer rebates to the government in order to participate in the Medicaid program.

Q 26.46.3   Are there any AKS risks involved with the manufacturer's offer of rebates to entities in the pharmaceutical supply chain?

Manufacturer discounts and rebates, if offered on products reimbursable by a federal healthcare program, must comply with the AKS. While the current version of the discount safe harbor shields properly disclosed manufacturer discount and rebate arrangements,[256] on January 31, 2019, the U.S. Department of Health and Human Services' (HHS) Office of the Inspector General (OIG) issued a proposed rule that sought to dramatically alter the scope of permissible conduct under the AKS.[257] Specifically, the proposed rule would eliminate safe harbor protection for rebates offered by manufacturers to PBMs and replace them with discounts provided to beneficiaries at the point of sale. To do so, the rule would:

- revise the existing discount safe harbor to prohibit the payment of discounts to plan sponsors under Medicare Part D, Medicaid managed care organizations, pharmacy benefit managers under contract with Part D sponsors, or Medicaid MCOs;[258]

- add a safe harbor for flat service fees from manufacturers to PBMs;[259] and

- add a safe harbor for point of sale reductions in price for prescription pharmaceutical products.[260]

Although the Trump administration officially withdrew the proposed rule on July 10, 2019,[261] similar legislation or rule making may be forthcoming as the administration remains committed to combatting rising drug costs.

Q 26.46.4   Are there any other risks associated with a manufacturer offering rebates or discounts to entities in the pharmaceutical supply chain?

State Attorneys General and the private plaintiffs' bar, in a series of class action lawsuits against insulin manufacturers,[262] have established a framework for alleging state consumer protection and Racketeer Influenced and Corrupt Organizations Act (RICO) violations against drug manufacturers that: (1) raise a drug's list price, (2) offer increasing rebates to PBMs for that drug, but nonetheless (3) keep the drug's net price relatively constant.[263] According to plaintiffs, PBMs base their formulary placement decisions of therapeutically equivalent drugs solely on manufacturer rebate offers. This practice incentivizes manufactures to raise the list prices of their drugs and use this price increase to offer PBMs larger rebates. Because manufacturers raise their list prices and PBM rebates in tandem, Plaintiffs assert that the drug's "real price" or "net price" (defined by plaintiffs as the price the health plan pays for the medication after applying all PBM rebates) remains constant.

Plaintiffs posit that the resulting disparity between the drug's inflated list price and its relatively static "real price" indicates that list prices no longer reasonably approximate the true price of prescription medications.[264] Since consumers expect a drug's list price to be the market price of the drug, plaintiffs conclude that manufacturers commit fraud whenever they publish these artificially inflated list prices and represent them as the drug's "true price."

Government Price Reporting

Q 26.47   What is government price reporting?

Government price reporting refers to a manufacturer's legal obligation to report certain sales and pricing data to either federal or state agencies. The major federal healthcare programs that impose price reporting requirements on manufacturers include:

- Medicaid;
- Medicare Part B;
- the 340B Program; and
- the Veterans Health Care Act pharmaceutical programs.

Failure to comply with these reporting requirements may result in:

- Termination of a manufacturer's agreement to participate in Medicaid;

- The obligation to refund to the government any overpayment, with interest, caused by the failure to accurately report the requisite pricing information;

- The imposition of civil monetary penalties—up to $10,000 per day[265]—at the NDC level;[266] and

- Liability under the federal civil False Claims Act, certain criminal statutes prohibiting false claims, and analogous state false claims laws.

The Medicaid Drug Rebate Program

Q 26.48   What is the Medicaid Drug Rebate Program?

Although classified as an optional benefit, all state Medicaid programs currently offer some form of outpatient prescription drug[267] coverage.[268] To partially offset the cost of providing prescription drug coverage, Congress enacted the Medicaid Drug Rebate Program (the "Program") under the Omnibus Budget Reconciliation Act of 1990.[269] The Program conditions Medicaid payment for a manufacturer's drug product(s) on the manufacturer entering into an agreement, known as a Medicaid National Drug Rebate Agreement, with the Secretary of the HHS.[270]

Pursuant to these rebate agreements, manufacturers agree to pay quarterly rebates to state Medicaid programs in exchange for the state's coverage of the manufacturer's products.[271] These rebates, which are calculated based on the prices manufacturers charge to wholesalers and retail pharmacies, ensure that Medicaid receives a net price for each drug that approximates the lowest or best price for which manufacturers sold that drug, inclusive of most discounts, rebates or other price concessions. The state then shares a portion of these rebates with the federal government.[272]

Q 26.48.1   How does the Medicaid Drug Rebate Program work?

Manufacturers are required to calculate and pay rebates on a quarterly basis to state Medicaid agencies pursuant to their Medicaid National Drug Rebate Agreements.[273] Although manufacturers retain ultimate responsibility for calculating their quarterly rebate payments,[274] in practice, CMS calculates the rebate amount based on regulatory formulas[275] and manufacturer-reported drug pricing and product data.[276] CMS then provides this information to the state, and the state invoices manufacturers for these rebates.[277]

The two primary components of the rebate calculation are the manufacturer's "average manufacturer price" (AMP) and the manufacturer's "best price" for a given drug.[278]

Q 26.48.2   What is AMP?[279]

AMP is defined, for a covered outpatient drug, as "the average price paid to the manufacturer for the drug in the United States by wholesalers for drugs distributed to retail community pharmacies and retail community pharmacies that purchase drugs directly from the manufacturer."[280] Accordingly, to calculate a drug's AMP a manufacturer averages the prices it received when selling a specific drug to:

- retail community pharmacies, including sales received by, paid by, or passed through to retail community pharmacies;[281]

- wholesalers[282] for drugs distributed to retail community pharmacies;[283] and

- other manufacturers who act as wholesalers for drugs distributed to retail community pharmacies[284] (collectively, "AMP-eligible sales").

Importantly, the prices used to calculate AMP must include certain "associated" manufacturer discounts or rebates, "which reduce the price received by the manufacturer for drugs distributed to retail community pharmacies."[285] As CMS explained, "it is the sales themselves, as well as the discounts, rebates, payment or financial transactions associated with the sales that are included in the AMP calculation."[286] Such rebates or discounts include, but are not limited to: cash discounts; free goods that are contingent on a purchase requirement; volume discounts; chargebacks; other financial incentives; and any administrative, distribution or other service fee that does not qualify as a bona fide services fee.[287]

Conversely, a number of common price concessions are excluded from the determination of AMP, such as:

- Sales, associated rebates, discounts, or other price concessions paid directly to insurers;[288]

- Customary prompt pay discounts extended to wholesalers;[289]

- Payments received from and rebates and discounts provided to pharmacy benefit manufacturers;[290]

- Free goods, not contingent upon any purchase requirement;[291]

- Manufacturer-sponsored drug discount card programs;[292]

- Manufacturer-sponsored programs that provide free goods, including but not limited to voucher or patient assistance programs;[293]

- Manufacturer-sponsored patient refund/rebate programs;[294] and

- Manufacturer copayment assistance programs.[295]

Q 26.48.3   What is best price?

Best price means "the lowest price available from the manufacturer during the rebate period to any wholesaler, retailer, provider,[296] health maintenance organization, nonprofit entity, or governmental entity in the United States in any pricing structure (including capitated payments[297]), in the same quarter for which the AMP is computed."[298] Accordingly, the best price for a specific covered drug is net of any discounts or rebates that "reduce the price of a drug," which are not otherwise excluded from the best price determination. Rebates or discounts that must be included in a drug's best price determination include: cash discounts, free goods that are contingent on any purchase requirement, volume discounts, customary prompt pay discounts, chargebacks, incentives, promotional fees, administrative fees, service fees (except bona fide service fees), distribution fees, and any other discounts or price reductions and rebates.[299]

Notably, much like the AMP determination described above, there are a number of price concessions excluded from a manufacturer's calculation of a drug's best price. Excluded price concessions include, but are not limited to:

- Manufacturer-sponsored drug discount card programs;[300]

- Manufacturer coupons to a consumer redeemed by a consumer, agent, pharmacy, or another entity acting on behalf of the manufacturer;[301]

- Manufacturer copayment assistance programs;[302]

- Manufacturer-sponsored patient refund or rebate programs;[303]

- Manufacturer-sponsored programs that provide free goods, including but not limited to vouchers and patient assistance programs;[304]

- Free goods, not contingent upon any purchase requirement;[305] and

- PBM rebates, discounts, or other financial transactions except their mail-order pharmacy's purchases or where such rebates, discounts, or other financial transactions are designed to adjust prices at the retail or provider level.[306]

Moreover, sales of a covered outpatient drug at a nominal price[307] are excluded from best price calculations if made to:

- A covered entity as described in section 340B(a)(4) of the Public Health Services Act;

- An Intermediate Care Facilities for Individuals with Intellectual Disabilities providing services identified at 42 C.F.R. § 440.150;

- A state-owned or operated nursing facility providing certain services identified at 42 C.F.R. § 440.155;

- A public or non-profit entity, or an entity based at an institution of higher learning whose primary purpose is to provide healthcare services to students of that institution, that provides family planning services; or

- A section 501(c)(3) entity exempt from tax under section 501(a) of the Internal Revenue Code of 1986 that provides the same services as a covered entity under section 340B(a)(4) of the Public Health Services Act.[308]

Q 26.48.4   How are Medicaid Drug Rebates calculated?

As explained above, the Medicaid Drug Rebate ("MDR") for covered outpatient drugs is calculated according to two formulas: one for brand name[309] drugs and a second for generic[310] drugs.[311]

Q 26.48.5   How is the MDR calculated for brand name drugs?

The MDR for a brand name drug has two components: the basic rebate amount and the "additional rebate" amount.[312] The basic rebate amount equals "the total number of units of each dosage form and strength paid for under the State plan in the rebate period"[313] multiplied by the greater of:

- The difference between the AMP and the best price for the dosage form and strength of the drug; or

- The AMP for the dosage form and strength of the drug multiplied by either 17.1% for a clotting factor or a drug approved exclusively for pediatric indications or 23.1% for all other brand name drugs.[314]

The additional rebate amount is an inflationary adjustment that is added to the basic rebate amount if the drug's AMP exceeds the increase in the Consumer Price Index for All Urban Consumers for the relevant time period.[315] The inflationary amount is meant to limit the increase in the net price of any drug to the rate of inflation.[316]

Q 26.48.6   How is the MDR calculated for generic drugs?

The MDR for generic drugs is calculated by multiplying 13% of that drug's AMP with "the total number of units of such dosage form and strength for which payment was made under the State plan for the rebate period."[317] Similar to brand drugs, an inflationary adjustment may be added to this rebate amount if the drug's AMP exceeds the increase in the Consumer Price Index for All Urban Consumers for the relevant time period.[318]

Q 26.48.7   What are a manufacturer's quarterly requirements under the MDR Program?

In addition to calculating and paying quarterly rebates to Medicaid, the MDR Program mandates that manufacturers submit quarterly pricing reports for covered outpatient drugs to CMS no later than thirty days after the end of a calendar quarter. These quarterly pricing reports must include the following information for each dispensed covered outpatient drug, identified by that drug's nine-digit NDC:

- The classification of the covered outpatient drugs (i.e., brand or generic);[319]

- The package size of the covered outpatient drugs dispensed to the beneficiary;[320]

- Quarterly AMP calculations;

- Best price calculations;

- Customary prompt pay discounts, which are to be reported as an aggregate dollar amount for each covered outpatient drug at the nine-digit NDC level, provided to all wholesalers in the rebate period; and

- Prices that fall within the nominal price exclusion, which are reported as an aggregate dollar amount and include all sales of single source and innovator multiple source drugs to the entities listed in 42 C.F.R. § 447.508(a) for the rebate period.[321]

These pricing reports must be certified by either the manufacturer's CEO, CFO, or an individual with the directly delegated authority to certify these reports on behalf of the CEO or CFO.[322] Lastly, manufacturers must report any revisions to these figures within twelve quarters from the quarter in which the reported figure was submitted.[323]

Q 26.48.8   What are a manufacturer's monthly requirements under the MDR Program?

Manufacturers must supplement their quarterly reports with monthly AMP reports.[324] The monthly AMP reports must be submitted to CMS within thirty days after the last day of the prior month.[325] The reports must include both the manufacturer's calculated monthly AMP and the manufacturer's monthly AMP unit data.[326] Revisions to monthly AMP reports must be received by CMS no later than thirty-six months after the report was initially due.[327] As with the quarterly reports, these monthly AMP reports must be certified by the manufacturer's CEO, CFO, or an individual with the directly delegated authority to certify these reports on behalf of the CEO or CFO.[328]

Q 26.48.9   What penalties do manufactures face if they do not report the required data?

Pursuant to section 1927(b)(3)(C)(i) of the Social Security Act, a manufacturer that fails to timely submit and certify its monthly or quarterly AMP data to CMS will be referred to OIG and may be subject to civil monetary penalties for each product not reported. It is OIG, and not CMS, that will investigate the matter and determine if civil monetary penalties are warranted.[329] Civil monetary penalties may be imposed if: (1) the manufacturer failed to provide the information required by the specified deadlines;[330] or (2) the manufacturer knowingly[331] provides any false information.[332] Additionally, manufacturers' failure to properly disclose accurate best price figures, i.e., to misrepresent the true amount of discounts given to purchasers, whether intentionally, recklessly, negligently or through clerical error, has been the basis of numerous False Claims Act *qui tam* actions.[333]

Medicare Part B

Q 26.49   What drugs does Medicare Part B cover?

Medicare Part B provides coverage for drugs and biologics administered by infusion or injection in a physician's office or hospital outpatient department as well as certain drugs furnished by suppliers. CMS reimburses providers for these drugs according to formulas that vary by drug type.[334] Generally, the reimbursement rate is equal to 106% of a drug's average sales price (ASP).[335]

Q 26.49.1   What is average sales price?

ASP is the average of nearly all sales a manufacturer has made to any purchaser in the United States over a given quarter for a particular drug. To calculate ASP, manufacturers divide the total sales of a drug (represented by a particular eleven-digit National Drug Code) by the total number of units sold by the manufacturer for the relevant time frame.[336] Similar to their AMP calculations, manufacturers include certain price concessions in their ASP determinations, such as:

- Volume discounts;

- Prompt pay discounts;

- Cash discounts;

- Free goods that are contingent on any purchase requirement;

- Chargebacks and rebates (other than rebates under the Medicaid program).[337]

Additionally, ASP excludes the following:

- prices charged to certain federal agencies including the Indian Health Service, the Department of Veterans Affairs, the Department of Defense, the Public Health Service, or a covered entity as defined by the Public Health Service Act;

- prices charged under the Federal Supply Schedule of the General Services Administration;

- prices used under a state pharmaceutical assistance program;

- any depot prices and single award contract prices;

- the prices negotiated from drug manufacturers for covered discount card drugs under an endorsed discount card program;

- prices with a Part D prescription drug plan;[338] and

- certain sales that are merely nominal in amount.[339]

Q 26.49.2   Are there any ASP reporting requirements?

Manufacturers must calculate their ASP on a quarterly basis and submit their ASP calculations to CMS within thirty days after the close of the quarter.[340] If data on the relevant price concessions is only available on a lagged basis, then the manufacturer must estimate the impact of its lagged price concessions on its ASP calculations.[341] Manufacturers do so according to the same methodology described above with regard a manufacturer's calculation of its monthly AMP data.[342]

Each report also must be certified by one of the following: the manufacturer's CEO; the manufacturer's CFO; or an individual who has delegated authority to sign for, and who reports directly to, the manufacturer's CEO or CFO.[343]

Q 26.49.3   What are the penalties for not reporting quarterly ASP data?

A manufacturer that fails to either timely or accurately submit its quarterly AMP data may be subject to civil monetary penalties.[344] If the Secretary determines that the manufacturer made a misrepresentation when reporting its ASP data, then "civil money penalty in an amount of up to $10,000 may be applied for each price misrepresentation and for each day in which the price misrepresentation was applied."[345] Additionally, a manufacturer's failure to account for all discounts offered to providers in their calculation of ASP, whether intentionally, recklessly, negligently or through clerical error, may also be the basis for potential FCA liability.[346]

340B Drug Pricing Program

Q 26.50   What is the 340B Drug Pricing Program?

The Veterans Health Care Act of 1992 established the 340B Discount Drug Pricing Program.[347] The 340B program is meant to help participating providers, referred to as covered entities, "stretch scarce Federal resources as far as possible, reaching more eligible patients and providing more comprehensive services."[348] To do so, section 340B of the Public Health Services Act instructs HHS to enter into pharmaceutical pricing agreements (PPA) with drug manufacturers.[349] When a drug manufacturer signs a PPA, it opts into the 340B Program and agrees that the prices it charges for covered outpatient drugs[350] to covered entities[351] will not exceed 340B ceiling prices.[352]

Although participation in the 340B program is optional, entering into a PPA is a precondition for a manufacturers' participation in the Medicaid Drug Rebate Program.[353] As a consequence, manufacturers generally participate in the MDR and 340B Programs.

Q 26.50.1   What is the ceiling price?

The 340B ceiling price is the maximum statutory price a manufacturer can charge a covered entity for the purchase of a covered outpatient drug.[354] The ceiling price is equal to a given drug's AMP from the preceding calendar quarter "for the smallest unit of measure" minus the drug's unit rebate amount (URA) for that quarter.[355] A drug's 340B URA is calculated by dividing that drug's average MDR amount by the drug's AMP.[356] Expressed formulaically, the ceiling price is calculated as follows:

$$AMP - \frac{Average\ MDR\ Amount}{AMP} = 340B\ Ceiling\ Price$$

Q 26.50.2   Do manufacturers have reporting requirements under the 340B program?

Pursuant to their PPAs, manufacturers must "furnish the Secretary with reports, on a quarterly basis, that include the price of each covered outpatient drug that is subject to the Agreement, that according to the manufacturer, represents the maximum price that covered entities may permissibly be required to pay for the drug," i.e., the drug's ceiling price.[357] Manufacturers fulfill this requirement by submitting quarterly pricing reports to the Health Resources and Services Administration (HRSA) through HRSA's 340B Office of Pharmacy Affairs Information System.[358] Manufacturer may only upload their pricing data during a two-week window that generally begins on the forty-fifth day of the quarter.[359]

Notable data points that a manufacturer must include in its quarterly report are, for each covered outpatient drug:

- AMP;
- 340B URA;
- Calculated ceiling price; and
- Package size and case package size.[360]

HRSA will compare the data it receives from manufacturers with the AMP and URA data it receives from CMS and the package size and case package size information it receives from First Databank.[361] HRSA will identify any discrepancies between the two data sets and ask the manufacturer to reconcile any differences.[362]

Q 26.50.3   What are the penalties for not reporting the applicable quarterly data?

Unlike AMP and ASP reporting, the failure to timely file 340B data does not result in the imposition of civil monetary penalties. Rather, a manufacturer faces civil monetary penalties only if it "knowingly and intentionally charges a covered entity more than the ceiling price."[363]

The Veterans Health Care Act

Q 26.51   What is the Veterans Health Care Act?

The Veterans Administration (VA) offers healthcare services to qualified veterans. Unlike the federal prescription drug benefit programs discussed above, the veterans' healthcare system is a closed system, meaning that the VA provides care directly to veterans through employed healthcare professionals. Consequently, the VA purchases pharmaceutical medications directly from manufacturers and dispenses these medications to veterans through its own pharmacies.

The Veterans Health Care Act[364] (VHCA), much like the MDR Program described above, requires that manufacturers offer statutorily defined rebates to the VA, the Department of Defense, the Public Health Services, and the Coast Guard (generally referred to as the "Big Four" federal agencies).[365] These rebates ensure that the Big Four federal agencies receive prices for pharmaceuticals that are commensurate with the lowest prices manufacturers charge commercial customers. To effectuate these statutory requirements, the VHCA mandates that manufacturers enter into a Master Agreement and Pharmaceutical Pricing Agreement with the VA.[366] If the manufacturer does not execute these agreements with the VA, it cannot participate in Medicaid program or the 340B program, and cannot sell its medications to Big Four federal agencies.[367]

Pursuant to these arrangements, manufacturers agree to make their "covered drugs"[368] available for sale on the Federal Supply Schedule (FSS).[369] Additionally, these contracts establish a maximum price that manufacturers may charge the Big Four federal agencies for covered drugs.[370] This cap is referred to as the Federal Ceiling Price (FCP).[371]

Q 26.51.1   How do you calculate the FCP?

In the first year of the contract, the federal ceiling price may not exceed 76% of a manufacturers' non-federal average manufacturer price (non-FAMP) less an "additional discount" meant to account for inflation.[372]

$$FCP \leq (Non\text{-}FAMP \times 0.76) - Additional\ Discount$$

In subsequent years, the FCP may not exceed the prior year's FCP increased by the percentage increase in the Consumer Price Index for all Urban Consumers (CPI-U) during the prior year.[373]

Q 26.51.2   What is non-FAMP?

The VHCA defines the non-FAMP as the weighted average price[374] of a single form and dosage unit of a covered drug, as identified by that covered drug's eleven-digit National Drug Code, that is paid by wholesalers in the United States to the manufacturer, taking into account any cash discounts or similar price reductions during that period, but not taking into account:

- Direct sales to the federal government; and

- Any prices found by the Secretary to be merely nominal in amount.[375]

Accordingly, much like AMP, non-FAMP is "net of all cash discounts, i.e. prompt payment and similar price reductions including rebates, free goods (excluding bona fide drug samples allowed by 21 U.S.C. § 353), chargebacks and incentive use based reductions or credits (where a buyer realizes a net reduced price with increased utilization of a product)."[376]

Q 26.51.3   What is the additional discount?

The additional discount represents the dollar amount of any increase in a product's price that exceeds the percentage increase in the CPI-U during the prior year.[377] To calculate the additional discount, a manufacturer must first determine the drug's "change in non-federal price" by subtracting the drug's non-FAMP for the third quarter of the current year with the non-FAMP from the third quarter of the prior year.[378] The resulting change in non-federal price is subtracted from the product of multiplying the non-FAMP from the third quarter of the prior year with the percentage increase in CPI-U.[379]

Change in Non-Federal Price =
Current Year Q3 Non-FAMP – Prior Year Q3 Non-FAMP

Additional Discount =
Change in Non-Federal Price – (Prior Year Q3 Non-FAMP × CPI-U %)

Q 26.51.4   What are the reporting requirements under the VHCA?

Under the VHCA, non-FAMP must be calculated and reported on both a quarterly and annual basis.[380] The non-FAMP quarterly reports are due within thirty days after the last day of the quarter[381] whereas the annual reports are due on or before November 15.[382]

Q 26.51.5   What are the penalties for not reporting the applicable quarterly data?

Pursuant to the Master Services Agreement and the Pharmaceutical Pricing Agreement, the VA may impose civil monetary penalties for each day the submission is late. Similarly, the manufacturer could be exposed to penalties if it knowingly provided false pricing data to the government. Lastly, a manufacturer that falsifies any of its non-FAMP calculations, either intentionally, recklessly, negligently or through clerical error, may be subject to liability under the FCA.

Notes to Chapter 26

1.   *See* U.S. DEP'T OF JUSTICE, EVALUATION OF CORPORATE COMPLIANCE PROGRAMS at 4–5 (2017), www.justice.gov/criminal-fraud/page/file/937501/download (an effective compliance program requires, among other things, effective identification and management of legal risks); *see also* U.S. DEP'T OF HEALTH & HUMAN SERVS., OFFICE OF INSPECTOR GEN., ET AL., PRACTICAL GUIDANCE FOR HEALTH CARE GOVERNING BOARDS ON COMPLIANCE OVERSIGHT (2015), https://oig.hhs.gov/compliance/compliance-guidance/docs/practical-guidance-for-health-care-boards-on-compliance-oversight.pdf (providing an in-depth discussion of how governing boards should discharge their compliance responsibilities).

2.   PHARM. RESEARCH & MFRS. OF AM., PRINCIPLES ON CONDUCT OF CLINICAL TRIALS: COMMUNICATION OF CLINICAL TRIAL RESULTS (Dec. 2014), http://phrma-docs.phrma.org/sites/default/files/pdf/042009_clinical_trial_principles_final_0.pdf.

3.   *See* 42 C.F.R. § 50.601 *et seq.*

4.   42 C.F.R. § 50.602.

5.   *Id.*

6.   *Id.* § 50.603.

7.   *Id.* § 50.602.

8.   *Id.* § 50.604.

9.   *Id.* § 50.603.

10.   *Id.*

11.   *Id.*

12.   *Id.* § 50.605(a).

13.   *Id.* § 50.603.

14.   *Id.* § 50.605(a).

15.   *Id.* § 50.606(a).

16.   *Id.*

17.   *Id.* § 50.606(c).

18.   *Id.* § 50.606(b).

19.   *Id.* § 50.607; 45 C.F.R. § 79.3.

20.   45 C.F.R. § 75.213.

21.   The National Science Foundation's *Grant Policy Manual* is available online at www.nsf.gov/pubs/manuals/gpm05_131/gpm05_131.pdf.

22.   *Developing Sponsored Research Agreements: Considerations for Recipients of NIH Research Grants and Contracts*, 23 NIH GUIDE, no. 25, July 1, 1994 [hereinafter NIH GUIDE]. The NIH published a proposed draft at 59 Fed. Reg. 55,673 (June 27, 1994).

23.   *Id.*

24.   Pub. L. No. 96-517, ch. 38, 94 Stat. 3015 (1980).

25.   NIH GUIDE, *supra* note 22.

26. The Department of Commerce regulations are at 37 C.F.R. pt. 401 and supersede applicable portions of 45 C.F.R. pts. 6 & 8.

27. NIH GUIDE, *supra* note 22.

28. *Id.*

29. *Id.*

30. *See* Financial Disclosure by Clinical Investigators, 21 C.F.R. § 54.1 *et seq.*

31. 21 C.F.R. § 54.4(a).

32. *Id.* § 54.2(e).

33. *Id.* § 54.2(a).

34. *Id.* § 54.2(b).

35. *Id.* § 54.2(c).

36. *Id.* § 54.2(f).

37. *Id.* § 54.4(b).

38. *Id.* § 54.5(b).

39. *Id.* § 54.4(c).

40. *Id.* § 54.5(c).

41. 45 C.F.R. pt. 46, subpt. A.

42. Agency for International Development (22 C.F.R. pt. 225); Department of Agriculture (7 C.F.R. pt. 1c); Consumer Product Safety Commission (16 C.F.R. pt. 1028); Department of Commerce (15 C.F.R. pt. 27); Department of Defense (32 C.F.R. pt. 219); Department of Education (34 C.F.R. pt. 97, subpt. A); Department of Energy (10 C.F.R. pt. 745); Department of Health and Human Services (45 C.F.R. pt. 46, subpt. A); Department of Housing and Urban Development (24 C.F.R. pt. 60); Department of Justice (28 C.F.R. pt. 46); Department of Veterans Affairs (38 C.F.R. pt. 16); Department of Transportation (49 C.F.R. pt. 11); Environmental Protection Agency (40 C.F.R. pt. 26); National Aeronautics and Space Administration (14 C.F.R. pt. 1230); and Central Intelligence Agency (Executive Order 12333).

43. 21 C.F.R. pt. 50 (protection of human subjects); 21 C.F.R. pt. 56 (Institutional Review Boards).

44. *See* Erin Williams, Federal Protection for Human Research Subjects: An Analysis of the Common Rule and Its Interactions with FDA Regulations and the HIPAA Privacy Rule, Congressional Research Service, Report for Congress (June 2, 2005).

45. 21 C.F.R. § 50.24.

46. 45 C.F.R. § 46.101(i).

47. 45 C.F.R. § 46.107(d) (HHS); 21 C.F.R. § 56.107(e) (FDA).

48. 21 C.F.R. pt. 54. See also the discussion above in this chapter of conflict-of-interest rules.

49. 45 C.F.R. § 46.101(h).

50. 21 C.F.R. § 312.120(a)(i).

51. *Id.* § 50.55(e) (FDA); 45 C.F.R. § 46.408(b) (HHS).

52. 45 C.F.R. § 46.408(c).

53. The official website of the International Conference on Harmonisation of Technical Requirements for Registration of Pharmaceuticals for Human Use is www.ich.org.

54. *See Mission, Harmonisation for Better Health*, ICH, www.ich.org/about/mission.html.

55. The guidance is published at 83 Fed. Reg. 8882 (Mar. 1, 2018) and is available at https://www.fda.gov/media/93884/download.

56. ICH E6, ch. 3.

57. *Id.* § 4.8.

58. *Id.* § 8.1.

59. WORLD MED. ASS'N, DECLARATION OF HELSINKI: ETHICAL PRINCIPLES FOR MEDICAL RESEARCH INVOLVING HUMAN SUBJECTS (Oct. 2013), www.wma.net/policies-post/wma-declaration-of-helsinki-ethical-principles-for-medical-research-involving-human-subjects/.

60. 45 C.F.R. § 46.116; 21 C.F.R. § 50.20.

61. 21 C.F.R. § 50.24(a)(1), (a)(4).

62. *Id.* § 50.24(a)(2), (a)(3).

63. *Id.* § 50.24(a)(5), (a)(6).

64. *Id.* § 50.24(a)(7).

65. *Id.* § 50.23(a).

66. *Id.* § 50.23(b).

67. 45 C.F.R. § 46.101(i).

68. *Id.* § 46.116(e)(3).

69. *Id.* § 46.116(f)(3).

70. *Id.* § 46.107; 21 C.F.R. § 56.107; Williams, *supra* note 44, at 2–3.

71. 45 C.F.R. § 46.108(b); 21 C.F.R. § 56.108(c).

72. 45 C.F.R. § 46.108(a)(3); 21 C.F.R. § 56.108(a).

73. 45 C.F.R. § 46.108(a)(4); 21 C.F.R. § 56.108(b).

74. Williams, *supra* note 44, at 3–4; 45 C.F.R. § 46.111; 21 C.F.R. § 56.109.

75. 45 C.F.R. § 46.110; 21 C.F.R. § 56.110(b).

76. 45 C.F.R. § 46.110(b)(2); 21 C.F.R. § 56.110(b).

77. 45 C.F.R. § 46.102(j); 21 C.F.R. § 56.102(i).

78. 45 C.F.R. § 46.103(a).

79. 21 C.F.R. § 312.8.

80. *Id.* § 312.8(c).

81. *Id.* § 312.8.

82. *Id.* § 312.320.

83. *Id.* § 312.305.

84. NCD for Routine Costs in Clinical Trials, Pub. L. No. 100-3 (July 9, 2007) (MEDICARE COVERAGE MANUAL § 310.1), http://www.cms.hhs.gov/ClinicalTrial Policies/ (follow "Current Policy—July 2007 NCD" hyperlink).

85. *Id.*

86. *Id.*

87. *Id.*

88. *Id.*
89. *Id.*
90. *Id.*
91. *See* 21 U.S.C. § 321(p).
92. *See* 21 C.F.R. § 312.
93. *Id.* § 312.23.
94. 21 C.F.R. § 314.50.
95. 21 C.F.R. § 314.92.
96. 21 C.F.R. § 314.94(a).
97. *See* Pub. L. No. 98-417 (1984).
98. 21 C.F.R. § 314.94(a).
99. 21 C.F.R. § 314.110.
100. FDA, Drug Applications for Over-the-Counter (OTC) drugs.
101. *See* 21 C.F.R. pt. 330.
102. *See* 21 C.F.R. § 207.20.
103. 42 U.S.C. § 262(i).
104. 42 U.S.C. pt. 262.
105. 21 U.S.C. § 321(g)(1).
106. 42 U.S.C. 262(a); 21 C.F.R. § 601.2.
107. *Id.*
108. 21 C.F.R. § 601.2.
109. 21 C.F.R. pt. 207.
110. 21 C.F.R. § 860.7(b).
111. 21 C.F.R. § 860.3(c)(1).
112. 21 C.F.R. § 860.3(c)(2).
113. 21 C.F.R. § 860.3(c)(3).
114. 21 C.F.R. § 814.20.
115. 21 C.F.R. § 814.42.
116. 21 C.F.R. § 814.44.
117. 21 U.S.C. § 360e(d)(2).
118. 21 C.F.R. § 814.45.
119. FDA, Policy for Device Software Functions and Mobile Medical Applications, Guidance for Industry and Food and Drug Administration Staff, issued Sept. 27, 2019, https://www.fda.gov/media/80958/download.
120. *Id.*
121. *Id.*
122. 42 U.S.C. § 282; FDA, Changes to Existing Medical Software Policies Resulting from Section 3060 of the 21st Century Cures Act, Guidance for Industry and Food and Drug Administration Staff, issued Sept. 27, 2019, https://www.fda.gov/media/109622/download.
123. FDA, Policy for Device Software Functions and Mobile Medical Applications, Guidance for Industry and Food and Drug Administration Staff, issued Sept. 27, 2019, https://www.fda.gov/media/80958/download.
124. *Id.*

125. *Id.*

126. 21 U.S.C. § 321(m).

127. United States v. Kordel, 335 U.S. 345, 350 (1948).

128. United States v. Urbuteit, 355 U.S. 355 (1948); *Kordel*, 355 U.S. at 345.

129. 21 C.F.R. § 202.1(*l*)(2).

130. *Id.*

131. *See* Wilson v. Frito-Lay N. Am., Inc., No. 12-1586, slip op. at 12–13 (N.D. Cal. Oct. 24, 2013) (describing FDA's practice in this regard).

132. 21 C.F.R. § 201.66.

133. 21 U.S.C. § 352(a), (c).

134. *Id.* § 352(f).

135. *Id.* § 331(a).

136. *Id.* § 333(a).

137. *Id.*

138. *Id.* § 333.

139. *Id.* § 332(a).

140. *Id.* § 334.

141. *Id.* § 352(n).

142. *See* 31 U.S.C. § 3729.

143. *See* Friedman v. Sebelius, 755 F. Supp. 2d 98 (D.D.C. 2010).

144. Transcript of Record at 10, United States v. Stevens, 771 F. Supp. 2d 556 (D. Md. 2011).

145. *See* 21 C.F.R. § 202.1(*l*)(1).

146. 21 U.S.C. § 352(n); 21 C.F.R. § 202.1(e)(1).

147. 21 C.F.R. § 202.1(e)(1).

148. *See* U.S. FOOD & DRUG ADMIN., GUIDANCE FOR INDUSTRY: BRIEF SUMMARY AND ADEQUATE DIRECTIONS FOR USE: DISCLOSING RISK INFORMATION IN CONSUMER-DIRECTED PRINT ADVERTISEMENTS AND PROMOTIONAL LABELING FOR PRESCRIPTION DRUGS (rev. Aug. 2, 2015), www.fda.gov/downloads/drugs/guidancecomplianceregulatoryinformation/guidances/ucm069984.pdf; *see also* Example of Fictional Highlights of Prescribing Information (Based on Proposed Physician Labeling Rule) Translated in Consumer-Friendly Language and Formatted for Use in Consumer-Directed Advertisement, www.fda.gov/downloads/Drugs/GuidanceComplianceRegulatory Information/Guidances/ucm069987.pdf (for mock Brief Summary); Example of Fictional Highlights of Prescribing Information (Based on Proposed Physician Labeling Rule), www.fda.gov/downloads/Drugs/GuidanceComplianceRegulatory Information/Guidances/ucm069985.pdf (for mock "Highlights" section).

149. 21 C.F.R. § 202.1(e)(1).

150. U.S. FOOD & DRUG ADMIN., GUIDANCE FOR INDUSTRY: CONSUMER-DIRECTED BROADCAST ADVERTISEMENTS (Aug. 1999), www.fda.gov/downloads/Drugs/Guidance ComplianceRegulatoryInformation/Guidances/UCM070065.pdf.

151. 21 C.F.R. § 202.1(e)(6).

152. *Id.* § 202.1(e)(7).

153. *Id.* § 202.1(e)(2)(1).

154. *Id.*

155. *Id.* § 202.1(e)(2).

156. *Id.* § 202.1(j)(4).

157. *Id.* § 202.1(j)(1).

158. *Id.* § 202.1(j)(2).

159. *Id.* § 202.1(j)(5).

160. *Id.* § 314.550.

161. 21 U.S.C. § 355(o).

162. U.S. FOOD & DRUG ADMIN., DRAFT GUIDANCE: GUIDANCE FOR INDUSTRY: DIRECT-TO-CONSUMER TELEVISION ADVERTISEMENTS—FDAAA DTC TELEVISION AD PRE-DISSEMINATION REVIEW PROGRAM at 2 (Mar. 2012), www.fda.gov/downloads/drugs/guidancecomplianceregulatoryinformation/guidances/ucm295554.pdf.

163. 21 C.F.R. § 314.81(b)(3).

164. *See* U.S. FOOD & DRUG ADMIN., GUIDANCE FOR INDUSTRY: FULFILLING REGULATORY REQUIREMENTS FOR POSTMARKETING SUBMISSIONS OF INTERACTIVE PROMOTIONAL MEDIA FOR PRESCRIPTION HUMAN AND ANIMAL DRUGS AND BIOLOGICS (Jan. 2014), www.fda.gov/downloads/Drugs/GuidanceComplianceRegulatoryInformation/Guidances/UCM381352.pdf.

165. U.S. FOOD & DRUG ADMIN., GUIDANCE FOR INDUSTRY: INTERNET/SOCIAL MEDIA PLATFORMS WITH CHARACTER SPACE LIMITATIONS—PRESENTING RISK AND BENEFIT INFORMATION FOR PRESCRIPTION DRUGS AND MEDICAL DEVICES (June 2014), https://www.fda.gov/media/88551/download.

166. 21 U.S.C. § 352.

167. *Id.* § 352(n) (prescription drug advertising); *id.* § 352(q), (r) (restricted medical devices).

168. *Id.* § 333(a).

169. *Id.*

170. *Id.* § 333.

171. *Id.* § 332(a).

172. *Id.* § 334.

173. Government Brief at 51, United States v. Caronia, No. 09-5006 (2d Cir. Oct. 8, 2010).

174. In 2017, the FDA published a lengthy defense of its skepticism toward promotion of off-label uses. *See* U.S. Food & Drug Admin., Memorandum: Public Health Interests and First Amendment Considerations Related to Manufacturer Communications Regarding Unapproved Uses of Approved or Cleared Medical Products (Jan. 2017); *see also* 82 Fed. Reg. 6367 (Jan. 19, 2017).

175. 21 C.F.R. § 312.7(a).

176. *See* U.S. FOOD & DRUG ADMIN., GUIDANCE FOR INDUSTRY: DISTRIBUTING SCIENTIFIC AND MEDICAL PUBLICATIONS ON UNAPPROVED NEW USES—RECOMMENDED PRACTICES (Feb. 2014), http://tinyurl.com/mqbn9zv.

177. 21 U.S.C. § 355(d).

178. *See* Decision in Washington Legal Foundation v. Henney, 65 Fed. Reg. 14,286 (Mar. 16, 2000). Adequate directions are "directions under which the layman can use a drug safely and for the purpose for which it is intended." 21 C.F.R. § 201.5.

179. *See* Decision in Washington Legal Foundation v. Henney, 65 Fed. Reg. 14,286 (citing United States v. Articles of Drug, 625 F.2d 665, 673 (5th Cir. 1980)).

180. 65 Fed. Reg. 14,286; 21 U.S.C. § 321(p)(1). "Intended use" is discussed at Q 26.39 *et seq.*

181. 21 C.F.R. § 201.128; *see also* 62 Fed. Reg. 64,074.

182. 21 C.F.R. § 201.128; 62 Fed. Reg. 64,074.

183. 21 U.S.C. § 352(f); 65 Fed. Reg. 14,286.

184. 21 C.F.R. § 201.128.

185. *Id.* § 801.4.

186. *See* Kolender v. Lawson, 461 U.S. 352 (1983); Skilling v. United States, 561 U.S. 358 (2010).

187. 42 U.S.C. § 1320a-7b(b).

188. *Id.*

189. *Id.*

190. PHARM. RESEARCH & MFRS. OF AM., CODE ON INTERACTIONS WITH HEALTHCARE PROFESSIONALS (July 2008) [hereinafter PhRMA Code], www.phrma.org/sites/default/files/108/phrma_marketing_code_2008.pdf.

191. Advanced Med. Tech. Ass'n, Code of Ethics on Interactions with Health Care Professionals (2020) [hereinafter AdvaMed Code], https://www.advamed.org/resource-center/advamed-us-code-ethics-final-eff-jan-1-2020 (the new version of the AdvaMed Code is effective January 1, 2020, and the current version is the 2009 version).

192. OIG Compliance Program Guidance for Pharmaceutical Manufacturers [hereinafter OIG Guidance], 68 Fed. Reg. 23,731, 23,734 (May 5, 2003).

193. *Id.*

194. *See* United States Statement of Interest at 2, United States v. Coloplast Corp., Civil Action No. 11-12131-RWZ, 2016 WL 4409272 (D. Mass. Aug. 8, 2016).

195. OIG Guidance, 68 Fed. Reg. at 23,738.

196. *See* OIG Advisory Opinion No. 06-16.

197. 42 C.F.R. § 1001.952.

198. AdvaMed Code, *supra* note 191, at 17.

199. AdvaMed Code, *supra* note 191, at 16 (examples of permissible items include modest meals, refreshments, and educational items).

200. OIG Guidance, 68 Fed. Reg. at 23,735.

201. PhRMA Code, *supra* note 190, at 9.

202. AdvaMed Code, *supra* note 191, at 20.

203. OIG Guidance, 68 Fed. Reg. at 23,735.

204. *Id.* at 23,736.

205. *Id.*

206. AdvaMed Code, *supra* note 191, at 13, 25.

207. PhRMA Code, *supra* note 190, at 9.

208. AdvaMed Code, *supra* note 191, at 13.

209. *Id.*

210. PhRMA Code, *supra* note 190, at 51.

211. AdvaMed Code, *supra* note 191, at 9.

212. *Id.*

213. *Id.*

214. *Id.* at 8.

215. PhRMA Code, *supra* note 190, at 19, 25.

216. AdvaMed Code, *supra* note 191, at 27.

217. *See* 42 U.S.C. § 1320a-7a(a)(5).

218. 31 U.S.C. § 3729.

219. *Id.* The False Claims Act is also discussed in chapters 12 and 25.

220. *See* 81 Fed. Reg. 42,491, 42,501 (June 30, 2016).

221. 15 C.F.R. § 6.3(a)(3).

222. *See* DEP'T OF HEALTH & HUMAN SERVS., OFFICE OF INSPECTOR GEN., CRITERIA FOR IMPLEMENTING SECTION 1128(B)(7) EXCLUSION AUTHORITY (Apr. 18, 2016), https:// oig.hhs.gov/exclusions/files/1128b7exclusion-criteria.pdf (risk of exclusion or burdensome monitoring requirements can be reduced by voluntarily disclosing violations).

223. *See* 42 U.S.C. § 1320a-7b(g).

224. This list includes the Prescription Drug Amendments' changes to the PDMA. *See* Pub. L. No. 102-353, 106 Stat. 941 (1992). The changes were to FDCA §§ 301, 303, 503, and 801 (21 U.S.C. §§ 331, 333, 353, and 381).

225. OIG Guidance, 68 Fed. Reg. at 23,739.

226. 42 C.F.R. § 403.904(a)(1).

227. 42 C.F.R. § 403.906(a)(1).

228. 42 C.F.R. § 403.912(a)–(b).

229. *Id.*

230. *Id.*

231. 42 C.F.R. § 403.902.

232. *Id.*

233. *Id.*

234. Ctrs. for Medicare & Medicaid Servs., *Glossary and Acronyms* (July 27, 2016), https://www.cms.gov/OpenPayments/About/Glossary-and-Acronyms.html# physician.

235. *Id.*

236. Ctrs. for Medicare & Medicaid Servs., *Natures of Payment* (Sept. 24, 2014), https://www.cms.gov/OpenPayments/About/Natures-of-Payment.html.

237. 42 C.F.R. § 403.904(c).

238. 42 C.F.R. § 403.902.

239. *Id.*

240. 42 C.F.R. § 403.904(h)(2).

241. Ctrs. for Medicare & Medicaid Servs., *Data Collection for Applicable Manufacturers and GPOs* (Sept. 6, 2018), https://www.cms.gov/openpayments/ program-participants/applicable-manufacturers-and-gpos/data-collection.html.

242. *See* 42 C.F.R. § 403.904(h)(2)(i).

243. 42 C.F.R. § 403.904(h).

244. 42 C.F.R. § 403.914.

245. *See* VT. STAT. ANN. tit. 18, § 4632. Starting January 1, 2022, the federal law will expand to include other types of healthcare providers, such as physician assistants, nurse practitioners, and certified nurse anesthetists. *See* Pub. L. No. 115-271, 132 Stat. 3894 (Oct. 24, 2018).

246. 84 Fed. Reg. 2340, 2341 (Feb. 6, 2019).

247. *Id.*

248. 42 U.S.C. § 1395w-3a(c)(6)(B).

249. 84 Fed. Reg. 2340, 2341 (Feb. 6, 2019).

250. *Id.*

251. *Id.*

252. Although the specifics of pharmacy reimbursement are outside the scope of this chapter, in our experience, the basis for these payments is typically "average wholesale price" or AWP. AWP is not a statutorily defined term, but is usually calculated as WAC + 20%. A pharmacy's reimbursement rate generally is a discount off of AWP plus a dispensing fee. The prices a pharmacy pays to acquire drug products, inclusive of discounts, rebates or other price concessions, is known as the pharmacy's "actual acquisition cost" (AAC). 42 C.F.R. § 447.502. State Medicaid program typically use AAC when calculating a pharmacy's reimbursement rates under fee-for-service Medicaid programs. *See* 42 C.F.R. § 447.518(a)(2).

253. Office of the Insurance Commissioner, *Washington State, Study of the Pharmaceutical Chain of Supply* 21–22 (June 2017), https://www.insurance.wa.gov/sites/default/files/2017-06/pharmacy-supply-chain-study_0.pdf; PHRMA, *Follow the Dollar: Understanding How the Pharmaceutical Distribution and Payment System Shapes the Prices of Brand Medicines* 3–4 (Nov. 2017), http://phrma-docs.phrma.org/files/dmfile/Follow-the-Dollar-Report.pdf.

254. *Id.*

255. Fed. Trade Comm'n, *Pharmacy Benefit Managers: Ownership of Mail-Order Pharmacies* 10–11 (2005), https://www.ftc.gov/sites/default/files/documents/reports/pharmacy-benefit-managers-ownership-mail-order-pharmacies-federal-trade-commission-report/050906pharmbenefitrpt_0.pdf.

256. See Q 26.46.3 for a more fulsome description of the AKS's discount safe harbor.

257. 84 Fed. Reg. 2340, 2343–44 (Feb. 6, 2019).

258. 84 Fed. Reg. 2340, 2347–48 (Feb. 6, 2019).

259. The safe harbor would require a written agreement between the PBM and manufacturer; compensation that is fixed, for fair market value and not based on the volume or value of referrals; and annual disclosures by the PBM to each of its health plan clients regarding the services performed by the PBM for the manufacturer. 84 Fed. Reg. 2340, 2349–50 (Feb. 6, 2019).

260. The safe harbor would require that the reduction be set in advance; be completely reflected in the price the pharmacy charges the beneficiary at the time of sale; and the total payment to the pharmacy be at least equal to the price agreed upon between the manufacturer of that drug and the Part D Plan or Medicaid MCO. 84 Fed. Reg. 2340, 2348–49 (Feb. 6, 2019).

261. Office of Mgmt. & Budget, Exec. Office of the President, OIRA Conclusion of EO 12866 Regulatory Review (July 10, 2019), https://www.reginfo.gov/public/do/eoDetails?rrid=129208.

262. Minnesota v. Sanofi-Aventis U.S. LLC, Novo Nordisk, Inc., & Eli Lilly & Co., No. 3:18-cv-14999-BRM-LHG (D.N.J. Oct. 16, 2018); *In re* Insulin Pricing Litig., No. 3:17-cv-00699-BRM-LHG (D.N.J. Mar. 29, 2018).

263. For instance, Manufacturers *A* and *B* each offer therapeutically equivalent drugs with a net cost of $90. Nonetheless, Manufacturer *A*'s drug has a higher list price ($110) than Manufacturer *B*'s drug ($100). According to plaintiffs, the difference in list price allows Manufacturer *A* to offer a larger rebate to PBMs than Manufacturer *B*, in this example, a $20 rebate instead of a $10. Plaintiffs believe that the larger rebate ensures that the PBM will place Manufacturer *A*'s drug on its formulary. In response, Manufacturer *B* may raise its drug's list price to $120 and offer a $30 rebate to the PBM. Plaintiffs conclude that this type of rebate based competition leads to ever increasing list prices while the drug's net price (the drug's "real price" according to plaintiffs) remains constant.

264. With regard to *In re Insulin*, the plaintiffs alleged that the list price of insulin increased by approximately 250% to 350% over the past fifteen years, while insulin's net price only rose by 3% to 57%.

265. 42 C.F.R. § 1003.1210(b).

266. *See* 81 Fed. Reg. 88,334, at 88,352–53 (Dec. 7, 2016). For instance, "a manufacturer that fails to provide the information required . . . for five separate NDCs may be penalized for each NDC, in an aggregate amount of not more than $50,000 per day for each day that the information is not provided. If, after 2 days, the manufacturer in this example submitted information for two of the missing NDCs, the manufacturer would be subject to an aggregate penalty of not more than $30,000 per day for each additional day that information was not provided for the remaining three NDCs." *Id.*

267. 42 C.F.R. § 447.502 defines covered outpatient drugs as "those drugs which are treated as a prescribed drug for the purposes of section 1905(a)(12) of the Act, a drug which may be dispensed only upon a prescription," which meet certain requirements enumerated by the definition, such as, being approved for safety and efficacy by the FDA. *See also* 42 U.S.C. § 1396r-8(k)(2)–(3). Typically covered outpatient drugs are those medications obtained by prescription and dispensed by pharmacies. 42 C.F.R. § 447.502. The term generally does not include drugs provided and billed pursuant to an inpatient hospital or nursing facility stay. *Id.*

268. U.S. Gov't Accountability Off., GAO-07-481T, Prescription Drugs: Oversight of Drug Pricing in 4 (Feb. 9, 2007); *see also* 42 U.S.C. §§ 1396a(a)(10), 1396a(a)(54), 1396d(a)(12).

269. Pub. L. No. 101-508.

270. 42 U.S.C. § 1396r-8(a)(1), (b)(1).

271. *See* 83 Fed. Reg. 12,770, 12,771 (Mar. 23, 2018).

272. *Id.*

273. 83 Fed. Reg. 12,770, 12,781 (Mar. 23, 2018).

274. 83 Fed. Reg. 12,770, 12,785 (Mar. 23, 2018).

275. *See generally* 42 C.F.R. § 447.509(c).

276. *See* U.S. Gov't Accountability Off., GAO-OEI-03-17-00100, Potential Misclassifications Reported by Drug Manufacturers May Have Led to $1 Billion in Lost Medicaid Rebates 1 (Dec. 2017).

277. 83 Fed. Reg. 12,770, 12,785 (Mar. 23, 2018).

278. *See* 42 C.F.R. § 447.509(a)(1)(i).

279. Note that the following discussion applies to the calculation of AMP for drugs dispensed by retail community pharmacies. A separate AMP must be calculated for inhalation, infusion, instilled, implanted, or injectable drugs (referred to in the relevant regulations as "5i" drugs) that are not generally dispensed through retail community pharmacies. The AMP of a 5i drug includes a number of transactions excluded from the retail AMP calculation. *Compare* 42 C.F.R. § 447.504(b), *with* 42 C.F.R. § 447.504(d) (setting forth AMP-eligible sales). Similarly, there are a number of exclusions from the 5i AMP calculation that are included when determining retail AMP. *Compare* 42 C.F.R. § 447.504(c), *with* 42 C.F.R. § 447.504(e) (identifying exclusions to AMP determinations). Although the sales included and excluded in the AMP determination vary, the two AMPs are calculated on a quarterly and monthly basis according to the same formulas discussed below.

280. 42 C.F.R. § 447.504(a).

281. *See id.* (defining "retail community pharmacy" as "an independent pharmacy, a chain pharmacy, a supermarket pharmacy, or a mass merchandiser pharmacy that is licensed as a pharmacy by the State and that dispenses medications to the general public at retail prices. Such term does not include a pharmacy that dispenses prescription medications to patients primarily through the mail, nursing home pharmacies, long-term care facility pharmacies, hospital pharmacies, clinics, charitable or not-for-profit pharmacies, government pharmacies, or pharmacy benefit managers").

282. 42 C.F.R. § 447.502 (defining "wholesaler" as "a drug wholesaler that is engaged in wholesale distribution of prescription drugs to retail community pharmacies").

283. A manufacturer may presume that all sales to a wholesaler that are not identified as going to purchasers other than retail community pharmacies are being made for drugs distributed to retail community pharmacies. 81 Fed. Reg. 5170, 5210 (Feb. 1, 2016).

284. 42 C.F.R. § 447.504(b)(1)–(3). Specifically excluded from the calculation of AMP are prices offered to federal agencies, such as Indian Health Services, the Department of Defense, and the Department of Veteran Affairs; sales to State Pharmaceutical Assistance Programs; sales outside the United States; sales directly to patients or certain providers, such as physicians, hospitals, hospices, clinics, long-term care providers, or other outpatient facilities; and sales to certain pharmacies, such as mail-order pharmacies, HMO or MCO operated pharmacies, not-for-profit pharmacies, or government-owned pharmacies.

285. 42 C.F.R. § 447.504(f); *see also* 77 Fed. Reg. 5318, 5327 (Feb. 2, 2012) ("[M]anufacturers are to include in the determination of AMP for a covered outpatient drug any other discounts, rebates, payments, or other financial transactions that are received by, paid by, or passed through to retail community pharmacies.").

286. 81 Fed. Reg. 5170, 5218 (Feb. 1, 2016).

287. 42 C.F.R. § 447.504(f); *see also* 42 C.F.R. § 447.502 (defining "bona fide service fee" as "a fee paid by a manufacturer to an entity that represents fair market value for a bona fide, itemized service actually performed on behalf of the manufacturer that the manufacturer would otherwise perform (or contract for) in the absence of the service arrangement, and that is not passed on in whole or in part to a client or customer of an entity, whether or not the entity takes title to the drug").

288. 42 C.F.R. § 447.504(c)(13).

289. 42 C.F.R. § 447.504(c)(15).

290. 42 C.F.R. § 447.504(c)(18).

291. 42 C.F.R. § 447.504(c)(24).

292. 42 C.F.R. § 447.504(c)(27) (only if the discount is passed on to the consumer, and the pharmacy, its agent or other AMP-eligible entity does not receive any price concession).

293. 42 C.F.R. § 447.504(c)(26) (only if the program is not contingent on any other purchase requirement; the full value the benefit is passed on to the consumer; and the pharmacy or any other AMP eligible entity does not receive any price concession).

294. 42 C.F.R. § 447.504(c)(28) (only if the full or partial refund or rebate is received by the patient for his or her out-of-pocket costs, and the pharmacy, agent, or other AMP eligible entity does not receive any price concessions).

295. 42 C.F.R. § 447.504(c)(29).

296. Provider is defined as "hospital, HMO, including an MCO, or entity that treats or provides coverage or services to individuals for illnesses or injuries or provides services or items in the provision of health care." 42 C.F.R. § 447.504(a).

297. Capitated payments refer to prospective periodic (generally monthly) per patient payments made by health plans. Capitated payments are usually based on the expected healthcare utilization of the patient.

298. 42 C.F.R. § 447.505(a). Specifically excluded from the determination of best price are, amongst other exclusions, prices charged to certain federal agencies, sales to State Pharmaceutical Assistance Programs, prices negotiated with Part D plan sponsors, prices charged to covered entities as defined by section 1927(a)(5)(B) of the SSA, and direct sales to patients. *See generally* 42 C.F.R. § 447.505(c)(1)–(19).

299. 42 C.F.R. § 447.505(d); 42 C.F.R. § 447.505(b).

300. 42 C.F.R. § 447.505(c)(8).

301. 42 C.F.R. § 447.505(c)(9).

302. 42 C.F.R. § 447.505(c)(10).

303. 42 C.F.R. § 447.505(c)(11).

304. 42 C.F.R. § 447.505(c)(12).
305. 42 C.F.R. § 447.505(c)(13).
306. 42 C.F.R. § 447.505(c)(14).
307. 42 C.F.R. § 447.502 (defining nominal price as "a price that is less than 10 percent of the average manufacturer price in the same quarter for which the AMP is computed").
308. 42 C.F.R. § 447.508(a)(1)–(5).
309. 42 C.F.R. § 447.504 (defining "brand name drug" as "single source or innovator multiple source drug").
310. 42 C.F.R. § 447.504 (defining "authorized generic drug" as an FDA-approved drug that is not a brand name drug).
311. *Compare* 42 C.F.R. § 447.509(a)(1), *with* 42 C.F.R. § 447.509(a)(6).
312. 42 C.F.R. § 447.509(a)(3). There exists a separate rebate methodology for drugs that are considered to be line extensions of brand drugs that are in an oral solid dosage form. *See generally* 42 C.F.R. § 447.509(a)(4).
313. 42 C.F.R. § 447.509(a)(1)(i).
314. 42 C.F.R. § 447.509(a)(1)(ii).
315. *See* 42 C.F.R. § 447.509(a)(2).
316. *Id.*
317. 42 C.F.R. § 447.509(a)(6).
318. Pub. L. No. 114-74.
319. U.S. Gov't Accountability Off., GAO-OEI-03-17-00100, Potential Misclassifications Reported By Drug Manufacturers May Have Led to $1 Billion in Lost Medicaid Rebates 1 (Dec. 2017).
320. 83 Fed. Reg. 12,770, 12,785 (Mar. 23, 2018).
321. 42 C.F.R. § 447.510(a)(1)–(4).
322. 42 C.F.R. § 447.510(e).
323. 42 C.F.R. § 447.510(b).
324. 42 C.F.R. § 447.510(d). This monthly AMP data is used by CMS to set federal upper limits for certain multiple source drugs. *See* 42 C.F.R. § 447.514(b).
325. *Id.*
326. 42 C.F.R. § 447.510(d)(6) (monthly AMP unit data means "total number of units that are used to calculate the monthly AMP in the same unit type as used to compute the AMP").
327. 42 C.F.R. § 447.510(d)(3).
328. 42 C.F.R. § 447.510(e).
329. 81 Fed. Reg. 5276.
330. 42 C.F.R. § 1003.110 defines "knowingly" as "a person, with respect to an act, has actual knowledge of the act, acts in deliberate ignorance of the act, or acts in reckless disregard of the act, and no proof of specific intent to defraud is required."
331. 42 C.F.R. § 1003.1200(b)(1).
332. 42 C.F.R. § 1003.1200(b)(2).

333. *See, e.g.*, Press Release, Dep't of Justice, GlaxoSmithKline to Plead Guilty and Pay $3 Billion to Resolve Fraud Allegations and Failure to Report Safety Data (July 2, 2012), https://www.justice.gov/opa/pr/glaxosmithkline-plead-guilty-and-pay-3-billion-resolve-fraud-allegations-and-failure-report.

334. *See generally* 42 C.F.R. § 414.904. Preventive vaccines, certain blood products, radiopharmaceuticals in physician offices, and compounded drug are examples of drugs paid for under alternate methodologies.

335. 42 C.F.R. § 414.904(a).

336. 42 C.F.R. § 414.804(a).

337. 42 C.F.R. § 414.804(a)(2)(A)–(E).

338. 42 C.F.R. § 414.804(a)(4)(i) (citing 42 U.S.C. § 1396r-8(c)(1)(C)(i)).

339. 42 C.F.R. § 414.804(a)(4)(ii) (citing 42 U.S.C. § 1396r-8(c)(1)(C)(ii)(III)). The nominal value exclusion works in the same way as the nominal value exclusion described above with regard to a manufacturer's calculation of best price under the MDR Program, i.e., it excludes nominal value sales, which are sales that are less than 10% of a manufacturer's ASP, that are made to the statutorily enumerated entities listed at 42 U.S.C. § 1396r-8(c)(1)(D)(i)(I)–(VI).

340. 42 C.F.R. § 414.804(a)(5).

341. *See generally* 42 C.F.R. § 414.804(a)(3).

342. 42 C.F.R. § 414.804(a)(3)(iv).

343. 42 C.F.R. § 414.804(a)(7).

344. 42 C.F.R. § 414.806.

345. *Id.*

346. *See, e.g.*, Press Release, Dep't of Justice, Sanofi US Agrees to Pay $109 Million to Resolve False Claims Act Allegations of Free Product Kickbacks to Physicians (Dec. 19 2012) ("The settlement also resolves allegations that Sanofi US submitted false average sales price (ASP) reports for Hyalgan that failed to account for free units distributed contingent on Hyalgan purchases. The government alleges that the false ASP reports, which were used to set reimbursement rates, caused government programs to pay inflated amounts for Hyalgan and a competing product.").

347. Pub. L. No. 102-585, § 602.

348. H.R. REP. NO. 102-384(II), at 12 (1992).

349. 42 U.S.C. § 256b(a)(1); *see* 42 C.F.R. § 10.2.

350. A "covered outpatient drug" has the same meaning under the 340B program as it does under the Medicaid Drug Rebate Program. *See* 42 C.F.R. § 10.3 (citing 42 U.S.C. § 1396r-8(k)(2)).

351. A "covered entity" is a defined term that includes federally funded clinics and hospitals that furnish care to large numbers of underserved or vulnerable individuals. *See* 42 U.S.C. § 256b(a)(4) (listing other types of covered entities).

352. *Id.*

353. 83 Fed. Reg. 12,770, 12,771 (Mar. 23, 2018).

354. 42 C.F.R. § 10.3.

355. 42 C.F.R. § 10.10(a).

356. 42 U.S.C. § 256b(a)(2)(i).

357. HRSA, Template 340B Drug Pricing Program Pharmaceutical Pricing Agreement Addendum § 1, https://www.hrsa.gov/sites/default/files/hrsa/opa/pdf/ppa-addendum-example.pdf.

358. HRSA, 340B Manufacturer Update (Dec. 2018), https://www.hrsa.gov/opa/updates/2018/december.html.

359. HRSA will send an email alert to the manufacturers notifying them that the two-week reporting window is open. HRSA, 340B Pricing Program: FAQs (Jan. 2019), https://www.hrsa.gov/opa/faqs/index.html.

360. HRSA, 340B Manufacturer Update (Dec. 2018), https://www.hrsa.gov/opa/updates/2018/december.html. First Data Bank is a third-party commercial data broker which tracks information relating to prescription medications.

361. *Id.*

362. *Id.*

363. 42 C.F.R. § 10.11.

364. Pub. L. No. 102-585, 106 Stat. 4943 (1992).

365. *See generally* 38 U.S.C. § 8126(a)–(b).

366. 38 U.S.C. § 8126(a)(2).

367. 38 U.S.C. § 8126(a)(4); *see also* 83 Fed. Reg. 12,770, 12,771 (Mar. 23, 2018).

368. 38 U.S.C. § 8126(h)(2) (defining covered outpatient drug to include innovator multiple source drugs, single source drugs and biologics).

369. 38 U.S.C. § 8126(a)(2).

370. *Id.* The VA guidelines permit pharmaceutical manufacturers to choose either a single or dual pricing model under these agreements. In a single pricing agreement, all FSS purchasers (which include the Big Four federal agencies and numerous other governmental agencies) may buy the manufacturer's products at the drug's FCP. Under a dual pricing agreement, the manufacturer sets two prices: the FCP for the Big Four, and a FSS list price for all other government agencies. The FSS list price for all other government agencies is a negotiated price where "the Government will seek to obtain the offeror's best price (the best price given to the most favored customer). However, the Government recognizes that the terms and conditions of commercial sales vary and there may be legitimate reasons why the best price is not achieved." 42 C.F.R. § 538.270-1(b).

371. 38 U.S.C. § 8126(h)(2).

372. 38 U.S.C. § 8126(a)(2).

373. 38 U.S.C. § 8126(d)(1).

374. 38 U.S.C. § 8126(h)(5). *See also* 38 U.S.C. § 8126(h)(5) (defining "weighted average price" as "the sum of the products of the average price per package unit of each quantity of the drug sold during the period and the number of package units of the drug sold during the period; divided by the total number of package units of the drug sold during the period").

375. 38 U.S.C. § 8126(h)(5).

376. *See* VA Master Agreement, § II(B)(7).

377. *See* 38 U.S.C. § 8126(c).

378. 38 U.S.C. § 8126(h)(1).
379. 38 U.S.C. § 8126(c).
380. 38 U.S.C. § 8126(e).
381. 38 U.S.C. § 8126(e)(1)(B).
382. 38 U.S.C. § 8126(e)(1)(A).

27

HIPAA Security and Privacy

Shannon B. Hartsfield

Health information privacy is a topic that affects every individual and many corporations, including those that are not in the healthcare industry. Federal regulations[1] implementing the Health Insurance Portability and Accountability Act of 1996 (HIPAA)[2] govern a subset of health data and specify how health data of certain patients or health plan enrollees may be used, disclosed, or retained. These regulations affect health plans, most healthcare providers, sponsors of self-insured health plans, and a number of other organizations and entities. Every entity that handles such information should be aware of these federal privacy and security rules. This chapter focuses on what compliance officers and in-house counsel should know about HIPAA's Privacy Rule and Security Rule (the "HIPAA Rules"), discusses the types of entities that are required to comply with HIPAA, and outlines some fundamental compliance activities that entities should undertake or periodically review and audit.

In 2009, Congress passed the American Recovery and Reinvestment Act. A portion of this act is known as the Health

Information Technology for Economic and Clinical Health (HITECH) Act.[3] The HITECH Act and its implementing regulations[4] made several changes to HIPAA. For example, it created an obligation to notify individuals if the privacy or security of their individually identifiable health information is compromised. The Department of Health and Human Services (HHS) must also receive notice of breaches, and the media must be notified in certain cases. The HITECH Act increases penalties for violations of HIPAA. These penalties can exceed $1.7 million for multiple violations of a particular requirement in a calendar year. The HITECH Act also gives state attorneys general the power to bring enforcement actions, and included new restrictions on selling information.

One of the more significant changes brought about by the HITECH Act is the fact that it broadened HIPAA's scope to apply to a greater number of individuals and entities. The HITECH Act made it clear that individuals can be held liable for HIPAA violations. Additionally, the HITECH Act expanded obligations imposed on business associates. Final regulations regarding those business associate requirements became enforceable in 2013.[5] HIPAA still does not apply to all health data, however. Because it only applies to certain covered entities and business associates, health information held by medical app developers and others may be subject to Federal Trade Commission regulations and various state laws instead, rather than HIPAA.

Applicability of HIPAA

Q 27.1 Who must comply with HIPAA?

HIPAA applies to "covered entities." Many of HIPAA's requirements also extend to "business associates" and "subcontractors" of those business associates.

Covered entities include health plans, healthcare clearinghouses, and most healthcare providers when they transmit protected health information (PHI) in connection with certain standard electronic transactions (such as payment or claims attachments).[6] (PHI is discussed in more detail at Q 27.2 below.) Under the HITECH Act, business associates and subcontractors must comply with particular provisions of the HIPAA rules.[7]

On January 25, 2013, the U.S. Department of Health and Human Services' Office for Civil Rights published a final rule, sometimes referred to as the "megarule"[8] or "omnibus rule,"[9] expanding many of HIPAA's requirements to business associates and their subcontractors. A business associate includes an entity that, on behalf of a covered entity or organized healthcare arrangement, "creates, receives, maintains, or transmits protected health information." The definition also specifically includes health information organizations, entities that offer personal health records on behalf of a covered entity, and subcontractors that create, receive, maintain, or transmit PHI on behalf of a business associate.[10]

Q 27.1.1   What is meant by "health plan"?

A "health plan" means an individual or group plan that provides or pays the cost of medical care, and includes group health plans, health insurance issuers, HMOs, and certain other plans and government programs.[11] A health plan does not include certain policies, plans, or programs that pay for "excepted benefits."[12] These excepted benefits include, among other things, coverage for accident or disability income insurance, workers' compensation insurance, and automobile liability or medical payment insurance.[13]

Covered Entities

Q 27.1.2   Are employers considered covered entities?

Although employers as such are not covered entities,[14] an employer's group health plan, including a welfare plan governed by ERISA that pays health benefits, is a covered entity; therefore, employers, especially those with self-insured group health plans, will need to take steps to ensure that those health plans comply with HIPAA. While some employers rely on their third-party administrators for HIPAA compliance, the employer, if it is a sponsor of a self-insured plan, flexible spending account, health savings account, or certain employee assistance plans, must also make sure that the plan is using and disclosing PHI in accordance with HIPAA.

With certain exceptions, group health plans, if they are going to disclose PHI to the plan sponsor, must ensure that the plan documents are amended to restrict how that plan sponsor can use and disclose the information.[15] The plan documents need not be amended if the group health plan, health insurance issuer, or HMO is disclosing only summary information to the sponsor for purposes of obtaining premium bids from health plans or modifying, amending, or terminating the group health plan.[16] The health plan may disclose enrollment and disenrollment information to the plan sponsor as well.[17] Summary information includes information that summarizes claims history, claims, expenses, or types of claims experienced by covered individuals, and from which all identifiers have been removed, except a five-digit ZIP code.[18] If the plan sponsor needs other PHI, the plan documents must contain a number of specific privacy protections outlined in the regulation.[19] Plan sponsors with fully insured plans should make sure that third parties, such as brokers, are not obtaining PHI on behalf of the plan, other than enrollment, disenrollment, and summary data. If they are, then it may trigger significant additional HIPAA compliance obligations for the plans.

Business Associates

Q 27.1.3   What is a business associate?

A "business associate" is a person or entity that, on behalf of a covered entity, creates, receives, maintains, or transmits PHI for a function or activity regulated by the HIPAA Rules.[20] Business associates include a wide variety of individuals and entities, including billing services, health information organizations, e-prescribing gateways, personal health record vendors that operate on behalf of a covered entity, practice and medical management companies, third-party administrators, and even lawyers and accountants.

A business associate also includes a subcontractor that creates, receives, maintains, or transmits PHI on behalf of the business associate.[21]

What Is a Covered Entity?

Example 1. ACME Corp. operates a continuing care retirement community where residents receive long-term care in exchange for an up-front entrance fee and monthly service fee. ACME Corp. does not do any Medicare or Medicaid billing, nor does it transmit PHI electronically in connection with one of the "standard transactions" listed in HIPAA. ACME Corp. is licensed by the agency in its state that regulates insurers. ACME Corp. is authorized to engage in the business of insurance only for the purpose of selling its continuing care retirement community contracts. ACME Corp. would not be a covered healthcare provider under HIPAA because it does not engage in standard transactions. It is likely, however, that ACME Corp. would be covered under HIPAA as

---

a "health plan" because it meets HIPAA's definition of a "health insurance issuer."

Example 2. Newco has a number of self-insured employee benefit plans, including a health plan. Newco's health plan is a covered entity; therefore, Newco must ensure that its health plan, as a covered entity, complies with HIPAA, and that PHI held by that plan is not used for its other benefit plans (absent compliance with certain HIPAA exceptions, or patient authorization). Newco itself would not be a covered entity unless, aside from its self-insured employee health plan, it meets HIPAA's definition of a health plan, a covered healthcare provider, or a healthcare clearinghouse.

Subcontractors

Q 27.1.4   Does HIPAA apply to business associates and their subcontractors?

Prior to the HITECH Act, HIPAA allowed covered entities to disclose PHI to business associates as long as written, HIPAA-compliant business associate agreements were in place. If a business associate failed to comply with an agreement, the business associate may have been guilty of a breach of contract, but the business associate was not directly subject to HIPAA. That changed with the HITECH Act, which makes business associates subject to many of HIPAA's requirements. The HITECH Act became effective on February 17, 2010, and final rules implementing many provisions of the HITECH Act became enforceable on September 23, 2013.

HIPAA's provisions regarding administrative, physical, and technical safeguards for PHI "shall apply to a business associate of a covered entity in the same manner that such sections apply to the covered entity."[22] Business associates must also document their policies and procedures relating to compliance with these requirements.[23] Business associates must also have written, HIPAA-compliant agreements with their subcontractors that also fall within HIPAA's definition of a business associate.[24] Covered entities can be business associates of other covered entities. A healthcare provider would not be a business associate just because a covered entity makes disclosures to the provider for treatment purposes.[25]

What Is a Business Associate?

Example 1. XYZ, Inc. provides disease management services to health plans. XYZ, Inc. does not transmit PHI electronically in connection with standard transactions, nor is it an individual or group plan that provides or pays for the cost of medical care. Instead, XYZ, Inc. assists health plans with their case management, utilization review, and other healthcare operations functions. XYZ, Inc. requires access to the health plans' PHI in order to perform these functions. XYZ, Inc. is a business associate.

Example 2. ABC, Inc. provides software used by hospitals to manage certain medical records and occasionally needs access to the hospitals' PHI to assist with troubleshooting, system setup, or other functions. ABC, Inc. is a business associate.

Example 3. ACME Corporation provides certain recordkeeping and other administrative functions to XYZ, Inc., the disease management company referenced in Example 1. In order to provide services to XYZ, Inc., ACME needs access to PHI that XYZ, Inc. receives from its covered entity clients. ACME Corporation is a business associate and a subcontractor.

Example 4. Dr. Smith is on the medical staff of the hospital. The hospital and the medical staff are part of an "organized health care arrangement." In her role on the medical staff, Dr. Smith sometimes provides input on administrative matters. Dr. Smith is not a business associate merely by virtue of the functions or activities she engages in for the organized healthcare arrangement as a member of the medical staff.

Privacy Overview

Q 27.2   What is the Privacy Rule?

HIPAA's Privacy Rule[26] is a set of federal regulations that restrict the use and disclosure of PHI, and provide patients with certain rights, including the right to access and amend medical information.

Protected Health Information (PHI)

Q 27.2.1   What is PHI?

"Protected health information" includes individually identifiable health information transmitted or maintained in any form or medium.[27] Individually identifiable health information is information that identifies the individual and is created or received by a healthcare provider, health plan, employer, or healthcare clearinghouse, and relates to the past, present, or future payment for the provision of healthcare to the individual.[28] It includes information that a layperson may not consider to be health-related, including demographic information, email addresses, and Internet protocol (IP) address numbers.

Q 27.2.2   How are use and disclosure of PHI restricted by the Privacy Rule?

Generally, absent an individual's written authorization, PHI may be used and disclosed only for purposes relating to treatment, payment, or healthcare operations,[29] or as required by law.[30] In order to comply with the Privacy Rule, covered entities must develop appropriate administrative, technical, and physical safeguards relating to PHI.

Security Overview

Q 27.3   What is the Security Rule?

The Security Rule, which became enforceable for most covered entities in April 2005, governs electronic protected health information (ePHI).

Electronic Protected Health Information (ePHI)

Q 27.3.1   What is considered ePHI?

Electronic PHI is individually identifiable health information transmitted or maintained in electronic media.[31] The Security Rule applies to ePHI that is stored or at rest, as well as PHI that is transmitted. The rule does not cover communication of information that is not in electronic form prior to transmission, such as person-to-person telephone calls, videoconferencing, paper-to-paper faxes, and voicemail messages.

Q 27.3.2   What are covered entities and business associates required to do under the Security Rule?

Covered entities and business associates must comply with four primary requirements:

(a) Ensure the confidentiality, integrity, and availability of all ePHI created, received, maintained, or transmitted;

(b) Protect against reasonably anticipated integrity or security threats or hazards;

(c) Protect against reasonably anticipated use or disclosures of ePHI that are not allowed or required under the Privacy Rule; and

(d) Ensure workforce compliance.

When it designed the Security Rule, HHS had as one of its goals to "frame the standards in terms that are as generic as possible and which, generally speaking, may be met through various approaches or technologies."[32]

HIPAA Compliance

Q 27.4   As a covered entity or a business associate, where do we begin when approaching compliance measures?

You should conduct a documented risk analysis and risk mitigation plan, and develop policies and procedures to comply with HIPAA's requirements. Your workforce members must be trained on those policies and procedures. You should design your security compliance program in light of its size, complexity, technical infrastructure, and probability of risk to critical PHI.[33] The National Institute of Standards and Technology has developed a HIPAA Security Toolkit application[34] to help organizations assess and understand HIPAA's security requirements. Likewise, HHS has useful online resources that provide basic information about various HIPAA-related topics, including numerous "frequently asked questions."[35] HHS has also developed an audit protocol that serves as a useful checklist of the major requirements of the HIPAA Rules.[36]

Risk Analysis

Q 27.4.1   What does a risk analysis involve?

Under the Security Rule, a risk analysis involves an accurate and thorough assessment of the potential risk and vulnerabilities to the integrity, confidentiality, and availability of ePHI.[37] An assessment of risks under the Privacy Rule should involve analyzing:

- how PHI flows into, through, and out of the organization;
- where it is stored;
- how it is used;
- who receives it; and
- why it is disclosed.

Conducting a risk analysis is important not only for entities just starting business, but also for existing entities that want to improve their privacy and security compliance.

On March 28, 2014, HHS released a tool that could be used by covered entities to conduct a "security risk assessment."[38] This tool, designed for "small to medium sized offices,"[39] contains a number of questions and enables a covered entity to assess and document the security risks that their organizations may face under the HIPAA Security Rule.

Once an entity identifies and assesses its risks, HIPAA also requires that the entity take measures to reduce those risks and vulnerabilities to a reasonable and appropriate level.[40] The entity's risk mitigation efforts must be geared toward ensuring the confidentiality, integrity, and availability of all ePHI the entity creates, receives, maintains, or transmits. This requires protecting against reasonably anticipated hazards and threats, as well as reasonably anticipated impermissible uses or disclosures, and ensuring workforce compliance.[41] Risk mitigation efforts must be documented.

Assigned Security/Privacy Responsibility

Q 27.4.2   Who oversees these compliance tasks?

Under the Privacy Rule and Security Rule, covered entities must appoint individuals to serve as privacy[42] and security officials.[43] Business associates are also required to appoint a security official[44] and should strongly consider appointing a privacy official if the business associate will be handling any privacy-related responsibilities on behalf of a covered entity. These officials can assist the business associate in fulfilling its privacy-related obligations. These individuals will oversee compliance with standards and specifications, as well as develop and implement policies and procedures to protect PHI.

Key Documents

Q 27.5   What are some of the key documents that a covered entity or business associate needs?

1.   Risk analysis and risk mitigation plan

Covered entities and business associates must have documentation of their risk analysis, as well as their plan to mitigate those risks. The Office for Civil Rights routinely requests a copy of the risk analysis when conducting compliance investigations.

2.   Policies and procedures

Every entity that handles PHI needs written policies and procedures to protect the data.[45] The Security Rule indicates that entities may change their policies and procedures at any time, provided that those changes comply with the regulations and are documented.[46] Policies and procedures must be retained six years from the date they were created or six years from the date they were last in effect, whichever is later.[47]

A critical aspect of a privacy and security compliance program is employee training. Employees must be trained not only on HIPAA's general requirements, but on the entity's actual policies and procedures.[48] Entities must document this training.

On April 7, 2014, the Office for Civil Rights publicized the availability of computer-based training modules it developed to help covered entities comply with the privacy, security, and breach notification rules.[49]

3.   Business associate agreements

Both the Security Rule and the Privacy Rule impose specific requirements for the written agreements between covered entities and business associates. For example, the Security Rule requires these agreements to provide that the business associate will implement administrative, physical, and technical safeguards to protect ePHI.[50] The Privacy Rule lists numerous specific provisions that the contract must contain.[51] The HITECH Act requires that the additional provisions of the act related to privacy and security that apply to business associates be incorporated into the business associate agreements.[52] It would be helpful for covered entities and business associates to maintain a comprehensive inventory of their business associate and subcontractor agreements.

4.   Notice of privacy practices

Virtually everyone who has been a patient of any kind or who has patronized a physician's office or pharmacy since 2003 has been made to sign an acknowledgment indicating that they have received a "Notice of Privacy Practices." Under the Privacy Rule, covered entities, but not business associates, must develop these notices to allow the general public to understand how their PHI may be used or disclosed. The Privacy Rule contains specific provisions regarding what these notices must contain[53] and how they must be provided to patients and the general public. For example, if the covered entity has a website, the notice must be prominently displayed on the site.[54] Final rules implementing the HITECH Act of 2009 required a number of changes to the Notice of Privacy Practices. For example, the notice must describe the types of uses and disclosures that require an authorization. The notice must also indicate that individuals have the right to opt out of fundraising communications. If a health plan intends to use PHI for underwriting purposes, its notice must include a statement indicating that the covered entity may not use genetic information for underwriting. The notice must also explain that covered entities must agree to certain restrictions on disclosure of PHI when a patient has paid out-of-pocket for a service in full.

To assist covered entities with developing their notices, on September 13, 2013, HHS issued model forms, which are also available in Spanish.[55]

5. Documentation demonstrating adherence to policies and procedures

The Office for Civil Rights audit protocols[56] suggest that, if they are audited, covered entities will be expected to produce documentation that they are following their policies and procedures. For example, in order to verify that a covered entity or business associate is properly following its policies regarding verification of the identity of persons requesting PHI, the auditor is instructed to obtain and review documentation of how the covered entity has verified the identity of several recent requestors of PHI.

Ongoing Compliance

Q 27.6   As a covered entity, we implemented a compliance program several years ago, so we're all set, right?

HIPAA compliance requires ongoing attention. You need to revisit your compliance efforts periodically. Employees should receive periodic privacy and security reminders. Policies and procedures should be reviewed to ensure that they continue to reflect your actual day-to-day operations. Privacy and security measures should be incorporated into a comprehensive and documented corporate compliance program. The final regulations implementing portions of the HITECH Act of 2009 required changes to a number of documents, including Notices of Privacy Practices, business associate agreements, policies and procedures, and employee training.

Practice Tips

Q 27.7   Do we need to be concerned about state law?

State law still applies to PHI unless it is impossible to comply with both sets of laws and regulations and state law is less stringent than HIPAA. Therefore, state law will often contain requirements that will apply to a covered entity. For example, Florida law requires that physicians or other owners of records obtain a patient's written consent prior to disclosing medical records for certain purposes allowed by HIPAA, such as for payment or healthcare operations purposes.[57] Entities attempting to comply with HIPAA must also examine state law.

Q 27.8   As a covered entity, how should we handle subpoenas?

HIPAA allows covered entities to disclose PHI pursuant to a subpoena, but only if certain requirements are met.[58] Specifically, you must receive "satisfactory assurances" that the individual who is the subject of the information has been given notice of the request and the opportunity to object, or the party seeking the PHI has requested a protective order from the court.[59] You should also ensure that the party seeking the information has followed applicable state law. "Satisfactory assurances" require both a written statement and documentation supporting the statement.[60]

Q 27.9   What should happen if there is an improper use or disclosure?

If a covered entity or business associate makes an improper use or disclosure of PHI, quick action is critical. The entity needs to determine what information has been disclosed, and what action should be taken to mitigate any potential harm to the individual. Notice to law enforcement may be a reasonable and appropriate step to try to prevent further improper use or disclosure of the information. State law may also require notification to the individual if certain identifying information was stolen, such as Social Security numbers or driver's license numbers. Business associates must notify covered entities of the improper use of disclosure as required by the business associate agreement.

Q 27.10   What constitutes a "breach"?

Under the regulations implementing the HITECH Act of 2009, a "breach" is defined to include acquiring, accessing, using, or disclosing PHI in a manner not permitted under the Privacy Rule "which compromises the security or privacy of the protected health information."[61] A "breach" does not include "[a]ny unintentional acquisition, access, or use of protected health information by a workforce member or person acting under the authority of a covered entity or a business associate, if such acquisition, access, or use was made in good faith and does not result in further use or disclosure in a manner not permitted under" the Privacy Rule.[62] The rule contains other exceptions to the breach definition. An impermissible acquisition, access, use, or disclosure of PHI is presumed to be a breach unless the covered entity or business associate can demonstrate "that there is a low probability that the protected health information has been compromised based on an analysis of at least four factors."[63] These factors include:

- the extent and nature of the PHI involved in the incident, including the types of identifiers and how likely it is that the information could be used to identify someone;

- the identity of the unauthorized person to whom the disclosure was made or who used the PHI;

- whether the PHI was actually viewed or acquired; and

- the extent to which any risk to the PHI has been mitigated.[64]

Q 27.10.1   What should happen if there is a breach?

Under the HITECH Act, if there is a breach, the covered entity must notify each individual whose unsecured PHI has been, or is reasonably believed to have been, compromised.[65] "Unsecured" PHI means PHI that is not rendered unreadable, unusable, or indecipherable to unauthorized persons through the use of a methodology or technology specified by the Secretary of HHS in guidance issued under section 13402(h)(2) of Public Law 111-5.[66] If a business associate discovers a breach, that business associate must report the breach to the covered entity.[67] If a breach involves 500 or more individuals, the breach must be reported immediately to the Secretary of HHS.[68] If the breach involves less than 500 people, the covered entity may maintain a log of the breaches and report the log annually to the Secretary.[69]

FIGURE 27-1

Job Aid: Key Considerations for Business Associate Agreements

The Job Aid below discusses factors that both covered entities and business associates should consider when negotiating the terms of their business associate agreements. This is not a comprehensive list. For example, the nature of the entity's business may dictate the need for very stringent parameters on how data are used or disclosed. Business associate agreements involving a health plan may require additional terms. This checklist does not address indemnification or insurance. Furthermore, these agreements must comply with state law.

I. **Required Provisions for All Business Associate Agreements (BAAs)**[70]

- The BAA must establish the permitted and required uses and disclosures of PHI by the business associate.

- The BAA may not allow the business associate to use or further disclose PHI in a manner that would not be permitted under HIPAA if done by the covered entity, except:

    - The BAA may allow the business associate to use and disclose PHI for the proper management and administration of business associate, as provided in 45 C.F.R. § 164.504(e)(4).

    - The BAA may allow the business associate to provide data aggregation services relating to the healthcare operations of the covered entity.

- The BAA must provide that the business associate will:

    - not use or further disclose PHI other than as permitted or required by the BAA or as required by law;

- use appropriate safeguards and comply, where applicable, with the HIPAA Security Rule with respect to ePHI, to prevent use or disclosure of the information other than as provided for by the BAA;

- report to the covered entity any use or disclosure of PHI not provided for by the BAA of which business associate becomes aware, including breaches of unsecured PHI as required by 45 C.F.R. § 164.410;

- ensure that any subcontractors that create, receive, maintain, or transmit PHI on behalf of the business associate agree to the same restrictions and conditions that apply to the business associate with respect to such information;

- make available protected health information to individuals requesting access to their own PHI, in accordance with 45 C.F.R. § 164.524;

- make available PHI for amendment and incorporate any amendments to PHI in accordance with 45 C.F.R. § 164.526;

- make available information required to provide an accounting of disclosures in accordance with 45 C.F.R. § 164.528;

- to the extent the business associate is to carry out a covered entity's obligation under the Privacy Rule, comply with the requirements of the Privacy Rule that apply to the covered entity in the performance of such obligation;

- make its internal practices, books, and records relating to the use and disclosure of PHI received from, or created or received by the business associate on behalf of, the covered entity available to the Secretary of HHS for purposes of determining the covered entity's compliance with HIPAA;

- at termination of the BAA, if feasible, return or destroy all PHI received from, or created or received by the business associate on behalf of, the covered entity that the business associate still maintains in any form and retain no copies of such information or, if such return or destruction is not feasible, extend the protections of the contract to the information and limit further uses and disclosures to those purposes that make the return or destruction of the information infeasible.

- The BAA must authorize termination of the contract by the covered entity, if the covered entity determines that the business associate has violated a material term of the BAA.

- If the arrangement involves ePHI, the BAA must provide that the business associate will:[71]

    - comply with the applicable requirements of the Security Rule;

    - in accordance with 45 C.F.R. § 164.308(b)(2), ensure that any subcontractors that create, receive, maintain, or transmit ePHI on behalf of the business associate agree to comply with the applicable requirements of the Security Rule by entering into a contract or arrangement that complies with this section;

    - report to the covered entity any security incident of which it becomes aware, including breaches of unsecured PHI.

- If the business associate commits a "breach," as defined in the HITECH Act, that compromises the privacy or security of PHI, the covered entity generally has only sixty days to notify individuals of a breach. If the business associate is an agent of the covered entity, rather than an independent contractor, the sixty-day clock starts ticking on the day the business associate discovered the breach, rather than on the day the business associate notified the covered entity. The parties should consider whether the agreement should state that the business associate is an independent contractor, although the contract language likely will not be determinative if the business associate is really an agent. The agreement should also give the business associate a reasonable timeframe within which to notify the covered entity.[72]

- If the business associate will be de-identifying or aggregating PHI, or creating limited data sets, that should be addressed in the agreement.

II. **Suggested Additional Considerations for Business Associates**

- The business associate should ensure that the BAA allows own proper management and administration, and to carry out the business associate's legal responsibilities.

- The BAA should allow the business associate to disclose PHI if the disclosure is required by law or the business associate obtains reasonable assurance from the recipient that the PHI will be held confidentially and used or further disclosed only as required by law or for the purpose for which it was disclosed, and the recipient notifies the business associate of any instances of which it is aware in which the confidentiality of the information has been breached.

- If the business associate knows that return or destruction of certain PHI will be infeasible, business associate should consider whether to address that situation in the BAA.

- The business associate should consider whether it would be reasonable for the BAA to enable the business associate, rather than the covered entity, to determine whether a breach has occurred.[73]

- The business associate should consider whether the BAA should include a provision indicating that, if a security incident results in an unauthorized access, use, disclosure, modification, destruction of information, or interference with system operations, it shall be reported to the covered entity as soon as practicable. For security incidents that do not result in such an outcome ("Unsuccessful Security Incidents"), however, the business associate should consider whether the BAA could contain a provision containing language that serves as notice of Unsuccessful Security Incidents. By way of example, the parties could consider such Unsuccessful Security Incidents not requiring special notice to include pings on a firewall, attempts to log on to a system with an invalid password or user name, malware, and denial-of-service attacks that do not result in a server being taken off-line.[74]

- The BAA should address state law. The business associate should consider requiring the covered entity to obtain any patient authorizations or consents that may be required under state law.

- If the business associate will be using a subcontractor to assist in performing the services that require the use or disclosure of PHI, the provisions of the BAA will need to flow down to that subcontractor agreement.

III. **Suggested Additional Considerations for Covered Entities**

- The business associate should be required to mitigate, to the extent practicable, any harmful effect that is known to business associate relating to a use or disclosure of PHI in violation of the BAA.

- The covered entity may want to have the option to require the business associate to notify individuals if business associate commits a breach, or at least be responsible to pay for costs associated with such breach.

- The covered entity may want to have the ability to decide whether return or destruction of PHI is feasible at the termination of the contract.

- If the covered entity is a health plan or another entity that is using the business associate to help submit claims, the covered entity should consider requiring the business associate to comply with HIPAA transaction standards.

- Business associates should be required to provide the covered entity with full information regarding any breaches within a short period of time, such as five business days.

Notes to Chapter 27

1. 45 C.F.R. pts. 160, 162, 164.
2. Pub. L. No. 104-191, 110 Stat. 1936 (Aug. 21, 1996).
3. 42 U.S.C. §§ 17921–53.
4. *See* Office for Civil Rights, Dep't of Health & Human Servs., Modifications to the HIPAA Privacy, Security, Enforcement, and Breach Notification Rules Under the Health Information Technology for Economic and Clinical Health Act and the Genetic Information Nondiscrimination Act; Other Modifications to the HIPAA Rules, 78 Fed. Reg. 5566 (Jan. 25, 2013) (final rule).
5. *See id.*
6. 45 C.F.R. §§ 160.102, 160.103.
7. 42 U.S.C. § 17931.
8. ABA Health eSource, vol. 9, Jan. 29, 2013.
9. U.S. Dep't of Health & Human Servs., Omnibus HIPAA Rulemaking, https://www.hhs.gov/hipaa/for-professionals/privacy/laws-regulations/combined-regulation-text/omnibus-hipaa-rulemaking/index.html.
10. 45 C.F.R. § 160.103.
11. *Id.*
12. *Id.*
13. 42 U.S.C. § 300gg-91(a)(2).
14. *See, e.g.*, Office of Sec'y, Dep't of Health & Human Servs., Standards for Privacy of Individually Identifiable Health Information, 65 Fed. Reg. 82,462, 82,485 (Dec. 28, 2000) (final rule) ("Employers are not covered entities under the privacy regulation.").
15. 45 C.F.R. § 164.504(f)(1).
16. *Id.* § 164.504(f)(1)(ii).
17. *Id.* § 164.504(f)(1)(iii).
18. *Id.* § 164.504(a).
19. *Id.* § 164.504(f)(2).
20. 45 C.F.R. § 160.103.
21. *Id.*
22. 42 U.S.C. § 17931(a) (referencing 45 C.F.R. §§ 164.308, 164.310, 164.312, and 164.316).
23. *Id.*
24. 45 C.F.R. § 160.103.
25. *Id.*
26. *See id.* pts. 160, 164 (subpts. A, E).
27. *Id.* § 160.103.
28. *Id.*
29. *Id.* § 164.502.

30. *Id.* § 164.512(a).
31. *Id.* § 160.103.
32. 68 Fed. Reg. 8336.
33. 45 C.F.R. § 164.306(b).
34. *HIPAA Security Rule Toolkit*, NAT'L INST. OF STANDARDS & TECH. (June 2, 2016), http://scap.nist.gov/hipaa.
35. *Health Information Privacy*, U.S. DEP'T OF HEALTH & HUMAN SERVS., www.hhs.gov/ocr/privacy; *HIPAA FAQs for Professionals*, U.S. DEP'T OF HEALTH & HUMAN SERVS., www.hhs.gov/hipaa/for-professionals/faq.
36. *Audit Protocol—Updated April 2016*, U.S. DEP'T OF HEALTH & HUMAN SERVS., www.hhs.gov/hipaa/for-professionals/compliance-enforcement/audit/protocol-current/index.html.
37. 45 C.F.R. § 164.308(a)(1)(ii)(A) (setting forth the risk analysis requirement under the Security Rule).
38. *Security Risk Assessment: What Is Risk Assessment?*, HEALTHIT.GOV (May 2, 2014), www.healthit.gov/providers-professionals/security-risk-assessment.
39. Press Release, U.S. Dep't of Health & Human Servs., HHS Releases Security Risk Assessment Tool to Help Providers with HIPAA Compliance (Mar. 28, 2014).
40. *See* 45 C.F.R. § 164.308(a)(1)(ii)(B).
41. *See id.* § 164.306(a).
42. *Id.* § 164.530(a)(1)(i).
43. *Id.* § 164.308(a)(2).
44. 42 U.S.C. § 17931(a) (requiring business associates to comply with specific HIPAA provisions, including 45 C.F.R. § 164.308, which, among other things, requires the appointment of a security official); *see also* 45 C.F.R. § 164.308(a)(2).
45. 45 C.F.R. § 164.530(i).
46. *Id.* § 164.316(a).
47. *Id.*
48. *See id.* § 164.530(b).
49. *Training Materials: Helping Entities Implement Privacy and Security Protections*, U.S. DEP'T OF HEALTH & HUMAN SERVS., www.hhs.gov/hipaa/for-professionals/training/index.html.
50. *Id.* § 164.314.
51. *Id.* § 164.504(e).
52. *See* 42 U.S.C. §§ 17931(a) and 17934(a).
53. 45 C.F.R. § 164.520.
54. *Id.* § 164.520(c)(3).
55. *Model Notices of Privacy Practices*, U.S. DEP'T OF HEALTH & HUMAN SERVS., www.hhs.gov/hipaa/for-professionals/privacy/guidance/model-notices-privacy-practices/index.html.
56. *Audit Protocol—Updated April 2016*, U.S. DEP'T OF HEALTH & HUMAN SERVS., www.hhs.gov/hipaa/for-professionals/compliance-enforcement/audit/protocol-current/index.html.

57.   *See* FLA. STAT. § 456.057 (2012) (listing the specific limited situations in which medical information may be disclosed absent a patient's written consent).

58.   45 C.F.R. § 164.512(f).

59.   *Id.* § 164.512(e)(1)(ii).

60.   *Id.* § 164.512(e)(1)(iii).

61.   *Id.* § 164.402.

62.   *Id.*

63.   *Id.*

64.   *Id.*

65.   42 U.S.C. § 17932(a).

66.   45 C.F.R. § 164.402.

67.   42 U.S.C. § 17932(b).

68.   *Id.* § 17932(e)(3).

69.   *Id.*

70.   *See* 45 C.F.R. § 164.504(e).

71.   *See id.* § 164.314(a)(2)(i).

72.   *See* 42 U.S.C. § 17932 (outlining notification requirements in the event that there is a breach).

73.   *See id.* § 17921 (defining "breach"); *see also* 45 C.F.R. § 164.402 (indicating that an incident is "presumed to be a breach unless the covered entity or business associate, as applicable, demonstrates that there is a low probability that the protected health information has been compromised").

74.   The HHS Office for Civil Rights has not published guidance specifying whether such a provision is fully compliant with the Security Rule, which requires reporting of Security Incidents.

28

The Affordable Care Act:
Employer Obligations

Kenneth A. Jenero

The Patient Protection and Affordable Care Act (ACA)[1] creates a multi-faceted and complex set of compliance issues for employers. This chapter discusses the ACA's employer shared responsibility penalties, notice obligations, reporting requirements, health insurance plan changes, taxes, anti-retaliation obligations, and other key provisions affecting employers. It also sets forth steps that employers should take to ensure compliance with the provisions of the ACA.

Overview

The Patient Protection and Affordable Care Act

Q 28.1   What is the ACA?

The ACA establishes a comprehensive system of healthcare reform with significant implications for individuals, employers, healthcare providers, and health plans. As originally enacted, the ACA:

(1) required most Americans to purchase health insurance;[2]

(2) established state-run insurance exchanges through which low-income individuals and qualifying businesses can purchase health insurance meeting minimum federal standards;

(3) created premium tax credits and cost-sharing reductions to subsidize the purchase of certain health insurance through an exchange;

(4) imposed several new requirements for and potential penalties on employers and employer-sponsored insurance plans; and

(5) created a variety of new or increased taxes to fund the reformed healthcare system.

This chapter reviews the key provisions of the ACA that impact employers.

Employers' Healthcare-Related Obligations

Q 28.1.1   What are the principal ways in which the ACA affects employers?

While the ACA makes many changes that affect an employer's healthcare-related obligations to its employees, the following are especially important for employers to consider from the standpoint of legal compliance. The ACA:

(1) imposes "shared responsibility penalties" on large employers that fail to offer qualifying health insurance coverage to eligible full-time employees and their dependents;

(2) creates related notice and reporting requirements for employers;

(3) mandates significant substantive and procedural changes in the scope, terms, and conditions of health insurance coverage provided by employers;

(4) creates health-related taxes, penalties, and fees that will impact employers' healthcare costs;

(5) makes it unlawful for employers to engage in retaliation against whistleblowers and employees who receive health coverage assistance under the ACA; and

(6) requires employers to provide reasonable breaks and private space for nursing mothers to express milk at work.

Each of these is discussed in the sections that follow.

Employer Shared Responsibility

Shared Responsibility Penalties

Q 28.2   What are shared responsibility penalties, and how are they calculated?

While the ACA does not require employers to offer health insurance coverage to their employees, it imposes "shared responsibility penalties" on large employers that (1) fail to provide minimal essential coverage for full-time employees (and their dependents) under an employer-sponsored plan, or (2) offer full-time employees (and their dependents) only the opportunity to enroll in minimal essential coverage that is either unaffordable or fails to provide minimum value under applicable federal standards.[3]

A large employer that does not provide its full-time employees (and their dependents) with the opportunity to enroll in minimum essential coverage under an employer-sponsored plan will be subject to a shared responsibility penalty if at least one full-time employee is certified to the employer as having (1) purchased qualified health insurance through a state exchange, and (2) received a related premium tax credit or cost-sharing reduction (together referred to as "health coverage assistance").[4] This is referred to as a "4980H(a) penalty."[5] In 2021, the 4980H(a) penalty for any month is equal to the number of full-time employees employed during the month (excluding the first thirty employees), multiplied by one-twelfth of $2,700 ($225), regardless of how many employees actually received health coverage assistance.[6] The multiplier adjusts for inflation annually.[7]

A large employer that offers its full-time employees (and their dependents) the opportunity to enroll in minimum essential coverage that is unaffordable or does not provide minimum value also will be subject to a shared responsibility penalty if at least one full-time employee declines to enroll in the coverage and is certified to the employer as having (1) purchased alternative qualified health insurance through a state exchange, and (2) received related health coverage assistance. This is referred to as the "4980H(b) penalty."[8] In 2021, the applicable penalty for any month is equal to the number of employees who purchased the alternative coverage and received health coverage assistance, multiplied by one-twelfth of $4,060 ($338.33). The multiplier adjusts for inflation annually. The aggregate amount of the penalty for any month cannot exceed the penalty that would have been imposed on the employer if it had not offered minimum essential health coverage at all.[9]

Under the ACA, the Department of Health and Human Services (HHS) is responsible for determining whether employees applying for insurance through a state exchange and seeking related health coverage assistance meet the applicable eligibility requirements. If the Secretary of HHS notifies a state exchange that an employee is eligible for health coverage assistance (for example, because the employer does not provide minimum essential coverage through an employer-sponsored plan or offers coverage that does not provide minimum value), the exchange must notify the employer of that fact and that the employer may be liable for shared responsibility penalties.[10] The notice also must explain the appeals process established for employers notified of potential liability for shared responsibility penalties[11] and inform the employer that discriminating against or terminating an employee because he or she received health coverage assistance is a violation of the ACA's anti- retaliation provision.[12]

Minimum Essential Coverage

Q 28.3 What is "minimum essential coverage" for purposes of the shared responsibility penalties?

For purposes of the shared responsibility penalties, "minimal essential coverage" means health coverage under any of the following programs or plans that offers a core package of items and services, known as "essential health benefits":

(1) certain government-sponsored programs, such as Medicare Part A, Medicaid, the CHIP program, and the TRICARE program;

(2) an eligible employer-sponsored plan;[13]

(3) a health plan offered in the individual market within a state;

(4) a grandfathered health plan;[14] or

(5) other health benefits programs, such as a state health benefits risk pool, as the Secretary of HHS recognizes for purposes of the ACA.[15]

Under the ACA, "essential health benefits" must include items and services within at least the following ten categories:

(1) ambulatory patient services;

(2) emergency services;

(3) hospitalization;

(4) maternity and newborn care;

(5) mental health and substance use disorder services, including behavioral health treatment;

(6) prescription drugs;

(7) rehabilitative and habilitative services and devices;

(8) laboratory services;

(9) preventive and wellness services and chronic disease management; and

(10) pediatric services, including oral and vision care.[16]

Q 28.3.1 What kinds of benefits are not treated as minimum essential coverage?

The ACA provides that certain "excepted benefits" may not be treated as minimum essential coverage. Therefore, if the only coverage offered by an employer consists of these benefits, the employer could be subject to shared responsibility penalties. These excepted benefits include:

(1) coverage only for accident or disability income insurance, or any combination thereof;

(2) liability insurance, including general and automobile liability insurance;

(3) coverage issued as a supplement to liability insurance;

(4) workers' compensation or similar insurance;

(5) automobile medical payment insurance;

(6) credit-only insurance;

(7) coverage for on-site medical clinics; and

(8) other similar insurance coverage, specified in regulations, under which benefits for medical care are secondary or incidental to other insurance benefits.[17]

The following benefits also may not be treated as minimum essential coverage if they are provided under a separate policy, certificate, or contract of insurance (that is, as independent, non-coordinated benefits):

(1) limited-scope dental or vision benefits;

(2) benefits for long-term care, nursing home care, home healthcare, community-based care, or any combination thereof;

(3) other similar, limited benefits specified in regulations;

(4) coverage only for a specified disease or illness;

(5) hospital indemnity or other fixed indemnity insurance; and

(6) Medicare supplemental health insurance or other similar coverage provided as a supplement to coverage under a group health plan.[18]

Q 28.3.2 When is minimum essential coverage considered to be "unaffordable" or to provide less than "minimum value" for purposes of the shared responsibility penalties?

For purposes of the shared responsibility penalties, minimum essential coverage is considered to be "unaffordable" if the employee's required contribution for self-coverage under the employer's plan exceeds a certain indexed percentage of his or her household income.[19] In 2021, the indexed percentage is 9.83% of the employee's household income, up from 9.78% in 2020. Recognizing that it may be difficult for an employer to know an employee's household income, the IRS's Shared Responsibility Rule also permits employers to base the affordability test on the employee's W-2 wages for the calendar year or the employee's base rate of pay, using the same indexed percentages.[20]

Minimum essential coverage fails to provide "minimum value" if the plan's share of the total allowed cost of benefits is less than 60% of the total cost of benefits provided under the plan.[21] In other words, for the employer to avoid penalties, the plan must pay at least 60% of the total expected cost of benefits for the year, leaving no more than 40% to be paid by the participant in the form of deductibles, co-payments, and co-insurance (but not the participant's premium contribution). The IRS has identified four methods by which an employer-sponsored plan can determine whether it meets the minimum value requirement:[22]

(1) A plan may use the minimum value calculator ("MV calculator") released by HHS, which permits plans to enter information about the plan's benefits, coverage of services, and cost-sharing to determine whether the plan provides minimum value.

(2) A plan may compare its coverage to design-based safe harbors, in the form of checklists issued by HHS and IRS, to determine whether the plan provides minimum value.

(3) A plan may seek certification by an actuary that it provides minimum value based on an analysis performed in accordance with generally accepted actuarial principles and methodologies.

(4) Any qualified health plan available in the small group market
that meets the ACA's prescribed "metal levels" of coverage
(bronze, silver, gold, or platinum) provides minimum value.[23]

Large Employers and Full-Time Employees

Q 28.4   Who are covered "large employers" for purposes of the shared responsibility penalties?

For purposes of the shared responsibility penalties, "large
employers" are those who employ an average of at least fifty full-time
employees (including full-time equivalent employees) on business
days during the preceding calendar year.[24]

Q 28.5   Who are "full-time" employees and "full-time equivalent employees" for purposes of the shared responsibility penalties?

"Full-time" employees generally are those who are employed for
an average of at least thirty hours of service per week. With limited
exceptions, employers are permitted to treat 130 hours of service in
a calendar month as the monthly equivalent of at least thirty hours of
service per week.[25]

The term "full-time equivalent employees" (FTEs) means a combination of employees, each of whom individually is not treated as a
full-time employee because he or she is not employed on average at
least thirty hours of service per week with an employer, who, in combination, are counted as the equivalent of a full-time employee solely
for purposes of determining whether the employer is an ACA-covered
"large employer."[26]

Q 28.5.1   How is the number of full-time employees calculated?

When calculating the number of full-time employees, an employer
must include for each month (1) the number of full-time employees
(i.e., those who are regularly scheduled to work an average of at least
thirty hours per week), plus (2) the number of additional FTEs (if any),

arrived at by dividing the aggregate number of hours of service of employees who are not full-time employees (up to a maximum of 120 hours of service per employee), by 120. As noted above, FTEs are counted only for purposes of determining whether the employer is a covered large employer. Covered large employers are not subject to shared responsibility penalties with respect to FTEs.[27]

An employer will not be considered to employ more than fifty full-time employees if (1) the employer's workforce exceeds fifty full-time employees for 120 days or less during the calendar year, and (2) the employees in excess of fifty during the maximum 120-day period are seasonal workers. A "seasonal worker" is one who performs labor of a kind that is performed exclusively during certain seasons or periods of the year and which, by its nature, may not be carried on throughout the year. Seasonal agricultural laborers and retail workers who are employed exclusively during holiday seasons would qualify as seasonal workers.[28]

All persons treated as a "single employer" under IRS aggregation rules (for example, commonly controlled corporations, partnerships, proprietorships, and affiliated service groups) are treated as one employer.[29] Accordingly, the employees employed by each of the aggregated entities must be included when determining the single employer's status as a "large employer" under the ACA.

The ACA does not specify the time period to be used (a month, a year, etc.) to determine if an employee is full-time. However, this subject is addressed at length in the Shared Responsibility Rule. The rule includes a "measurement" or "look-back" period that allows an employer to measure how many hours an employee averaged per week during a defined period of not less than three and not more than twelve consecutive months. If an employee is determined to have worked full-time during the measurement period, an employer will then have the option of entering an "administrative" period during which the employee may be enrolled in a health plan. Following the administrative period (if any), the employee will be treated as a full-time employee during a corresponding "stability" period. The full-time classification will remain in place during the stability period so long as the worker remains an employee, regardless of how many hours he or she works.[30]

The Shared Responsibility Rule specifies, in detail, how the measurement, administrative, and stability periods are determined for three groups of employees:

(1) ongoing employees,

(2) new employees who are reasonably expected to work full-time, and

(3) new employees who are seasonal or variable hour employees.

An "ongoing employee" is one who has been employed for at least one complete standard measurement period."[31] A "new employee" is one who has not been employed for at least one complete standard measurement period.[32] A "seasonal employee" is one who is hired into a position for which the customary annual employment is six months or less.[33] A "variable-hour employee" is one for whom the employer cannot determine, based on the facts and circumstances at the employee's start date, whether he or she is reasonably expected to be employed on average at least thirty hours of service per week during the initial measurement period because the employee's hours are variable or otherwise uncertain.[34]

The Shared Responsibility Rule permits employers to use measurement periods and stability periods that differ either in length or in their starting and ending dates for the following categories of employees, provided that the employees in each category are treated consistently:

(1) collectively bargained employees and non-collectively bargained employees;

(2) each group of collectively bargained employees covered by a separate collective bargaining agreement;

(3) salaried employees and hourly employees; and

(4) employees whose primary places of employment are in different states.[35]

Offer of Coverage

Q 28.6   What is an "offer of coverage" for purposes of the shared responsibility penalties?

To avoid shared responsibility penalties under the ACA, a covered large employer must offer its full-time employees (and their dependents) the opportunity to enroll in minimum essential coverage under an eligible employer-sponsored plan. The Shared Responsibility Rule provides that an employer will not be treated as having made an offer of coverage to a full-time employee for a plan year if the employee (1) does not have an effective opportunity to elect to enroll in the coverage at least once with respect to the plan year, or (2) does not have an effective opportunity to decline to enroll if the coverage offered is unaffordable or does not provide minimum value.[36]

The Shared Responsibility Rule provides that for purposes of assessing a 4980H(a) penalty, an applicable large employer is treated as offering minimum essential coverage to its full-time employees (and their dependents) for a calendar month, if, for that month, it offers such coverage to all but 5% (or, if greater, five) of its full-time employees, provided that an employee is treated as having been offered coverage only if the employer also offers coverage to that employee's dependents.[37]

Under the ACA, a "dependent," to whom an employer must offer minimum essential coverage or be subject to a related shared responsibility penalty, is a biological or adopted child of an employee who has not attained age twenty-six.[38] The definition does not include the spouse of an employee, a stepson or stepdaughter, or a foster child. To avoid shared responsibility penalties, a large employer must offer minimum essential coverage to the dependents of full-time employees, but is not required to pay for dependent coverage. Also, as noted above, whether minimum essential coverage is affordable is based on the employee's required contribution for self-coverage only.

Multi-Employer Health Plans

Q 28.7 Are there any special rules applicable to employers who contribute to multi-employer health plans?

The Shared Responsibility Rule continued certain interim guidance that simplified compliance with the ACA's requirements for large employers that are required by a collective bargaining agreement or related participation agreement to make contributions to a multi-employer plan that offers qualifying health coverage to individuals who satisfy the plan's eligibility requirements. Under this interim guidance, employers that contribute to multi-employer plans will not be subject to shared responsibility penalties with respect to employees for whom they are making contributions under the plan, as long as the plan:

(1) provides coverage that is affordable,

(2) provides minimum value coverage, and

(3) offers coverage to the employee's dependents.[39]

For purposes of determining whether coverage under a multi-employer plan is affordable, employers may use any of the affordability safe harbors included in the Shared Responsibility Rule (for example, the employee's W-2 wages or the base rate of pay). Coverage under a multi-employer plan also will be considered affordable if the employee's required contribution (if any) toward self-only coverage under the plan does not exceed the applicable indexed percentage of the wages reported to the plan.

According to the Shared Responsibility Rule, employers may rely on this interim guidance until it is modified. In addition, any future guidance that limits the scope of the interim guidance will be applied prospectively and will take effect no earlier than January 1 of the calendar year beginning at least six months after the date of issuance of the new guidance.[40]

Implementation

Q 28.8   When did the shared responsibility penalties take effect?

The shared responsibility penalties originally were scheduled to take effect on January 1, 2014. However, on July 9, 2013, the IRS issued Notice 2013-45, which provided transition relief pursuant to which no shared responsibility penalties would apply for 2014. This transition relief was adopted in the Shared Responsibility Rule.[41] Therefore, covered large employers generally did not become subject to shared responsibility penalties until January 1, 2015.[42]

Employer Notice and Reporting Requirements

Written Notice to Employees

Q 28.9   What notice requirements does the ACA impose on employers?

Employers covered by the Fair Labor Standards Act (FLSA)[43] are required to provide each current and newly hired employee with written notice regarding the existence of a state insurance exchange, including a description of the services provided by the exchange and the manner in which the employee may contact the exchange to request assistance.[44] The notice also must inform the employees that (1) under certain circumstances (such as if the employer's share of the total allowed costs of benefits provided under the plan is less than 60% of the costs), they may be eligible for health coverage assistance (premium tax credits and cost-sharing reductions) to subsidize the purchase of a qualified health plan through the exchange,[45] and (2) they may lose the employer contribution to their health plan benefit if they purchase coverage through the exchange.[46]

Employer Reporting Requirements

Q 28.10 What reporting requirements does the ACA impose on employers?

The ACA imposes the following requirements on employers:

(1) reporting the cost of employer-sponsored health coverage;

(2) reporting by employers subject to shared responsibility penalties; and

(3) reporting by insurers providing minimum essential coverage.

Q 28.10.1 What are the requirements for reporting the cost of employer-sponsored health coverage?

The ACA requires most employers to report on employees' W-2 forms the aggregate cost of benefits provided to each employee under applicable employer-sponsored group health coverage.[47] Pursuant to interim relief provided by the IRS, this reporting requirement is optional for employers that filed fewer than 250 W-2s in the prior year. However, this optional status could be changed or limited by future IRS guidance.[48]

The total cost of the coverage provided to the employee must be reported, whether paid by the employer or the employee. For this purpose, the "aggregate cost" is determined under rules similar to those in IRC section 4980B(f)(4), dealing with the cost of coverage for COBRA purposes. The employer may use the COBRA applicable premium method, the premium charged method, or the modified COBRA premium method under the COBRA regulations. However, the additional 2% allowed to be added to the applicable premium charged to COBRA beneficiaries is not included in the reportable cost.

"Applicable employer-sponsored coverage" means, with respect to any employee, coverage under any group health plan made available to the employee by the employer that is excludable from the employee's gross income under IRC section 106, or would be so excludable if it were employer-provided coverage for purposes of section 106. "Applicable employer-sponsored coverage" generally does not include any of the "excepted benefits" that may not be treated as minimum essential coverage under the ACA.[49]

In addition, the cost of coverage does not include contributions to health savings accounts (HSAs) of the employee or the employee's spouse, contributions to a health reimbursement arrangement (HRA), salary reduction contributions to health flexible spending arrangements (Health FSAs), or contributions to Archer medical savings accounts (MSAs). Also excluded are the costs of self-insured plans not subject to the COBRA requirements (such as a self-insured church plan), multi-employer plans to which the employer contributes, and plans provided by governmental employers to members of the military or their families.

Q 28.10.2 What are the requirements for reporting by employers subject to shared responsibility penalties?

Every large employer that is subject to the ACA's shared responsibility penalties must report certain health insurance coverage information to both its full-time employees and the IRS on an annual basis.[50] A "large employer" generally is one that employs an average of at least fifty full-time employees during the preceding calendar year.[51] The information provided to employees will help them determine whether they may claim a premium tax credit on their individual tax returns. The information provided to the IRS is designed to facilitate administration of the ACA's shared responsibility provisions.

Every large employer must submit an information return to the IRS with respect to each full-time employee. Under the general reporting method set forth in the Employer Information Reporting Rule, each information return must show:

(1) the employer's name, address, and employer identification number (EIN);

(2) the name and telephone number of the employer's contact person;

(3) the calendar year for which the information is reported;

(4) a certification as to whether the employer offered to its full-time employees (and their dependents) the opportunity to enroll in minimum essential coverage under an eligible employer-sponsored plan, by calendar month;

(5) the months during the calendar year for which minimum essential coverage under the plan was available;

(6) each full-time employee's share of the lowest cost monthly premium for self-only coverage providing minimum value that was offered to the full-time employee under an eligible employer-sponsored plan, by calendar month;

(7) the number of full-time employees for each month during the calendar year;

(8) the name, address, and taxpayer identification number (TIN) of each full-time employee during the calendar year and the months, if any, during which the employee was covered under the plan; and

(9) any other information specified in forms, instructions, or published guidance.[52]

Each employer who is required to submit an information return to the IRS also must furnish each full-time employee identified on the return a written statement showing:

(1) the employer's name, address, and EIN; and

(2) the information required to be shown on the IRS information return with respect to the employee.[53]

The foregoing information must be provided in the form and by the annual deadline prescribed by the IRS. The IRS information return generally must be filed on or before February 28 (or March 31, if filed electronically) of the year succeeding the calendar year to which it relates. The written statements to employees generally must be furnished by no later than January 31 of the year succeeding the calendar year to which they relate.[54]

Employers are permitted to contract with and use third parties to facilitate filing information returns and employee statements. This includes an administrator of a multi-employer plan in which the employer participates. However, the employer remains responsible for compliance with the reporting requirements. It may not use contractual arrangements to transfer potential liability for non-compliance to a third party.[55]

Q 28.10.3 What are the requirements for reporting by insurers providing minimum essential coverage?

Covered entities that provide minimum essential coverage to an individual during a calendar year, including health insurance issuers and large employers providing coverage under a self-insured health plan, must report certain information to the IRS and the individuals to whom the coverage is provided.[56]

The following information must be provided to the IRS for the calendar year of coverage:

(1) the name, address, and EIN of the reporting entity required to file the return;

(2) the name, address, and TIN, or date of birth (if a TIN is not available), of each individual enrolled in the minimum essential coverage;

(3) the name and TIN, or date of birth (if a TIN is not available), of each individual who is covered under the policy or program;

(4) for each covered individual, the months for which the individual was enrolled in coverage and entitled to receive benefits; and

(5) any other information specified in forms, instructions, or published guidance.[57]

IRS information returns that report minimum essential coverage provided to an individual by a health insurance issuer through a group health plan must include the following additional information:

(1) the name, address, and EIN of the employer sponsoring the plan;

(2) whether the coverage is a qualified health plan enrolled in through the Small Business Health Options Program (SHOP) and the SHOP's unique identifier; and

(3) other information specified in forms, instructions, or published guidance.[58]

Each entity required to submit an information return to the IRS also must furnish each individual who was enrolled in the minimum essential coverage a written statement showing:

(1) the phone number for a person designated as the reporting entity's contact person;

(2) the health plan policy number, if any; and

(3) the information required to be shown on the IRS information return with respect to the individual.[59]

This information must be provided in the form and by the annual deadline prescribed by the IRS. The IRS information return generally must be filed on or before February 28 (or March 31, if filed electronically) of the year following the calendar year in which the minimum essential coverage was provided. The written statements to individuals generally must be furnished by no later than January 31 of the year following the calendar year in which the coverage was provided.[60]

Large employers that provide minimum essential coverage on a self-insured basis are subject to the reporting requirements applicable to both insurers (as discussed above) and employers (as discussed in the preceding section of this chapter). The IRS's rules permit such employers to file combined returns and statements that satisfy both sets of reporting requirements.[61]

Substantive and Procedural Changes in Health Insurance Coverage

Q 28.11 How does the ACA change the scope, terms, and conditions of health insurance provided by employers?

The ACA mandated the following significant substantive and procedural changes in the scope, terms, and conditions of health insurance coverage provided by employers:

(1) expanded coverage for dependent children;

(2) a ban on annual and lifetime limits;

(3) extension of nondiscrimination rules to fully insured plans; and

(4) a limit on waiting periods.[62]

The ACA also includes a number of other provisions applicable to all plans, as well as additional provisions applicable to grandfathered plans and to collectively bargained grandfathered plans.

Coverage for Dependent Children

Q 28.11.1   How does the ACA expand coverage for children?

The ACA requires group health plans that provide coverage for dependent children to continue to make such coverage available to adult children (regardless of marital status) until they reach twenty-six years of age. However, employers are not required to offer coverage to an adult child's spouse or children. Adult child coverage must be offered at the same level and the same cost as coverage for other dependents under the group health plan. Employers also must offer a special enrollment period for adult children eligible for coverage under the plan, as well as for employees not currently covered under the plan who may have eligible adult children.[63]

Annual and Lifetime Limits

Q 28.11.2   How does the ACA change the ability of health plans and insurance issuers to impose limits on coverage and benefits?

The ACA prohibits group health plans and health insurance issuers offering group health coverage from imposing lifetime limits on the dollar value of essential health benefits provided to plan participants and beneficiaries, and from placing unreasonable annual limits on the dollar value of benefits provided to participants and beneficiaries.[64]

The ACA also bans annual limits on the dollar value of coverage of participants and beneficiaries.[65] However, benefit-based annual and lifetime limits are still permitted for benefits that are not included within minimum essential coverage. The ban on annual limits also does not apply to health flexible spending accounts that are offered through a Code section 125 plan.[66]

Nondiscrimination Rules

Q 28.11.3   How does the ACA affect nondiscrimination rules?

As enacted, the ACA requires non-grandfathered fully insured group health plans to satisfy the same nondiscrimination rules previously applied only to self-insured group health plans.[67] These rules prohibit plan sponsors of group health plans from (1) establishing requirements relating to eligibility for healthcare coverage that are based on an employee's total hourly or annual salary, and (2) discriminating in favor of "highly compensated individuals," which generally includes the five highest-paid officers, any 10% owners, and the highest-paid 25% of all employees.[68] The nondiscrimination rules preclude employers from providing special health insurance coverage to their executives and other highly compensated employees on a pre-tax basis. Employers who violate the nondiscrimination rules are subject to potentially substantial excise taxes.[69]

The extension of the nondiscrimination rules to non-grandfathered fully insured plans originally was set to take effect for plan years beginning on and after September 23, 2010. However, in December 2010, the IRS announced that the extension was delayed indefinitely pending the issuance of regulations or other administrative guidance on how to comply with the new requirement.[70] To date, no such regulations or guidance have been issued.

Waiting Periods

Q 28.11.4   How does the ACA affect waiting periods?

The ACA prohibits any group health plan or health insurance issuer from applying a waiting period in excess of ninety days.[71] For this purpose, a "waiting period" is the period that must pass before the individual is eligible to be covered for benefits under the terms of the plan.[72]

Additional Provisions

Q 28.11.5   What additional substantive and procedural changes made by the ACA apply to all plans?

The following additional provisions apply to all group health plans under the ACA:

(1) Employers and insurers may not retroactively cancel coverage except in limited circumstances, including situations involving fraud.[73]

(2) Employers generally may not exclude coverage for pre-existing conditions for dependents under age nineteen.[74]

(3) Employers may not exclude coverage for pre-existing conditions for any individuals.[75]

(4) Employers must provide coverage for clinical trials for life-threatening diseases.[76]

(5) The caps on wellness program incentives generally increased from 20% to 30% of the cost of coverage. Employers may encourage employees to participate in wellness programs through premium assistance, waiver of cost-sharing and other incentives, provided that alternative arrangements are made available for individuals who are unable to participate in wellness programs because of certain limitations.[77]

Q 28.11.6   What additional substantive and procedural changes made by the ACA apply to all non-grandfathered plans?

The additional provisions set forth below apply to all non-grandfathered plans under the ACA:[78]

(1) Group health plans must provide certain preventive care, including immunizations, breast cancer screenings, and other services recommended by the Preventive Services Task Force, and are prohibited from imposing any cost-sharing requirements on such preventive care.[79]

(2) Cost-sharing for emergency services must be the same for in-network and out-of-network services, and emergency services also must be covered under a group health plan without pre-authorization.[80]

(3) Group health plans that require participants to select a primary care provider must allow those participants to select among any available provider that participates in the plan's network.[81]

(4) Group health plans must allow female participants to obtain OB/GYN services without first obtaining a referral.[82]

(5) Group health plans must have an effective internal appeals process, must provide participants with information about the process, and must have an external appeals process that meets minimum uniform external review model reform standards established by the National Association of Insurance Commissioners.[83]

(6) Employers may not impose cost-sharing in amounts greater than the then-current out-of-pocket limits for high deductible health plans.[84]

Grandfathered Plans

Q 28.12 What additional substantive and procedural changes made by the ACA apply to grandfathered plans?

The ACA contains special provisions for group health plans in effect as of March 23, 2010, referred to as "grandfathered plans." These plans are exempt from certain provisions of the ACA, including those:

(1) extending the nondiscrimination rules to fully insured plans;

(2) mandating first-dollar coverage for certain preventive care;

(3) requiring equal cost-sharing for in-network and out-of-network emergency services;

(4) requiring coverage for emergency services without prior authorization;

(5) permitting individuals participating in plans requiring selection of a primary care provider to select any provider participating in the plan's network;

(6) prohibiting pre-authorization or referral as a condition of securing professional OB/GYN care; and

(7) requiring the development of effective internal and external appeal processes.[85]

The ACA does not specify what will cause a plan to lose grandfathered status, other than to say that enrolling new employees or adding family members will not affect grandfathered status, provided that the plan included dependent coverage as of March 23, 2010.[86] However, this subject is addressed in final rules issued by the IRS.[87] The rules were written with the intent that only reasonable changes routinely made by plan sponsors would allow the plan to retain its grandfathered status and that, over time, most grandfathered plans would lose their status and be required to comply with all of the changes required by the ACA.

Q 28.12.1 What requirements must a plan satisfy in order to maintain its grandfathered status?

Under the final rules, the following conditions must be satisfied to maintain status as a grandfathered plan:

(1) The plan must include, in plan materials provided to participants or beneficiaries describing the benefits provided under the plan, a statement that the plan believes it is a grandfathered plan and contact information for questions and complaints. The rule includes model language to be used for this purpose.

(2) The plan must maintain records documenting the terms of the plan that were in effect on March 23, 2010, and any other documents necessary to verify, explain, or clarify its status as a grandfathered plan.

(3) The terms of coverage under the plan may be modified only within the parameters prescribed in the rules.[88]

The rules provide that a grandfathered plan will lose its status if it makes any of the following changes to terms that were in effect on March 23, 2010:

(1) elimination of all or substantially all of the benefits to diagnose or treat a particular condition (for example, the plan decides to no longer cover care for people with diabetes or HIV/AIDS);

(2) any increase in a percentage cost-sharing requirement (such as an individual's co-insurance requirement) for health insurance or benefits;

(3) any increase in a fixed-amount cost-sharing requirement other than a co-payment (such as a deductible or out-of-pocket limit) if the total percentage increase exceeds the greater of the government's prescribed consumer price index measure of medical inflation or the premium-adjustment percentage that HHS publishes in its annual notice of benefits and payment parameters; provided, however, that high-deductible health plans (HDHPs) may increase fixed amount cost-sharing requirements as long as the changes are necessary to comply with HDHP rules under section 223(c)(2)(A) of the Internal Revenue Code;[89]

(4) any increase in a fixed-amount co-payment if the increase exceeds the greater of $5.00, as adjusted annually for medical inflation, or the medical inflation rate plus 15%;

(5) a decrease in the percentage the employer pays of the cost of any tier of coverage (for example, single coverage or family coverage) by more than 5%, as calculated with the following formula: (COBRA rate—employee premium) divided by the COBRA rate; and

(6) imposition of a new annual limit on the dollar value of benefits, imposition of an annual limit at a dollar value that is lower than the pre-existing dollar value of the lifetime limit, or reduction in the dollar value of the annual limit.[90]

As provided in the rules, the following changes will not cause a grandfathered plan to lose its status:

(1) changes in the dollar amount of deductibles, out-of-pocket limits or co-payments that are smaller than those that will trigger a loss of grandfathered status (as provided above);

(2) changes to comply with the ACA or other federal or state legal requirements;

(3) one or more individuals enrolled in the plan on March 23, 2010, cease to be covered by the plan, provided that the plan has continuously covered at least one person since March 23, 2010;

(4) normal enrollment of employees and family members who were not enrolled on March 23, 2010, and employees' normal election changes;

(5) for insured plans, entering into a new policy, certificate, or contract of insurance, provided that there are no other changes that would trigger a loss of grandfathered status;

(6) for insured plans, renewing the current carrier; and

(7) for self-insured plans, changing third-party administrators.[91]

If a plan does not meet the requirements to maintain grandfathered status, that status will be lost as of the effective date of the impermissible change, regardless of when the change was adopted. At that point, the plan immediately will become subject to all of the ACA's mandates and the employer (or the plan, in the case of a multi-employer plan) will be subject to potentially substantial excise taxes for each affected individual up to the date of correction. Once grandfathered status is lost, there is no opportunity to cure the loss.

Q 28.12.2   What rules apply to collectively bargained grandfathered plans?

A grandfathered collectively bargained plan is one that was ratified before March 23, 2010. Under the final rules issued by the IRS, collectively bargained grandfathered plans generally are subject to the same rules applicable to all other grandfathered plans (as discussed above). Therefore, all of the ACA changes that took effect for other grandfathered plans generally applied to collectively bargained plans as well.[92]

The rules provide that an insured collectively bargained grandfathered plan will not lose its grandfathered status until the termination of the last collective bargaining agreement relating to the coverage (the "Last CBA"). This means that an insured collectively bargained plan will not lose grandfathered plan status during the term of the Last CBA even if changes are made to the cost or coverage provisions of the plan that otherwise would cause a non-collectively bargained insured plan to lose its grandfathered status. However, the insured collectively bargained plan does not get a "free pass" for any cost and coverage changes made during the term of the Last CBA. The potential loss of grandfathered status is simply delayed until the termination of the Last CBA.

After the date on which the Last CBA terminates, the changes made to the plan after March 23, 2010, will be compared to the terms of the plan as they existed on March 23, 2010, to determine if the insured plan retains its grandfathered status. If non-permitted changes were made to the plan, then it will lose its grandfathered status effective as of the date on which the Last CBA terminated. If no non-permitted changes were made to the plan, then it will retain its grandfathered status following the expiration of the Last CBA. Thereafter, it will lose its grandfathered status immediately (as opposed to at the end of the new collective bargaining agreement) upon making any of the changes that generally will cause a loss of grandfathered status.

The final rules clarify that a change in insurance issuers during the term of the Last CBA, by itself, will not affect grandfathered plan status. An insured collectively bargained plan may enter into a new group health insurance policy during the term of the Last CBA, and may renew that policy after the collective bargaining agreement expires, without adversely affecting grandfathered status, provided that no changes have been made to the cost and coverage terms that would independently affect grandfathered status. However, any change to a new group insurance policy after the expiration of the Last CBA will result in loss of grandfathered plan status.

The final rules also clarify that the addition of new contributing employers or new groups of employees of an existing contributing employer to a grandfathered multi-employer health plan will not affect the plan's grandfathered status, provided that the plan has not made any other changes that would cause the plan to relinquish its grandfathered status.

Healthcare-Related Taxes, Penalties, and Revenue-Raisers

Q 28.13   What other health-related taxes, penalties, and fees does the ACA create that will impact employers' healthcare costs?

Among the health-related taxes, penalties, and fees created by the ACA that will impact employers' healthcare costs are the following:

(1) an additional hospital insurance tax for high-wage workers;
(2) a surtax on unearned income;
(3) provisions affecting HSAs, Archer MSAs, and FSAs; and
(4) elimination of the deduction for employer Part D.[93]

Q 28.13.1   What additional hospital insurance taxes are high-wage workers required to pay?

The ACA increased the Medicare Hospital Insurance (MHI) tax rate component of FICA wages in excess of $250,000 in the case of a married couple filing a joint return, $125,000 in the case of a married taxpayer filing a separate return, and $200,000 in all other cases. The MHI tax rate also increased for self-employment income in excess of the same taxpayer dollar thresholds. These thresholds are not indexed for inflation.[94] The employer is liable for the amount of the additional MHI tax and related penalties if it fails to withhold the tax on wages that it pays to an employee in excess of the applicable dollar thresholds.[95]

Q 28.13.2   What is the ACA's surtax on unearned income?

The ACA imposed a surtax (called the "Unearned Income Medicare Contribution") on net investment income of higher-income taxpayers.[96]

The threshold amount for the surtax is $250,000 for a married couple filing a joint return or a surviving spouse, $125,000 for a married individual filing a separate return, and $200,000 in all other cases. For surtax purposes, "investment income" generally includes interest, dividends, royalties, rents, gross income from a trade or business involving passive activities, and net gain from disposition of property (other than property held in a trade or business). "Net investment income" is arrived at by subtracting properly allocable deductions from investment income.[97]

Q 28.13.3   How are health savings accounts, Archer medical savings accounts, and flexible spending accounts affected by the ACA?

The ACA increased the penalty on nonqualified distributions from health savings accounts (HSAs), as well as the penalty on nonqualified distributions from Archer medical savings accounts ("Archer MSAs"). In addition, distributions from HSAs, Archer MSAs, and health flexible spending accounts (FSAs) for medicines or drugs are considered "nonqualified" unless the medicine or drug is prescribed or is insulin.[98]

The ACA also placed an annual limit on the amount an employee may contribute by salary reduction to an FSA maintained under a cafeteria plan, which adjusts annually for inflation.[99]

Q 28.13.4   What effect does the ACA have on the deduction for employers who maintain prescription drug plans for their Medicare Part D–eligible retirees?

The ACA eliminated the deduction for employers who maintain prescription drug plans for their Medicare Part D–eligible retirees.[100]

Anti-Retaliation Provisions

Q 28.14   What anti-retaliation protections does the ACA provide for?

The ACA amended the FLSA by adding an anti-retaliation provision that protects whistleblowers and employees who receive health coverage assistance.[101] Specifically, the new provision makes it unlawful for an FLSA-covered employer to discharge or in any manner discriminate against any employee with respect to his or her compensation, terms, conditions, or other privileges of employment because the employee, or an individual acting at the request of the employee, has:

(1) received health coverage assistance in the form of a premium tax credit or cost-sharing reduction;

(2) provided, caused to be provided, or is about to provide or cause to be provided to the employer, the federal government, or the attorney general of a state information relating to any violation of, or any act or omission the employee reasonably believes to be a violation of, any provision of Title 29 of the U.S. Code (the "Labor Code");

(3) testified or is about to testify in a proceeding concerning such violation;

(4) assisted or participated, or is about to assist or participate, in such a proceeding; or

(5) objected to, or refused to participate in, any activity, policy, practice, or assigned task that the employee (or other such person) reasonably believed to be in violation of any provision of the Labor Code, or any related order, rule, regulation, standard, or ban.[102]

Q 28.14.1 How is the ACA's anti-retaliation provision enforced?

An employee who believes that he or she has been discharged or otherwise discriminated against by any employer in violation of the anti-retaliation provision may seek relief in accordance with the procedures, notifications, burdens of proof, remedies, and statutes of limitation set forth in the Consumer Product Safety Improvement Act of 2008.[103] An aggrieved individual may file a complaint with the Secretary of Labor within 180 days of the alleged violation. The secretary thereafter conducts an investigation and makes a determination of whether there is reasonable cause to believe that the complaint has merit. Upon the request of either party, the secretary will convene a formal administrative hearing to address the allegations in the complaint. Under certain circumstances, the aggrieved individual may pursue his or her complaint in federal district court.

In order to prevail, the complainant must demonstrate that his or her protected behavior was a contributing factor in the challenged employment action. The employer may avoid liability by demonstrating by clear and convincing evidence that it would have taken the same employment action in the absence of the employee's protected behavior. If a violation is established, the available relief includes reinstatement to the employee's former position with compensation (including back pay), compensatory damages, and an award of attorney fees and costs.

The ACA provides that nothing in the new anti-retaliation provision shall be deemed to diminish any rights, privileges, or remedies of any employee under any federal or state law or under any collective bargaining agreement. In addition, the rights and remedies established by the anti-retaliation provision may not be waived by any agreement, policy, form, or condition of employment.[104]

Breaks for Nursing Mothers

Q 28.15   What rights does the ACA create for nursing mothers?

The ACA amended the FLSA by adding a provision requiring FLSA-covered employers to provide reasonable unpaid breaks to a non-exempt employee who is breastfeeding and needs to express milk for her nursing child who is up to one year old.[105] Employers are required to provide a reasonable amount of time to express milk as frequently as needed by an eligible nursing mother. According to the U.S. Department of Labor (DOL), the frequency of breaks needed to express milk, as well as the duration of each break, will likely vary from person to person.

The new provision requires employers to furnish a private space, other than a restroom, for employees to express milk in the workplace. The space must be shielded from view and free from intrusion by co-workers and the public. If the space is not dedicated to the nursing mother's use, it must be available when needed in order to meet the statutory requirement. A space temporarily created or converted into a space for expressing milk, or made available when needed by the nursing mother, is sufficient provided that it is shielded from view and free from intrusion.

Only employees who are not exempt from the FLSA's minimum wage and overtime provisions are entitled to breaks to express milk under the ACA. However, the ACA's mandated break provisions do not preempt state laws covering expressing of breast milk. Accordingly, employers may be required to provide breaks to exempt employees who are nursing mothers under applicable state laws.

Employers with fewer than fifty employees are not subject to the ACA's mandated break provisions if they can demonstrate that complying would "impose an undue hardship by causing the employer significant difficulty or expense." Whether compliance would be an "undue hardship" is determined by looking at the difficulty and expense of compliance for a specific employer in comparison to the size, financial resources, nature, and structure of the employer's business. All employees who work for the covered employer, regardless of work site, are counted when determining whether this exemption applies.[106]

The ACA does not require employers to compensate nursing mothers for breaks taken for the purpose of expressing milk. However, according to the DOL, where employers already provide compensated breaks, an employee who uses that break time to express milk must be compensated in the same way that other employees are compensated for break time. In addition, the FLSA's general requirement that the employee must be completely relieved from duty in order for the time to be non-compensable applies. Employers also may be obligated to provide paid breaks for nursing mothers under more beneficial state laws.[107]

Compliance Steps

Q 28.16   What steps should employers take to ensure compliance with the provisions of the ACA?

The impact of the ACA's healthcare reforms on employers is multi-faceted and complex. Most of the ACA's provisions (including the shared responsibility penalties) already have taken effect. By now, employers should have determined how the ACA affects their businesses and developed effective compliance strategies; should have trained the personnel responsible for ensuring that compliance is achieved; and should be maintaining regular and informed communications with all affected employees. Taking these steps will help to protect employers from potentially significant costs and penalties, as well as adverse employee relations consequences.

The following are recommended steps for employers to take to ensure compliance with the ACA and minimize the risks to their businesses:

(1) Employers must determine whether they qualify as large employers subject to shared responsibility penalties and other mandates.

(2) Covered large employers must determine whether they are going to "pay," "play," or "play and pay" (as explained in further detail below).

(3) Employers must determine whether their existing health insurance plans qualify for grandfathered plan status.

(4) Employers should determine the nature and timing of the ACA's mandates and other changes that will apply to their plans, along with applicable notice, record-keeping, and reporting obligations.

(5) Employers should consider adjustments to the affordability contribution percentages and other indexed provisions of the ACA when developing a compliance strategy.

(6) Employers should be transparent and prepare employees for the possible need to offset increased healthcare costs.

(7) Small employers should assess how the ACA will affect their businesses.

(8) Employers should be careful to respond to IRS shared responsibility letters within the thirty-day timeframe.

Q 28.16.1   What should employers take into consideration when determining whether they qualify as large employers subject to shared responsibility penalties?

In making this determination, employers must follow the provisions of the ACA and applicable IRS rules regarding which employees and hours are included in the "large employer" calculation. Employers also must consider the potential application of the IRS's aggregation rules. Employers with multiple small businesses (that is, each with fewer than fifty FTEs) may find that all of the businesses are subject to the ACA's mandates, including the shared responsibility penalties, because they are included in an aggregated "single employer" group.

Q 28.16.2   What is the "pay," "play," or "pay and play" determination that covered large employers need to make?

Covered large employers must determine whether they are going to:

(1)   provide minimum essential coverage to full-time employees and their dependents, and avoid all of the ACA's shared responsibility penalties (sometimes referred to as "playing");

(2)   provide no healthcare coverage at all and pay the full 4980H(a) penalty (sometimes referred to as "paying"); or

(3)   provide something less than qualifying minimum essential coverage (for example, coverage that is either unaffordable or does not provide minimum value under applicable ACA rules) and pay the potentially lower 4980H(b) penalty based on the number of employees who actually purchase health insurance through a state exchange and receive related health coverage assistance (sometimes referred to as "playing and paying").

Which option to select will depend on an analysis of a number of factors, including the following:

(1)   the type of insurance (if any) that the employer is providing to its employees;

(2)   the cost of any such insurance;

(3) the comparative cost of insurance available through a state-run exchange;

(4) the cost of providing minimum essential coverage compared with the amount of the potential "pay" or "play and pay" penalties;

(5) the impact of applicable union contracts and collective bargaining obligations on the employer's ability to implement health insurance changes;

(6) the employer's employee relations goals and objectives; and

(7) the projected impact of each of the available options on employee recruitment, retention, and morale.

Employers should consider possible ways of reducing the number of full-time employees for whom they may be subject to shared responsibility penalties. This includes, for example, using a greater number of part-time employees (that is, those who are not employed for an average of at least thirty hours of service per week) or outsourcing work to legitimate independent contractors. When doing so, however, employers should not ignore the impact that this may have on scheduling, productivity, customer service, employee satisfaction, and exposure to union organizing efforts. Employers also should be aware that converting existing employees from full-time to part-time status (as opposed to hiring new part-time employees) in order to avoid the increased costs associated with the ACA could expose the employer to a viable interference claim under section 510 of ERISA.

Q 28.16.3 What are the implications of qualifying or not for grandfathered plan status?

If an employer determines that its existing health insurance plan qualifies for grandfathered plan status, the employer should evaluate the importance of maintaining grandfathered status. Whether and when to relinquish grandfathered status will depend on whether the rules applicable to grandfathered plans are more or less favorable and/or costly than those applicable to non-grandfathered plans. Employers will need to evaluate the costs and administrative burdens associated with maintaining a grandfathered plan and balance them against the cost-savings and other benefits associated with grandfathered status.

The financial implications of maintaining a plan's grandfathered status may not prove worthwhile if, for example, structural plan changes are needed to avoid significant premium increases.

In any event, employers must carefully plan any changes to their health insurance coverage to achieve their desired objective regarding grandfathered plan status. This requires a thorough knowledge and understanding of the types of changes that will and will not cause a loss of grandfathered status under the ACA and applicable rules. Employers who decide to retain the grandfathered status of their health plans also must carefully document the plan's terms as of March 23, 2010, and include the model grandfathered plan statement in plan materials distributed to participants and beneficiaries.

Q 28.16.4   What factors should employers take into consideration in determining the nature and timing of ACA mandates, including notice, record-keeping, and reporting obligations?

As noted above, certain mandates apply to all health insurance plans; certain mandates apply only to non-grandfathered plans; and other mandates have delayed effective dates for grandfathered plans. Employers should assess their group health plans to determine which of the applicable mandates will require plan changes and the related costs. Employers with union contracts also should determine if their contracts contain language allowing them to secure relief from any added costs associated with the required plan changes during the term of the contracts (for example, healthcare or economic re-opener provisions, management rights clauses, or other contractual reservations of rights).

Q 28.16.5   What should an employer's concerns be regarding transparency?

Employers should create an environment of transparency regarding the financial impact of healthcare reform and prepare employees for the possible need to offset increased healthcare costs with decreases in wages or other benefits. Employers also should ensure that they have communication channels in place to fulfill their obligations to educate employees about available insurance exchanges, how to access them, and the impact of doing so on their ability to participate in an employer-sponsored health plan. In addition, employers should properly train managers, supervisors, and other personnel on the ACA's requirements in order to ensure compliance and avoid liability under the whistleblower and anti-retaliation provisions.

Q 28.16.6 What compliance concerns are particular to small employers?

Small employers should assess how the ACA will affect their businesses. Employers with fewer than fifty full-time employees are not subject to the ACA's shared responsibility penalties. Accordingly, they are not required to offer health insurance to their employees and will not owe the ACA penalties if they fail to do so. However, even small employers must provide notice to their employees about insurance exchanges. In addition, small employers who offer health insurance will be affected by the ACA's benefit, coverage, and testing requirements, including (but not limited to) the bans on annual and lifetime limits, extension of coverage to dependent children up to age twenty-six, required coverage for persons with pre-existing conditions, limits on maximum waiting periods, and application of the nondiscrimination rules to insured plans. These and other ACA mandates may significantly increase the cost of continuing to provide health coverage under an employer-sponsored plan.

Notes to Chapter 28

1. Pub. L. No. 111-148 (ACA), 124 Stat. 119 (2010).

2. On December 22, 2017, President Donald Trump signed the Tax Cuts and Jobs Act of 2017, which effectively repealed the ACA's "individual mandate" (i.e., the provision subjecting individuals to penalties if they failed to purchase required health insurance) effective 2019.

3. ACA § 1513(a), amending Internal Revenue Code of 1986, 26 U.S.C. § 4980H. The Internal Revenue Service (IRS) issued a final rule regarding the ACA's shared responsibility provisions on February 12, 2014. Shared Responsibility for Employers Regarding Health Coverage, 79 Fed. Reg. 8544, 8597–8601 (Feb. 12, 2014) [hereinafter Shared Responsibility Rule].

4. Health coverage assistance generally is available to qualified low-income individuals and families. This includes individuals whose household income is not less than 100%, nor more than 400%, of the federal poverty line, and who are not eligible for qualified employer-sponsored health insurance or Medicaid. ACA § 1401(a), adding I.R.C. § 36B(c)(1).

5. ACA § 1401(a), adding I.R.C. § 36B(c)(2)(A), (B); 26 C.F.R. § 54.4980H-4(a), Shared Responsibility Rule, 79 Fed. Reg. at 8597.

6. The Shared Responsibility Rule also provides various circumstances in which an employer will not be subject to a shared responsibility penalty for a certain period of time. The term "limited non-assessment period for certain employees" is used to describe these periods. The term includes (1) certain limited periods of time during an employer's first year as a covered large employer, (2) the three-full-calendar-month period beginning with the first full calendar month in which an employee is first otherwise eligible for an offer of coverage under the monthly measurement method, (3) the initial three full calendar months of employment for an employee reasonably expected to be a full-time employee at the start date under the look-back measurement method, (4) certain limited periods during the initial measurement period for a new variable hour employee, seasonal employee, or part-time employee determined to be employed on average at least thirty hours of service per week under the look-back measurement method, (5) certain limited periods of time following an employee's change in employment status to a full-time employee during the initial measurement period under the look-back measurement method, and (6) the calendar month in which an employee's start date occurs on a day other than the first day of the calendar month. Shared Responsibility Rule, 79 Fed. Reg. at 8580. The various measurement methods for determining an employee's status as a full-time employee are discussed in Q 28.5.1, *infra*.

7. ACA § 1513, amending I.R.C. § 4980H(a), (d)(2).

8. ACA § 1401(a), adding I.R.C. § 36B(c)(2)(C); 26 C.F.R. § 54.4980H-4(b), Shared Responsibility Rule, 79 Fed. Reg. 8598–8601.

9. ACA § 1513, amending I.R.C. § 4980H(c), (d)(1).

10. ACA § 1411(e)(4)(B)(iii), citing I.R.C. § 4980H.

11. ACA § 1411(e)(4)(C), citing ACA § 1411(f), which sets forth the appeals and redeterminations process.

12. ACA § 1558, adding new Fair Labor Standards Act (FLSA) § 18C. The anti-retaliation provision is discussed in Q 28.14 *et seq., infra.*

13. An "eligible employer-sponsored plan" includes (1) a governmental plan (within the meaning of section 2791(d)(8) of the Public Health Services Act), (2) any other plan or coverage offered in the small or large group market within a State, and (3) a grandfathered health plan offered in a group market. ACA § 1513(f)(2). This list does not specifically include a self-funded plan. However, on August 30, 2013, the IRS issued a final rule regarding shared responsibility payment for not maintaining minimum essential coverage, which clarifies that an "eligible employer-sponsored plan" includes "[a] self-insured group health plan under which coverage is offered by, or on behalf of, an employer to the employee." Shared Responsibility Payment for Not Maintaining Minimum Essential Coverage, 78 Fed. Reg. 53,658 (Aug. 30, 2013) [hereinafter Minimum Essential Coverage Rule]; *see also* Preamble, Shared Responsibility Rule, 79 Fed. Reg. at 8545.

14. Grandfathered plans are discussed in Q 28.11.7 *et seq., infra.*

15. ACA § 1513(f)(1).

16. *See* Ctr. for Medicare and Medicaid Servs., Essential Health Benefits Standards: Ensuring Quality, Affordable Coverage, https://www.cms.gov/CCIIO/Resources/Fact-Sheets-and-FAQs/ehb-2-20-2013.

17. *Id.* § 1513(f)(3)(A), referencing the excepted benefits described in paragraph (1) of section 2791 of the Public Health Services Act, 42 U.S.C. § 300gg-91(c)(1).

18. ACA § 1513(f)(3)(B), referencing the excepted benefits described in paragraphs (2), (3), and (4) of section 2791 of the Public Health Services Act, 42 U.S.C. § 300gg-91(c)(2), (3), (4).

19. *Id.* § 1401(a), adding I.R.C. § 36B(c)(2)(C)(i).

20. Shared Responsibility Rule, 79 Fed. Reg. at 8599–8601.

21. ACA § 1401(a), adding I.R.C. § 36B(c)(2)(C)(ii).

22. The methods for determining minimum value are set forth in the IRS's final rule regarding standards related to essential health benefits, actuarial valuation, and accreditation. Patient Protection and Affordable Care Act; Standards Related to Essential Health Benefits, Actuarial Value, and Accreditation, 78 Fed. Reg. 12,834, 12,834–72 (Feb. 25, 2013).

23. The ACA requires non-grandfathered individual and small group market plans offered on and off the exchange to provide coverage at specific actuarial value categories. Categories are defined by the average share of total health spending on essential benefits paid for by the plan. The ACA identifies specific actuarial value categories as "metal levels" specified as bronze, silver, gold, and platinum. Bronze plans have the least generous cost coverage and platinum plans have the most generous cost coverage. Coverage levels are as follows: bronze—60%; silver—70%; gold—80%; and platinum—90%.

24. ACA § 1513, amending I.R.C. § 4980H(d)(2); Shared Responsibility Rule, 79 Fed. Reg. at 8578. The definitions of "full-time employees" and "full-time equivalent employees" are discussed in Q 28.5 below.

25. Shared Responsibility Rule, 79 Fed. Reg. at 8579–80. The rule defines an "hour of service" as each hour for which (1) an employee is paid or entitled to payment for the performance of duties for an employer, and (2) an employee is paid or entitled to payment by the employer for a period of time during which no duties are performed due to vacation, holiday, layoff, jury duty, military duty, or certain qualifying leaves of absence. *Id.* at 8580.

26. ACA § 1513, amending I.R.C. § 4980H(d)(2); Shared Responsibility Rule, 79 Fed. Reg. at 8580.

27. ACA § 1513, amending I.R.C. § 4980H(d)(4); Shared Responsibility Rule, 79 Fed. Reg. at 8579–80, 8582.

28. ACA § 1513, amending I.R.C. § 4980H(d)(2)(B); Shared Responsibility Rule, 79 Fed. Reg. at 8581–82; *see* 29 C.F.R. § 500.20(s)(1).

29. ACA § 1513, amending I.R.C. § 4980H(d)(2)(C); Shared Responsibility Rule, 79 Fed. Reg. at 8579.

30. Shared Responsibility Rule, 79 Fed. Reg. at 8584–97.

31. *Id.* at 8580.

32. *Id.* at 8580–81.

33. *Id.* at 8581.

34. *Id.* at 8581–82.

35. *Id.* at 8587.

36. *Id.* at 8597–98.

37. *Id.* at 8597.

38. *Id.* at 8579.

39. *Id.* at 8576.

40. *Id.*

41. *Id.* at 8569; *see also* I.R.S. Notice 2013-45 (July 9, 2013).

42. The Shared Responsibility Rule provided additional transition relief protecting certain large employers (i.e., those with fewer than 100 full-time employees during 2014) from exposure to shared responsibility penalties in 2015 and a portion of 2016. 79 Fed. Reg. at 8574. To give employers sufficient time to expand their health plans to add dependent coverage, the rule also provided transition relief from shared responsibility penalties in 2014 and/or 2015 to employers who took steps during those years to extend coverage under the plan to dependents who were not offered coverage during the 2013 and/or 2014 plan years. 79 Fed. Reg. at 8573, 8597–99.

43. 29 U.S.C. § 201 *et seq.*

44. ACA § 1512(a)(1). The original effective date for providing the notice was March 1, 2013. The DOL extended the effective date to October 1, 2013, in Dep't of Labor, Technical Release 2013-02 (May 8, 2013).

45. *Id.* § 1512(a)(2).

46.   *Id.* § 1515(a)(3). The DOL has issued model notices that satisfy the applicable content requirements. The notices are available on the DOL's website, www. dol.gov/agencies/ebsa/laws-and-regulations/laws/affordable-care-act/for-employers-and-advisers/coverage-options-notice.

47.   *Id.* § 9002, amending I.R.C. § 6051(a)(14). This reporting requirement has been in effect since 2012. On January 23, 2012, the IRS issued Interim Guidance on Informational Reporting to Employees of the Cost of Their Group Health Insurance Coverage, I.R.S. Notice 2012-9 (Jan. 23, 2012). On February 15, 2012, the IRS issued updated Frequently Asked Questions (FAQs) on reporting the cost of employer-provided healthcare coverage, which reflect the information included in the Interim Guidance.

48.   *Id.*

49.   See the discussion of "minimum essential coverage" and "excepted benefits" in Q 28.3 and Q 28.3.1, *supra.*

50.   ACA § 1514(a), adding I.R.C. § 6056. This information reporting requirement originally was scheduled to take effect on January 1, 2014. However, the effective date was delayed several times. The first information reports were not required until March 31, 2016 (for calendar year 2015). *See* IRS. Notice 2013-45; Information Reporting by Applicable Large Employers on Health Insurance Coverage Offered Under Employer-Sponsored Plans, 79 Fed. Reg. 13,231 (Mar. 10, 2014) [hereinafter Employer Information Reporting Rule]; and IRS Notice 2016-04, 2016-3 I.R.B. 279.

51.   *See* Q 28.4 *et seq., supra.*

52.   Employer Information Reporting Rule, 79 Fed. Reg. at 13,248.

53.   *Id.*

54.   *Id.*

55.   *Id.* at 13,245–46.

56.   ACA § 1502(a), adding I.R.C. § 6055(a). This information reporting requirement originally was scheduled to take effect on January 1, 2014. However, the IRS extended the reporting deadlines for insurers and self-insuring employers to the same dates as those applicable to large employers (i.e., March 31, 2016). *See supra* note 50; IRS Notice 2013-45; Information Reporting of Minimum Essential Coverage, 79 Fed. Reg. 13,220 (Mar. 10, 2014); and IRS Notice 2016-04, 2016-3 I.R.B.

57.   Information Reporting of Minimum Essential Coverage at 13,228–29.

58.   *Id.* at 13,229.

59.   *Id.*

60.   *Id.*

61.   *Id.* at 13,224–25; Employer Information Reporting Rule, 79 Fed. Reg. at 13,235–36.

62.   As originally enacted, the ACA required employers that (1) were covered by the FLSA, (2) had more than 200 full-time employees, and (3) offered one or more employer-sponsored health plans, to automatically enroll new full-time employees in one of the plans offered, subject to any waiting period authorized by law. ACA § 1511. However, the automatic enrollment provisions were repealed in

November 2015. Employers may choose to voluntarily continue with automatic enrollment options (such as "default" or "negative" elections), but there is no obligation to do so.

63.   ACA § 2714. These provisions took effect for plan years beginning on or after September 23, 2010. However, they did not take effect for "grandfathered plans" until plan years beginning on or after January 1, 2014. (Grandfathered plan status is discussed in Q 28.11.8 *et seq., infra.*) On November 18, 2015, the IRS issued final rules for dependent coverage (80 Fed. Reg. 72,192–294 (Nov. 18, 2015)), which became effective on January 19, 2016.

64.   ACA § 2711. These provisions took effect for plan years beginning on or after September 23, 2010. The IRS issued final rules for lifetime and annual limits (80 Fed. Reg. 72,192–294 (Nov. 18, 2015)), which became effective on January 19, 2016.

65.   *Id.* This ban took effect for plan years beginning on and after January 1, 2014.

66.   *Id.*

67.   ACA § 2716(a). These changes do not apply to "grandfathered plans," which are discussed in Q 28.11.8 *et seq., infra.*

68.   *Id.* § 2716(a).

69.   *Id.* § 9001.

70.   I.R.S. Notice 2011-1 (Dec. 22, 2010).

71.   ACA §§ 2708, 2704(b)(4) (effective for plan years beginning on or after January 1, 2014). The IRS issued a final rule on the ninety-day waiting period limitation on June 25, 2014 (79 Fed. Reg. 35,943 (June 25, 2014)), which became effective on January 19, 2016.

72.   *Id.*

73.   ACA § 2712 (effective for plan years beginning on or after September 23, 2010). The IRS issued final rules for rescissions (80 Fed. Reg. 72,192–294 (Nov. 18, 2015)).

74.   *Id.* (effective for plan years beginning on or after September 23, 2010). The final rules for rescissions (*see supra* note 73) also covered preexisting condition exclusions. 80 Fed. Reg. 72,192–294.

75.   *Id.* (effective for plan years beginning on or after January 1, 2014).

76.   ACA § 2709(b) (effective for plan years beginning on or after January 1, 2014).

77.   *Id.* § 2705(a) (effective for plan years beginning on or after January 1, 2014). On June 10, 2013, the IRS issued Incentives for Nondiscriminatory Wellness Programs in Group Health Plans, 78 Fed. Reg. 33,158 (June 10, 2013) (final rule). The rule addresses the 10% increase in the maximum permissible reward under a health-contingent wellness program offered in connection with a group health plan (from 20% to 30%). It also further increases the maximum permissible reward to 50% for wellness programs designed to prevent or reduce tobacco use. In addition, the rule includes clarifications regarding the reasonable design of health-contingent wellness programs and the reasonable alternatives they must offer in order to avoid prohibited discrimination.

78. "Grandfathered plans" generally are those that existed as of March 23, 2010. Although the vast majority of the ACA's provisions apply to all group health plans, grandfathered plans are exempt from certain provisions of the ACA and have the benefit of delayed effective dates with respect to other provisions. See discussion of grandfathered plans in Q 28.11.7 *et seq., infra.*

79. ACA § 2713(a) (effective for plan years beginning on or after September 23, 2010). On July 2, 2013, the IRS issued Final Rules, Coverage of Certain Preventive Services Under the Affordable Care Act, 78 Fed. Reg. 39,870 (July 2, 2013). A final rule authorizing the exemption of group health plans and group health insurance coverage sponsored by certain religious employers from having to cover certain preventive health services (contraceptive services) was issued on February 15, 2012, and took effect on April 16, 2012. Group Health Plans and Health Insurance Issuers Relating to Coverage of Preventive Services Under the Patient Protection and Affordable Care Act, 77 Fed. Reg. 8725 (Feb. 15, 2012).

80. ACA § 1302(b)(4)(E) (effective for plan years beginning on or after September 23, 2010).

81. *Id.* § 2719A(a) (effective for plan years beginning on or after September 23, 2010).

82. *Id.* § 2719A(d) (effective for plan years beginning on or after September 23, 2010).

83. *Id.* § 2719(a), (b) (effective for plan years beginning on or after September 23, 2010). The IRS issued final rules for appeals and patient protections (80 Fed. Reg. 72,192–294 (Nov. 18, 2015)), which became effective on January 19, 2016.

84. *Id.* § 1302 (effective for plan years beginning on or after January 1, 2014).

85. *See* IRS final rules for grandfathered plans (80 Fed. Reg. 72,192–294 (Nov. 18, 2015)), which became effective on January 19, 2016 [hereinafter Grandfather Rules]. In other areas, grandfathered plans benefit from delayed effective dates. For example, the provision of the ACA requiring plans to provide coverage for dependents up to age twenty-six (which generally took effect for plan years beginning on or after September 23, 2010), did not apply to grandfathered plans until plan years starting on or after January 1, 2014.

86. ACA § 1251.

87. *See* Grandfather Rules, *supra* note 85.

88. *Id.* at 72,238–39.

89. The alternative use of the greater of the consumer price index measure or the premium-adjustment percentage, and the special rule for HDHPs, were included in the Final Rule on Grandfathered Group Health Plans and Grandfathered Group Health Insurance Coverage, with an effective date of January 14, 2021, and an applicability date of June 15, 2021; 85 Fed. Reg. 81097 *et seq.*

90. *Id.* at 72,240–42. The Grandfather Rules provide that if any of the foregoing changes were made prior to the effective date of the rules, they will not result in loss of grandfathered status if they were revoked or modified, as of the first day of the first plan year on or after September 23, 2010, and the plan, as modified, otherwise complied with the requirements for maintaining grandfathered status as of such date.

91. *Id.* at 72,193, 72,238; *see also* Interim Final Rules, 75 Fed. Reg. 34,558–60 (June 17, 2010).

92. ACA § 1251(d). However, the rules provided limited relief for insured (as opposed to self-insured) single-employer and multi-employer plans maintained pursuant to a collective bargaining agreement. Grandfather Rules, 80 Fed. Reg. at 72,198, 72,240.

93. As enacted, the ACA also imposed a significant excise tax on certain high-cost insurance plans referred to as "Cadillac plans." This tax originally was scheduled to take effect in 2018, but its implementation date was delayed several times until it was fully repealed in December 2019.

94. I.R.C. § 911(a)(1). The increased MHI tax rate began in 2013.

95. ACA § 9015, amending I.R.C. § 3101(b).

96. I.R.C. § 1411(d). The surtax began in 2013.

97. I.R.C. § 1411(c)(1)(A)(iii).

98. ACA § 9003, amending I.R.C. §§ 220(d)(2) and 223(d)(2). These changes began in 2011.

99. ACA § 9005, amending I.R.C. § 125. This limitation began in 2013.

100. ACA § 9012 (effective January 1, 2013).

101. ACA § 1558, amending the FLSA, 29 U.S.C. § 218 *et seq.*

102. *Id.* On October 13, 2016, the U.S. Department of Labor's Occupational Safety and Health Administration (OSHA) published a final rule governing employee retaliation claims under the ACA. 81 Fed. Reg. 70,607–26 (Oct. 13, 2016). The final rule includes procedures and time frames for filing and handling employee complaints, investigations by OSHA, appeals of OSHA determinations to an administrative law judge (ALJ), review of ALJ decisions by the Administrative Review Board (ARB), judicial review of the ARB's final decision, and interpretations of certain terms used in the ACA's anti-retaliation provisions. The final rule also clarifies the broad range of activities protected by the ACA, the relatively low burden of proof for employees asserting claims under the ACA, and the potentially significant liability to which employers are exposed for engaging in unlawful retaliation. For more information on the final rule, see Kenneth A. Jenero, *OSHA Issues Final Rule on Complaints Under Affordable Care Act's Anti-Retaliation Provision*, 42 EMP. RELATIONS L.J. No. 4 (Spring 2017).

103. 15 U.S.C. § 2087(b).

104. ACA § 1558, adding I.R.C. § 125(j). *See supra* note 102, regarding OSHA's final rule governing employee retaliation claims under the ACA.

105. ACA § 4207, amending 29 U.S.C. § 207(r)(1). The Wage and Hour Division of the U.S. Department of Labor has issued a Fact Sheet and a series of Frequently Asked Questions on this topic. *See Fact Sheet No. 73: Break Time for Nursing Mothers Under the FLSA*, U.S. DEP'T OF LABOR (rev. Aug. 2013), www.dol.gov/whd/regs/compliance/whdfs73.htm; *Frequently Asked Questions—Break Time for Nursing Mothers*, U.S. DEP'T OF LABOR, www.dol.gov/whd/nursingmothers/faqBTNM.htm.

106. ACA § 4207, amending 29 U.S.C. § 207(r)(1).

107. *Id.*

29

Anti-Money Laundering

*Gabriel Caballero, Jr.**

Money laundering is the general term used to describe the process of concealing the true source, origin, ownership, destination, or use of money or property. It "is the criminal practice of processing ill-gotten gains, or 'dirty' money, through a series of transactions; in this way, the funds are 'cleaned' so that they appear to be proceeds from legal activities."[1] The "dirty" money may have come from virtually any illegal activity, or it may be planned for an illicit purpose, like terrorism, but in every case it has one thing in common: to give money the appearance of having come from a legitimate source or being used for a legitimate purpose.

Many companies are required by law to implement anti-money laundering programs. Even for companies not required to have programs, the best defense against becoming unwittingly involved in a possible violation of the Money Laundering

*   The author wishes to acknowledge Gregory Baldwin, Steven D. Gordon and Christopher A. Myers for their contributions to this chapter.

Control Act is to have an effective anti-money laundering compliance program. Such a program can be used to demonstrate that the business is a "good corporate citizen" that took reasonable steps to avoid involvement (through willful blindness or otherwise) in criminal money laundering activity.

Introduction

Q 29.1   What are the goals of money laundering?

For the average criminal, money laundering is the process by which his or her criminal proceeds are made to look legitimate. For the average terrorist, money laundering is the process used to fund terrorist activity without revealing the true source, destination, or purpose of the money. These funds can only be used safely if the criminal or terrorist is able to place funds into the legitimate financial system, efficiently and securely move those funds in order to cover their source, ownership, or purpose, and then use the funds—all without attracting unwanted attention to the underlying criminal activity or purposes involved. Money laundering provides the vehicle for criminals and terrorists to operate and expand their criminal enterprises. To do so, they must exploit legitimate businesses. This is the only way they can make their money and themselves look legitimate.

> **money laundering,** *n.* The act of transferring illegally obtained money through legitimate people or accounts so that its original source cannot be traced.[2]

Q 29.1.1   How does money laundering work?

The methods and means of laundering money are limited only by the imagination of the money launderer. Although there are many different methods money launderers may use, there are three generally recognized and independent steps that can often occur simultaneously:

- placement
- layering
- integration[3]

Q 29.1.2   What is placement?

A great deal of criminal activity generates cash. Of course, criminal activity can also generate proceeds in forms other than cash, but if the proceeds are large amounts of cash, that creates a major problem for the criminal. Large amounts of cash can be hard to spend without attracting a lot of unwanted attention, hard to move around because cash is so bulky, and very difficult to hide. Regardless of the form of the proceeds, however, it is important for the criminal to disguise the true source and ownership of the money. The criminal has only one solution to these problems: get the criminal proceeds into the financial system, where it will be safer and much easier to move and disguise. The essential process of getting criminal proceeds into the financial system is known as the "placement" stage of money laundering. It is during the placement stage that criminal proceeds are most vulnerable to being identified and seized by law enforcement authorities.

Q 29.1.3   What is layering?

Once illicit funds have been placed into the financial system, the money launderer needs to conceal them as completely as possible. To accomplish this, the launderer moves the funds that have been placed in the financial system from business to business (often, but not always, a phony business), country to country, and continent to continent. This creates a trail that is extremely difficult and time-consuming for law enforcement to follow—which is the entire point of the effort. Layering is the process of moving the money through a complicated, extended trail in order to conceal its source, ownership, or purpose.

Q 29.1.4   What is integration?

Once illicit funds have been hidden through the layering process, the money launderer is ready to use the money. To accomplish this, the money launderer will seek ways to efficiently "resurface" the money so that it looks completely legitimate—such as from the legal sale of products, employment, or consulting fees from apparently legitimate businesses, or the return on legal investments. This process of making the illicit funds available so that they look "clean" is known as the "integration" stage of money laundering.

Q 29.1.5   What forms aside from cash can funds for laundering take?

Money laundering and terrorist financing can involve every possible form that money and property can take in addition to cash:

- money orders
- checks
- cashier's checks
- bank drafts
- wire transfers
- traveler's checks
- letters of credit
- credit cards
- life insurance annuities
- real property
- precious stones and metal
- jewelry
- prepaid access cards[4]

The most common form for the funds in the placement stage is cash, although placement can also involve the deposit of checks and other fraudulently obtained monetary instruments. The layering and integration stages most commonly involve monetary instruments (such as wire transfers) and other forms of property.

The Legal Framework

Q 29.2   What are the federal anti-money laundering statutes?

There are several key federal statutes that together aim to detect and deter money laundering. Some apply only to certain types of businesses. Others apply to all businesses and all persons in the United States and, in some cases, even to persons and businesses located *outside* the United States.

The key laws are:

(1) the Money Laundering Control Act of 1986, as amended (MLCA);

(2) Currency and Foreign Transactions Reporting Act, commonly known as the Bank Secrecy Act, as amended (BSA);

(3) 1992 Annunzio–Wylie Anti-Money Laundering Act;

(4) Uniting and Strengthening America by Providing Appropriate Tools Required to Intercept and Obstruct Terrorism Act of 2001 (USA PATRIOT Act);

(5) the federal laws requiring the reporting of large cash transactions; and

(6) the federal laws prohibiting transactions with "specially designated" persons, such as narcotics trafficking "kingpins," terrorists, and supporters of terrorist activity.

There are also special laws regarding "Money Services Businesses" (MSBs).

COMPLIANCE FACT

MSBs include: currency dealers or exchangers; check cashers; issuers, sellers, or redeemers of cashier's checks, traveler's checks or money orders; money transmitters; and providers and sellers of prepaid access.[5]

Q 29.2.1   To whom do these AML laws apply?

Some apply only to certain types of businesses. Others apply to all businesses and all persons in the United States and, in some cases, even to persons and businesses located *outside* the United States. But with all of these laws, it is important to keep in mind the general legal principle of "corporate liability." Under the law of the United States, every business is legally responsible for the acts or omissions of its employees and agents, as long as those employees or agents: (a) were acting within the scope of their employment; and (b) were acting for at least the partial benefit of their employer.

Thus, if the law requires some act to be performed and an employee purposely fails to perform that act because he or she thinks it may help the business, both that employee *and* the business can be criminally prosecuted for the failure to perform the act. Conversely, if the law prohibits some act and an employee performs that act anyway, then again, both that employee *and* the business itself can be criminally prosecuted for the employee's actions. It is therefore essential that every business and its employees scrupulously comply with the anti-money laundering laws.

The Money Laundering Control Act of 1986

Q 29.3   What does the MLCA provide?

The MLCA consists of two criminal statutes, 18 U.S.C. §§ 1956 and 1957. Generally, the MLCA makes it a federal crime to launder money. Violation of this law can result in up to twenty years' imprisonment for an individual and substantial fines for both an individual and a business. The MLCA applies not only to the person(s) who committed the underlying crime and are seeking to launder the illicit funds, but also to any person or business that knowingly assists or attempts to assist in the laundering. The MLCA applies to all persons and businesses in the United States. In addition, certain provisions of the MLCA are applicable to persons and businesses *outside* the United States.

As discussed below, the MLCA is complicated and involves numerous elements. Stripped to its barest essentials, however, the MLCA imposes liability on any person or business that "knows" or is "willfully blind" to the fact that funds or property involved in "a financial transaction" come from "some form of unlawful activity," and then engages in or attempts to engage in the financial transaction involving those funds or property, or transports, transmits, or transfers such funds or property, if the funds or property in fact come from or are intended to further a "specified unlawful activity."

Many of the terms used in both sections of the MLCA are specifically defined in the statute, and it is essential to understand those definitions in order to understand the scope of activity that can be considered criminal money laundering.

Key Definitions

Q 29.3.1   What does "some form of unlawful activity" mean under the MLCA?

"Some form of unlawful activity" means any activity that constitutes a felony under *any* federal law, *any* state law, or *any* law of a foreign country. All a person needs to know is that the funds or property have come from some illegal activity, even if he or she is ignorant or mistaken about the exact nature of the illegal activity. The law provides that no person or entity may get involved with funds or property they know is "dirty" money; it does not say the person or entity involved needs to know where the "dirt" came from.[6]

Q 29.3.2   What constitutes "knowledge" under the MLCA?

As interpreted by the case law, "knowing" the property comes from "some form of illegal activity" means not only *actual* knowledge but also "*deliberate indifference*," or "*willful blindness*." The term "deliberate indifference" is defined as "[t]he careful preservation of one's ignorance despite awareness of circumstances that would put a reasonable person on notice of a fact essential to a crime."[7] "Willful blindness" is the "[d]eliberate avoidance of knowledge of a crime, [especially] by failing to make a reasonable inquiry about suspected wrongdoing despite being aware that it is highly probable."[8]

Willful blindness occurs in situations in which one is aware of facts that would cause a reasonable person's suspicions to be aroused, but further inquiry is deliberately omitted because one wishes to remain in ignorance of the true facts.[9] It is the intentional "cutting off of one's normal curiosity by an effort of the will."[10] A person may not escape criminal liability by pleading ignorance "if he . . . strongly suspects he is involved with criminal dealings but deliberately avoids learning more exact information about the nature or extent of those dealings."[11] Willful blindness creates an inference of *actual* knowledge of the factual element in issue. If a jury concludes that a person deliberately ignored the warning signs or "red flags" that funds or property involved in a transaction were derived from some form of illegal activity, the law will permit that jury to infer that the person *actually knew* that the funds or property were criminally derived.

In sum, one may not, simply to avoid learning the truth, turn a blind eye or ignore "red flags" indicating that funds or property are derived from some unlawful activity. Putting one's head ostrich-like in the sand will not provide a defense later.

Q 29.3.3 What is a "specified unlawful activity" for purposes of the MLCA?

Specified unlawful activities include violations of approximately 250 federal criminal laws as well as violations of certain *foreign* laws.[12] Given the broad definition, virtually any federal criminal offense can constitute "specified unlawful activity." The particular *foreign* laws that constitute "specified unlawful activity" include:

(1) violations of foreign drug laws;

(2) crimes of violence, such as murder, kidnapping, extortion, and terrorism;

(3) fraud by or against a foreign bank;

(4) public corruption, such as bribery, misappropriation or embezzlement of public funds;

(5) illegal arms dealing;

(6) sexual exploitation of children and "trafficking in persons" in general; and

(7) any act for which the United States would be obligated to extradite a person under a treaty with the nation in question.

Q 29.3.4   What are "financial transactions"?

A "financial transaction" is defined by the MLCA to include virtually every type of transaction that can be imagined. Specifically, the term covers: (1) a transaction that affects interstate or foreign commerce involving the movement of funds by wire, involving monetary instruments, or involving the transfer of title of any real property, vehicle, vessel, or aircraft; or (2) a transaction involving the use of a financial institution engaged in, or whose activities affect, interstate commerce.[13]

Q 29.3.5   What are "monetary instruments"?

Monetary instruments are defined, for purposes of the MLCA, as: (i) coin or currency of the United States or of any other country, traveler's checks, personal checks, bank checks and money orders, or (ii) investment securities or negotiable instruments, in bearer form or otherwise in such form that title thereto passes upon delivery.[14]

Q 29.3.6   What are "financial institutions"?

As used in the MLCA, the term "financial institution" means *much more than just banks*, although banks (including *foreign* banks) are certainly included. The term also includes all businesses listed as "financial institutions" under the BSA,[15] thus extending the meaning to include a host of other businesses as well.[16]

Laundering of Money Instruments

Q 29.4   What does section 1956 of the MLCA prohibit?

Section 1956 of the MLCA, entitled the "Laundering of Monetary Instruments,"[17] criminalizes three types of activity, which can generally be described as

(1)   transaction money laundering,
(2)   transportation money laundering, and
(3)   transactions involving money used in sting operations.

Q 29.4.1   What is "transaction money laundering"?

The MLCA prohibits any person or entity from engaging or attempting to engage in a "financial transaction":

(1)   "knowing" that the property involved in the transaction represents the proceeds of "some form of unlawful activity," and with

    (a)   the intent to promote a "specified unlawful activity," tax evasion,[18] or fraud and false statements on a tax return or related documents,[19] or

    (b)   the knowledge that the transaction is at least partly designed to conceal the true nature, location, source, ownership or control of the proceeds of a "specified unlawful activity," or to avoid a state or federal transaction reporting requirement;

(2)   if the funds or property are in fact derived from a specified unlawful activity.[20]

Q 29.4.2   What is "transportation money laundering"?

Section 1956 of the MLCA prohibits any person or entity from transporting, transmitting or transferring, or attempting to do so, any "funds" or "monetary instrument" into, out of, or through the United States:

(1)   with the intent to promote a "specified unlawful activity"; or

(2)   knowing that the funds or instrument represent the proceeds of some form of unlawful activity, and that the movement is designed at least in part to either:

    (A)   conceal the true nature, location, source, ownership or control of the proceeds of a "specified unlawful activity," or

    (B)   avoid a federal or state transaction reporting requirement.[21]

Q 29.4.3   What are the prohibitions related to "sting" operations?

Section 1956 of the MLCA makes it a crime for any person or entity to conduct or attempt to conduct a "financial transaction" involving property "represented to be" the proceeds of a "specified unlawful activity," or property used to conduct or facilitate a "specified unlawful activity" with the intent to:

(1) promote the "specified unlawful activity";

(2) conceal the true nature, location, source, ownership or control of the proceeds of the "specified unlawful activity"; or

(3) avoid a federal or state transaction reporting requirement.[22]

The phrase "represented to be" means any representation made by a law enforcement officer or another person at the direction or with the approval of a federal law enforcement officer. Thus, funds in an undercover "sting" operation are considered to be the proceeds of a "specified unlawful activity" even if they are *not* derived from such activity, but an undercover agent *says* they are.

Q 29.4.4   What are the MLCA penalties for violation of section 1956?

Criminal: Any person or entity convicted of violating section 1956 of the MLCA may be sentenced to twenty years in prison and/or a criminal fine of $500,000 or twice the value of the property, whichever is *greater*.[23]

Civil: Section 1956 of the MLCA may also be enforced by civil penalty in the amount of $10,000 or twice the value of the property, whichever is *greater*.[24]

Forfeiture: Any real or personal property involved in a transaction or attempted transaction in violation of section 1956 or 1957 of the MLCA, or any property traceable to such property, is subject to civil or criminal forfeiture by the United States.[25]

However, "tracing" the property to the offense is *not* required:

- if funds subject to forfeiture are deposited at a foreign bank and that foreign bank has an "interbank account" with a U.S.

bank, a branch or agency of a foreign bank in the United States, or a broker or dealer registered with the SEC. In such cases, funds may be seized directly from the "interbank account," and neither the foreign bank nor the U.S. entity holding the "interbank account" has standing to contest the forfeiture.[26]

- in a civil forfeiture action in which the subject property consists of cash or monetary instruments in bearer form deposited into a financial institution, if the forfeiture action is commenced within one year of the offense that is the basis for the forfeiture.[27]

Q 29.4.5 What extraterritorial jurisdiction does section 1956 of the MLCA have?

The criminal provisions of section 1956 of the MLCA apply not only to persons and entities inside the United States, but also, under certain circumstances, to persons and entities located *outside* the United States.[28] The MLCA confers jurisdiction over criminal conduct that occurs in foreign countries if:

(1) the conduct is by a U.S. citizen, or is by a non-U.S. citizen and occurs at least in part in the United States; and

(2) the transaction or series of related transactions involves funds or monetary instruments of a value exceeding $10,000.

In addition, the U.S. government may initiate a civil action against any domestic or foreign person or entity for violation of section 1956 or section 1957 (discussed below) of the MLCA.[29] The civil penalty is the greater of (i) the value of the property or funds involved in the transaction; or (ii) $10,000. Federal courts have *personal* jurisdiction over the foreign person or entity when that person or entity:

(1) commits one of the three criminal offenses (*see* QQ 29.4.1–29.4.3, *supra*) involving a financial transaction that occurs in whole or in part in the United States;

(2) converts to his, her, or its own use property that has been forfeited to the United States by court order; or

(3) is a "financial institution" that maintains a bank account at a financial institution in the United States.[30]

The term "financial institution" includes any of the several dozen types of businesses defined as such in the BSA,[31] or any foreign bank.[32] For purposes of enforcing section 1956 of the MLCA, a U.S. court may issue a restraining order to ensure that any bank account or other property held in the United States by a defendant is available to satisfy a judgment. The courts have the authority to appoint a "federal receiver" to find and collect all of a defendant's assets, wherever located, to satisfy a civil or criminal judgment, or an order of forfeiture. The federal receiver is granted substantial powers to accomplish this task.[33]

Engaging in Monetary Transactions in Property Derived from Specified Unlawful Activity

Q 29.5   What does section 1957 of the MLCA provide?

Section 1957 of the MLCA[34] makes it illegal for any person or entity to knowingly engage or attempt to engage in a "monetary transaction" in "criminally derived property" of a value over $10,000, if the property is, in fact, derived from a "specified unlawful activity." The definition of "knowing" applicable to section 1957 of the MLCA applies also to this section of the MLCA. A "specified unlawful activity" has the same meaning as that used for purposes of section 1956 of the MLCA.[35]

Q 29.5.1   What is a "monetary transaction"?

It is the deposit, withdrawal, transfer, or exchange of funds or monetary instruments by, through, or to a "financial institution."[36] This provision essentially makes it illegal to *spend* funds in excess of $10,000 derived from "specified unlawful activity" without regard for the intent or purpose of the transaction.

Further, the government need not prove that the defendant knew that the offense from which the funds were derived was a "specified unlawful activity." It is enough for the defendant to know only that the funds were "criminally derived." Thus, any "financial institution" which *receives* funds in a transaction and knows, or is "willfully blind" to the fact that the funds come from criminal activity, potentially violates section 1957 of the MLCA.

Q 29.5.2   What is "criminally derived property"?

Any property, in whatever form, constituting or derived from proceeds obtained from a criminal offense.[37]

Q 29.5.3   Does the government have extraterritorial jurisdiction to prosecute violations of section 1957 of the MLCA?

A violation of section 1957 occurring *outside* the United States may be prosecuted if the defendant is a "United States person." A "United States person" includes a national of the United States, any resident alien, any person within the United States, any entity composed principally of nationals or permanent resident aliens of the United States, or any corporation organized under the laws of the United States, any state, the District of Columbia, or any territory or possession of the United States.[38]

Q 29.5.4   What are the penalties for violations of section 1957 of the MLCA?

Violations of this section are punishable by imprisonment for up to ten years and a fine of up to twice the amount of the value of the criminally derived property involved in the transaction. In addition, the forfeiture provisions described above also apply to violations of this section.

The Bank Secrecy Act

Q 29.6   What is the BSA?

The BSA is basically a *regulatory* statute that seeks to deter money laundering through regulations requiring certain business practices.[39] Unlike the MLCA, the BSA applies only to certain types of businesses. The types of businesses it applies to are further limited by the implementing regulations issued by the Secretary of the Treasury. The Treasury regulations issued under the BSA are issued by the Financial Crimes Enforcement Network (FinCEN), a bureau within the Treasury Department whose mission is to deter and detect money laundering and terrorist financing. Although the BSA is a regulatory statute, violations of the BSA can be enforced through criminal prosecution against individuals and businesses.[40]

Q 29.6.1   To whom does the BSA apply?

With the exception of the cash reporting requirements (*see* Q 29.12.2, *infra*), the BSA applies only to businesses classified as "financial institutions." It authorizes the U.S. Treasury Department to require those businesses to take certain anti-money laundering actions, including reporting large cash transactions (those over $10,000), making and keeping certain records, implementing a formal, written "anti-money laundering compliance program," and mandatory reporting of "suspicious activity" to the federal government.

Q 29.6.2   What is the definition of "financial institutions" for purposes of the BSA?

Under the BSA, the term "financial institution" includes *much more than banks*. The term is defined[41] to include the following (however, not all of these businesses have yet been regulated pursuant to the BSA (see below)):

(1)   an insured bank;[42]

(2)   a commercial bank or trust company;

(3)   a private banker;

(4)   an agency or branch of a foreign bank in the United States;

(5)   any credit union;

(6)   a thrift institution;

(7)   a broker or dealer registered with the SEC under the Securities Exchange Act of 1934;

(8)   any futures commission merchant, commodity trading advisor, or commodity pool operator registered or required to be registered under the Commodity Exchange Act;

(9)   a broker or dealer in securities or commodities;

(10) an investment banker or investment company;[43]

(11) a currency exchange;

(12) MSBs;[44]

(13) an operator of a credit card system;

(14) an insurance company;

(15) a dealer in precious metals, stones, or jewels;

(16) a pawnbroker;

(17) a loan or finance company;

(18) a travel agency;

(19) funds transmitters, both licensed businesses as well as informal networks of people engaged in facilitating domestic or international transfers outside the conventional financial system;

(20) a telegraph company;

(21) a business engaged in the sale of vehicles (including automobiles, airplanes, and boats);

(22) persons involved in real estate closings and settlements;

(23) the U.S. Postal Service;

(24) an agency of the U.S. government or of a state or local government carrying out a power or duty of a business described in 31 U.S.C. § 5312;

(25) a casino, a gambling casino, or gaming establishment with an annual gaming revenue of more than $1 million;

(26) any business engaging in an activity the secretary determines by regulation to be similar to, related to, or a substitute for any business described in 31 U.S.C. § 5312; and

(27) any other business designated by the secretary whose cash transactions have a high degree of usefulness in criminal, tax, or regulatory matters.

Anti-Money Laundering Program Requirements

Q 29.7   Which financial institutions must implement AML compliance programs, and which are exempted?

The Secretary of the Treasury has issued regulations implementing the BSA. All of those regulations are published at 31 C.F.R. part 1010 *et seq.* The regulations are organized by financial industry.[45]

The regulations issued by the Secretary only apply to *some* of the "financial institutions" listed in the BSA. Other BSA "financial institutions" have been exempted from regulation.

Currently, the "financial institutions" subject to specific implementing regulations are:

- all banks regulated by a federal regulatory agency;

- businesses regulated by the SEC;

- futures commissions merchants and introducing brokers in commodities;

- casinos and card clubs;

- credit unions regulated by the National Credit Union Administration;

- mutual funds;[46]

- MSBs;

- businesses engaged in vehicle sales, including automobile, airplane, and boat sales;

- operators of credit card systems;

- some dealers in precious metals, precious stones, or jewels;

- residential mortgage lenders and originators;

- certain life insurance companies; and[47]

- housing government-sponsored enterprises.[48]

All other businesses that fall within the definition of "financial institution" have been temporarily exempted from the provisions of the BSA, except for government agencies, which have been permanently exempted.[49]

A careful reading of the BSA regulations is important for all "financial institutions" because some types of businesses that fall within the general BSA description of "financial institution" (particularly life insurance companies and dealers in precious metals, stones, or jewels) may be excluded from the regulatory definitions.[50]

Q 29.7.1   What are the general regulatory requirements for subject financial institutions?

(1) Implementation of an anti-money laundering program;

(2) Implementation of customer identification programs (CIPs);

(3) Reporting of "suspicious transactions" to the Treasury Department;

(4) Reporting "large cash transactions"; and

(5) Certain record-keeping requirements.

Not all of these requirements are equally applicable to regulated "financial institutions," and accordingly, careful review of the applicable regulations is necessary.

Q 29.7.2   What are the BSA's requirements for anti-money laundering programs?

(1) An anti-money laundering program must be in writing.

(2) The "financial institution" must:

   (a) formally appoint an "anti-money laundering compliance officer" who is in overall charge of the program;

   (b) conduct periodic training of appropriate employees about the institution's anti-money laundering policies and procedures; and

   (c) conduct a periodic independent audit of the program to ensure it has been implemented and is being followed.[51]

(3) Anti-money laundering programs must be "risk-based."

Q 29.7.3   What is a "risk-based" anti-money laundering program?

This means that each institution must carefully consider its customer base, products, services, geographic areas of operation, and market area in order to determine the degree of money laundering risk the institution faces and the degree of risk associated with each of these various categories. As a practical matter, this involves the preparation of a written "Risk Assessment" covering each of the factors just noted. Then, based upon that assessment, the institution must develop written policies and procedures specifically designed to address the degree of risk and detect, deter, and report money laundering or terrorist financing activity.

Customer Identification Programs (CIPs)

Q 29.8   What are the BSA's requirements regarding CIPs?

CIPs are required only for some "financial institutions." These include:

- banks;
- savings associations;
- credit unions;
- securities broker-dealers;
- futures commission merchants and introducing brokers; and
- mutual funds.[52]

The CIP must be in writing and, if the institution is also required to have an anti-money laundering program, the CIP must be included as part of that program. The CIP must include, at a minimum, procedures to verify the name, date of birth, address or principal place of business, and identification number of the customer. Verification may be done through documents specifically set forth in the program (generally, a government-issued photo identification for persons, or documents showing the legal existence of an entity). Verification may be made through non-documentary procedures, but the specific procedures to be followed must be specified in the program. The CIP must also prescribe the procedures to be followed by the institution when verification cannot be accomplished, including the circumstances under which an account must be closed for lack of verification. The institution must maintain copies of all records and documents used in the verification process.

"Suspicious Transactions"

Q 29.9   What is a "suspicious transaction"?

Generally, transactions are considered to be "suspicious" and subject to the reporting requirement where the institution knows, suspects, or has reason to suspect that a transaction:

(1) involves funds derived from illegal activities;

(2) is intended or conducted in order to hide or disguise funds or assets derived from illegal activities;

(3) is designed to evade any reporting or other requirements of the BSA or the BSA regulations;

(4) has no business or apparent lawful purpose;

(5) is not normal for the customer involved, and the institution knows of no reasonable explanation for the transaction; or

(6) involves the use of the financial institution to facilitate criminal activity.

Q 29.9.1   Who must report suspicious transactions?

Some financial institutions must so report. Those required to report suspicious transactions in writing to the Treasury Department (specifically, to FinCEN) are:

(1) banks;[53]

(2) mutual funds;

(3) insurance companies covered under 31 C.F.R. § 1025 (formerly 31 C.F.R. § 103.137);

(4) brokers or dealers in securities;

(5) futures commission merchants and introducing brokers in commodities;

(6) MSBs;

(7) residential mortgage lenders and originators; and

(8) casinos.[54]

No financial institution (or any officer, director, employee, or agent) may disclose a suspicious activity report (SAR), or any information that would reveal the existence of a SAR. Any financial institution that is subpoenaed or otherwise requested to disclose a SAR or any information that would reveal the existence of a SAR must refuse to provide that information and must notify FinCEN.[55]

However, *provided no person involved in the transaction is notified that the transaction has been reported*, disclosures *may* be made to

(1) FinCEN;

(2) any federal, state, or local law enforcement agency;

(3) any federal regulatory authority that examines the financial institution for compliance with the BSA; or

(4) any self-regulatory organization that examines the financial institution for compliance with its SAR reporting requirements, upon the request of the federal agency responsible for its oversight.

The regulations also allow: (i) the disclosure of the underlying facts, transactions, and documents upon which a SAR is based, including, but not limited to, disclosures related to filing a joint SAR and in connection with certain employment references or termination notices; and (ii) the sharing of a SAR, or any information that would reveal the existence of a SAR, within the corporate organizational structure of a financial institution for purposes consistent with the BSA, as determined by regulation or FinCEN guidance.[56]

Q 29.9.2 Doesn't reporting a suspicious transaction expose me and/or my company to legal risk?

The BSA provides a "safe harbor" for financial institutions (and their officers, directors, employees, and agents) reporting suspicious transactions or activity. No financial institution may be held liable to any person or entity under any federal statute or regulation, or under the constitution, law, or regulation of any state or political subdivision, for disclosing suspicious activity or for failing to notify the person or entity who is the subject of, or named in, the report.[57]

Q 29.9.3 What are the filing requirements for reports of suspicious transactions?

Suspicious activity reports may only be filed electronically on FinCEN Form 111.[58] In all cases, however, the report must be filed within thirty days after the date of the detection of the facts that constitute grounds for filing. Filing may be delayed an additional thirty days in order to enable the institution to identify a suspect, but in no case may filing be delayed more than sixty days. Transactions involving ongoing money laundering schemes or terrorist financing must be verbally reported immediately upon suspicion to an appropriate law enforcement agency.

Uniting and Strengthening America by Providing Appropriate Tools Required to Intercept and Obstruct Terrorism Act of 2001 (USA PATRIOT Act)

Q 29.10 General Information

In response to the September 11, 2001, terrorist attacks, Congress passed the Uniting and Strengthening America by Providing Appropriate Tools Required to Intercept and Obstruct Terrorism Act of 2001 (USA PATRIOT Act).[59] The purpose of the USA PATRIOT Act is to deter and punish terrorist acts in the United States and around the world, and to enhance law enforcement investigatory tools.[60] While the BSA remains the primary U.S. law regarding Anti-Money Laundering, the USA PATRIOT Act criminalized the financing of terrorism and amends the anti-money laundering provisions of the BSA to include certain provisions with regard to financial institutions, some of which are summarized below.

Section 311: Special Measures for Jurisdictions, Financial Institutions, or International Transactions of Primary Money Laundering Concern	Under Section 311, the Secretary of the Treasury is authorized to designate a foreign jurisdiction, institutions, classes of transactions, or accounts as a "primary money laundering concern" and to require U.S. financial institutions to take certain "special measures" against the primary money laundering concern.[61]
Section 312: Special Due Diligence for Correspondent Accounts and Private Banking Accounts	Section 312 amends the BSA by imposing specific, risk-based, and enhanced due diligence requirements on U.S. financial institutions that maintain correspondent accounts for foreign financial institutions or private banking accounts for non-U.S. persons.[62] The due diligence program must be reasonably designed to detect and report any known or suspected money laundering or other suspicious activity.[63]
Section 313: Prohibition on U.S. Correspondent Accounts with Foreign Shell Banks	Section 313 of the USA PATRIOT Act specifically prohibits banks and broker-dealers from opening or maintaining any correspondent accounts for any foreign bank that does not have a physical presence in any country.[64] The statute further requires financial institutions to take reasonable steps to ensure any existing correspondent accounts are not used to indirectly provide correspondent services to any shell bank.[65]

Section 314: Cooperative Efforts to Deter Money Laundering	Section 314 is divided into two sections (described in more detail infra) which assists in identifying, disrupting, and preventing terrorist acts and money laundering activities. The section requires financial institutions to share information regarding those suspected of being involved in terrorism or money laundering (see QQ 29.11–29.11.2).
Section 319(b): Bank Records Related to Anti-Money Laundering Programs	This section authorizes the Secretary of the Treasury or the Attorney General to issue a summons or subpoena to any foreign bank that maintains a correspondent account in the U.S. for records related to those accounts.[66]
Section 325: Concentration Accounts at Financial Institutions	Section 325 allows the Secretary of the Treasury to issue regulations to govern accounts controlled by financial institutions to verify the identity of the customer who is the direct or beneficial owner of the funds being moved through the account.
Section 326: Verification of Identification	Section 326 grants authority to the Secretary of the Treasury to issue regulations that set minimum standards for identifying a customer prior to opening an account at a financial institution (see Q 29.8).[67]
Section 351: Amendments Relating to Reporting of Suspicious Activities	This section expands immunity from liability for reporting suspicious activities and expands prohibition against notification to individuals of SAR filing. This section also enhanced confidentiality of SARs.[68]

The USA PATRIOT Act and its implementing regulations also:

- Expanded the AML program requirements to all financial institutions[69] (*see* Q 29.7, *supra*).

- Increased the civil and criminal penalties for money laundering.

- Facilitated records access and required banks to respond to regulatory requests for information within 120 hours.[70]

- Required federal banking agencies to consider a bank's AML record when reviewing bank mergers, acquisitions, and other applications for business combinations.

Information Sharing

Q 29.11   What is "information sharing"?

Information sharing, authorized by section 314 of the USA PATRIOT Act,[71] was designed to develop cooperative efforts among certain financial institutions, regulatory authorities, and federal law enforcement agencies through the exchange of information concerning possible participants in money laundering and terrorist financing. It consists of two distinct types, each subject to different regulations:

- Section 314(a) "mandatory information sharing" between financial institutions and federal law enforcement agencies; and

- section 314(b) "voluntary information sharing" between financial institutions alone.

Q 29.11.1   What is section 314(a) mandatory information sharing?

Generally, section 314(a) mandatory information sharing consists of federal, state, local, or foreign law enforcement agencies[72] requesting, through FinCEN, financial institutions to state whether particular individuals, entities, or organizations:

(i)   maintain a current "account" with the institution;

(ii) have maintained an "account" with the institution during the preceding twelve months; or

(iii) have been involved in any "transaction" or transmittal of funds by or through the institution during the preceding six months.

Law enforcement agencies are limited to requesting information only for investigations of terrorist activity or money laundering.[73] Section 314(a) requests for information may be made to financial institutions only through FinCEN, and a financial institution's response is provided to FinCEN only. Information provided to FinCEN in response to a section 314(a) request is reported by FinCEN to the law enforcement agency that initiated the FinCEN request.

Q 29.11.2   Who is subject to section 314(a) mandatory information sharing?

Mandatory information sharing applies to all "financial institutions" as defined by the BSA.[74] In practice, however, the financial institutions subject to section 314(a) mandatory information sharing requests from FinCEN are limited to banks, credit unions, securities and commodities broker-dealers, MSBs, residential mortgage lenders and originators, and casinos.[75]

Q 29.11.3   What must a financial institution do upon receipt of a section 314(a) mandatory information sharing request?

Financial institutions are required to immediately check their records upon receipt of the request and promptly respond within the time frame specified by FinCEN in the request (generally fourteen days).[76] Unless otherwise instructed in the request, the search must include:

(1) deposit account records;

(2) funds transfer records maintained pursuant to 31 C.F.R. § 103.33 to determine whether a suspect was an originator/transmitter or beneficiary/recipient of a funds transfer;

(3) records of the sale of monetary instruments (for example, cashier's checks, money orders, or traveler's checks) kept pursuant to 31 C.F.R. § 103.29;

(4) loan records;

(5) trust department account records;

(6) records of accounts to purchase, sell, lease, hold, or maintain custody of securities;

(7) commodity futures, options, or other derivatives account records; and

(8) safe deposit box records (but only if such safe deposit box records are searchable electronically).[77]

Positive matches must be reported directly and only to FinCEN. If the search does not uncover any matching account or transaction, the financial institution should not reply to the request. A positive report must include:

(i)   the name of the individual, entity, or organization matched;

(ii) the number of each account or, in the case of a transaction, the date and type of the transaction; and

(iii) any Social Security or taxpayer identification number, passport number, date of birth, address, or other similar identifying information provided by the named suspect.

Reports should not provide any other details to FinCEN other than the fact that the financial institution has a match, together with the required information.[78]

Q 29.11.4   Should a positive response to a section 314(a) mandatory information sharing request include records?

No. A section 314(a) request is not a substitute for a subpoena or other legal process. But a financial institution submitting a positive report to FinCEN can expect to receive a grand jury subpoena or other legal process for documents relating to the suspect named in that report.

Q 29.11.5   Are section 314(a) mandatory information sharing requests and responses confidential?

Yes. Except to the extent necessary to comply with the request, a financial institution may not disclose to any person the fact that FinCEN has requested or obtained information. Each institution should have appropriate policies and procedures in place to ensure confidentiality.

Section 314(a) requests may, however, be disclosed to the institution's primary regulator, a *domestic* parent or holding company, and *domestic* subsidiaries and affiliates if those entities offer "account" or "transaction" services and are financial institutions as described in 31 U.S.C. § 5312(a)(2). The domestic parent or affiliate must maintain the confidentiality of the section 314(a) request.

Q 29.11.6   Should a section 314(a) mandatory information sharing request trigger the filing of a suspicious activity report if there is a positive match?

No. Mere inclusion in a section 314(a) list should not be the sole factor (but it may be one factor) used to determine whether to file a SAR.[79] However, a financial institution that has a section 314(a) account or transaction should review that customer's activity in light of the section 314(a) request to decide whether to keep or close an account, engage in a proposed transaction, or file a SAR.

Q 29.11.7   What is section 314(b) voluntary information sharing?

Voluntary information sharing is the sharing of information between financial institutions about individuals, entities, organizations, or countries for the purposes of identifying and reporting activities that a financial institution suspects may involve possible terrorist activity or money laundering.[80]

Q 29.11.8   What information may be shared among financial institutions under section 314(b) voluntary information sharing?

The only information that may be exchanged under section 314(b) is information relating to identifying and reporting money laundering or terrorist activity. Section 314(b) may not be used to exchange information about other suspected criminal activity, or for general business purposes such as credit or lending decisions, locating defaulting borrowers or their assets, and so on.[81]

Q 29.11.9   Who may share information under section 314(b)?

Only those financial institutions that are required by regulation to have anti-money laundering programs are eligible to participate in voluntary information sharing.[82] This includes all banks and credit unions regulated by a federal regulatory agency, securities broker dealers, futures commissions merchants, and originating brokers in commodities, mutual funds, MSBs, casinos, operators of credit card systems, dealers in precious metals, precious stones or precious jewels, residential mortgage lenders and originators, and certain life insurance companies.[83]

Q 29.11.10   How does one participate in section 314(b) voluntary information sharing?

If a financial institution is eligible to participate, it must first submit a notification to FinCEN.[84] The notification is effective immediately and authorizes participation in voluntary information sharing for one year from the date of the notification. It must be renewed annually in order to continue to participate.

Q 29.11.11   Who may information be shared with?

Financial institutions may only share information with other eligible financial institutions that have themselves already filed the FinCEN notification.[85] Before engaging in voluntary information sharing, a financial institution must take reasonable steps to determine that the entity it is sharing with has also submitted the required notification to FinCEN.[86]

Q 29.11.12   Is information shared under 314(b) confidential?

Yes. Participating institutions must establish appropriate procedures to protect shared information, both internally and externally.

Q 29.11.13   Should a section 314(b) voluntary information sharing request trigger the filing of a SAR?

A financial institution may use information obtained under section 314(b) to determine whether to file a SAR, but the intention to prepare or file a SAR may not be shared with another financial institution. If a financial institution shares information under section 314(b), it should not include any reference to any SAR filing.

Q 29.11.14   May a financial institution that shares information under section 314(b) be sued civilly by the subject of the information?

Section 314(b) provides financial institutions with a "safe harbor" from civil liability for sharing information, and for not providing notice of such sharing to any person identified in the information shared if, and only if, the institution has fully complied with all of the voluntary information sharing regulations in 31 C.F.R. § 103.110(b)(2), (b)(3), and (b)(4).[87]

Reporting Large Cash Transactions

Q 29.12   Why does the government require large cash transactions to be reported?

Because cash transactions leave little or no documentary trail. Credit card transactions and check purchases leave records identifying the date and nature of the transaction as well as the names of the persons or entities involved. When a person engages in a cash transaction, there is rarely any record (other than a personal receipt) of the transaction's occurrence. A record showing the nature of the transaction or, more importantly, the persons involved in it, is even rarer still. Thus, in an effort to overcome this absence of a paper trail in cash transactions, federal laws require virtually all businesses in the United States to file reports with the federal government on all cash transactions over $10,000.

Q 29.12.1   What forms are used to report large cash transactions?

- Currency Transaction Report
- IRS/FinCEN Form 8300

Currency Transaction Reports

Q 29.12.2   What are the requirements for filing a Currency Transaction Report (CTR)?

The BSA authorizes the Secretary of the Treasury to require domestic financial institutions to report all cash transactions in excess of $10,000 that occur within a single business day by or on behalf of the same person.[88] "Cash transactions" are those involving the coin or paper money of the United States, as well as foreign currency.[89] A reportable cash transaction includes the aggregate of multiple cash transactions conducted at all of a reporting institution's branches and agencies on a single day if the transactions are conducted by or on behalf of the same person/entity. Reports must be made within fifteen days of the transaction to the IRS on a "Currency Transaction Report," FinCEN Form 104.[90] As of July 1, 2012, CTRs must be filed electronically.

The financial institutions required to report such transactions on a CTR include depository institutions such as banks, credit unions and thrift institutions, broker-dealers in securities, mutual funds, commodities futures traders, MSBs (that is, currency dealers or exchangers; check cashers; issuers or sellers of cashier's checks, traveler's checks, or money orders; providers or sellers of prepaid access; and money transmitters), and casinos and card clubs.[91]

It is illegal to structure a cash transaction for the purpose of evading the reporting requirement.[92] It is illegal to fail to file a CTR, or to intentionally file one that is inaccurate or purposely omits required information. Negligent violations may be punished civilly; intentional failures may be punished civilly or criminally as violations of the BSA.

IRS Form 8300

Q 29.12.3   What are the requirements for filing an IRS Form 8300?

Both the BSA[93] and the Internal Revenue Code[94] require that any person who is engaged in a trade or business and who, in the course of such trade or business, receives more than $10,000 in currency in one transaction, or in two or more "related" transactions, is required to file a report of the transaction with FinCEN and the IRS. This requirement includes *all other* "financial institutions" not otherwise required to file CTRs, as well as *all other persons and businesses* in the United States, if they receive over $10,000 in "currency" in the course of their trade or business.[95]

Although required by two separate statutes, and subject to two separate (but virtually identical) sets of regulations,[96] reports are made on a single form, an IRS/FinCEN Form 8300, which is transmitted to the IRS.[97] A Form 8300 must be filed within fifteen days of the receipt of over $10,000 in currency, unless the fifteenth day falls on a holiday, Saturday or Sunday, then the business must file the next business day.[98] On February 24, 2012, FinCEN announced that businesses may electronically file their Form 8300 using the Bank Secrecy Act Election Filing System ("BSA E-Filing") or may also continue to be filed on paper.[99]

It is illegal to structure a cash transaction for the purpose of evading the reporting requirement.[100] It is illegal to fail to file a Form 8300, or to intentionally file one that is inaccurate or purposely omits required information. Negligent violations may be punished civilly, and intentional violations may be punished civilly and criminally, as violations of the BSA. Violations may also be punished civilly or criminally under the Internal Revenue Code.[101]

In addition to reporting currency transactions, every business must furnish a single, annual written statement to each person named on a Form 8300 that includes the name and address of the business, the total amount of currency reported to have been received in the calendar year from or on behalf of the person named in the form, and a statement saying that the information was reported to the IRS. The statement must be sent to each person named in the form on or before

January 31 of the year following the calendar year in which the currency was received.[102]

Q 29.12.4   What constitutes "currency" for purposes of Form 8300?

Just as in the case of CTRs, "currency" includes U.S. currency, and the currency of any other country.[103] Unlike CTRs, however, "currency" for Form 8300 reporting purposes is not limited just to cash. "Currency" has a different meaning when the transaction involves the retail sale of a "consumer durable" or a travel or entertainment activity.[104] It includes cashier's checks (by whatever name called, including "treasurer's checks" and "bank checks"), bank drafts, traveler's checks, or money orders, *with a face value of under $10,000.*[105] The term does not include a personal check, regardless of the face value.

Q 29.12.5   What is a reportable transaction?

The law requires that if a business receives more than $10,000 in "currency" in one transaction or in two or more "related" transactions, it is required to file a Form 8300 with the IRS. A "transaction" means the underlying event precipitating the payer's transfer of currency to the recipient. This includes, but is not limited to the:

- sale of goods or services;
- sale of real property;
- sale of intangible property;
- rental of real or personal property;
- exchange of currency for other currency;
- establishment or maintenance of a custodial, trust, or escrow arrangement;
- payment of a pre-existing debt;
- conversion of currency into a negotiable instrument;
- reimbursement for expenses paid; or
- making or repayment of a loan.[106]

Any transactions between a business and the same customer that occur within a twenty-four-hour period are considered to be one transaction for reporting purposes.[107]

Q 29.12.6   When are transactions considered "related"?

Transactions are considered "related" for reporting purposes even if they occur over a period of more than twenty-four hours, if the receiving business knows or has reason to know that each transaction is one of a series of connected transactions.[108]

Q 29.12.7   How are multiple-payment transactions handled?

The receipt of "currency" deposits or installment payments for a single transaction is reported differently, depending on the amounts of cash paid in the initial and subsequent payments.[109]

If a customer's initial payment in one transaction is over $10,000 in "currency," that payment must be reported on Form 8300 within fifteen days of the transaction. If the initial payment is in "currency" but does not exceed $10,000, then the initial payment must be combined with subsequent "currency" payments made within one year. As soon as the total of "currency" payments on the transaction exceeds $10,000, a Form 8300 must be filed. If more "currency" payments on that transaction are later received within the one-year period, they must be separately reported every time they total over $10,000.

BSA Record-Keeping Requirements

Q 29.13   What records must be made and kept under the BSA?

The BSA requires certain records of particular types of transactions must be made and kept. The record-keeping requirements of the BSA generally fall into three categories:

- those applicable to all businesses in general;
- those applicable to "all financial institutions"; and
- those applicable only to specific "financial institutions."

In general, the only record-keeping requirement applicable to all businesses in general is that copies of all reports of transactions involving "currency" over $10,000 (which are filed on IRS Form 8300) (*see* Q 29.12.3, *supra*) must be maintained for five years from the date of filing.[110] It is important to note here that "currency" has a unique meaning that involves more than just cash; it can also include certain types of monetary instruments (*see* Q 29.12.4, *supra*).

The BSA regulations also require that "all financial institutions" must keep records of:

- each extension of credit over $10,000 that is not secured by real property; and

- each advice, request, or instruction received or given that results in the transfer of funds, securities, or credit to or from any person, account, or place outside the United States.

These records must be kept for a period of five years.[111]

Although the record-keeping regulations apply to "all financial institutions," the regulatory definition of "financial institution" differs from the BSA statutory definition. For purposes of the regulations, "financial institutions" are banks, credit unions, MSBs, a telegraph company, brokers or dealers in securities, mutual funds, casinos and card clubs, futures commission merchants, and introducing brokers in commodities.[112]

FIGURE 29-1

Example: Multiple-Payment Transactions and Form 8300

Joe Customer intends to purchase a $45,000 necklace from a business and pay over a five-month period. The $45,000 is a single transaction for cash reporting purposes. Joe pays $9,000 each month for five months; thus, if any part of any of the payments is made in cash, once the cash portions total over $10,000, a Form 8300 must be filed on the cash payments.

Monthly Payment	Form of Payment	File Form 8300?	Why/Why Not?
1	$9,000 personal check	No	A personal check is not cash.
2	$9,000 cash	No	The amount of cash received by the company is still under $10,000.
3	$9,000 cashier's check	Yes	The business has now received, in one transaction, over $10,000 in cash—$9,000 in currency and $9,000 in a cashier's check (a "monetary instrument" that is the equivalent of cash).
4	$9,000 cash	No	After filing the first Form 8300, the $10,000 count starts over again.
5	$9,000 traveler's check	Yes	The business has again received, in one transaction (the original $45,000 transaction), over $10,000 in cash—$9,000 in currency and $9,000 in the traveler's check (again, the "monetary instrument" equivalent of cash).

The BSA record-keeping requirements applicable only to specific "financial institutions" apply to banks and credit unions, currency dealers or exchangers, brokers or dealers in securities, casinos, and MSBs.[113]

"Bulk Cash Smuggling"

Q 29.14   What is "bulk cash smuggling"?

It is the act of physically transporting, mailing, shipping, or causing the same, of any cash or "monetary instrument" into or out of the United States without filing the required report. For U.S. purposes, aggregate amounts exceeding $10,000 into or out of the United States must be reported to the U.S. Customs Service. The report must be made on a "Report of International Transportation of Currency or Monetary Instruments," also known as a "CMIR" or FinCEN Form 105.[114] On February 24, 2012, FinCEN announced that businesses may electronically file their CMIR using BSA E-Filing or may also continue to file on paper.[115]

Q 29.14.1   What are the filing requirements for FinCEN Form 105?

The report must be filed before or at the time of the entry or departure into or from the United States. It may also be made by mail on or before the date of entry, departure, mailing, or shipping. However, as a practical matter, the report should be filed directly with U.S. Customs at the time or entry or departure.

A person or entity *receiving* cash or monetary instruments from outside the United States must file a FinCEN Form 105 within fifteen days of receipt if the form has not already been filed by the person sending or causing the sending of the funds.[116]

Q 29.14.2   What are the consequences of bulk cash smuggling?

The knowing and intentional failure to file this report may result in the seizure and civil or criminal forfeiture of the currency and monetary instruments being transported. If the currency or monetary instrument is concealed for the purpose of avoiding a report, the container or conveyance carrying the funds may also be seized. A knowing and intentional failure to report can be also punished criminally by imprisonment for up to five years.[117]

Q 29.14.3 For purposes of bulk cash smuggling, what are "currency" and "monetary instruments"?

For purposes of this law, "currency" means the coin or paper money of the United States, as well as the coin or paper money of a foreign country. Thus, the import or export of foreign currency whose value in U.S. dollars exceeds $10,000 must be reported.

The term "monetary instrument" means:

- currency;

- traveler's checks in any form;

- all forms of negotiable instruments (including personal and business checks) that are either in bearer form, that may be endorsed without restriction, that are made out to a fictitious payee, or that are in any other form such that title passes upon delivery;

- incomplete instruments that are signed but with the payee's name left out; and

- securities or stocks in bearer form or whose title passes on delivery.[118]

Q 29.14.4 Are there any exceptions to this reporting requirement?

There are a number of them, including:

(1) banks, foreign banks, and securities broker-dealers shipping by mail or by common carrier;

(2) certain overland shipments by a domestic commercial bank or trust company for an established customer;

(3) common carriers of passengers with respect to funds carried by passengers;

(4) common carriers of goods with respect to funds shipments not declared to the common carrier;

(5)   a non-U.S. citizen or resident for funds mailed or shipped from abroad to a bank or broker-dealer by mail or common carrier; and

(6)   issuers of traveler's checks.[119]

Structuring

Q 29.15   What is structuring?

In order to avoid the large cash transaction reporting requirements, money launderers and terrorists frequently attempt to disguise one single cash transaction that exceeds $10,000 as multiple, separate transactions, each under $10,000. This type of activity, when designed to avoid the filing of applicable reports, is called "structuring."

Q 29.15.1   What are the penalties for structuring violations?

Structuring is illegal and punishable by imprisonment up to five years. Structuring violations, if committed while violating another law of the United States or as part of a pattern of any illegal activity involving over $100,000 in a one-year period, are punishable by a fine of up to $500,000 and imprisonment for up to ten years for an individual and a fine of up to $1 million for a corporation.[120]

Transactions with Specially Designated Persons

Q 29.16   Who are the "specially designated persons" that federal AML statutes prohibit transactions with?

A number of federal laws impose severe restrictions and sanctions against:

(1)   persons, groups, entities, and countries deemed to be supporters of terrorist activity;

(2)   terrorists; and

(3)   international narcotics traffickers and "kingpins."

The U.S. Treasury Department's Office of Foreign Assets Control (OFAC) maintains a list of these "Specially Designated Nationals"

(SDNs) on its "OFAC List" (or "SDN List"). These sanctions are implemented through regulations issued by OFAC and apply to all "United States persons."

Q 29.16.1   Who is considered a "United States person"?

Generally, a "United States person" includes:

*   a national of the United States anywhere in the world;

*   any resident alien;

*   any person within the United States;

*   any entity composed principally of nationals or permanent resident aliens of the United States; or

*   any corporation organized under the laws of the United States, any state, the District of Columbia, or any U.S. territory or possession.

Generally, for anti-money laundering and anti-terrorist financing purposes, the term does not include foreign subsidiaries of U.S. entities. However, the term *does* include, and the prohibitions *do* directly apply to, individual United States persons located anywhere in the world, regardless of who their employer is.[121]

Q 29.17   What kinds of transactions with SDNs are prohibited?

Generally, the OFAC regulations prohibit any United States person from conducting any business transaction or transfer of any funds or property, facilitating any business transaction, or providing any service to any person, group, or organization on the OFAC List. The regulations further generally require either that all property and assets of SDNs be "blocked" (that is, placed in an interest-bearing account not accessible to the SDN), or that any transaction involving any property or funds belonging to an SDN be rejected and promptly reported to OFAC. However, the precise prohibitions imposed by OFAC regulations against SDNs and the specific requirements imposed on United States persons vary according to the particular reason why the person, group, entity, or country has been placed on the OFAC List.[122] Accordingly, the names found on the list also refer to the particular reason for inclusion. It is thus important not only to identify SDNs, but also to know their specific designation in order to determine the precise requirements and prohibitions imposed on United States persons by the regulations.

Q 29.17.1   What are the consequences of conducting business with an SDN?

Violations can be punished by severe fines and imprisonment, depending upon the statute and sanctions program involved. Civil fines imposed by OFAC against United States persons violating OFAC regulations can be substantial, frequently involving hundreds of thousands—and in some cases millions—of dollars.[123]

Special Rules for MSBs

Q 29.18   What are the AML requirements for MSBs?

In addition to maintaining formal anti-money laundering programs and reporting "suspicious transactions," all MSBs are required to register with FinCEN.[124] Operating as an MSB without registering is a federal felony punishable by fine and imprisonment for up to five years.[125]

In addition, many states also require MSBs to register. Failure to register with a state, if required by state law, would likewise be considered both a state and a federal felony, regardless of whether the MSB knew about the licensing requirement.[126] It is, therefore, essential for every such business not only to comply with the federal registration regulations, but also to check the laws of each state in which it does business. In some cases, an MSB may have to file multiple registrations. Care must be taken to closely examine the definition of the term "MSBs" under both the federal regulations and local state law, because they frequently differ. This can result in a business having to register in some states but not others, or with FinCEN but not with the state, or with the state but not with FinCEN.

Agents and branches of MSBs are not required by federal regulation to register with FinCEN, although the business must report information about its branch locations or offices, and must maintain a list of its agents. This list must include each agent's name, address, telephone number, type of service provided by the agent, the agent's bank, the year the agent first became an agent, the number of branches or sub-agents the agent has, and a listing of the months in the preceding twelve months in which the agent's gross transaction amount exceeded $100,000.[127]

Registration is valid for a two-year period, and a copy of the registration must be kept at a location in the United States for five years. If, however, the business is subject to a state registration requirement, then a change in control that requires re-registration with the state requires re-registration with FinCEN. In addition, the federal regulations also require re-registration with FinCEN if there is a transfer of more than 10% of the voting power or equity interest of the business. Further, if the business experiences a more than 50% increase in the number of its agents during any registration period, the business must re-register with FinCEN. Re-registration must be done within 180 days of the event triggering the re-registration requirement.[128]

Q 29.19   What are the AML requirements for *foreign* MSBs?

On July 21, 2011, FinCEN issued a final rule (effective in September 2011) clarifying the definition of MSBs to include *foreign* MSBs as well as domestic ones.[129] Specifically, FinCEN revised 31 C.F.R. § 1010.100(ff) so that an entity qualifies as an MSB based on its activity within the United States, not the physical presence there of one or more of its agents, agencies, branches, or offices. The new definition now states (in relevant part) that an MSB includes: "[a] person wherever located doing business ... wholly or in substantial part within the United States. . . ."

The phrase "wholly or in substantial part within the United States" requires more than mere maintenance of a bank account in the United States by a foreign-located person or entity.[130] FinCEN has made it clear, however, that whether a foreign-located person's MSB activities occur within the United States depends on all of the facts and circumstances of each case, *including whether persons in the United States are obtaining MSB services from the foreign-located person, such as sending money to or receiving money from third parties through the foreign-located person.*[131] The new definition does not include foreign banks or broker dealers. The new definition provides that foreign banks—as well as other foreign financial agencies that engage in financial activities that, if conducted in the United States, would require that agency to be registered with the SEC or CFTC—are not included in the new definition of MSB.[132]

As a result of the new definition, foreign MSBs will have the same registration, reporting, and record-keeping requirements as MSBs physically located in the United States and will be subject to the same civil and criminal penalties.[133] Foreign MSBs will also be required to designate a person who resides in the United States to act as an agent to accept service of legal process, including with respect to BSA compliance.[134]

AML Compliance Programs

Compliance and Your Company

Q 29.20   Why should my company care about having an anti-money laundering compliance program?

Any business that is a "financial institution" under the BSA and that is required to implement an anti-money laundering compliance program *must* care, because failure to implement the program could expose the business to criminal, civil, and administrative penalties.[135] For such businesses, it is equally important to monitor changes in, or additions to, that requirement (for example, a requirement to report "suspicious transactions" or maintain certain types of records may be added to an already-existing compliance program requirement). Failure to comply with the applicable Treasury regulations can be punished both civilly and criminally under the BSA and may also subject regulated "financial institutions" to severe administrative penalties imposed by their federal regulatory agency for failure to comply, or even for failure to fully and sufficiently comply.

Regardless of whether a business is a BSA "financial institution," for all businesses, the best defense against becoming unwittingly involved in a possible violation of the MLCA is to have an effective anti-money laundering compliance program. Such a program can be used to demonstrate that the business is a "good corporate citizen" that took reasonable steps to avoid involvement (through willful blindness or otherwise) in criminal money laundering activity.

Finally, the board of directors and senior management of every corporation, regardless of whether it is a BSA "financial institution," should consider whether it has a fiduciary duty to include anti-money laundering policies and procedures as part of its overall compliance program.[136] Management should consider the risk that money launderers may attempt to engage in laundering activities with the corporation.

Q 29.20.1 Our institution is currently exempted from anti-money laundering compliance program requirements. How can we keep track of changing regulations should our status change?

Businesses that are "financial institutions" under the BSA but that are exempt under 31 C.F.R. § 103.170 should closely monitor the *Federal Register* or FinCEN's website, www.fincen.gov, in order to determine whether the Treasury Department intends to issue regulations removing it from that exemption. In such cases, Treasury normally will issue a Notice of Proposed Rule Making in the *Federal Register*, explaining and stating the proposed regulations and inviting public comment. A Notice of Proposed Rule Making is a clear indication that the status of an exempted "financial institution" is about to change, although a substantial amount of time may elapse before a *proposed* rule is made a *final* rule. Further, sometimes a proposed rule imposing anti-money laundering requirements may be withdrawn by Treasury.[137]

Components of an Effective Compliance Program

Q 29.20.2 What are the elements of an effective anti-money laundering compliance program?

To restate the BSA's minimal requirements for a *mandatory* anti-money laundering program:

(1) An anti-money laundering program must be in writing.

(2) The financial institution must:

    (a) formally appoint an "Anti-Money Laundering Compliance Officer" who is in overall charge of the program;

    (b) conduct periodic training of appropriate employees about the institution's anti-money laundering policies and procedures; and

    (c) conduct a periodic independent audit of the program to ensure it has been implemented and is being followed.[138]

(3) Anti-money laundering programs must be "risk-based."[139]

In addition, a key element for the prevention and detection of money laundering and terrorist financing is to develop effective "Know Your Customer" procedures. In every transaction, each business should be diligent in knowing who it is dealing with and have reasonable grounds to believe that each customer is entirely legitimate and using funds derived from legitimate activity. This includes confirming an individual customer's true identity and, for customers that are businesses, ensuring that every entity with which one does business is, in fact, a legally established entity.

Customer Due Diligence Requirements for Financial Institutions

Q 29.20.3   What are the Customer Due Diligence Requirements for Financial Institutions?

On May 11, 2016, FinCEN revised the BSA regulations to improve financial transparency through the Customer Due Diligence Requirements for Financial Institutions ("CDD Rule").[140] The primary purpose of the CDD Rule is to require covered financial institutions to establish and maintain written procedures that allow the institution to identify and verify the "beneficial owners" of legal entity customers.[141] Among other things, the CDD Rule requires that financial institutions:

    (1) identify and verify the identity of their customers;

    (2) identify and verify the identity of the beneficial owners of companies opening accounts;

    (3) understand the nature and purpose of customer relationships to develop customer risk profiles; and

(4)   conduct ongoing monitoring to identify and report suspicious transactions and, on a risk basis, to maintain and
update customer information.[142]

In addition to the CDD Rule requirements, the Federal Financial
Institutions Examination Council (FFIEC) published two new chapters of the BSA/AML Examination Manual entitled "Examination Procedures"[143] and "Beneficial Ownership Requirements for Legal Entity
Customers—Overview,"[144] which address examination procedures
and regulatory expectations relating to the CDD Rule and the beneficial ownership requirements.

Q 29.20.4   When is the CDD Rule effective?

The CDD Rule became effective on May 11, 2018.

Q 29.20.5   Who is subject to the CDD Rule?

The CDD Rule only applies to "covered financial institutions."[145]
For purposes of the CDD Rule, "covered financial institutions" are
federally regulated banks and federally insured credit unions, mutual
funds, brokers or dealers in securities, futures commission merchants,
and introducing brokers in commodities.[146]

Q 29.20.6   Who qualifies as a legal entity customer?

"Legal entity customer" means a "corporation, limited liability
company, or other entity that is created by the filing of a public document with a Secretary of State or similar office, a general partnership,
and any similar entity formed under the laws of a foreign jurisdiction
that opens an account."[147]

However, there are certain entities that are explicitly excluded
from the definition of a "legal entity customer." Under 31 C.F.R.
§ 1010.230(e)(2), a "legal entity customer" does not include:

*   A financial institution regulated by a federal functional regula-
    tor or a bank regulated by a state bank regulator;

*   A person as described in 31 §§ C.F.R. 1020.315(b)(2) through (5);

*   An issuer of a class of securities;

- An investment company;

- An exchange or clearing agency;

- An issuer of a class of securities registered under the Securities Exchange Act of 1934;

- An investment company, investment adviser, an exchange or clearing agency, or any other entity that is registered with the SEC;

- A registered entity, commodity pool operator, commodity trading advisor, retail foreign exchange dealer, swap dealer, or major swap participant that is registered with the Commodity Futures Trading Commission;

- A public accounting firm registered under section 102 of the Sarbanes-Oxley Act;

- A bank holding company or savings and loan holding company;

- A pooled investment vehicle that is operated or advised by an excluded financial institution;

- An insurance company that is regulated by a state;

- A financial market utility designated by the Financial Stability Oversight Council;

- A foreign financial institution established in a jurisdiction where the regulator of such institution maintains beneficial ownership information regarding such institution;

- A non-U.S. governmental department, agency, or political subdivision that engages only in governmental rather than commercial activities; and

- Any legal entity only to the extent that it opens a private banking account subject to 31 C.F.R. § 1010.620.

Q 29.20.7   Which accounts or relationships are exempted from the CDD Rule?

FinCEN had previously provided temporary exceptive relief to covered financial institutions that offer certain accounts or maintain certain relationships.[148] While most of the temporary exceptive relief provided has since expired, FinCEN still provides relief for premium finance lenders whose payments are remitted directly to the insurance provider or broker, including certain situations where such lending involves the potential for cash refunds.[149]

Notwithstanding the foregoing, FinCEN retains the right to revisit any exceptive relief or provide additional exceptive relief in the future.

Q 29.20.8   Who is a "Beneficial Owner" for purposes of the CDD Rule?

A "beneficial owner" means:

(1) Each individual, if any, who, directly or indirectly, through any contract, arrangement, understanding, relationship or otherwise, owns 25% or more of the equity interests of a legal entity customer; and

(2) A single individual with significant responsibility to control, manage, or direct a legal entity customer, including:

    (i) An executive officer or senior manager (e.g., a Chief Executive Officer, Chief Financial Officer, Chief Operating Officer, Managing Member, General Partner, President, Vice President, or Treasurer); or

    (ii) Any other individual who regularly performs similar functions.[150]

The "beneficial ownership" analysis is separated into two categories in order to evaluate who is in fact the beneficial owner of an account—the control prong and the ownership prong. Under the control prong, the beneficial owner is a single individual with significant responsibility to control, manage or direct a legal entity customer.[151] Under the ownership prong, a beneficial owner is each individual which owns 25% or more of the equity interests of a legal entity customer, either directly or indirectly.[152]

Q 29.20.9   How does an entity verify the identity of a customer?

The covered financial institution is required to establish and maintain written procedures to identify information that must be obtained for new account openings on or after the CDD Rule's Effective Date. At a minimum, the covered financial institution must obtain the name, date of birth, address, and Tax Identification Number or Social Security Number for each beneficial owner of a legal entity customer.

However, the covered financial institution does not need to show the correctness of each element of the verifying identity. They must, however, verify enough information to form a reasonable belief that it knows the true identity of the beneficial owner of the legal entity customer prior to account opening.[153]

Q 29.20.10   What are the key issues regarding beneficial ownership?

A key component of the CDD Rule is the written "risk-based" policy that describes, at a minimum, the level of information needed prior to opening a new account after May 11, 2018.[154] The institution's policy must outline and plan for instances where the institution will not be able to confirm the beneficial owner of an account. The policies, procedures, and processes should describe:

- Circumstances in which the covered financial institution should not open an account.

- Which terms, if any, will allow a customer to use an account while the covered financial institution attempts to verify the identity of the beneficial owner(s) of a legal entity customer.

- When the covered financial institution should close an account, if unable to confirm the identity of the beneficial owner(s) of a legal entity customer.

- When the covered financial institution should file a SAR.[155]

Q 29.20.11   How does the CDD Rule affect companies and businesses that are not financial institutions?

Companies and businesses that are not considered "covered financial institutions" under the CDD Rule are not required to comply with the CDD Rule. However, the CDD Rule does have practical implications for these parties. For example, in the maintenance of their accounts or while dealing with their financial intermediaries, they may be asked to provide information or documentation regarding their beneficial owners. Additionally, legal representatives of these parties (including their senior executive officers) may be required to issue certifications in favor of such financial institutions or intermediaries regarding the company's beneficial ownership.

AML Compliance Officers

Q 29.20.12   What are the key considerations in appointing a compliance officer?

The compliance officer should be appointed by the board of directors or senior management. Although the actual title is not important, the compliance officer must have a level of authority and responsibility in the company sufficient to implement, supervise, and enforce the compliance program on a daily basis, and sufficient resources (budgetary and personnel) to perform his or her function.

The compliance officer must be a qualified person who is knowledgeable about money laundering and the Money Laundering Control Act. For "financial institutions," it is critical that the compliance officer also be fully knowledgeable about the BSA and the implementing regulations that apply to the particular business. The compliance officer should also have a full knowledge of the business, its products, services, operations, general customer base, and money laundering risk assessment.

Finally, it is imperative that the compliance officer be of the highest integrity. Bad actors must be kept out of the position, and out of the overall supervision and operation of the compliance program. The board and senior management must take reasonable steps to screen out persons whom the company knows, or should know through the exercise of due diligence, have a history of engaging in illegal activity or other misconduct.

Employee Training

Q 29.20.13   What are the key considerations when approaching employee training?

For all BSA "financial institutions" that are required to maintain anti-money laundering programs, periodic employee training is mandatory. Periodic employee training is also necessary for any other business with an anti-money laundering compliance program because the failure to conduct periodic training will render the program ineffective.

All appropriate employees should be trained on money laundering in general and on the company's anti-money laundering policies and procedures. Who the "appropriate" employees are will vary from business to business and will also depend on the company's risk assessment, but at a minimum should include all employees whose duties could expose them to money laundering. Generally, this will include management, sales, finance, and accounting personnel. Training should be tailored to the person's specific responsibilities. In addition, new staff should be given an overview of the compliance program during employee orientation. For "financial institutions," it is critical that employees be trained about the BSA and the implementing regulations that apply to the particular business.

Training should be periodic (generally, annually) and include not only training on basic policies and procedures, but also current anti-money laundering developments and changes to any company policies and procedures. Important developments and changes should be disseminated on an ongoing basis, as needed.

The company should document its training program and keep accurate records of the dates of the periodic employee training, the content of the training, training and testing materials, and attendance records.

Independent Audit

Q 29.20.14   What are the key considerations regarding independent audits?

An anti-money laundering compliance program should be periodically tested independently to ensure it has been implemented, followed, and enforced. For all BSA "financial institutions" that are required to maintain anti-money laundering programs, periodic independent auditing of the program is mandatory. While the frequency of the independent audit is not prescribed, even for "financial institutions," it is generally a sound practice to conduct independent testing annually.

The periodic audit must be "independent" in the sense that it is conducted by persons who are not involved in or responsible for the program's operation. Thus, it may be conducted by the internal audit department, outside auditors, consultants, or other qualified persons.

The persons conducting the independent audit should be knowledgeable about the program, the policies and procedures included in the program, the business and its operations, and the company's money laundering risk assessment. For all BSA "financial institutions," the auditor(s) should also be knowledgeable about the BSA and the regulations applicable to the company. They should also be familiar with the company's money laundering risk assessment, because the audit should be "risk-based" and evaluate the quality of risk management for all operations and departments involved in applying the program's policies and procedures.

The persons conducting the independent audit should report directly to the company board of directors, or to a designated board committee. Deficiencies and corrective recommendations should then be conveyed to senior management and the compliance officer for correction and follow-up. Senior management should ensure, through the compliance officer, that identified deficiencies are promptly addressed and corrective recommendations implemented.

"Know Your Customer" Procedures

Q 29.20.15   How can we confirm a customer's identity?

For individual customers, verifying identity is normally done by means of a government-issued photo identification, and in appropriate cases by determining the customer's source of funds or wealth. For business customers, it normally means securing a copy of articles of incorporation, government-issued licenses, government tax identification numbers, trust documents, partnership registrations, or the like. It can also include procedures to verify business information by telephone or through publicly available information.

Q 29.20.16   What if verifying a customer's identity is not possible?

For some businesses, it is neither possible nor practical, from a cost or customer relations point of view, to secure such documentation for *every* customer. This is where the risk assessment comes into play. Depending upon the degree and type of risk, a business should determine when to require identification, what type of identification to secure, and what follow-up procedures are appropriate. The point to keep in mind is that, depending on the degree of risk and the volume of business being done, each business should attempt to establish, as effectively and efficiently as it can, that the individual or business it is doing business with is who it claims to be, is engaged in legitimate business activities, is using funds derived from legitimate business or legitimate sources of wealth and income.

Creating and Administering a Program

Q 29.20.17   What are the actual steps a company must take to create an effective anti-money laundering compliance program?

The regulations provide no guidance on *how* to create an effective anti-money laundering program. The U.S. Sentencing Guidelines, however, provide some direction that, at a minimum, a company should take:[156]

(1) Establish policies, standards, and procedures to prevent and detect money laundering.

(2) Ensure that the company's board of directors and senior management understand the content and operation of the compliance program and exercise reasonable oversight with respect to its implementation and effectiveness. Specific senior manager(s) should have overall responsibility to ensure the implementation and effectiveness of the program. A compliance officer should be delegated at the outset to conduct or supervise the risk assessment, develop appropriate procedures, and oversee the drafting, implementation and day-to-day operation of the program. This person should be afforded adequate resources and authority to accomplish these tasks.

(3) Take reasonable steps to ensure that the compliance officer and his or her staff are adequately knowledgeable about the business, money laundering, and applicable statutes and regulations. Also ensure that company management and the compliance officer and staff are of the highest integrity by screening out persons whom the company knows, or should know through the exercise of due diligence, have a history of engaging in illegal activity or other misconduct.

(4) Conduct a risk assessment based on the company's products, services, customer base and geographic location(s); prepare a written risk assessment; and develop specific risk-based procedures to meet the perceived risk areas. A risk assessment is *not* a one-time-only exercise. It is a continuing process that continually takes into account changes in methods of money laundering, new products or services offered by the company, changes in the company's customer base and geographic areas of operation, and changes in the law or applicable regulations.

(5) Take reasonable steps to communicate periodically and in a practical manner the company's standards and procedures to all officers, employees, and, as appropriate, agents, through effective training programs and otherwise disseminating information.

(6) Take reasonable steps to

    (a) ensure that the program is followed, including using monitoring and auditing to detect misconduct;

    (b) evaluate periodically the program's effectiveness; and

    (c) have a system in which employees and agents may report or seek guidance regarding potential or actual misconduct without fear of retaliation (although a mechanism for anonymous reporting is not required).

(7) Promote and enforce the program through appropriate incentives and disciplinary measures for engaging in misconduct and for failing to take reasonable steps to prevent or detect misconduct.

(8) Take reasonable steps to respond appropriately to money laundering by customers and to prevent further similar conduct, including making any necessary modifications to the compliance and ethics program.[157]

Q 29.20.18 What is the relationship between a compliance program under the U.S. Sentencing Guidelines and an anti-money laundering compliance program?

Since enactment of the USA PATRIOT Act, bank regulators have focused heavily on BSA/anti-money laundering compliance. The regulatory focus on BSA compliance has steadily evolved, and BSA compliance has become a primary element of the regulatory strategy and expectations in bank examinations. For banks in particular, the FFIEC published the *Bank Secrecy Act/Anti-Money Laundering Examination Manual* in 2007, as amended in 2014,[158] which institutionalizes this primary focus through its detailed, coordinated guidance, and with its emphasis on regular risk assessments.

The logical extension is the expansion of supervisory attention to other compliance areas. The Board of Governors of the Federal Reserve System has recognized this expansion, and the Board's Division of Banking Supervision and Regulation now organizes its Risk

Section to include both BSA/AML compliance risk and *other* compliance risk. The Board expects banks to have effective *comprehensive* compliance and ethics programs as an essential component of the safety and soundness of their operations. These expectations are consistent with guidance from other regulatory agencies, including the SEC. Thus, BSA "financial institutions" are increasingly expected to have the overall comprehensive compliance program encouraged by chapter 8 of the U.S. Sentencing Guidelines *in addition to* their BSA anti-money laundering compliance programs.

Q 29.20.19 Is there a standard anti-money laundering compliance program that my company can effectively use?

There is no such thing as a one-size-fits-all anti-money laundering compliance program. An effective program must be based on a risk assessment that is specific to each company. Each company must examine the nature of its business, its products and services, its customer base, and the areas in which it operates in order to determine and prioritize its potential exposure to money laundering, and the policies and procedures it adopts must be designed based on that company-specific analysis.

Q 29.20.20 How do we go about designing an anti-money laundering compliance program?

Initially, the company should determine whether the company is *required* to have an anti-money laundering compliance program. If so, it must satisfy the requirements of the applicable BSA regulations. Compliance with those regulations should result in a basically sound compliance program that can then be tweaked and improved over time based upon the company's experience.

Even if the company is a "financial institution" that is not yet regulated under the BSA or is not a "financial institution," the regulations still provide a good starting point for designing a compliance program. Although the specifics of the regulations vary somewhat from one industry to another, they are generally similar and provide overall guidance on what constitutes an effective program.

In addition to using the regulations as a blueprint for a compliance program, the following steps are essential:

Step One: Secure the support of the board of directors. This can be done by educating board members generally on the MLCA and, for "financial institutions," on the BSA. The board should be made to understand that the best defense against involvement in criminal money laundering is an effective anti-money laundering compliance program.

Step Two: Have appropriate policies issued by the board directing senior management to publish company-wide policies and procedures stating the senior management's determination to comply with the law, to avoid involvement with money laundering, and to issue policies and procedures specifically designed to detect and deter such activity. These policies may provide for direct supervision and reporting to the board itself, or to a specially designated board committee.

Step Three: Develop, in association with outside consultants as deemed necessary, the specific duties, responsibilities, and authority of both senior management and the compliance officer regarding the implementation, operation, and enforcement of the compliance program.

Step Four: The board (or the designated board committee), in conjunction with senior management, should select and appoint a qualified anti-money laundering compliance officer and provide him or her with sufficient resources to implement, operate, and enforce a compliance program. The appointment of the compliance officer should be announced to all levels of management and to all employees. The announcement should make clear the compliance officer's scope of authority, as well as the board's and senior management's full support for the compliance officer in the performance of his or her mission.

Step Five: Under the supervision of the compliance officer, and in association with outside consultants as deemed necessary, prepare a written risk assessment which takes into account the areas of the business most vulnerable to money laundering activity. This should specifically include an analysis of the company's products, services, customer base, geographic locations and overall operations, and develop a risk assessment for each category. The results of the risk assessment should be reported to the board or the designated board committee.

It bears repeating that risk assessment is *not* a one-time-only exercise. It is a continuing process that takes into account changes in methods of money laundering, new products or services offered by the company, changes in the company's customer base and geographic areas of operation, and changes in the law or applicable regulations.

Step Six: Prepare a written set of procedures (based directly on the results of the risk assessment) that are specifically designed to deter and detect money laundering and that are practical in light of actual company operations and are as cost-efficient as possible. This process should occur under the supervision of the compliance officer and/or senior management, and in association with outside consultants as deemed necessary.

Step Seven: Issue a company-wide announcement of the compliance program, the appointment of the compliance officer, his or her duties, responsibilities and authority, and senior management's full expectation that every employee will fully comply with the program.

Step Eight: Conduct company-wide mandatory education of appropriate employees (as selected by the compliance officer) on money laundering, the company's anti-money laundering policies, and the company's specific anti-money laundering procedures contained in the compliance program. Employee training should be periodic and ongoing.

Step Nine: Establish a clear schedule for reporting by the compliance officer to the board and senior management on the progress of the implementation of the compliance program. Keep the board informed of the progress of the implementation of the program through direct reports to either the board or a designated board committee.

Step Ten: Select the independent audit team and establish dates for the commencement and completion of the initial periodic audit. For a newly established program, audits should be more frequent— about every six months until the program has been in place for a year or two. Well-established programs may be audited about every twelve to eighteen months.

Q 29.20.21 What are the basic considerations for the ongoing administration and enforcement of an anti-money laundering compliance program?

First, an effective compliance program changes with the environment in which the company operates; it is not static. Thus, one foundation of the program is ongoing risk assessment, which takes into account changes in methods of money laundering, new products or services offered by the company, changes in the company's customer base and geographic areas of operation, and changes in the law or applicable regulations. As new areas of vulnerability are identified, the program itself must evolve.

The second part of the foundation for an effective program is how the company administers and enforces it.

(1) The company must conduct effective, periodic training programs and otherwise disseminate information about the compliance program to both officers and appropriate employees.

(2) The company must establish and publicize a system by which employees know how to report not only suspected money laundering, but also internal violations of program policies and procedures.

(3) The company must promptly and carefully investigate any reports of suspected money laundering or internal misconduct, and take corrective action as appropriate. This is particularly important for those BSA "financial institutions" that are required to report "suspicious transactions" to FinCEN. Failure to identify and report such transactions can result in severe administrative, civil, and even criminal penalties.

(4) The company also should provide feedback to employees who have reported suspected internal misconduct so that they know that their allegations were taken seriously and that an appropriate resolution was reached. Employees who believe that their complaints have been ignored by the corporation are far more likely to become "whistleblowers" who initiate litigation against the company than employees who believe that their complaints have been considered and addressed.[159]

(5) The company should document suspected instances of money laundering and suspected violations of the program procedures *and* the steps that it takes to address them. Failure to keep such records makes it difficult or impossible to audit the operation of the program and severely hinders the company's ability to demonstrate its good faith and diligence should it ever become the target of scrutiny or accusation.

Q 29.20.22 Who should administer the anti-money laundering compliance program?

Several different departments within the company may have significant roles to play in the day-to-day operation of the compliance program, including the company audit or accounting department, the security department, human resources, and the legal department. However, their various compliance efforts must be coordinated as part of a single program, so the compliance officer should be responsible and accountable for overseeing the company's compliance efforts. Again, in order to accomplish this task and ensure the smooth and effective operation of the compliance program, the compliance officer needs to have sufficient line authority and resources.

Q 29.20.23 What role does top management have in administering the program?

The success of any compliance program depends upon the support and involvement of top management. Not surprisingly, the Treasury Department regulations requiring "financial institutions" to implement anti-money laundering programs expect the company's board of directors and senior management to issue the policies and procedures designed to implement the compliance program itself, as well as those designed to deter and detect money laundering. Top management is also expected to monitor, at least through the periodic independent audit, the operation of the program. While clearly not applicable to all businesses, the regulations establish a basic standard for the role of top management.

In addition to establishing the program and issuing the appropriate policies and procedures, the board of directors, or at least the senior management, should appoint the compliance officer. The compliance officer should report directly to senior management and the board.

It is the duty of the board and senior management to ensure that the compliance officer is qualified and that he or she has the necessary resources (in terms of budget and staff) to perform the assigned duties. The board and senior management need to understand the content and operation of the compliance program and exercise reasonable oversight with respect to its implementation and effectiveness. The board and senior management should supervise the compliance officer and receive periodic reports from him or her concerning the operation of the compliance program and any updates or changes needed in company policies and procedures. The individual delegated day-to-day operational responsibility should report periodically to senior management and should have direct access to the board of directors.

Again, because an effective compliance program is the best defense against becoming unwittingly involved in possible money laundering violations, senior management of every corporation—regardless of whether it is a "financial institution" required by law to comply— should consider the risk that money launderers may attempt to engage in laundering activities with the corporation, and thus whether to include anti-money laundering policies and procedures as part of its overall compliance program.[160]

Notes to Chapter 29

1.   FEDERAL FINANCIAL INSTITUTIONS EXAMINATION COUNCIL, BANK SECRECY ACT/ ANTI-MONEY LAUNDERING EXAMINATION MANUAL 7 (2014) [hereinafter BSA/AML EXAMINATION MANUAL].

2.   BLACK'S LAW DICTIONARY (10th ed. 2014).

3.   *See, e.g.*, BSA/AML EXAMINATION MANUAL 7–8 (2014).

4.   Prepaid access is "access to funds or the value of funds that have been paid in advance and can be retrieved or transferred at some point in the future through an electronic device or vehicle, such as a card, code, electronic serial number, mobile identification number, or personal identification number." *See* 31 C.F.R. § 1010.100(ww).

5.   31 C.F.R. § 1010.100(ff)(2)–(7).

6.   18 U.S.C. § 1956(c)(1).

7.   *Indifference*, BLACK'S LAW DICTIONARY (10th ed. 2014).

8.   BLACK'S LAW DICTIONARY (10th ed. 2014).

9.   United States v. Murray, 154 F. App'x 740, 744 (11th Cir. 2005).

10.   United States v. Leahy, 464 F.3d 773, 796 (7th Cir. 2006).

11.   United States v. Craig, 178 F.3d 891, 896 (7th Cir. 1999).

12.   18 U.S.C. § 1956(c)(7).

13.   *Id.* § 1956(c)(4).

14.   *Id.* § 1956(c)(5).

15.   31 U.S.C. § 5312(a)(2).

16.   18 U.S.C. § 1956(c)(6); *see also* Q 29.6.2 (for the list of BSA "financial institutions").

17.   18 U.S.C. § 1956.

18.   26 U.S.C. § 7201.

19.   *Id.* § 7206.

20.   18 U.S.C. § 1956(a)(1).

21.   *Id.* § 1956(a)(2). In addition, for purposes of subsection (2), a defendant's knowledge can be established if: (i) a law enforcement agent states that the funds or monetary instruments represent the proceeds of "some form of unlawful activity"; and (ii) the defendant's subsequent statements or actions indicate that the defendant believed this to be true. *See id.* § 1956(a)(2).

22.   18 U.S.C. § 1956(a)(3).

23.   *Id.* § 1956(a).

24.   *Id.* § 1956(b)(1).

25.   18 U.S.C. § 981(a)(1)(A).

26.   *Id.* § 981(k). An "interbank account" means any account held by a foreign bank in the United States primarily for the purpose of facilitating customer transactions. *See id.* §§ 981(k)(4)(a), 984(c)(2)(B).

27. *Id.* § 984.
28. *Id.* § 1956(f).
29. *Id.* § 1956(b)(1).
30. *Id.* § 1956(b)(2). On the key issue of federal *subject matter* jurisdiction over foreign entities, see United States v. Lloyds TSB Bank PLC, 639 F. Supp. 2d 314 (S.D.N.Y. 2009) (holding that the court lacked subject matter jurisdiction over a foreign bank sued by the United States for violation of the MLCA and dismissing the complaint).
31. 31 U.S.C. §§ 5312(a)(2), 5312(c).
32. 18 U.S.C. § 1956(c)(6).
33. *Id.* § 1956(b)(3)–(4).
34. *Id.* § 1957.
35. *Id.* § 1957(f)(3).
36. *Id.* § 1957(f)(1). The term specifically excludes, however, paying an attorney for representation in a criminal matter.
37. *Id.* § 1957(f)(2).
38. *Id.* §§ 1957(d)(2), 3077(2).
39. 31 U.S.C. § 5311 *et seq.* The BSA can be enforced criminally, but it is more common for it to be enforced through the imposition of civil penalties.
40. A willful violation of the BSA or a regulation prescribed under the BSA is punishable by a fine of up to $250,000 and imprisonment for up to five years. Such violations, if committed while violating another law of the United States or as part of a pattern of any illegal activity involving over $100,000 in a one-year period, are punishable by a fine of up to $500,000 and imprisonment for up to ten years. Violations of section 5318(i) or (j) (relating to private banking and correspondent accounts), or any regulations or special measures imposed under section 5318(A), are punishable by a fine equal to not less than two times the amount of the transaction, but not more than $1 million. 18 U.S.C. § 5322(d).
41. *See* 31 U.S.C. § 5312(a)(2), (c).
42. See section 3(h) of the Federal Deposit Insurance Act, 12 U.S.C. § 1813(h), for the definition of insured bank.
43. FinCEN has included mutual funds as investment company "financial institutions," effective May 14, 2010. *See* 75 Fed. Reg. 19,241 (Apr. 14, 2010). Mutual funds are now included in the general definition of "financial institution" at 31 C.F.R. § 1010.100(t)(10). FinCEN has also included residential mortgage lenders and originators as investment company "financial institutions," effective April 16, 2012. *See* 77 Fed. Reg. 8148 (Feb. 14, 2012). Residential mortgage lenders and originators are now included in the general definition of "financial institution" at 31 C.F.R. § 1010.100(*lll*).
44. MSBs include: dealers in foreign exchange; check cashers; issuers or sellers of traveler's checks or money orders; providers and sellers of prepaid access; money transmitters; the U.S. Postal Service; and sellers of prepaid access. 31 C.F.R. § 1010.100(ff). On July 18, 2011, FinCEN issued a final rule (effective on September 19, 2011) clarifying the definitions of each of these terms. The definitions now include *foreign* MSBs as well as domestic ones, which means that

foreign MSBs are now required to register with FinCEN and are subject to the same BSA/AML requirements as their domestic counterparts. *See* Final Rule: Bank Secrecy Act Regulations, Definitions and Other Regulations Relating to MSBs, 76 Fed. Reg. 43,585, 43,589 (July 21, 2011). For further discussion on this rule, see also Q 29.19.

    45.   Chapter X is organized as follows:

Section 1010	GENERAL PROVISIONS
Section 1020	RULES FOR BANKS
Section 1021	RULES FOR CASINOS AND CARD CLUBS
Section 1022	RULES FOR MONEY SERVICE BUSINESSES
Section 1023	RULES FOR BROKERS OR DEALERS IN SECURITIES
Section 1024	RULES FOR MUTUAL FUNDS
Section 1025	RULES FOR INSURANCE COMPANIES
Section 1026	RULES FOR FUTURES COMMISSION MERCHANTS AND INTRODUCING BROKERS IN COMMODITIES
Section 1027	RULES FOR DEALERS IN PRECIOUS METALS, PRECIOUS STONES OR JEWELS
Section 1028	RULES FOR OPERATORS OF CREDIT CARD SYSTEMS
Section 1029	RULES FOR LOAN OR FINANCE COMPANIES
section 1030	RULES FOR HOUSING GOVERNMENT-SPONSORED ENTERPRISES

    46.   Although FinCEN has issued rules that apply to mutual funds (specifically, maintaining anti-money laundering programs, CIPs, and due diligence programs for correspondent and private banking accounts, and reporting suspicious transactions), FinCEN did not include mutual funds within the original definition of "financial institution" until April 2010. *See* 75 Fed. Reg. 19,241 (Apr. 14, 2010). Mutual funds are now required to file CTRs (instead of IRS Forms 8300, *see* Q 29.12.3, *infra*), as previously required, and comply with other BSA record-keeping regulations such as the "Travel Rule" (*see* 31 C.F.R. § 1024.410 and other record-keeping and retention rules).

    47.   See variously subsection .210 of each of 31 C.F.R. §§ 1020–29.

    48.   "Housing government sponsored enterprises" are the Federal National Mortgage Association, the Federal Home Loan Mortgage Corporation, and each Federal Home Loan Bank.

    49.   31 C.F.R. § 1010.205. These include businesses such as agencies of federal, state, or local government carrying out a duty or power described in the definition of "financial institution."

50.   Regulations applicable to "dealers in precious metals, stones and jewels" are of limited application and generally exempt retail businesses. *See* 31 C.F.R. § 1027.100. With regard to insurance companies, only those companies that are engaged within the United States as a business in the issuing of a permanent life insurance policy (other than group policies), annuity contracts (other than group contracts), and "any other insurance product with features of cash value or investment" are required to implement anti-money laundering programs. *See* 31 C.F.R. § 1025.100.

51.   31 U.S.C. § 5318(h).

52.   See variously subsection .220 of each of 31 C.F.R. §§ 1020, 1023, 1024, and 1026.

53.   "Banks" include all commercial banks, trust companies, savings or building and loan institutions and credit unions organized under federal or state law; private banks; institutions insured under the National Housing Act; savings banks; and foreign banks operating in the United States. 31 C.F.R. § 1010.100(d).

54.   See variously subsection .320 of each of 31 C.F.R. §§ 1020–26 and 31 C.F.R. § 1029.

55.   See subsection .320(e)(1)(i) of each of 31 C.F.R. §§ 1020–26 and 31 C.F.R. § 1029.

56.   See subsection .320(e)(1)(ii) of each of 31 C.F.R. §§ 1020–26 and 1029. With regard to disclosure to corporate affiliates, see also FinCEN Guidance FIN-2010-G005 (Nov. 23, 2010), which can be found on FinCEN's website, www.fincen. gov.

57.   31 U.S.C. § 5318(g)(3). The "safe harbor" applies to any "financial institution" that makes either a mandatory or a "voluntary" disclosure. *Id.* Therefore, the "safe harbor" applies to *all* "financial institutions," even including those that are not *required* by regulation to make such reports.

58.   Financial institutions required to file SARs can access the SAR form on the BSA E-Filing System. *See* BSA E-FILING SYSTEM, http://bsaefiling.fincen.treas. gov/main.html.

59.   BSA/AML EXAMINATION MANUAL 3 (2014).

60.   *See* FinCen.gov.

61.   31 U.S.C. § 5318A.

62.   31 U.S.C. § 5318.

63.   31 C.F.R. § 1010.610(a); 31 U.S.C. § 5318(i).

64.   Title III, sec. 313, Pub. L. No. 107-56, 115 Stat. 307.

65.   *Id.*

66.   Title III, sec. 319, Pub. L. No. 107-56, 115 Stat. 307.

67.   31 U.S.C. § 5318.

68.   31 C.F.R. § 1010.320.

69.   31 U.S.C. § 5312(a)(2).

70.   31 U.S.C. § 5318(k)(2).

71.   Uniting and Strengthening America by Providing Appropriate Tools Required to Intercept and Obstruct Terrorism Act of 2001 (USA PATRIOT Act), Pub. L. No. 107-56, 115 Stat. 272. While Section 314 was not included by Congress

as a formal part of the BSA's inception, on February 5, 2010, FinCEN amended the regulations to allow state, local, and certain foreign law enforcement agencies access to the information sharing program. *See, e.g.*, BSA/AML EXAMINATION MANUAL 92 (2014), https://www.ffiec.gov/bsa_aml_infobase/documents/BSA_AML_Man_2014_v2.pdf. The full text of section 314 is also available as part of the Historical and Statutory Notes following 31 U.S.C. § 5311. *See also* 75 Fed. Reg. 6560 (Feb. 10, 2010).

72. *See* 31 C.F.R. § 1010.520(a)(2). Only foreign law enforcement in a country that provides U.S. law enforcement agencies reciprocal access to information may participate.

73. 31 C.F.R. § 1010.520(b)(1).

74. 31 U.S.C. § 5312(a)(2); *see also* Q 29.6.2, *supra.* This is unusual in that BSA regulations generally apply only to "financial institutions" as defined in 31 C.F.R. § 1010.100(t), which is substantially narrower than the definition of "financial institution" found in 31 U.S.C. § 5312(a)(2) and (c).

75. Under 31 C.F.R. § 103.100(b)(1), section 314(a) requests may only ask whether an institution maintains or has maintained an "account" (as defined in 31 C.F.R. § 1010.505(a)) or has engaged in a "transaction" (as defined in 31 C.F.R. § 1010.505(d)) for, with or on behalf of a specified person or entity. Consequently, mandatory information sharing is limited to financial institutions that provide such services.

76. 31 C.F.R. § 1010.520(b)(3)(ii). See also FinCEN General Instructions and Frequently Asked Questions [hereinafter FinCEN FAQs] for section 314(a) requests, available to financial institutions on the FinCEN section 314(a) Secure Information Sharing System.

77. *See also* FinCEN FAQs.

78. 31 C.F.R. § 1010.520(b)(3)(v).

79. *Id.*; *see also* FinCEN FAQs; BSA/AML EXAMINATION MANUAL, *supra* note 71, at 94.

80. *Id.* § 1010.540(b).

81. *Id.* § 1010.540(b)(4).

82. *Id.* § 1010.540(a)(1).

83. *Id.* § 1010.520(a)(1), (b). Only insurance companies that are engaged within the United States as a business in the issuing of a permanent life insurance policy (other than group policies), annuity contracts (other than group contracts) and "any other insurance product with features of cash value or investment" are required to implement anti-money laundering programs. *See id.* § 1025.100.

84. *Id.* § 1010.540(b)(2). The notice is available on FinCEN's website, www.fincen.gov.

85. This does not include *foreign* financial institutions, even if they are parents, subsidiaries or affiliates of a participating financial institution because they do not meet the eligibility requirement of having to have an anti-money laundering program under the BSA regulations.

86. 31 C.F.R. § 1010.540(b)(3). A list of participating institutions, including their related contact information, is periodically posted by FinCEN, and checking that list is deemed by the regulations to satisfy the verification requirement.

87. *Id.* § 1010.540(b)(5). Specifically, section 314(b) of the USA PATRIOT Act provides that a financial institution that "transmits, receives, or shares . . . information for the purposes of identifying and reporting activities that may involve terrorist acts or money laundering activities shall not be liable to any person under any law or regulation of the United States, any constitution, law or regulation of any State or political subdivision thereof, or under any contract or other legally enforceable agreement (including any arbitration agreement)" for disclosing information regarding possible terrorist activity or money laundering, or for failing to provide notice of the disclosure to the person who is identified in it. Pub. L. No. 107-56, tit. III, § 314(b), 115 Stat. 307 (Oct. 26, 2001).

88. 31 U.S.C. § 5313; 31 C.F.R. § 1010.310.

89. 31 C.F.R. § 1010.100(m). Note that the definition of "currency" does *not* include monetary instruments such as cashier's checks, money orders, traveler's checks, or personal checks.

90. Casinos are required to use FinCEN Form 103.

91. Reporting for certain customers may be exempted under Treasury regulations. *See* 31 C.F.R. § 1020.315. While the *reporting* requirement applies to all "financial institutions," the reporting *form* to be used differs. Only the businesses listed in the text above should file Currency Transaction Reports (CTRs), and all of those businesses should use FinCEN Form 104, except for casinos and card clubs, which should use FinCEN Form 103. All other businesses, including those that are technically "financial institutions" under section 5312 of the BSA, and including insurance companies, dealers in precious metals, stones or jewels, and credit card operators, are required to report large cash transactions, but on IRS/FinCEN Form 8300.

92. 31 U.S.C. § 5324(a).

93. *Id.* § 5331.

94. 26 U.S.C. § 6050I.

95. *See generally* 31 C.F.R. § 1010.330. Insurance companies, dealers in precious metals, stones or jewels, and credit card operators should refer to subsection .330 of 31 C.F.R. §§ 1025, 1027, or 1028, respectively. All other businesses that are not included in the BSA regulatory definition of "financial institution" at 31 C.F.R. § 1010.100(t) should follow the cash transaction reporting regulations at 26 C.F.R. § 1.6050I.

96. The BSA regulations for reporting large cash transactions by businesses other than those required to file CTRs are found at 31 C.F.R. § 1010.330. The Internal Revenue Code regulations for reporting large cash transactions by businesses other than those required to file CTRs are found at 26 C.F.R. § 1.6050I-1.

97. 31 C.F.R. § 1010.330(e); 26 C.F.R. § 1.6050I-1(e)(2).

98. 31 C.F.R. § 1010.330(e); 26 C.F.R. § 1.6050I-1(e).

99. *See* Press Release, FinCEN, FinCEN Announces Electronic Filing for Form 8300 (Sept. 19, 2012), https://www.fincen.gov/news/news-releases/fincen-announces-electronic-filing-form-8300; *see also* FinCEN, BSA E-FILING SYSTEM, http://bsaefiling. fincen.treas.gov/main.html.

100. 31 U.S.C. § 5324(b); 26 U.S.C. § 6050I(f).

101. 26 U.S.C. § 6721.

102. 26 C.F.R. § 1.6050I-1(f); the BSA regulations do not include this obligation.

103. 31 C.F.R. § 1010.330(c)(1)(i); 26 C.F.R. § 1.6050I-1(c)(1)(i).

104. A "consumer durable" means "an item of tangible personal property of a type that is suitable under ordinary usage for personal consumption or use, that can reasonably be expected to be useful for at least one year . . . and has a sales price of more than $20,000." 31 C.F.R. § 1010.330(c)(7); 26 C.F.R. § 1.6050I-1(c)(2).

105. 31 C.F.R. § 1010.330(c)(1)(ii); 26 C.F.R. § 1.6050I-1(c).

106. 31 C.F.R. § 1010.330(c)(12)(i); 26 C.F.R. § 1.6050I-1(c)(7).

107. 31 C.F.R. § 1010.330(c)(12)(ii); 26 C.F.R. § 1.6050I-1(c)(7)(ii).

108. *Id.*

109. 31 C.F.R. § 1010.330(b); 26 C.F.R. § 1.6050I-1(b).

110. 31 C.F.R. § 1010.330(e).

111. *Id.* § 1010.410.

112. *Id.* § 1010.100(t).

113. *See id.* §§ 1010.415, 1020.410, .33(e), .34, respectively (banks); *id.* § 1023.410 (brokers or dealers in securities); *id.* § 1021.410 (casinos); *id.* § 1022.410 (currency dealers or exchangers).

114. *Id.* § 1010.340(a).

115. *See supra* note 99.

116. *Id.* § 1010.340(b).

117. 31 U.S.C. § 5332.

118. 31 C.F.R. § 1010.100(dd).

119. *Id.* § 1010.340(c). However, all exempted persons would be well advised to file the FinCEN Form 105 regardless of any supposed exemption, in order to avoid erroneous seizures by U.S. Customs officials. In addition, if an exempted business receives over $10,000 cash or monetary instruments from outside the United States, that business must report the receipt regardless of the exemption. *See id.* § 1010.340(b).

120. 31 U.S.C. § 5324; 18 U.S.C. § 3571(b)(3), (c)(3).

121. *See generally* 18 U.S.C. § 3077(2). However, the specific OFAC regulations should be checked for the precise application of the OFAC regulations, as they may be different depending upon the sanction program involved.

122. The OFAC regulations, which are voluminous, are generally found at 31 C.F.R. pts. 500–598. A useful reference for finding the specific regulatory prohibitions and requirements for specific sanctions programs can be found at 31 C.F.R. pt. 500, app. A to ch. V, located immediately following 31 C.F.R. § 598.

123. OFAC has issued a final rule entitled "Economic Sanctions Enforcement Guidelines" as guidelines for persons subject to the requirement of U.S. sanctions statutes, which became effective on November 9, 2009. *See* 74 Fed. Reg. 57,593 (Sept. 8, 2008); *see also* 31 C.F.R. pt. 501 (app. A).

124. 31 C.F.R. § 1022.380(a). Any person who owns or controls an MSB is responsible for registering the business, although only one registration for an MSB is required. *See id.* § 103.41(c).

125. 18 U.S.C. § 1022.380(c). On July 18, 2011, FinCEN issued a final rule (effective in September 2011) extending the registration requirement to *foreign-located* MSBs "doing business . . . wholly or in substantial part within the United States. . . ." *See* Final Rule: Bank Secrecy Act Regulations, Definitions and Other Regulations Relating to MSBs, 76 Fed. Reg. 43,585, 43,589 (July 21, 2011). For further discussion on this rule, see also Q 29.19.

126. 18 U.S.C. § 1960(b).

127. 31 C.F.R. § 1022.380(d).

128. *Id.* § 1022.380(b).

129. Bank Secrecy Act Regulations, Definitions and Other Regulations Relating to MSBs, 76 Fed. Reg. 43,585, at 43,589 (July 21, 2011).

130. *See* FinCEN Clarifies MSBs Definitions Rule Includes Foreign-Located MSBs Doing Business in U.S. (July 18, 2011), https://www.fincen.gov/sites/default/files/shared/20110715.pdf (a foreign-located currency exchanger whose only presence in the United States was a bank account was not deemed an MSB when the currency exchange transactions occurred solely in a foreign country for foreign-located customers and the use of the U.S. bank account was limited to issuing and clearing dollar-denominated monetary instruments); *see also* 76 Fed. Reg. 43,585, at 43,588 (July 21, 2011).

131. 76 Fed. Reg. at 43,588 (emphasis added).

132. 31 C.F.R. § 1010.100(ff)(8).

133. 76 Fed. Reg. at 43,589.

134. 31 C.F.R. § 1022.380(a)(2).

135. For businesses required to implement AML compliance programs, see Q 29.7, *supra*.

136. *See In re* Caremark Int'l, Inc. Derivative Litig., 698 A.2d 959, 970 (Del. Ch. 1996); *see also* Miller v. McDonald (*In re* World Health Alternatives, Inc.), 385 B.R. 576 (Bankr. D. Del. 2008) (applying *Caremark* duties to senior officers and in-house counsel).

137. See the discussion in Q 29.7 and at *supra* note 49.

138. 31 U.S.C. § 5318(h). For "financial institutions" *required* to have such programs, essential elements may also include CIPs and procedures for identifying and reporting "suspicious transactions."

139. *See* QQ 29.7.2 and 29.7.3, *supra* ("risk-based" programs). *See* BSA/AML EXAMINATION MANUAL 11–23 (2014) (offering an excellent overview of the components of an anti-money laundering program). Although specifically addressed to banks and credit unions, it offers "best practices" applicable to any business. The manual is available online at www.ffiec.gov.

140. 81 Fed. Reg. at 29,398; *see also* https://www.fincen.gov/resources/statutes-and-regulations/cdd-final-rule.

141. See FIN-2016-G003, Frequently Asked Questions Regarding Customer Due Diligence Requirements for Financial Institutions, https://www.fincen.gov/sites/default/files/2016-09/FAQs_for_CDD_Final_Rule_%287_15_16%29.pdf.

142. *Id.*

143. BSA/AML EXAMINATION MANUAL (EXAMINATION PROCEDURES) (2018), https://bsaaml.ffiec.gov/manual/RegulatoryRequirements/02_ep.

144. BSA/AML EXAMINATION MANUAL (BENEFICIAL OWNERSHIP REQUIREMENTS FOR LEGAL ENTITY CUSTOMERS—OVERVIEW) (2018), https://bsaaml.ffiec.gov/manual/RegulatoryRequirements/03.

145. 31 U.S.C. § 5312(a)(2), (c)(1).

146. *See* FIN-2016-G003, Frequently Asked Questions Regarding Customer Due Diligence Requirements for Financial Institutions, https://www.fincen.gov/sites/default/files/2016-09/FAQs_for_CDD_Final_Rule_%287_15_16%29.pdf.

147. 31 C.F.R. § 1010.230(e)(1).

148. *See* FinCEN, Information on Complying with the Customer Due Diligence (CDD) Final Rule, https://www.fincen.gov/resources/statutes-and-regulations/cdd-final-rule.

149. However, covered financial institutions still have an obligation to comply with all other applicable BSA requirements, including the filing of SARs. *See Premium Finance Cash Refunds and Beneficial Ownership Requirements for Legal Entity Customers*, FIN-2018-R001 (May 11, 2018), https://www.fincen.gov/sites/default/files/administrative_ruling/2018-05-11/FIN-2018-R001.pdf.

150. 31 C.F.R. § 1010.230(d).

151. 31 C.F.R. § 1010.230(d)(2); *see also* BSA/AML EXAMINATION MANUAL (BENEFICIAL OWNERSHIP REQUIREMENTS FOR LEGAL ENTITY CUSTOMERS—OVERVIEW) (2018), https://bsaaml.ffiec.gov/manual/RegulatoryRequirements/03.

152. 31 C.F.R. § 1010.230(d)(1).

153. *See* BSA/AML EXAMINATION MANUAL (BENEFICIAL OWNERSHIP REQUIREMENTS FOR LEGAL ENTITY CUSTOMERS—OVERVIEW) (2018), https://bsaaml.ffiec.gov/manual/RegulatoryRequirements/03.

154. *Id.*

155. *Id.*

156. U.S. SENTENCING GUIDELINES MANUAL § 8B2.1 (Nov. 2008, as amended Nov. 1, 2018).

157. *Id.* § 8B2.1(b).

158. The BSA/AML EXAMINATION MANUAL was further amended on April 15, 2020. The updates offer further transparency into the examination process and establish no new requirements. *See* https://www.ffiec.gov/press/PDF/FFIEC%20BSA-AML%20Exam%20Manual.pdf.

159. The BSA specifically provides for "whistleblower" protection. *See* 31 U.S.C. § 5328; *see also* Miller v. McDonald (*In re* World Health Alternatives, Inc.), 385 B.R. 576 (Bankr. D. Del. 2008).

160. *See Caremark*, 698 A.2d at 970.

30

Sarbanes-Oxley Act of 2002

Jerome W. Hoffman & John A. Canale*

Following the scandalous collapse of Enron and WorldCom and the attendant whirlwind of criticism by angry shareholders, Congress passed the Public Company Accounting Reform and Investor Protection Act of 2002 ("Sarbanes-Oxley" or SOX).[1] Its purpose was to restore investor confidence by improving the quality and transparency in financial reporting.

Congress intended for SOX to strengthen the authority and duties of boards of directors and their audit committees and make corporate management more accountable. It was anticipated that SOX would impose new regulations and obligations on attorneys and auditors, improve the quality of financial reporting, protect employee whistleblowers, and strengthen the powers of the U.S. Securities and Exchange Commission (SEC).

*   The authors would like to acknowledge Richard T. Williams for his contribution to this chapter.

The core requirements, enhanced in SOX, that companies registering securities in the United States maintain accurate financial records and devise, implement, and maintain adequate internal financial controls originated in the Foreign Corrupt Practices Act of 1977,[2] alongside its more widely known anti-bribery provisions, themselves adopted in response to widely publicized bribery and accounting scandals involving Lockheed, Northrop, Gulf Oil and others.[3] The accuracy and internal controls provisions were carried forward, with additional requirements and enhanced penalties in SOX.

Most sections of SOX remain unchanged; limited amendments to it were adopted as part of the massive Dodd-Frank Wall Street Reform and Consumer Protection Act of 2010 (Dodd-Frank),[4] and refined in the Jumpstart Our Business Startups Act of 2012 (the JOBS Act).[5]

Civil enforcement is principally accomplished today through SEC administrative and litigation proceedings and litigation brought by whistleblowers; criminal enforcement is managed by the Department of Justice.

In addition to describing the principal provisions of SOX, this chapter reviews how SOX has been enforced over the past two decades and what lies ahead.

Overview

Q 30.1   To whom does SOX apply?

All SOX provisions apply to "issuers."[6] Issuers are entities that have registered (or are presently registering) securities with the SEC, or that are required to file periodic reports with the SEC.

Some SOX provisions also apply to privately held companies and to all persons.[7] These include the following:

- obstruction of any federal investigation;[8]

- protection of employee whistleblowers;[9]

- penalty enhancement provisions for white collar crimes;[10]

- debts incurred in connection with violation of securities laws are no longer dischargeable in bankruptcy.[11]

Q 30.2   Which companies are "issuers"?

Issuers include:

- all public companies in the United States whose securities are listed on any stock exchange or are otherwise publicly traded;

- all companies whose securities are registered under the Securities Exchange Act of 1934, regardless of whether or not they are listed on any stock exchange;

- all foreign companies whose securities are listed or traded in the United States;

- private companies whose debt securities are publicly offered; and

- all investment companies, mutual funds, closed-end investment companies, unit investment trusts, and issuers of asset-backed securities.

Q 30.3   Generally, what does SOX require?

SOX requires companies to adopt codes of ethics, and it increases the oversight responsibilities of directors, especially members of a board's audit committee. Particular types of loans and stock transactions are prohibited with respect to senior managers and directors. The chief executive officer and chief financial officer are required to certify the accuracy of financial reports and the fair presentation of other public disclosure. Jointly, the officers and directors must implement and maintain extensive disclosure controls and internal accounting controls. General counsel and legal departments are subject to SEC rules imposing investigative, reporting, and disclosure obligations upon them. Outside auditors must examine and certify management's representations concerning the adequacy and effectiveness of internal accounting controls.[12]

Codes of Ethics

Q 30.4   What should a company put in its code of ethics?

There are no specific language requirements. The SEC defines the term "code of ethics" broadly as:

> ... such standards as are reasonably necessary to promote—
>
> (1) honest and ethical conduct, including the ethical handling of actual or apparent conflicts of interest between personal and professional relationships;
>
> (2) full, fair, accurate, timely, and understandable disclosure in reports and documents that a company files with, or submits to, the SEC and in other public communications made by the company;

    (3)   compliance with applicable governmental laws, rules and regulations;

    (4)   the prompt internal reporting of violations of the code to appropriate person(s) identified in the code; and

    (5)   accountability for adherence to the code.[13]

The scope and particular details of corporate codes of ethics and business conduct vary widely, as a review of websites shows; see current examples for Amazon, Alphabet and Google, Hewlett Packard, Verizon, Citigroup and Sanofi.[14] (See also chapter 2 above, which extensively discusses compliance programs.)

Q 30.4.1   What does a company do with its code of ethics once it is adopted by the board?

The code must be filed with the SEC and also must be made publicly available, including being posted on the corporate Internet website.[15] The New York Stock Exchange (NYSE) and NASDAQ have adopted listing requirements that include a code of ethics.[16]

Companies must adhere to their codes of ethics, and any amendment to or waiver of provisions of the code must be promptly disclosed in a Form 8-K that must be filed with the SEC within four business days. Note that failure to "take action within a reasonable period of time regarding a material departure from a provision of the code of ethics that has been made known to an executive officer" would be deemed an implicit waiver of the code.

Boards of Directors/Audit Committees

Q 30.5   How does SOX affect boards of directors?

The boards of directors of issuers are now required to have a majority of their members be "independent."[17] An independent member is one who has not been employed or compensated by an issuer within the three years preceding his or her service on the board of directors. The exchanges have additional criteria for defining "independence."[18]

Q 30.5.1   Do boards have to act in a manner different from the way they did before SOX?

Boards of directors must now conduct executive sessions outside the presence of management and ensure that the audit committee, compensation committee, and nominating and governance committees are composed exclusively of independent directors.

Increasingly since 2009, the SEC has reminded audit committee members and independent directors of the importance of their work to investors and has brought enforcement actions against them for recklessly failing to heed "red flag" warnings of corporate fraud.[19]

Q 30.6   What does an audit committee do?

The audit committee meets with external auditors and recommends approval of financial statements to the full board of directors. The audit committee has the authority to engage and remove auditors. The audit committee and external auditors are required to meet to confirm the terms and scope of the audit engagement and to discuss material issues identified by the auditors in the course of their work.[20] The SEC adopted rules directing the nation's stock exchanges to prohibit the listing of any security of a company that is not in compliance with the SOX audit committee requirements.[21]

COMPLIANCE FACT

Audit committee members and their general responsibilities must be disclosed in annual reports or proxy statements of issuers.

Q 30.6.1   How does SOX affect the make-up of the audit committee?

Each member of an audit committee must now be an independent member of the board of the directors and may not receive any other compensation from the corporation, except for that given to any member of the board of directors and its committees. All members must be financially literate (able to read and understand the fundamental financial statements, including a company's balance sheet, income statement, and cash flow statement), and at least one member of the audit committee must be an "independent financial expert" (a person who has experience as a public accountant or auditor, or as a principal financial officer, comptroller, or principal accounting officer of a public company).

Q 30.6.2   What if no one in the company is an independent financial expert?

Individual companies may find it difficult to locate an independent financial expert among the ranks of their present directors or to be able to recruit quickly an appropriate candidate for election to their board of directors. In that case, the audit committee may engage appropriate professional experts as advisors for an interim period; without the obligations of decision-making imposed on board members, candidates for advisors to audit committees may be more plentiful.

COMPLIANCE FACT

Companies must disclose their audit committee financial expertise (or lack thereof) in their annual report.[22]

Q 30.6.3   Does SOX change the audit committee's responsibilities?

The audit committee is now directly responsible for the engagement and removal of any registered public accounting firm employed for the purpose of preparing or issuing audit reports. The audit committee is also responsible for conferring with the auditors about material issues identified during an audit and for resolving disagreements between management and auditors regarding financial reporting.[23] The audit committee has to establish procedures for dealing with complaints from employees about its accounting procedures. The audit committee must be given the authority to engage independent counsel and other advisors. Issuers are obligated to provide appropriate funding to compensate public accounting firms for their audit reports, and to pay advisors and counsel hired by the audit committee.

Officers and Directors

Q 30.7   What are the SOX requirements for officers and directors?

Congress included in SOX a series of specific prohibitions and requirements upon the conduct of officers and directors of issuers:

- prohibition of insider trading during pension fund blackout periods;[24]

- prohibition on certain personal loans;[25]

- prompt disclosure of insider stock transactions;[26] and

- prohibition on fraudulently influencing, coercing, manipulating, or misleading any independent auditors.[27]

Penalties

Q 30.8   What are the SEC's penalties for officers and directors if they violate SOX?

If restatement of financial statements occurs due to material non-compliance with SOX, the CEO and CFO may have to forfeit their bonuses and profits made on the sale of the company's securities.[28] In addition, they may be barred from serving as directors or officers of any public company.[29] In this regard, Congress has significantly lowered the standard for misconduct necessary to disqualify officers and directors.[30]

Q 30.8.1   Do officers and directors face any penalties beyond those imposed by the SEC?

SOX includes a significant number of civil and criminal penalty provisions. SOX encompasses a number of criminal statutes related to document destruction.[31] In addition, SOX has amended the Federal

Sentencing Guidelines, extended statutes of limitation and dramatically increased fines and prison terms, which now reach up to twenty-five years.[32] Finally, the SEC has been given the power to petition for a judicial freeze of corporate assets in order to avoid last-minute looting by directors and officers.

Q 30.8.2   Have the SEC and law enforcement actually used these SOX powers?

The high-profile cases involving executives at Enron, WorldCom, HealthSouth, Gateway, Adelphia, Rite Aid, etc., are emblematic of the SEC's zealous pursuit of corporate malfeasance. In addition, the SEC has moved aggressively against overseas issuers and auditors such as the Italian company Parmalat, and the U.K. accounting firm Moore Stephens.[33]

Insurance

Q 30.9   Are violations of SOX by officers and directors generally covered by liability insurance?

Historically, private securities lawsuits have been alleged against issuers, directors, and officers with the expectation that a settlement will be funded from directors-and-officers liability insurance proceeds and corporate funds. Nowadays, directors and officers need greater insurance coverage as a result of their greater responsibilities imposed upon them by SOX; and, at the same time, insurers are more wary of providing such coverage. Far greater disclosure is necessary in the application and renewal process seeking insurance coverage. Moreover, constraining the insurer's ability to rescind coverage becomes of paramount importance to directors, although such restrictions in policy language are generally available only at additional cost.

Q 30.9.1   Other than insurers, who else is concerned with the effect SOX could have on officers and directors?

Underwriters also seek to develop an understanding and assess the quality of directors' and management's decision-making. The greater the commitment of an issuer to the "tone at the top" of its ethical conduct and its responsiveness to auditor and whistleblower allegations, the more comfortable an underwriter can be with an issuer's risk profile. Supplementing its evaluation by scrutinizing external business forecasts and analysis of finances and of corporate governance is very useful for underwriters, as are interviews of an issuer's senior management.

Whistleblowers

Q 30.10   How does SOX protect whistleblowers?

SOX is meant to encourage and protect employees[34] who file complaints, give testimony, provide information or otherwise assist or participate in an internal corporate investigation[35] or an SEC, congressional, or law enforcement investigation.[36] Under SOX, no issuer may discharge, demote, suspend, threaten, harass, or, in any other manner, discriminate against an employee in the terms and conditions of employment because of any lawful act done by the whistleblower.

In FY 2016, the SEC received 4,218 whistleblower tips concerning potential securities law violations, an increase of 300 tips over the prior year. During FY 2016, the greatest number of tips originated in California (547 tips), followed by New York, Florida, Ohio, Texas, Illinois, Washington, and New Jersey, each with more than 100 tips. Internationally, more than thirty tips each originated in Canada (sixty-eight), followed by the United Kingdom, Australia, China, and Mexico. Of the total tips, 938 involved claims of improper corporate disclosures and financial reporting, a category increasing in each of the past four years. The SEC has awarded more than $111 million to thirty-four whistleblowers, whose information and assistance led to SEC enforcement actions in which over $584 million in financial sanctions were ordered. The whistleblower program has evolved to become an important enforcement tool for the SEC.[37]

> **TIP:** An employee who believes he or she has been retaliated against in violation of this section may file a complaint with the Occupational Safety and Health Administration (OSHA) of the Department of Labor and, eventually, in federal court.

Q 30.10.1 What does a whistleblower employee need to show to prove that the company is taking retaliatory action against him or her?

The employee must show his or her specific whistleblowing activities, that unfavorable personnel action was taken against him or her, and that whistleblowing behavior was "a contributing factor" to the adverse personnel action.

SOX section 806 limits protected whistleblowing to specific federal statutes (mail fraud, wire fraud, bank fraud, securities fraud), SEC rules and regulations, and federal laws relating to fraud against shareholders.[38] These violations must occur in the United States.[39]

Company Action

Q 30.10.2 What procedures should be in place to help stave off successful legal action by whistleblowers?

A company should have an effective corporate code of conduct in place that includes information on making anonymous reports of questionable accounting or securities disclosure matters and that affirms that the company will not retaliate against employees for making such reports. Furthermore, the company should train supervisors and managers, both in the human relations and financial management areas, on recognizing and responding to such complaints.

TIP: It is important to always document performance failures that lead to employee discipline. This will help the employer demonstrate that the penalty imposed on an employee was not retaliatory and not related to his or her complaints under SOX.

Q 30.10.3   What should the company do once a complaint is filed?

Once a legitimate complaint is filed within the company, the employer must thoroughly—and immediately—investigate; typically, this is done by coordinated effort among the company's human resources staff, SOX compliance officer, and outside counsel. The accuracy and completeness of this investigation will pay great dividends in dealing with OSHA and the SEC and in restraining the potential for collateral damage to the company's reputation among investors. Records must be preserved concerning the investigation and underlying issues.

TIP: In preparing investigation reports, keep in mind that both SEC staff and OSHA staff are likely to review the reports.

Consequences of Whistleblower Prevailing

Q 30.10.4   What happens if the whistleblower wins the case?

In the event the employee prevails, he or she may be awarded reinstatement with seniority (or front pay if reinstatement is not feasible), back pay with interest, compensation for special damages including for litigation costs, expert witness fees, and attorney fees.[40]

Q 30.10.5   Are there any repercussions beyond what is owed to the whistleblower?

SOX provides for numerous civil remedies.[41] In addition, Congress adopted a broad criminal statute.[42] This statute punishes whoever knowingly and with the intent to retaliate takes action, including interference with employment, against any person "for providing to a law enforcement officer any truthful information relating to the commission or possible commission of any Federal offense." Violations are punishable by fines or imprisonment for up to ten years or both.

State Law

Q 30.10.6   Do states have similar protections for whistleblowers?

At the state level in the United States, individual states vary in their protection for whistleblowers, although forty-two states claim to have recognized at least some claims for retaliatory discharges. Some states are restrictive in their protection, such as in New York where financial improprieties are carved out of the protections.[43] In other jurisdictions, such as New Jersey, extensive litigation by whistleblowers is already occurring.

Outside Auditors

Q 30.11   The landscape has changed for public companies, but what about for accounting firms?

Congress dramatically overhauled the regulatory landscape for public accounting firms in SOX, creating an independent federal Public Company Accounting Oversight Board (PCAOB) and requiring accounting firms to register with it to be eligible to prepare audit reports of issuers.[44] Registrants promise to be governed by the PCAOB's accounting standards, approved by the SEC, and which take precedence over Generally Accepted Accounting Principles (GAAP).[45]

As of the end of 2016, the PCAOB expected to employ 876 staff, financed by a $253 million budget approved by the SEC and funded by fees paid by issuers, broker-dealers, and 2,107 registered public accounting firms. In 2015, the PCAOB issued 218 reports of its audits of large and small public accounting firms, both domestic and foreign; in the course of these audits, the PCAOB examined portions of each of more than 800 audits by these firms of issuers. The PCAOB enforces its accounting standards with monetary penalties, censure, suspension, and revocation of registration. Its largest enforcement action was the levy of a $2 million penalty against Deloitte & Touche LLP in October 2013 for permitting a former partner to remain associated with that firm after being suspended by the PCAOB.[46]

COMPLIANCE FACT

The PCAOB periodically inspects the performance of auditors and may discipline individual accountants as well as accounting firms.

Companies and Auditors

Q 30.12   Has SOX affected the relationship between the companies and auditors?

In a seismic shift from the past, Congress has prohibited auditors of an issuer from providing other services to their audit clients. The responsibilities of an issuer's management to install and maintain appropriate accounting systems and internal controls for the reliability of financial reporting have been underscored. Any former coziness between auditors and issuers is replaced by enforced independence and distance. In fact, the auditors are required under the PCAOB's Ethics and Independence Rules 3501–3526 and Interim Independence Standards ET-1, ET-2 and ET-191 to provide issuers' audit committees written disclosure about their provision of tax and other non-audit-related services, and their independence from the issuer.[47]

Q 30.12.1   What about "one-stop shopping" for financial and accounting services?

No longer are public accounting firms permitted to be "one-stop shopping" venues for audit clients also desiring accounting, planning, information technology, control, and consulting services.[48] SOX flatly prohibits registered firms who are preparing audit reports for an issuer from contemporaneously providing "non-audit service," such as bookkeeping, designing or implementing financial information systems, rendering appraisal and valuation services, giving fairness opinions, providing actuarial or internal audit services, performing management or human resources functions,[49] broker-dealer services,[50] legal services,[51] or expert services unrelated to an audit.

Audit Committees and Auditors

Q 30.13   What is the relationship between the audit committees and the auditors?

All audit services must be pre-approved by the issuer's audit committee every five years; in addition, the audit report must expressly name the audit firm's lead partner on the engagement.[52] An audit committee may delegate to one or more designated independent director's authority to pre-approve work by an audit firm, subject to ratification by the audit committee at its next scheduled meeting. The audit committee's approval must be disclosed in periodic reports to investors. The audit firm is required to communicate with the audit committee concerning an overview of the overall audit strategy, all critical accounting policies and practices used in the audit, the auditor's evaluation of the quality of the issuer's financial reporting, significant risks the auditor identified, difficult or contentious matters for which the auditor consulted outside the audit engagement team, information related to significant unusual transactions, and any expected departures from the auditor's standard report.[53]

Q 30.13.1   Can a company keep using audit partners with whom it has an established relationship?

An audit firm's lead partner on the engagement and the audit partner responsible for reviewing the audit must rotate out of the engagement at least once every five years.[54] In addition, a registered audit firm may not provide new audit services if an issuer's CEO, CFO, controller, or chief accounting officer was employed by that audit firm, and participated in any capacity at all in the audit of that issuer, during the preceding year.

Procedures

Q 30.14 What are new procedures that auditors must follow?

Congress specified certain requirements be included in PCAOB rules in SOX section 103:

- Audit firms must prepare and maintain for at least seven years audit work papers in sufficient detail to support the conclusions reached in a given audit report;

- A second partner who was not in charge of the audit must approve each audit report;

- In each audit report concerning an issuer's internal controls, the audit firm is to:

  - describe the scope of its testing of an issuer's structure and procedures for internal controls and present the findings from such testing, along with an evaluation of the internal controls and a description of material weaknesses in such internal controls, and of any material non-compliance found;

  - evaluate an issuer's maintenance of records that accurately and fairly reflect the transactions and disposition of its assets;

  - provide reasonable assurance that transactions are recorded as necessary to permit preparation of financial statements in accordance with GAAP; and

  - provide reasonable assurance that receipts and expenditures of the issuer are being made only in accordance with authorizations of management and directors of the issuer;

- Audit firms are to monitor their professional ethics and independence from issuers; and

- Audit firms are to provide:

  - procedures for internal consultation on accounting and audit questions;

  - for the supervision of audit work on behalf of which the firm issues audit reports;

  - for hiring and professional development of personnel;

- procedures and standards for the acceptance and continuance of engagements; and

- procedures for internal inspections.

PCAOB

Q 30.15   What powers does the PCAOB have over the auditors?

The PCAOB obtains regular and special reports from registered audit firms and has investigatory and disciplinary powers over them.[55] Those powers include requiring testimony from registered firms or their associated persons and the production of audit work papers and other documents from firms or associated persons. The PCAOB may sanction firms or associated persons who do not cooperate by suspending them from practice or suspending or revoking their registration with the PCAOB.[56]

COMPLIANCE FACT

The PCAOB coordinates its investigations with the SEC and may seek SEC subpoenas to compel testimony or documents from any person, including audit clients.

Q 30.15.1   What can the PCAOB do if it uncovers a violation?

The PCAOB is authorized to impose disciplinary or remedial sanctions, including temporary suspension or permanent revocation of registration, suspension or bar of a person from further association with any registered firm, temporary or permanent limitations on the activities of a firm or person, and a civil penalty of up to $750,000 for an individual or $15 million for a firm.[57] These sanctions are available in cases of reckless or intentional misconduct. Censure and a requirement for additional professional training may be imposed for lesser violations.

Q 30.15.2   How have the new PCAOB rules changed audits?

Overall, these standards have emphasized the tightening of internal controls and proper documentation for transactions, more than making substantive changes in accounting principles. The relative frequency of enforcement actions by the SEC involving improper revenue recognition practices and misuse of reserves serves as a warning to issuers to be more cautious and conservative in applying and interpreting GAAP than before SOX. The vigor of the enforcement program, along with the pervasive impacts of this SOX revolution in the regulation of public accounting firms, has greatly altered the business, business methods, and even the daily professional activities of auditors. The combination of market scandals and SOX is forcing accountants to become gatekeepers for the public and the SEC.[58]

Foreign Auditors

Q 30.16   What effect does SOX have on foreign auditors?

Foreign public accounting firms who prepare and furnish audit reports for issuers are subject to SOX to the same extent as U.S. public accounting firms, including registration with the PCAOB and inspections and discipline by PCAOB.[59]

Q 30.16.1   What if a U.S. accounting firm relies in part upon a foreign accounting firm?

If a registered U.S. public accounting firm, in issuing an audit report, chooses to rely in part upon an opinion or other material services furnished by a foreign public accounting firm, then the U.S. public accounting firm is deemed to have consented to supply the audit work papers of that foreign accounting firm to U.S. regulators on demand, and to have secured the agreement of that foreign public accounting to produce such work papers. Unless the U.S. public accounting firm secures such arrangements, it may not rely upon the work of a foreign public accounting firm in issuing audit reports.

Lawyers

Q 30.17   How does SOX affect lawyers for issuers?

While SOX does not impose a new oversight body upon the legal profession comparable to the PCAOB, the issuance and enforcement of rules for attorneys emanate directly from the SEC. Moreover, SEC standards preempt state bar regulation. Without formally deputizing attorneys as law enforcement employees of the federal government, the SEC nonetheless intrudes on traditional attorney-client relationship, privilege and even asserts the authority to second-guess the content and quality of a lawyer's legal advice.

Q 30.17.1   What responsibilities does the SEC impose upon lawyers under SOX?

The SEC views lawyers as gatekeepers. The SEC believes that lawyers, in particular in-house counsel, are in the best position to detect and stop fraudulent conduct by corporate managers and employees.

COMPLIANCE FACT

Lawyers are monitored by the SEC for their work in fraud prevention, not for their customary role as advocates for corporations.

Q 30.17.2   Which lawyers are affected by SOX?

The SEC's assertion of applicability of its rules to attorneys is very broad. Attorneys are not only persons who are admitted to practice law in the various states, but also include any person holding himself out as a lawyer and anyone otherwise qualified to be an attorney.[60] Likewise, the scope of work performed by attorneys that is subject to Rule 205 is defined very expansively. The preparation of documents to be filed with the SEC is covered, as is contributing information to such documents or advising issuers about them. Investigating a matter that is a subject of SEC reporting is also a form of practice before the SEC, as is formally appearing and representing a corporate client before the SEC.

Q 30.17.3   Are there any limitations on the applicability of the SEC rules on attorney conduct?

A few limitations are recognized, and the rules ordinarily do not apply to:

- attorneys who do not have an attorney-client relationship with an issuer; for example, attorneys performing a non-legal function or simply speaking before an audience of business persons who are not clients;

- attorneys for underwriters or other third persons are generally not considered attorneys for issuers;

- attorneys performing work for non-public clients who are not issuers or affiliates of issuers;

- foreign attorneys practicing foreign law in consultation with U.S. attorneys who are themselves appearing before the SEC.[61]

"Up-the-Ladder" Reporting

Q 30.18   What is "up-the-ladder" reporting?

If an attorney has identified "credible evidence" of a "material violation," he or she must report it to the top of the issuer corporation. The rules provide for a two-step internal reporting process regarding material violations.[62] First, a subordinate attorney must report the evidence to his or her supervisory attorney.[63] Second, a supervisory attorney must report evidence of a material violation up-the-ladder within the issuer company to the chief legal counsel (for example, the company's general counsel or chief legal officer (CLO)) or to the CEO.[64]

Q 30.18.1   Do the requirements depend on whether the attorney is in a supervisory position?

Although the scope of their "up-the-ladder" reporting obligations vary, both supervisory and subordinate attorneys, both inside an issuer and in law firms providing services to issuers, are subject to the rules.[65]

Q 30.18.2   What if an attorney has reason to believe that reporting to the CEO or CLO would be futile?

If the CEO or the chief legal counsel does not respond appropriately to the evidence or if the attorney reasonably believes that reporting to the chief legal counsel would be futile, the attorney must report the evidence to one of the following:

(1)   the audit committee of the board of directors of the company;
(2)   a committee of independent directors; or
(3)   the full board of directors.[66]

Q 30.18.3   How do these requirements apply to outside counsel?

Outside counsel is also subject to this reporting duty. An attorney retained or directed by the chief legal officer to litigate a reported violation does not have a reporting obligation so long as he or she is able to assert a colorable defense on behalf of the issuer and the chief legal officer provides reports on the progress and outcome of the litigation to the issuer's board of directors.[67]

Supervisory and Subordinate Attorneys

Q 30.19   Who is a "supervisory attorney"?

Supervisory attorneys are those who oversee or direct another attorney in performing a task that is within the scope of practicing before the SEC on behalf of an issuer. A supervisory attorney is the one responsible for complying with the reporting requirements when he or she has received a report of evidence of a material violation from a subordinate attorney. A supervisory attorney who reasonably believes that information received from a subordinate attorney does not constitute evidence of a material violation need not report it to the issuer and has no further obligation under the SEC rules.

Q 30.20   Who is a "subordinate attorney"?

A subordinate attorney is one who is supervised by another attorney in performing a task that is part of practicing before the SEC. A subordinate attorney who reports evidence of a material violation, as described below, to his or her supervisory attorney has no further obligation under the SEC rules. If a subordinate attorney reasonably believes that the supervisory attorney to whom he or she reported the evidence has failed to comply with the SEC rules, then he or she is permitted to report the evidence directly to the issuer, thereby bypassing the supervisory attorney.

Q 30.20.1   As long as there is an attorney above you on the chain, are you a subordinate attorney?

An attorney (such as an assistant general counsel) who operates under a chief legal officer's supervision or direction is not considered a subordinate attorney under the rules. Such an attorney must go beyond reporting to a superior attorney and comply with the full panoply of rules.[68]

Q 30.20.2   Are the definitions of supervisory and subordinate attorney static?

Except for a corporation's chief legal officer and his or her direct reporting attorneys, one may be a supervising attorney for one task or matter and a subordinate attorney for another. To minimize confusion, it may be helpful for an issuer or its law firm to designate a formal chain of command within its legal department.

Required Action

Q 30.21 What do SOX and the SEC require of a lawyer?

Lawyers who practice before the SEC and become aware of credible evidence that any material violation of any federal securities law, or other federal or state law or breach of fiduciary duty, has taken place, is taking place, or is about to take place, must report it up the ladder until the lawyer receives an appropriate response.[69] If there is no appropriate response, the lawyer must take further reporting or action, including a "noisy withdrawal" (withdraw representation and notify the SEC of the withdrawal and the basis of its withdrawal, which is related to professional considerations), if necessary.

Q 30.21.1 How does this affect the attorney-client relationship?

Unquestionably, the SEC rules impose greater obligations upon lawyers with respect to public disclosure by issuers. In brief, they tend to command a lawyer: "When in doubt, report; when in doubt, disclose." They intend to narrow the confidences that issuer's counsel may protect, in what SOX and the SEC perceive as the greater objective of transparency and completeness in communications with investors.

Q 30.21.2 What sanctions are there for violations by an attorney of the SEC rules under SOX?

A violation of any rule issued by the SEC under SOX constitutes a violation of the Exchange Act.[70] Accordingly, a violation of the rule subjects the violator to all the remedies and sanctions available under the Exchange Act, including injunctions, and cease-and-desist orders. The SEC may deny, temporarily or permanently, the privilege of appearing or practicing before the SEC, including preparing and filing documents with the SEC.[71] The SEC may also bar an attorney from serving as an officer or director of a public company. Finally, a violation of disciplinary rules is routinely reported to other jurisdictions where the attorney is admitted, usually resulting in disciplinary proceedings in those jurisdictions as well.[72]

Credible Evidence and Material Violation

Q 30.22   What does "becoming aware of credible evidence" actually mean?

The information assessed by the attorney is credible evidence concerning a "material violation" if it would be unreasonable, under the circumstances, for a prudent and competent attorney not to conclude that it is "reasonably likely" (that is, more than a mere possibility, less than a probability) that a material violation has occurred or is about to occur.[73] The amount of information a reasonable and prudent attorney may determine to establish "credible evidence" may vary according to a given attorney's background, experience, seniority, and professional skills; the time constraints under which the attorney is acting; the attorney's previous experience and familiarity with the client; and the availability of other attorneys with whom he or she may consult.[74]

Q 30.22.1   How should companies define "credible evidence"?

Internally, an issuer or its outside law firm may elect to adopt a lower threshold for attorney reporting simply to assure that higher authority does not miss the opportunity to meet the minimum standards of the SEC.

Q 30.23   What constitutes a "material violation"?

What is to be reported upward is credible evidence concerning a material violation. What is "material" should be understood from the viewpoint of a reasonable investor. If there is a substantial likelihood that such an investor would see given information as significantly altering the total mix of information before him, that given information is material.

Information relating to integrity of management is always material, as are intentional misstatements, even a quantitatively small and nonintentional misstatement of a financial statement item, including:

- where a misstatement arises from an item capable of precise measurement or whether it arises from an estimate and, if so, the degree of imprecision inherent in the estimate;

- where a misstatement masks a change in earnings or other trends;

- whether a misstatement hides a failure to meet analysts' consensus expectations for the enterprise;

- where a misstatement changes a loss into income or vice versa;

- where a misstatement concerns a segment or other portion of the registrant's business that has been identified as playing a significant role in the registrant's operations or profitability;

- where a misstatement affects the registrant's compliance with regulatory requirements;

- where a misstatement affects the registrant's compliance with loan covenants or other contractual requirements; and

- where a misstatement has the effect of increasing management's compensation—for example, by satisfying requirements for the award of bonuses or other forms of incentive compensation.

Q 30.24 At what stage must a future possible violation be reported?

No case law or SEC guidance limits the prospective time horizon for incipient violations. The requirements for credible evidence and the reasonable likelihood of a material violation will provide screens to filter out speculation or gossip. However, the pressure upon attorneys for issuers deputizing them to report potential violations to top management, audit committees, or boards of directors is clear.

Qualified Legal Compliance Committees

Q 30.25   What is a qualified legal compliance committee (QLCC)?

An issuer may, but need not, establish a qualified legal compliance committee. A QLCC is a committee of the issuer's board of directors, consisting of at least one member of the audit committee (or its equivalent if the issuer does not have one) and two or more other independent members of the issuer's board who are not employed, directly or indirectly, by the issuer.

TIP: The QLCC need not be a separate committee; the audit committee or another committee of the board of directors, appropriately composed, may be designated as the QLCC.[75]

Q 30.25.1   How is a QLCC established?

The QLCC must be formally established and must adopt written procedures for the confidential receipt, retention, and consideration of any report of evidence of a material violation. The QLCC must be established *before* receiving its first report of a material violation. If it is established in response to a report, it is not qualified to act with respect to that report. A QLCC acts by majority vote; upon receiving any report, it may initiate an investigation, will engage independent counsel to it, and may recommend that an issuer implement an appropriate response. If an issuer fails to implement an appropriate response recommended by the QLCC, the QLCC has authority to notify the SEC of the matter.

Q 30.25.2   How does the QLCC operate?

Typically, a QLCC will engage counsel to investigate on its behalf. An attorney retained or directed by a QLCC to investigate a reported violation has no reporting obligations other than to the QLCC. Similarly, an attorney retained or directed by a QLCC to litigate a reported violation has no reporting obligations except to the QLCC, provided he or she may assert a colorable defense on behalf of the issuer.

CLO Responsibilities and Appropriate Responses

Q 30.26   What steps must a CLO take when presented with a report of evidence of a material violation?

The CLO is obligated to cause an inquiry to be conducted that he or she believes is appropriate to determine whether the reported material violation has occurred, is ongoing, or is about to occur. If the CLO determines there is no material violation, he or she must so notify the reporting attorney of the basis for such determination. If the CLO determines there is a material violation, he or she must take reasonable steps to ensure that the issuer adopts an appropriate response (which may include remedial measures and/or sanctions, and appropriate disclosures) and advise the reporting attorney accordingly. Alternately, the CLO or another supervising attorney may refer the report of a material violation to a QLCC. If the CLO makes such referral, the CLO must inform the reporting attorney of the referral. Once the report and referral occur, the CLO and supervising attorney are relieved of any further obligation (but also lose further control over the matter).[76]

Q 30.26.1   What kind of paper trail should the inquiry have?

The SEC excluded from its final rules requirements for documentation of reports of material violations, finding, for the present, that the risks and burdens associated with preparing and preserving documentation may outweigh the benefits. Probably, a determination by an attorney to report a material violation should be documented in writing to a higher authority. A preparatory inquiry or consideration of appropriate responses may be necessary. At this stage, excessive documentation may interfere with candid communications and/or impede the process and objective of ultimate transparency the rules seek to promote. It is likely this will be an unsettled area for the foreseeable future.

Q 30.26.2   What would be considered an "appropriate response"?

Following receipt of a report of a material violation, the CLO, CEO, audit committee, or QLCC must make an appropriate response. The response may take one of several forms:

- A determination that no material violation has occurred or is about to occur;

- The adoption of appropriate remedial measures to prevent any material violation that has yet to occur; or

- The issuer retains or directs an attorney to review the reported evidence of a material violation and either has implemented remedial recommendations made by such attorney or has been advised that such attorney may assert a colorable defense on behalf of the issuer.[77]

Q 30.26.3   How does a reporting attorney determine whether the response was appropriate?

Whether a response is appropriate must be evaluated under the particular circumstances of each report, considering the amount and weight of evidence of a material violation, the severity of the material violation, and the scope of the investigation that has been made following the report. In forming a belief concerning the appropriateness of a response, a reporting attorney may rely upon reasonable factual representations and legal determinations made by persons upon whom a reasonable attorney would rely.

Q 30.26.4   What does a reporting attorney do after the company has responded?

An attorney who receives what he or she believes is an appropriate response to a report need do nothing more.[78] However, an attorney who does not reasonably believe that the issuer has made an appropriate response, or who has not received an appropriate response within a reasonable time, must explain his or her reasons for disputing the appropriateness of the response to the CLO, CEO, or directors to whom the attorney first made his or her report.[79]

Q 30.26.5 In the absence of an appropriate response to a report of a material violation, what should a conscientious counsel do?

Initially, the SEC proposed a noisy withdrawal. As of today, the SEC has not adopted any final rules requiring further action by the reporting attorney.

Q 30.26.6 What options do lawyers currently have when a SOX violation may be occurring?

Apart from withdrawal, and breaking sharply from state regulations and case law, the SEC's rule authorizes an attorney to reveal facts to the SEC that the attorney believes are necessary to prevent an issuer from committing a material violation that would cause substantial injury, to prevent an issuer from committing perjury, or to rectify consequences of a material violation by the issuer.[80] An attorney may also use records made in the course of fulfilling reporting obligations to defend himself or herself against charges of misconduct.

Foreign Lawyers

Q 30.27 Does SOX also apply to foreign lawyers?

Foreign lawyers who assist companies issuing securities for sale in the United States with reporting documents to be filed with the SEC are practicing before the SEC and, in doing this work, they are subject to SOX and to the obligation to comply with the Rules of Professional Practice adopted by the SEC.

State Rules

Q 30.28 How do the SEC rules compare with American Bar Association and state rules?

The SEC views its rules as preemptive of any conflicting state provisions concerning lawyer behavior. Shortly after SOX, the American Bar Association amended its Model Rule 1.13 ("Organization as Client"). The amended rule is more general in content but closer in concept to SOX Rule 205. Model Rule 1.13(b) imposes an up-the-ladder reporting duty upon an attorney engaged by an organization who knows that an officer or employee is acting or intends to act in violation of law likely to result in substantial injury to the organization. The attorney "shall proceed as is reasonably necessary in the best interest of the organization" to refer the matter to higher authority in the organization, including to its highest authority.

COMPLIANCE FACT

More than forty states have included up-the-ladder reporting in adopting local versions of the model rules, but Delaware has not and the adopting states vary in the details of their requirement.

Q 30.28.1   What is the difference between the SEC and ABA and state rules?

Generally, Rule 205 is broader and more detailed than the model rules or states' disciplinary rules for lawyers. For example, some state provisions, such as California's Rule 3-100 of its Rules of Professional Conduct, do not permit a lawyer to report a client's fraud or imminent violation of law (unless it will cause death or severe bodily harm to an individual) outside the organization. Model Rule 1.13(f) parallels the provisions in SOX Rule 205 emphasizing that a lawyer for an organization represents the organization, which may have interests adverse to those of individual officers, directors, or employees. In dealing with those individuals, an attorney is required to explain to them who his or her client is—and who is not.

Q 30.28.2   What is the relationship between the SEC and state rules?

Rule 205 supplements, but does not replace, most state rules of professional conduct for attorneys. It specifically permits additional and more rigorous regulation of lawyers by the states. Although there are no federal court decisions yet on the application of Rule 205, in analogous circumstances, it has been held that federal law regulating NASD arbitration preempts California's ethical standards for arbitrators.[81] By analogy, it is likely that the standards implementing SOX section 307 preempt inconsistent state ethical and disciplinary rules.

Law Firm Training

Q 30.29   How should law firms and lawyers adjust to the new standards?

The ever-changing and enlarging requirements of corporate compliance impose obligations on lawyers and their public companies and law firms for mandatory regular training. Given the breadth of the definition of practice before the SEC in the SEC's Rule 205, all attorneys should attend. Participants, whether in-house or in law firms, whether newly hired or long-tenured, should file written certifications of completion of training for inclusion in compliance files of the general counsel.

TIP: Training should take place at least once every year.

Q 30.29.1   What should the training entail?

The subjects of training should include at the very minimum:

- familiarization with the company's most updated compliance policy, governance documents, and code of ethics, including the availability of anonymous telephone hotlines and websites and the protection afforded to whistleblowers;

- review of SEC rules, procedures, and enforcement actions, including the attorney conduct rules and enforcement actions. Lawyers must know the penalties for failures of compliance, including corporate disciplinary procedures for failure to perform up-the-ladder reporting; and

- review recent key disclosure documents for accuracy, completeness, and to make personnel aware of the scope of required disclosures.

Punishment

Q 30.30   Has the SEC punished lawyers for misconduct?

Yes. The SEC has proceeded vigorously against lawyers engaged directly in fraudulent or dishonest conduct. The SEC has named lawyers as respondents or defendants in more than thirty enforcement actions.

Q 30.30.1   How has the SEC punished lawyers?

Civil actions commenced by the SEC against attorneys for violation of its attorney conduct rules have sought injunctive relief and monetary civil penalties, and administrative cease-and-desist proceedings. The SEC may notify a state bar of its disciplinary proceedings against an attorney. Beyond enforcing its rules of professional conduct, the SEC has also disciplined lawyers for inadequacy in the quality of their legal advice.[82]

Insurance

Q 30.31   How do the new SEC rules affect insurance for lawyers?

The gatekeeper responsibilities thrust upon lawyers by SOX and by the SEC's rules of attorney conduct make the general counsel and his staff more prominent to disgruntled investors and in greater need of insurance protection. Attraction and retention of capable legal officers requires an issuer to provide adequate insurance. Where the general counsel is covered, he or she should be protected even if other officers may have committed misconduct. Thus, the inability for the insurance company to rescind the coverage is especially important for the legal staff (and independent directors), as is severability (so that coverage of a class of insureds is not voided by allegations against one or more officers or directors). Separate and distinct policy limits for payment of defense expenses, and for settlements or judgments, are necessary.

General Counsel

Q 30.32   What should the role of the general counsel be in the new environment?

Under the collaborative model of corporate governance envisioned by COSO,[83] and assumed by the SEC in its SOX rulemakings, it is more important for an issuer than ever for the general counsel to be viewed as an advisor, with a greater range of topics on which he or she must present legal options to management and the directors. SOX compliance anticipates increasing communication among officers and directors, some of it formal (such as meetings with an audit committee), and much of it informal (such as designing, testing, and utilizing disclosure controls).

Q 30.32.1   How have the SEC rules changed the relations among general counsel, directors, and management?

SOX has substantially increased the accountability of directors and general counsel for oversight and disclosures of conduct by an issuer, necessarily adjusting the formal and informal relationships among them. In particular, these new responsibilities affect the functioning of the general counsel. Therefore, when speaking with individual officers, managers, and directors, the general counsel represents the issuer, whose interests may differ from, or even be adverse to, interests of those individuals. Depending on the circumstances, the general counsel may also be obligated under SOX to communicate with the board of directors over the objection of the CEO.

Q 30.32.2   How does the new environment affect the CEO vis à vis the general counsel?

With multiple dimensions ranging from SOX obligations, to certification programs for quality standards, such as ISO 9000, to due diligence reviews by insurers, lenders, regulators and in connection with business combinations, corporate compliance is becoming perpetual and pervasive. The independent obligations of directors, CEO, CFO, and the general counsel are forcing collaboration to accomplish effective corporate oversight. Accordingly, and at different paces in different companies but especially in larger public companies, the extent of the CEO's individual dominance is receding.

SOX Effect

Q 30.32.3   How has SOX changed the role of the general counsel?

Historically, general counsel often served as confidential advisors to management, counseling on strategy and business issues beyond questions of law. Under SOX, the general counsel's obligations for disclosure and for up-the-ladder reporting of evidence of material violations have caused some officers to view their general counsel as a deputy cop who cannot keep secrets, and whose first loyalty is external, rather than to his fellow officers. This can lead the general counsel sometimes to be informally screened from participating in strategic discussions.

Q 30.32.4   What new tasks does the general counsel have under SOX?

SOX prescribes an extensive list of tasks that will require intense involvement by an issuer's general counsel, some of which are new and others of which have wider scope of applications. The availability of electronic communications and the regulatory requirements for real-time disclosures pressure a general counsel for speedy handling of these tasks, which may reduce the time available for careful deliberation:

- Documenting corporate governance procedures—for example, charters for the audit committee, adoption of a code of ethics;

- Implementing rules against prohibited loans to officers;

- Investigating comments and complaints submitted via hotlines and websites;

- Assisting the CEO and CFO in acquiring and evaluating information from which they can determine whether to certify periodic financial reports under SOX sections 302 and 906;

- Assuring that internal controls for financial reporting have been documented, tested, and are being monitored;

- Preparing text for management's discussion and analysis of operations for investors and the SEC, and assuring the accuracy, fairness of presentation, and completeness of these disclosures;

- Overseeing the establishment, content, documentation, testing, monitoring, and improvement of disclosure controls;

- Administering nuts and bolts elements of the issuer's compliance program, including coordinating the performance of risk assessments and the evaluation of loss contingencies for audit and disclosure purposes;

- Communicating with internal auditors, external auditors, the CEO, CFO, and directors about a myriad of matters concerning independence of auditors, pre-approval of auditors' work, communications for audit verifications with third parties, and about credible evidence of material violations of law (if any);

- Dealing with external auditors and counsel on attestations under SOX section 404 and the recognition and amelioration of material weaknesses and significant deficiencies in the effective functioning of controls;

- Dealing, as appropriate, with regulators such as the SEC;

- Coordinating and dealing with corporate responses to data security breaches.[84]

Q 30.32.5   How do SOX requirements interact with the need to protect privileged communications?

Because the general counsel sometimes fulfills executive functions apart from the performance of legal services, and because privilege often will not extend to non-legal tasks (unless incidental and ancillary to legal work), the organization of the legal function at an issuer in the post-SOX era is particularly important. It is increasingly appreciated that the risk assessment tasks that are part of the development and testing of internal controls and disclosure controls are appropriately performed by specialized professionals outside the law department of an issuer but communicating frequently with the general counsel, in a dotted-line relationship.

Tools

Q 30.32.6   What organizational steps and tools are out there to assist the general counsel?

Protection of a general counsel's scarce time can be improved through several mechanisms:

- Delegation of preparation of periodic report information and updates to a compliance officer;

- Assignment of a junior lawyer or legal assistant to initial review and investigation of hotline and anonymous complaints on the corporate website, reporting to the general counsel with summaries on a regular basis;

- Assignment of a liaison to the information technology department to provide access for the general counsel to automated reports on the operation of significant internal controls;

- Arranging for separate electronic mailboxes for strategic communications among senior management, for compliance communications with outside counsel and auditors, for compliance communications with directors and audit committee members;

- Regular meetings with operating and key administration department leaders to verify progress on development, testing, improvement of controls, and status of pending or potential reportable events;

- Assignment of a manager or officer to conduct and oversee risk assessments, taking guidance and providing reports to the general counsel, so that a broader span of loss contingencies and of operating, legal and financial risks are monitored, from overtime pay compliance, to environmental contamination and cleanup responsibilities, to adherence to domestic and foreign regulatory directives, etc.;

- Engaging outside specialist consultants to assist the risk assessment officer in undertaking specialized risk assessments, such as those involving evaluation of environmental liability exposure;

- Requiring monthly and quarterly sub-certificates from managers of significant divisions, departments, and staff functions of the same attestations contained in SOX 302, with opportunities for comments and notes to be attached, so that compliance topics requiring the general counsel's attention will arrive earlier at his or her desk;

- Requiring all personnel to be familiar with up-the-ladder reporting and, in that connection, requiring quarterly sub-certificates that none have failed to report information concerning potential violations of law or of compliance policies to the legal department, with the assurance that compliance in good faith will not subject the employee to discipline or dismissal;

- Requiring outside counsel to make quarterly certifications to the general counsel with respect to up-the-ladder reporting and any information or awareness of potential violations of law or of compliance policies;

- Instructing outside counsel as to the form and procedures for making reports to the general counsel and others within the company;

- Regular meetings with the CEO, CFO, and audit committee members reporting upon and discussing compliance topics so that an appropriate tone at the top is reinforced, a collaborative atmosphere is encouraged, and the risks of unanticipated crises minimized;

- Designing in advance, with the CEO and senior management, broad contingency plans so that, should crises arise, calm implementation of important early steps in investor and public communications, internal investigation and maintaining as much as possible business as usual in unaffected areas of corporate operations.

Q 30.32.7   How does a general counsel determine the best interests of the corporation?

The complexity inherent for a public company in competing in multiple product or service categories in domestic and overseas markets, each with multiple and evolving regulators, adds difficulty to a general counsel's fulfilling the fiduciary responsibility to recommend decisions in the best interests of the corporation. These matters illustrate the ever-increasing importance of involving the general counsel in strategic discussions at a public company, and the need for collaboration among management and directors, notwithstanding the disclosure obligations to regulators of the participants.

Investigations

Q 30.33   What factors are relevant to the SEC in the course of an investigation?

A general counsel should be mindful of guidance the SEC has published on how corporate behavior and cooperation influence its enforcement decisions:

1. What is the nature of the misconduct involved? Did it result from inadvertence, honest mistake, simple negligence, reckless or deliberate indifference to indicia of wrongful conduct, willful misconduct, or unadorned venality? Were the company's auditors misled?

2. How did the misconduct arise? Is it the result of pressure placed on employees to achieve specific results, or a tone of lawlessness set by those in control of the company? What compliance procedures were in place to prevent the misconduct now uncovered? Why did those procedures fail to stop or inhibit the wrongful conduct?

3. Where in the organization did the misconduct occur? Who knew about, or participated in, the misconduct? How high up in the chain of command were they? Did senior personnel participate in, or turn a blind eye toward, obvious indicia of misconduct? How systemic was the behavior? Is it symptomatic of the way the entity does business, or was it isolated?

4. How long did the misconduct last? Was it a one-quarter, or one- time, event, or did it last several years? In the case of a public company, did the misconduct occur before the company went public? Did it facilitate the company's ability to go public?

5. How much harm has the misconduct inflicted upon investors and other corporate constituencies? Did the share price of the company's stock drop significantly upon its discovery and disclosure?

6. How was the misconduct detected and who uncovered it?

7. How long after discovery of the misconduct did it take to implement an effective response?

8. What steps did the company take upon learning of the misconduct? Did the company immediately stop the misconduct? Are persons responsible for any misconduct still with the company? If so, are they still in the same positions? Did the company promptly, completely, and effectively disclose the existence of the misconduct to the public, to regulators, and to self-regulators? Did the company cooperate completely with appropriate regulatory and law enforcement bodies? Did the company identify what additional related misconduct is likely to have occurred? Did the company take steps to identify the extent of damage to investors and other corporate constituencies? Did the company appropriately recompense those adversely affected by the conduct?

9. What processes did the company follow to resolve many of these issues and ferret out necessary information? Were the audit committee and the board of directors fully informed? If so, when?

10. Did the company commit to learn the truth, fully and expeditiously? Did it do a thorough review of the nature, extent, origins, and consequences of the misconduct and related behavior? Did management, the board, or committees consisting solely of outside directors oversee the review? Did company employees or outside persons perform the review? If outside persons, had they done other work for the company?

Where the review was conducted by outside counsel, had management previously engaged such counsel? Were scope limitations placed on the review? If so, what were they?

11. Did the company promptly make available to our staff the results of its review and provide sufficient documentation reflecting its response to the situation? Did the company identify possible violative conduct and evidence with sufficient precision to facilitate prompt enforcement actions against those who violated the law? Did the company produce a thorough and probing written report detailing the findings of its review? Did the company voluntarily disclose information the SEC did not directly request and otherwise might not have uncovered? Did the company ask its employees to cooperate with our staff and make all reasonable efforts to secure such cooperation?

12. What assurances are there that the conduct is unlikely to recur? Did the company adopt and ensure enforcement of new and more effective internal controls and procedures designed to prevent a recurrence of the misconduct? Did the company provide our staff with sufficient information for it to evaluate the company's measures to correct the situation and ensure that the conduct does not recur?

13. Is the company the same company in which the misconduct occurred, or has it changed through a merger or bankruptcy reorganization?[85]

Q 30.33.1 Has the SEC indicated the areas of greatest concern?

The SEC has underscored the foregoing guidelines in recently announcing its intention to monitor closely the conduct of attorneys in their handling of internal investigations of alleged corporate wrongdoing. Internal investigations are typically performed under considerable time pressure and logistical obstacles by overworked teams of honest, bright, and diligent lawyers. It is, unfortunately, a further consideration in planning and conducting such an investigation to bear in mind that it may later be reviewed with the benefit of hindsight by the SEC.

In effect, the investigating lawyers must plan and document their audit program, double-check their facts and files, examining themselves while they investigate the conduct of others.

Q 30.33.2   What are the biggest obstacles to cooperation?

The management of archived computerized documents and of electronic mail presents logistics obstacles in every company. During an SEC inquiry, general counsel and outside counsel must make it a priority to retrieve such documents and to be candid with the SEC about its progress in responding to document requests. Delay, obfuscation, and unfounded excuses will frustrate the SEC and can only exasperate the situation.

    CASE STUDY: *In re Lucent Techs., Inc.*[86]

The SEC's May 2004 enforcement settlement with Lucent Technologies demonstrates the seriousness of inadequate attention to an investigation and the potential repercussions of delay in compliance with an SEC investigation. Lucent agreed to pay a $25 million penalty for its non-cooperation with an SEC investigation.

Certification of Financial Statements

Requirements for Certification

Q 30.34   What are SOX's certification requirements?

To enhance confidence in the reliability of financial reports and to place accountability squarely on the CEO and CFO of issuers, Congress required two certifications of financial statements and expressed the sense of the Senate that corporate tax returns should be signed by the CEO and CFO.[87] In addition, Congress required disclosure of accounting in an issuer's financial reports that does not correspond with GAAP.[88]

Q 30.34.1   What must the SOX section 906 certificate contain?

The SOX section 906 certificate must be signed by the CEO and the CFO attesting that the report containing the financial statements fully complies with the reporting requirements in section 13(a) or 15(d) of the Securities Exchange Act of 1934[89] and the information contained in the report "fairly presents, in all material respects, the financial condition and results of operations of the issuer."

Q 30.34.2   What is the test for liability under the financial certificate requirements?

A corporate officer who knowingly makes a false certification by certifying a periodic report filed with the SEC that contains material false statements the officer knew to be false may be liable as a primary violator for securities fraud under section 10(b) of the Exchange Act as well as for criminal penalties.

Q 30.34.3   What else must the CEO and CFO do under SOX section 302?

SOX requires that the CEO and CFO have personal knowledge of the financial statements and impose responsibility on these executives to have established appropriate internal accounting controls and disclosure controls so that reliable financial statements may be prepared by the issuer. Under this requirement, the specificity of the promises and their basis in personal knowledge make it easier to demonstrate a violation.[90]

Q 30.34.4   What must the CEO and CFO actually certify under SOX section 302?

(1) He or she has reviewed the report being filed;

(2) Based on his or her knowledge, the report does not contain any untrue statement of a material fact or omit to state a material fact necessary to make the statements made, in light of the circumstances under which such statements were made, not misleading with respect to the period covered by the report;

(3) Based on his or her knowledge, the financial statements, and other financial information included in the report, fairly present in all material respects the financial condition, results of operations and cash flows of the issuer as of, and for, the periods presented in the report;

(4) He or she and the other certifying officers are responsible for establishing and maintaining disclosure controls and procedures for the issuer and have:

   (i) Designed such disclosure controls and procedures to ensure that material information relating to the issuer, including its consolidated subsidiaries, is made known to them by others within those entities, particularly during the period in which the periodic reports are being prepared,

   (ii) Evaluated the effectiveness of the issuer's disclosure controls and procedures as of a date within ninety days prior to the filing date of the report ("Evaluation Date"), and

   (iii) Presented in the report their conclusions about the effectiveness of the disclosure controls and procedures based on their evaluation as of the evaluation date;

(5) He or she and the other certifying officers have disclosed, based on their most recent evaluation, to the issuer's auditors and the audit committee of the board of directors (or persons fulfilling the equivalent function):

   (i) All significant deficiencies in the design or operation of internal controls which could adversely affect the issuer's ability to record, process, summarize, and report financial data, and have identified for the issuer's auditors any material weaknesses in internal controls, and

   (ii) Any fraud, whether or not material, that involves management or other employees who have a significant role in the issuer's internal controls; and

(6) He or she and the other certifying officers have indicated in the report whether or not there were significant changes in internal controls or in other factors that could significantly

affect internal controls subsequent to the date of their most recent evaluation, including any corrective actions with regard to significant deficiencies and material weaknesses.[91]

Q 30.34.5 Does the CEO have to sign the company's federal tax returns?

SOX section 1001 only sets forth the sense of the Senate that federal income tax returns of any corporation should be signed by the CEO.

Pre-Certification

Q 30.34.6 What should the CEO and CFO do prior to certifying a report under SOX?

Consistent with their affirmative responsibilities, before certifying a report under SOX section 302 or 906, a CEO and CFO should do no less than the following:

- Personally study the proposed report, looking closely at the financial statements, notes, and the discussion of financial matters and risk assessments, both financial and operating, in Management's Discussion and Analysis section;

- Require each member of the company's disclosure committee also to study personally the proposed report, thinking critically about the disclosures and notifying the CEO and CFO promptly of areas for consideration of further or modified discussion;

- With assistance from the disclosure committee, compare the proposed report with the company's recent filings with the SEC to identify instances where further amplification is appropriate in the proposed report;

- Specifically inquire of the disclosure committee and of all other members of management, the company's internal auditors, and outside auditors to report on the current status of any material weaknesses, significant deficiencies, and potential significant deficiencies, both financial and non-financial, in internal controls and disclosure controls that might impact the completeness and accuracy of the proposed report, including corrective steps planned or under way to relieve the weaknesses and deficiencies;

- Personally review with management and with outside auditors the current procedures undertaken to prepare the proposed report and to identify any issues appropriate for discussion in the report that were not raised by those procedures, as well as improvements in the information-gathering procedures;

- Obtain from other members of management and confirm with the audit partner(s) from outside auditors that none of them are aware of any material misrepresentations or omissions in the proposed report and, further, that the proposed report fairly presents the financial condition, results of operations, and cash flows of the issuer, apart from the requirements of GAAP; and that the proposed report addresses every requirement for the particular report in SEC regulations and rules; and

- Meet with the audit committee to identify and resolve any disagreements regarding disclosures in the proposed report, and explain to the audit committee the due diligence performed by the CEO and CFO to enable their certification of the proposed report.

Non-GAAP Reporting

Q 30.35   What is non-GAAP reporting?

A non-GAAP financial measure is a numerical measure of a registrant's historical or future financial performance, financial position, or cash flow that (1) actually or effectively excludes amounts that are included in the most directly comparable measure calculated and presented in accordance with GAAP in the statement of income, balance sheet or statement of cash flows (or equivalent statements) of the issuer, or (2) actually or effectively includes amounts that are excluded from the most directly comparable GAAP measure that is so calculated and presented. Excluded from the definition of a "non-GAAP financial measure" are

(i)   operating and other statistical measures; and

(ii)   ratios or statistical measures calculated exclusively comprised of components calculated under GAAP.[92]

Q 30.35.1   How must a company report a non-GAAP financial measure?

The regulations require public companies that disclose or release non-GAAP financial measures to include in the disclosure (1) a presentation of the most directly comparable GAAP financial measure, and (2) a reconciliation of that measure with a GAAP measure.[93] A registrant must disclose its reasons why management believes that presentation of the non-GAAP measure is useful along with any additional purposes. The regulations prohibit any misleading use of non-GAAP measures or using titles or descriptions of non-GAAP financial measures that are the same as, or confusingly similar to, titles or descriptions used for GAAP financial measures.

TIP: If a non-GAAP financial measure is released orally, telephonically, or by webcast or broadcast, the issuer may provide the required accompanying information by (a) the availability of the required accompanying information during its presentation, and (b) posting that information on its Internet website.[94]

Enforcement

Q 30.36   What enforcement action can the SEC take upon discovery of false certifications?

In addition to civil penalties and injunctions to cease and desist from violations, specific and significant governance requirements have been imposed by the SEC in its proceedings against issuers for false certifications of financial statements and periodic reports. The most extensive governance provisions to date were announced as part of a settlement with HealthSouth Corporation, following suits against fifteen officers of HealthSouth in which individual penalties were obtained. Along with a $100 million settlement was an unusually detailed permanent injunction.[95]

Internal Controls

Q 30.37   What internal controls does SOX require?

SOX section 404, as implemented by the SEC's rules,[96] requires that a public company's annual report include an internal control report of management that contains:

- A statement of management's responsibility for establishing and maintaining adequate internal control over financial reporting for the company;

- A statement identifying the framework used by management to conduct the required evaluation of the effectiveness of the company's internal control over financial reporting;

- Management's assessment of the effectiveness of the company's internal control over financial reporting as of the end of the company's most recent fiscal year, including a statement as to whether or not the company's internal control over financial reporting is effective;

- The assessment must include disclosure of any material weaknesses in the company's internal control over financial reporting identified by management. Management may not qualify its conclusions with respect to the effectiveness of the company's internal control over financial reporting. Rather, management must take those problems into account when concluding whether the company's internal control over financial reporting is effective; and

- A statement that the registered public accounting firm that audited the financial statements included in the annual report has issued an attestation report on management's assessment of the registrant's internal control over financial reporting.[97]

Q 30.37.1   What is the scope of internal controls over financial reporting?

The SEC has summarized the scope of internal controls over financial reporting for this purpose, as including policies and procedures that:

- pertain to the maintenance of records that in reasonable detail accurately and fairly reflect the transactions and dispositions of the assets of the registrant;

- provide reasonable assurance that transactions are recorded as necessary to permit preparation of financial statements in accordance with GAAP, and that receipts and expenditures of the registrant are being made only in accordance with authorizations of management and directors of the registrant; and

- provide reasonable assurance regarding prevention or timely detection of unauthorized acquisition, use or disposition of the registrant's assets that could have a material effect on the financial statements.[98]

Q 30.37.2   What are the elements and scope of internal controls?

The COSO framework for internal controls consists of five very general components:

(1) the control environment;
(2) risk assessment;
(3) control activities;
(4) information and communication; and
(5) monitoring.[99]

Q 30.37.3   Is there a specified process for designing, monitoring, or testing internal controls?

The PCAOB and SEC have explained that controls must be customized to the individual business operations of each public company and are expected, therefore, to vary from one company to the next. The audit standards and rules implementing SOX do not prescribe any method or procedure to be followed by an issuer in designing its internal controls, nor in testing them, nor in evaluating their effectiveness.

Q 30.37.4   What can be expected from internal controls?

No matter how comprehensive an issuer's internal controls, nor how well they function, there are genuine, and often inadequately appreciated, limits to their effectiveness. Accordingly, the PCAOB and SEC limit their requirements for an effective internal control system to its providing reasonable assurance of reliability in financial statements.

Q 30.37.5   What is a "reasonable assurance"?

The concept of reasonable assurance is built into the definition of internal control over financial reporting and also is integral to the auditor's opinion. Reasonable assurance includes the understanding that there is a remote likelihood that material misstatements will not be prevented or detected on a timely basis. Although not absolute assurance, reasonable assurance is, nevertheless, a high level of assurance.[100]

Q 30.37.6   Whose responsibility is it to design and develop internal controls?

Under SOX section 404, it is management's responsibility to determine accounting principles, to design and implement internal controls, and to prepare financial statements. However, an auditor's giving advice to management, and even limited assistance, does not violate the auditor-independence rules. The SEC has acknowledged that "both common sense and sound policy dictate that communications must be ongoing and open in order to create the best environment for producing high quality financial reporting and auditing."[101]

Q 30.37.7   How do auditors advise on internal controls without violating the stringent requirements of auditor independence?

An issuer must keep in mind these basic principles on auditor independence:

(1) an auditor cannot function as management for an issuer,

(2) an audit firm cannot audit its own work,

(3) an audit firm cannot be an advocate for the issuer, and

(4) an auditor may not have a conflict of interest impairing its independence with respect to a client issuer.

Accordingly, the development of internal controls and internal audit work cannot be outsourced by the issuer to the auditor.[102] However, an auditor's discussing and exchanging views with management does not in itself violate the independence principles, nor does it fall into a prohibited category of services. An auditor may even assist management in documenting internal controls, provided management is actively involved in the process.[103]

Q 30.37.8   What are the processes for developing internal controls for financial reporting?

Conceptually, the design of individual controls for accuracy and reliability, however diverse their subject matter, involves the same steps:

(1) Specifying a clear purpose for a process or procedure;

(2) Mapping each step in that process or procedure to show the sources, travel, processing, and output of information, identifying each document and department through whose hands it passes;

(3) Declaring business rules to assure the consistency in the information and its processing; and

(4) Preparing tests and reports that monitor the application and enforcement of the business rules.

Manipulation of Financial Reports

Q 30.38   What areas of financial reporting appear to be most vulnerable to manipulation?

The SEC's enforcement activities reveal that certain parts of financial statements are especially vulnerable to manipulation and fraudulent schemes. *Repeatedly*, similar issues arise at different companies for the same elements of financial reporting. Accordingly, a public company should give special attention to strong internal controls in the areas of:

(1) revenue recognition;
(2) expense disclosure and recognition;
(3) asset valuations;
(4) contingent liability valuations; and
(5) transactions with special-purpose entities.

Q 30.38.1   What aspects of revenue recognition should be considered in particular?

Companies have recorded revenues from fictitious transactions or expired agreements. They have also improperly accelerated the timing of revenue recognition, bringing future revenues into the current period. Some have entered into round-trip transactions with customers or vendors to stuff distribution channels in the current period, inflating revenues, and then secretly reversing or writing off the transactions in future periods.

Other companies have falsely represented that one-time transactions would yield recurring revenues in future periods, inflating revenues and earnings projections. In other cases, senior management has required that unsubstantiated adjustments be made, inflating revenues and earnings. There have also been instances of inflated promotional allowances and discounts from vendors, inflating revenues, sometimes including inducing vendors to sign false confirmation letters to auditors attesting to the enhanced allowances. Finally, companies have improperly treated revenues resulting from improper formation or non-consolidation of special-purpose entities, inflating revenues and profits.

CASE STUDY: *SEC v. Quattrone*

In January 2004, the SEC charged former executives and five customers of Suprema Securities in a $700 million fraud.[104] The heart of the Suprema scheme involved round-tripping transactions, in which Suprema, together with certain customers and vendors, created fictitious sales through false invoices and other fraudulent documentation. The effect of these transactions was to give the appearance that sales were made, when in actuality no products had been sold or shipped at all. The SEC went after both the issuer and the third parties.

Q 30.38.2   What aspects of expense accounting should be considered in particular?

It is not unusual for companies not to document or falsely support personal expenses. Some companies make improper overseas payments in violation of the Foreign Corrupt Practices Act. Companies also often fail to disclose payments to entities controlled by officers, directors, or their immediate family members. Companies may improperly capitalize operating expenses over several years, rather than charging in current period, thus reducing the charge against earnings in current period. Companies commonly fail to disclose payments for non-competition promises by officers and directors.

Q 30.38.3   What aspects of asset valuations should be considered in particular?

Companies use valuation methods not in compliance with GAAP resulting in values exceeding fair value, so as to avoid recognizing asset impairments and resulting write-downs. They also divert cash from proceeds of asset sales to officers and directors as well as understate expenses from acquisitions and restructuring.

Q 30.38.4 What aspects of contingent liability valuations should particularly be considered?

Companies have sometimes decreased values of reserves to inflate earnings. Valuation of balance sheet assets and liabilities necessarily involves judgments and may be devilishly complicated. Rendering them transparent in financial reporting can be quite difficult, the more so if not all levels of management are committed to such transparency.

Q 30.38.5 What aspects of special-purpose entities should particularly be considered?

Especially since the collapse of Enron with its extensive use of mysterious complex special-purpose entities, the use of special-purpose entities has become a red flag for investors and the SEC. If issuers choose to use a special-purpose entity, they must provide the following disclosure:

- The nature and business purpose of the issuer's off-balance-sheet arrangements;

- The importance of the off-balance-sheet arrangements to the issuer for liquidity, capital resources, market risk or credit risk support, or other benefits;

- The financial impact of the arrangements on the issuer (e.g., revenues, expenses, cash flows, or securities issued) and the issuer's exposure to risk as a result of the arrangements (e.g., retained interests or contingent liabilities); and

- Known events, demands, commitments, trends, or uncertainties that affect the availability or benefits to the issuer of material off-balance-sheet arrangements.

Q 30.38.6 How should companies document internal controls?

Management of a public company must compile and maintain evidential matter including documentation, regarding both the design of internal controls and the testing processes to provide reasonable support for management's assessment of the effectiveness of internal control over financial reporting. This evidential matter should provide "reasonable support for the evaluation of whether the control is designed to prevent or detect material misstatements or omissions; for the conclusion that the tests were appropriately planned and performed; and that the results of the tests were appropriately considered."[105]

TIP: The form and extent of documentation will vary from company to company but include paper and electronic files, policy manuals, process models, flowcharts, job descriptions, forms, and reports.

Q 30.38.7 What else is management required to do beyond developing, documenting, putting into operation, and using internal controls?

Under SOX section 404, management is also required to:

- accept responsibility for the effectiveness of the company's internal control over financial reporting;

- evaluate the effectiveness of the company's internal control over financial reporting using suitable control criteria;

- support its evaluation with sufficient evidence, including documentation; and

- present a written assessment of the effectiveness of the company's internal control over financial reporting as of the end of the company's most recent fiscal year.

Q 30.38.8 What should management use to assess their internal controls?

One way to understand the scope of management's assessment of the effectiveness of an issuer's financial controls is to examine what the PCAOB and SEC have prescribed for an outside auditor to do in evaluating management's assessment. Management should anticipate these audit steps, undertake many of them itself in addition to studying what self-assessment and ongoing monitoring of controls is done by its employees already.

Auditing Standards

Q 30.39   What are the auditing standards?

Auditors performing a SOX evaluation must first examine management's handling of each of the following elements:

- Determining which controls should be tested, including controls related to all significant accounts at all significant business units, locations, and activities, and disclosures in the financial statements, including:

  - controls over initiating, authorizing, recording, processing, and reporting significant accounts and disclosures in the financial statements,

  - controls over the selection and application of accounting policies consistent with GAAP,

  - antifraud programs and controls,

  - controls, such as computerized software, on which other controls are dependent,

  - controls over significant non-routine and non-systematic transactions, involving judgments and estimates,

  - company level controls including the control environment, and

  - controls over the financial reporting process, including controls over procedures used to close the books; to enter transaction totals into the general ledger; to initiate, authorize, record, and process journal entries in the general ledger; and to record adjustments to the financial statements (for example, consolidating adjustments, report combinations, and reclassifications);

- Evaluating the likelihood that failure of the control could result in a misstatement, the magnitude of such a misstatement, and the degree to which other controls ("compensating controls"), if effective, achieve the same control objectives;

- Evaluating the design effectiveness of controls;

- Evaluating the operating effectiveness of controls based on testing, internal audit, inspection of evidence of the application of controls, self-assessment, and ongoing monitoring, some of which might occur as part of management's ongoing monitoring activities;

- Identifying and determining deficiencies that are of such a magnitude and likelihood of occurrence that they constitute significant deficiencies or material weaknesses in internal control over financial reporting; and

- Documenting the foregoing process.[106]

Q 30.39.1   What should testing encompass?

The procedures for testing controls should include inquiry, observation, inspection of relevant documentation, and re-performance of the application of the control. Testing should include "walkthroughs" of a process described by an individual internal control. Most importantly, the person doing the testing should ask:

- What do employees do to determine if there is an error in the process?

- What is done when they find an error?

- What kind of errors have they found so far?

- What happened as a result of finding the errors?

- How were the errors resolved?

Q 30.39.2   What other inquiries should be made?

Management should also review all internal audit reports for the year related to internal controls as well as all complaints of violations of the code of ethics and other similar policy statements at the company. Management should also look back at what training employees were given with respect to the code of ethics. Finally, management should ascertain whether the audit committee acted independently during the year.

Problems

Q 30.40   What should management do if it finds problems with the internal controls?

Shortcomings in internal controls must be disclosed by management to the auditors and the more serious among them must be reflected in the public disclosure of an issuer. These shortcomings are graduated, and may be categorized as "control deficiencies," "significant deficiencies," and gravest of all, "material weaknesses" in internal controls.

Q 30.40.1   What is a "control deficiency"?

A control deficiency exists when the design or operation of a control does not allow management or employees, in the normal course of performing their assigned functions, to prevent or detect misstatements on a timely basis. A deficiency in *design* exists when (a) a control necessary to meet the control objective is missing or (b) the control operates as designed and the control objective is not always met. A control is deficient in *operation* when it does not operate as designed, or when the person assigned to perform it has not the qualifications or authority to do so effectively.

Q 30.40.2   What is a "significant deficiency"?

A significant deficiency is a control deficiency, or combination of control deficiencies, that adversely affects the company's ability to record, process, or report external financial data reliably in accordance with GAAP so there is more than a remote likelihood that a misstatement of the company's financial statements, that is more than inconsequential, will not be prevented or detected. A misstatement is *inconsequential* if a reasonable person would conclude, after considering the possibility of further undetected misstatements, that the misstatement, either individually or when aggregated with other misstatements, would clearly be immaterial to the financial statements.

> **TIP:** If a reasonable person could not reach such a conclusion regarding a particular misstatement, that misstatement is more than inconsequential.

Q 30.40.3   What is a "material weakness"?

A material weakness is a significant deficiency, or combination of significant deficiencies, that results in more than a remote likelihood that a material misstatement of the annual or interim financial statements will not be prevented or detected. In determining whether a control deficiency or combination of deficiencies is a significant deficiency or a material weakness, the auditor should evaluate the effect of compensating controls and whether such compensating controls are effective. The importance of categorizing a shortcoming as a material weakness is that the SEC requires that management and auditors disclose to the public each material weakness. Thus, an auditor may issue an unqualified opinion only when there are no identified material weaknesses and when there have been no restrictions on the scope of the auditor's work. The existence of a material weakness requires the auditor to express an adverse opinion on the effectiveness of internal control over financial reporting. Significant deficiencies should be disclosed to the Audit Committee and Board of Directors for remediation.

Categorizing Problems

Q 30.40.4   What factors should be considered in categorizing a shortcoming?

- The likelihood that a deficiency, or a combination of deficiencies, could result in a misstatement of an account balance or disclosure, and the magnitude of such a potential misstatement;

- The nature of the financial statement accounts; for example, suspense accounts and related-party transactions involve greater risk;

- The susceptibility of the related assets or liability to loss or fraud; that is, greater susceptibility increases risk;

- The subjectivity, complexity, or extent of judgment required to determine the amount involved (that is, greater subjectivity, complexity, or judgment, like that related to an accounting estimate, increases risk);

- The cause and frequency of known or detected exceptions for the operating effectiveness of a control;

- The interaction or relationship of the control with other controls (that is, the interdependence or redundancy of the control);

- The interaction of the deficiencies (for example, when evaluating a combination of two or more deficiencies, whether the deficiencies could affect the same financial statement accounts, amplifying or compensating for one another);

- The possible future consequences of the deficiency; and

- The dollar amounts or total number of transactions exposed to the deficiency.

Q 30.40.5   What kinds of deficiencies are least likely to be considered significant?

Deficiencies in the following areas are least likely to be considered significant:

(1) Controls over the selection and application of accounting policies that are in conformity with GAAP;

(2) Antifraud programs and controls;

(3) Controls over non-routine and non-systematic transactions; and

(4) Controls over the period-end financial reporting process, including controls over procedures used to enter transaction totals into the general ledger (that is, initiate, authorize, record, and process journal entries into the general ledger and record recurring and nonrecurring adjustments to the financial statements).

Q 30.40.6   What kinds of deficiencies are likely to be considered material?

(1) Restatements of previously issued financial statements to reflect the correction of an error or fraud;

(2) Identification by the auditor of a material misstatement in financial statements in the current period that was not initially found by management; and

(3) Whether the audit committee is evaluated as being ineffective.

Q 30.40.7   What should accompany the disclosure of material weaknesses?

Disclosure of material weaknesses by management should be accompanied by information about plans for remediation and also by contextual information. A disclosure will likely be more useful to investors if management differentiates the potential impact and importance to the financial statements of the various identified material weaknesses, distinguishing those material weaknesses that may have a pervasive impact on internal control over financial reporting from those material weaknesses that do not.

PCAOB Standards

Q 30.41   What are the PCAOB's auditing standards?

The PCAOB adopted, and the SEC approved, eighteen audit standards; effective December 31, 2016, those standards were reorganized into a single set numbered AS 1001 through AS 6115.[107]

Q 30.41.1   How important is documentation to an audit?

The PCAOB believes that the quality and integrity of an audit depends, in large part, on the existence of a complete and understandable record of the work the auditor performed, the conclusions the auditor reached, and the evidence the auditor obtained that supports those conclusions. Meaningful reviews, whether by the board in the context of its inspections or through other reviews, such as internal quality control reviews, would be difficult or impossible without adequate documentation.

Documentation

Q 30.42   What is the proper standard for documentation?

A proper standard is reviewability (keeping enough documentation to facilitate an external review). "Audit documentation related to planning, conducting, and reporting on the audit should contain sufficient information to enable an experienced auditor who has had no previous connection with the audit to ascertain from the audit documentation the evidence that supports the auditors' significant judgments and conclusions."[108] An experienced auditor is one who has a reasonable understanding of audit activities and has studied the company's industry as well as the accounting and auditing issues relevant to the industry.

Q 30.42.1   What are the relevant subjects for which management's records should be retained?

- Documenting testing of accounts, details, design of controls, operating effectiveness of controls, including walkthroughs;

- Documenting the inspection of terms and administration of significant contracts or agreements;

- Documenting related to significant complex or unusual transactions, accounting estimates, and uncertainties as well as related management assumptions;

- Sufficient information supporting conclusions of assessment;

- Significant information inconsistent with or contradicting conclusions of assessment;

- Selecting, applying, and consistency of accounting principles, including related disclosures;

- Scheduling of audit adjustments, including the nature and cause of each misstatement;

- Representations and communications between management and auditors;

- Communications with the audit committee; and

- Identifying significant deficiencies and, separately, material weaknesses and including bases for determining these items to be deficient.

Continuing SOX Compliance

Q 30.43   What should a company do to sustain SOX compliance?

Beginning the second year of compliance with SOX, three project-like tasks must be given priority:

(1) Correction of material weaknesses reported in existing controls (these are disclosure events, as are the plan and progress for their remediation, and significant deficiencies that could become material weaknesses also need remedial attention);

(2) Establishment of an orderly process to assure that basic controls are in place for all significant locations, activities, and processes and that they are integrated into company-level controls; and

(3) Required quarterly reporting of disclosures of material changes in controls.

Q 30.43.1   What specific expectations does the SEC have regarding companies' ongoing compliance efforts?

Apart from clearing the decks with the foregoing tasks, sustainable compliance is the main task. The SEC envisions compliance as an ongoing, unending *process*, exactly like each of the traditional management functions and processes at a company. Every year, there should be a plan and budget, objectives, and staffing goals for the management of internal controls, just as there are for the managers of manufacturing and the managers of sales.

More specifically:

- The formal permanent organization structure of the issuer includes positions and committees for the oversight of compliance and risk assessment;

- The responsibilities of accounting, finance, information technology, internal audit, legal and general management functions, and personnel for developing, testing, monitoring, and assessing internal controls are specified in great detail and are closely coordinated;

- Adequate increased budget resources are routinely devoted to the work of these internal functions and personnel with respect to disclosure controls (smaller specific tasks will be outsourced to specialists and consultants);

- All employees are trained in their respective personal responsibilities in the compliance process (providing timely and accurate information, reporting mistakes and unauthorized behavior, and suggesting ways to optimize the processing of information); and

- Periodic objectives for improving the quality of controls are set, and progress toward their attainment is monitored.

Q 30.43.2   What approach should a company take to achieve "optimization"?

Optimization includes pervasive integration of controls, quantitative monitoring, and feedback leading to continuous process improvement. The culture of the organization promotes continual improvement and change in all its processes, including controls. Management should apply a top-down approach, identifying from its knowledge, experience, and judgment the areas of financial statements for its business most susceptible to risk of material misstatement, and designing and testing controls at those levels. In performing future assessments, management may move back from a focus on individual controls to study the objective for batches of controls, testing their effectiveness in combination in meeting a broad control objective. It need not be the case that every individual step in a complex control is required to be tested in order to determine that the overall control is operating effectively.

Q 30.43.3   What is the advantage of a top-down approach?

A top-down approach prevents a management assessor or an auditor from spending unnecessary time and effort understanding a process or control that does not affect the likelihood that the company's financial statements could be materially misstated. Because of the pervasive effect of company-level controls, in this top-down approach, the auditor tests and evaluates the effectiveness of company-level controls first, because the results of this work will affect the auditor's testing strategy for controls at the process, transaction, and application levels.

Q 30.43.4   What can a company use to augment the top-down approach?

Risk assessment techniques should also be used, by management and auditors alike, in their respective work under SOX section 404. A direct relationship is meant to exist between the degree of risk that a material weakness could exist or arise in a particular area of the company and the amount of assessment attention by management and audit attention by the auditor that should be devoted to that area. Identifying and discussing the areas of greatest risk will improve the focus and efficiency of both management's assessment and the auditor's evaluation of internal controls.

Q 30.43.5   What kinds of risk analysis should be used?

Both quantitative and qualitative methods for risk analysis may be applied. For valuing material loss contingencies, quantitative risk analysis identifies various potential outcomes, using a decision tree, for example, and assigns to each a probability of occurrence and an estimate of potential loss. Multiplying each potential loss by its probability and summing the results for a given topic (for example, a lawsuit, or a potential dispute) will provide an overall loss expectancy. Events can be ranked by the magnitude of this overall risk expectancy. The obvious limitations of the process are the difficulties of assigning appropriate probabilities and omitting potential outcomes for evaluation.

Disclosure Controls

Q 30.44   What are disclosure controls?

Controls and procedures that are designed to ensure that information required to be disclosed in the reports filed under the Exchange Act is timely recorded, processed, summarized, and reported. Disclosure controls incorporate a broader concept of controls and procedures designed to ensure compliance with disclosure requirements generally. Disclosure controls address the quality and timeliness of disclosure.

Q 30.44.1   What are the certification requirements related to disclosure controls?

In quarterly and annual reports to the SEC on Forms 10-Q and 10-K, respectively, and on amendments to these reports, corporate CEOs and CFOs are each required by SOX section 302 to certify that he or she and the other certifying officers:

(1) are responsible for establishing and maintaining *disclosure controls* and procedures for the issuer and have:

  • designed such *disclosure controls* and procedures to ensure that material information relating to the issuer, including its consolidated subsidiaries, is made known to them by others within those entities, particularly during the period in which the periodic reports are being prepared;

  • evaluated the effectiveness of the issuer's *disclosure controls* and procedures as of a date within ninety days prior to the filing date of the report ("Evaluation Date"); and

  • presented in the report their conclusions about the effectiveness of the *disclosure controls* and procedures based on their evaluation as of the Evaluation Date;

(2) have disclosed, based on their most recent evaluation, to the issuer's auditors and the audit committee of the board of directors (or persons fulfilling the equivalent function):

- all significant deficiencies in the design or operation of internal controls that could adversely affect the issuer's ability to record, process, summarize, and report financial data, and have identified for the issuer's auditors any material weaknesses in internal controls; and

- any fraud, whether or not material, that involves management or other employees who have a significant role in the issuer's internal controls; and

(3) have indicated in the report whether or not there were significant changes in internal controls or in other factors that could significantly affect internal controls subsequent to the date of their most recent evaluation, including any corrective actions with regard to significant deficiencies and material weaknesses.

Q 30.44.2   What exactly must the CEO and CFO certify about the disclosure controls?

An issuer must give reasonable assurance that the disclosure controls and procedures will meet their objectives.[109] If reasonable assurances cannot be given, then the issuer must clarify in Item 307 that the procedures are *designed* to give reasonable assurance.

Q 30.44.3   What is the purpose of disclosure controls?

Disclosure controls exist to require fair presentation in reports, which may require going beyond presenting financial information in conformity with GAAP. The essential elements include whether the accounting principles selected are appropriate in the circumstances and whether the disclosure is informative and reasonably reflects the underlying transactions and events.

Q 30.44.4   Is the procedure for disclosure important?

The SEC has emphasized that the procedure for disclosure is as important as the content of disclosure. In designing their disclosure controls, companies are expected to make judgments regarding the processes on which they will rely to meet applicable requirements. Some companies might design their disclosure controls and procedures so that certain components of internal control over financial reporting pertaining to the accurate recording of transactions and disposition of assets or to the safeguarding of assets are not included. Many companies will design their disclosure controls and procedures so that they do not include all components of internal control over financial reporting.

Q 30.44.5   What should the disclosure contain?

In content and subject matter, disclosure controls should identify and assure discussion of:

(1) known trends or known demands, commitments, events, or uncertainties that will result in or that are reasonably likely to have a material effect on financial condition, operating performance, or result in the registrant's liquidity increasing or decreasing in any material way;

(2) key performance indicators, including non-financial performance indicators, that their management uses to manage the business and that would be material to investors;

(3) a view of the company through the eyes of management, providing both a short- and long-term analysis of the business; and

(4) an assessment and evaluation of operational and regulatory risks may be necessary, along with disclosure of circumstances indicating a material violation of law.

Q 30.44.6   How should a company handle disclosure?

The very breadth of disclosure controls makes it prudent for compliance to be done through a company's disclosure committee, including the general counsel and other executive and financial officers designated as responsible for designing, maintaining, and evaluating disclosure controls. Such a committee should regularly meet with the CEO, CFO, and audit committee. The committee can prioritize its work and delegate responsibility for particular areas of controls.

Q 30.44.7   What should the disclosure controls consist of?

- Self-assessments at company and subordinate levels to identify and describe economic, financial, and operating trends and indicators used by management and to be considered for disclosure by the disclosure committee;

- Assessments by managers with the general counsel and risk assessment personnel of legal and regulatory risks, describing pending, threatened and potential claims, disputes, and proceedings, as well as those circumstances that present potential exposure for the company;

- Assessments and evaluation of contingencies and threats to company assets and operations from natural forces, man-made events (for example, power interruptions and competitors' behaviors);

- Procedures for communicating relevant information in timely fashion to the disclosure committee for review and transmittal to the CEO and CFO and, as appropriate, the audit committee; and

- Drafting and review procedures to assure that discussion in proposed disclosure documents of the foregoing is accurate, adequate, and clearly articulated.

Q 30.44.8   How should a company sustain and enhance disclosure controls and enterprise risk management?

The same priority tasks as internal controls are needed beginning the second year of compliance with SOX:

(1) remediation of material weaknesses;

(2) checking the adequacy of disclosure controls for all significant locations, activities, and processes to address any situations neglected in the tumult of initial compliance; and

(3) disclosing material changes in controls and new controls.

The SEC

Q 30.45   How has SOX enhanced the powers of the SEC?

Congress has given the SEC the power to "promulgate such rules and regulations, as may be necessary or appropriate in the public interest or for the protection of investors, and in furtherance of this Act."[110] In addition, and no less sweeping, SEC was given power over the PCAOB. The SEC may review the discipline given by the PCAOB to auditors and accountants registered before it, and may deny them the privilege of practice before the SEC.[111] It may do the same with lawyers.[112] Congress also authorized that any violation of SOX or of the rules of the SEC thereunder and of the PCAOB may be treated as a violation of the Securities Exchange Act of 1934.[113]

Q 30.45.1   How much has the SEC grown under SOX?

Not surprisingly, the enactment of SOX in 2002 resulted in massive increases in budget and personnel at the SEC:

Fiscal Year	Budget (in millions)
2002	$514.0
2003	$745.5
2017	$1,781.0
2022	$1,993.0

The staff of the SEC has also increased significantly since 2002:

Fiscal Year	Full-Time Equivalent Employees
2003	3,200
2017	4,870
2022	4,658

Of these positions, for 2022 the SEC has requested a total of 1,330 positions in enforcement, 1,088 positions in examinations, 409 in corporate finance, 275 in trading and markets, 218 in investment management, 158 in economic and risk analysis, 148 in the Office of General Counsel, 53 in the Office of Inspector General and 979 other support staff.

The scale of the SEC's responsibilities has grown even more. The SEC oversees nearly 14,000 investment advisers, 14,000 mutual funds and exchange traded funds, over 3,500 broker dealers, 300 transfer agents, twernty-four national securities exchanges, nine credit rating agencies, seven clearing agencies, the PCAOB, the Financial Industry Regulatory Authority (FINRA), Municipal Securities Rulemaking Board (MSRB), the Securities Investor Protection Corporation (SIPC), and the Financial Accounting Standards Board (FASB). In addition, the SEC selectively reviews the disclosures and financial statements of over 7,400 reporting companies. Trading volume in equity markets is now over $100 trillion; assets under management of registered advisers are more than $97 trillion; and assets in mutual funds now exceed $27 trillion.[114]

Q 30.45.2   How has the increased budget affected enforcement?

These resources have permitted an enlarged level of reviews of disclosure reports filed by public companies and of enforcement investigations. In FY 2005, 4,500 reviews of reporting companies' filings were conducted, roughly 38% of all reporting companies. The SEC reported in 2006 that it was on track to review the filings of all public companies at least once every three years, as required by SOX section 408; in FY 2008, the SEC reviewed 39% of companies making disclosures; in FY 2013, this rose to 52%; and in FY 2018, this again rose to 57%.[115]

In 2013, the SEC's Enforcement Division created the Financial Reporting and Audit Task Force, dedicated to detecting fraudulent or improper financial reporting and concentrating on high-risk areas of the market.[116]

The average number of months between the SEC's opening an investigation and commencing an enforcement action was twenty-two in FY 2011,twenty-one in FY 2013, and twenty-four in FY 2015.[117]

Q 30.45.3   Has the SEC expanded into any new areas?

In July 2004, the SEC established its Office of Risk Assessment, reporting to the chairman. That office and the Office of Compliance Inspections and Examinations have been identifying new or resurgent forms of fraud or questionable activities. More recently, an upgrade of information technology systems at the SEC has resulted in more than 90% of required forms from regulated persons now being filed electronically. Risk assessment techniques have been integrated into the examination of electronically filed disclosure documents, enhancing the SEC's enforcement and disclosure review programs. As a result of the enactment in late 2010 of Dodd-Frank, the SEC has been instructed by Congress to regulate certain derivatives, hedge funds and other transactions and to increase its investor protection responsibilities.

Private Rights of Action

Q 30.46   Are there any express private rights of action under SOX?

In contrast to its aggressive empowerment of the SEC, Congress largely avoided creating new private causes of action under SOX. Indeed, Congress specifically forswore doing so in SOX section 804. Only two private rights of action were elsewhere established in SOX:

- SOX section 306 authorizes public companies, and their shareholders, to recover the proceeds from insider trading by officers and directors during pension blackout periods. Subject to a two-year statute of limitations, if an issuer fails to file suit against a violator within sixty days of being asked to do so, shareholders may bring a derivative action for recovery. This section responded to insider trading at Enron but has provoked few lawsuits, as most pension plans include blackout periods applicable to management, directors, and also to all participant employees.

- SOX section 806 protects whistleblowers, providing employees the opportunity for suits to recover compensatory damages, including back pay, and attorney fees for retaliatory termination, demotion, or ill treatment against employees who report fraudulent conduct (mail fraud, wire fraud, bank fraud, or securities fraud) or give testimony to state or federal law enforcement agencies. This provision is not limited to securities laws, or to public companies. Employees must first present a claim to the Secretary of Labor and may not commence litigation until a statutory period has elapsed or the Secretary has undertaken enforcement of the claim. Congress reinforced the private right of action with criminal penalties against those who interfere with whistleblowers.[118]

Q 30.46.1   Did SOX enhance any existing private rights of action?

In SOX section 804, Congress enlarged the statute of limitations applicable to securities litigation claims for "fraud, deceit, manipulation or contrivance" from one year after discovery of facts amounting to fraud to two years, and from three years after the alleged violation took place to five years. It should be noted, however, this amendment does not extend the limitations period for other litigation under the Securities Act of 1933, the Investment Company Act of 1940, or the Investment Advisers Act of 1940. As a further limit, this amendment applied to actions commenced on or after SOX was enacted and did not revive expired claims.

Q 30.46.2   Does SOX have any effect on private 10b-5 litigation?

SOX affected 10b-5 liabilities in a few ways. Certification by CEOs and CFOs of financial reports under SOX improves the ability of plaintiffs to allege specific facts that give rise to a strong inference that defendants making false statements acted with scienter. Moreover, the detailed disclosure mandated by SOX, including discussions of material weaknesses and significant deficiencies in internal controls, will provide more information to plaintiffs to identify misleading statements in financial reports and to demonstrate their materiality.

Further, it is likely that the particular standards prescribed for officers and directors in SOX will be imported into additional requirements of fiduciary duties for defendants in shareholder suits, whether in state courts or as ancillary claims to federal securities cases. Faulty or outright false certifications of financial reports by a CEO may

have greater traction in proving a breach of fiduciary duty than sur-
mounting the pleading barriers of Rule 10b-5 litigation created by the
Private Securities Litigation Reform Act of 1995.[119]

Q 30.46.3 Does SOX create a private right under which investors can file claims against the issuer's attorneys?

The SEC's Rules of Professional Conduct for lawyers apply to attorneys who assist in the preparation of documents filed with the SEC
and made public, and prescribe obligations for the attorney. Though
this should occur only in the most extreme circumstances, the knowledge possessed by an attorney, and the depth of his or her involvement in drafting and verifying registration statements, annual reports,
and similar documents, all the time failing to correct misrepresentations, may implicate that attorney as the speaker making false representations to the public, or causing them to be made through the
issuer. This drafting, reviewing, and commenting on a public company's statements was found sufficient to permit the law firm of Vinson
& Elkins to be alleged to be a primary violator of the securities laws
in the Enron litigation.[120] Quite apart from the risk that lawyers will be
alleged to be primary actors and direct participants in private securities fraud cases, there is an additional risk of exposure for secondary
actors: Racketeer Influenced and Corrupt Organizations (RICO) Act
claims.

SOX Provisions That Apply to Companies Other Than Issuers

Q 30.47 What are the SOX penalty provisions that apply to also-private companies?

SOX provides new penalties for the destruction, alteration, or fal-
sification of records in federal investigations and bankruptcies. Penalties include up to twenty years' imprisonment, fines, or both.[121] SOX
further provides that any person who *attempts* to commit securities
law crimes can be punished as if they had committed the crime.[122]
SOX also increases the maximum penalty for mail and wire fraud from
five to twenty years' imprisonment.[123] In addition, SOX requires that

anyone who obstructs or tampers with an official proceeding be fined, imprisoned up to twenty years, or both.[124] Finally, SOX provides for a fine, imprisonment up to ten years, or both for retaliating against any corporate whistleblower.[125]

Q 30.48   What are the SOX record retention requirements that apply to all companies and persons?

SOX requires accountants conducting audits of any issuer to retain all audit or review paperwork for a period of five years. Penalties for violations include imprisonment up to ten years, fines, or both.[126]

Q 30.49   What are SOX's requirements for ERISA and notice of pension-fund blackout periods?

SOX increases penalties for ERISA violations. The maximum penalty for individual violations is increased from a $5,000 to a $100,000 fine and from one year to ten years' imprisonment. The maximum penalty for businesses is increased from a $100,000 to a $500,000 fine.[127] SOX requires employers to give employees thirty days' advance written or electronic notice of any pension-fund blackout period.[128]

Almost-Public Companies

Q 30.50   Does SOX apply to almost-public companies?

In addition to public companies for whom SOX is mandatory, many private companies are almost-public and should carefully consider acting as if SOX is mandatory for themselves, such as:

- private companies preparing for an initial public offering of securities;
- private companies preparing to sell divisions or affiliates to public companies;
- private companies with registered debt or equity securities;
- foreign operations of U.S. public companies; and

- U.S. operations of foreign public companies whose securities are traded in the United States.

Q 30.50.1   How does SOX affect almost-public companies?

In order to complete a successful initial public offering, a private company will need to document and demonstrate its corporate governance consistent with SOX and its preparedness for SOX certifications and assessments of its internal controls and disclosures. Likewise, to make a division or part of its operations marketable at the highest price, a private company must consider preparing it for sale to a public company and facilitating the transition for that division to a SOX-compliant environment.

Non-Public Banks and Insurance Companies

Q 30.51   Does SOX cover non-public banks?

SOX applies, of course, to banks that are issuers of securities. Larger banks with assets of $500 million or more, regardless of whether they qualify as issuers, are subject to section 36 of the Federal Deposit Insurance Act and the FDIC's implementing regulations and guidelines. The FDIC's implementing guidelines reference and incorporate SOX provisions relating to auditor independence. Smaller, non-public banks are not subject to most SOX provisions, but the FRB and its fellow financial supervising agencies have long endorsed sound corporate governance practices and existing banking laws and guidelines already require or encourage all banking organizations to adhere to corporate governance and auditing practices that are similar in many respects to those reflected in SOX.

Q 30.52   Does SOX affect non-public insurance companies?

SOX enforcement has spilled over into insurance regulations applicable beyond public companies. For example, in the wake of American International Group's disclosure in April 2005 of finite reinsurance transfers admitted to be improperly accounted for, the New York Insurance Department has adopted and implemented a new rule requiring CEOs in such transactions to certify that legitimate risk transfer occurred, a SOX-like certification.[129] The National Association of Insurance Commissioners (NAIC) promptly thereafter agreed on new model disclosure standards for finite reinsurance transactions for individual states to adopt.

SOX and International Companies

Q 30.53   What problems has SOX caused for international companies?

International public companies have faced very difficult compliance challenges with SOX:

- The adoption of SOX by Congress was done speedily and with little consultation with the European Union (EU) or its member states, notwithstanding that SOX provisions and implementing rules were broad and clearly would apply to EU companies and EU operations of U.S. companies;

- Corporate governance in the EU's member states is different structurally and culturally from that found in the United States. For example, directors may be collectively responsible for company management, but are not individually responsible; related-party transactions and off-balance-sheet transactions with special-purpose entities need not be publicly disclosed; further, company law varies among the member states;

- Accounting principles differ in numerous details between the EU and the United States; and

- Audit firms are not required to have the same independence or responsibilities in the EU as in the United States, and EU firms have not been subject to extra-territorial inspection or investigation.

Q 30.53.1   Has the EU responded to SOX with a law of its own?

The EU has recently passed the Eighth Company Law Directive, which prescribes audit committees, with independent members, to hire the auditors, oversee them, and communicate directly with auditors without going through management. Auditors would be given help in resisting inappropriate pressure from management during an audit. Auditors would follow new international auditing standards to be endorsed by the EU Commission; audit firms and staff would undergo compulsory continuing education in the new standards. Auditors and audit firms would undergo quality assurance reviews; audit firms for listed companies would issue annual reports including a description of the audit firm's operations, a governance statement, and a description of the internal quality control system and a confirmation of its effectiveness by the management of the audit firm.

Q 30.53.2 How has the EU coped with SOX?

The EU negotiated with the SEC for exemptions from SOX provisions covering overseas auditors. Particular points of contention have been the imposition on EU auditors of another layer of regulation—by the PCAOB—which was inconsistent with the laws in some EU member states and which could hinder the fulfillment of EU requirements based on emerging international standards. The EU has largely been unsuccessful in obtaining exemptions from SOX, though several provisions have been delayed in their implementation for foreign auditors and public companies.[130] PCAOB authorized itself to assist EU home country regulators in conducting inspections and investigations of auditors registered with PCAOB but located in the EU.

Q 30.53.3 Is there any hope for a convergence of EU and SEC standards?

On April 25, 2006, the EU Council of Ministers adopted the Statutory Audit Directive,[131] which somewhat parallels SOX and strengthens the EU framework of standards and public oversight for the audit profession. It replaces the Eighth Company Law Directive of 1984 (Directive 84/253/EC) and also amends the Fourth and Seventh Company Law Directives (Directives 78/660/EEC and 83/349/EEC) by introducing additional EU rules on the audit of company accounts. By 2010, the Statutory Audit Directive was implemented by national legislation and financial resources in all EU member countries.[132]

Among other things, the Statutory Audit Directive introduces a requirement that European companies with transferable securities admitted to trading on a regulated market in any EU member state have an audit committee that meets certain requirements and performs certain functions set out in the directive. As to accounting standards, the FASB and the International Accounting Standards Board have aggressively pursued convergence for several years in drafting International Financial Reporting Standards (IFRS), with support from the SEC.[133]

In December 2013, the European Parliament and EU member states agreed upon further audit reform rules, including more detailed audit reports, closer supervision of auditors by audit committees, mandatory rotation of audit firms after ten years, and tools limiting potential conflicts of interest, including caps and limits on non-audit services.[134]

Non-Profit Organizations

Q 30.54   How are non-profit governmental organizations treated under SOX?

Private non-profit organizations are not subject to most SOX requirements. The principal regulation for such organizations has come from the IRS's regulation and monitoring to assure each such organization operates as a legitimate charity, and from state laws and regulations, generally enforced by states' attorneys general, and, to an extent, through private litigation. Federal legislation, however, is likely to be forthcoming to regulate further the governance and financial reporting by non-profit organizations. New SOX-like regulations will likely cover:

(1) financial statements;
(2) Form 990 series tax returns;
(3) executive compensation;
(4) loans;
(5) related-party transactions;
(6) conflicts of interest;
(7) independent directors;
(8) bars to serving on boards of directors; and
(9) protection of whistleblowers.

Q 30.55   Does SOX apply to colleges and universities?

A particularly complex environment for compliance is presented by the subset of non-profits that are colleges and universities. Higher-education institutions are subject only to those sections of SOX applicable to all persons, and not to those portions regulating public companies. However, SOX concepts have permeated a dizzying array of compliance programs that do apply to colleges and universities. Thus, most colleges and universities receive some funding from state or federal agencies for research and programs, for which they are subject to audits and extensive requirements for internal controls.

Retrospective and Future Outlook

Q 30.56   How has SOX impacted the markets since its enactment?

It is widely recognized that SOX has improved the quality of financial reporting. A 2013 Government Accountability Office survey of 746 public companies, to which 25% responded, focused specifically on SOX section 404 requirements of auditor attestation. Eighty percent of respondents viewed section 404 as benefiting the quality of the company's controls; 53% viewed the requirement as benefiting their company's financial reporting; 46% viewed their ability to prevent and detect fraud as improved; and 52% reported greater confidence in the financial reports of other section 404–compliant companies.[135]

Other countries have adopted SOX-similar statutes or regulations, including Japan and the European Union.[136]

Compliance costs are manageable. A 2013 study of 300 executives and professionals found that 65% of the organizations surveyed plan to spend $500,000 or less on SOX compliance and 75%, including many large companies, will spend less than $1 million.[137]

Research has shown that investors react negatively to company disclosures of weaknesses in internal controls, as shown by increases in both the cost of debt and of equity.[138]

However, a number of U.S. public companies disclose persistent weaknesses in internal controls, even three years after initially disclosing them.[139] Other companies fail to report timely weaknesses in internal controls until compelled by an earnings restatement to do so.[140]

Q 30.57   What lies ahead for SOX enforcement?

In the near future, the performance of audit committees and of outside auditors, and the effectiveness of internal corporate controls continue to be of paramount concerns for SOX enforcement; monitoring revenue recognition practices will continue to be a staple of the SEC's financial fraud caseload.[141]

The SEC's increased focus on internal controls was apparent in its settlement of *In the Matter of JPMorgan Chase & Co.*[142] in September 2013 in which the financial institution acknowledged its ineffective controls resulted in violations of federal securities laws and agreed to pay a $200 million civil penalty. Although the SEC alleged public filings misstated financial results, the thrust of the proceeding emphasized ineffectual internal controls, and failures of numerous bank managers to bring concerns about risks in investment activities to the attention of senior management and the Audit Committee. The SEC has stated internal controls are a particular focus to its current enforcement efforts.[143]

Cybersecurity has become a prominent new emphasis at the SEC, beginning with the issuance of disclosure guidance on October 13, 2011,[144] and continuing with a public roundtable and webinar on March 26, 2014, likely a prelude to further SEC guidance and enforcement activities.[145]

The 2011 disclosure guidance addressed accounting for costs of prevention of cyber attacks and incidents, mitigation of damages from cyber incidents (whether the result of hacking attacks, natural disasters, or otherwise), and treatment of losses and of diminished future cash flows and other risks to the business appropriately disclosed in SEC filings. The SEC has indicated that an issuer's disclosure controls should encompass cybersecurity: "To the extent cyber incidents pose a risk to a registrant's ability to record, process, summarize, and report information that is required to be disclosed in Commission filings, management should also consider whether there are any deficiencies in its disclosure controls and procedures that would render them ineffective."[146]

Just as the COSO framework for internal controls for financial reporting were subsequently approved by the SEC as one mechanism for implementation of SOX requirements, the "Framework for Improving Critical Infrastructure Cybersecurity," issued February 12, 2014, by the National Institute of Standards and Technology, and its companion "Roadmap"[147] may become a valuable resource for issuers developing appropriate internal and disclosure controls with respect to their computer systems and assets.

Finally, on August 13, 2013, in its massive Release No. 2013-005,[148] the PCAOB proposed two major rules for public comment: (1) Adding specific informational content to an auditor's report and unqualified opinion on financial statements; and (2) Enlarging the responsibilities of auditors to comment on "other information" in documents containing audited financial statements and the related auditor's report.

The form of auditor's reports has not changed substantially since the 1940s, but the scope of work performed and of information examined by auditors in their work on a company's financial statements has exploded. The proposed auditor reporting standard would require the auditor to communicate in the auditor's report "critical audit matters" that would be specific to each audit.

> The auditor's required communication would focus on those matters the auditor addressed during the audit of the financial statements that involved the most difficult, subjective, or complex auditor judgments or posed the most difficulty to the auditor in obtaining sufficient appropriate audit evidence or forming an opinion on the financial statements.[149]

The required procedures under the proposed other information standard would

> focus the auditor's attention on the identification of material inconsistencies between the other information and the company's audited financial statements and on the identification of material misstatements of fact, based on relevant evidence obtained and conclusions reached during the audit. When evaluating the

other information, the auditor would be in a position to identify potential inconsistencies between the other information and the company's financial statements that could be difficult for investors and other financial statement users to identify when analyzing the company's financial performance. Such inconsistencies could occur for a number of reasons, including unintentional error, managerial biases, or intentional misreporting. As a result of the auditor's evaluation of other information and communication of any potential material inconsistencies or material misstatements of fact to the company's management, the proposed other information standard could promote consistency between the other information and the audited financial statements, which in turn could increase the amount and quality of information available to investors and other financial statement users.[150]

If adopted in toto as proposed, these rules would lead to sea changes in the working relationships between auditors and management of public companies and would make auditing more expensive and contentious a process. However, it should be noted that the International Auditing and Assurance Standards Board (IAASB), the United Kingdom's Financial Reporting Council (FRC), and the European Commission (EC) have been working on similar projects to change the auditor's report.[151] In the global economy, changes adopted by these bodies to audit reports will increase pressure for accommodating changes in the United States.

Notes to Chapter 30

1. Sarbanes-Oxley Act of 2002 (SOX), Pub. L. No. 107-204, 116 Stat. 745.
2. 15 U.S.C. § 78m(b)(2).
3. *See* M. Koehler, *The Story of the Foreign Corrupt Practices Act*, 73 OHIO STATE L.J. 930, 934, 954 (2012).
4. Dodd-Frank Wall Street Reform and Consumer Protection Act of 2010 (Dodd-Frank), Pub. L. No. 111-203, 124 Stat. 1376.
5. Jumpstart Our Business Startups Act of 2012 (JOBS Act), Pub. L. No. 112-106, 126 Stat. 306.
6. 15 U.S.C. § 78c(a)(8). Dodd-Frank section 989G permanently exempts public corporations with a market capitalization below $75 million from the internal controls provisions of SOX § 404(b). In April 2011, an SEC staff study required by the same section of Dodd-Frank recommended that public corporations with a market capitalization between $75 and $250 million continue to be subject to SOX § 404(b). In 2012, the JOBS Act was signed into law; among other provisions, it exempted "emerging growth companies" from complying with SOX § 404(b) for the first five years after becoming a public company, so long as it remains below a revenue threshold of $1 billion.
7. *See infra* QQ 30.47–30.48.
8. SOX §§ 802, 1102.
9. *Id.* §§ 806, 1107.
10. *Id.* §§ 807, 902.
11. *Id.* § 803.
12. SOX § 404 requires management of issuer companies to include an assessment of their internal financial controls in their financial reporting and requires outside auditors to attest to, and report on, management's assessment.
13. 17 C.F.R. § 229.406(b). An issuer may adopt separate codes of ethics for different officers. *Id.* §§ 229.406(d), 228.406(d).
14. *See Code of Business Conduct and Ethics*, AMAZON, http://phx.corporate-ir. net/phoenix.zhtml?c=97664&p=irol-govconduct; *Code of Conduct*, ALPHABET INVESTOR RELATIONS, https://abc.xyz/investor/other/code-of-conduct.html; *Google Code of Conduct*, ALPHABET INVESTOR RELATIONS, https://abc.xyz/investor/other/google-code-of-conduct.html; *Corporate Ethics*, HEWLETT PACKARD, www8.hp.com/us/en/hp-information/global-citizenship/governance/ethics.html (HP's codes for employees, U.S. public employees, contingent workers, suppliers, and business partners); VERIZON, OUR CODE OF CONDUCT (2017), www.verizon.com/about/sites/default/files/Verizon-Code-of-Conduct.pdf; *Investor Relations*, CITIGROUP, www.citigroup. com/citi/investor/corporate_governance.html; *see also Corporate Governance*, SANOFI, http://en.sanofi.com/investors/corporate_governance/corporate_governance. aspx (Sanofi's 2017 Corporate Code of Ethics, Financial Code of Ethics and Corporate Responsibility).

15. *Id.* §§ 229.601(b)(14), 228.601(b)(14), 229.406(c)(2), 228.406(c)(2), 229.406(c)(3), 228.406(c)(3).

16. *Id.* §§ 228.406(a), 229.406(a).

17. SOX § 301.

18. *See* Standards Relating to Listed Company Audit Committees, SEC Release Nos. 33-8820, 34-47654, and IC-26001 (Apr. 9, 2003), 68 Fed. Reg. 18,788 (Apr. 16, 2003).

19. *See In re* Deloitte & Touche LLP, ALPS Fund Servs., Inc. & Andrew C. Boynton, SEC Accounting and Auditing Enforcement Release No. 3668 (July 1, 2015) (audit firm consultant and audit firm penalized for his committee memberships on boards of directors of three audit clients, compromising independence of committee and of audit firm); *In re* MusclePharm Corp., SEC Administrative Proceedings File No. 3-16788 (Sept. 8, 2015); *In re* Donald W. Prosser, CPA, SEC Accounting and Auditing Enforcement Release No. 3687 (Sept. 8, 2015) (audit committee chairman wrongly substituted incorrect personal interpretation of SEC rules for treatment of executive perquisites for views of experts hired by company). In *In re* Shirley Kiang, Exchange Act Release No. 71,824 (Mar. 27, 2014), the SEC issued as cease-and-desist order against the audit committee chair, who was a director of a Seattle-headquartered coal company with all its operations in China. Shirley Kiang, a U.S. citizen living in Thailand, certified falsely that any fraud involving management had been disclosed to the company's auditors and the audit committee. Kiang knew that an individual named in public filings with SEC as CFO had not performed any work as the CFO, but she did not disclose that in her own Sarbanes-Oxley certification of Form 10-K or disclose that external auditors were not informed of this. On March 11, 2014, the SEC charged the audit committee chairman and several senior executives of AgFeed Industries, Inc. with falsifying sales invoices and sales revenues and with concealing separate accurate accounting records from auditors to avoid disclosure of accounting fraud during a campaign to raise capital. *See* Press Release No. 2014-47, U.S. Sec. & Exch. Comm'n, SEC Charges Animal Feed Company and Top Executives in China and U.S. with Accounting Fraud (Mar. 11, 2014), www.sec.gov/News/PressRelease/Detail/PressRelease/1370541102314. Prior actions were taken against the audit committee chairman of Cycle Country, Exchange Act Release No. 64,513 (May 18, 2011); Director of Goldman Sachs Group, Inc. and Proctor & Gamble Co., Exchange Act Release No. 63,995, Securities Act Release No. 9192, Investment Advisers Act Release No. 3167, Investment Company Act Release No. 29,590 (Mar. 1, 2011); Three Audit Committee Members of DHB Indus., Litigation Release No. 21,867 (Feb. 28, 2011); Audit Committee Chairman of InfoGroup, Inc., Litigation Release No. 21,451 (Mar. 15, 2010).

20. SOX § 204; *see* PCAOB Auditing Standard No. 16, Communications with Audit Committees, PCAOB Release No. 2012-004 (Dec. 15, 2012).

21. *Id.*

22. 17 C.F.R. § 229.401(h).

23. *See* Information for Audit Committees About the PCAOB Inspection Process, PCAOB Release No. 2012-003 (Aug. 1, 2012), and PCAOB Auditing Standard No. 16, Communications with Audit Committees, PCAOB Release No. 2012-004 (Dec. 15, 2012).

24. SOX § 306.

25. *Id.* § 402.

26. *Id.* § 403.

27. *Id.* § 303.

28. *Id.* § 304; *see* Press Release No. 2016-25, U.S. Sec. & Exch. Comm'n, Monsanto Paying $80 Million Penalty for Accounting Violations (Feb. 9, 2016) (CEO and former CFO were found not to have engaged in personal misconduct but reimbursed company for $3.1 million and $0.7 million in cash bonuses and stock awards they received during period the company committed violations, averting necessity for formal clawback proceeding); Press Release No. 2016-97, U.S. Sec. & Exch. Comm'n, Mortgage Company and Executives Settle Fraud Charges (May 31, 2016) (company, president and five other senior officers paid civil penalties; president disgorged cash compensation of $411,000 and paid penalty of $200,000 in lieu of formal clawback after mis-accounting on mortgage-backed securities); *see also* Press Release No. 2015-28, U.S. Sec. & Exch. Comm'n, SEC Announces Half-Million Dollar Clawback from CFOs of Silicon Valley Company That Committed Accounting Fraud (Saba Software) (Feb. 10, 2015); Litigation Release No. 21149A, SEC v. Maynard L. Jenkins (July 23, 2009) (first clawback lawsuit seeking $4 million in bonuses and stock sale profits from company's overstating income in accounting fraud) (litigation settled for $2.8 million disgorgement, *Ex-CSK Auto CEO Giving Back $2.8 M in SEC Accord*, SAN DIEGO UNION TRIB., Nov. 15, 2011); Litigation Release No. 20,387, SEC v. William W. McGuire MD (Dec. 6, 2007) (former CEO of United Healthcare Group settled clawback action and reimbursed company for $448 million in cash bonuses and profits from stock options, disgorged further $11 million and paid a civil penalty of $7 million for backdating stock options); *In re* Babak ("Bobby") Yazdani, Exchange Act Release No. 73,201 (Sept. 24, 2014) (ex-CEO of Saba Software ordered to reimburse company $2.57 million in bonuses, incentive compensation and stock profits).

29. 15 U.S.C. § 78u(d); *see* Press Release No. 2010-197, U.S. Sec. & Exch. Comm'n, Former Countrywide CEO Angelo Mozilo to Pay SEC's Largest Ever Financial Penalty Against a Public Company's Senior Executive (Oct. 15, 2010) (in addition to $45 million in disgorgement and $22.5 million in civil penalties, ex-CEO was permanently barred from being an officer or director of a public company); Litigation Release No. 22,903, SEC v. Innovida Holdings, LLC et al., 2014 WL 117595 (Jan. 13, 2014) (former CEO permanently barred from being officer or director of a public company); SEC v. Subaye, Inc., 2014 WL 4652578 (S.D.N.Y. Sept. 18, 2014) (approving lifetime ban of former CFO). Shorter bar periods, such as five years, have been imposed in less egregious cases; *see, e.g.*, SEC Litigation Release No. 22,940, SEC v. Alternative Green Techs., Inc. (Mar. 12, 2014) (former CEO barred for five years); *In re* Edward L. Cummings, CPA, Exchange Act Release No. 72,722 (July 30, 2014) (former CFO barred for five years).

30. SOX §§ 303, 1105; *see also* SEC v. Levine, Fed. Sec. L. Rep. (CCH) ¶ 94,320 (D.D.C. May 8, 2007).

31. SOX §§ 802, 1102; 18 U.S.C. §§ 1519, 1520. On February 15, 2015, in Yates v. United States, 135 S. Ct. 1074 (2015), a majority of the Supreme Court reversed the conviction of a fisherman for violation of section 1519 for dumping overboard undersized fish identified by a federal inspector, concluding that the statutory prohibition on destruction of "tangible objects" was limited to objects used to record or preserve information, based upon its adoption as part of the SOX anti-fraud provisions. Noting that this section permits a penalty of twenty years' imprisonment, four dissenting Justices argued that the statute was adopted by Congress to be broad, while criticizing the statute as giving prosecutors too much leverage, sentencing authorities too much discretion, and calling section 1519 an "emblem of a deeper pathology in the federal criminal code." *Id.* at 1101.

32. SOX §§ 804, 805, 807.

33. *See* SEC v. Parmalat Finanziaria, S.p.A., Litigation Release No. 18,803 (July 28, 2004); Moore Stephens Chartered Accountants (United Kingdom) & Peter D. Stewart, Litigation Release No. 18,695 (May 5, 2004); *see also* SEC v. Koninklijke Ahold N.V. (Royal Ahold), Litigation Release No. 18,929 (Oct. 13, 2004); SEC v. Nortel Networks Corp. & Nortel Networks Ltd. (Nortel Networks Pays $35 Million to Settle Financial Fraud Charges), Litigation Release No. 20,333 (Oct. 15, 2007); *In re* NEC Corp., Exchange Act Release No. 57,974 (June 17, 2008) (registration of securities revoked); SEC v. Urs Kamber, et al., Litigation Release No. 20,605 (May 30, 2008) (CFO of U.S. divisions of Centerpulse Ltd. settled overstatement of corporate income charges with disgorgement, civil penalty, pre-judgment interest, and a five-year bar from serving as a public company officer or director). In addition, SEC has pursued actions for FCPA violations (bribery and failure of internal controls) against foreign issuers, including: *In re* Orthofix Int'l N.V, Accounting and Auditing Enforcement Release Nos. 3845 (Jan. 18, 2017) and 3851 (Jan. 18, 2017) (disgorgement of $2.9 million for bribery, civil penalties of $11 million, pre-judgment interest of $263,000, and engagement of independent consultant to evaluate and monitor adequacy of internal controls); *In re* Sociedad Quimica Y Minera de Chile, S.A., SEC Administrative Proceeding File No. 3-17774 (Jan. 13, 2017) ($15 million civil penalty); *In re* Cadbury Ltd. & Mondolez Int'l, SEC Administrative Proceeding File No. 3-17759 (Jan. 6, 2017) ($13 million civil penalty); Press Release 2016-277, U.S. Sec. & Exch. Comm'n, Teva Pharm. Indus., Ltd. (Dec. 22, 2016) ($236 million in disgorgement and interest, $283 million penalties).

34. Protection of whistleblowers extends to employees of privately held contractors and subcontractors, including employees of investment advisers, law firms, accounting companies, who perform work for public companies. Lawson v. FMR LLC, 134 S. Ct. 1158 (2014). In the mutual fund industry that is the subject of *Lawson*, "virtually all mutual funds are structured so that they have no employees of their own; they are managed, instead, by independent investment advisers." *Id.* at 1171. SOX has been held not to be limited to instances where a public company—either acting on its own or acting through its contractors—makes material

misrepresentations about its financial picture in order to deceive its shareholders; it is not a general anti-retaliation statute applicable to any private company doing business with a public company. Gibney v. Evolution Mktg. Research, LLC, 25 F. Supp. 3d 741 (E.D. Pa. 2014).

35. SOX § 302 requires each audit committee to establish procedures for the confidential, anonymous submission by employees of "concerns regarding questionable accounting or auditing matters."

36. *Id.* §§ 806, 1107. For more detailed information, see Moy, Neilan, Blostein & Kelley, *Whistleblower Claims Under the Sarbanes-Oxley Act of 2002, in* UNDERSTANDING THE SECURITIES LAWS 2009, at 573 (PLI Corp. Law & Practice, Course Handbook Ser. No. 1756, 2009). Whistleblower disclosures are protected when made to law enforcement or public authorities, but not when made to the press. *See* Tides v. Boeing Co., 2011 WL 1651245, 94 Empl. Prac. Dec. (CCH) ¶ 44,168 (9th Cir. May 3, 2011). Where an employee removes confidential documents from a company for use in presenting a whistleblower complaint to the SEC or under the False Claims Act, his conduct may be protected. *See* SEC Rule 21F-17(a), 17 C.F.R. § 240.21(F)-17(a); Vannoy v. Celanese Corp., 2008-SOX-00064, ARB No. 09-118, 2011 WL 4690624 (Sept. 28, 2011); *see also* U.S. *ex rel.* Grandeau v. Cancer Treatment Ctrs. of Am., 350 F. Supp. 2d 765, 773 (N.D. Ill. 2004); U.S. *ex rel.* Head v. Kane Co., 668 F. Supp. 2d 146, 152 (D.D.C. 2009). *But cf.* U.S. *ex rel.* Cafasso v. Gen. Dynamics C4 Sys., Inc., 634 F.3d 1047 (9th Cir. 2011).

37. *See* U.S. SEC. & EXCH. COMM'N, 2016 ANNUAL REPORT TO CONGRESS ON THE DODD-FRANK WHISTLEBLOWER PROGRAM (Nov. 15, 2016), www.sec.gov/whistleblower/reportspubs/annual-reports/owb-annual-report-2016.pdf. Detailed rules administering the whistleblower program were published in Exchange Act Release No. 64,545 (May 25, 2011). For interpretive guidance, see Resources, SEC Office of Whistleblower, www.sec.gov/about/offices/owb/owb-resources.shtml; *see also* 80 Fed. Reg. 47,829 (Aug. 10, 2015).

38. 18 U.S.C. § 1514A(a)(1); *see also* Lockheed Martin Corp. v. Admin. Review Bd., 717 F.3d 1121 (10th Cir. 2013); Ellington v. Giacoumakis, 977 F. Supp. 2d 42 (D. Mass. 2013). Protected conduct requires that employee complaints concern violations of specific U.S. statutes, SEC rules or allege securities fraud. Other complaints fall outside SOX section 806. *See* Villanueva v. U.S. Dep't of Labor, 743 F.3d 103 (5th Cir. 2014) (complaints about fraudulent tax reporting in Colombia not protected conduct); Reamer v. U.S. Dep't of Labor, 505 F. App'x 439, 441 (6th Cir. 2012) (employee's email about FBI conducting a frivolous fraud investigation of a dealership neither stated nor suggested securities fraud); Boyd v. Accuray, Inc., 873 F. Supp. 2d 1156 (N.D. Cal. 2012) (on a "termination track" for a year for poor performance, employee's discussion of incorrect numbering of a product in inventory records with the employer did not mention or indicate fraud or a violation of securities laws; first complaint to SEC about the same conduct occurred nine days after employee was terminated and played no role in termination). For a recent comprehensive analysis of pleading the elements of a retaliation claim, see Wood v. Dow Chem. Co., 2014 WL 7157100 (E.D. Mich. Dec. 15, 2014).

39. SOX is not extra-territorial. *See* Liu Meng-Lin v. Siemens A.G., 763 F.3d 175 (2d Cir. 2014); Carnero v. Bos. Sci. Corp., 433 F.3d 1, 6–19 (1st Cir. 2006).

40. If reinstatement with seniority is not feasible in a given case, front pay may be awarded. *See* Perez v. Progenics Pharm., Inc., 204 F. Supp. 3d 528 (S.D.N.Y. Aug. 30, 2016). Special damages for retaliation may include compensation for reputational injury and emotional distress. Halliburton, Inc. v. Admin. Review Bd., 771 F.3d 254 (5th Cir. 2014); Lockheed Martin Corp. v. Admin. Review Bd., 717 F.3d 1121 (10th Cir. 2013).

41. SOX § 806.

42. 18 U.S.C. § 1513(e).

43. N.Y. LAB. LAW § 740.

44. In Free Enter. Fund v. Pub. Co. Accounting Oversight Bd., 561 U.S. 477 (2010), the U.S. Supreme Court found that SEC appointment of members to the PCAOB was lawful and that severing one part of a two-level provision for removal of such members, leaving removal in the hands of the SEC, would avoid a violation of the president's powers; the PCAOB was found otherwise constitutional.

45. *See* Order Granting Approval of Proposed Rules to Require Disclosure of Certain Audit Participants on a New PCAOB Form and Related Amendments to Auditing Standards, Exchange Act Release No. 77,787, File No. PCAOB-2016-01 (May 9, 2016).

46. *See* PUB. CO. ACCOUNTING OVERSIGHT BD., 2015 ANNUAL REPORT (Sept. 21, 2016), https://pcaobus.org/About/Administration/Documents/Annual%20Reports/2015.pdf.

47. PCAOB has issued and enforces four sets of standards: Accounting standards, Ethics and Independence standards, Quality Control standards and Attestation standards; these are available, along with interpretative guidance and pending updates. *See Standards*, PCAOB, https://pcaobus.org/standards.

48. SOX § 201.

49. 17 C.F.R. § 210.2-01(c)(4)(vi).

50. *Id.* § 210.2-01(c)(4)(vii).

51. *Id.* § 210.2-01(c)(4)(ix).

52. SOX §§ 201(h), 202, 205(a).

53. *See* Public Company Accounting Oversight Board; Order Granting Approval of Proposed Rules on Auditing Standard No. 16, Communications with Audit Committees, and Related and Transitional Amendments to PCAOB Standards Exchange Act Release No. 68,453 (Dec. 17, 2012); *see also* PCAOB Auditing Standard No. 16, http://pcaobus.org/Standards/Auditing/Pages/default.aspx.

54. SOX § 203.

55. *Id.* § 105; *see also* Exchange Act Release No. 60,497 (Aug. 13, 2009) (approving PCAOB Rules 2200-2207 concerning annual and special reporting by audit firms).

56. On January 22, 2014, an SEC administrative law judge suspended the Chinese affiliates of the "Big Four" audit firms from practicing before the SEC for six months, after the affiliates declined to provide audit work papers from audits

of certain Chinese issuer companies being investigated by the SEC, as required by SOX § 106. *See In re* BDO China Dahua CPA Co., Ltd.; Ernst & Young Hua Ming LLP; KPMG Huazhen (Special General Partnership); Deloitte Touche Tohmatsu Certified Public Accountants Ltd.; PricewaterhouseCoopers Zhong Tian CPAs Limited, Initial Decision Release No. 553, File Nos. 3-14872 and 3-15116 (May 9, 2014). A settlement of this matter was approved by the SEC; *see* Exchange Act Release No. 72,417 (Feb. 6, 2014). Pursuant to the settlement, each of the Chinese affiliates agreed to pay $500,000 and agreed to follow detailed procedures to give the SEC access to audit documents via the China Securities Regulatory Commission; a six-month suspension of their right to audit U.S. traded firms was stayed for four years; noncompliance could lead to penalties or a renewal of the enforcement case.

57. SOX § 106 prescribes these limits on civil penalties for intentional and knowing violations; smaller civil penalties of up to $100,000 per individual and up to $2 million per firm may be ordered for other violations. PCAOB has issued sixty- five settled disciplinary orders and eleven adjudicated disciplinary orders. Examples of PCAOB's major sanctions include the following: *In re* Deloitte & Touche LLP, PCAOB Release No. 105-2013-008 (Oct. 22, 2013) (censure, civil money penalty of $2 million and specific remedial actions required with respect to oversight of audit engagement leaders); *In re* Ernst & Young LLP, et al., PCAOB Release No. 105-2012-001 (Feb. 8, 2012) (censure, two employees barred from association with a registered public accounting firm, civil money penalties of $2 million against the firm and of $50,000 and $25,000 against the individual employees); *In re* Price Waterhouse, Bangalore, et al., PCAOB Release No. 105-2011-002 (Apr. 5, 2011) (censure, prohibiting Indian affiliate from accepting SEC issuer engagement for new clients for six months, requiring an independent monitor, specific remedial quality control and training actions, and civil money penalty of $1,500,000).

58. The Big 4 audit firms feel competitive pressure to perform well on PCAOB inspections. This can lead to inappropriate conduct. KPMG fired its vice chairman, its top executive overseeing U.S. audit practice, and national managing partner for audit quality and professional practice, and other partners and employees for improperly obtaining information from a PCAOB employee about which audits the regulator planned to inspect. Having such information in advance would permit polishing of particular audit files to improve inspection results. *See KPMG Fires Partners over Leak*, WALL ST. J. (Apr. 12, 2017), at B1–B2.

59. *See* Rule 2105, Exchange Act Release No. 48,180; File No. PCAOB-2003-03 (July 16, 2003).

60. *See* 17 C.F.R. § 205.2(b).

61. *See id.* § 205.2(a)(2).

62. *Id.* § 205.3(b)(1).

63. *Id.* § 205.5.

64. *Id.* § 205.3(b)(2).

65. SOX § 307.

66. 17 C.F.R. § 205.3(b)(3), (4).

67. *Id.* § 205.3(b)(7).
68. *Id.* § 205.5.
69. SOX § 307.
70. *Id.* § 3; 17 C.F.R. § 205.6.
71. *See* 17 C.F.R. § 201.102(a).
72. *Id.* § 205.6.
73. *Id.* § 205.2(e).
74. *Id.* § 205.2(m).
75. *Id.* § 205.2(k).
76. *Id.* § 205.3(c).
77. *Id.* § 205.1(b).
78. *Id.* § 205.3(b)(8).
79. *Id.* § 205.3(b)(9).
80. *Id.* § 205.3(d).
81. *See* Credit Suisse First Bos. Corp. v. Grunwald, 400 F.3d 1119, Fed. Sec. L. Rep. (CCH) 93,125 (9th Cir. 2005).
82. Since 2015, the SEC has brought and resolved multiple enforcement actions against lawyers and law firms who were not registered with the SEC as brokers but who received commissions for selling and recommending EB-5 visa investments. *See* Press Release No. 2015-274, U.S. Sec. & Exch. Comm'n, SEC: Lawyers Offered EB-5 Investments as Unregistered Brokers (Dec. 7, 2015); *see also* Gregory Bartko, Exchange Act Release No. 71,666 (Mar. 7, 2014) (attorney who was CEO and chief compliance officer of registered broker-dealer criminally convicted of mail fraud and illegal sales of unregistered securities, was barred from association with any broker, dealer, investment adviser or ratings organization); Leaddog Capital Mkts., LLC, et al., Initial Decision Release No. 468, 2012 WL 4044882 (Sept. 14, 2012) (attorney-general partner ordered to cease and desist from violations of antifraud provisions and, jointly and severally, with partner and firm, to disgorge gains of $220,572, pay a civil money penalty of $130,000, be barred from association with any broker, dealer, investment adviser, or investment company and be permanently barred from practice before the SEC as an attorney); Steven Altman, Esq., Exchange Act Release No. 63,306 (Nov. 10, 2010) (commercial litigator permanently denied right to practice before the SEC as an attorney because of violations of New York state bar ethics disciplinary rules, including seeking financial benefits for his client, a prospective witness in SEC proceedings, in exchange for her false testimony); Chris G. Gunderson, Esq., Exchange Act Release No. 61,234 (Dec. 23, 2009) (application for reinstatement by former general counsel of penny stock issuer, who engaged in scheme to sell unregistered securities, was enjoined from further violations, barred by the SEC from practice before it, found in civil contempt of the court injunction, was denied); David J. Lubben, Esq., SEC News Digest 2009-33-2, 2009 WL 424436 (Feb. 20, 2009) (former general counsel of public issuer UnitedHealth Group, Inc. suspended from practicing before SEC as an attorney for three years, following his consent to permanent injunction by district court enjoining violations of antifraud provisions, barring him from serving as officer or director of public

companies for five years, paying a $575,000 civil penalty, repricing stock options reducing their value by $2.7 million, and paying $630,000 in settlements of private derivative and shareholder lawsuits, relating to backdating of options); SEC v. John E. Isselmann, Jr., No. CV 04-1350 MO (D. Or.), Litigation Release No. 18,896 (Sept. 24, 2004); *see also* SEC v. Henry C. Yuen, Civil Action No. CV 03-4376 MRP (PLAX) (C.D. Cal.), Litigation Release No. 19,047 (Jonathan B. Orlick) (Jan. 21, 2005). *But cf.* Scott G. Monson, Investment Company Act Release No. 28,323 (June 30, 2008) (SEC affirmed dismissal by administrative law judge of complaint against a former general counsel for legal advice not found to be negligent); *see also* Tonya M. Grindon, *Regulating Ethics: A Review of Recent SEC Enforcement Actions Against Attorneys, in* SECURITIES FILINGS 2009, at 707 (PLI Corp. Law & Practice, Course Handbook Ser. No. 1767, 2009).

83.   COSO refers to The Committee of Sponsoring Organizations (COSO) of the Treadway Commission, author of Internal Control—An Integrated Framework (1992) (the "COSO Report"). The COSO Report provides a widely accepted framework for the development and improvement of internal controls for financial reporting. In May 2013, an updated Framework was issued by COSO, retaining the five main components of the original framework—control environment, risk assessment, control activities, information and communication, and monitoring activities—while articulating seventeen specific principles, each with explicit points of focus to guide companies in applying the framework. The framework provides a "top-down" and "risk-adjusted" technique that permits management and auditors to focus on key controls. *See* News Release, COSO, *COSO Issues Updated Internal Control-Integrated Framework and Related Illustrative Documents* (May 14, 2013), www.coso.org/documents/COSO%20Framework%20Release%20PR%20May%2014%202013%20Final%20PDF.pdf. *See generally* COSO, www.COSO.org.

84.   *See, e.g.*, Yahoo, Inc., Form 10-K (Mar. 1, 2017), at 5, 44–47, disclosing an adverse $350 million purchase price adjustment in its sale to Verizon Communications, Inc. and its payment of $16 million in legal and related expenses incurred in 2016 resulting from two major data breaches (2013 affecting one billion user accounts and 2014 affecting 500 million customer email accounts, and disclosing forty-eight class action and other lawsuits and multiple investigations relating to the data breaches. The legal department was faulted for inadequate analysis and legal advice concerning the data breaches, and the general counsel resigned. *Id.* at 47.

85.   *See* Report of Investigation Pursuant to Section 21(a) of the Securities Exchange Act of 1934 and Commission Statement on the Relationship of Cooperation to Agency Enforcement Decisions, Exchange Act Release No. 44,969; SEC Accounting and Auditing Enforcement Release No. 1470 (Oct. 23, 2001).

86.   *See* Lucent Techs., Inc., Litigation Release No. 18,715 (May 17, 2004); SEC Accounting and Auditing Enforcement Release No. 2016 (May 17, 2004).

87.   SOX §§ 302, 906.

88.   *Id.* § 401.

89.   15 U.S.C. § 78m or 15 U.S.C. § 78o(d).

90.   *See, e.g.*, Masterson v. Commonwealth Bankshares, Inc., 2014 WL 930854, at *5–6 (E.D. Va. Mar. 10, 2014) (certifications of fraudulent official financial reports of a company's financial performance plausibly show CEO and CFO were responsible for and had control over the accuracy of public disclosures); *In re* Symbol Techs., Inc. Sec. Litig., 2013 WL 6330665, at *11 (E.D.N.Y. Dec. 5, 2013) (admissions in amended reports to prior false certifications under SOX §§ 302, 404, and 906 tended to support allegations of falsity and of scienter in Rule 10(b)(5) class action complaint); *see also* Adams v. Kinder-Morgan, Inc., 340 F.3d 1083, 1109 (10th Cir. 2003); *In re* Enron Corp. Sec., Derivative & ERISA Litig., 258 F. Supp. 2d 576, 598 (S.D. Tex. 2003).

91.   17 C.F.R. § 240.13a-15.

92.   *Id.* §§ 228.10(h)(2), (4), 229.10(e)(2) (Regs. S-K and S-B).

93.   *Id.* § 244.100(a).

94.   *Id.* § 244.100 (Reg. G), at n.1.

95.   SEC v. HealthSouth Corp., 261 F. Supp. 2d 1298 (N.D. Ala. 2003).

96.   For exemptions from SOX section 404, see Final Rule, Internal Control over Financial Reporting in Exchange Act Periodic Reports of Non-Accelerated Filers, Securities Act Release No. 9142, Exchange Act Release No. 62,914 (Sept. 21, 2010), www.sec.gov/rules/final/2010/33-9142.pdf. The SEC adopted amendments to the definitions for "accelerated filer" and "large accelerated filer" in order to provide a narrow carve-out for qualifying "smaller reporting companies" that reported less than $100 million in annual revenues in the most recent fiscal year for which audited financial statements were available. Under the amendments, companies qualifying for the carve-out will no longer be subject to the requirement under SOX section 404(b) to have an auditor attestation report on internal control over financial reporting, a requirement that applies to accelerated and large accelerated filers. *See* Final Rule, Accelerated Filer and Large Accelerated Filer Definitions, Securities Act Release No. 88365 (Apr. 27, 2020), https://www.sec.gov/rules/final/2020/34-88365.pdf.

97.   *See* 17 C.F.R. §§ 240.13a-15(c), 240.15d-15(c).

98.   *Id.* § 240.13a-15(f).

99.   *See* COSO, Internal Control—Integrated Framework (1992), at Executive Summary.

100. PCAOB Rulemaking: Public Company Accounting Oversight Board; Notice of Filing of Proposed Rule on Auditing Standard No. 2, An Audit of Internal Control Over Financial Reporting Performed in Conjunction with an Audit of Financial Statements, Exchange Act Release No. 49,544, File No. PCAOB-2004-03 (Apr. 8, 2004).

101. *See* Securities Act Release No. 8183 (Jan. 28, 2003).

102. *See* Item 2-01(c)(4) of Regulation S-X, 17 C.F.R. § 210.2-01(c)(4); Exchange Act § 10A(g).

103. *See* Securities Act Release No. 8183 (Jan. 28, 2003).

104. *See* SEC v. Quattrone, Civil Action No. 04-33(SRC) (D.N.J.); SEC Sues 10 Defendants for Securities Fraud Arising from $700 Million Round-Tripping Scheme at Suprema Specialties, Litigation Release No. 18,534; SEC Accounting and Auditing Enforcement Release No. 1938 (Jan. 7, 2004).

105. *See* Final Rule: Management's Reports on Internal Control over Financial Reporting and Certification of Disclosure in Exchange Act Periodic Reports, Securities Act Release No. 8238, Exchange Act Release No. 47,986, at 15 (June 11, 2003).

106. PCAOB's Audit Standard No. 2.

107. The PCAOB auditing standards are available on the PCAOB website. *See Auditing Standards*, PCAOB, https://pcaobus.org/Standards/Auditing/Pages/default.aspx; *see also* Reorganization of PCAOB Auditing Standards and Related Amendments to PCAOB Standards and Rules, PCAOB Release No. 2015-002 (Mar. 31, 2015), https://pcaobus.org/Rulemaking/Docket040/Release_2015_002_Reorganization.pdf.

108. U.S. Gen. Accounting Office, Government Auditing Standards, Field Work Standards for Financial Audits (2003 Revision), ¶ 4.22.

109. *See* Item 307 of Regulations S-K and S-B (Forms 10K) and Item 15 of Form 20-F and General Instruction B(6) to Form 40-F.

110. SOX § 3.

111. *Id.* §§ 107(c), 602.

112. *Id.* § 307.

113. *Id.* § 3(b).

114. *See* U.S. SEC. & EXCH. COMM'N, FY 2022 CONGRESSIONAL BUDGET JUSTIFICATION, FY 2022 ANNUAL PERFORMANCE PLAN, FY 2020 ANNUAL PERFORMANCE REPORT, https://www.sec.gov/files/FY%202022%20Congressional%20Budget%20Justification%20Annual%20Performance%20Plan_FINAL.pdf.

115. *See* U.S. SEC. & EXCH. COMM'N, FY 2020 CONGRESSIONAL BUDGET JUSTIFICATION, FY 2020 ANNUAL PERFORMANCE PLAN, FY 2018 ANNUAL PERFORMANCE REPORT, https://www.sec.gov/secfy20congbudgjust_0.pdf.

116. *See* Press Release No. 2013-121, U.S. Sec. & Exch. Comm'n, SEC Announces Enforcement Initiatives to Combat Financial Reporting and Microcap Fraud and Enhance Risk Analysis (July 2, 2013), www.sec.gov/News/PressRelease/Detail/PressRelease/1365171624975#.U9EmZUHD_cs.

117. *See* U.S. SEC. & EXCH. COMM'N, FY 2017 CONGRESSIONAL BUDGET JUSTIFICATION, FY 2017 ANNUAL PERFORMANCE PLAN, FY 2015 ANNUAL PERFORMANCE REPORT, www.sec.gov/about/reports/secfy17congbudgjust.pdf.

118. SOX § 1107.

119. Pub. L. No. 104-67, 109 Stat. 737 (2004).

120. *See* Judge Harmon's denial of a motion to dismiss complaint as against Vinson & Elkins in *In re* Enron Corp. Sec., Derivative & ERISA Litig., 235 F. Supp. 2d 549, 704–05 (S.D. Tex. 2002).

121. SOX § 802(a) (codified at 18 U.S.C. §§ 1519–20). The Supreme Court interpreted these sections broadly to include any tangible objects in Yates v. United States, 135 S. Ct. 1074 (2015).

122. *Id.* § 902(a) (codified at 18 U.S.C. § 1349).

123. *Id.* § 903(a)–(b) (codified at 18 U.S.C. §§ 1341, 1343).

124. *Id.* § 1102 (codified at 18 U.S.C. § 1512).

125. *Id.* § 1107(a) (codified at 18 U.S.C. § 1513(e)).

126. *Id.* § 306(b) (codified at 29 U.S.C. § 1021(i)).

127. *Id.* § 904 (codified at 29 U.S.C. § 1131).

128. *Id.* § 306 (codified at 29 U.S.C. § 1021).

129. *See AIG Reinsurance Problems Likely to Spur Vast Changes in Industry Practices, Experts Say,* BESTWIRE, Apr. 11, 2005.

130. *See, e.g.,* PCAOB, Final Rules Relating to the Oversight of Non-U.S. Public Accounting Firms, PCAOB Release No. 2004-005 (June 9, 2004), in which the PCAOB agreed it may—but need not—rely on a European home country for inspections or investigations of auditors in the EU.

131. Council Directive 2006/43/EC, of the European Parliament and of the Council of 17 May 2006 on statutory audits of annual accounts and consolidated accounts, amending Council Directives 78/660/EEC and 83/349/EEC and repealing Council Directive 84/253/EEC (Text with EEA relevance), 2006 O.J. (L 157) 87–107, https://eur-lex.europa.eu/legal-content/EN/TXT/?uri=CELEX%3A32006L0043.

132. *See* Scoreboard on the Transposition of the Statutory Audit Directive (2006/43/EC) (Sept. 1, 2010); *see also* Scoreboard on the Transposition of the Statutory Audit Directive (2006/43/EC) (July 31, 2008), https://www.iasplus.com/en/binary/europe/0807statutoryauditscoreboard.pdf.

133. *See* Concept Release on Allowing U.S. Issuers to Prepare Financial Statements in Accordance with International Financial Reporting Standards (Aug. 14, 2007), 72 Fed. Reg. 45,600. For recent developments, see www.IFRS.com.

134. *See* Press Release No. MEMO/13/1171, European Commission, Commissioner Michel Barnier Welcomes Provisional Agreement in Trilogue on the Reform of the Audit Sector (Dec. 17, 2013), http://europa.eu/rapid/press-release_MEMO-13-1171_en.htm?locale=en.

135. *See* U.S. GOV'T ACCOUNTABILITY OFFICE, REPORT TO CONGRESSIONAL COMMITTEES, INTERNAL CONTROLS: SEC SHOULD CONSIDER REQUIRING COMPANIES TO DISCLOSE WHETHER THEY OBTAINED AN AUDITOR ATTESTATION (GAO-13-582) (July 2013), http://gao.gov/assets/660/655710.pdf.

136. *See* E. Han Kim & Yao Lu, *Corporate Governance Reforms Around the World and Cross-Border Acquisitions,* 22 J. CORP. FIN. 236–53 (2013).

137. *See* Protiviti, Inc., Building Value in Your SOX Compliance Program: Highlights from Protiviti's 2013 Sarbanes-Oxley Compliance Survey (May 2013), https://www.protiviti.com/sites/default/files/united_states/insights/2013-sox-compliance-survey-protiviti.pdf.

138. *See* Jeong-Bon Kim, Byron Y. Song & Liandong Zhang, *Internal Control Weakness and Bank Loan Contracting: Evidence from SOX Section 404 Disclosures*, 86 ACCT. REV. 1157–88 (2011); J. Hammersley, L. Myers & C. Shakespeare, *Market Reactions to the Disclosure of Internal Control Weakness and to the Characteristics of those Weaknesses under Section 302 of the Sarbanes Oxley Act of 2002*, 13 REV. ACCT. STUDIES 141–65 (2008); J.C. Coates, & S. Srinivasan, *SOX After Ten Years: A Multidisciplinary Review* (Jan. 2014) (forthcoming in *Accounting Horizons*, available on SSRN).

139. *See* K. Johnstone, C. Li & K. Rupley, *Changes in Corporate Governance Associated with the Revelation of Internal Control Material Weaknesses and their Subsequent Remediation*, 28 CONTEMP. ACCT. RES. 331–83 (2011).

140. *See* S. Rice, D. Weber & B. Wu, *Does SOX 404 Have Teeth? Consequences of the Failure to Report Existing Internal Control Weaknesses* (2013). An abstract of this paper is available on the Social Science Research Network website. *See* https://papers.ssrn.com/sol3/papers.cfm?abstract_id=2506896.

141. *See* Andrew Ceresney, Co-Dir., SEC Div. of Enf't, Address at the American Law Institute Continuing Legal Education: Financial Reporting and Accounting Fraud (Sept. 19, 2013), www.sec.gov/News/Speech/Detail/Speech/1370539845772; *see also* 45 Sec. Reg. & L. Rep. (BNA) 1759 (Sept. 18, 2013).

142. *See* JPMorgan Chase & Co., Exchange Act Release No. 70,458, Accounting and Auditing Enforcement Release No. 3490 (Sept. 19, 2013).

143. "We continue to spend time with staff in our Enforcement Division on investigations that involve internal control considerations, and I think you should expect that financial reporting and disclosure investigations going forward are likely to continue to include taking a close look at the adequacy of internal accounting controls as well as evaluations and conclusions about both internal control over financial reporting and disclosure controls and procedures. We're also beginning to see some of our first auditor cases related to audits of internal control over financial reporting." Brian T. Croteau, Deputy Chief Accountant, Office of Chief Accountant, SEC, Remarks Before the 2013 AICPA National Conference on Current SEC and PCAOB Developments—Audit Policy and Current Auditing and Internal Control Matters, www.sec.gov/News/Speech/Detail/Speech/1370540472057; *see also* News Release, PCAOB, PCAOB Issues Staff Audit Practice Alert in Light of Deficiencies Observed in Audits of Internal Control Over Financial Reporting (Oct. 24, 2013), http://pcaobus.org/News/Releases/Pages/10242013_Practice_Alert.aspx.

144. *See CF Disclosure Guidance: Topic No. 2—Cybersecurity*, U.S. SEC. & EXCH. COMM'N (Oct. 13, 2011), www.sec.gov/divisions/corpfin/guidance/cfguidance-topic2.htm.

145. *Cybersecurity Roundtable*, U.S. SEC. & EXCH. COMM'N (May 14, 2014), www.sec.gov/spotlight/cybersecurity-roundtable.shtml.

146. *See CF Disclosure Guidance: Topic No. 2—Cybersecurity*, U.S. SEC. & EXCH. COMM'N (Oct. 13, 2011), www.sec.gov/divisions/corpfin/guidance/cfguidance-topic2.htm.

147. *See* NAT'L INST. FOR STANDARDS & TECH., FRAMEWORK FOR IMPROVING CRITICAL INFRASTRUCTURE CYBERSECURITY, VERSION 1.0 (Feb. 12, 2014), https://www.nist.gov/sites/default/files/documents/cyberframework/cybersecurity-framework-021214.pdf; NIST Roadmap for Improving Critical Infrastructure Cybersecurity (Feb. 12, 2014), www.nist.gov/cyberframework/upload/roadmap-021214.pdf (the "Roadmap"); *see also* PCAOB, PUBLIC COMPANY ACCOUNTING OVERSIGHT BOARD STRATEGIC PLAN: IMPROVING THE QUALITY OF THE AUDIT FOR THE PROTECTION AND BENEFIT OF INVESTORS 2013–2017 (Nov. 26, 2013), http://pcaobus.org/About/Ops/Documents/Strategic%20Plans/2013-2017.pdf.

148. *See* Proposed Auditing Standards—The Auditor's Report on an Audit of Financial Statements When the Auditor Expresses an Unqualified Opinion; The Auditor's Responsibilities Regarding Other Information in Certain Documents Containing Audited Financial Statements and the Related Auditor's Report; and Related Amendments to PCAOB Standards PCAOB Release No. 2013-005 (Aug. 13, 2013), http://pcaobus.org/Rules/Rulemaking/Docket034/Release_2013-005_ARM.pdf.

149. *Id.* at 6.

150. *Id.* at 7.

151. See the proposed new and revised international standards for public comment in July 2013. *Reporting on Audited Financial Statements: Proposed New and Revised International Standards on Auditing*, INT'L FED'N OF ACCOUNTANTS, https://www.ifac.org/publications-resources/reporting-audited-financial-statements-proposed-new-and-revised-international.

31

SEC Investigations of Public Companies

*Stephen P. Warren & Allison Kernisky**

The U.S. Securities and Exchange Commission ("SEC" or "Commission") is the law enforcement agency specifically charged by Congress with civil enforcement of the federal securities laws.[1] The SEC has authority to investigate all violations of the securities laws by any person or entity it believes may have committed a violation, including individuals, public companies, securities exchanges, broker-dealers, investment advisers, and mutual funds.[2]

This chapter explains how the SEC conducts investigations of public companies and their directors and officers and will help you understand what to expect during the course of such

*   The authors would like to thank Mitchell E. Herr, the original author of this chapter, for many years of well-reasoned and principled guidance.

an investigation. While this chapter will help orient a non-specialist to the process, the defense of an SEC investigation is best directed by an attorney with substantial experience in this specialty practice area.

Overview of SEC Investigations

The Basics

Q 31.1   What does the SEC investigate?

The SEC will initiate an enforcement investigation of a public company when it has reason to suspect that the company has violated the federal securities laws.[3] For instance, the SEC investigates potential securities fraud—that is, the making of false or misleading statements to the public through a company's financial statements, its periodic public disclosures (such as SEC Forms 10-Q and 10-K), or its press releases.

Any public company that restates its financial statements can expect an enforcement inquiry.[4] Financial reporting violations are always a high priority for the SEC's Division of Enforcement.[5] The SEC also may investigate a public company suspected of violating various other federal securities statutes or SEC regulations such as the registration requirements for the public issuance of new securities, the required disclosure of payments that violate the Foreign Corrupt Practices Act (FCPA), and the prohibition against the selective disclosure of material information to the marketplace. In the last decade, the SEC has significantly ramped up its enforcement efforts against insider trading.[6]

Q 31.1.1   What individuals are subject to investigation?

An SEC investigation of a public company typically involves scrutiny of all persons involved in the conduct in question. For example, in an investigation related to a company's financial statements, the SEC will examine the officers involved in the underlying conduct, the officers responsible for the financial statements (such as the Controller and the CFO), and the CFO and CEO who certified those financial statements under sections 302 and 906 of the Sarbanes-Oxley Act of 2002 (SOX).[7]

The SEC views attorneys as "gatekeepers" to our nation's financial markets and scrutinizes the role of corporate counsel. In a January 2018 speech, former SEC Chairman Jay Clayton explained his "expectations for market professionals," noting that:

Market professionals, especially gatekeepers, need to act responsibly and hold themselves to high standards. . . . Our securities laws—and 80 plus years of practice—assume that securities lawyers, accountants, underwriters, and dealers will act responsibly. It is expected that they will bring expertise, judgment, and a healthy dose of skepticism to their work. Said another way, even when the issue presented is narrow, market professionals are relied upon to bring knowledge of the broad legal framework, accounting rules, and the markets to bear.[8]

Q 31.1.2   Who at the SEC is responsible for conducting investigations?

SEC investigations are conducted by its Division of Enforcement. The SEC's 2022 budget request calls for a budget to support 1,372 professional enforcement staff, 1,330 of which would be full-time employees.[9] Less than half of the SEC's Enforcement staff work in its home office in Washington, D.C.; the majority work in eleven regional offices around the country (Atlanta, Boston, Chicago, Denver, Fort Worth, Los Angeles, Miami, New York, Philadelphia, Salt Lake City, and San Francisco).[10] Typically, the Enforcement Division office that begins an investigation sees it through to its conclusion, including the settlement or trial of any resulting enforcement action.

As part of efforts to revitalize the Division of Enforcement, in 2009 former Director Robert Khuzami eliminated an entire level of management (Branch Chiefs), allowing the Enforcement Division to devote additional seasoned attorneys to line investigative duties. In early 2010, former Director Khuzami created specialized units to focus the Division's enforcement efforts in particular areas; each unit is headed by a unit chief and staffed by enforcement personnel who have the relevant expertise.[11] The specialized units are:

(1) Asset management: issues involving investment advisers, investment companies, hedge funds, and private equity funds;

(2) Market abuse: large-scale market abuses and complex manipulation schemes by institutional traders and market professionals;

(3) Complex Financial Instruments (formerly known as structured and new products): complex derivatives and financial

products including credit default swaps, collateralized debt obligations, and securitized products;

(4) Foreign corrupt practices: violations of the FCPA, which prohibits U.S. companies from bribing foreign officials; and

(5) Municipal securities and public pensions: issues concerning offering and disclosure fraud, tax or arbitrage-driven fraud, pay-to-play and public corruption violations, and pension accounting, disclosure, valuation, and pricing fraud.

These specialized units continue to interact with the SEC's existing supervisory and reporting structure as these six areas continue to receive priority focus from the Enforcement Division. The six units have developed several proactive initiatives that have resulted in multiple enforcement actions as they bring to bear their respective expertise.

In September 2017, the SEC announced the creation of a Cyber Unit to focus on targeting cyber-related misconduct.[12] This unit has been active in the cryptocurrency space, which includes initial coin offerings (ICOs) and tokens. While there remains no definitive guidance on which digital assets are securities, in July 2017 the Commission issued an investigative report (the "DAO Report"), which concluded that some, but not all, digital assets were securities and explained that issuers of certain digital asset securities must register offers and sales of such securities unless a valid exemption applies.[13]

The number of enforcement actions involving cryptocurrency is on the rise. The SEC brought just over a dozen enforcement actions involving digital assets in FY 2018, twenty-one actions in FY 2019, twenty-three actions in FY 2020, and five actions in the first part of FY 2021 alone.[14] For example:

- In October 2019, the SEC announced an emergency action halting an unregistered ICO by a mobile messaging company.[15]

- In December 2019, the SEC filed an action in the Southern District of New York, charging the founder of a digital-asset issuer and the issuer itself with defrauding investors in connection with an ICO.[16]

- In February 2020, the SEC settled a cease-and-desist proceeding against a blockchain technology company for conducting an unregistered ICO of digital tokens.[17]

- In September 2020, the SEC filed a settled cease-and-desist proceeding against a blockchain lending company for conducting an unregistered ICO of digital tokens.[18]

As the availability and use of digital assets increases, the SEC's interest in pursuing enforcement actions in this space will likely continue to grow. Because this is a rapidly evolving area of the law, it would be wise to consult with experienced SEC counsel for the most up-to-date guidance.

Q 31.1.3   What triggers an SEC investigation?

The Enforcement Division obtains investigatory leads from a wide variety of sources, including electronic and traditional news media, investor complaints, internal referrals from other SEC offices,[19] and referrals from self-regulatory organizations and other state and federal law enforcement and regulatory authorities. Section 408 of SOX required the SEC to review a public company's disclosures at least once every three years, which is considerably more frequently than in the past. These more frequent reviews of corporate filings by the Division of Corporation Finance have led to an increased number of referrals to the Enforcement Division. For example, in fiscal year 2018 (the last year for which the SEC released such data), the SEC reviewed the public filings of 57% of public companies.[20] The SEC's whistleblower program also has become a powerful source of investigative leads for its Division of Enforcement (*see* Q 31.1.4). And the SEC is increasingly using sophisticated data analytics to identify and prosecute misconduct (*see* Q 31.1.5). For example, the SEC recently disclosed an "EPS Initiative" that uses data analytics to detect statistical anomalies in public companies' earnings results. In September 2020, the SEC announced the first two settlements with companies targeted by the EPS Initiative. Both companies had patterns of meeting or slightly exceeding consensus EPS (earnings per share) estimates for consecutive quarters, followed by significant drops in EPS.[21]

Q 31.1.4   What is the SEC's whistleblower program?

Section 922 of the Dodd-Frank Act ("Dodd-Frank") directed the SEC to make monetary awards to eligible individuals who voluntarily provide original information that leads to successful Commission enforcement actions, resulting in the imposition of monetary sanctions over $1 million, and certain related successful actions. The SEC can make awards ranging from 10% to 30% of the monetary sanctions collected. In addition, section 924(d) of Dodd-Frank directed the SEC to establish a separate office within the SEC to administer the whistleblower program; in February 2011, the SEC established the Office of the Whistleblower (OWB).

The SEC has developed a sophisticated system for processing and evaluating whistleblower tips, and its whistleblower program has become a powerful source of generating investigative leads. Since the program's inception, the Division has received over 42,200 whistleblower tips, resulting in the award of more than $562 million to whistleblowers, including $175 million in FY 2020 alone.[22] In FY 2020, the SEC received 6,900 whistleblower complaints, a 31% increase from 2019 and the largest number received in a fiscal year.[23] The SEC made awards to thirty-nine individuals in FY 2020.[24]

The largest award to date is a $114 million award to a whistleblower authorized on October 22, 2020.[25] The second largest award to date for $50 million was announced in June 2020.[26] In announcing this award, Jane Nordberg, Chief of the SEC's Office of the Whistleblower, stated: "Whistleblowers have proven to be a critical tool in the enforcement arsenal to combat fraud and protect investors."

COMPLIANCE FACT

During FY 2020, the SEC filed 715 cases, a 17% decrease from the prior year. The decrease may be explained in part on the disruptive impact of the COVID pandemic. The 715 cases consisted of 405 standalone actions filed in federal court or brought as administrative proceedings, 180 follow-on administrative proceedings, and 130 proceedings to de-register public companies that were delinquent in their SEC filings. In FY 2020, the SEC obtained over $4.68 billion in monetary sanctions, an 8% increase from FY 2019.[27]

Q 31.1.5   How does the SEC use data analytics in the enforcement process?

The Division of Enforcement program is increasingly being supported—at all stages from case identification to trial—by sophisticated data analytics. The SEC's Division of Enforcement is often assisted by the Division of Economic and Risk Analysis (DERA). DERA—staffed primarily by non-lawyer quantitative, financial, and industry experts—integrates sophisticated analysis of economic, financial, and legal disciplines with data analytics and quantitative methodologies in support of the SEC's various missions, including enforcement.

The SEC has noted that:

> DERA's continued development of customized analytic tools and analyses enable the proactive detection of market risks indicative of possible violations of the federal securities laws. For example:
>
> - The Corporate Issuer Risk Assessment (CIRA) dashboard was designed to provide SEC staff with a comprehensive overview of the financial reporting environment of Commission issuer filers, and to assist Enforcement in detecting aberrant patterns in financial statements that may warrant additional inquiry. CIRA now produces over 200 customized metrics that the staff can use to analyze issuer behavior;
>
> - The Investment Company Risk Assessment was operationalized in FY 2016, and creates a system of risk rankings based

on detecting anomalous investment company characteristics, allowing Enforcement and OCIE to dig deeper and determine if specific, violative conduct might be occurring at a fund; and

- The Broker-Dealer Risk Assessment tool was developed in conjunction with OCIE and helps prioritize and support examinations in that area and provide key insights into the market. New metrics were added and new examination findings were integrated into the model.

DERA also continues to directly support Enforcement in investigating and prosecuting wrongdoing through rigorous, quantitative analyses that help identify violations of securities laws and measure harm to investors. For example, DERA has developed new methods for analyzing accounts to identify advisers engaged in "cherry picking" and for identifying potential market manipulation through high-frequency trading in U.S. Treasuries.[28]

Confirming the Division of Enforcement's increasing use of data analytics, former Commissioner Michael S. Piwowar spoke in 2018 about some of the latest technological tools used by the Division of Enforcement, including:

- Advanced Relational Trading Enforcement Metric Investigation System (ARTEMIS), designed by the Market Abuse Unit Analysis and Detection Center, to combine historical trading and account holder data with other data sources to enable longitudinal, multi-issuer, and multi-trader data analyses to detect insider trading and market manipulation activities;

- Market Information Data Analytics System (MIDAS) to analyze big data generated by the U.S. equity markets through the daily collection and processing of about 4 billion records from the proprietary feeds of the national equity exchanges and the consolidated tape, time-stamping each record with microsecond granularity, and enabling the Division of Trading and Markets to monitor market behavior, understand market events, and test hypotheses about the equity markets with a high level of precision; and

- Other cutting-edge data analytics technologies being developed internally and in partnership with the private sector to "root out fraud in the securities markets and protect investors."[29]

Former Chairman Clayton reiterated that data analytics are "more important than ever," to the SEC and help it to use its "existing resources more efficiently and effectively."[30] He also noted that the SEC's Retail Strategy Task Force, established in 2018 with the dual objectives of "develop[ing] data-driven, analytical strategies for identifying practices in the securities markets that harm retail investors and generating enforcement matters in these areas," and "collaborat[ing] within and beyond the SEC on retail investor advocacy and outreach," has "undertaken a number of lead-generation initiatives built on the use of data analytics."[31]

Q 31.2 What is the difference between a "preliminary" investigation and a "formal" investigation?

The SEC may gather facts and make a charging decision either through a "preliminary" (or "informal") investigation or through a "formal" investigation. Both are serious. Indeed, preliminary investigations that never reach the formal stage may still result in SEC enforcement charges.

At the preliminary investigation stage, requests for documents or witness testimony are voluntary.[32] Of course, given the SEC's emphasis on cooperation, a corporation is likely to conclude that it is in its interests to respond to the staff's voluntary requests.

When the SEC staff wants authority to subpoena documents or take witness testimony, it obtains a Formal Order of Investigation,[33] which identifies the securities laws that may have been violated and designates the SEC officers who are authorized to compel documents and testimony. The Commission has delegated authority to approve Formal Orders of Investigation to the Director of the Division of Enforcement.[34] The Director of Enforcement also has delegated authority to file an action in federal district court to enforce subpoenas issued pursuant to Formal Orders of Investigation.[35]

Under the Commission's Rules Relating to Investigations, a person who is compelled to produce documents or testify has the right to be shown the Formal Order of Investigation; however, furnishing a copy of the formal order rests in the discretion of senior enforcement personnel.[36]

> **TIP:** When compelled to produce documents or testify, it is useful to request a copy of the Formal Order of Investigation, as it may give some insight into the staff's concerns. While the formal order indicates, at a high level, the staff's concerns at the time it was issued, the staff subsequently may develop investigatory concerns that are not reflected in the formal order.

Q 31.2.1   Are all SEC investigations private?

Regardless of whether they are preliminary or formal, all SEC investigations are "non-public," meaning that neither the Commission nor the staff should acknowledge or comment on the investigation unless and until charges are brought.

However, parties under investigation may, and are sometimes obligated to, disclose the pendency of the investigation. SEC disclosure counsel may advise disclosing the investigation in the company's SEC filings, and companies may have to disclose the SEC investigation in response to other regulatory matters or in response to requests for proposals or in a due diligence process.

Statistics

Q 31.3   How many enforcement actions does the SEC bring, how long does the process take, and how successful is the SEC when it brings actions?

In 2020, the SEC brought 715 enforcement actions, and obtained over $4.68 billion in monetary sanctions, consisting of disgorgement of ill-gotten gains and penalties.[37]

In 2020, the SEC opened close to 1,200 new inquiries and investigations.[38] In 2020, the average time between opening a matter under inquiry (the first step in the Division of Enforcement's investigative process) and commencing an enforcement action was 21.6 months.[39] The SEC has identified reducing the time it takes from opening a matter under inquiry or investigation and commencing an enforcement action to be one of its "top priorities," recognizing that enforcement actions "have the greatest impact when filed as close in time to the conduct as possible."[40]

In 2020, the Division of Enforcement obtained relief on one or more of its claims in 93% of its enforcement actions; its success rate had ranged from 92%–97% in the preceding five years (2015–2019).[41] During former Chairman Clayton's tenure, the SEC often articulated that its focus is on qualitative measures of performance and not merely statistics alone. As he noted in his December testimony to the Senate Banking Committee, "purely quantitative measures alone cannot adequately measure the effectiveness of Enforcement's work, which can be evaluated better by assessing the nature, quality and effects of each of the Commission's enforcement actions with an eye toward how they further the agency's mission."[42]

Cooperation in Investigations

Q 31.4   What are a company's obligations to its SEC defense counsel?

The company must be entirely candid with its SEC defense counsel. Counsel cannot adequately defend the company's interests (or the interests of its directors, officers, or employees) without the benefit of the complete, unvarnished truth.

It is critical that counsel know all of the relevant facts from the beginning. The company's SEC defense counsel may make certain factual representations to the SEC early in the investigation. If these representations turn out to be inaccurate, the company will lose credibility and possibly be branded as uncooperative or obstructive. Thus, the company should disclose the full and complete truth—including facts that may be inconvenient or embarrassing—to its SEC defense counsel.

Q 31.5   What role does cooperation play in SEC enforcement investigations?

The SEC has repeatedly stressed the value of cooperation with its investigations. In its October 23, 2001, "Report of Investigation

Pursuant to Section 21(a) of the Securities Exchange Act of 1934 and Commission Statement on the Relationship of Cooperation to Agency Enforcement Decisions" (the "Seaboard Report"),[43] the SEC articulated the role of self-policing, self-reporting, remediation, and cooperation with its investigations in its enforcement decisions relating to corporate actors.

In order to give proper consideration to a company's cooperation or lack thereof, senior Enforcement Division staff have publicly stated that they keep a running "scorecard" of cooperation during an investigation. In an April 29, 2004, speech, the SEC's then-Director of Enforcement explained how cooperation can lead to more favorable outcomes for companies:

> The . . . core factor, which will often prove decisive in our analysis [regarding what, if any, penalty to seek], is the extent of a violator's cooperation, as measured by the standards set forth in the Commission's 21(a) Report. . . . [T]he provision of extraordinary cooperation . . . including self reporting a violation, being forthcoming during the investigation, and implementing appropriate remedial measures (including, in the case of an entity, appropriate disciplinary action against culpable individuals), can contribute significantly to a conclusion by the staff that a penalty recommendation should be more moderate in size or reduced to zero.[44]

Similarly, in a January 4, 2006 statement concerning financial penalties, the SEC reiterated that "[t]he degree to which a corporation has . . . cooperated with the investigation and remediation of the offense, is a factor that the Commission will consider in determining the propriety of a corporate penalty."[45] More recently, former Co-Director of Enforcement Steven Peikin noted, "not every case warrants a penalty."[46] As such, he stated, "[t]he SEC has a robust program that is intended to encourage cooperation in SEC investigations and enforcement actions. The program provides incentives to those who come forward and provide valuable information to SEC staff."[47]

Q 31.6   What are the potential benefits of cooperation with the SEC?

In many instances, cooperation with an SEC investigation undoubtedly has mitigated what otherwise would have been a harsher outcome for the corporation. Of course, when the SEC believes that a corporate actor has been affirmatively uncooperative, it will mete out even harsher penalties than might otherwise be warranted by the underlying conduct.[48]

In the matter that gave rise to the Seaboard Report on cooperation discussed above at Q 31.5, the SEC explained that it refrained from taking any enforcement action against the company in light of its complete cooperation with the SEC investigation:

> We are not taking action against the parent company, given the nature of the conduct and the company's responses. Within a week of learning about the apparent misconduct, the company's internal auditors had conducted a preliminary review and had advised company management who, in turn, advised the Board's audit committee, that Meredith had caused the company's books and records to be inaccurate and its financial reports to be misstated. The full Board was advised and authorized the company to hire an outside law firm to conduct a thorough inquiry. Four days later, Meredith was dismissed, as were two other employees who, in the company's view, had inadequately supervised Meredith; a day later, the company disclosed publicly and to us that its financial statements would be restated. The price of the company's shares did not decline after the announcement or after the restatement was published. The company pledged and gave complete cooperation to our staff. It provided the staff with all information relevant to the underlying violations. Among other things, the company produced the details of its internal investigation, including notes and transcripts of interviews of Meredith and others; and it did not invoke the attorney-client privilege, work product protection or other privileges or protections with respect to any facts uncovered in the investigation.

> The company also strengthened its financial reporting processes to address Meredith's conduct—developing a detailed closing process for the subsidiary's accounting personnel, consolidating subsidiary accounting functions under a parent company CPA, hiring three new CPAs for the accounting department responsible for preparing the subsidiary's financial statements, redesigning the subsidiary's minimum annual audit requirements, and requiring the parent company's controller to interview and approve all senior accounting personnel in its subsidiaries' reporting processes.[49]

The Seaboard Report describes a level of self-policing, self-reporting, remediation, and cooperation that only a few companies have been able to achieve. The SEC has made clear that only the most complete cooperation will warrant a pass from any enforcement action.

 CASE STUDY: *Harris Corp.*[50]

In 2016, the SEC declined to charge Harris Corp. in a Foreign Corrupt Practices Act investigation due to its exemplary cooperation. While the SEC charged the former chairman and CEO of the Chinese subsidiary of Harris Corp. with FCPA violations that occurred prior to Harris's acquisition of the subsidiary, the SEC determined not to bring charges against Harris in consideration of the company's efforts at self-policing that led to the discovery of this misconduct shortly after the acquisition, self-reporting, thorough remediation, and exemplary cooperation with the SEC's investigation. This was the first time that a large public multinational corporation obtained a full declination in a situation where an employee of the company suffered an FCPA enforcement action involving factual allegations that created potential FCPA liability for the company.

 CASE STUDY: *Credit Suisse Group*

On February 1, 2012, the SEC charged four former investment bankers and traders at Credit Suisse for their roles in a complex scheme to fraudulently overstate $3 billion worth of subprime bonds to boost their own profitability to reap substantial year-end bonuses and other rewards. The SEC entered into a cooperation agreement with Credit Suisse whereby it decided not to charge the investment bank for several reasons, including:

> the isolated nature of the wrongdoing and Credit Suisse's immediate self-reporting to the SEC and other law enforcement agencies as well as prompt public disclosure of corrected financial results. Credit Suisse voluntarily terminated the four investment bankers and implemented enhanced internal controls to prevent a recurrence of the misconduct. Credit Suisse also cooperated vigorously with the SEC's investigation of this matter, providing SEC enforcement officials with timely access to evidence and witnesses.

Q 31.7   What are the potential benefits to an individual of cooperation with the SEC?

Although the SEC articulated standards for *corporate* cooperation in its October 2001 Seaboard Report, the SEC had not systematically addressed the question of *individual* cooperation. This led many practitioners to question whether the SEC would give cooperating individuals appropriate credit. In January 2010, the Commission issued a formal policy statement on individual cooperation that set forth the analytical framework that it will use to balance the tension between the objectives of holding individuals fully accountable for their misconduct and providing incentives for individuals to cooperate with law enforcement.

The framework sets forth four considerations that the SEC will examine:

(1) the assistance provided, which will include the quality of the information divulged and the amount of time and resources saved as a result of the cooperation;

(2) the nature of the individual's cooperation, including whether it was voluntary and whether the revealed information was requested or might not have been otherwise discovered;

(3) the importance of the underlying matter, including the character and importance of the investigation and the dangers to investors from the violations; and

(4)   the societal interest in holding the individual accountable, including the severity of the individual's misconduct and the culpability of the individual.[51]

This framework signals the Commission's clear intent to appropriately reward individuals who cooperate with its enforcement investigations. The Enforcement Division is implementing the Commission's cooperation policy through an initiative that former Director Khuzami stated "has the potential to be a game-changer for the Enforcement Division."[52] The Enforcement Division's November 2017 *Enforcement Manual*[53] sets forth eight mechanisms that provide the enforcement staff with a wide range of tools for facilitating and rewarding cooperation:

- cooperation agreements;
- deferred prosecution agreements;
- non-prosecution agreements;
- immunity requests;
- oral assurances;
- termination notices;
- settlement recommendations; and
- publicizing the benefits of cooperation.

In employing each of these tools, the manual directs the staff to apply the analytic framework for cooperation described above.

In 2015, five years after the Division of Enforcement launched its cooperation program, it had entered into just five deferred prosecution agreements and six non-prosecution agreements but had signed over eighty cooperation agreements.[54]

Q 31.7.1   What is a cooperation agreement?

A cooperation agreement is a written agreement with the division in which the Division agrees to recommend to the Commission that the cooperator receive credit for cooperation in the enforcement action; in some cases, the Division may make specific enforcement recommendations to the Commission. Cooperation agreements do not formally bind the Commission.

Q 31.7.2   ... a deferred prosecution agreement?

A deferred prosecution agreement is a written agreement with the Commission in which it agrees to forego an enforcement action if the cooperator complies with express prohibitions or undertakings during a specified period of time, generally not to exceed five years. Deferred prosecution agreements and non-prosecution agreements formally bind the Commission.

Q 31.7.3   ... a non-prosecution agreement?

A non-prosecution agreement is a written agreement in which the Commission agrees not to bring an enforcement action against the cooperator; the *Enforcement Manual* notes that such an agreement will almost never be proper for a recidivist and should not be entered at an early stage of the litigation. A non-prosecution agreement offers the greatest credit with respect to potential SEC civil liability.

Q 31.7.4   ... an immunity request?

The Enforcement Division's ability to encourage cooperation by individuals was further enhanced by the Commission's delegation to it of authority to seek immunity from criminal prosecution from the Department of Justice (DOJ). With this authority, the Division can offer a potential cooperator the prospect of immunity from federal criminal prosecution as well as specified relief from SEC civil liability.

Q 31.7.5   ... an oral assurance?

Where the available evidence indicates that an individual or company has not violated the federal securities laws such as to warrant an enforcement action, Division of Enforcement staff may orally inform the individual or company that the Division does not anticipate recommending an enforcement action against the individual or company based upon the evidence currently known to the staff. Oral assurances are only given when the investigative record is adequately developed.

Q 31.7.6   ... a termination notice?

When an investigation has been completed as to a potential cooperator and the Division has determined, for any reason, not to recommend to the Commission an enforcement action against the potential cooperator, the staff may—and in some cases is required to—send a letter informing the potential cooperator of the determination. These notices may be provided before the Commission's investigation is closed or before a determination has been made as to every other potential defendant or respondent.

Q 31.7.7   ... a settlement recommendation?

Even in the absence of a cooperation agreement, the staff may take an individual's or company's cooperation into account in connection with recommending sanctions or charges associated with the alleged misconduct and, under certain circumstances, forgoing enforcement actions against a cooperating individual or company.

Q 31.7.8   ... publicizing the benefits of cooperation?

The Commission's enforcement program may be enhanced by publicizing the benefits associated with cooperating in a Commission investigation or related enforcement actions. Nevertheless, the staff retains discretion regarding whether and how to disclose the fact, manner, and extent of an individual or company's cooperation.

 CASE STUDY: *Goodyear Tire & Rubber Co.*

In 2015, the SEC settled an FCPA case with Goodyear Tire & Rubber Co.[55] The SEC typically requires a company settling such a case to pay disgorgement in the amount of its illicit profits, plus a civil money penalty in the same amount. Here, in light of the company's "self-reporting, prompt remedial acts, and significant cooperation with the SEC's investigation," the SEC did not impose any monetary penalty on the company, making this its first disgorgement-only FCPA settlement.

CASE STUDY: *Akamai Technologies and Nortek, Inc.*

In 2016, the SEC entered non-prosecution agreements with two companies in FCPA matters pursuant to which the companies agreed to disgorge their ill-gotten gains connected to bribes paid to Chinese officials by their foreign subsidiaries.[56] Both companies self-reported the misconduct promptly, and cooperated extensively with the ensuing SEC investigations. The non-prosecution agreements stipulate that the companies are not charged with FCPA violations and do not pay additional monetary penalties. In announcing these agreements, the former Director of Enforcement stated:

> When companies self-report and lay all their cards on the table, non-prosecution agreements are an effective way to get the money back and save the government substantial time and resources while crediting extensive cooperation.[57]

These non-prosecution agreements reflect that the companies:

- self-reported to the SEC in the early stages of their internal investigations;

- shared detailed findings of their internal investigations and provided timely updates to enforcement staff;

- provided summaries of witness interviews and voluntarily made witnesses available for interviews;

- voluntarily translated documents from Chinese into English;

- terminated employees responsible for the misconduct; and

- strengthened their anti-corruption policies and conducted extensive mandatory training with employees around the world.[58]

Related Investigations

Coordination with Other Agencies

Q 31.8   Does the SEC coordinate investigations with other law enforcement authorities?

Yes. The SEC can share investigative information and coordinate its efforts with any number of foreign, federal, state, and local criminal, civil, or regulatory agencies.[59] In the post-Enron era, it has become common for the SEC to coordinate its investigations with other law enforcement authorities, both civil and criminal. In FY 2020, law enforcement offices and other regulators requested and obtained access to materials in the SEC's investigative files in more than 475 SEC investigations, some of which resulted in parallel criminal actions.[60]

COMPLIANCE FACT

Many recent FCPA cases have been prosecuted both civilly and criminally:

- Och-Ziff (2016)
- JP Morgan (2016)
- Teva Pharmaceutical (2016)
- Biomet (2017)
- Sociedad Quimica y Minera de Chile S.A. (2017)
- Panasonic Corp. (2018)
- Legg Mason, Inc. (2018)
- Fresenius Medical Care AG & Co KGaA (2019)
- Mobile TeleSystems PJSC (2019)

Active coordination with enforcement authorities is not limited to major corporate fraud cases. For instance, in 2007 the SEC began a sweeping investigation in conjunction with the DOJ, FBI, IRS, the Board of Governors of the Federal Reserve System, the Office of the Comptroller of the Currency, and a coalition of state attorneys general into anticompetitive practices in the municipal reinvestment industry involving bidding practices related to Guaranteed Investment Contracts (GICs). The investigative team collected $743 million from several settlements, including with UBS Financial Services, Inc., J.P. Morgan Securities, LLC, Banc of America Securities, LLC, Wachovia Bank, N.A., and GE Funding Capital Market Services.[61] Eighteen individuals were also indicted.[62]

The SEC also coordinates its investigations with various civil authorities. For instance, in the fall of 2014, the SEC charged Bank of America Corporation with violating the internal controls and record-keeping provisions of the federal securities laws after it took over a large portfolio of structured notes and other financial instruments as part of its acquisition of Merrill Lynch. The SEC acknowledged the assistance of the Board of Governors of the Federal Reserve System and the Public Company Accounting Oversight Board (PCAOB) in its investigation.[63] Similarly, in the spring of 2014, the SEC announced two separate cases against men who profited by insider trading on confidential information they learned from their wives about Silicon Valley–based tech companies. In that announcement, the SEC thanked the Financial Industry Regulatory Authority and the Options Regulatory Surveillance Authority.[64]

The SEC's coordination with criminal prosecutors has also resulted in the use of new tools to combat securities fraud. For instance, the Galleon hedge fund insider trading ring case of 2009 marked the first time that criminal authorities (working closely with the SEC) used wiretaps (which previously had been reserved for investigating organized crime and narcotics cases) to investigate insider trading.[65]

As noted earlier, the SEC does not have the authority to pursue criminal actions under the securities laws; those are handled by the DOJ. The DOJ and the SEC continue to work closely, and the use of wiretaps is now more common in insider trading investigations. While the SEC does not have the statutory authority to ask a court to authorize the use of wiretaps in a civil investigation, in its civil case against Raj Rajaratnam and others involved in the Galleon hedge fund insider trading ring, the SEC procured the U.S. attorney's office wiretap evidence by serving document requests directly on Rajaratnam. In affirming the district court's order compelling Rajaratnam to turn over that wiretap evidence to the SEC, the U.S. Court of Appeals for the Second Circuit noted that as long as a wiretap was legally obtained, the SEC could get the wiretap evidence directly from the defendant in a criminal proceeding for use in its civil proceeding.[66]

Parallel Civil and Criminal Investigations

Q 31.8.1   Do parallel civil and criminal investigations present additional risks?

The prospect of coordination between the SEC and other prosecutorial or regulatory authorities substantially increases the complexity of and risks attendant to an SEC investigation. These risks are often difficult to assess because, as discussed in the next section (Q 31.8.2), the SEC will not confirm or deny whether parallel investigations are being conducted, but will direct counsel to inquire with whatever other prosecutorial authority she may be concerned about.[67] Additionally, in many cases the SEC will conclude its investigation and resulting enforcement action before the first sign of any criminal interest in the matter becomes apparent.

As a practical matter, if the circumstances might be attractive to a criminal prosecutor (for example, if there is intentionally fraudulent conduct and significant investor losses), a company's safest course is to assume that there is or will be a parallel criminal investigation. In these circumstances, SEC defense counsel will often bring white-collar criminal defense counsel into the matter to help navigate the difficult issues raised by parallel civil and criminal investigations.[68]

Q 31.8.2   Must the government disclose that there are parallel civil and criminal investigations?

It is well-accepted that the government's civil (SEC) and criminal (DOJ) authorities may conduct parallel investigations of conduct that potentially violates the federal securities laws.[69] There are limits, however, to the degree that the SEC and the DOJ may coordinate. The courts have long held that the "[g]overnment may not bring a parallel civil proceeding and avail itself of civil discovery devices to obtain evidence for subsequent criminal production."[70] Be aware, however, that an April 4, 2008, decision by the Ninth Circuit[71] holds that the government has extremely wide latitude in conducting parallel investigations:

- The government may use the SEC investigation as a stalking horse to obtain information for use in the criminal prosecution as long as it does not engage in outright deceit.

- SEC Form 1662 provides sufficient notice of the possibility of criminal prosecution, even if the government actively conceals that a criminal investigation is underway.

- If the SEC investigation is commenced first, no amount of DOJ involvement with that investigation will justify a finding that the SEC investigation is being used impermissibly to obtain evidence for DOJ's criminal investigation.

In practice, the Ninth Circuit decision makes it very difficult for defendants to successfully argue that the government's conduct of an undisclosed parallel criminal investigation violated their rights.

TIP: In any SEC investigation of conduct that might be of interest to a criminal prosecutor (all securities violations are *potentially* criminally prosecutable), defense counsel should assume that there is a parallel criminal investigation. Accordingly, defense counsel and their clients must make informed decisions as to whether witnesses should waive their Fifth Amendment rights.

Q 31.8.3   Will both the criminal and civil proceedings proceed simultaneously?

After the investigation phase is complete, the government often will announce joint civil and criminal prosecutions, and then move to stay the civil case to prevent the defendant from using civil discovery to gain a purportedly unfair advantage in the criminal case in which it would not otherwise have broad discovery rights. Some federal courts have criticized this practice, holding that the usual rationales in favor of staying a civil case in favor of a pending criminal proceeding do not apply where the government has initiated both the civil and criminal proceedings.[72] For instance, in *SEC v. Saad*, in denying the government's motion to stay the SEC's civil case, the court observed that it was:

> strange[ ] . . . that the U.S. Attorney's Office, having closely coordinated with the SEC in bringing simultaneous civil and criminal actions against some hapless defendant, should then wish to be relieved of the consequences that will flow if the two actions proceed simultaneously.[73]

Directors' and Officers' Insurance Policies

Coverage for Investigation-Related Expenses

Q 31.9   Do directors' and officers' insurance policies cover the costs of responding to an SEC investigation?

A company's directors' and officers' (D&O) insurance policy potentially could cover the costs of defending an SEC investigation of an insured person.[74] Whether such coverage exists will depend on the precise policy language and, possibly, the type of investigation at issue. Covered "claims" under some policies may not include government investigations, and most policies exclude coverage for preliminary (or informal) investigations.[75] Because coverage may exist, however, the company should give timely notice to its D&O carriers of any investigation, including all excess layer carriers.

TIP: *D&O Coverage Before a Formal SEC Investigation Is Opened.* Companies should be mindful of the language in their D&O policies regarding coverage for expenses incurred in responding to an informal SEC investigation. Typically, D&O policies do not cover SEC investigations until the SEC issues a Formal Order of Investigation. Two cases drive home this point:

> *MBIA, Inc.*: In July 2011, the U.S. Court of Appeals for the Second Circuit affirmed that MBIA's D&O insurance policies covered the company's expenses incurred in responding to regulatory investigations by the SEC and the New York attorney general, which included fees paid to an independent auditor and expenses incurred by a special litigation committee that the company formed to respond to a related shareholder derivative action. The court noted that all of this activity occurred *after* the SEC instituted formal proceedings and thus triggered the definition of a "Securities Claim" under the policy.[76]
>
> *Office Depot*: In an unpublished opinion issued later that year, the U.S. Court of Appeals for the Eleventh Circuit held that Office Depot's D&O policy did not cover defense costs associated with an informal SEC investigation because coverage did not arise until the investigation became formal through the issuance of subpoenas or a Wells Notice.[77]

D&O insurance is explicitly available for SEC investigations, but it is expensive and to date has not been widely used.

SEC investigations often proceed simultaneously with related shareholder litigation, typically a class action lawsuit alleging violations of the federal securities laws. When they do, both defenses become inextricably intertwined. For instance, the document productions will overlap, and inadequate preparation of witnesses for SEC testimony can create an evidentiary record that could prejudice the defense of the shareholder litigation. In these circumstances, even if the policy does not cover the SEC investigation, at least some of the expenses related to the SEC investigation might be covered under policy language that defines a claim to include "costs, charges, and expenses incurred . . . *in connection with* any Claim," which generally includes shareholder litigation.

In purchasing D&O coverage, companies should pay special attention to the policy language regarding coverage for SEC investigations and shareholder actions. To negotiate policy language that will provide the desired coverage, companies often work with attorneys and brokers who specialize in D&O coverage.

TIP: Coverage questions can be complex. Even if, on the face of the policy, an SEC investigation does not appear to be covered, a company may have substantial arguments in favor of coverage. Thus, the company should engage an expert in D&O coverage issues to review its policies at the outset of the SEC investigation.

Q 31.9.1   What kinds of expenses related to an enforcement action might not be covered by a D&O policy?

D&O coverage may not extend to all of the relief that the SEC seeks in an enforcement action. For instance, many D&O policies do not cover penalties paid to the SEC or disgorgement of ill-gotten gains. Likewise, many policies exclude coverage for intentional misconduct, fraud, dishonest or criminal acts, or acts that were undertaken for personal profit. But, because these exclusions do not apply unless there has been a final adjudication by a finder of fact (i.e., a judge or jury), defense costs incurred before a final adjudication should be covered. However, if a settling party is required to admit wrongdoing under the SEC's admissions policy (*see* Q 31.31.1), such an admission may trigger the denial of D&O coverage in the SEC investigation or any related shareholder litigation.

Rescission of Coverage

Q 31.9.2   What other D&O policy issues/considerations are raised by SEC investigations?

The conduct underlying an SEC investigation can give rise to a risk that the company's D&O coverage may be rescinded. D&O policy applications often require the company's officers to make representations concerning their knowledge of wrongful acts. If the SEC's investigation uncovers evidence that the officer who signed the application committed (and, therefore, was aware of) wrongful acts that were not disclosed on the application, the carrier may have grounds to rescind the policy.

There is also a risk of rescission if the company restates its financial statements. Because the carrier is, in effect, underwriting the ability of the company to indemnify its directors and officers, the carrier may argue that it relied upon the company's financial statements (whether attached to the policy application or filed with the SEC before policy renewal) in determining whether to underwrite the risk. If the financials are restated, the carrier could argue that the original (but now admittedly incorrect) financial information was material to its underwriting decision, meaning that there was no "meeting of the minds" and, hence, no valid contract for insurance.

Q 31.9.3   How can a company mitigate the risks of rescission of the D&O policy?

Consider obtaining expert assistance to negotiate the policy with a view to minimizing these risks. Furthermore, under the cooperation clause of most D&O policies, carriers can demand that their insureds turn over information relating to the SEC investigation which potentially could give rise to grounds for rescission. Additionally, providing such information to the carrier could waive the attorney-client privilege or work-product immunity, potentially prejudicing the company's defense of the SEC investigation as well as any shareholder or derivative action. For these reasons, a company must walk a fine line between sufficiently cooperating with its carrier to maintain coverage and not handing the carrier grounds to rescind the policy or prejudicing its defenses to the underlying action.

The Process of an SEC Investigation

Q 31.10   How is an SEC investigation conducted?

Typically, SEC investigations follow a predictable course, in this order:

- document requests;
- witness testimony;
- Wells Notice and Wells Submission; and
- settlement negotiations.

Document requests. Most SEC investigations of public companies begin with a request for documents.[78] In an investigation of any consequence, the enforcement staff likely will make several sets of document requests.

Witness testimony. If the enforcement staff, after reviewing the company's document productions, continues to have an investigatory interest in the company, it will request sworn witness testimony.

Wells Notice and Wells Submission. After witness testimony has been completed, the enforcement staff will review the evidentiary record to determine whether to recommend that the Commission institute charges.[79] If the staff tentatively decides to make an enforcement recommendation to the Commission, in non-emergency cases it issues (typically by telephone and a follow-up letter) a so-called "Wells Notice" to the proposed defendant.[80] The proposed defendant is given an opportunity (typically, about three weeks) to respond with a "Wells Submission," which is a memorandum explaining its position (videotaped submissions are also permitted, but rarely made).

Settlement negotiations. If defense counsel does not succeed in convincing the staff through submission of the Wells Submission that no enforcement action is warranted, counsel typically will engage the staff in settlement discussions to determine whether the matter can be resolved on mutually agreeable terms.

Q 31.10.1   Has the SEC disclosed how it conducts its investigations?

On November 28, 2017, the SEC's Division of Enforcement publicly released a revised version of its *Enforcement Manual.*[81] The *Enforcement Manual* provides valuable insight into the SEC's investigatory process and is required reading for any attorney dealing with an SEC enforcement investigation. Among other things, the *Enforcement Manual* explains how the Enforcement Division:

- ranks investigations and allocates scarce enforcement resources;

- reviews the status of pending investigations;

- handles referrals from the public, the PCAOB, state regulators, Congress, and self-regulatory organizations such as the NYSE;

- opens and closes investigations; and

- obtains formal orders of investigations.

The *Enforcement Manual* also explains:

- the Wells Process;

- how the Commission considers enforcement recommendations;

- various investigative practices, including:

  - communications with senior SEC staff;

  - tolling agreements;

  - handling of parallel investigations;

  - document requests and subpoenas;

  - the requirement that settling parties confirm the completeness of document production;

  - procedures for taking testimony;

  - witness assurance letters, immunity orders, and proffer agreements;

  - attorney-client, work-product, and Fifth Amendment assertions;

  - inadvertent production or productions without privilege review;

  - requests for waiver of the attorney-client privilege; and

  - confidentiality agreements;

- informal referrals to federal or state criminal agencies or others including state bars.

Finally, the *Enforcement Manual* contains a detailed explanation of how the Enforcement Division will employ the analytic framework for individual cooperation and cooperation tools described above at QQ 31.7.1 to 31.7.8.

Document Requests

Obligation to Preserve Documents

Q 31.11   What are a company's obligations regarding documents?

After learning of a *potential* SEC investigation, a company's foremost obligation is to preserve, without alteration, *all* potentially relevant documents, in both hard copy and electronic formats. The company and its employees must ensure that no copies of relevant electronic files, including emails, word-processing and spreadsheet files, and backups, are destroyed or overwritten, even inadvertently. The company must preserve all documents within its custody or control including, for instance, documents in the custody of its outside professionals, such as legal counsel.

Q 31.11.1   Are there special considerations for preserving electronic documents?

Electronic documents are particularly problematic because they are easily altered or deleted, often through a company's routine electronic data retention policies. For example, a company might routinely delete emails of a certain age or recycle backup media, both of which destroy potentially relevant data.

In addition, often it is not obvious where relevant electronic documents may reside. Among the many possible places such documents might reside are:

- file, email, and voicemail servers;
- desktop computers, laptops, and tablets;
- cell phones;
- temporary storage devices (e.g., portable hard drives, USB flash drives); and
- backup media.

Q 31.11.2   What are the consequences of inadequate document preservation?

First, SOX provides for serious criminal penalties for document destruction that was intended to interfere with a governmental investigation. Section 802 of SOX provides for criminal penalties of up to twenty years' imprisonment for anyone who:

> knowingly alters, destroys, mutilates, conceals, covers up, falsifies, or makes a false entry in any record, document, or tangible object with the intent to impede, obstruct, or influence the investigation . . . of any matter within the jurisdiction of any department or agency of the United States. . . .[82]

Importantly, section 802 does not require that there be a pending investigation at the time of the conduct; a person can violate this section if he or she is aware of a *potential* governmental investigation. This prohibition applies to all persons; namely, companies, their employees, their directors, their legal counsel, their accountants, and other representatives. Section 802 of SOX also provides for fines of up to $10 million.

Entirely apart from these criminal sanctions, the SEC can impose significant monetary penalties on companies that do not preserve and timely produce relevant documents.

Accordingly, a senior company official (preferably the general counsel) should instruct its IT department to ensure that no potentially relevant electronic files, including backup media, are overwritten. These preservation efforts might well require alteration of the company's routine electronic data retention policies.[83] Similarly, company employees should be instructed to preserve all relevant electronic files, regardless whether they reside on their desktop or laptop computers, home computers, personal digital assistants, or temporary storage devices. Companies should also keep a record of all document preservation instructions and efforts, in case questions later arise about what was done to comply with the obligation to preserve documents.

Q 31.11.3   Should we preserve everything or only those documents we think the SEC will want produced?

Your document preservation efforts should be broad and inclusive. However, just because potentially relevant documents are being preserved does not mean they necessarily will be produced to the SEC. The company's SEC defense counsel will negotiate the scope of production with enforcement staff and will review the company's and its employees' documents for responsiveness and privilege before producing any documents to the SEC.

    CASE STUDY: *Lucent Technologies, Inc.*

Further underscoring the seriousness with which the SEC approaches this subject, in a May 17, 2004, settlement with Lucent Technologies, Inc., the SEC imposed a $25 million penalty for various acts of "non-cooperation," including incomplete document preservation and production in an enforcement proceeding.[84]

    CASE STUDY: *China-Based Associates of "Big Four" Accounting Firms*

In 2015, the SEC imposed $500,000 in penalties on four China-based accounting firms that had refused to turn over documents during the course of enforcement investigations.[85] The firms had registered with the U.S. Public Company Accounting Oversight Board, obligating them to produce documents to the SEC upon request. The SEC's Division of Enforcement served the four firms with requests for audit work papers and related documents. The firms responded by asserting that People's Republic of China law prevented them from producing documents directly to the Division of Enforcement. The SEC then commenced proceedings

---

against the firms pursuant to SEC Rule of Practice 102(e), under which the SEC has disciplinary authority against accounting firms that practice before it, charging that the firms had willfully refused to provide the SEC with work papers and related documents. The four firms eventually settled with the SEC, agreeing, among other things, to each pay a penalty of $500,000.

Document Requests and Production

Q 31.12   What can we expect during the document request process?

In SEC investigations, the enforcement staff routinely asks companies to produce a broad range of documents. The staff typically requests production of electronic data,[86] such as documents from the company's file and email servers, hard drives, and other storage media. It may even request that the company restore certain backup media. It is often possible to negotiate the scope and sequence of a document production with the enforcement staff.

At the beginning of the production, it can be difficult to accurately project a reasonable schedule for the document production because there are many difficult-to-estimate variables that must be taken into consideration, including the size of the document collection, the number of duplicates that will be eliminated, and the number of documents that will be responsive to key-word searches. If a company finds that it is falling behind its production schedule due to unforeseen circumstances, it is important to notify the enforcement staff to avoid appearing dilatory or uncooperative.

It is vital that the SEC staff regard the producing party as making a timely and complete production of all non-privileged, responsive documents.[87] In larger document productions, the staff usually prefers to get the production started early and that it be produced on a rolling basis. It is often easiest to begin the production with hard-copy documents.

The enforcement staff frequently will follow up its initial document requests with additional document requests directed to individual directors, officers, and third parties that it believes may have relevant information (for example, auditors and parties to transactions that are under review), as well as with supplemental requests to the company. The staff routinely requires company witnesses to testify to the completeness of the document production and their roles in the production process. Additionally, the staff frequently requires producing parties to certify the adequacy of their searches for documents and the completeness of their productions.

TIP: Given the importance of complete document preservation and production, it is sound practice to document the steps that the company and its counsel have taken to preserve and produce documents.

Q 31.13   Can we negotiate with the SEC about our document production?

Counsel should negotiate the scope, sequence, and timing of a document production with the enforcement staff. Particularly in the case of an electronic document production, counsel should have a firm grasp of where and how documents are stored, the likely relevance of documents in various data sources, and the costs and time required to produce those documents. Armed with those facts, counsel can press the staff for reasonable limits on the scope and timing of a document production.

Counsel should consider whether it is in the company's interest to agree with the staff on a production protocol that addresses which data sources and email accounts and folders will be produced,[88] which backup media will be restored, the search terms or other search methodology that will be used to screen the data for relevance, and the format in which the data must be delivered. Agreement on these parameters will reduce the likelihood that the staff will find the production inadequate, deeming the company to be "uncooperative" and forcing it to bear the expense of a costly supplementation of its electronic production.

On the other hand, counsel may conclude that it is unwise to allow the SEC to dictate which data sources should be reviewed and which search terms should be used. Counsel may feel that opening these subjects to negotiation may result in the company being required to engage in a more sweeping document production than it would otherwise have to make.

There is certainly no "one-size-fits-all" solution to this quandary. Counsel will be guided by many factors, including her perceptions of the seriousness of the investigation, the availability and relevance of various data sources, and the staff's attitude toward the company.

Q 31.14   What are the advantages of hiring an outside e-discovery vendor?

Because electronic data productions are complex, expensive, and time-consuming, an outside vendor that is expert in electronic discovery can provide invaluable assistance. The vendor can help the company identify and preserve relevant data sources, copy electronic data in a forensically sound manner (with no alteration of metadata), eliminate duplicates, search the remaining document collection by key words, run preliminary privilege screens, host the electronic document collection online, provide a web-based review tool to facilitate attorney review, and, finally, properly format the documents for production to the SEC.[89]

Additionally, most e-discovery vendors now provide some form of predictive coding. Predictive coding is a preliminary processing tool that is endorsed by an increasing number of courts[90] to find key documents electronically without requiring manual review, thus potentially saving the often significant expenses of attorney document review.

Selective Disclosure of Privileged Information in SEC Investigations

Q 31.15   Why is the question of selective disclosure in SEC investigations important?

The question of whether a company can "selectively disclose" privileged information to governmental authorities without waiving the privilege with respect to other parties has come to the fore in recent years, largely because of the confluence of two factors. SOX has put pressure on companies to uncover potential wrongdoing, resulting in an unprecedented number of internal investigations. At the same time, government enforcement authorities (such as the DOJ and SEC) have rewarded companies that "cooperate" by sharing their internal investigative findings. Indeed, in cases where the SEC has spared a company from any enforcement action, the company's cooperation included sharing the results of its internal investigation with its enforcement staff.[91]

Q 31.16   Can privileged information be selectively disclosed to the SEC without waiver?

The DOJ and SEC have supported selective disclosure through various means. They have entered into confidentiality agreements with the disclosing company that purport to maintain the privilege with respect to third parties; they have accepted disclosures in forms that do not leave paper trails (such as oral disclosures or opportunities to review documents, but not retain, copies of them); and they have supported the principle of selective disclosure in *amicus* briefs filed in private litigation.

The principle of selective disclosure garnered early support from the Eighth Circuit, which in 1978 held that the production of documents to the SEC did not result in a general waiver of the privilege despite the lack of a written confidentiality agreement.[92] Following this decision, several other courts of appeal indicated that they might apply the selective waiver principle where the producing party had entered a written confidentiality agreement with the government.[93]

However, by 2002, the Sixth Circuit described the law governing selective disclosure as being in a state of "hopeless confusion" and rejected the doctrine, refusing to limit waivers despite the existence of a written confidentiality agreement.[94] Since then, the trend has been decidedly against allowing companies to selectively disclose privileged information to government agencies without generally waiving privilege, even if there was a written confidentiality agreement in place.[95] In 2017, a federal magistrate judge held that a law firm waived work product protection for its witness interview memoranda after counsel provided oral summaries of the interviews to the SEC staff.[96]

CASE STUDY: *United States v. Reyes*[97]

In this particularly notable rejection of selective disclosure, the court rejected the principle even though confidentiality agreements were in place and the disclosing party did not produce any documents to the government, but limited its disclosures to oral briefings concerning witness interviews and investigative findings. The court noted that its rejection of the principle was "[i]n accord with every appellate court that has considered the issue in the last twenty-five years."[98]

Q 31.16.1   What is the outlook for selective disclosure?

Proponents of selective disclosure had hoped that the issue would be resolved by an amendment to the Federal Rules of Evidence. However, at its April 2007 meeting, the Advisory Committee on Evidence Rules to the U.S. Judicial Conference rejected an amendment to Rule 502 that would have protected selective disclosures to the government. The committee's report noted that the selective disclosure proposal was "very controversial" and "raised questions that were essentially political in nature."[99] Accordingly, the committee prepared language to assist Congress should it decide to proceed with legislation on selective disclosure, but refrained from recommending such an amendment to the Rules of Evidence. Rule 502, as adopted on

September 19, 2008, does not speak to the question of selective disclosure.

Q 31.16.2   Should we consider disclosing privileged information?

Given the current state of the case law, the absence of rules or legislation that resolve the issue, and the fact that most companies can be subject to litigation in almost any jurisdiction in the country, companies should assume that *any* disclosure of privileged information to the government—regardless of whether a confidentiality agreement is in place and regardless of the form of the disclosure—runs a severe risk of waiving the attorney-client privilege and work-product immunity.

Witness Testimony

SEC Requests for Testimony

Q 31.17   From whom is sworn testimony likely to be requested?

The SEC's enforcement staff likely will take sworn testimony from current and former employees, contractual counter-parties, and outside professionals, such as auditors. The staff often begin with lower-level employees who can explain the organizational structure, the availability and location of potentially relevant documents, and basic information concerning the transactions or other matters under investigation. The staff will then proceed up the corporate hierarchy, finishing with those witnesses whose actions can be imputed to the company and who themselves might be personally liable.

Q 31.17.1   Should witnesses speak informally with SEC enforcement staff?

SEC enforcement staff occasionally try to engage unrepresented witnesses, such as former employees, in substantive discussions early in the investigation, often by telephone. Witnesses should be wary of engaging in any such discussions. These conversations often take place before the witness understands what is at issue and has had an opportunity to refresh her memory. The witness also will not have the benefit of representation by defense counsel.

Unfortunately, a witness's ill-advised comments made at this preliminary stage are not "off the record." Typically, several SEC enforcement staff will participate in the conversation and will make detailed notes of the witness's statements, essentially locking in her testimony. Additionally, any inaccurate responses could later be interpreted as uncooperative conduct. Inaccurate responses, even though unsworn, might also expose the witness to criminal charges under 18 U.S.C. § 1001, which prohibits materially false statements to government officials.

> **TIP:** If SEC enforcement staff contact former employees and try to engage them in discussions, those former employees should politely but firmly make clear that they will need to consult with counsel before speaking with the staff.

Witness Examination

Q 31.18   How should we respond after a subpoena for sworn witness testimony has been issued?

Preparing a witness for sworn testimony is perhaps the most important aspect of defending an SEC investigation. Sworn testimony is often a witness's best opportunity to explain her (and the company's) side of the story to SEC enforcement staff. The testimony will factor significantly in the staff's formulation of a charging decision and will lock in the witness's testimony.

Before holding preparation sessions with the witness, defense counsel will review all relevant documents that were written or received by the witness or which might help refresh the witness's memory (if that is prudent). Experienced SEC defense counsel can anticipate the staff's lines of inquiry and can help the witness put herself and the company in the best possible light, offering testimony that is both credible and consistent with the documents and other testimony the staff is likely to hear.

Q 31.19   What can we expect when a witness testifies before the SEC?

Typically, several SEC enforcement staff participate in examining a witness. A staff attorney (the line-level investigator) usually leads the examination, with a supervisor and other enforcement staff (such as accountants) asking follow-up questions to ensure that a thorough record has been made. SEC investigative testimony is given under oath and on the record.[100]

Q 31.20   What rights do witnesses have?

Witnesses have the right to:

- obtain a copy of their transcript on payment of the appropriate fee (unless the Commission denies the request for good cause) and to inspect the official transcript of their own testimony;[101]

- see the formal order of investigation;[102] and

- be represented, accompanied, and advised by counsel.[103]

Witnesses should be aware that their sworn testimony is subject to both the penalty for perjury[104] as well as to the penalties for making false statements to the government.[105]

Q 31.20.1   Can a witness refuse to testify?

Witnesses have the right to refuse, under the Fifth Amendment to the U.S. Constitution, to give any information that may tend to incriminate her or subject her to a fine, penalty, or forfeiture. Witnesses should be aware, however, that the government will draw an "adverse inference" of wrongdoing from a refusal to testify, which will prejudice the witness's ability to defend against SEC civil charges.

Q 31.20.2 What are some important considerations in deciding whether or not to refuse to testify?

The decision as to whether a witness should testify in the SEC's civil investigation often comes down to a choice between the lesser of two evils. For example, a witness who is asked to testify in a civil proceeding may assert her Fifth Amendment rights to protect herself from criminal exposure, but doing so risks that the SEC will draw an adverse inference of wrongdoing from her refusal to testify. Conversely, testifying holds risks for the witness. The witness may not be able to satisfactorily explain her conduct, thereby further exposing her to both civil and criminal charges for the underlying substantive offense. Or the witness may make statements that—unbeknownst to her or her defense counsel—support a prosecutorial theory of which counsel is unaware. And, if the witness testifies inaccurately (even if due to a faulty memory or inadequate preparation, rather than an intent to mislead), she may be exposed to criminal perjury or obstruction of justice charges.

Q 31.20.3 What is a witness's counsel permitted to do during testimony?

Counsel may:

(1) advise the witness before, during, and after the conclusion of such examination;

(2) briefly ask clarifying questions of the witness at the conclusion of the examination; and

(3) make summary notes during the examination.[106]

Q 31.21 What other important considerations should we keep in mind regarding sworn testimony?

Because SEC investigations are fact-finding inquiries rather than evidentiary proceedings, the staff takes the view that it has greater latitude in examining the witness (particularly in calling for speculation and opinion) than would be permitted under the Federal Rules of Evidence.

While a company may wish to cooperate with the staff's investigation, allowing speculation and lay opinion to creep into the record creates risks. While such testimony may be inadmissible in court, it can be used to support the staff's charging recommendation to the Commission. SEC defense counsel can minimize the amount of such prejudicial testimony through proper witness preparation and representation during the testimony.

Representation by Counsel

Q 31.22   Should the same counsel represent the company and its employees?

A company will often want the same counsel to represent both it and its current and former employees, but there are risks.

Q 31.22.1   What are the advantages of using the same counsel?

In a corporate investigation of any complexity, it is expensive for counsel to become sufficiently familiar with the issues, relevant documents, and witness testimony to be able to competently represent a single employee in sworn testimony. It could be unduly costly if the company were required to obtain separate counsel for each of its present or former employee witnesses. For this reason, the company typically will offer, at its expense, to have its defense counsel (in its capacity as the company's counsel) represent its employee witnesses during their sworn testimony.

Multiple representations also have the advantage of making company counsel privy to the testimony of all commonly represented employees. Because SEC investigations are confidential, only the counsel who represented the witness in testimony can order a copy of the witness's transcript. If company counsel did not represent an employee during testimony, the staff usually will not allow company counsel to review that witness's testimony unless and until a Wells Notice (discussed at Q 31.25, *infra*) has been issued.

Q 31.22.2   Are there any limitations on using the same counsel?

Counsel may represent multiple witnesses in testimony provided that there are no actual or potential conflicts of interest among the company and each commonly represented employee witness.[107] The SEC's cooperation tools, however, may have an impact on multiple-representation scenarios. Unlike the white collar world, where it is rare for a criminal defense counsel to represent more than a single person, it has been common in SEC enforcement practice for a single defense lawyer to represent multiple witnesses, as long as no conflicts of interest between them existed. With the SEC's cooperation policies in effect, regardless of whether there are conflicts between witnesses, it may be in the interest of one client to be the first to report the misconduct to the SEC and offer cooperation. The SEC's cooperation program is bound to heighten the ethical concerns of defense counsel and may lead to fewer multiple representations. It also may have the unintended consequence of driving up the cost of SEC investigations to corporations that are responsible for indemnifying the defense costs of their employees. While the SEC will permit counsel, acting strictly in her capacity as company counsel, to represent present and former employees during their investigative testimony, the SEC typically advises witnesses at the beginning of their testimony that they have a right to be represented during their testimony by their own personal counsel.[108]

Joint Defense Agreements

Q 31.23   What if an employee decides to retain separate personal counsel?

In the event that a present or former employee retains personal counsel, the company might secure many of the informational advantages of a multiple representation through a joint defense agreement (JDA). Provided that the parties have a common interest in defending an SEC investigation, a JDA allows parties—even those who have potentially or actually conflicting interests—to share privileged communications and work product without fear of privilege waiver. Thus, through a JDA, company counsel can help a separately represented employee more efficiently prepare for her SEC testimony by sharing

work product with her counsel; company counsel can even participate in the preparation sessions. Likewise, through a JDA, company
counsel may learn the substance of the testimony of a separately represented witness.

Q 31.24   What are the opportunities for informal advocacy during the investigation?

During the investigation, SEC enforcement staff typically will not
share their concerns with counsel. Nevertheless, there are numerous
opportunities for informal advocacy during the course of the
investigation.

Near the outset of the investigation, company counsel may decide
to give the staff an overview of the matter, possibly even providing
the staff with key documents. A presentation must be accurate and
balanced if the company and its defense counsel are to have credibility with the staff. Such a presentation can demonstrate a company's
cooperation and, at the same time, present the company's views at an
early date to SEC decision-makers who are more senior than the line-
level investigators who will be responsible for the day-to-day conduct
of the investigation.[109]

As the investigation unfolds, counsel may find that the staff is
laboring under a misapprehension of law, fact, or expert knowledge
(for example, an arcane facet of Generally Accepted Accounting Principles). Counsel might find it advantageous to correct this misapprehension early in the investigation.

If, at the conclusion of the testimonial phase of the investigation,
SEC staff makes a preliminary determination to recommend charges
to the Commission, it will issue a Wells Notice (discussed at Q 31.25,
infra) to the proposed subject of such charges. On the other hand, if
the staff does not issue a Wells Notice, a company may hear nothing
about the status of the investigation for a long time, and can only
guess the staff's intentions.[110]

Typically, after the apparent close of testimony, a company will
simply await further contact from the staff. However, in cases where
the company believes that it has an especially strong position or where
it is concerned that lower-level staff might not accurately summarize

the investigatory record to their superiors, a company may consider providing more senior staff with its views on what the investigative record has established. This kind of "pre-Wells" submission must be approached cautiously, because the staff could re-open the record to fill any holes that the company has identified in the investigatory record.

Although a Wells Submission is the only opportunity for advocacy formally identified in the SEC's rules, experienced defense counsel will find ample opportunities during the investigative process to advance the client's views.

Wells Notice and Wells Submission

Wells Notice

Q 31.25   What is a Wells Notice?

A Wells Notice outlines the legal charges that the staff is prepared to recommend to the Commission and, sometimes, but only at a high level, the factual basis for those charges. Although not required by the SEC's rules, the staff will usually give the proposed subject of charges an opportunity to review all relevant testimony and exhibits. Under Dodd-Frank, not later than 180 days after the SEC staff provides a written Wells Notice to any person, the staff must either file an action against the person or provide notice to the Director of Enforcement of its intent not to file an action.[111]

In 2015, the U.S. Court of Appeals for the D.C. Circuit held that the 180-day rule did not act as a statute of limitations, and instead accepted the SEC's position that the provision was "intended to operate as an internal-timing directive, designed to compel [the] staff to complete investigations, examinations, and inspections in a timely manner."[112]

Wells Submission

Q 31.26   What is a Wells Submission?

A Wells Submission is an opportunity for the proposed defendant to explain its position via a memorandum (forty pages maximum) or (less commonly) videotape. A Wells Submission may argue that no enforcement action is warranted or that lower-level charges and less severe relief are appropriate; it may also argue in favor of a proposed settlement.[113] Because the SEC takes the position that Wells Submissions are admissible at trial (*see* Q 31.26.1, below), it is prudent to confine concessions and settlement offers to a separate settlement offer document, which will be an inadmissible settlement communication under Federal Rule of Evidence 408.

Q 31.26.1   Should a Wells Submission automatically follow a Wells Notice?

No. While Wells Submissions can be effective defense tools, they must be approached with care. The SEC warns that "[t]he staff of the Commission routinely seeks to introduce [Wells] submissions . . . as evidence in Commission enforcement proceedings."[114] Additionally, they may be discoverable in civil litigation with third parties.[115] The SEC generally refuses to accept Wells Submissions under claims of privilege or as settlement materials.

Charges, Forum, and Remedies

Q 31.27   What kind of charges can the SEC bring?

Broadly speaking, the SEC can bring two types of charges against a public company and its directors and officers: the SEC can charge the defendants either as primary violators (i.e., persons who directly commit the violation) or as secondary violators (i.e., persons who assist the primary violation of another person). The SEC's ability to pursue aiding-and-abetting charges was significantly enhanced by Dodd-Frank. Prior to Dodd-Frank, the SEC could only bring aiding-and-abetting charges under the Securities Exchange Act of 1934. Dodd-Frank allows the SEC to also bring aiding-and-abetting charges under both the Securities Act of 1933 and the Investment Company Act of 1940.[116] Dodd-Frank also made it easier for the SEC to prove aiding-and-abetting liability. Prior to Dodd-Frank, the SEC had to show that the defendant had "actual knowledge" that she was involved in improper activity; Dodd-Frank reduced this state of mind requirement to "knowingly or recklessly."[117] Dodd-Frank also made clear that the SEC has authority to charge "control persons" with liability,[118] enabling the SEC to charge corporate officers for their employees' violations.

The SEC can bring a wide variety of charges against a public company, ranging from scienter-based fraud charges under section 10(b) of the Exchange Act and section 17(a)(1) of the Securities Act (both of which require fraudulent intent or severely reckless conduct) to charges that do not require any intent, such as failures to maintain accurate books and records and delinquent SEC filing.[119]

Fraud charges. To sustain fraud charges against a public company, the SEC must show that the company, through its directors or officers, made material misrepresentations or omissions (for which there must be a duty to speak) in the company's public statements, such as its SEC filings (including its financial statements) and in its press releases. A financial fraud charge is significant not only because of its greater stigma, but because it also serves as the predicate for heavier penalties (discussed below) and other sanctions, including director and officer bars. The statute of limitations for an SEC claim for civil penalties is five years.[120] In 2017, a unanimous Supreme Court held that the five-year statute of limitations also applies to SEC claims for disgorgement.[121]

Violating the "books and records" and internal control provisions of the securities laws. These provisions require public companies to maintain accurate books and records and adequate internal control systems, and to file accurate periodic reports with the Commission. Unlike a financial fraud charge, these provisions generally do not require the SEC to prove that the company acted with bad intent or severe recklessness. When the SEC believes that it can prove financial fraud, it will invariably also charge books and records violations. However, where the evidence does not support a financial fraud charge, the SEC will limit the charges to books and records and internal control violations. The SEC is increasingly bringing stand-alone internal control cases—that is, cases in which the only violation charged is a lack of adequate internal controls.[122]

Q 31.28   Where can the SEC file an enforcement action?

The SEC can bring actions to enforce the federal securities laws both in federal court and in administrative cease-and-desist proceedings before its own administrative law judges (ALJs). Historically, however, the SEC could only impose civil money penalties in administrative proceedings against those persons who had voluntarily associated themselves with regulated entities such as brokerage firms, investment advisers, and investment companies (for example, mutual funds); the SEC could only obtain civil money penalties against public companies and their officers and directors through federal court proceedings.

In 2010, however, section 929(P) of Dodd-Frank authorized the SEC to impose civil money penalties in cease-and-desist proceedings against *all* persons, regardless of whether they were associated with a regulated entity. With this new authority, the Division of Enforcement began to bring an increasing percentage of its cases administratively. For instance, as recently as 2005, SEC federal court actions outnumbered administrative proceedings.[123] But in FY 2020, the SEC initiated 510 administrative proceedings, or 71% of all cases filed that year, but only 205 federal court actions.[124] Relatedly, 89% of the sixty-one cases the SEC initiated against public companies and related subsidiaries in FY 2020 were filed as administrative proceedings and only 11% were federal court actions, consistent with the 10% average over the last five fiscal years.[125]

It soon began to appear that the SEC enjoyed a "home court" advantage before its ALJs. For instance, from October 2010 through March 2015, the Division of Enforcement won 90% of its contested administrative cases, but only 69% of its contested federal court cases.[126] Recent academic scholarship, however, casts doubt on whether the SEC enjoys a "home court advantage" in its administrative proceedings. One study reports that between 2007 and 2015, there was no statistically significant difference between its success rate in administrative proceedings (89.8%) and in federal court (87.8%).[127]

Q 31.28.1 What are the differences between bringing an enforcement action in an administrative proceeding and bringing an enforcement action in federal court?

Although the SEC recently revised its procedural rules for its in-house administrative proceedings,[128] the rules still do not offer the same procedural safeguards to which defendants are entitled in federal court. The amendments provide, among other things, the following:

- SEC administrative hearings proceed along a much faster track than federal court trials—administrative hearings are held within ten months from initiation of the proceeding.

- Discovery is limited in SEC administrative hearings, with no depositions permitted in the simplest cases; in the most complex cases, only three depositions are allowed as of right per side if there is a single respondent, and only five depositions allowed as of right per side if there are multiple respondents.

- Hearsay evidence will be admitted if it is "relevant, material and bears satisfactory indicia of reliability so that its use is fair."

- Factual findings are made by the ALJ, eliminating any right to jury trial. Additionally, appeals are to the SEC, which usually affirms its ALJs; from there, appeals are to the federal courts of appeals, which apply *Chevron* deference to the SEC's interpretations of the securities laws.

SEC administrative proceedings disadvantage individual respondents in another way. Many SEC requirements, such as the books-and-records and internal control requirements, apply directly only to companies; individuals can only be charged as secondary actors with respect to such provisions. When the SEC charges an individual as a secondary actor in federal court, it must proceed on an aiding and abetting theory, which requires the SEC to prove intent or recklessness. However, the SEC can charge an individual as a secondary actor in an administrative proceeding under a "causing" theory for which mere negligence will suffice.

With the SEC's increased use of administrative proceedings, the perception that the SEC enjoys a "home court advantage" in such proceedings, and the procedural disadvantages of administrative proceedings to the defense, a number of litigants challenged the constitutionality of such proceedings. The challenge that gained the most traction contended that the SEC ALJs law judges are "inferior officers" who were not appointed by the president, the SEC commissioners, or a court as required by the Appointments Clause in Article II of the U.S. Constitution. In *Lucia v. SEC*,[129] the Supreme Court agreed, holding that SEC ALJs are "inferior officers" under the U.S. Constitution's Appointments Clause,[130] and, therefore, must be appointed by the President or the SEC itself (and not, as they had been, by SEC staff). The SEC has since reappointed its ALJs in compliance with the Appointments Clause and the SEC remanded approximately 200 cases previously before ALJs or on appeal to the SEC to different, properly appointed ALJs for reconsideration. In 2019, many of the matters were resolved without the need for a rehearing.[131]

Q 31.29 What remedies can the SEC obtain against a company?

Regardless of the nature of the charges it brings, the SEC may seek two kinds of relief against a public company:

(1) A federal court injunction or an administrative cease-and-desist order obligating the company to obey the law in the future.

(2) Two forms of monetary relief:

(a) Equitable disgorgement (including pre-judgment interest); and

(b) A civil money penalty.[132]

An order of equitable disgorgement requires a company to pay back any ill-gotten gains that it received as a result of its illegal conduct. Because it is usually difficult to quantify the company's receipt of ill-gotten gains in a financial reporting case, disgorgement usually is not a significant factor in these kinds of cases.[133] Civil money penalties, however, have become a much more prominent feature of financial reporting cases.

Q 31.29.1   How large are civil monetary penalties?

While the SEC was not in the habit of seeking large penalties against public companies in financial fraud cases in the past, this has changed. Until 2002, the SEC's largest penalty was for $10 million against Xerox Corp. Since then, SEC penalties have increased exponentially. For instance, in 2003 the SEC obtained $750 million in total relief against WorldCom.[134] The SEC has garnered well over 100 penalties for $10 million or more since SOX was enacted in 2002, including more than a dozen penalties of over $100 million each.[135] The largest monetary relief to date is $800 million against AIG, followed by VimpelCom at $795 million (jointly with the DOJ), followed by WorldCom at $750 million, then the $600 million in total relief the SEC obtained in 2013 against SAC Capital Advisors, followed by 2010's penalty against Goldman, Sachs & Co. for $550 million.[136]

The enforcement climate in the wake of the last decade of corporate scandals incentivized the SEC to obtain large penalties from public companies, in large part due to SOX. The "fair funds" provision of SOX (section 308(a)) allows the SEC to add any penalties that it collects to a disgorgement fund for the benefit of the "victims" of the violation.[137]

The securities laws provide a three-tiered penalty scheme, which is periodically increased to account for inflation. The tiers are set forth in Table 31-1.[138]

Because these penalties apply to each "violation" (which is not defined in the securities statutes), the enforcement staff has flexibility in arguing how many violations occurred; for instance, the staff can argue that every refiling or republication of a misstated financial statement constituted a separate violation.

TABLE 31-1

Monetary Penalties Against Corporations
for Securities Violations

Tier	Penalty per violation	When available
1	Not to exceed greater of gain to defendant* or **$97,523**	Any violation
2	Not to exceed greater of gain to defendant or **$487,616**	Violations involving fraud, deceit, manipulation, or deliberate or reckless disregard of a regulatory requirement
3	Not to exceed greater of gain to defendant or **$975,230**	Same as Tier 2 *and* when such violation directly or indirectly resulted in substantial losses or created a significant risk of substantial losses

* The gain measure applies only if the SEC sues in federal court.

Q 31.29.2   What factors does the SEC consider when deciding whether to assess a penalty on a company?

In January 2006, the SEC issued guidance regarding civil penalties against corporations. The SEC acknowledged that:

> The question of whether, and if so to what extent, to impose civil penalties against a corporation raises significant questions for our mission of investor protection. The authority to impose such penalties is relatively recent in the Commission's history, and the use of very large corporate penalties is more recent still. Recent cases have not produced a clear public view of when and how the Commission will use corporate penalties, and within the Commission itself a variety of views have heretofore been expressed, but not reconciled.[139]

After reviewing the legislative history of the Securities Enforcement Remedies and Penny Stock Reform Act of 1990, which gave the Commission authority generally to seek civil money penalties in enforcement cases, the SEC announced that the appropriateness of a penalty on a corporation turns principally on two considerations:

(1) *The presence or absence of a direct benefit to the corporation as a result of the violation.* The SEC explained that "the strongest case for the imposition of a corporate penalty is one in which the shareholders of the corporation have received an improper benefit as a result of the violation; the weakest case is one in which the current shareholders of the corporation are the principal victims of the securities law violation."[140]

(2) *The degree to which the penalty will recompense or further harm the injured shareholders.* The SEC explained that "[t]he presence of an opportunity to use the penalty as a meaningful source of compensation to injured shareholders is a factor in support of its imposition. The likelihood a corporate penalty will unfairly injure investors, the corporation, or third parties weighs against its use as a sanction."[141]

In its statement, the SEC identified the following additional factors that are properly considered in determining whether to impose a penalty on a corporation:

COMPLIANCE FACT

Since passage of the "fair funds" provision, the SEC has obtained a number of settlements in financial fraud cases that dwarf all prior civil monetary penalties. In 2020, the SEC's enforcement cases resulted in a total of more than $4.68billion in disgorgement and penalties.[142]

The total monetary relief of some of the biggest settlements include:

AIG: $800 million in disgorgement and penalties, which they agreed in 2006 to pay and which will be returned to investors through a "fair fund."

VimpelCom: $795 million (jointly with DOJ)

WorldCom: $750 million

SAC Capital Advisors: $600 million

Goldman Sachs: $550 million

Fannie Mae: $350 million penalty as well as an additional $50 million to the Office of Federal Housing Enterprise Oversight, with whom the SEC jointly brought the case.

- the need to deter the particular type of offense;

- the extent of the injury to innocent parties;

- whether complicity in the violation is widespread throughout the corporation;

- the level of intent on the part of the perpetrators;

- the degree of difficulty in detecting the particular type of offense;

- presence or lack of remedial steps by the corporation; and

- extent of cooperation with Commission or other law enforcement.[143]

 CASE STUDY: *SAC Capital Advisors, LP*

In March 2013, the SEC settled an insider trading case against an affiliate of SAC Capital Advisors, LP, hedge fund advisory firm CR Intrinsic Investors, in which the firm agreed to pay more than $600 million ($275 million penalty, $275 million disgorgement, and $51.8 million in interest). The SEC initially brought charges in November 2012 against the firm for allegations that one of its portfolio managers, Matthew Martoma, illegally obtained information regarding a confidential clinical trial for an Alzheimer's drug being jointly developed by two pharmaceutical companies.[144]

As Sanjay Wadhwa, Senior Associate Director of the SEC's New York Regional Office, stated:

> A robust culture of compliance and zero tolerance toward employee misconduct can help other firms avoid the severe financial consequences that CR Intrinsic is facing for its misconduct.[145]

Q 31.29.3　Does the SEC ever seek other remedies?

While the SEC is statutorily authorized to seek only the foregoing remedies against public companies, it frequently seeks other relief as a condition of settlement. For instance, the SEC may require a company to retain and follow the recommendations of an independent consultant charged with reviewing its accounting policies and procedures and internal control systems. The SEC will sometimes accept such undertakings in mitigation of the civil money penalty that it would otherwise require.

Q 31.30　What remedies can the SEC seek against directors and officers?

The SEC can seek both injunctive and monetary relief against individual corporate actors, including directors and officers.[146]

Q 31.30.1　What monetary penalties can the SEC seek against directors and officers?

The penalty amounts applicable to individuals are considerably lower than those against corporations. The tiers are as follows:[147]

TABLE 31-2

Monetary Penalties Against Individuals for Securities Violations

Tier	Penalty per violation	When available
1	Not to exceed greater of gain to defendant* or **$9,753**	Any violation
2	Not to exceed greater of gain to defendant or **$97,523**	Violations involving fraud, deceit, manipulation, or deliberate or reckless disregard of a regulatory requirement
3	Not to exceed greater of gain to defendant or **$195,047**	Same as Tier 2 *and* when such violation directly or indirectly resulted in substantial losses or created a significant risk of substantial losses
* The gain measure applies only if the SEC sues in federal court.		

The largest civil penalty the SEC has obtained against an individual is $92.8 million against Galleon Management LP hedge fund manager Raj Rajaratnam for insider trading,[148] followed by $67.5 million against former Countrywide Financial CEO Angelo Mozilo.[149] Mozilo was also barred for life from serving as a director or officer of a public company.

Q 31.30.2   What other kinds of relief can the SEC seek against directors and officers?

Where an individual has violated section 10(b) of the Exchange Act or any of the rules thereunder, the SEC can bar the individual (temporarily or permanently) from serving as a director or officer of a public company (a "D&O bar"). Prior to SOX, D&O bars were used sparingly in only the most egregious cases. However, section 305 of SOX reduced the standard for imposing D&O bars from "substantially unfit" to serve as a director or officer of a public company to merely "unfit." Additionally, while the SEC previously could seek a D&O bar only in a federal court proceeding, section 1105 of SOX empowers the SEC to impose this remedy in an administrative cease-and-desist proceeding. In a February 11, 2004, speech, the SEC's then-Director of Enforcement warned, "[Y]ou can expect us to continue to use this remedy aggressively."[150] In FY 2020, the SEC obtained 475 D&O bars against individuals.[151]

Under section 304 of SOX, if a company is required to restate its financials as a result of "misconduct," the CEO and CFO can be required to reimburse the company for (1) all bonuses and incentive- or equity-based compensation the officer received during the year following issuance of the restated document and (2) any profits from the sale of the issuer's securities during that year. Under section 304, the CEO and CFO need not have personally engaged in any misconduct to be liable; rather, the misconduct may be committed by lower level employees. In 2009, the SEC first used SOX section 304 to "claw back" compensation from an executive not charged with any violation of the securities laws.[152] Because section 304 applies to incentive- based compensation, it does not apply to a CEO's or CFO's salary.

Under section 1103 of SOX, the SEC is authorized during the course of an investigation to seek a forty-five-day freeze (which may be extended to ninety days) of any "extraordinary payments (whether compensation or otherwise)" to any of the company's directors, officers, partners, controlling persons, agents, or employees. If such an order is entered, the company is required to escrow those payments into an interest-bearing account. If the company or person is charged with a securities violation, the freeze remains in effect during the pendency of that proceeding.

Finally, if the subject of an investigation is a CPA who "appeared or practiced before the Commission" (for example, prepared or signed the company's SEC filings), the individual could be subject to a proceeding under SEC Rule of Procedure 102(e) to censure the individual or deny her, temporarily or permanently, the privilege of appearing or practicing before the Commission. In egregious circumstances, Rule 102(e) proceedings have been brought against attorneys.

Settlement Negotiations

Q 31.31   How does the SEC approach settlements?

A party can discuss settlement with the enforcement staff at almost any time, including during the fact-gathering stage, in connection with or following a Wells Submission, and even after an enforcement action has been commenced.

While the staff does not have independent authority to accept a settlement, settlement offers that do not have staff support are rarely accepted by the Commission.

A settlement reached prior to the commencement of an enforcement action often results in a reduction of the charges or relief that the staff would otherwise seek, whereas the range of compromise available after commencement of an enforcement action is usually more limited.

The SEC routinely issues press releases when it brings and settles enforcement actions. Thus, when a matter is settled before an enforcement action is commenced, there is a single press event. When a matter is settled post-commencement, there are two press events: first, when the enforcement action is brought; and second, when it is settled.

Q 31.31.1   Is a party that settles with the SEC required to admit liability?

Historically, the SEC's policy has been to allow a party to settle with the SEC without admitting or denying the SEC's allegations. Under this long-standing policy, when a party settles a federal injunctive action, neither the court nor the SEC makes any factual finding. The SEC files a complaint making its allegations, and the court enters a final judgment enjoining the defendant from future violations and usually ordering other relief (such as disgorgement and penalties), but makes no factual findings. However, when a party settles an SEC administrative action, the settling party (albeit without admitting or denying the SEC's charges) allows the SEC to make certain factual findings and conclusions of law. In "no admit/no deny" settlements, the settling party is prohibited from publicly denying the SEC's charges, but is permitted to defend itself in litigation with parties other than the SEC.[153]

Faced with criticisms that the SEC's "no admit/no deny" policy was too lenient and failed to impose accountability on settling parties, the SEC changed its policy to require certain settling parties to admit liability in order to settle with the SEC. In January 2012, former Director of Enforcement Khuzami announced that a party that admits guilt in order to resolve a parallel criminal prosecution, including non-prosecution agreements or deferred prosecution agreements that include admissions or acknowledgments of criminal conduct, must admit liability in any SEC settlement. Former SEC Chair White announced a further change in the SEC's settlement policy in June 2013 to require certain settling parties to admit wrongdoing even if there has been no admission of guilt in a related criminal proceeding. The types of cases that might have required such an admission of wrongdoing included those where:

(a) a large number of investors were harmed, or the market or investors were placed at risk of serious harm;

(b) obtaining an admission of wrongdoing would serve a protective purpose, such as where the settling party engaged in egregious intentional misconduct; or

(c) the settling party unlawfully obstructed the SEC's investigative process.[154]

From FY 2010 through FY 2017, the SEC obtained admissions in ninety-six stand-alone settlements.[155] However, under former Chairman Jay Clayton, the SEC returned to its historic no admit/no deny policy.[156] Time will tell how the SEC treats admissions under new Chair Gary Gensler.

Notes to Chapter 31

1. *See* Securities Act of 1933 (Securities Act) §§ 19, 20, 15 U.S.C. §§ 77s, 77t; Securities Exchange Act of 1934 (Exchange Act) § 21, 15 U.S.C. § 78u. Violations of the federal securities laws may also constitute criminal offenses. *See* Securities Act § 24, 15 U.S.C. § 77x; Exchange Act § 32(a), 15 U.S.C. § 78ff. However, the SEC does not have statutory authority to bring criminal prosecutions; all criminal prosecutions for federal securities offenses are handled by the U.S. Department of Justice ("DOJ"). *See* Securities Act § 20(b), 15 U.S.C. § 77t(b); Exchange Act § 21(d), 15 U.S.C. § 78u(d).

2. The SEC's civil enforcement jurisdiction extends beyond public companies to any person or entity that violates the federal securities laws. For example, the SEC has authority to enforce the securities antifraud rules against all issuers of securities, including private companies, partnerships, and individuals. The term "security" encompasses far more than stock; it also includes mutual funds, variable annuities, promissory notes, and investment contracts. Similarly, the SEC may and does enforce the nation's securities laws against individuals, such as persons who engage in insider trading.

3. *See, e.g.*, Exchange Act § 21(a), 15 U.S.C. § 78u(a) ("The Commission may, in its discretion, make such investigations as it deems necessary to determine whether any person has violated, is violating, or is about to violate any provision of this chapter.").

4. If, following a financial restatement, the company experiences a drop in its stock price, it can also expect to become the target of a securities class action and, possibly, a shareholder derivative suit. Accordingly, companies planning to restate their financial statements often retain experienced securities class action and SEC enforcement defense counsel to manage the restatement process to minimize such exposures.

5. *See* U.S. SEC. & EXCH. COMM'N, FISCAL YEAR 2020 AGENCY FINANCIAL REPORT 145 (Nov. 12, 2020), https://www.sec.gov/files/sec-2020-agency-financial-report-_1.pdf.

6. In FY 2020, the SEC brought thirty-three insider trading cases against fifty-nine parties; this was 8% of the SEC's enforcement caseload. The SEC continues to use its proprietary analytic tools to conduct sophisticated data analysis to identify and pursue insider trading cases. U.S. SEC. & EXCH. COMM'N, DIVISION OF ENFORCEMENT 2020 ANNUAL REPORT 29 (Nov. 2, 2020), https://www.sec.gov/files/enforcement-annual-report-2020.pdf.

7. Pub. L. No. 107-204, §§ 302, 906, 116 Stat. 745.

8. Jay Clayton, Chairman, U.S. Sec. & Exch. Comm'n, Opening Remarks at the Securities Regulation Institute (Jan. 22, 2018), https://www.sec.gov/news/speech/speech-clayton-012218.

9.   *See* U.S. SEC. & EXCH. COMM'N, FY 2022 CONGRESSIONAL BUDGET JUSTIFICATION, FY 2022 ANNUAL PERFORMANCE PLAN, at 14 [hereinafter SEC 2022 CONGRESSIONAL BUDGET JUSTIFICATION], https://www.sec.gov/files/FY%202022%20Congressional%20 Budget%20Justification%20Annual%20Performance%20Plan_FINAL.pdf.

10.   *Id.* at 12.

11.   Press Release No. 2010-5, U.S. Sec. & Exch. Comm'n, SEC Names New Specialized Unit Chiefs and Head of New Office of Market Intelligence (Jan. 13, 2010), www.sec.gov/news/press/2010/2010-5.htm.

12.   Press Release No. 2017-176, U.S. Sec. & Exch. Comm'n, SEC Announces Enforcement Initiatives to Combat Cyber-Based Threats and Protect Retail Investors (Sept. 25, 2017), https://www.sec.gov/news/press-release/2017-176.

13.   Report of Investigation Pursuant to Section 21(a) of the Securities Exchange Act of 1934: The DAO (July 25, 2017), https://www.sec.gov/litigation/ investreport/34-81207.pdf.

14.   SEC Spotlight on Cyber Enforcement Actions, https://www.sec.gov/spot light/cybersecurity-enforcement-actions.

15.   SEC Halts Alleged $1.7 Billion Unregistered Digital Token Offering (Oct. 11, 2019), https://www.sec.gov/news/press-release/2019-212.

16.   SEC Charges Founder, Digital-Asset Issuer With Fraudulent ICO (Dec. 11, 2019), https://www.sec.gov/news/press-release/2019-259.

17.   Press Release, U.S. Sec. & Exch. Comm'n, ICO Issuer Settles SEC Registration Charges, Agrees to Return Funds and Register Tokens As Securities (Feb. 19, 2020), https://www.sec.gov/news/press-release/2020-37.

18.   Press Release, U.S. Sec. & Exch. Comm'n, SEC Charges Blockchain Lending Company in Connection with Unregistered ICO (Sept. 30, 2020), https:// www.sec.gov/enforce/33-10865-s.

19.   Internal SEC referrals most often come from the Division of Corporation Finance (which reviews corporate disclosures), the Division of Trading and Markets (which regulates major market participants such as broker-dealers, self-regulatory organizations and transfer agents), the Division of Investment Management (which regulates investment companies such as mutual funds, closed-end funds, UITs, ETFs, and interval funds, as well as variable insurance products and federally registered investment advisers), and the Office of Compliance Inspections and Examinations (OCIE) (which conducts examinations of registered entities, including self-regulatory organizations, broker-dealers, transfer agents, investment companies and investment advisers).

20.   U.S. SEC. & EXCH. COMM'N, FY 2020 CONGRESSIONAL BUDGET JUSTIFICATION 128 (Mar. 2019), https://www.sec.gov/files/secfy20congbudgjust_0.pdf.

21.   Press Release No. 2020-226, U.S. Sec. & Exch. Comm'n, SEC Charges Companies, Former Executives as Part of Risk-Based Initiative (Sept. 28, 2020), https://www.sec.gov/news/press-release/2020-226.

22.   *See* U.S. SEC. & EXCH. COMM'N, WHISTLEBLOWER PROGRAM 2020 ANNUAL REPORT TO CONGRESS, at 2 (Nov. 16, 2020), https://www.sec.gov/files/2020%20Annual% 20Report_0.pdf.

23. *Id.* at 27.

24. *Id.* at 2.

25. Press Release No. 2020-266, U.S. Sec. & Exch. Comm'n, SEC Issues Record $114 Million Whistleblower Award (Oct. 22, 2020), https://www.sec.gov/news/press-release/2020-266.

26. Press Release No. 2020-126, U.S. Sec. & Exch. Comm'n, SEC Awards Record Payout of Nearly $50 Million to Whistleblower (June 4, 2020), https://www.sec.gov/news/press-release/2020-126.

27. *See* U.S. SEC. & EXCH. COMM'N, DIVISION OF ENFORCEMENT 2020 ANNUAL REPORT 16-17 (Nov. 2, 2020), https://www.sec.gov/files/enforcement-annual-report-2020.pdf.

28. U.S. SEC. & EXCH. COMM'N, AGENCY FINANCIAL REPORT: FISCAL YEAR 2016, at 24–25 (Nov. 14, 2016), https://www.sec.gov/about/secpar/secafr2016.pdf.

29. Michael S. Piwowar, Comm'r, U.S. Sec. & Exch. Comm'n, Remarks at the 2018 RegTech Data Summit—Old Fields, New Corn: Innovation in Technology and Law (Mar. 7, 2018), https://www.sec.gov/news/speech/piwowar-old-fields-new-corn-innovation-technology-law.

30. Jay Clayton, Chairman, U.S. Sec. & Exch. Comm'n, Keynote Remarks at the Mid-Atlantic Regional Conference (June 4, 2019), https://www.sec.gov/news/speech/clayton-keynote-mid-atlantic-regional-conference-2019.

31. *Id.*

32. Persons or entities regulated by the SEC, such as broker-dealer firms and investment advisers, however, must respond to preliminary requests for information.

33. *See* Exchange Act § 21(b), 15 U.S.C. § 78u(b); 17 C.F.R. § 202.5(a).

34. 17 C.F.R. § 200.30-4(a)(13).

35. *Id.* § 200.30-4(a)(10).

36. *Id.* § 203.7(a).

37. *See* U.S. SEC. & EXCH. COMM'N, DIVISION OF ENFORCEMENT 2020 ANNUAL REPORT 16-17 (Nov. 2, 2020), https://www.sec.gov/files/enforcement-annual-report-2020.pdf.

38. *Id.* at 7.

39. *Id.* at 6.

40. *Id.*

41. SEC 2022 CONGRESSIONAL BUDGET JUSTIFICATION, *supra* note 9, at 108.

42. Testimony of Chairman Jay Clayton before the U.S. Senate Cmte. on Banking, Housing, and Urban Affairs (Dec. 10, 2019), https://www.banking.senate.gov/imo/media/doc/Clayton%20Testimony%2012-10-191.pdf.

43. Exchange Act Release No. 44,969 (Oct. 23, 2001), www.sec.gov/litigation/investreport/34-44969.htm.

44. Stephen M. Cutler, Dir., Div. of Enforcement, U.S. Sec. & Exch. Comm'n, Remarks Before the 24th Annual Ray Garrett, Jr. Corporate & Securities Law Institute (Apr. 29, 2004), www.sec.gov/news/speech/spch042904smc.htm.

45. Press Release No. 2006-4, Statement of the Securities and Exchange Commission Concerning Financial Penalties, U.S. Sec. & Exch. Comm'n (Jan. 4, 2006), www.sec.gov/news/press/2006-4.htm. This statement discusses what factors the SEC will consider in connection with imposing a penalty on a company.

46. Steven Peikin, Co-Dir., Div. of Enforcement, U.S. Sec. & Exch. Comm'n, "Remedies and Relief in SEC Enforcement Actions" (Oct. 3, 2018), https://www.sec.gov/news/speech/speech-peikin-100318.

47. Steven Peikin, Co-Dir., Div. of Enforcement, U.S. Sec. & Exch. Comm'n, Keynote Address at the New York City Bar Association's 7th Annual White Collar Crime Institute (May 9, 2018), https://www.sec.gov/news/speech/speech-peikin-050918.

48. Similarly, in its April 11, 2002, settlement with Xerox Corporation, the SEC imposed a $10 million penalty, noting that "[t]he penalty . . . reflects, in part, a sanction for the company's lack of full cooperation in the investigation." Press Release No. 2002-52, U.S. Sec. & Exch. Comm'n (Apr. 11, 2002), www.sec.gov/news/headlines/xeroxsettles.htm.

49. Exchange Act Release No. 44,969 (Oct. 23, 2001).

50. *See* Administrative Proceeding File No. 3-17535, SEC Charges Former Information Technology Executive with FCPA Violations; Former Employer Not Charged Due to Cooperation with SEC (Sept. 12, 2016), www.sec.gov/litigation/admin/2016/34-78825.pdf.

51. 17 C.F.R. § 202.12.

52. Robert Khuzami, Dir., Div. of Enforcement, U.S. Sec. & Exch. Comm'n, Remarks at SEC Press Conference (Jan. 13, 2010).

53. SEC, DIV. OF ENFORCEMENT, ENFORCEMENT MANUAL (2017) [hereinafter SEC ENFORCEMENT MANUAL], www.sec.gov/divisions/enforce/enforcementmanual.pdf; *see also* Spotlight on Enforcement Cooperation Program, https://www.sec.gov/spotlight/enforcement-cooperation-initiative.shtml.

54. Andrew Ceresney, Dir., Div. of Enforcement, U.S. Sec. & Exch. Comm'n, The SEC's Cooperation Program: Reflections on Five Years of Experience (May 13, 2015), https://www.sec.gov/news/speech/sec-cooperation-program.html.

55. *See* Press Release No. 2015-38, U.S. Sec. & Exch. Comm'n, SEC Charges Goodyear with FCPA Violations (Feb. 24, 2015), www.sec.gov/news/pressrelease/2015-38.html.

56. *See* Press Release No. 2016-109, U.S. Sec. & Exch. Comm'n, SEC Announces Two Non-Prosecution Agreements in FCPA Cases (June 7, 2016), www.sec.gov/news/pressrelease/2016-109.html.

57. *Id.*

58. *Id.*

59. Indeed, the standard form that the SEC provides to every individual and entity from whom it seeks either documents or testimony (Form 1662: "Supplemental Information for Persons Requested to Supply Information Voluntarily or Directed to Supply Information Pursuant to a Commission Subpoena") warns that "[t]here is a likelihood that information supplied by you will be made available to such agencies [federal and state prosecutors] where appropriate." The form goes

on to list twenty-three categories of routine uses that the SEC might make of the supplied information. *See also* 17 C.F.R. § 240.24c-1 (2006) ("[t]he Commission may, in its discretion and upon a showing that such information is needed, provide nonpublic information in its possession to any of the following persons if the person receiving such nonpublic information provides such assurances of confidentiality as the Commission deems appropriate . . . federal, state, local or foreign government[s] or any political subdivision, authority, agency or instrumentality of such government. . . ."). The securities statutes expressly authorize the SEC to share investigative information with the DOJ. *See* 15 U.S.C. §§ 77t(b), 78u(d)(1).

60. *See* SEC 2022 CONGRESSIONAL BUDGET JUSTIFICATION, *supra* note 9, at 93.

61. *See* Press Release No. 2011-276, U.S. Sec. & Exch. Comm'n, SEC Charges GE Funding Capital Market Services with Fraud Involving Municipal Bond Proceeds (Dec. 23, 2011), www.sec.gov/news/press/2011/2011-276.htm.

62. *Id.*

63. Press Release No. 2014-220, U.S. Sec. & Exch. Comm'n, SEC Charges Bank of America with Securities Laws Violations in Connection with Regulatory Capital Overstatements (Sept. 29, 2014), www.sec.gov/News/PressRelease/Detail/Press Release/1370543065483.

64. Press Release No. 2014-61, U.S. Sec. & Exch. Comm'n, SEC Charges Two Men with Insider Trading on Confidential Information from Their Wives (Mar. 31, 2014), www.sec.gov/News/PressRelease/Detail/PressRelease/1370541344904.

65. *See* Amended Complaint, SEC v. Galleon Mgmt. LP, 2009 WL 4837219 (S.D.N.Y. filed Nov. 5, 2009). The use of wiretaps in insider trading prosecutions was sanctioned by the U.S. Court of Appeals for the Second Circuit in its June 2013 opinion affirming Raj Rajaratnam's conviction. *See* United States v. Rajaratnam, 719 F.3d 139 (2d Cir. 2013).

66. *See* SEC v. Rajaratnam, 622 F.3d 159, 165 (2d Cir. 2010). Former Director of Enforcement Robert Khuzami made clear in a 2009 speech that the SEC will continue to embrace a prosecutorial mindset and use wiretap evidence as a useful tool in future enforcement actions involving insider trading. "The use of [wiretaps] underscores the view that large scale insider trading by industry professionals is as serious as organized crime, extortion and similar misconduct where wiretaps commonly are used. Persons involved in illegal insider trading schemes now must rightly consider whether their conversations are under surveillance." *See* Robert Khuzami, Dir., Div. of Enforcement, U.S. Sec. & Exch. Comm'n, Remarks at AICPA National Conference on Current SEC and PCAOB Developments (Dec. 8, 2009), www.sec.gov/news/speech/2009/spch120809rsk.htm.

67. In a 2006 *amicus curiae* brief to the U.S. Court of Appeals for the Ninth Circuit, the SEC advised, "When defendant Stringer's attorney asked whether the SEC was working in conjunction with the U.S. Attorney's Office of any jurisdiction, he was correctly advised that the SEC's policy was not to comment on such issues, but to direct the witness to inquire of the U.S. Attorney's Office if he chose to." Brief of the Securities and Exchange Commission, *Amicus Curiae*, in Support of Appellant's Brief Seeking Reversal and Remand, United States v. Stringer, 2006 WL 3225567 (9th Cir. Sept. 13, 2006).

31–65

68. *See* Q 31.20.2 (discussing one such issue: the decision as to whether or not a witness should testify in a civil investigation).

69. *See, e.g.*, United States v. Kordel, 397 U.S. 1 (1970) (there is no departure from the proper administration of justice where the defendant had to choose between either asserting Fifth Amendment rights or answering interrogatories, the responses to which were later used to convict him); SEC v. First Fin. Grp. of Tex., Inc., 659 F.2d 660, 666–67 (5th Cir. 1981) ("'There is no general federal constitutional, statutory, or common law rule barring the simultaneous prosecution of separate civil and criminal actions by different federal agencies against the same defendant involving the same transactions. . . . The simultaneous prosecution of civil and criminal actions is generally unobjectionable because the federal government is entitled to vindicate the different interests promoted by different regulatory provisions even though it attempts to vindicate several interests simultaneously in different forums.'"); SEC v. Dresser Indus., Inc., 628 F.2d 1368 (D.C. Cir. 1980) (holding that courts should not intervene in parallel investigations unless the nature of the proceedings prejudices substantial rights).

70. United States v. Parrott, 248 F. Supp. 196, 202 (D.D.C. 1965).

71. United States v. Stringer, 535 F.3d 929 (9th Cir. 2008). The Ninth Circuit's opinion expressly overruled United States v. Stringer, 408 F. Supp. 2d 1083 (D. Or. 2006), and rejected the reasoning of United States v. Scrushy, 366 F. Supp. 2d 1134, 1140 (N.D. Ala. 2005), two lower court cases that had sharply criticized the government's conduct in conducting surreptitious parallel criminal investigations.

72. Judge Rakoff of the Southern District of New York has termed the practice of the government initiating civil charges with the intent to stay those charges in favor of a parallel criminal proceeding as "a misuse of the processes" of the judicial system. *See* SEC v. Oakford Corp., 181 F.R.D. 269, 273 (S.D.N.Y. 1998); *see also* SEC v. Kornman, 2006 WL 1506954, at *4 (N.D. Tex. May 31, 2006) (following denial of motion to stay SEC civil action, SEC moved for voluntary dismissal without prejudice; court granted dismissal motion but allowed defendant to conduct requested discovery finding that requested dismissal was "an attempt to circumvent" the denial of the stay motion); SEC v. Yuen, No. 03-4376, slip op. at 5, 11–13 (C.D. Cal. Oct. 2, 2003) (denied motion to stay, in part, because government had chosen to bring both proceedings simultaneously); SEC v. Poirier, No. 97-3478, slip op. at 5 (N.D. Ga. Feb. 13, 1998) (same); SEC v. Tucker, 130 F.R.D. 461, 463 (S.D. Fla. 1990) (same).

73. SEC v. Saad, 229 F.R.D. 90, 91 (S.D.N.Y. 2005).

74. *See, e.g.*, Nat'l Stock Exch. v. Fed. Ins. Co., 2007 WL 1030293 (N.D. Ill. Mar. 30, 2007) (finding coverage for defense costs of officers from date of SEC's issuance of formal order of investigation to company).

75. A company might consider requesting that the SEC proceed by formal process to trigger its D&O coverage. Of course, the desire for D&O coverage must be balanced against the concern that formal investigations may be more likely to result in enforcement action because they have received attention both at high levels within the Enforcement Division, as well as from the Commission.

76. *See* MBIA, Inc. v. Fed. Ins. Co., 652 F.3d 152 (2d Cir. 2011).

77. *See* Office Depot, Inc. v. Nat'l Union Fire Ins. Co., 453 F. App'x 871 (11th Cir. 2011).

78. Occasionally, the SEC's initial contact with a company will be a request for an explanation of certain events, such as a financial restatement. The company's response could be in the form of either a written submission or a personal meeting. It is critical that counsel thoroughly prepare the company's response to ensure that its representations will withstand further investigative scrutiny. If the company's initial representations are discredited, both the company and its counsel will have credibility problems with the enforcement staff, which will make the investigation more protracted and costly.

79. The SEC has five commissioners who are appointed by the President for five-year terms.

80. *See* 17 C.F.R. § 202.5(c).

81. *See* SEC ENFORCEMENT MANUAL, *supra* note 53.

82. 18 U.S.C. § 1519. Similarly, section 1102 of SOX makes it punishable by up to twenty years' imprisonment to "corruptly" alter, destroy, mutilate, or conceal a record to impair its integrity or availability for use in an official proceeding. 18 U.S.C. § 1512.

83. See chapter 5 for a full discussion of records management programs and policies.

84. Litigation Release No. 18,715 (May 17, 2004), www.sec.gov/litigation/litreleases/lr18715.htm. The SEC also made substantive allegations against Lucent in this matter.

85. *See* Press Release No. 2015-25, U.S. Sec. & Exch. Comm'n, SEC Imposes Sanctions Against China-Based Members of Big Four Accounting Networks for Refusing to Produce Documents (Feb. 6, 2015), www.sec.gov/news/pressrelease/2015-25.html.

86. See chapter 7 for an extensive discussion of e-discovery.

87. While a company may choose to disclose certain privileged documents to SEC staff in the interest of cooperating with the investigation, as discussed in Q 31.15 *et seq.*, the case law has become increasingly hostile to selective disclosures, holding that a disclosure to the SEC waives the attorney-client privilege with respect to all third parties.

88. One of the most efficient methods for managing e-discovery costs is to confine the number of sources, or custodians, to only those key individuals that are likely to have relevant electronic information.

89. The SEC's technical data delivery standards are constantly evolving. If the staff does not include its current data standards in its request for an electronic production, the responding party should request them.

90. *See, e.g., In re* Biomet M2a Magnum Hip Implant Prods. Liab. Litig., 2013 WL 1729682 (N.D. Ind. Apr. 18, 2013); Nat'l Day Labor Org. Network v. ICE, 877 F. Supp. 2d 87 (S.D.N.Y. 2012); Glob. Aerospace, Inc. v. Landow Aviation, L.P., No. CL-61040, slip op. (Va. Cir. Ct. Apr. 23, 2012); Da Silva Moore v. Publicis Groupe, 287 F.R.D. 182 (S.D.N.Y. Feb. 24, 2012).

91. The SEC's then-Enforcement Director stated on May 4, 2007, however, that the SEC does not request waivers of the attorney-client privilege:

> First, we do not—indeed we cannot—require waiver of the attorney/client privilege. Second, waiver of a privilege or protection is not a pre-requisite to obtaining credit in a Commission investigation. The credit given is based on, among other things, the factual information given, the timeliness of the provision of information and the usefulness of the information. Waivers may be, and often are, a means to that end but are not an end in and of themselves.

Linda Chatman Thomsen, Dir., Div. of Enforcement, U.S. Sec. & Exch. Comm'n, Remarks Before the 27th Annual Ray Garrett, Jr. Corporate and Securities Law Institute (May 4, 2007), www.sec.gov/news/speech/2007/spch050407lct.htm. Indeed, the *SEC Enforcement Manual* expressly directs that *"[t]he staff should not ask a party to waive the attorney-client or work product privileges and is directed not to do so."* SEC ENFORCEMENT MANUAL § 4.3. Nonetheless, it remains to be seen whether any company that does not share the work product of its internal investigation will get a complete pass from any enforcement action.

92. *See* Diversified Indus., Inc. v. Meredith, 572 F.2d 596, 611 (8th Cir. 1978) (en banc).

93. *See, e.g., In re* Sealed Case, 676 F.2d 793, 824 (D.C. Cir. 1982); *In re* Steinhardt Partners, L.P., 9 F.3d 230, 236 (2d Cir. 1993); United States v. Billmyer, 57 F.3d 31, 37 (1st Cir. 1995); Dellwood Farms, Inc. v. Cargill, Inc., 128 F.3d 1122, 1127 (7th Cir. 1997); *In re* Keeper of Records, 348 F.3d 16, 28 (1st Cir. 2003).

94. *See In re* Columbia/HCA Healthcare Corp. Billing Practices Litig., 293 F.3d 289, 294–95 (6th Cir. 2002).

95. *See, e.g., In re* Qwest Commc'ns Int'l, Inc. Sec. Litig., 450 F.3d 1179 (10th Cir. 2006) (declining to allow selective disclosure even where a confidentiality agreement is in place); McKesson HBOC, Inc. v. Superior Court, 9 Cal. Rptr. 3d 812 (Ct. App. 2004) (rejecting selective disclosure under California law); McKesson Corp. v. Green, 597 S.E. 2d 447, 454 (Ga. Ct. App. 2004) (rejecting selective disclosure under Georgia law); United States v. Bergonzi, 216 F.R.D. 487, 498 (N.D. Cal. 2003) (rejecting selective disclosure under federal common law). *But see* Aronson v. McKesson HBOC, Inc., 2005 WL 934331, at *10 (N.D. Cal. May 31, 2005) (allowing selective disclosure under federal common law where there was a written confidentiality agreement); Saito v. McKesson HBOC, Inc., 2002 WL 31657622, at *15 (Del. Ch. Nov. 13, 2002) (same).

96. Order on Defendants' Motion to Compel Production from Non-Party Law Firm, SEC v. Herrera, No. 17-20301 (S.D. Fla. Dec. 5, 2017), https://static.reuters.com/resources/media/editorial/20171207/secvherrera–waiveropinion.pdf.

97. United States v. Reyes, 239 F.R.D. 591 (N.D. Cal. 2006).

98. *Id.* at 603.

99. Report of the Advisory Committee on Evidence Rules (May 15, 2006), www.uscourts.gov/file/14810/download.

100. *See* 17 C.F.R. § 203.6.

101. *Id.*

102. *Id.* § 203.7(a).

103. *Id.* § 203.7(b).

104. 18 U.S.C. § 1621.

105. *Id.* § 1001.

106. 17 C.F.R. § 203.7(c).

107. Sometimes conflicts (or simply the advisability of having personal counsel) do not emerge until after the witness testifies or until after the SEC staff issues a Wells Notice advising of its preliminary charging recommendation. For this reason, certain witnesses may obtain personal counsel after testifying.

108. Indeed, SEC Form 1662, shown to every witness at the start of testimony, warns that multiple representations present a potential conflict of interest if one client's interests are or may be adverse to another's.

109. While testimony typically is not attended by senior staff, overview presentations frequently will be attended by an Assistant Director or higher.

110. If the staff reaches a firm conclusion that it will not recommend enforcement charges, it has the discretion to advise the party that the investigation has been terminated. *See* 17 C.F.R. § 202.5(d). It is a matter of Enforcement Division policy to issue such letters, but its practice is not uniform. When they come at all, closing letters typically come long after (often more than a year) the conclusion of witness testimony.

111. Dodd-Frank Wall Street Reform and Consumer Protection Act of 2010 (Dodd-Frank), Pub. L. No. 111-203, § 929U, 124 Stat. 1326. Certain complex actions may be extended 180 days with the approval of the Director of Enforcement and notice to the Chairman of the Commission; a further 180-day extension may be granted by the Chairman.

112. Montford & Co. v. SEC, 793 F.3d 76 (D.C. Cir. 2015).

113. *See* Mitchell E. Herr, *SEC Enforcement: A Better Wells Process*, 32 SEC. REG. L.J. 1, 56 (Spring 2004), www.hklaw.com/content/whitepapers/SECEnforcement ABetterWells.pdf.

114. *See* SEC Form 1662. On the other hand, the SEC's then Chief Administrative Law Judge held that Wells Submissions are inadmissible as protected settlement materials under Rule 408 of the Federal Rules of Evidence. *See In re* Allied Stores Corp., 52 SEC Docket 451, 451–52 (1992).

115. *See In re* Initial Pub. Offering Sec. Litig., 2003 U.S. Dist. LEXIS 23102 (S.D.N.Y. Dec. 24, 2003).

116. Dodd-Frank § 929M.

117. *Id.* §§ 929M, 929O.

118. *Id.* § 929P(c).

119. Although less commonly invoked, the SEC may also charge non-scienter fraud under Securities Act § 17(a)(2) and (3), 15 U.S.C. § 77a(a)(2), (3), for merely negligent conduct.

120. *See* Gabelli v. SEC, 133 S. Ct. 1216, 1224 (2013) (rejecting the so-called discovery rule and holding that the clock begins running when the fraud occurred, not when it was or should have been discovered).

121. Kokesh v. SEC, 137 S. Ct. 1635 (2017) (applying the five-year statute to SEC claims for civil penalties and disgorgement).

122. *See, e.g., In re* JDA Software Grp., Inc., Exchange Act Rel. No. 73,209 (Sept. 25, 2014) (stand-alone internal control charges settled for $750,000); *In re* Stein Mart, Inc., Exchange Act Rel. No. 75,958 (Sept. 22, 2015) (stand-alone internal control charges settled for $800,000); *In re* Idle Media, Inc. & Marcus Frasier, Exchange Act Rel. No. 75,963 (Sept. 22, 2015) (stand-alone internal control charges settled for $50,000).

123. Steinway, *SEC "Monetary Penalties Speak Very Loudly," But What Do They Say? A Critical Analysis of the SEC's New Enforcement Approach*, 124 YALE L.J. 1 (Oct. 2014).

124. *See* SEC 2022 CONGRESSIONAL BUDGET JUSTIFICATION, *supra* note 9, at 23.

125. Cornerstone Research, SEC Enforcement Activity: Public Companies and Subsidiaries, Fiscal Year 2020 Update 6, https://www.cornerstone.com/Publica tions/Reports/SEC-Enforcement-Activity-FY-2020-Update.

126. *See* Jean Eaglesham, *SEC Trims Use of In-House Judges*, WALL ST. J., Oct. 11, 2015.

127. Urska Velikonja, *Are the SEC's Administrative Law Judges Biased? An Empirical Investigation*, 92 WASH. L. REV. 315, 356 (2017).

128. *See* Amendments to the Commission's Rules of Practice, Release No. 34-78319 (July 13, 2016).

129. Lucia v. SEC, 138 S. Ct. 2044 (2018).

130. U.S. CONST. art. II, § 2, cl. 2.

131. U.S. SEC. & EXCH. COMM'N, DIVISION OF ENFORCEMENT 2019 ANNUAL REPORT 21 (Nov. 6, 2019), https://www.sec.gov/files/enforcement-annual-report-2019.pdf.

132. Dodd-Frank authorizes the SEC to impose monetary penalties in administrative cease-and-desist proceedings. *Id.* § 929P(a). This significantly enhances the SEC's enforcement options, because administrative proceedings are faster than federal court actions and do not allow for the expansive discovery available in federal district court.

133. In a footnote in the *Kokesh* decision, the Supreme Court explained that it was not deciding whether the SEC is authorized to obtain disgorgement. Kokesh v. SEC, 137 S. Ct. 1642 n.3 (2017). The Court took up that issue in November 2019, however, when it granted certiorari in an enforcement action in which a defendant was ordered to pay disgorgement as part of a final judgment entered by the district court. Liu v. SEC, 140 S. Ct. 451 (2019). In June 2020, the Supreme Court issued an 8-1 opinion, holding that the SEC could obtain disgorgement as a form of equitable relief in an amount not to exceed the wrongdoer's illicit profits, after deducting "legitimate expenses", and that the returned money must flow back to harmed investors, to the extent possible. Liu v. SEC, 140 S. Ct. 1936, 1950 (2020).

134. *See* SEC v. Worldcom, Inc., 273 F. Supp. 2d 431, 435–36 (S.D.N.Y. 2003).

135. *See Top 10 SEC Settlements*, NERA ECONOMIC CONSULTING, www.securitieslitigationtrends.com/top10.asp.

136. *Id.*

137. The SEC has distributed these amounts of Fair Funds: FY 2013, $251 million, FY 2014, $424 million, FY 2015, $158 million, FY 2016, $140 million, FY 2017, $1.073 billion, FY 2018, $794 million, FY 2019, $1.197 billion, FY 2020 $602 million. *See* SEC 2020 CONGRESSIONAL BUDGET JUSTIFICATION, at 126; U.S. SEC. & EXCH. COMM'N, DIVISION OF ENFORCEMENT 2020 ANNUAL REPORT 18 (Nov. 2, 2020), https://www.sec.gov/files/enforcement-annual-report-2020.pdf.

138. 17 C.F.R. § 201.1005; *see also* https://www.sec.gov/enforce/civil-penalties-inflation-adjustments.htm.

139. Press Release No. 2006-4, U.S. Sec. & Exch. Comm'n, Statement of the Securities and Exchange Commission Concerning Penalties, www.sec.gov/news/press/2006-4.htm.

140. *Id.*

141. *Id.*

142. *See* U.S. SEC. & EXCH. COMM'N, DIVISION OF ENFORCEMENT 2020 ANNUAL REPORT 16-17 (Nov. 2, 2020), https://www.sec.gov/files/enforcement-annual-report-2020.pdf.

143. *See* Press Release No. 2006-4, *supra* note 139.

144. *See* Press Release No. 2013-41, U.S. Sec. & Exch. Comm'n, CR Intrinsic Agrees to Pay More Than $600 Million in Largest-Ever Settlement for Insider Trading Case (Mar. 15, 2013), www.sec.gov/News/PressRelease/Detail/PressRelease/1365171513308#.UfnmpRaG6-I.

145. *Id.*

146. A director or officer cannot be held liable merely as a result of his or her position. To be held liable as a principal, the director or officer must have personally acted with the requisite scienter (i.e., state of mind). Similarly, a director or officer cannot be held liable as a "control person" if he or she acted in good faith and did not directly or indirectly induce the violation.

147. 17 C.F.R. § 201.1005; *see also* https://www.sec.gov/enforce/civil-penalties-inflation-adjustments.htm.

148. *See* Press Release No. 2011-233, U.S. Sec. & Exch. Comm'n, SEC Obtains Record $92.8 Million Penalty Against Raj Rajaratnam (Nov. 8, 2011), www.sec.gov/news/press/2011/2011-233.htm. In the parallel criminal prosecution, Rajaratnam was convicted on fourteen counts of securities fraud, sentenced to eleven years in prison and ordered to pay $63.8 million in forfeiture and fines. *Id.*

149. *See* Press Release No. 2010-197, U.S. Sec. & Exch. Comm'n, Former Countrywide CEO Angelo Mozilo to Pay SEC's Largest-Ever Financial Penalty Against a Public Company's Senior Executive (Oct. 15, 2010), www.sec.gov/news/press/2010/2010-197.htm.

150. Stephen M. Cutler, Dir., Div. of Enforcement, U.S. Sec. & Exch. Comm'n, Remarks Before the District of Columbia Bar Association (Feb. 11, 2004), www.sec.gov/news/speech/spch021104smc.htm.

151. *See* U.S. SEC. & EXCH. COMM'N, DIVISION OF ENFORCEMENT 2020 ANNUAL REPORT 7 (Nov. 2, 2020), https://www.sec.gov/files/enforcement-annual-report-2020.pdf..

152. *See* Complaint for Violations of Section 304 of the Sarbanes-Oxley Act of 2002, SEC v. Jenkins, 2009 WL 2350797 (D. Ariz. July 22, 2009) (No. CV 09-1510-PHX-JWS).

153. 17 C.F.R. § 202.5(e).

154. These types of cases were reportedly identified in an internal email dated June 17, 2013, from former Co-Directors of Enforcement Canellos and Ceresney and distributed to Enforcement Staff. *See, e.g.*, Dina ElBoghdady, *SEC to Require Admissions of Guilt in Some Settlements*, WASH. POST (June 18, 2013), www.washingtonpost.com/business/economy/sec-to-require-admissions-of-guilt-in-some-settlements/2013/06/18/9eff620c-d87c-11e2-a9f2-42ee3912ae0e_story. html; Marc Fagel, *The U.S. Securities and Exchange Commission's Troubling New Policy Requiring Admissions*, BLOOMBERG BNA (June 30, 2013), www.bna.com/us-securities-exchange-n17179875550/.

155. *See* VERITY WINSHIP & JENNIFER K. ROBBENNOLT, AN EMPIRICAL STUDY OF ADMISSIONS IN SEC SETTLEMENTS, 60:1 ARIZ. L. REV. 15 (2018), www.arizonalawreview.org/pdf/60-1/60arizlrev1.pdf.

156. During an October 2017 panel discussion, former Co-Director of Enforcement Steven Peikin indicated that the Division may pull back from requiring admissions. *See* Dave Michaels, *SEC Signals Pullback from Prosecutorial Approach to Enforcement*, WALL ST. J. (Oct. 26, 2017), https://www.wsj.com/articles/sec-signals-pullback-from-prosecutorial-approach-to-enforcement-1509055200.

32

Directors and Officers Liability Insurance

Thomas H. Bentz, Jr.

Directors and officers operate under closer scrutiny today than ever before. Extreme volatility in the stock market, a suffering economy, COVID-19 related concerns, and alleged and real corporate scandals have encouraged an active plaintiffs' bar. These realities, combined with increased governmental regulation, have put the actions of directors and officers under a microscope.

Faced with the real and ever-increasing risk of significant litigation judgments, defense costs and damage to their reputations, many directors and officers have begun to focus on how to best protect their personal assets, careers, and livelihoods in the event of a serious claim. For many, this has meant a fresh look at their directors and officers (D&O) liability insurance.

D&O insurance is often the last line of defense for the personal assets of a director or officer. As such, directors and officers cannot leave to chance whether this multimillion-dollar asset will protect them if their company fails to provide advancement or indemnification. Directors and officers who assume that they are protected just because their company has D&O insurance may find out the hard way that their protection is inadequate.

Fortunately, there are a number of D&O insurance policies available, and D&O insurance policies are highly negotiable. Although a D&O insurance policy cannot protect against every risk, a comprehensive and properly negotiated D&O policy can help significantly reduce the chance that a director or officer will suffer severe personal loss. By taking the time to negotiate improvements to the D&O policies and ensuring that the coverage is appropriate for the insured's risk profile, directors and officers can greatly improve the chances that their policy will protect them when they need it most.

This chapter is intended to provide a basic understanding of the complexities of D&O insurance and to offer some tips to help insureds obtain the strongest possible protection. As described in more detail below, D&O insurance policies vary widely, with dramatic differences in coverage. As a result, the information below cannot and should not replace consultation with an experienced D&O insurance broker *and* an insurance attorney specializing in D&O insurance policy reviews.

Overview: D&O Liability Insurance As a Risk-Transfer Device

Q 32.1   Where does D&O insurance fit with other liability protections?

D&O insurance provides coverage for directors and officers who are alleged to have breached their fiduciary duties to the company that they serve. While D&O insurance is important for protecting the personal assets of directors and officers, it is often an individual insured's last line of defense. For most directors and officers, statutory protections, corporate charters/bylaws, and/or individual indemnification agreements will provide the first line of defense. Only if these protections fail would a director or officer need to turn to his or her D&O insurance policy for protection.

To be fully protected, individual directors and officers need all of these protections to work together. Corporate indemnification and D&O insurance should complement each other: In some situations, indemnification rights will protect the insured persons (for example, if the company's insurance limit has been exhausted or if an exclusion applies); in other situations, D&O insurance will provide the protection (for example, if the company is insolvent, if there is a derivative claim, or if there is a legal principle that prohibits the company from indemnifying the individual). While indemnification rights and D&O insurance both play key roles in protecting directors and officers, neither provides complete coverage on its own.

State Indemnification Statutes

Q 32.1.1   What statutory protections exist for D&O liability?

For most companies, state law governs indemnification, granting corporations the authority to indemnify and limiting the circumstances in which they may do so. As an example, Delaware law states that, subject to certain restrictions,

> a corporation shall have power to indemnify any person who was or is a party or is threatened to be made a party to any threatened, pending or completed action, suit or proceeding, whether civil, criminal, administrative or investigative (other than an action by

or in the right of the corporation) by reason of the fact that the person is or was a director, officer, employee or agent of the corporation, . . . against expenses (including attorneys' fees), judgments, fines and amounts paid in settlement.[1]

FIGURE 32-1

Hierarchy of Liability Protection

Statutory Protection

⇩

Corporate Bylaws

⇩

Individual Indemnification Agreements

⇩

Traditional D&O Insurance

It is important to note that this provision *does not* require companies to indemnify their directors; it merely gives them the power to do so. In fact, Delaware law requires companies to indemnify their directors only when the director has been successful in a proceeding and only when the losses they are reimbursing are attorney fees and expenses.[2]

Indemnification statutes such as the one described above are often viewed as insufficient for several reasons. The Delaware statute, like many others, leaves the determination of whether a director or officer should be indemnified in most situations to a majority vote of non-interested directors, a majority vote of the shareholders, or the opinion of independent, outside legal counsel. Obtaining any of these can be difficult due to political pressures, changes in management, etc. Likewise, most state statutes do not require the company to advance defense costs prior to the resolution of the litigation. This can force a director or officer to front such costs for months or even years. Given the ever-rising cost of defense, this could place quite a burden on an individual director or officer and could negatively impact the director's or officer's ability to mount a proper defense.

Corporate Charters/Bylaws

Q 32.1.2   How do corporate charters/bylaws typically provide protection for D&O liability?

To ameliorate the insufficiencies of a permissive indemnification statute, many companies include mandatory indemnification or advancement provisions in their bylaws or other governing documents. Unfortunately, these provisions often do nothing more than track the language of the governing state statute or simply set forth that the company shall indemnify its directors and officers "to the fullest extent allowed by law." While better than silence, such provisions do not offer directors and officers the protection they need in today's market. For example, simply stating that the company will indemnify a director or officer "to the fullest extent permitted by law" is insufficient because this language does not necessarily include the right to advancement of defense costs and because the company may change or delete this protection from the bylaws in the future. The latter is exactly what happened in *Schoon v. Troy Corp.*

 CASE STUDY: *Schoon v. Troy Corp.*[3]

In *Schoon*, the Troy Corporation changed its bylaws to eliminate advancement of defense costs to former directors. One such former director was then sued and sought advancement. The Delaware Chancery Court held that the company had the right to amend its bylaws and eliminate the right to the advancement up until the point that there was an actual claim brought against the director. Since the claim came after the amendment to the bylaws, the company was free to amend its bylaws as it saw fit. As a result, the former director was left without the protection he thought he had under the bylaws that were effective when he served the company. *Schoon* was overturned by the Delaware General Assembly. H.B. 19, 145th Del. Gen. Assem. (2009). The new law, which became effective on August 1, 2009, addresses both advancement and indemnification and provides that once the act or omission that is the subject of the action for which a corporate official seeks advancement or indemnification has occurred, the right to advancement or indemnification cannot be eliminated or "impaired," unless the provision granting the right explicitly permitted otherwise. Keep in mind, however, that this legislative change only affects companies incorporated in Delaware.

Q 32.1.3   What kinds of indemnification provisions should a company's bylaws include?

Instead of boilerplate provisions, directors and officers should insist that their bylaws provide broad protection that cannot be altered in the future except as required by law. For example, such provisions should:

- mandate indemnification (instead of simply allowing it);

- mandate advancement of defense costs on a current basis;

- state that indemnification will be provided to the fullest extent permitted by law;

- provide that the right to indemnification and advancement is a contractual right that cannot be amended in the future;

- provide strong disincentives for the board to vote against indemnification if a state statute permits it; and

- include protections if the director or officer invokes their Fifth Amendment rights as part of the defense strategy.

To illustrate the benefits of such detailed provisions, consider the issue of advancement of defense costs during a lawsuit. Advancement provides the funds a director or officer needs to retain legal counsel and to vigorously defend against a lawsuit. An advancement provision not only should require such advancement but also should specify a time frame within which the company must respond after receiving a reimbursement request. Without a set time frame, a company may delay advancement for months or even years. This delay could prove devastating. Insureds could find themselves waging a war on two fronts: in the courtroom defending a securities class action lawsuit or a criminal charge and in the boardroom seeking defense cost advancement. An insured can avoid this bind if the insured entity's bylaws provide that defense costs shall be advanced on a current basis, or within sixty days of receipt of a reimbursement request and without the director or officer having to provide information or evidence that may jeopardize a legal privilege.

Individual Indemnification Agreements

Q 32.1.4   How do individual indemnification agreements protect directors and officers?

Amending a company's bylaws or other governing documents can be a difficult task. In addition, some companies are reluctant to insert the level of detail necessary to provide optimal indemnification rights in their bylaws and/or are reluctant to provide such broad advancement and indemnification rights to all directors and officers. In these situations, an individual indemnification agreement may be appropriate. Like D&O insurance policies, indemnification agreements come in many shapes and sizes. They can be as simple as a one-page document stating that the company shall indemnify its directors and officers to the fullest extent permitted by law, or fifteen or more pages detailing substantive and procedural rights to indemnification.

The specificity of a well-drafted indemnification agreement can provide answers and peace of mind. It can also allow directors or officers to determine whether or not serving on the board of a particular company is worth the potential risks.

D&O Insurance

Q 32.1.5   How does D&O insurance protect directors and officers?

Even the broadest state statutes, corporate bylaws, and indemnification agreements cannot provide absolute protection. For example, even where there is a broad indemnification agreement in place, if the company lacks sufficient funds, it cannot extend the protection. Even if sufficient funds are available, a company may simply refuse to provide an innocent director or officer with contracted-for protection for reasons of public or shareholder relations or to show cooperation with prosecutors. Similarly, a bylaw provision will not prevent funds from being frozen by a court during a bankruptcy proceeding. A strong D&O insurance program, however, can help fill in these and other potential gaps.

A D&O policy can also respond to the following:

- Claims arising out of the Securities Act of 1933. The Securities and Exchange Commission takes the position that indemnification for liabilities arising under the Securities Act of 1933 is against public policy and therefore unenforceable but that such claims are insurable; or

- A derivative claim against the directors or officers. Many statutes prohibit indemnification in derivative claims but will allow a D&O insurance policy to respond.

In addition, because the D&O insurance policy is a contract, it cannot be unilaterally altered once the parties are bound.

In short, although it is often the last line of defense for directors and officers, D&O insurance is a critical component in any comprehensive plan of executive protection.

How Typical D&O Insurance Policies Work

Scope of Coverage

Q 32.2   What type of coverage do D&O insurance policies typically offer?

The insuring agreements are the heart of the D&O policy, setting forth the basic scope of the coverage provided. Typically, D&O insurance policies provide three main types of coverage set forth in three distinct insuring agreements:

- Non-indemnifiable (or "Side A") coverage, which protects directors and officers when the company may not indemnify its directors or officers by law or for public policy reasons or cannot indemnify its directors or officers due to financial insolvency;

- Corporate reimbursement (or "Side B") coverage, which protects the company by reimbursing the company for amounts it pays to its directors and officers as indemnification and advancement; and

- Entity protection (or "Side C") coverage, which protects the company for its own wrongful acts—Side C coverage is typically limited to securities actions in public company D&O insurance policies, but may provide broader protection in private company and nonprofit company policies.

In addition to these three main areas of protection, some D&O insurance policies include agreements covering other risks and exposures:

- employment practices liability coverage;
- crisis coverage;
- derivative investigation coverage;
- employed lawyers' coverage;
- first-dollar e-discovery consultant services;
- personal reputation coverage;
- asset protection coverage;
- coverage for U.K. Corporate Manslaughter Act defense costs;
- extradition costs;
- cyber liability coverage; and
- Sarbanes-Oxley Act section 304 costs.

Q 32.2.1   What are the advantages and disadvantages of Side A, B, and C coverage?

Until the mid-1990s, D&O insurance typically only provided Side A and Side B coverage (that is, there was no coverage provided for any direct liability of the company). This changed because the vast majority of the lawsuits included allegations against the company as well as the directors and officers. The lack of entity coverage typically resulted in an argument between the insurer and the insured about how to properly allocate the defense costs and other liability between the covered individual insureds and the uncovered corporate entity. Insurers added entity coverage in an attempt to solve this problem.

However, the addition of entity coverage created different issues. For example, it allowed company losses to dilute the protection offered to the directors and officers. Although most claims are paid under either the Side B or Side C coverage, having Side B and Side C coverage can have some real disadvantages from the perspective of the directors and officers. Chief among the disadvantages is that covered company losses can erode or exhaust the limit of the policy, leaving the directors and officers underinsured or completely uninsured. This risk has become more severe as settlements and judgments against companies have increased in size. The increasing popularity of partial settlements and opt-outs has also exacerbated this problem (for example, those left out of an early settlement may not have sufficient policy limits to cover the remaining claims).

Another shortcoming in a traditional side A, B, and C D&O insurance policy is that it may be considered an asset of the company for bankruptcy purposes (*see* Q 32.38 *et seq.*). In that event, the bankruptcy court could freeze the policy limits during the bankruptcy proceeding forcing the directors and officers to pay their own defense costs during what could be a multi-year lawsuit. Worse yet, the bankruptcy court could make the limits of a traditional D&O insurance policy available to creditors. Either way, this could leave individual directors and officers without insurance protection when they need it most.

To help avoid the shortcomings of the traditional D&O insurance policy, insurers developed the dedicated-limit policy, discussed in further detail below (*see* Q 32.11 *et seq.*).

Q 32.3   Who is insured?

D&O insurance policies typically cover the directors and officers of the company, the company itself, and the company's subsidiaries. However, many policies go well beyond this to include individuals serving outside entity organizations, a debtor-in-possession in a bankruptcy context, or other high-profile individuals such as the general counsel or risk manager. Some policies will also insure employees of the company generally.

A broad definition of "insured" can increase the likelihood that the policy will respond in the event of a claim—however, it also dilutes the protection for key individuals, since those individuals share the protection with everyone included in the broad definition. Thus, a company must balance the desire to have a broad definition with the desire to ensure adequate protection for key individuals.

D&O insurance policies also typically cover claims against a spouse, estate, heir, legal representative, or assign of any individual insured provided that the claim is made solely as a result of such spouse's, estate's, heir's, legal representative's, or assign's status. Many D&O insurance policies extend similar coverage to domestic partners. This coverage extension typically does not extend to a claim against such persons for their own wrongful acts unrelated to the business of the corporate insured.

Q 32.4   What constitutes a claim?

A pivotal term in a D&O insurance policy is "claim." In order to trigger coverage, a claim must have been made against an insured. What constitutes a claim is generally defined by the D&O policy itself; however, the definition of a claim varies significantly between different D&O policies, while some D&O policies do not define the term at all. What is important to remember is that a claim is not limited to a lawsuit. It can include a written demand for monetary or other relief; a civil, criminal or administrative proceeding or investigation; or even a written notice that an investigation has or may be commenced against an insured person.

Negotiating the definition of a claim is discussed at Q 32.16. Reporting claims and defending claims are discussed in further detail at Q 32.16 *et seq.*

Q 32.5   What qualifies as a "wrongful act"?

Most D&O policies define a "wrongful act" broadly to include any breach of duty, neglect, error, misstatement, misleading statement, omission, or act by an insured. Because D&O insurance is typically considered an "all-risk" policy (meaning that an act will be covered unless it is specifically excluded by the policy), generally the only limitation on the definition is that the act must have been committed by an insured while acting in a business-related capacity.

Q 32.6   What is a "loss"?

A typical definition of "loss" includes damages, judgments, settlements and defense costs incurred on account of a covered claim. Most definitions of loss exclude civil or criminal fines or penalties, taxes, amounts for which the insureds are not financially liable, employment- related benefits, or other losses uninsurable as a matter of law. Depending upon the policy, the definition of loss may or may not include punitive, exemplary and multiple damages if insurable under the applicable law.

Negotiating the definition of the term "loss" is discussed below at Q 32.19.

Q 32.7   What is typically excluded from coverage?

Most D&O insurance policies will cover a claim unless there is a specific exclusion eliminating coverage. There are four general categories of exclusions in the typical D&O policy, all of which should be considered for negotiation:

1.   *Illegal conduct exclusions:* claims arising out of illegal or fraudulent conduct (for example, illegal profits, criminal acts, fraudulent or intentionally dishonest acts, and medical malpractice, if proven). Generally, a D&O policy will provide defense costs coverage for such claims unless and until the illegal or fraudulent conduct is proven;

2. *Other-insurance exclusions:* claims that should be covered by other types of policies (for example, claims for property damage, bodily injury, and workers' compensation, which are covered by different types of insurance policies);

3. *Timing exclusions:* claims that occurred prior to the policy period and/or were not reported properly (for example, late notice, claims made on a previous policy, and claims where the risk was known prior to the inception of the policy); and

4. *The insured-versus-insured exclusion:* claims where one insured brings suit against another insured (this type of claim is excluded due to its potentially collusive nature).

"Non-Duty-to-Defend" Coverage

Q 32.8   What is "non-duty-to-defend" coverage?

Under a "non-duty-to-defend" D&O insurance policy, the insurer is not required to defend a covered claim; instead, it is the duty of insureds to retain and pay for counsel to defend a claim, and the insurer is only required to reimburse the insured for those expenses. Defense costs incurred by an insured to defend a claim may be covered by the insurer on either a reimbursement or advance basis.

Unlike many other types of insurance policies, D&O policies typically do *not* require the insurer to defend a covered claim. Defending claims is discussed below (*see* Q 32.43).

Q 32.8.1   What are the advantages and/or disadvantages of a non-duty-to-defend policy?

Many insureds prefer a non-duty-to-defend policy because it gives the insureds more control of the defense of the claim. However, this additional control comes with insurer oversight. The non-duty-to-defend policy also requires the insureds to obtain the insurers' consent prior to incurring defense costs and/or agreement to a settlement. Failure to obtain that consent can leave insureds responsible for paying all or a portion of their expenses. In short, although the insured controls the defense, the insured must still work with its insurers if it hopes to have its expenses covered by the insurance policy.

Defending claims is discussed below (*see* Q 32.43 *et seq.*).

Q 32.8.2   What is the difference between reimbursing and advancing the costs for defending a claim?

The reimbursement approach requires the insured to pay expenses and then ask the insurer to reimburse them. This can put a burden on some insureds to front defense costs for several months until the insurer pays the reimbursement. For this reason, many insureds prefer advancement policies. With an advancement policy, the insurer pays the expenses directly to the defense firms so that the insured does not have to pay and then wait to be reimbursed. However, many insurers will require the use of a pre-selected "panel counsel" law firm before it will agree to advance defense costs. Some insureds like this, others do not.

Most reimbursement and advancement clauses are subject to two conditions:

(1)   The parties must agree to an appropriate allocation of the defense costs (that is, covered and uncovered losses), with only covered losses subject to reimbursement/advancement; and

(2)   The insurance company must receive the insureds' agreement to repay the insurance company if it is determined that the insureds' losses are not covered by the policy.

Q 32.8.3   How is allocation of defense costs decided?

Allocation is necessary if a lawsuit involves both covered and uncovered claims. Similarly, allocation is necessary if a lawsuit names both insured and uninsured persons as defendants and both parties are represented by the same law firm. For this reason, a common reimbursement/advancement clause provides that if the insureds and the insurance company can agree on an allocation between covered and uncovered losses, the insurer will advance, on a current basis, the amount allocated to covered loss. If the parties are unable to agree, a typical reimbursement/advancement clause will require the insurance company to pay only the portion of defense costs it deems "reasonable" until a different allocation is determined by negotiation, arbitration or a judicial proceeding. Some parties will give the insured the option of submitting an allocation dispute to binding arbitration.

Q 32.8.4   How do repayment clauses work?

Most D&O policies require an insured to repay any defense costs that are advanced if it later turns out that the insured is not entitled to indemnification under the insurance policy. The mechanism used for this guarantee of repayment is called an "undertaking." Some D&O policies require the insured to guarantee the undertaking. For example, one D&O insurance policy provides as follows:

> As a condition of any advancement of defense expenses, the Insurer may require a written undertaking on terms and conditions satisfactory to the Insurer guaranteeing the repayment of defense expenses paid on behalf of the Insured if it is finally determined that Loss incurred by such Insured would not be covered by this policy [emphasis added].

An insurer could argue that the *guarantee* of repayment translates into the need to *collateralize* the advancement. Obviously, this could be problematic, as many insureds may lack sufficient collateral to support the advancement of what could be millions of dollars' worth of defense fees. Although it is debatable whether an insurer would be successful with this argument, insureds should be cautious about agreeing to such a provision.

Q 32.8.5   Do defense costs erode the policy limit?

Yes. It is important to remember that defense costs generally erode the policy limit. Thus, every dollar spent defending a claim reduces the limit available to resolve the matter.

"Claims-Made" Coverage

Q 32.9   What is "claims-made" coverage?

D&O insurance policies are nearly all written on a claims-made basis. This means that for a claim to be covered, it must be made during the policy period and the "wrongful act" must occur after a preset retroactive date (generally the inception date of the first D&O policy provided by the insurer) but before the end of the policy term. Even within the policy period, insureds are generally required to give notice "as soon as practicable" and often within a set number

of days. Although some policies may relax (or restrict) these requirements, claims-made policies are extremely time-sensitive. Thus, it is
imperative that insureds recognize when a claim has been made and
report such a claim promptly. Failure to do so may result in a denial
of coverage.

In addition to requiring notice of a claim, many policies permit
an insured to provide notice of any "circumstance" that may give rise
to a claim in the future. Giving notice of a circumstance is generally
discretionary, but it can have some advantages. For example, if a company properly notices a circumstance during the policy period, the
insurer will generally consider a subsequent claim that arises from
that circumstance to be "made" during the policy period in which the
insured provided the notice. This can allow a claim that is not actually made until after the policy period has expired to be covered by
the policy nonetheless. The benefit of this is that subsequent policy
limits will not be impaired by any claims arising from the noticed
circumstances.

On the other hand, because giving notice of a circumstance creates a potential increase in exposure for the insurer, most policies
demand a high degree of specificity about the circumstance in order
for coverage to apply. Failure to provide sufficient details can result
in coverage being denied by the current insurer and may trigger an
exclusion in a future policy. This complicates the decision to report a
circumstance, especially if the company is changing insurers or relevant coverage terms, including limit. In addition, it is possible that the
insurer will count the potential increased exposure from the notice
of circumstances against the insureds. This could result in a higher
renewal quote or, in a worst-case scenario, the refusal to quote the
risk going forward.

D&O Insurance Program Structure

Q 32.10   What is a typical structure for a D&O insurance program?

Few insurers today are willing to provide more than $10 to $15 million of coverage for any one risk. So insureds who seek more than
$10 to $15 million in D&O insurance coverage often must purchase
multiple insurance policies.

In the United States, insureds that desire more than $10 to $15 million in coverage typically "layer" or "stack" insurers. The first layer (or primary policy) will set forth the general terms and conditions for the entire program. Excess policies provide any needed additional limit. In this model, the primary insurer bears 100% of the risk of loss up to its limit. Then, the first excess insurer will bear 100% of its layer on, and so on.

One alternative to the layered structure is a "quota share" program. Popular in Europe but rarely seen in the United States, a quota share program allows the insurers to share the risk across a program in proportion to the premium they receive. This may be easiest to understand graphically:

FIGURE 32-2

D&O Liability Insurance Program Structures: Layered Versus Quote Share

Traditional U.S. Model Layered (or Stacked) Insurance	
Excess Insurer 4	$10M excess $40M
Excess Insurer 3	$10M excess $30M
Excess Insurer 2	$10M excess $20M
Excess Insurer 1	$10M excess $10M
Primary Insurer	$10M primary limit

Traditional U.K. Model Quota Share Insurance	
$50M	Insurer E—20% of loss
	Insurer D—20% of loss
	Insurer C—20% of loss
	Insurer B—20% of loss
	Insurer A—20% of loss

Negotiating excess policies is discussed below at Q 32.35.

Dedicated-Limit Insurance

Q 32.11   What is dedicated-limit insurance?

As discussed above (*see* Q 32.2.1), the dedicated-limit policy, commonly referred to as a "Side A–Only," or a "difference-in-conditions" policy, was developed to help avoid the shortcomings of the traditional D&O insurance policy.

Dedicated-limit policies can simultaneously sit both on top of and alongside a traditional D&O insurance program. They can drop down to cover cases of company and insurer insolvency and/or can provide excess coverage in the event of exhaustion of the underlying limits. Dedicated-limit policies can also drop down to provide "first-dollar" protection in certain circumstances. It is important to remember, however, that dedicated-limit policies are typically triggered only if a claim is non-indemnifiable or if all other sources of indemnification have failed.

The following are some examples of "non-indemnifiable" claims:

- derivative actions where the company is not permitted by law or public policy to indemnify directors or officers for judgments or settlements;

- certain securities registration and anti-fraud suits under the federal securities laws where indemnification is against public policy;

- any claim where the company is financially unable to fund the advancement or indemnification; and

- any claim where the applicable law prohibits advancement and indemnification.

By limiting its coverage to only these "non-indemnifiable" claims, the dedicated limit policy avoids some of the main disadvantages of traditional D&O insurance. For example, since the policy does not cover the company, company losses cannot erode or exhaust the limit. For the same reason, a dedicated limit policy cannot be treated as an asset of the bankruptcy estate. Thus, it will remain beyond the reach of the bankruptcy court and any creditors of the company.

Another advantage of a dedicated-limit policy is that it generally provides broader coverage than a traditional D&O insurance policy. For example, a typical dedicated-limit policy will be completely non-rescindable and non-cancelable once the insureds (or the insureds' company) pay the premium. Many of the exclusions generally found in a traditional D&O insurance policy—such as the ERISA, failure to maintain insurance, pollution, libel/slander, and defamation exclusions—are not included in a typical dedicated-limit policy. Moreover, the dedicated-limit policy generally has several more insured-friendly exclusions, including the insured-versus-insured (*see* Q 32.25.1) and employment practices exclusions. Some newer policies will even delete these exclusions completely.

The main purpose of D&O insurance is to protect the personal assets of the directors and officers. By adding a dedicated limit policy on top of a traditional D&O insurance program, a company can fill potential coverage gaps in its overall executive protection program. This can help the company retain and attract directors and officers. More importantly, it can help ensure that innocent directors and officers will be protected should the potentially catastrophic claim occur.

Q 32.11.1   How is a dedicated-limit policy structured?

Yet another advantage of a dedicated-limit policy is that it can be structured to best meet the risk transfer needs of management. The following are three examples of ways a dedicated-limit policy can be structured:

(1)   Some policies can be structured simply as a follow-form Side A excess policy, which will cover directors and officers on an excess basis above a company's traditional D&O insurance program. This structure tends to be less expensive, but offers less protection than other types of dedicated limit policies.

(2)   More commonly these days, a company can select a Side A difference-in-conditions (DIC) policy, which can serve as an excess policy or drop down to the primary position if the underlying traditional D&O insurance program and/or the company cannot or fails to respond (rightly or wrongly) due to: (i) rescission by the underlying insurers; (ii) wrongful refusal or financial inability of the underlying insurers or the

company to advance defense costs or indemnify a loss; and/ or (iii) denial of coverage by the underlying insurers due to coverage exclusions that are not contained in the dedicated limit policy.

(3) A company may also select an independent directors liability (IDL) policy. This policy is similar to a Side A DIC policy except that an IDL policy only protects the independent or outside directors. The main advantage of an IDL policy (as opposed to a Side A or Side A DIC policy) from the perspective of the independent directors is that the limit of an IDL policy cannot be eroded or exhausted by officers who typically face a greater risk of large defense costs, settlement amounts and judgments because they were personally involved in the conduct alleged in the claim.

Considerations in Selecting an Insurance Policy

Q 32.12   What factors should be considered when purchasing D&O insurance?

The are several important factors to consider when purchasing a D&O insurance policy, including:

- policy limit;
- retention;
- terms and conditions;
- claims handling;
- financial ratings; and
- insurer's longevity in the industry.

Policy Limit

Q 32.12.1   How do insureds determine the right policy limit?

There is no fool-proof way to determine the perfect amount of D&O insurance to purchase for any particular year. Nonetheless, there are many factors that can inform insureds as to the proper amount of insurance they need to feel comfortable:

- *Claim studies.* Perhaps the most scientific way to determine the appropriate D&O insurance limit is to consider a claims study by NERA, Cornerstone, or a similar economic consulting firm. These studies consider the mean and average settlement values for class action settlements controlling for factors such as market cap, industry, and insider and institutional investor holdings. The studies project a range of probable losses for various stock drops based on historical trends. For example, if a company's stock dropped 20%, the expected loss would be X. If the company's stock dropped 40%, the expected loss would be Y. While these studies can be informative, they cannot predict the size of a future stock drop or whether the losses relating to such a drop will fall within historical trends.

- *Benchmarking studies.* Benchmarking studies provide an insured with information about what limit the insured's "peer companies" are purchasing. Again, this can be helpful, but there is no guarantee that the insured's peer companies are purchasing the right limit. Moreover, such studies are typically limited to one broker's experience, which may or may not include a statistically significant sampling of peer companies.

- *What the directors want.* Sometimes, directors or officers will insist on a certain amount of insurance regardless of any claim studies or benchmarking data. Failure to provide the desired limit may mean that the company will be unable to attract or retain directors or officers.

- *What the insured can afford.* What the insureds can afford is another very real factor in determining what limit insureds should purchase.

- *Public perception.* Some companies fear that a high D&O insurance limit may attract lawsuits and/or increase the size of settlements. Most studies do not support this conclusion.

When deciding the appropriate limit to purchase, insureds should also consider that defense costs are usually (but not always) included within the limit of liability. Thus, insureds also need to factor in the cost of defending a lawsuit when determining the appropriate limit.

Retention

Q 32.12.2   How do insureds determine the right retention?

A retention is the amount of risk retained by the insured before the insurance policy will begin to provide coverage. A retention is similar to a deductible. Selecting the right retention is also a complicated decision. Generally, an insured should select a retention that is above what it takes to resolve a typical "cost of doing business" type claim but below the point where satisfying the retention would have a significant negative impact on the insured's operations. Within that range, the insured must balance the cost of a policy with the lower retention amount against the cost of a policy with a higher retention amount.

Other Factors

Q 32.12.3   To what extent should an insured consider terms and conditions?

Perhaps the most important factor to consider when deciding which D&O policy to purchase are the terms and conditions of the policy itself. Terms and conditions in D&O policies are not standard. An insured who saves a few dollars in premium by selecting an inferior policy may find themselves "penny-wise but pound-foolish."

Q 32.12.4   ... claims handling?

An insured purchases a D&O policy to pay claims. Different insurers handle claims very differently. Before deciding to purchase a D&O policy, it is important to know the insurer's reputation for paying claims. Insureds may also find it helpful to know whether the insurer has its own experienced claims staff or whether it uses outside law firms for its claims.

Q 32.12.5   ... financial ratings?

The financial strength of an insurer is important. One way to determine the financial strength of a company is to consider its rating from A.M. Best or a similar rating agency.

Q 32.12.6   ... an insurer's longevity in the industry?

Some insurers try to time their entry and exit from particular areas of insurance to coincide with the hard and soft market cycle. While such an insurer may be able to offer lower prices during "good times," it is typically better for an insured to work with an insurer who will remain in the market in both good and bad times.

Q 32.12.7   How important is price in choosing an insurer and policy?

There are a large number of D&O insurers to choose from. Insureds that consider only price may find out too late that price is not the most important factor to consider when purchasing insurance. While price is important when selecting the right D&O policy limit, retention, and insurer, it is only one factor to consider, and it is usually the least reliable factor in determining the *right* policy limit, retention, or insurer for insureds.

Negotiating Key Provisions of a D&O Policy

Overview

Q 32.13   Why do D&O insurance policies need to be negotiated?

D&O policies are unlike many other types of insurance policies. There is no standard D&O insurance form. There is a lack of uniformity in terms and conditions, as well as in scope of coverage. As a result, comparing the premiums of D&O insurance is not informative. Instead, insureds must compare and contrast each D&O policy to ensure that it meets their risk transfer needs. Today, some forty insurers offer a total of more than eighty different D&O insurance policies. Even the simplest of these policies has an intimidating number of detailed definitions, terms and conditions, and exclusions, with nuances of wording that can have very costly consequences. Narrow definitions and overly broad exclusions found in many "off-the-shelf" policies can mean the difference between a policy covering a multimillion-dollar loss or one that leaves insureds to pay the tab.

Fortunately, D&O insurance policy forms are not cast in stone. There is sufficient competition in the marketplace that many D&O insurers are willing to consider suggestions and, in varying degrees, to tailor policies to meet the insureds' needs by means of endorsements. In fact, D&O insurance policies are among the most negotiable forms of insurance coverage. Too few insureds avail themselves fully of this opportunity, and many discover shortfalls only after a claim arises.

Q 32.13.1   Should counsel or consultants be hired to negotiate a D&O policy?

Negotiating enhanced coverage is a formidable challenge for insureds. D&O insurance policy negotiation requires the knowledge and experience of defense counsel, a claims expert, and a wordsmith for the following reasons:

1. A standard D&O insurance policy form does not exist. D&O insurance policy forms vary significantly from one insurance company to the next. Some insurance companies offer, in addition to a general corporate form, different forms for financial institutions, healthcare organizations, mutual funds, and other specialized markets.

2. The frequency of new policy forms is increasing. Each new policy has new language that may impact the coverage.

3. The meaning of policy language frequently is unclear. The movement for plain-English contracts has not been widely embraced by D&O insurers.

4. Few buyers have a full appreciation of the many built-in pitfalls in standard policies. Until insureds have been through the complete cycle of working with an insurer—from negotiating policy terms, to making a claim and receiving a "reservation of rights" letter, to working through a coverage dispute—they cannot foresee many of the issues that an insurance company may raise to limit or deny coverage under a policy.

For all of these reasons, it is unrealistic for insureds to expect a risk manager who reviews one D&O insurance policy per year to obtain top coverage. And unless a broker specializes in D&O insurance, it is nearly impossible to stay on top of all of the market changes and the endorsements offered by each insurer. Insureds should engage a team of professionals. Otherwise, what they save now, they may pay for many times over in the future.

Q 32.13.2   What parts of the policy should be negotiated?

Broadly speaking, insureds should negotiate:

- definitions;
- exclusions; and
- terms and conditions.

Each of these areas is discussed in further detail in the following questions.

Negotiating Definitions

Q 32.14   Which definitions should an insured negotiate?

Insureds often overlook the definitions in a D&O insurance policy. However, the definitions are what most often determine the coverage. To illustrate this point, a few years ago, an insurer issued a policy with no exclusions. Of course, this did not mean all risks were covered by the policy. Instead, the insurer narrowly defined terms such as "Claim" and "Loss" to exclude the risks it did not want to cover. Given that there is a myriad of definitions in each D&O insurance policy and that each can impact coverage, insureds should carefully review and negotiate the definitions in light of the insureds' specific risk transfer needs. Some of the definitions that insureds should focus on include:

- "application";
- "claim";
- "insured";
- "insured person";
- "loss"; and
- "securities claim."

Q 32.15   What are the important factors to consider when negotiating the definition of the term "application"?

The definition of "application" is important because the application is the basis for coverage. If material information is omitted or misstated in the application, this may constitute application fraud, which could result in rescission of the policy. Consequently, it is in the insured's best interest to keep the definition as narrow as possible.

D&O policies often define the term "application" to include, in addition to the application form itself, any public document filed by the named insured with any federal, state, local, or foreign regulatory agency at any time. This definition is overly broad and can have a devastating effect on coverage. For example, an insurer should generally not be allowed to rely on a document filed with the Securities and Exchange Commission many years ago to deny coverage today. One way to limit this risk is to narrow the definition of "application." By limiting the documents considered part of the application to only those documents filed with the SEC in the twelve months prior to the inception date of the policy, directors and officers may reduce the chance that irrelevant, old, and potentially stale information could affect their coverage.

TIP: Directors and officers should take the time to review the application each year (not just the quote or proposal for insurance). The application is the basis of the insurance contract and a careful review of the application can minimize the risk of rescission later.

Q 32.16   ... the definition of the term "claim"?

What constitutes a "claim" as defined by a D&O insurance policy is critical. It impacts the scope of coverage and triggers several obligations of the insurer and the insured. A claim is not limited to a lawsuit. It can include a written demand for monetary or other relief; a civil, criminal, or administrative proceeding or investigation; and even a written notice that an investigation has or may be commenced against an individual insured. For example, an Equal Employment Opportunity Commission complaint (regardless of merit) may constitute a claim and, as with any claim, an insured must report it promptly.

Some D&O insurance policies use an unreasonably narrow definition of a claim. Consider the following definition:

> A claim shall mean any adjudicatory proceeding in a court of law or equity brought against any Insured Person, including any appeal from such adjudicatory proceeding.

This definition is highly objectionable because it is limited to proceedings brought in court. It does not cover administrative or other governmental proceedings or the investigative stage of such proceedings. It also does not include arbitration or other alternative dispute resolution proceedings.

Another unreasonably narrow definition of "claim" in a D&O insurance policy currently being offered excludes criminal proceedings. Defense costs for such proceedings should be covered by the policy (at least until the insured is convicted of the offense). In addition, insureds should be sure that a criminal proceeding commenced by both an *indictment* or by an *information* are covered by the policy. An indictment is the product of a grand jury, whereas an information is the product of a prosecutor. Many policies today include only criminal proceedings commenced by an indictment. Since both an indictment and an information can commence a criminal proceeding, the definition of claim should refer to both.

Insureds should also consider whether they have coverage for an SEC investigation. Companies can spend millions of dollars defending an SEC investigation before the SEC ever files a lawsuit. Whether a D&O policy will cover these expenses typically depends on the definition of "claim" within the policy. For the broadest coverage possible, the definition of claim should include any administrative or regulatory proceeding against the insured company as well as any *investigation* of the company. Many insurers will not provide such broad protection or will attempt to limit the definition of claim to only "formal" investigations or only formal investigations that also name a director or officer as well as the company. Either restriction could limit the insureds' potential recovery.

Although it is generally desirable to have a broad definition of "claim," too broad a definition can also be problematic. For example, some policy forms define "claim" to include both written and *oral* demands for monetary damages. The addition of an oral demand to the definition might seem like a desirable expansion of coverage; however, this addition may create coverage problems for the insureds. An officer who receives an oral demand might not recognize it as a claim and, thus, may not report it to the insurer in a timely manner. No timely notice, no coverage.

In addition, there is the problem of proof. Trying to establish what a disgruntled stockholder said to an officer of the company at a cocktail party three years ago and trying to determine if it constituted a reportable demand for monetary damages could be a difficult task. To avoid potential coverage issues, it is generally better for insureds to ask their insurer to delete oral demands from the definition of "claim."

Q 32.17   ... the definition of the term "insured"?

The definition of "insured" may seem straightforward. However, the standard definition can omit key entities that the company intended to cover, so insureds may need to amend the definition to ensure that all appropriate entities have coverage.

The term "insured" typically includes a "named insured entity, its subsidiaries, and certain insured persons." One example of how this definition may be lacking is that it does not clearly cover a "debtor in possession." When a company files for protection from its creditors under Chapter 11 of the Bankruptcy Code, the company becomes a debtor in possession. A debtor in possession is considered a separate legal entity from the company despite the fact that many of the same directors and officers may still be involved in running the entity. The problem is that the definition above may not include a debtor in possession as an "insured." This could leave a serious hole in the company's insurance protection. Fortunately, most insurers will amend the definition of insured to include a debtor in possession upon request.

Another potential shortcoming of the standard definition of insured is that many companies are part of a complicated structure that may include parent and subsidiary companies, "sibling" companies, unrelated companies who work closely together or even share resources or work, joint ventures, for-profit entities, and non-profit entities sponsored by a for-profit entity. Often, insureds desire to insure the collective risk of some mix of companies, some of which have relationships more complicated than parent and subsidiary. In this case, it is critical that the company amend the definition of insured to include all entities that do not clearly fall under the standard definition.

Finally, it is important to determine what entity to list as the named insured or parent company. Coverage in a D&O policy typically flows down from the parent, not up the corporate chain. If the named insured is the parent company, the policy should cover all of the parent's subsidiaries. The reverse is not true. Sometimes companies name a subsidiary as the named insured for tax purposes or because the subsidiary is where most of the business risk lies, only to find out later that, in doing so, the parent company lacks coverage. Since the parent company is often named in a lawsuit regardless of whether it was ultimately responsible for the alleged action, it is generally not advisable to use a subsidiary as the named insured.

Q 32.18   ... the definition of the term "insured person"?

As implied by the name, D&O insurance policies cover "directors and officers," with the term "individual insured" typically being defined as "any past, present, or future *duly elected or appointed* directors or officers of the Company." Determining who is a duly elected or appointed *director* is generally straightforward. Determining who is a duly elected or appointed *officer* can be a bit more complicated. For example, companies must decide whether the definition above should cover individuals such as the general counsel, risk manager, or the assistant vice president of marketing.

Insurance companies will usually "schedule" additional members of management without additional premium. That said, each person added to the coverage has the potential to dilute and even exhaust the coverage. At some point, many directors and officers would prefer not to take the risk of a lower-level employee diluting or exhausting coverage that is intended to cover their own personal assets.

With regard to a company's controller and its chief accounting officer, it is important to keep in mind that these positions have high exposure, particularly in a publicly held company. For example, the controller or chief accounting officer must sign each registration statement filed with the SEC under the Securities Act of 1933. This exposes him or her to personal liability under section 11 of that act for material misstatements and omissions in the registration statement.

Once the universe of insured persons has been determined, there is also the issue of whether the insured is acting in his or her capacity as such. Two circumstances warrant extra attention:

(1)   when a company has in-house attorneys, and
(2)   when there is a controlling shareholder.

Some additional positions that companies often consider adding to the definition of "insured" include:

- directors that serve on the boards of outside entities;

- general counsel;

- risk manager;

- director of human resources;

- controller or chief accounting officer; and

- employees (including temporary employees, independent contractors and/or volunteers).

Q 32.18.1   Will D&O insurance cover in-house attorneys?

With regard to in-house attorneys, some argue that the capacity language in a D&O insurance policy means that the D&O policy will not cover the legal work performed by in-house attorneys because such work is not performed in the attorney's capacity as an officer of the company. In-house attorneys, on the other hand, typically argue that one of their duties as an officer of the company is to perform legal tasks and, thus, the policy should cover that work. Unfortunately, there is no hard-and-fast rule to determine whether a particular action is performed in the insured's capacity as an officer of the company or in some other capacity. Further, there is little, if any, case law or precedent that discusses in what capacity any particular action is performed. Thus, whether a D&O insurance policy will respond to a particular action will largely depend on the allegations in the complaint and how a particular claims adjuster handles the claim.

Q 32.18.2   Will D&O insurance cover controlling shareholders?

Under federal securities laws, a control person may be liable simply by virtue of their status as such. Thus, a person who is a substantial shareholder and a director or officer can be subject to claims in both their controlling shareholder capacity, as well as their managerial capacity as a director or officer. D&O insurance policies do not explicitly provide for coverage for claims against directors and officers as controlling shareholders. However, it is possible to obtain an endorsement to the D&O policy that states that the insurer will cover all losses arising from a claim made against a director or officer in their capacity both as a director or officer and as a controlling shareholder.

Q 32.19   What are the important factors to consider when negotiating the definition of the term "loss"?

The definition of "loss" is another important term in D&O insurance policies, since there must be a loss for coverage to attach. D&O insurance policies typically define loss to include damages, judgments, settlements, and defense costs incurred as a result of a covered claim. Loss typically excludes civil or criminal fines or penalties, taxes, amounts for which insureds are not financially liable, employment-related benefits, or other losses uninsurable as a matter of law. Depending upon the policy, the definition of "loss" may or may not include punitive, exemplary, and multiple damages if insurable under the applicable law.

Two important provisions for purchasers to consider with relation to what will constitute loss are "most favorable venue" provision and a "section 11, 12, and 15" carve-back endorsement.

Q 32.19.1   What is the benefit of a "most favorable venue" provision?

Coverage of punitive damages can be an important reason for purchasing a D&O insurance policy, but the insurability of such damages varies between jurisdictions. To maximize the chances that punitive damages will be covered by the policy, the policy should have a "most favorable venue" provision that provides that the applicable law that *most* favors the insurability of punitive damages will apply when determining coverage.

Some jurisdictions may require a more specific "most favorable venue" provision that limits the potential venues to those that have some relation to the claim and/or the insurance contract. Such a provision may state that the most favorable law of any of the following jurisdictions will apply to determine the insurability of punitive damages:

(1) the location of the named entity's headquarters or its principal place of business;

(2) where the insurer is located;

(3) where the alleged wrongful act took place;

(4) where the claim is brought; or

(5) any other jurisdiction that has a substantial relationship to the claim.

Q 32.19.2   What is the benefit of a "section 11, 12, and 15" carve-back?

In addition to negotiating for coverage of punitive, exemplary, and multiple damages, insureds should also request a "section 11, 12 and 15" carve-back endorsement. This endorsement addresses the fact that some courts have recently held that losses arising from claims alleging violations of section 11, 12 and 15 of the Securities Act of 1933 should be considered the return of ill-gotten gains and therefore do not constitute loss and are uninsurable as a matter of law.

Perhaps the most cited case for this concept is *Conseco, Inc. v. National Union Fire Insurance Co.* (see the Case Study below).[4] The *Conseco* decision was contrary to the expectations of most insureds and many insurers. As a result, many insurers will provide a section 11, 12, and 15 endorsement, which states that the insurer will not assert that the amounts incurred by insureds attributable to allegations of section 11, 12, and 15 violations are uninsurable loss.

Q 32.20   What are the important factors to consider when negotiating the definition of the term "securities claim"?

D&O insurance policies for public companies almost always limit coverage for company losses (Side C coverage) to those losses arising from "securities claims." In many policies, the definition also imposes a requirement that a securities claim arise out of, or be based upon, the purchase or sale of securities of an insured entity. This can be problematic because securities violations may result from other corporate conduct or the purchase or sale of the securities of a non-insured entity. Without negotiations, the D&O policy may not cover such conduct.

 CASE STUDY: *Conseco, Inc. v. Nat'l Union Fire Ins. Co.*

In *Conseco,* the underlying lawsuit alleged that Conseco had made "material misstatements and/or omissions" regarding the financial health of Conseco, thereby artificially inflating the price of the company's stock in the initial public offering. Plaintiffs who purchased stock in the IPO brought claims under section 11 of the Securities Act, which prohibits false or misleading statements in direct securities offerings. According to the court, section 11 claims divest a company of a specific sum of money that it improperly obtained as a result of false or misleading statements. In other words, section 11 requires the company to return money it had no right to possess in the first place. In contrast, other securities claims do not create "ill-gotten" gains for the company because,

---

although a company's shares may decline in value after a false or misleading statement is revealed, the company itself would not receive a direct monetary benefit from the artificial inflation of the stock price.

According to the court, allowing Conseco to recover that amount from its insurer would result in an improper windfall to Conseco; thus, the court concluded, the section 11 portion of the settlement represented a disgorgement of profits to which Conseco was never entitled. As such, the portion of the settlement attributable to the section 11 claims could not constitute a "loss" under the plain meaning of the D&O policy.[5]

To obtain broad protection, the definition of "securities claim" should at least cover the most frequent types of securities lawsuits brought against directors, officers, and their corporations. These include suits alleging violations of the Securities Act of 1933 (which includes sections 11, 12, and 15), the Securities Exchange Act of 1934 (which includes section 10(b), the general anti-fraud section), the rules promulgated thereunder (which includes Rule 10b-5, the popular general anti-fraud rule under federal securities laws), and the securities laws of any state or similar common law.

It is important that the definition of a "securities claim" cover actions under state securities laws and common law, particularly in light of the recent trend for plaintiffs to bring securities fraud litigation in state courts. In addition, many companies sell their securities abroad. For those who do and whose policies do not provide such coverage automatically, they should request that the definition of "securities claim" include actions alleging violations of foreign securities laws.

Negotiating Exclusions: Generally

Q 32.21   Which exclusions should an insured negotiate?

The exclusions found in most D&O insurance policies fall into four main categories, all of which should be considered for negotiation. They are:

(1) claims arising from illegal or fraudulent conduct (for example, illegal profits, criminal acts, fraudulent or intentionally dishonest acts, and medical malpractice, if proven);

(2) claims that are covered by other types of policies (for example, claims for property damage, bodily injury, and workers' compensation);

(3) claims that belong on previous policies due to timing issues (for example, matters where the risk was noticed on another policy, the risk was known prior to the inception of the policy, or the litigation had commenced prior to the inception of the policy); and

(4) insured-versus-insured exclusion for claims that are potentially collusive (for example, claims brought by or with the assistance of an insured).

Negotiating Exclusions: Illegal/Fraudulent Conduct Exclusion

Q 32.22   What are the important factors to consider when negotiating the illegal or fraudulent exclusions?

Suits brought by shareholders represent the largest category of D&O claims against public companies and the second largest category of D&O claims against private companies. Since most shareholder claims against directors and officers include allegations of fraud—which, if true, would exclude coverage under a D&O policy—how a policy determines whether a "conduct exclusion" applies, and who gets to make this determination, is extremely important.

Typical conduct exclusions exclude coverage for:

- intentional dishonest acts or omissions;
- deliberate fraudulent acts or omissions;
- deliberate criminal acts or omissions;
- willful violations of any statute, rule or law;
- receipt of illegal profits; and
- receipt of illegal remuneration.

For example, does the determination of whether a director or officer committed fraud have to be made by a court, or can the insurer make the determination? Similarly, assuming a court must make the determination, must the court make the determination in the underlying action, or can the insurance company bring a new and separate action to determine the fraud after the fact? An action against the insured by its insurance company, coming right behind a shareholder action, is a most unappealing prospect for many insureds.

For this reason, many insureds prefer a "final adjudication" standard. This standard provides directors and officers with the maximum coverage possible and requires a final, unappealable adjudication by a court in the underlying action to establish that the alleged wrongful conduct occurred. Without such a final adjudication of wrongful conduct, the exclusion does not apply (that is, there is coverage available from the policy).

A less preferable alternative is an "in fact" determination. It is not altogether clear what constitutes an "in fact" determination. However, it is certainly less than a final, unappealable adjudication by a court and, therefore, less desirable from the perspective of providing the maximum coverage possible to the individual insureds. Of course, as with many issues with D&O insurance coverage, providing the broadest coverage possible may make it possible for a "guilty" insured to dilute or exhaust the policy limit to the detriment of the other "innocent" insureds. As such, some insureds may prefer the "in fact" standard or some other hybrid of the "in fact" and final adjudication standards.

Negotiating Exclusions: Other-Insurance Exclusions

Q 32.23   What are the important factors to consider when negotiating other-insurance exclusions?

D&O policies contain a number of exclusions designed to ensure that risks that are more properly covered by a different type of insurance policy are not covered by the D&O policy. For example, most D&O policies exclude the following types of claims:

- property damage and bodily injury claims, which may be covered by general liability insurance;

- workers' compensation claims, which may be covered by workers' compensation insurance;

- losses related to the environment, which may be covered by environmental liability insurance; and

- ERISA claims, which may be covered by fiduciary liability insurance.

It is important to negotiate each of the exclusions identified above so that they are as narrow as possible. For instance, with regard to a property damage and bodily injury claim (a claim that should be covered by a general liability policy), some policies exclude coverage for any claim "arising out of, based upon or attributable to" property damage and bodily injury. This is too broad. Instead, the quoted language should be replaced with the word "for." This addresses the situation when there is an injury that is followed by a secondary lawsuit claiming a failure to supervise. A company's general liability policy might cover the direct liability associated with the injury, but it will not cover the subsequent lawsuit. With the change to "for," the company's D&O insurance policy could provide coverage.

A similar situation may arise with regard to environmental issues. Most D&O policies exclude coverage for claims "arising out of, based upon or attributable to" pollution. Again, such a broad exclusion could create gaps in coverage for the directors and officers. To fix the gap, the pollution exclusion should expressly carve out securities claims, as well as non-indemnifiable loss.

Negotiating Exclusions: Timing-Related Exclusions

Q 32.24   What are the important factors to consider when negotiating timing-related exclusions?

As discussed above, most D&O insurance policies are written on a "claims made and reported" basis (*see* Q 32.9), making timing critical to the determination of coverage. To emphasize this point, most D&O policies will contain several timing-related exclusions. The three most common of these exclusions are:

(1)   the prior-notice exclusion;
(2)   the pending and prior litigation exclusion; and
(3)   the prior-acts exclusion.

In order to obtain maximum coverage, an insured should negotiate each of these exclusions.

Q 32.24.1   What is a prior-notice exclusion?

A typical prior-notice exclusion excludes any claim arising out of, based upon, or attributable to any facts or circumstances alleged or contained in any claim that was previously reported by the insured under a previous insurance policy. The risk with this exclusion is that an insurer may reject a reported claim. In these situations, the insured may be left without coverage. As such, insureds should attempt to negotiate language that states that only those claims that are previously reported *and covered* by a previous insurance policy will be excluded by the new policy.

Q 32.24.2   What is a pending and prior litigation exclusion?

A typical pending and prior litigation exclusion excludes any pending or prior litigation and any new litigation that is based upon the same or essentially the same facts or circumstances as any pending or prior litigation. The intent of this exclusion is to ensure that the insurer does not get tricked into insuring a "burning building." Insureds should consider asking the insurer to remove this exclusion or to limit the scope of the exclusion so that only litigation known to a select control group of insureds (for example, the CEO, CFO and general counsel) will be excluded from coverage.

Q 32.24.3   What is a prior-acts exclusion?

A typical prior-acts exclusion excludes coverage for any claims based upon wrongful acts that occurred prior to a certain date—often the inception date of the policy. Given the claims-made nature of the D&O insurance policy, a prior-acts exclusion has the potential to strip the D&O policy of all or most of its value and insureds should avoid such an exclusion whenever possible.

Negotiating Exclusions: Insured-Versus-Insured Exclusion

Q 32.25   What is an "insured-versus-insured" exclusion?

In the mid-1980s, D&O insurers added an "insured-versus-insured" exclusion to bar claims brought by or on behalf of one insured against another insured. The purpose of the exclusion is to avoid covering collusive, inter-corporate disputes. For example, prior to the advent of the insured-versus-insured exclusion, Bank of America filed a lawsuit against certain of its loan officers and then turned the loss over to its D&O insurer. By doing so, Bank of America converted its D&O policy from third-party liability coverage into a policy that could cover first-party business risk.

Q 32.25.1   What are the important factors to consider when negotiating an insured-versus-insured exclusion?

While there is clearly a need for an insured-versus-insured exclusion in the example above, many insured-versus-insured exclusions cast too broad a net and can severely impair much needed coverage. For example, in the bankruptcy context, it is not uncommon for a bankruptcy trustee or a creditors' committee to bring suit against directors or officers on behalf of the debtor company. Although these suits are obviously not collusive, many insurers take the position that the bankruptcy trustee or creditors' committee stands in the debtor's shoes. As such, the insured-versus-insured exclusion can bar coverage for the suit.

To protect against this situation, it is necessary to modify the insured-versus-insured exclusion. Many insurers will agree to "carve back" claims by a bankruptcy trustee, examiner, receiver, liquidator, rehabilitator, creditors' committee, or any comparable authority from the insured-versus-insured exclusion upon request and without additional premium. (If the insured-versus-insured carve-back does not include each of the categories above—many carve-backs do not include suits by a creditors' committee—the policy does not fully protect the directors and officers.) Unfortunately, many companies do not request this change and only discover the limitation after it is too late.

TIP: Some newer insurance forms go further and only exclude claims by the insured entity against an insured. This is typically the best option for the insured when it is available.

Q 32.25.2   What other insured-versus-insured carve-backs are possible?

Other carve-backs that D&O insurance policies may provide, or that insureds may negotiate to include, are:

- cross-claims or third-party claims or other claims for contribution or indemnity by an insured person;

- employment-related claims brought by an insured person;

- claims brought by a former insured person who has not served for a certain amount of time (often more than three, four, or five years);

- claims brought by an insured person brought and maintained outside the United States, Canada, or any other common law country (including any territories thereof);

- securities claims, provided that they are instigated and continued totally independent of, and totally without the solicitation of, or assistance of, or active participation of, or intervention of, an insured; and

- whistleblower claims.

Even if a D&O insurance policy contains all of the available carve-backs, it will still address the original purpose of excluding potentially collusive claims. The impact of this exclusion comes as a surprise to many insureds, especially smaller companies. When determining whether to purchase D&O insurance and the amount of limit to buy, insureds should consider that, subject to the carve-backs discussed above, the D&O policy generally will not cover suits between insured persons or insured persons and the insured entity.

Q 32.25.3   What is the bodily injury and property damage exclusion?

Most D&O policies have a bodily injury and property damage exclusion to ensure that general liability or property losses do not end up eroding or exhausting the protections provided by the D&O coverage. While this makes sense, it is important to make sure that claims of negligence or breach of fiduciary duty against the directors or officers are still covered by the D&O policy even if the negligence or breach claims arise out of a bodily injury or property damage. This distinction is demonstrated by claims arising out of the COVID-19 pandemic. A claim to recover *for bodily injuries* that a plaintiff suffered as a result of COVID-19 exposure belongs on the general liability policy. However, a claim to recover *for damage to a company's stock price* because the board of directors were negligent in adopting or implementing policies to protect the company's employees or customers against COVID-19 related injuries, should be covered under a D&O policy.

To make sure that the D&O policy will cover the later claim, the bodily injury exclusion should state that only claims *for* bodily injury or property damage are excluded from the coverage—as opposed to any claim that is *based upon, arising out of, or attributable to* bodily injuries or property damage. This simple change can make a huge difference in coverage.

Q 32.26   How can an insured ensure that the acts of one insured person do not impact coverage for other, innocent insureds?

A D&O insurance policy should contain an exclusion severability provision stating that no wrongful act by any insured shall be imputed to any other insured for purposes of determining the applicability of any of the exclusions.

Negotiating Terms and Conditions

Q 32.27   Which terms and conditions should an insured negotiate?

Among the terms and conditions that should be negotiated are:

(1) allocation;
(2) the application severability clause;
(3) rescission;
(4) the forced settlement ("hammer") clause;
(5) the cancellation clause;
(6) the order-of-payments provision; and
(7) notice and claim reporting provisions.

Q 32.28   What are the important factors to consider when negotiating an allocation provision?

Allocation arises in two main contexts:

(i) claims against both insured and uninsured individuals or entities, and

(ii) claims for insured and uninsured matters.

The first can be understood by considering what happens when a public company and its directors and officers are the defendants in a non-securities claim. In this situation, particularly where one law firm represents all of the defendants, the issue that must be addressed is the extent to which the defense costs, awards, and settlements should be allocated between the insured directors and officers on the one hand and the uninsured corporation on the other. Subject to the terms of the D&O insurance policy, the insurance company will pay the portion of the covered losses allocated to the directors and officers, but not the portion allocated to the uninsured corporate entity.

Allocation is also an issue when a lawsuit includes covered and uncovered claims. One example is a suit against directors and officers that includes both counts for a breach of the duty of care (typically covered by a D&O insurance policy) and for libel and slander (typically not covered).

Most D&O insurance policies issued today address both of these allocation issues. Generally, the allocation provisions favor the insurance company by setting up a general framework for allocation that often is not as favorable to insureds as case law. The following is an example of such an allocation provision:

> If both Loss covered under this Policy and loss not covered under this Policy are incurred, either because a Claim against an Insured includes both covered and uncovered matters, or because a Claim is made against both a Director and Officer and the Company, the Insureds and the Insurer shall allocate such amount between covered Loss and uncovered loss based upon the *relative legal exposures* of such parties to such matters [emphasis added].

The italicized language seems fair on its face but, in many jurisdictions, it could produce a significantly less favorable result than would be obtained without the allocation provision in the policy. To illustrate, the rule established by a leading allocation case is that defense costs "reasonably related" to the defense of covered claims must be paid by the insurance company, even if such costs are partially related to the defense of an uncovered count. So long as the item of defense costs is reasonably related to defense of a covered claim, it may be apportioned wholly to the covered claim.[6] This rule can operate more favorably to an insured than the allocation test quoted above.

TIP: Differences of opinion over allocation are one of the most common reasons for disputes between insureds and insurance companies. This is understandable, considering that advancement typically is subject to issues regarding allocation. To avoid such disputes and provide as much protection to the insureds as possible, insureds should do their best to negotiate for the "reasonably related" test.

Q 32.29   What is the importance of an application severability clause?

An application severability clause helps ensure that "innocent" insureds do not lose their coverage. Absent such provision, if any insured had knowledge of a fact that was misstated in the D&O insurance application, coverage under the policy could be voided for *all* insureds. For instance, in *Cutter & Buck, Inc. v. Genesis Insurance Co.*,[7] the company's CFO pleaded guilty to fraud charges related to how the company was accounting for product sales. Because the CFO signed the D&O insurance application, Genesis imputed the CFO's knowledge of the fraud to all insureds under the policy and brought suit to rescind the coverage. The court found that Genesis was correct and allowed the insurer to void the policy—leaving all of the innocent insureds without coverage.

A strong application severability provision could have avoided this outcome by making it clear that the knowledge of an insured who knew of facts that were misrepresented in the application could not be imputed to any other insured person for the purpose of determining whether coverage is available under the policy.

Q 32.29.1   What does an application severability provision look like?

The following is an example of an insured-friendly application severability provision:

> Coverage under this Policy shall be void as to the following:
>
> (1) any Insured Person who knew, as of the Inception Date of the Policy Period, the facts that were not accurately and completely disclosed in the application;
>
> (2) the Company to the extent it indemnifies any Insured Person who knew that facts were not accurately and completely disclosed as of the inception date of the Policy Period; and
>
> (3) the Company if any past or present chief executive officer, chief financial officer, or chief operating officer of the Parent Company knew, as of the Inception Date of the Policy Period,

the facts that were not accurately and completely disclosed in the application.

Other than as provided above, the knowledge of an insured shall not be imputed to any other insured.

Q 32.30   What are the important factors to consider when negotiating a rescission provision?

"Rescission" is the act of completely voiding a policy due to a fraud or misrepresentation in the application for insurance. Rescission eliminates all coverage for all insureds back to the inception date of the policy.

Fortunately, rescinding a D&O insurance policy is not an easy task. Although the exact requirements vary by state, before an insurer can rescind a policy, the insurer must generally prove that there was a material misrepresentation in the application for insurance and that the insurer relied upon that misrepresentation when underwriting the risk. Since the insurer bears the burden of proof in establishing these elements, it will typically have to bring a successful lawsuit against its insured before it can rescind its policy. For many reasons, this is not something insurers want to do except in the most egregious of situations.

For this reason, among others, many insurers today will provide non- rescindable coverage upon request. However, insureds must be very careful here, as some non-rescindable endorsements may actually make it easier for insurers to deny coverage. For example, some endorsements make the policy fully non-rescindable, but then allow the insurer to determine whether there was a material misrepresentation in the application or whether the insurer relied upon such a misrepresentation. This type of language shifts the burden of disproving the insurer's position to the insured. Thus, instead of having to go to court to prove that there was a material misrepresentation *and* reliance on that misrepresentation, the non-rescindable endorsement allows the insurer to simply deny coverage for the claim. To dispute the insurer's position, the insured must then bring the lawsuit and bear the burden of proving that it did not make a misrepresentation in the application and/or that the insurer did not rely on the alleged misrepresentation.

For many insureds, such a provision would be less favorable and should be avoided. As with other provisions, this is an area where a review by a D&O insurance expert can be extremely helpful.

Q 32.31   What is a forced settlement clause?

A forced settlement (or "hammer") clause provides that if the insurer agrees to fund a settlement within the policy limit but the insured rejects the settlement, the insurer's liability is capped at the amount of the rejected settlement plus any defense costs incurred up to that date. Insurers include this provision in their D&O policies to prevent insureds from fighting on principle with the insurers' money. By forcing a settlement, the insurer is essentially saying that if the insured wants to continue to fight, it should bear the risk of a less favorable resolution to the case.

Q 32.31.1   What are the important factors to consider when negotiating a forced settlement clause?

While a hammer clause as described above may sound reasonable, there are many reasons why such a clause can be problematic. The following are some examples of how a hammer clause can be unfair:

Example 1: The insured is defending a claim where, if the case goes to trial, there is a 90% chance that the case would be resolved for $25,000 or less, but there is a 10% chance that the loss could be as much as $300,000. The plaintiff makes an offer to settle the claim for $250,000 (the amount of the policy's applicable retention). Using the hammer clause, the insurer "recommends" settlement to force the insured to accept the $250,000 settlement so that the claim could never reach the insurer's policy limit. Such a result is unfair since the insurer is forcing the insured to pay more than the claim is worth. To avoid this risk, the hammer clause must be limited so that the insurer can only enforce the hammer if the settlement exceeds the self-insured retention of the policy and/or the insurer is willing to fully fund the settlement.

Example 2: The plaintiff offers to settle a claim on the following terms: Director X pays $5 million, officer Y pays $5 million, and the insurer pays $1 million. Again, the insurer would have an incentive to "recommend" this settlement in order to limit its exposure. However, forcing the insured (and director *X* and officer *Y*) to accept this offer is unfair. To avoid this risk, the insurer should be required to fully fund any proposed settlement before it can use the hammer.

Example 3: The plaintiff offers to settle a claim with a nominal payment of $1,000, but the company must agree that it will no longer engage in a particular type of business practice. Clearly, enforcing the hammer clause without consideration of the value of discontinuing the business practice at issue is unfair. To ensure that an insurer cannot force this type of settlement, the hammer clause should be limited so that it can only apply if all damages are compensatory in nature.

Example 4: Finally, consider a situation where settling a lawsuit would require an admission of wrongdoing or would encourage other lawsuits. The cost of subsequent settlements could exceed the policy limit and the policy might not provide coverage. To avoid these problems, insureds should request that the insurer remove the hammer clause from the policy. If an insurer will not delete the hammer clause, the clause should be limited so that it only applies if:

(1)   the settlement exceeds the self-insured retention;

(2)   the insurer is willing to fully fund the settlement; and

(3)   the settlement only involves compensatory damages (that is, there is no non-monetary relief required by the settlement).

Another option is to "soften the hammer" so that the insured would only be liable for a small percentage above any settlement recommended by the insurer (typically 10%–25%).

Q 32.32   What does a typical D&O policy cancellation clause provide?

The cancellation clause in a D&O insurance policy establishes the circumstances in which an insurer may cancel its policy. Many D&O insurance policies allow the insurer to cancel a policy for any reason or for no reason at all. Obviously, directors and officers would not want their D&O insurance policy cancelled by an insurer that senses serious claims are coming (for example, when an insurer fears a bankruptcy filing may be in the company's future).

Many states have attempted to address this problem by requiring that all policies issued in their state include a "state amendatory endorsement," which limits how and when an insurer can cancel its policy. Unfortunately, few states have kept up with changing market conditions, and insurers are often willing to provide more protection against cancellation than the states require in their mandatory endorsements. In fact, many of the mandatory state endorsements actually reduce coverage for insureds today rather than increase it. State laws on cancellation were intended to protect insureds by providing a minimum, not a maximum, amount of protection.

Q 32.32.1   What are the important factors to consider when negotiating a cancellation clause?

To be sure that a D&O insurance policy has the broadest protection against cancellation possible, insureds should negotiate their D&O insurance policies so that:

(1) the D&O insurance policy only allows the insurer to cancel coverage if the company fails to pay the premium when due; and

(2) if the D&O insurance policy has a state-required endorsement that limits when the insurer may cancel coverage, it must also have a "state amendatory inconsistent" endorsement that states that, to the extent permitted by law, where there is an inconsistency between a state amendatory endorsement and any term or condition of the policy, the insurer shall apply the terms and conditions of either the amendatory endorsement or the policy that are more favorable to the insured.

Q 32.33   What does a typical "order-of-payments" provision provide?

A typical "order-of-payments" provision states that the D&O insurance policy limit should apply first to losses due under the Side A coverage (the coverage for directors and officers). Then, if any limit remains, the limit should apply to company losses under the Side B and/or Side C coverage. Some order-of-payments provisions go further and permit a senior officer of the named insured to defer any payments to the company until after potential payments are made under the Side A coverage.

Q 32.33.1   What are the important factors to consider when negotiating an order-of-payments provision?

An order-of-payments provision is an attempt to ensure that, in the event of a bankruptcy, the policy proceeds will be available to the directors and officers and not the debtor. The U.S. Bankruptcy Code prohibits clauses that trigger modifications to coverage upon:

(1)   the filing of a petition in bankruptcy;

(2)   insolvency; or

(3)   the financial condition of the company.

However, since it applies in all circumstances, some courts have cited the order-of-payments provision as evidence that the policy proceeds are intended to benefit the individual directors and officers as opposed to the company. Although not all courts agree with this conclusion, directors and officers should insist on an order-of-payments provision. Insureds should be forewarned that provisions that allow a senior officer to decide whether the proceeds should be held for the company or paid out to the individuals are likely to be unenforceable. If a senior officer waived the insured entities' right to insurance in favor of the directors and officers (including, potentially, themselves), it is likely that this action would conflict with the senior officer's fiduciary duties to the insured entities' shareholders and/or creditors.

Q 32.34   What is the importance of the notice and claim reporting requirements of a D&O policy?

Failure to give timely notice of a claim is one of the most common reasons insurers deny coverage for an otherwise covered matter. To avoid a denial of coverage, insureds should become very familiar with the reporting requirements of their D&O policies. In addition to addressing issues of timing for reporting claims (detailed below), insureds should also seek to limit the insured persons whose knowledge will trigger the reporting requirements.

Q 32.34.1 What do typical notice and claim reporting provisions look like?

The notice provisions in D&O policies can differ dramatically. The following are some of the many types of reporting requirements that exist:

Claims must be reported within the policy period. This is the traditional "claims made and reported" language—and it is undesirable. The problem with this language is that the policy will only cover a claim made the day before the policy is about to expire if the insured reports that claim before the policy expires. This puts an unreasonable burden on the insured. On the plus side, a claim made early in the policy period could be reported as late as the last day of the policy period (as much as a year later) without loss of coverage.

Claims must be reported as soon as practicable. This language softens the result above in that an insured would be allowed to report a claim that is made late in the policy period for some "reasonable" period after the policy expired (this language creates a "mini-tail" reporting period). However, this language may also require that a claim made early in the policy period be reported long before the expiration of the policy. How long "as soon as practicable" is will depend on the circumstances.

Claims must be reported as soon as practicable, but in all events within [a set number, usually thirty to ninety] days after the claim is made. This language is similar to the "as soon as practicable" language, except that it essentially defines "as soon as practicable" as a set number of days. Generally, insureds would do better with the ambiguity of the "as soon as practicable" language.

Claims must be reported as soon as practicable within the policy period, but if the claim is made within the last thirty days of the policy period, the insured will have an additional thirty [some policies will extend to as many as ninety] days after the policy period to report the claim. This language is the most insured-friendly, as it allows maximum flexibility as to when a claim may be reported.

Q 32.34.2   How do notice provisions address the reporting "trigger"?

Because the typical notice provision applies to all insureds (including *all* directors and *all* officers of *all* insured entities) and many of the insureds may not fully understand the D&O insurance reporting requirements, it is best to limit the reporting trigger to when the risk manager or general counsel of the parent company first learns of the claim.

For example, one insurer provides as follows:

> An Organization or an Insured shall, as a condition precedent to the obligations of the Insurer under this Policy, give written notice to the Insurer of a Claim made against an Insured as soon as practicable after the Named Entity's Risk Manager or General Counsel (or equivalent position) first becomes aware of the Claim, but in all events no later than either:
>
> (1)   the end of the Policy Period or the Discovery Period (if applicable); or
>
> (2)   within 30 days after the end of the Policy Period or the Discovery Period (if applicable), as long as such Claim was first made against an Insured within the final 30 days of the Policy Period or the Discovery Period (if applicable).

CASE STUDY: *Briggs Ave. LLC v. Ins. Corp. of Hannover*[8]

The need to negotiate the notice provision was recently highlighted by Second Circuit decision in which the insured's D&O insurance policy contained the "as soon as practicable" requirement. Briggs Ave. LLC, a one-member company and owner of a building in the Bronx, failed to update its address with the state. Thus, it did not become aware of a personal injury action being brought against it, or receive the summons and complaint that were served by notice to the secretary of state to the company's previous address, until months later. Although the company promptly notified its insurers after it discovered the complaint (when it was served directly with

---

a motion for default judgment), the insurers denied coverage on the basis that they did not receive notice as soon as practicable after the claim as made. The U.S. Court of Appeals for the Second Circuit agreed, finding that the insured could have "practicably" changed its address on file with the secretary of state and that the insured's notification of the lawsuit almost eight months after service of process was sent to the secretary of state was not "as soon as practicable."

Negotiating Excess Policies

Q 32.35   How do excess policies typically work with the primary policy?

Most D&O insurance programs with more than $10 million in limit will have a number of D&O insurance policies consisting of a primary policy and one or more excess policies. (See Q 32.10, *supra*, for further discussion of the structure of typical D&O insurance programs and for an illustration of two traditional models.)

Excess policies come in two general types: the "independent" (stand-alone) form and the "follow-form" policy. The independent-form policy has the full complement of policy provisions: coverage agreements, definitions, exclusions, and conditions. The follow-form policy, by contrast, adopts the terms of the underlying policy, but generally contains its own special provisions. Unfortunately, these special provisions can diminish overall coverage.

Insureds often fail to analyze or negotiate follow-form policies, which are far more prevalent than independent-form policies. This makes little sense because once the limit of liability of the primary policy is exhausted by the payment of losses, the excess policy will be very relevant as to whether a claim will continue to be paid. In fact, in a large D&O insurance program, the excess policies constitute the vast majority of the limit of coverage.

The failure to review and negotiate an excess policy may result in a loss of coverage, particularly as it relates to excess policies' provisions addressing:

- attachment/exhaustion;
- arbitration; and
- appeals.

Q 32.35.1   What factors should be considered when negotiating an excess policy's attachment/ exhaustion provision?

Perhaps the most important provisions in an excess policy are those that determine when that policy will begin to provide coverage. This is referred to as the "attachment" or "exhaustion" point. Some excess policies state that the excess insurer's liability for any covered loss will attach *only* after the *insurers* of the underlying policies have paid for loss equal to the full amount of the underlying limit. Such a provision could be interpreted to mean that payments by the insureds (or another source such as a Side A policy) to settle coverage disputes would not count toward the exhaustion of the underlying limit of liability. This is exactly what happened in the *Qualcomm* case.

 CASE STUDY: *Qualcomm, Inc. v. Certain Underwriters at Lloyd's, London*[9]

Qualcomm had a $20 million primary policy with AIG and an excess policy with Lloyd's of London (Lloyd's). In resolving the underlying lawsuit, Qualcomm incurred $28.6 million in defense and indemnity costs. In seeking insurance funding for the loss, Qualcomm settled a coverage controversy with AIG so that AIG paid $16 million of its $20 million limit. Qualcomm then sought to recover $8.6 million from its excess insurer Lloyd's (Qualcomm was willing to absorb the $4 million in costs between the $16 million paid by AIG and the $20 million limit). Lloyd's refused to pay any of the excess loss based on its attachment/exhaustion

---

provision. This provision stated that the "Underwriters shall be liable only after the insurers under each of the Underlying Policies [i.e., the AIG policy] have paid or have been held liable to pay the full amount of the Underlying Limit of Liability." Qualcomm sued and the court held in favor of Lloyd's. According to the court, since AIG did not pay its full $20 million limit and since AIG was never held liable to pay the limit, the terms of the exhaustion provision in the Lloyd's policy were not met and Lloyd's would not be required to pay any amounts to the insured.

Q 32.35.2   How can an insured negotiate an attachment provision to avoid an unfair result?

Because strict attachment/exhaustion provisions have the potential to gut coverage, as *Qualcomm* demonstrates, insureds need to negotiate excess insurance policies so that they recognize payments *made by the insureds*, as well as the other insurers. An example of such a provision might provide the following:

> Underwriters shall be liable only after the insurers of each of the Underlying Policies and/or the Insureds and/or any other source have paid or have been held liable to pay the full amount of the Underlying Limit of Liability.

If an insurer refuses to provide the preferred language above and there are no alternative insurers who are willing to do so, another option is a "shaving of limits" provision. Such a provision states that the excess insurer will attach once the underlying limit has been paid by the underlying insurers and/or the insureds, but that the excess insurer will receive the benefit of the underlying negotiations and will pay no greater a percentage of the excess limit than the lowest percentage paid by any underlying insurers. In other words, if the underlying insurer paid only 80% of its limit, the excess insurer would only have to pay 80% of its limit.

The problem with this solution is that there may be a reason to give a "discount" to an underlying insurer that does not exist with an excess insurer. For example, what if the reason for giving a discount to the underlying insurer is that the underlying policy had a different choice of law provision than the excess policy? In such a case, the reason to give a discount to the underlying insurer would not exist with the excess insurer. As such, it would be unfair for the excess insurer to benefit from the discount.

Q 32.35.3   What factors should be considered when negotiating an excess policy's arbitration provision?

Some D&O insurance policies require disputes between the insured and the insurer to be resolved by arbitration (as opposed to litigation). Many insureds consider this a problem: Because litigation tends to be more insured-friendly than arbitration, they would prefer to have the option to litigate coverage disputes. This issue can be even more problematic in large insurance programs that require multiple insurers to build the total limit of coverage. Large insurance programs may have multiple and potentially inconsistent arbitration provisions. This type of inconsistency could force an insured to fight multiple battles on multiple fronts with potentially inconsistent results. Clearly, this is not what an insured wants from its D&O insurance program.

To avoid this result, an insured should attempt to remove all arbitration requirements from its policies. If this is not possible, an insured should seek to have all of the insurers agree to one arbitration method with only one choice of law provision to resolve any potential coverage disputes. Which law is chosen and which jurisdiction should be specified as the judicial "seat" of the arbitration are likewise matters of significant concern; counsel experienced in such matters should be consulted.

Q 32.35.4   What factors should be considered when negotiating an excess policy's appeals provision?

Some D&O insurance policies allow an excess insurer to appeal an adverse judgment against an insured even if the insured has no desire to appeal. One reason an insurer may want to appeal a matter is if the insurer believes the jury awarded unreasonably high damages and that such damages might be reduced on appeal. By appealing the judgment, the insurer may be able to reduce its losses. The insured, on the other hand, may have no desire to appeal the jury award—especially if the insurer is fully covering the loss. Instead, the insured may prefer to leave the matter resolved and remove the distraction of the litigation.

Perhaps the most troubling aspect of an appeals provision, however, is that most appeals provisions do not make the insurer responsible for any additional losses above the insurer's policy limit incurred as a result of the appeal. Thus, if instead of reducing the jury award on appeal, the case is remanded and the new jury returns an even higher award—one that exceeds the insurer's policy limit—the insured could potentially be required to pay for the increased award.

To avoid this result, insureds should negotiate to delete the appeals provision from its program.

How D&O Insurance Works in Specific Situations

Mergers and Acquisitions

Q 32.36   What kinds of coverage issues arise where a new subsidiary is created or acquired?

D&O insurance policies customarily cover the entity named in the policy and any subsidiary in existence at the *inception* of the policy period. Most D&O policies define a "subsidiary" to include a corporation of which the insured parent owns more than 50% of the voting stock, either directly or through one or more subsidiaries. Based on this definition, a coverage issue can arise for a subsidiary created or acquired *during* the policy period.

The treatment of a new subsidiary varies widely from policy to policy. The most restrictive approach provides coverage for the directors and officers of a newly acquired subsidiary *only* if:

(1)   notice of the acquisition is given to the insurance company,

(2)   the insurance company agrees to provide coverage in its *sole discretion*, and

(3)   the named parent corporation accepts any special terms, conditions, exclusions, and *additional premium charges* required by the insurance company.

A somewhat less restrictive approach provides coverage for the directors and officers of the newly acquired subsidiary subject to premium and coverage revisions to the original policy. Although coverage is not at the sole discretion of the insurance company, it may require exclusions, an additional premium or both, which can put coverage out of reach as a practical matter.

The best provision affords *automatic* coverage, without any additional premium, for any new subsidiary below a specified size. Several insurers include such a provision in their D&O insurance policy form for a newly acquired or created subsidiary whose assets do not exceed 10%–25% of the *total consolidated assets* of the named entity and its subsidiaries as of the inception date of the policy. But not all policies providing automatic coverage compare assets this way. For example, a provision in one policy that can prove to be so restrictive as to be almost illusory compares the assets of the new subsidiary with the assets of the named entity only—not the consolidated assets of the named entity and its existing subsidiaries.

If the D&O insurance policy form does not include automatic coverage for a small newly acquired or created subsidiary without additional premium, insureds should request such coverage by endorsement. If the D&O insurance policy form provides such coverage, an insured should make sure its size test utilizes the *consolidated* financial picture of the named entity and its existing subsidiaries.

Sale of the Company

Q 32.37   What are the possible ramifications for a D&O insurance policy of the sale of a company?

The sale of a company can increase the risk of a claim dramatically. In the case of a sale, some shareholders may want to sell the company for top dollar, while others may feel that the value in keeping the business exceeds the proposed purchase price. Whoever loses the argument may sue the company and its directors for breach of the duty of care or loyalty. Another possibility is that employees or third parties may disapprove of the deal and bring suit. A transaction can even trigger the filing of latent claims. For instance, an employee who is the subject of harassment may take no action out of a sense of loyalty to the company. Once the owners decide to sell, the employee may feel the company is no longer loyal and decide to file suit. It is important to protect against these claims, which may not be filed until after the transaction closes.

At the same time that the risk is increasing, coverage under the D&O insurance policy is transitioning. When a company is purchased, its D&O insurance policies transition into run-off coverage. What this means is that the policy will only cover pre-sale wrongful acts for the remainder of the policy period. Typically, the purchaser's D&O insurance policies will begin covering post-sale wrongful acts immediately. The problem with this transition is that the remaining policy period is at most one year long (assuming the sale occurs the day after renewal). Claims for pre-closing wrongful acts may be brought years later.

As a result, without further action, insureds may be without coverage for claims with long statutes of limitations that can be filed *years* after a policy expires, such as fraud claims, which, under the Sarbanes-Oxley Act of 2002, may be filed by stockholders up to five years after the fraud was allegedly committed.[10] To protect against these claims, insureds may purchase additional run-off coverage, sometimes called a "tail" policy, for periods of one to six years. Tail policies are usually written as an endorsement to an existing D&O insurance policy, but also may be in the form of a policy newly issued by another insurer.

Q 32.37.1   What are the important factors to consider when purchasing run-off coverage?

As with other aspects of D&O insurance, insureds must consider many factors when purchasing run-off coverage, including the premium and duration of coverage, the remaining policy limit, and the adequacy of the terms and conditions of the expiring policy.

First, the insured should review the policy. Since it probably does not include a predetermined premium for a specified term of run-off coverage, the insured will need to negotiate those terms with the insurer before the acquisition is effective. The typical duration of run-off policies today is six years, for which the premium is likely to be 150%–250% of the expiring policy's annual premium.

Purchasing run-off insurance does *not* automatically reinstate the expiring policy's limit. Consequently, if all or most of the limit on the expiring policy has been eroded by payments of losses, run-off insurance will not provide the financial comfort an insured seeks unless a fresh limit is obtained.

Because run-off insurance is usually provided by an endorsement to an expiring D&O insurance policy, run-off insurance will inherit any coverage defects in that policy (such as an unduly narrow definition of claim or a lack of coverage for punitive damages) unless the terms of the expiring policy are negotiated. The insurer would prefer to confine negotiations to the premium and duration of the run-off endorsement, but an insured may push to widen the scope of the negotiations (especially given the substantial amount of premium involved). As noted, run-off coverage generally costs more than the premium on the expiring policy. If the insurer on the expiring policy is unwilling to negotiate to the insured's satisfaction, it is worth checking to see if another insurer is willing to provide run-off coverage on more acceptable terms.

Bankruptcy

Q 32.38   What kinds of coverage issues arise in a bankruptcy?

Although most claims are paid under either the Side B or Side C coverage of the D&O insurance policy, Side B and Side C coverage can have some real disadvantages from the perspective of directors and officers if their company becomes a debtor in bankruptcy. Chief among those disadvantages is that the bankruptcy court may consider the D&O insurance policy proceeds to be an asset of the bankruptcy estate. As such, the policy proceeds may be subject to the automatic stay imposed by the Bankruptcy Code[11] when a company files for bankruptcy. Since the automatic stay typically does not apply to individual directors and officers, they may be left self-funding any defense, settlement, and judgment until the bankruptcy case is resolved (a process that could take years). Worse yet, if the bankruptcy court ultimately decides that the policy proceeds are assets of the company's bankruptcy estate, the court could make those proceeds available to creditors to satisfy the company's liabilities, leaving the directors and officers with little or no coverage for their losses.

Q 32.38.1   Are D&O insurance proceeds typically considered property of the bankruptcy estate?

Courts are split on whether D&O insurance policy proceeds should be considered an asset of the bankruptcy estate. Although the proceeds of a D&O insurance policy are most likely to be considered an asset of the bankruptcy estate when the policy includes entity coverage (Side C coverage), some courts have ruled that the policy proceeds are part of the bankruptcy estate based solely on the existence of corporate reimbursement coverage (Side B coverage). Other courts have found that the policy proceeds should not be considered part of the bankruptcy estate regardless of whether there is corporate reimbursement or entity coverage.

With such inconsistency, insureds need to take steps to make sure that their D&O insurance policy will protect them if the company becomes a debtor in bankruptcy in the future.

Cyber Insurance

Q 32.39   Does a D&O policy cover cyber risk?

A security incident presents a host of risks to the directors and officers of a company. For example, a data breach may result in business interruption losses, loss of profits, loss of intellectual property, fines and penalties, and/or significant harm to a company's reputation. Each of these may result in claims against the individual directors and officers for their alleged failure to prevent a security incident.

For public companies, a security incident may also result in a shareholder derivative suit or class action securities claims against the directors and officers. Although lawsuits against directors and officers related to security incidents have had mixed success, the risk to directors and officers is real—as are the costs to defend the claims. In extreme cases, these claims can result in personal liability to the directors and officers.

For this reason, directors and officers need to have a strong cyber liability insurance policy in place to minimize their losses after a breach. To limit their individual exposure, they also need a strong D&O policy—one that does not exclude losses related to data security. Directors and officers also need to safeguard their business judgment rule protections by making and documenting their informed decisions about cyber security.

Changing Insurers

Q 32.40   What impact can changing insurers have on an insured's D&O coverage?

One reason companies change D&O insurance insurers is to save premium. A lower premium is a worthy goal. However, even if the terms offered by a competing insurer are identical to those of a company's current insurer, a switch can create a gap in coverage that puts the company's directors' and officers' personal assets at risk.

Key terms that insureds should negotiate to ensure that they are protected if their company files for bankruptcy:

- definition of "insured" (*see* Q 32.17);
- change-in-control provision;
- insured-versus-insured exclusion (*see* Q 32.25 *et seq.*);
- order-of-payments provision (*see* Q 32.33 *et seq.*);
- cancellation clause (*see* Q 32.32);
- non-rescindable coverage (*see* Q 32.30);
- definition of "application" (*see* Q 32.15); and
- application severability provision (*see* Q 32.29).

Before changing insurers, a company must evaluate the new policy and the application process to avoid or minimize the gap. In particular, a company should focus on:

(1) whether the new policy will provide continuity of coverage; and

(2)   the effect of any warranty statement required by the new insurer.

Q 32.40.1   How can insureds ensure continuity of coverage?

As discussed above, D&O insurance policies are generally written on a "claims-made" basis (*see* Q 32.9). This means that only claims that are made and reported during the policy period will be covered by the policy. In contrast, many other types of policies are written on an "occurrence" basis. With an occurrence policy, the policy in effect at the time the harm is caused is the policy that will respond. Claims-made and reported policies are extremely time-sensitive, and this sensitivity is particularly pronounced when an insured changes insurers.

Consider the following example: An insured purchased Policy *A* with *ABC* insurer with a policy period from January 1, 2014, to January 1, 2015. The next year, the insured decides to change insurers and purchased Policy *B* from *XYZ* insurer with a policy period from January 1, 2015, to January 1, 2016. One week before the end of Policy *A*'s policy period (on December 25), a claim is made against the insured. Unfortunately, the insured fails to report the claim for two weeks (until January 8). At that time, Policy *B* is in effect.

A possible result of this situation could be that *ABC* insurer would deny coverage for the claim as the claim was not reported during its policy period. In addition, *XYZ* insurer would deny coverage for the claim because the claim was not made during its policy period. In short, the insured has lost coverage for what should be a covered claim.

This problem can become even more pronounced with larger D&O insurance programs where there are multiple excess policies. For example, if it becomes necessary to replace an insurer in a multi-layer program, the continuity issue described above would likely affect not only the replaced insurer, but also all of the excess insurers above that insurer's layer as well.

Thus, when thinking about switching to another insurer, an insured should negotiate for "full continuity" on the new policy so the new policy will cover claims arising from wrongful acts that occurred after the continuity date of the *prior* policy. To do so, the prospective new insurer must either delete any prior acts exclusion it may have, or use the same continuity date as the old policy.

Q 32.40.2   What considerations does a warranty statement by the new issuer raise when changing insurers?

A similar gap in coverage can arise if a new insurer requires a warranty statement, either in response to a question in the application for insurance or in a stand-alone warranty letter. A warranty statement requires the insured to warrant that no proposed insured is aware of any facts or circumstances that could give rise to a claim. (Generally, insureds should not provide a warranty statement if renewing the same limit with the same insurer.) Similar to a prior-acts exclusion, such a warranty statement can produce a gap in coverage because claims arising from any listed circumstances will be not be covered by the new policy (the new insurer will exclude all known facts and circumstances), and such claims will not be covered by the old policy because it has already expired.

If the proposed insurer refuses to drop the warranty statement requirement, the insured should try to minimize the gap in coverage by:

(a)   negotiating the language of the warranty statement to narrow its exclusionary effect, and/or

(b)   providing a notice to the existing insurer of circumstances that could give rise to a claim.

Q 32.40.3   What does a typical warranty statement look like?

Standard warranty statements do not exist. Insureds must review and narrow overly broad language. For example, some warranty forms ask insureds to warrant that there is no "fact, circumstance or situation that *might* give rise to any claim." However, almost any fact, circumstance or situation, however remote, *might* give rise to a claim. If insureds list them all, they would gut the coverage provided by the proposed policy. If insureds fail to list them, they may be accused of application fraud and the insurer may attempt to rescind the policy or reject coverage of the undisclosed acts. In response to such a provision, insureds should negotiate a warranty statement along the following lines: "There are no facts, circumstances, or situations which the *insureds reasonably believe are likely to give rise to a claim.*"

Another way to try to avoid the gap caused by a warranty statement is to provide a notice of circumstances under the expiring policy. A notice-of-circumstances provision provides that if, during the policy period, an insured gives the insurer notice of circumstances that may give rise to a claim, any subsequent claim against the insured arising out of such circumstances shall be treated as if it was made during the policy period.

Proceed with caution, however. To be valid, a notice of circumstances must provide the information called for by the policy. Failure to be sufficiently specific may result in the insurer rejecting the notice. And unfortunately, even if the insurer rejects the notice, it may still trigger a prior notice exclusion in the new policy. As a result, neither policy would cover claims arising from such circumstances.

Claims

Reporting Claims

Q 32.41   When should an insured report a claim?

A claims-made-and-reported policy, by definition, requires that a claim be properly noticed "during the policy period." A strict reading of this language means that:

(1) a claim that arises a few days before a policy expires must still be reported before that policy expires for coverage to attach; and

(2) a claim that occurs in the first few days of a policy can still be covered even if it is not reported until just before the policy expires.

As discussed above (*see* Q 32.34.1), some D&O insurance policies attempt to soften the strict timing requirements by allowing claims to be reported "as soon as practicable" or as soon as practicable "but in no event more than 30 days after the claim is made." This type of language can create a "mini-tail" reporting period that allows a claim that occurs shortly before the policy expires to still be reported in a timely fashion after the policy expires. On the other hand, this type of language can exclude coverage on a claim that is not reported within the window set forth in the policy even if the policy has not yet expired.

Q 32.42   What details should be included in the notice of claim?

Once it is clear that notice of a claim or circumstance should be sent, it is important to ensure that proper notice is given. For a claim, it is generally necessary to forward the written demand for relief to the insurer. In addition, when noticing circumstances, the D&O insurance policy may require a description of:

(1)   the claim or circumstance;

(2)   the nature of the "wrongful act";

(3)   the nature of the alleged or potential damage;

(4)   the names of actual or potential claimants; and

(5)   how the company first became aware of the claim or circumstance.

CASE STUDY: *Westrec Marina Mgmt., Inc. v. Arrowood Indem. Co.*[12]

Insurers take the claim reporting timing requirement very seriously. For example, in *Westrec Marina Management, Inc. v. Arrowood Indemnity Co.*, the insured, Westrec, received a claim letter seven days before its D&O policy was to renew with the *same* insurer. Westrec failed to report the claim until the new policy period, and the insurer denied coverage. The court upheld the insurer's denial, explaining that Westrec had not properly made the claim during

---

the first policy period, since Westrec failed to report it within the allotted time set forth in the first policy. Further, the claim was not proper under the new policy because the claim was not first made during that policy period.

TIP: Given the obvious importance of ensuring a claim is reported in the appropriate time frame, it is vitally important that a company have a well-defined system in place for claims to be forwarded to the company's risk manager or general counsel and, ultimately, its insurer. Failure to provide clear direction to company managers can result in a delay in reporting and, in turn, a dispute or even a denial of coverage by the insurer.

The policy will also state where the insured should send the notice. The insured should send all insurers (primary and excess) notice of any claim or potential claim even if the insured does not expect the claim to exceed the primary insurer's limit.

In addition, different insurers on the same D&O insurance program may have different requirements. To obtain coverage at all layers, it is important to notice *each insurer* and follow the terms of *each policy*.

Q 32.43   Are there instances in which an insured should consider *not* reporting a claim?

Generally, reporting a claim under a D&O insurance policy is not discretionary. Thus, even if a claim does not appear to have any merit or is unlikely to exceed the company's deductible or retention, the insured should still normally report it promptly. That said, some companies are concerned that reporting such claims can potentially result in higher premiums and/or less favorable coverage when the policy is renewed and will either not report or defer reporting the claim.

However, the claims-made requirement of a D&O insurance policy does not afford a company the luxury of waiting to gauge the severity of a claim.

Q 32.43.1   What are the possible consequences of *not* reporting a claim?

Failure to promptly report a claim can result in an insurer denying coverage even if the claim later develops into a more substantive and insurable risk. This risk can be significant, as a claim that appears small or without merit may, nonetheless, result in large legal costs and/or liability. Hence, it is advisable to report all claims that are likely to fall within the ambit of coverage afforded by the D&O insurance policy and disregard any commercial consideration in connection with the claims reporting decision.

TIP: The true test of an insurance program is how it responds to a claim. Starting with the decision of whether to put insurers on notice of a D&O claim or a circumstance and continuing through the structuring of a settlement agreement, insureds get better results when they take an active role in the claims process.

Defending Claims

Q 32.44   How are D&O claims defended?

Most D&O policies are written on a "non-duty-to-defend" basis. A "non-duty-to-defend" policy (*see* Q 32.8) allows the insured (as opposed to the insurer) to manage and control the defense of the claim. This means that the insured can decide issues such as which defense counsel to retain and when and if it will settle the claim. Although a D&O insurer will still have a say in these important decisions (typically, such decisions are made with the consent of the insurer), a non-duty-to-defend policy is attractive to many D&O insureds given the types of claims that can be brought under a D&O policy.

Of course, some D&O insureds prefer a "duty to defend" policy. Typically, smaller companies or companies that do not have a legal department or other staff to manage a complex D&O claim will prefer such a policy.

Perhaps the best option, however, is a policy that allows the insured to choose whether it wants to run the defense for any particular claim. Many insurers today will allow the insured to choose whether any particular claim will be handled on a duty to defend or a non-duty-to-defend basis.

Post-Claim Issues

Q 32.45   What should an insured expect after reporting a claim?

Generally speaking, the insurer may respond with a "reservation-of-rights" letter, discussing potential coverage issues raised by the nature of the claim. It is also possible that the insurer will issue a "denial-of-coverage" letter.

Reservation of Rights

Q 32.45.1   What is a reservation-of-rights letter?

Shortly after an insured reports a claim, the insurer will typically respond with a reservation-of-rights letter. This letter will discuss potential coverage issues raised by the nature of the claim and will explain why the claim may not be covered. Because an insurer is often deemed to have waived any issues that are not raised in a reservation of rights letter, many reservation-of-rights letters are extremely broad.

Although a reservation-of-rights letter is obviously for the insurer's benefit, it should not necessarily create an adverse relationship between the insurer and insured. It is the insurer's initial response, not its final decision on coverage. The reservation-of-rights letter can be useful to the insured because it provides an early indication of the insurer's position. It also allows the insured to take necessary steps to protect its potentially uninsured interests.

Further, the reservation-of-rights letter allows the insurer to withhold a final coverage determination on certain allegations until sufficient facts have been developed. For example, most claims against directors and officers include allegations that the director or officer acted dishonestly, committed fraud, and/or acted in bad faith—all of which, if true, would likely nullify coverage under a D&O insurance policy. By issuing a reservation-of-rights letter, the insurer can advance defense costs and entertain settlement proposals, but withhold its final determination as to the merits of the plaintiff's allegations without prejudicing its own right to deny coverage if the allegations turn out to be true.

> **TIP:** Although a claim may put an insured at odds with an insurer, many insureds can benefit from working with an insurer as a business partner. Insurers can be a valuable source of knowledge and experience regarding a claim. For example, during the height of the stock option backdating claims, some insurers were sharing their experience about settlement ranges and terms with their insureds. This sharing of information allowed many insureds to resolve their claims more quickly and less expensively than they might have otherwise done.

Denial of Coverage

Q 32.45.2   What is a denial-of-coverage letter?

An insurer may also issue a denial-of-coverage letter denying coverage if the claim appears to be outside the scope of coverage provided by the policy or if the insureds have not complied with the terms and conditions of the policy.

TIP: In many jurisdictions, a denial-of-coverage or disclaimer letter will effectively terminate the obligation of the insured to keep the insurer informed of claim developments. Notwithstanding whether a duty exists, however, it may be wise to continue to keep the insurer informed of case developments, as later developments can alter the insurer's coverage position. In addition, keeping the insurer apprised of developments can assist the insured if the coverage dispute is later litigated.

Duties and Obligations of Insureds

Q 32.46   What are an insured's obligations with respect to the insurer after a claim has been reported?

Most D&O insurance policies impose a duty to cooperate and to provide such information as the insurer may reasonably require. Assuming that the insurer does not deny coverage at the outset, it is incumbent upon the insured to keep the insurer informed of significant developments as they occur. Generally, this means that the insured must forward copies of pleadings, settlement demands, and significant court orders to the insurance company. The insured's defense counsel may also be required to provide periodic updates or "case status reports" to the insurer.

Perhaps the most critical duty an insured has is to advise the insurer of any settlement negotiations at the time that they occur. Failure to keep the insurer advised of settlement talks will likely result in the insurer denying coverage even if the claim would have otherwise been covered.

Other duties of an insured include taking all reasonable steps to mitigate any damages.

     CASE STUDY: *Vigilant Ins. Co. v. Bear Stearns Cos.*[13]

In *Vigilant Insurance Co. v. Bear Stearns Cos.*, Bear Stearns failed to obtain its insurers' consent prior to settling a case. The insurers denied coverage, citing the consent provision in the policy that stated that "[t]he Insured agrees not to settle any Claim, incur any Defense Costs or otherwise assume any contractual obligation or admit any liability with respect to any Claim . . . without the insurer's consent."[14] The New York Court of Appeals held that the denial of coverage was proper, as Bear Stearns had clearly not obtained the consent of the D&O insurer prior to settlement. The result was a loss of $40 million of insurance coverage.

Privileges and Protections

Q 32.47   Are communications related to a claim protected by the attorney-client privilege and work-product doctrine?

A company and its directors and officers should be aware that not all communications between the insurer and the insured will be protected by the attorney-client privilege and work-product doctrine. In fact, the rules governing when a communication will be protected vary by jurisdiction; thus, an insured should always consult with legal counsel to determine the amount of protection afforded to a particular communication.

There may also be limits on the protection granted to communications between a director or officer and the company's in-house or outside counsel. Again, the amount of protection varies by jurisdiction, but communications between a director or officer and the corporate attorney may not be protected. This is of particular concern in derivative lawsuits or other matters where the company's interests may not align with the interests of the director or officer.

Issues concerning the attorney-client privilege and work-product doctrine sometimes arise when there are joint defense agreements. Since lawsuits often name multiple officers and directors and possibly other parties who are represented by more than one attorney, it is sometimes necessary to implement joint defense agreements so that the parties can present a united and cohesive front. Some jurisdictions recognize that communications between parties with a common legal purpose are protected. However, when the interests of the parties do not align legally, the protection may falter. Again, insureds should consult legal counsel on all matters pertaining to the attorney-client privilege and work-product doctrine.

FIGURE 32-3

Insureds' Checklist for Defending D&O Claims

❐ Promptly notice all claims to all insurers on your D&O program.

❐ Determine whether any other insurance policies might respond to the claim, and if so, notify those insurers as well.

❐ Once a claim is made, check to see if you are required to select from a list of pre-selected law firms (panel counsel) to defend the claim. Failure to use a panel counsel firm when required could result in a loss of coverage.

❐ Make sure all defense costs are "reasonable and necessary to the defense of the claim." Take an active role in managing defense costs. As soon as possible, inform all insurers of the name of the law firm selected as well as the hourly billing rates of the attorneys who will be defending the claim.

❐ Insurers must approve the use of multiple firms to defend a claim. Absent a conflict, all directors and officers should use the same counsel.

❐ Determine whether any litigation management guidelines will apply. If so, share these with defense counsel promptly.

❐ Provide all defense costs bills to the insurers on a monthly basis and push for prompt audits of such bills—even before the retention is exhausted.

❑   Know that defense costs typically erode the policy limit, which means every dollar spent defending a claim reduces the amount available to pay a settlement or judgment.

❑   Use your insurer's experience on coverage matters to your advantage.

❑   Know that you need to obtain consent before settling or offering to settle claims.

Notes to Chapter 32

1. DEL. GEN. CORP. LAW § 145(a).
2. *Id.* § 145(c).
3. Schoon v. Troy Corp., 948 A.2d 1157 (Del. Ch. 2008).
4. Conseco, Inc. v. Nat'l Union Fire Ins. Co., 2002 WL 31961447 (Ind. Ct. App. Dec. 31, 2002), *relying on* Level 3 Commc'ns, Inc. v. Fed. Ins. Co., 272 F.3d 908, 909–10 (7th Cir. 2001).
5. *See also* CNL Hotels & Resorts, Inc. v. Twin City Fire Ins. Co., 291 F. App'x 220 (11th Cir. 2008) (applying New York law, the court concluded that section 11 damages did not constitute loss and thus, such damages were not insurable under a D&O insurance policy). Although company losses under section 11 may not be insurable, some courts have concluded that losses incurred by non-issuers (e.g., individual directors and officers) in a section 11 class action are insurable. *See, e.g.*, Bank of Am. Corp. v. SR Int'l Bus. Ins. Co., SE, 2007 WL 4480057 (N.C. Super. Ct. Dec. 19, 2007) (concluding that where the insured did not receive any proceeds from the offering, the settlement payment should not be viewed as disgorgement and, thus, could be covered by insurance).
6. Cont'l Cas. Co. v. Bd. of Educ., 489 A.2d 536, 545 (Md. 1985).
7. Cutter & Buck, Inc. v. Genesis Ins. Co., 306 F. Supp. 2d 988 (W.D. Wash. 2004).
8. Briggs Ave. LLC v. Ins. Corp. of Hannover, 550 F.3d 246 (2d Cir. 2008).
9. Qualcomm, Inc. v. Certain Underwriters at Lloyd's, London, 73 Cal. Rptr. 3d 770 (Ct. App. 4th Dist. 2008).
10. Sarbanes-Oxley Act of 2002, Pub. L. No. 107-204, § 804, 116 Stat. 745; 28 U.S.C. § 1658.
11. *See* 11 U.S.C. § 362.
12. Westrec Marina Mgmt., Inc. v. Arrowood Indem. Co., 78 Cal. Rptr. 3d 264 (Ct. App. 2d Dist. 2008).
13. Vigilant Ins. Co. v. Bear Stearns Cos., 884 N.E.2d 1044 (N.Y. 2008).
14. *Id.*

Appendix 32A

Glossary of Common D&O Liability Insurance Terms

All-risk. A type of policy that provides protection against any claim that is not specifically excluded by the policy. The opposite type of coverage is a **named-peril** policy, which covers only those types of claims that are specifically listed in the policy.

Allocation. The split between covered and uncovered loss. Allocation usually occurs when there are covered and uncovered allegations in a claim or when there are allegations against covered and uncovered persons or entities.

Attachment/exhaustion. The attachment/exhaustion provision sets forth when an excess policy will provide coverage. Generally, this provision provides that the excess policy will only attach once the underlying policy limit is exhausted.

Captive. An insurance company that is owned by a parent company and used to insure the parent's own risks.

Change-of-control provision. Generally details how certain events/ transactions will impact the insurance coverage. For example, the change of control provision might state that if the parent company is sold, the insurance will cease to provide going forward insurance coverage.

Claim. Generally defines the events that will trigger coverage under the D&O liability insurance policy. Most D&O liability insurance policies will define a "claim" broadly to include litigation, arbitration, EEOC proceedings, criminal proceedings, formal SEC investigations, etc.

Claims-made. A type of policy that requires that a claim be made and reported during the policy period in order to be covered by the policy.

Coinsurance. Insurance that requires the insureds to retain some percentage of the risk of loss. For example, the D&O liability policy may provide that the insurer will pay 90% of a loss and that the insured will pay the remaining 10%.

Conduct exclusions. In the D&O insurance context, the conduct exclusions remove coverage for certain wrongful acts committed by the insureds (e.g., where the insured gains illegal profits or commits intentional misconduct or fraud).

Continuity date. Generally, the date on which the insureds first purchased D&O liability insurance from the insurer. D&O liability policies typically exclude coverage for any claims or circumstances that could give rise to claims that were known to the insureds as of the continuity date.

Continuity of coverage. A continuation of the representations and warranties given by the insureds in the insurance application. Continuity of coverage is very important to insureds as it allows them to avoid making new representations and warranties at the renewal or when the insured changes insurers. This is a particularly important issue in a **claims-made** policy.

Debtor in possession. A company that operates while under Chapter 11 bankruptcy protections.

Dedicated limit. A policy that dedicates its limit to only certain directors or only the directors and officers (as opposed to the entity). The most common dedicated limit policies are Side A–Only and Independent Directors Liability insurance policies. *See* **Side A** and **IDL.**

Derivative suit. An action brought on behalf of the corporation by its shareholders against the corporation's directors and officers.

DIC. Difference in conditions (typically a policy that simultaneously sits on top of and alongside of a traditional D&O policy), a policy that has the ability to "drop down" into a primary position in situations where the DIC policy provides broader coverage than the underlying policy or where the underlying policy does not respond. DIC policies generally provide only **Side A** coverage.

Difference in conditions. *See* **DIC.**

Diminishing-limits. A type of policy where defense costs incurred by the insureds reduce the limit of liability available to pay loss.

Discovery period. *See* **ERP.**

Disgorgement. A repayment of ill-gotten gains—money to which the insured did not have a right to in the first place. In the D&O liability insurance context, disgorgement most often arises in the context of the definition of "loss." Most D&O liability policies do not consider disgorgement to be a loss and, therefore, do not cover any disgorgement.

Duty-to-defend. A type of policy that requires the insurer to defend any covered lawsuit or claim brought against an insured.

Employee Retirement Income Security Act of 1974. *See* **ERISA**.

ERISA. Employee Retirement Income Security Act of 1974, the statutory scheme that regulates employee benefit plans.

ERP. Extended reporting period, an optional extension of coverage that allows insureds to report claims made during the ERP, provided that the wrongful act occurred prior to the expiration of the original policy period.

Extended reporting period. *See* **ERP**.

Final adjudication standard. Requires the insurer to cover allegations of fraud or illegal conduct against an insured unless and until there is a final, unappealable adjudication that determines that the insured committed the fraud or other illegal conduct alleged. *Compare* **Final determination standard**.

Final determination standard. Requires the insurer to cover allegations of fraud or illegal conduct against an insured unless and until there is a final determination by a court or other alternative dispute resolution proceeding that the insured committed the fraud or other illegal conduct alleged. The major difference between the final determination standard and the final adjudication standard is that with the final determination standard, the insurer would not be required to fund any appeals after a determination by a trial court that the insured committed the fraud or other illegal conduct.

Forced settlement clause. Provides that if the insurer agrees to fund a settlement within the policy limit but the insured rejects the settlement, the insurer's liability is capped at the amount of the rejected settlement plus any defense costs incurred up to that date. Insurers include this provision in their D&O liability policies to prevent insureds from fighting on principle with the insurers' money. By forcing a settlement, the insurer is essentially saying that if the insured wants to continue to fight, it should bear the risk of a potentially less favorable resolution to the case. Also called a "**hammer clause**."

Hammer clause. *See* **Forced settlement clause**.

IDL. Independent directors' liability, insurance coverage that protects only the independent (non-officer, non-employee) directors for non-indemnified acts.

In-fact standard. Requires the insurer to cover allegations of fraud or illegal conduct against an insured unless and until there is a determination that the insured in fact committed the fraud or other alleged illegal conduct. Who gets to determine whether the proscribed conduct in fact occurred, and what standard of proof is required, is not clear with this standard.

Indemnification. In the D&O context, the company's obligation to reimburse or compensate its directors and officers for any losses they incur as a result of their service to the company.

Independent directors' liability. *See* IDL.

Insured-versus-insured exclusion. Excludes coverage for claims brought by one insured against another insured. This exclusion is designed to prevent collusive lawsuits that would convert the third-party D&O coverage to a business risk coverage. Carve-backs from this exclusion are routinely obtained for derivative suits, certain bankruptcy claims, cross-claims, and employment practices claims.

Most-favorable-venue. In the D&O liability context, a clause that generally states that the parties should use the law of the venue most favorable to finding coverage to determine the insurability of punitive damages.

Named-peril. A type pf policy that covers only the hazards specifically named in the policy. Named-peril policies tend to be less expensive than **all-risk** policies, which cover all hazards unless the hazard is specifically excluded from coverage.

Non-indemnifiable. In the D&O context, acts for which the company may not indemnify its directors or officers by law or for public policy reasons or cannot indemnify its directors or officers due to financial insolvency.

Order of payments. The provision in a D&O policy that generally states that the policy limit shall be used first to cover the Side A or individual directors' and officers' losses. If any limit remains after such losses are paid, the policy shall be used to cover any Side B or company reimbursement losses. Finally, if any limit remains after the Side A and Side B losses have been paid, the limit shall be used to cover the Side C or entity losses. This provision is designed to help prevent the policy limit from being considered an asset of the bankruptcy estate.

Panel counsel. The list of pre-approved consultants, public relations firms, or law firms that some D&O liability insurance policies require be used for certain claims.

Pending and prior litigation exclusion. Eliminates coverage for any litigation or proceeding that relates to any litigation or proceeding pending on or prior to the inception of the policy (or some other designated date).

Presumptive indemnification. A provision that prevents the company and the insureds from taking advantage of the typically lower retention that is applicable under the Side A non-indemnifiable coverage insurance agreement by simply refusing to indemnify the directors and officers. Most D&O policies state that the company is presumed to indemnify its directors or officers to the fullest extent permitted or required by law (unless the company cannot do so due to bankruptcy) regardless of whether the company actually provides the indemnification.

Prior acts exclusion. Excludes claims arising from wrongful acts occurring before the prior acts date. Prior acts exclusions are strongly disfavored in a **claims-made** policy, as they tend to significantly reduce the protection provided by the policy.

Quota share. A type of program that spreads loss among two or more insurers in preset percentages.

Rescission. The act of completely voiding an insurance policy so that it is as if the policy had never been issued. Generally, the insurer returns any premium collected, and the insured returns to the position it would have been in if the insurance contract had never been bound. Rescission typically occurs only if there is a material misrepresentation in the application for insurance.

Reservation-of-rights letter. A letter from the insurer to the insured that sets forth all of the potential reasons why coverage may not apply to a particular claim.

Retention. The amount of risk retained by the insured before the insurance policy will begin to provide coverage. Similar to a deductible.

Retroactive date. Claims arising out of wrongful acts committed prior to the retroactive date are not covered by the D&O liability policy.

Section 11 and 12 claims. Claims alleging violations of sections 11 and 12 of the Securities Act of 1933, prohibiting false or misleading statements in a registration statement filed with the SEC or in a prospectus used in the offer or sale of securities.

Securities Act of 1933. Federal legislation that generally regulates the initial offering and sale of securities of a company.

Securities Exchange Act of 1934. Federal legislation that generally regulates secondary trading of securities. This act created the Securities and Exchange Commission and gave it broad investigative and regulatory powers to prevent fraud in the trading of securities.

Severability of exclusions. A provision that provides that the wrongful acts of one insured shall not be imputed to any other insured to determine the applicability of a given exclusion.

Severability of the application. Generally, all statements in the application for insurance are attributed to all insureds protected by the insurance contract. The severability-of-the-application provision limits this general rule so that the statements in the application are not imputed to all insureds, but are instead deemed binding only on the particular person or persons who were responsible for making the statements.

Side A. Coverage that protects directors and officers when the company may not advance or indemnify its directors or officers by law or for public policy reasons, or cannot advance or indemnify its directors or officers due to financial insolvency. Also called "non-indemnifiable loss" coverage.

Side B. Coverage that protects the company by reimbursing the company for amounts it pays to its directors and officers as indemnification. Also called "corporate reimbursement" coverage.

Side C. Coverage that protects the company against losses it is liable for as a result of wrongful acts by its directors, officers and representatives. Side C coverage is typically limited to securities actions in public company D&O insurance policies but may provide broader protection in private company and non-profit company policies. Also called "entity protection" coverage.

33

Cyber Liability Insurance

Thomas H. Bentz, Jr.

According to CSO Magazine, cyber crime damages will cost the world $6 trillion annually by 2021—up from $3 trillion in 2015. This represents the greatest transfer of economic wealth in history . . . and will be more profitable than the global trade of all major illegal drugs combined."

Florida International Bankers Association
"Regulators and Cybersecurity Audits, Are You Ready?,"
Webinar, May 16, 2018

My message for companies that think they haven't been attacked is: "You're not looking hard enough."

James Snook, Deputy Director,
Office for Cyber Security & Information Assurance,
Government Cabinet Office,
London, April 2016

The last several years have taught us that no matter how strong your IT defenses are, no matter how well you train your employees, and no matter how much time or money you spend on network security, you will experience a breach. It is not a matter of *if*; it is a matter of *when*.

> *JP Morgan is a company that has 2,000 people dedicated to cyber security. They have spent $250 million dedicated to cyber security. They did everything right, and they still got hacked.*
>
> Erik Avakian, Chief Information Security Officer, Commonwealth of Pennsylvania, September 2015

Data breaches are expensive. According to the 2019 IBM Ponemon Institute Cost of a Data Breach Study, the average cost of a data breach in the United States in 2018 was $8.19 million, up from $6.53 million in 2015.[1] A data breach may also result in business interruption losses, loss of intellectual property, fines and penalties, and significant harm to a company's reputation.

For this reason, many companies turn to cyber liability insurance to try to minimize losses in the event of a breach. Unfortunately, cyber insurance policies are both complicated and rapidly changing. There is no standard policy form, which means that the coverage offered by one insurer may (and often does) differ dramatically from that offered by another insurer. There is little agreement between insurers on what should be covered, when the coverage should be triggered or even how basic terms should be defined.

These differences make understanding what is and is not covered very difficult. It also makes it nearly impossible (or at least foolish) to purchase this coverage based on price alone. Notwithstanding, a strong cyber liability insurance policy may offer significant protection to companies. In some cases, it may even save a company from financial and reputational ruin.

The purpose of this chapter is to provide a basic understanding of the complexities of cyber liability insurance and to offer some tips to help insureds obtain the strongest possible protection. As described in more detail below, cyber liability insurance policies vary widely, with dramatic differences in coverage. As a result, the information below cannot and should not replace consultation with an experienced cyber liability insurance broker *and* an insurance attorney specializing in cyber liability insurance policy reviews.

Background

Q 33.1   How long has cyber insurance been around?

Cyber liability insurance is a relatively new concept. The first policies did not appear until the late 1990s, and there have been constant changes to the forms and the protections offered ever since. Today, there are approximately fifty insurers that offer some type of meaningful cyber risk and data privacy coverage. However, the coverage provided varies wildly from insurer to insurer. In addition, the market is in flux with new coverage types and new coverage forms appearing nearly as often as new cyber claims are reported.

The cyber insurance market has seen rapid growth over the past few years. Advisen estimates that in 2019, 77% of companies purchased some form of cyber insurance. This is a significant increase from 2011, when only 35% of companies purchased the coverage.[2]

COMPLIANCE TIP

Because there is so much difference in the coverage, it is imperative that insureds understand what coverage they need, what coverage is being offered, and what risks they will need to self-insure against even after they purchase coverage. Comparisons of cyber policies based on price alone are nearly meaningless for this line of coverage.

How Typical Cyber Liability Insurance Policies Work

Scope of Coverage

Q 33.2 What type of coverage do cyber liability insurance policies typically offer?

Cyber insurance policies generally contain both first-party and third-party coverage. First-party coverage insures against an insured's own losses (essentially, balance sheet protection for the company), such as loss of the insured's own data, an extortion demand, required notification costs, network/data restoration costs or lost business income resulting from a breach or cyberattack. Third-party coverage insures against liability to third parties caused by a breach or cyberattack such as defense costs (including attorney fees), settlements for claims and other damages resulting from a data breach or security incident.

Not all coverage grants are available to all insureds. For example, strong business interruption coverage may be extremely difficult to find for a large retail business. It is also important to note that the pricing for this coverage may vary significantly depending on the current market conditions. See the discussion of the price of insurance policies below at QQ 33.12.1–33.12.2.

Cyber liability insurance policies are nearly all written on a claims-made basis (*see* Q 33.5, *infra*). A cyber liability policy can be written on a "duty-to-defend" basis or as "non-duty-to-defend" (*see* Q 33.6, *infra*).

Q 33.2.1   What is typically *not* covered by cyber liability insurance policies?

Each coverage grant in a cyber liability insurance policy will have its own set of exclusions that will apply. Typical exclusions and tips on how to negotiate those exclusions are discussed in detail below (*see* QQ 33.16–33.16.1, *infra*). Exclusionary language, however, is not limited to the exclusions section; insureds must also consider a policy's definitions. In fact, the definitions section is often where many limitations on coverage appear in a policy. This makes comparing policies between insurers extremely difficult. It is further complicated by the fact that different insurers rarely use the same terms for a specific concept.

For example, in some policies the term "computer system disruption" is limited to a data breach. In other policies, this term also includes the introduction of a virus or spam-mail. This could have significant implications for coverage. Although not technically an exclusion, the narrower definition has the same effect. Similarly, one insurer may use the term "computer system disruption," whereas another uses "security failure." This lack of uniformity makes comparing terms and coverage grants very hard to do. Negotiating definitions is discussed in further detail below (*see infra* Q 33.15 *et seq.*).

Q 33.3   What are the typical coverage grants for a cyber policy?

The typical coverage grants for a cyber policy can be broken into three general categories: essential coverage grants; business interruption/expense coverage; and theft/property loss coverage. The first category contains the essential coverage grants—the coverage necessary to stop and contain a data breach and then respond to plaintiffs and regulators who allege they were injured by a data breach. The second category includes first-party losses to the insured company as a result of the breach (business interruption coverage). The final category of coverage grants includes coverage for theft/property loss. This category is similar in some respects to crime and general liability coverage.

FIGURE 33-1

Typical Coverage Grants for a Cyber Liability Insurance Policy

The following breakdown identifies three general categories of typical coverage grants for a cyber liability insurance policy and the protections each may include. Different insurers may label these coverage grants differently. Some will split them out into different coverage parts with different limits and retentions, and some will offer only some of the protections. The lack of uniformity is part of the reason that understanding cyber liability insurance is so difficult.

1. Essential Coverage Components

   - loss containment
   - third-party liability
   - regulatory defense and penalties
   - online media liability

2. Business Interruption/Expense Coverage

   - network/business interruption
   - extra expenses

3. Theft/Property Loss Coverage

   - data loss and restoration
   - cyber extortion
   - computer fraud
   - improper electronic transfer of funds

Essential Coverage Components

Q 33.3.1   What kind of protections do essential coverage components offer for "loss containment"?

Loss containment protections can include the following:

- Forensic investigation coverage: Covers the costs and expenses related to determining whether a cyberattack has occurred, how it occurred, and how to stop the attack/loss of data. Some policies also cover work needed to prevent future breaches.

- Crisis management costs. Covers crisis management and public relations expenses to assist in managing and mitigating a cyber event. Some policies will also cover the costs related to setting up a post breach call center.

Q 33.3.2   ... "third-party liability"?

Third-party liability protections can include the following:

- Notification/credit monitoring costs. Covers costs related to notifying customers and others about a cyber event as well as any mandatory credit/fraud monitoring expenses. Most policies will cover credit monitoring for one year. Some policies will also cover costs necessary to restore stolen identities.

- Litigation and privacy liability expenses. Covers defense costs, judgments, settlements and related liabilities caused by plaintiffs who bring suit against the insured for various theories of recovery due to the cyber event. Some policies provide coverage only if there is theft of data (for example, where a hacker obtains personally identifiable information). Other policies will provide coverage even if there is an intrusion without theft. This is an important distinction and may result in a significant difference in the coverage provided.

> **TIP:** An insured company should be sure that its policy covers damage inflicted on a third party—for example, transmitting a virus to a third-party computer system. Not all policies offer this, and some offer it only by endorsement.

Q 33.3.3 ... "regulatory defense and penalties"?

This includes coverage for defense costs to prepare for and defend against regulatory proceedings including legal, technical, and forensic work. Some policies also cover certain fines and penalties that may be assessed against the insureds, as well as costs related to responding to government inquiries about the cyber event.

Cyber liability insurance is one of the few insurance policies that will cover fines and penalties. This is extremely valuable when dealing with regulators from multiple states that are enforcing different and even inconsistent laws.

> **TIP:** The General Data Protection Regulation (GDPR) went into effect on May 25, 2018. The GDPR imposes new obligations on companies doing business in the European Union and allows fines and penalties up to 4% of the company's total global revenue for non-compliance. Although many cyber insurance policies provide coverage for fines and penalties, it is not clear whether fines and penalties assessed under the GDPR will be insurable. This is because the GDPR allows fines based on data storage and use of personal information regardless of whether there is a breach. Since most U.S. cyber policies require a breach to trigger coverage, it is not clear how those fines and penalties will be addressed. Fortunately, insureds may be able to negotiate coverage for GDPR fines and penalties from their insureds.

Q 33.3.4   ... "online media liability"?

Online media liability protection includes costs related to claims of defamation, copyright, and trademark infringement for material published on the insured company's website. This coverage is not for losses related to a data breach or intrusion; instead, it is for improper use of information by the insured company—for example, if the company's website uses a photo of a customer without the customer's permission.

The coverage is generally only available for website activities. It does not cover print or other types of media.

Business Interruption/Expense Coverage

Q 33.3.5   What does "network/business interruption" protection cover?

This covers lost income and operating expenses due to a "material interruption or suspension" of an insured's business caused by a "network security failure." Definitions of "material interruption" and "network security failure" vary greatly from policy to policy. For example, some policies will only include a data breach, whereas others will also include introduction of a virus or other type of disruption.

What is covered may also vary significantly. Depending on the policy, coverage may be available for:

(1) income lost when the insured cannot sell its product because its computer system failed;

(2) dependent business interruption; or

(3) extended business interruption.

Currently, only a few insurers offer dependent and extended business interruption coverage on their policy forms. Some insurers only offer these extensions by endorsement and some will not offer the coverage.

> **TIP:** Some insureds purchase business interruption protection because it provides an added incentive to the insurer to handle and resolve claims more expeditiously.

Q 33.3.6   What does "extra expenses" protection cover?

This protection covers certain expenses necessary to expedite recovery from an electronic disruption. Covered expenses are generally fairly limited and subject to lower limits of liability. Some policies cover these expenses only if the expense "reduces" the loss. This is tricky since it is often hard to know at the time the expense is incurred whether an extra expense will reduce the loss.

Theft/Property Loss Coverage

Q 33.3.7   What kind of protection does theft/property loss coverage offer against "data loss and restoration"?

Data loss and restoration coverage covers the costs of retrieving and restoring data, hardware, software, or other information damaged or destroyed in a cyberattack. Some policies will also cover damages caused when an employee accidently erases data. This coverage does not apply if the employee acted intentionally. It also does not typically cover costs for upgrading or otherwise improving the software during a restoration process.

Q 33.3.8   ... "cyber extortion"/ransomware?

Cyber extortion protection includes costs related to hackers who attempt to extort money by threatening to release sensitive information/data if a ransom is not paid, as well costs related to hackers who attempt to hold a network or data on the network hostage. Typically, this coverage will pay for:

(1) the money necessary to meet the extortion demand;

(2) the costs of a consultant/expert to negotiate with the extortionist; and

(3) the costs of an expert to stop the intrusion and block future extortion attempts.

This may be extremely valuable coverage since many companies have little or no experience negotiating with extortionists.

COMPLIANCE FACT

Symantec reports that for 2018, as compared to 2017, web attacks were up 56%, cryptojacking was up four times, supply chain attacks were up 78% over 2017, there was a 1,000% increase in malicious powershell scripts, and a 25% increase in the number of attack groups using destructive malware.[3]

According to the *McAfee Labs Threats Report*, a single ransomware crime organization netted $121 million during the first half of 2016.[4] In the first quarter of 2019, ransomware attacks grew by 118%.[5]

Q 33.3.9   ... "computer fraud"?

Computer fraud protection covers losses related to the loss or destruction of the insured's data as a result of criminal or fraudulent cyberattacks. A typical scenario is where a hacker obtains information about an insured company's client and uses that information to withdraw money from the client's bank account through an ATM. This coverage grant does not cover fraudulent acts of employees, independent contractors, or persons under the insured's supervision. Furthermore, it is increasingly difficult to obtain in off-the-shelf cyber liability forms.

Q 33.3.10   ... "improper electronic transfer of funds"?

This protection covers lost income and operating expenses due to a material interruption or suspension of an insured's business caused by a network security failure. This coverage grant requires the fraudulent transfer of funds from one financial institution to another. Like computer fraud protection, this coverage grant is increasingly difficult to obtain in off-the-shelf cyber liability forms.

Specialized Consultants/Panel Counsel

Q 33.4 What additional available protections should purchasers consider?

As the number of companies purchasing cyber liability insurance has increased significantly in the last several years, some insurers have started offering as part of their policies access by insureds to specialized consultants, such as data breach coaches, expert forensic and crisis management professionals, and attorneys. These specialized consultants and professionals are often the most important part of the protection available in the policy.

According to one study, companies that had insurance paid less than one-third as much to resolve claims as companies that did not have insurance. This may be because insured companies have access to these experienced professionals. The fact is that most companies are not set up to handle a data breach or other cyber-related claims on their own. Having access to known and vetted experts and professionals in the cyber/data breach fields may save an insured time and money and may reduce losses or even help prevent future losses from occurring.

TIP: Insurance companies are uniquely suited to help handle and resolve cyber liability claims. Their relationships with specialists and experts in this area often allow an insured company to resolve claims faster and for significantly less money than if the company had tried to handle a claim on its own.

Many policies also offer insureds access to IT assessment services, system audits, training and compliance forums, and even sample policies to respond to a data breach. Again, these "extra" coverage grants are often viewed as one of the most important reasons to purchase a cyber liability insurance policy.

Q 33.4.1   Should an insured retain its own experts?

Many companies are more proactive today in their approach to cyber risk and have retained their own computer/forensic experts and legal professionals to review and/or vet their computer systems, apps, and related services, and to assist them with their planning and crisis management needs. Companies that have done so should check their policies to ensure that they will be allowed to use their preferred experts and professionals in the event of a data breach or intrusion. Some policies will provide coverage only if the insured company uses one of the experts or professionals included on the policy's pre-approved "panel counsel" list. This may be extremely frustrating to insureds.

Fortunately, most insurers are willing to add an insured's preferred expert and/or professional to the policy by endorsement if this is negotiated prior to when a claim is made. The time to learn about and resolve these potential issues is before the policy is finalized. Insurers are often much more willing to endorse a coach or firm onto a policy at renewal or before the policy is purchased than to provide an exception at the time of the claim. In addition, the company will need to respond promptly to a breach and may not have time to seek an exception to the panel firm requirements after a breach is discovered.

TIP: Beware the "Double Secret" Panel Counsel Requirement

Some insurers will say that you may use whatever service provider that you want as long as that provider's hourly rates are "necessary and reasonable." That may sound attractive, but it is often difficult to find a top service provider that will work for what an insurer thinks is "necessary and reasonable." If your policy does not specify the service providers that you are required to use, we highly recommend that you endorse on your preferred service providers along with their agreed to hourly rates.

"Claims-Made" Coverage

Q 33.5   What is claims-made coverage?

Cyber liability insurance policies are nearly all written on a claims-made basis. This means that for a claim to be covered, it must be made during the policy period, and the wrongful act must occur after a preset retroactive date (generally the inception date of the first cyber liability policy provided by the insurer) but before the end of the policy term. Even within the policy period, insureds are generally required to give notice "as soon as practicable" and often within a set number of days. Although some policies may relax (or restrict) these requirements, claims-made policies are extremely time-sensitive. Thus, it is imperative that insureds recognize when a claim has been made and report such a claim promptly. Failure to do so may result in a denial of coverage.

> **TIP:** When purchasing cyber liability coverage, it is important to negotiate the retroactive date. Many policies only cover cyberattacks or data breaches occurring after the retroactive date. This may leave an insured without coverage for a network security breach that occurred but was undetected before the retroactive date.

In addition to requiring notice of a claim, many policies permit an insured to provide notice of any "circumstance" that may give rise to a claim in the future. Giving notice of a circumstance is generally discretionary, but it can have some advantages. For example, if a company properly notices a circumstance during the policy period, the insurer will generally consider a subsequent claim that arises from that circumstance to be "made" during the policy period in which the insured provided the notice. This may nonetheless allow a claim that is not actually made until after the policy period has expired to be covered by the policy. The benefit of this is that subsequent policy limits will not be impaired by any claims arising from the noticed circumstances.

On the other hand, because giving notice of a circumstance creates a potential increase in exposure for the insurer, most policies demand a high degree of specificity about the circumstance in order for coverage to apply. Failure to provide sufficient details may result in coverage being denied by the current insurer and may trigger an exclusion in a future policy. This complicates the decision to report a circumstance, especially if the company is changing insurers or relevant coverage terms, including limit. In addition, it is possible that the insurer will count the potential increased exposure from the notice of circumstances against the insureds. This could result in a higher renewal quote or, in a worst-case scenario, the refusal to quote the risk going forward.

"Duty-to-Defend" Coverage

Q 33.6   What is duty-to-defend coverage?

Some cyber liability policies are written on a "duty-to-defend" basis, while others are written as "non-duty-to-defend." A duty-to-defend policy means that the insurer (not the insured) controls the defense and claim strategy. Decisions such as which law firm to use, whether and how to defend a claim, and on what terms a claim should be settled are determined by the insurer in this type of policy.

A non-duty-to-defend policy requires the insureds to retain and pay for counsel to defend a claim. The insurer will then either reimburse the insured for its expenses or advance such costs to the insured. (Concerns about how and when the insurer will handle the expenses are discussed in more detail directly below.) Many insureds prefer a non-duty-to-defend policy because it gives the insureds more control of the defense of the claim; however, this additional control comes with insurer oversight. The non-duty-to-defend policy also requires the insureds to obtain the insurers' consent prior to incurring defense costs and/or agreement to a settlement. Failure to obtain that consent may leave insureds responsible for paying all or a portion of their expenses.

In short, although the insured controls the defense, the insured must still work with its insurers if it hopes to have its expenses covered by the insurance policy.

Some companies may prefer a duty-to-defend policy, especially if they feel unequipped to handle a data breach on their own. However, we generally recommend that insureds request at least the option to defend claims on their own. At a minimum, insureds should consider requesting the right to control the defense of regulatory proceedings that may be covered by the cyber liability policy.

Q 33.6.1   What is the difference between advancement and reimbursement of defense costs?

The reimbursement approach requires the insured to pay expenses and then ask the insurer to reimburse it. This may put a burden on some insureds to front defense costs for several months until the insurer makes the reimbursement. For this reason, many insureds prefer advancement policies.

With an advancement policy, the insurer pays the expenses directly to the defense firms so that the insured does not have to pay and then wait to be reimbursed. However, many insurers will require the use of a pre-selected "panel counsel" law firm before they will agree to advance defense costs. Some insureds like this; others do not.

> **TIP:** An insured should ensure that its reimbursement or advancement provision specifies when payment by the insurer must occur. Some forms say payment must be made within sixty days; others say only that payment must be made prior to the final resolution of the claim. The latter is much less preferable.

Most reimbursement and advancement clauses are subject to two conditions: (1) the parties must agree to an appropriate allocation of the defense costs (that is, covered and uncovered losses), with only covered losses subject to reimbursement/advancement; and (2) the insurance company must receive the insured's agreement to repay the insurance company if it is ultimately determined that the insured's losses are not covered by the policy.

Some cyber liability policies require the insured to guarantee the undertaking. For example, one advancement provision provides as follows:

> As a condition of any advancement of defense expenses, the Insurer may require a written undertaking on terms and conditions satisfactory to the Insurer *guaranteeing the repayment* of defense expenses paid on behalf of the Insured if it is finally determined that Loss incurred by such Insured would not be covered by this policy [emphasis added].

An insurer could argue that the *guarantee* of repayment translates into the need to *collateralize* the advancement. Obviously, this could be problematic as many insureds may lack sufficient collateral to support the advancement of what could be millions of dollars' worth of defense fees. Although it is debatable whether an insurer would be successful with this argument, insureds should be cautious about agreeing to such a provision.

Q 33.6.2   How and when is allocation of defense costs used?

Allocation is necessary if a lawsuit involves both covered and uncovered claims. Similarly, allocation is necessary if a lawsuit names both insured and uninsured persons as defendants, and both parties are represented by the same law firm. For this reason, a common reimbursement/advancement clause provides that if the insureds and the insurance company can agree on an allocation between covered and uncovered losses, the insurer will advance, on a current basis, the amount allocated to covered loss. If the parties are unable to agree, a typical reimbursement/advancement clause will require the insurance company to pay only the portion of defense costs it deems reasonable until a different allocation is determined by negotiation, arbitration or a judicial proceeding. Some parties will give the insured the option of submitting an allocation dispute to binding arbitration.

Q 33.6.3   How do defense costs affect the policy limit?

It is important to remember that defense costs generally erode the policy limit. Thus, every dollar spent defending a claim reduces the limit available to resolve any liability payments for the matter.

For example, if a policy has a $1 million limit and $400,000 is spent on defense costs, only $600,000 would be left to satisfy any judgment or settlement in the matter.

This is a particularly important point for cyber liability insurance policies because many cyber policies have multiple coverage grants with separate retentions, limits, and conditions. Insureds should keep this in mind when selecting what limits and what aggregate of coverage they need.

Cyber Liability Insurance Program Structure

Q 33.7 How should an insured structure its cyber insurance program?

Few insurers today are willing to provide more than $10 to $15 million of coverage for any one risk, so insureds that seek more than $10 to $15 million in cyber liability insurance coverage often must purchase multiple insurance policies. In the United States, such insureds typically layer or stack insurers. The first layer (or primary policy) will set forth the general terms and conditions for the entire program. Excess policies provide any needed additional limit. In this model, the primary insurer bears 100% of the risk of loss up to its limit. Then, the first excess insurer will bear 100% of its layer on, and so on.

One alternative to the layered structure is a quota share program. This is more popular in Europe and rarely used by most U.S.-based insurers. A quota share program allows the insurers to share the risk across a program in proportion to the premium they receive, as illustrated by Figure 33-2.

FIGURE 33-2

Cyber Insurance Program Structures: Layered Versus Quota Share

Traditional U.S. Model Layered (or Stacked) Insurance	
Excess Insurer 4	$10M excess $40M
Excess Insurer 3	$10M excess $30M
Excess Insurer 2	$10M excess $20M
Excess Insurer 1	$10M excess $10M
Primary Insurer	$10M primary limit

Traditional U.K. Model Quota Share Insurance	
	Insurer E—20% of loss
	Insurer D—20% of loss
$50M	Insurer C—20% of loss
	Insurer B—20% of loss
	Insurer A—20% of loss

Other Types of Insurance Policies

Q 33.8 What other types of insurance do insureds use to cover cyber events?

Cyber liability policies are not the only place where an insured might find coverage for a cyber event. Depending on the losses and/or allegations, several other types of insurance policies may also respond to a cyber-related claim, including:

- directors and officers insurance;
- errors and omissions/professional liability insurance;
- commercial general liability insurance;

- fiduciary liability insurance;
- employment practices liability insurance; and
- crime/fidelity insurance.

Q 33.8.1   How can an insured cover cyber events using directors and officers insurance?

One of the largest potential exposures in the wake of a cyber event has turned out to be derivative actions against the board of directors for failure to exercise proper business judgment in preparing for or dealing with a cyber event. These types of derivative claims may be covered under a directors and officers (D&O) policy (*see* chapter 32 for complete coverage). Other third-party claims against the directors and officers of the insured company may also be covered by a D&O policy.

Q 33.8.2   ... errors and omissions/professional liability insurance?

An errors and omissions/professional liability insurance (E&O) policy may provide some cross-over coverage for a cyber claim. For example, law firms have a duty to keep their clients' information confidential. Failure to keep personally identifiable information confidential as a result of a data breach may be covered by a law firm E&O policy. However, some insurers have denied such claims, arguing that a data breach is not caused by a wrongful act by the law firm. Regardless, even the broadest E&O policies are unlikely to provide notification/credit monitoring coverage or full coverage for forensic investigations. As such, a cyber policy will likely be needed for full protection.

Q 33.8.3   ... commercial general liability insurance?

Many commercial general liability (CGL) policies offered at least some coverage for a cyber event. For example, many CGL policies covered invasion of privacy or privacy/confidentiality allegations. Recently, however, the standard CGL form was changed to add an exclusion for cyber events. This may limit the amount of coverage available under a CGL policy going forward.

Q 33.8.4   ... fiduciary liability insurance?

Certain provisions of the Health Insurance Portability and Accountability Act (HIPAA) and the Health Information Technology for Economic and Clinical Health (HITECH) Act require prompt notice of a data breach or privacy event and provide strict penalties for failure to comply with the laws. A strong fiduciary liability (FI) policy may respond to some of the notice expenses as well as certain penalties from a cyber event. However, as noted with E&O coverage, it is unlikely that an FI policy would cover notification/credit monitoring or full, forensic investigations.

Q 33.8.5   ... employment practices liability insurance?

Employment practices liability insurance (EPLI) policies may cover certain allegations by employees that the company failed to protect their personally identifiable information. This is highly dependent on the allegations made by the employees. Some EPLI policies may also provide coverage for third parties, but these protections are generally available only where the plaintiff can show discrimination or harassment. EPLI policies are also unlikely to cover credit monitoring or notification costs.

Q 33.8.6   ... crime/fidelity insurance?

Finding some coverage for a cyber event/data breach under a crime/fidelity policy may be possible depending on the damages alleged. For example, some crime policies will include a computer fraud rider that may allow coverage for certain expenses related to customer communications, public relations, lawsuits, regulatory defense costs, and fines imposed by credit card vendors.

Coverage for Phishing Attacks/Social Engineering Fraud

Q 33.9   What are phishing attacks?

One of the more common and costly potential coverage gaps is the lack of coverage for "voluntary transfers" related to social engineering fraud or phishing attacks. There are many variations on this scam, but essentially, the CFO receives what appears to be a legitimate email from a client or vendor asking the CFO to wire money to an account. The email often looks completely real and, in fact, is often the result of a hacker breaking into the client or vendor's system, allowing the hacker to send messages from the client or vendor's actual email address. Only after wiring the money (often multiple transfers and increasingly larger sums) does the CFO learn that he or she has become a victim of fraud.

This type of fraud is increasingly common, hitting companies large and small and across several industries including banks, manufacturers, retailers and even several law firms. According to the FBI, phishing attacks have cost businesses more than $2.3 billion in losses in the last three years and there has been a 2,370% increase in losses from phishing scams between January 2015 and December 2016. In fact, Stu Sjouwerman, Founder and CEO of KnowBe4, estimates that phishing attacks are the number one penetration point for most Internet crime.

COMPLIANCE FACT

According to APWG's Phishing Activity Trends Report, November 2019, phishing attacks reached their highest level in three years in 2019.[6]

Q 33.9.1   How can insureds get coverage for phishing attacks?

Unfortunately, many companies are not covered for loss from phishing attacks even if they purchase cyber liability insurance coverage. Most cyber insurers will not cover this loss because it was not the insured's system that was hacked—instead, it was the insured's client's or vendor's system that was breached. Without a breach, there is no covered loss under the policy despite the obvious fraud on the insured.

In addition, the insured's crime/fidelity bond policy will typically not respond because there is no "theft." Generally, crime policies consider this type of social engineering fraud a "voluntary transfer," which is specifically excluded from coverage. This exclusion has applied even when the CFO was tricked into wiring the money.[7]

Coverage for this type of social engineering fraud is generally available upon request as an add-on for most crime policies and some cyber liability insurance policies. It is just that most companies do not know to ask for it.

Coordinating Multiple Policies

Q 33.10   How does an insured coordinate its cyber coverage with other types of insurance?

Coordinating the various types of coverages that may apply—differing limits, retentions/deductibles, and other coverage requirements—can be one of the most difficult things about a cyber event. In addition, because multiple types of policies may apply, there may be problems coordinating defense counsel (different insurers may not approve of a firm required by another insurer or there may be disagreement between insurers about reasonable hourly rates). The claims-made requirement of many of these policies may also present problems for insureds in the event of a claim. Insureds are well advised to coordinate their coverage in advance so they are not attempting to resolve these issues for the first time after a cyber event has occurred.

TIP: Consider the following when coordinating coverage:

- Priority of coverage (which policy goes first?);
- Potential allocation issues;
- Potential issues with choice of counsel;
- Potential issues with attorney hourly rates;
- Other insurance clauses.

Selecting an Insurance Policy

In General

Q 33.11   What are some general tips for buying cyber insurance policies?

Before buying a cyber insurance policy, a company should be sure to do the following:

1. Understand its risk. The first step in securing appropriate cyber liability insurance coverage is to understand the most significant risks facing the company. This is absolutely essential to the process of securing the best coverage possible. For some companies, the primary concern may be the costs resulting from the theft of personal financial information (notification costs, credit monitoring, etc.). For other companies, the main concern is the disruption of the business caused by attacks.

TIP: Many companies believe that they do not need cyber insurance because they do not "store" personally identifiable information. However, this may not be true as even companies that do not store this information can be included in lawsuits involving breaches. Since defense costs in these cases can be significant, deciding not to buy cyber insurance is risky. Moreover, cyber criminals have increasingly been targeting corporate, non-public information such as intellectual property and financials. As this trend develops, companies may see more need for the coverage.

---

2. Understand its existing coverage. As noted above, insureds may find coverage for a data breach or cyber claim in many different types of insurance policies (*see* Q 33.8). Knowing what its various insurance policies will and will not cover may significantly reduce the expense of an insured's cyber liability insurance policy. For example, if an insured already has third-party coverage through an E&O policy, it may be possible to reduce the premium for a cyber liability policy by removing duplicate coverage or by purchasing lower limits.

3. Match its risk transfer needs to the cyber liability policy. Once you have an understanding of your risk transfer needs, it is important to find a cyber liability policy that most closely aligns with those needs. There is no point in paying for coverage that you do not need. Likewise, there is little point in purchasing coverage that does not cover your most important concerns. Only a thorough review of the policy options will determine whether a particular policy provides a good fit for your risk transfer needs.

4. Involve the relevant parties at the company. One of the most common mistakes when purchasing cyber liability insurance is the failure to involve the relevant parties at the company in the key coverage decisions. For example, the risk manager may be very comfortable with the panel counsel requirement under the policy, but the general counsel may insist on using a non-panel firm for a particular claim. Using a non-panel firm may jeopardize the coverage or even void it altogether. (This is a common issue for cyber liability policies, which often require the use of a pre-approved breach coach, public relations firm, and law firm as a condition for coverage. See Q 33.4.1 for further discussion of specialized consultants and panel counsel.)

Specific Policy Considerations

Q 33.12   What factors should be considered when purchasing a cyber liability insurance policy?

Among the important factors to consider when purchasing a cyber liability insurance policy are:

- price;
- policy limit;
- retention;
- terms and conditions;
- claims handling;
- financial ratings; and
- the insurer's longevity in the industry.

Price

Q 33.12.1   How should price factor into a policy purchaser's decision?

Price is important when selecting the right cyber liability policy limit, retention, and insurer. However, price is just one factor to consider, and it is usually the least reliable factor in determining the *right* policy limit, retention, or insurer.

Companies cannot leave to chance whether this multimillion-dollar asset will protect them in the event of a data breach/claim. Companies that assume that they are protected just because their company has cyber liability insurance may find out the hard way that their protection is inadequate. By taking the time to consider the right policy limit, retention, and insurer for its risk transfer needs, a company may greatly improve the chances that its cyber liability policy will protect the company when it needs it most.

Q 33.12.2   Is cyber liability insurance expensive?

The pricing for typical cyber liability insurance coverage may vary significantly depending on the current market conditions. In fact, quoted premiums may vary significantly by insurer for the same risk. It is not uncommon to see quotes that are 20% to 30% higher for a risk from one insurance carrier to the next. Given this volatility, it is imperative that insureds work with an experienced advisor who knows which markets will be interested in and competitive for the risk.

COMPLIANCE FACT

The average cost of a data breach for a large company from 2014 to 2018 was $5.6M. The median total breach cost was $1M.

The average cost for crisis services (forensics, notification, credit monitoring, breach coach, etc.) was $3.8M. The median cost was $369,000.

The average legal defense costs were $1.4M. The median legal fees were $502,000.

The average regulatory defense costs and fines was $3.5M. The median was $3.5M.

The average cost for legal settlement was $2.6M. The median settlement was $1.2M.

The average number of records exposed was 19.6M. The median was 48,000.

The average cost per-record was $42,617. The median cost per-record was $15.[8]

Policy Limit

Q 33.12.3   How do insureds determine the right policy limit?

There is no fool-proof way to determine the perfect amount of cyber liability insurance to purchase for any particular year. Nevertheless, there are many factors that may inform insureds as to the proper amount of insurance they need to feel protected:

- *Claims studies.* Perhaps the most scientific way to determine the appropriate cyber liability insurance limit is to consider a claims study. Claims studies consider the mean and average settlement values for breaches compared to the number of records that may be jeopardized in the event of a breach. While these studies can be informative, they do have limitations.

- *Benchmarking studies.* Benchmarking studies provide an insured with information about what limit the insured's peer companies are purchasing. Again, this may be helpful, but there is no guarantee that the insured's peer companies are purchasing the right limit. Moreover, such studies are typically limited to one broker's experience, which may or may not include a statistically significant sampling of peer companies.

- *What the directors want.* Sometimes, directors or officers will insist on a certain amount of insurance regardless of any claim studies or benchmarking data. Failure to provide the desired limit may mean that the company will be unable to attract or retain directors or officers.

- *What the insured can afford.* What the insureds can afford is another very real factor in determining what limit insureds should purchase.

- *Public perception.* Some companies fear that a high cyber liability insurance limit may attract lawsuits and/or increase the size of settlements. Most studies do not support this conclusion.

- *Defense costs.* When deciding the appropriate limit to purchase, insureds should also consider that defense costs are usually (but not always) included within the limit of liability. Thus, insureds also need to factor in the cost of defending a lawsuit when determining the appropriate limit.

- *Other factors.* It is still unclear how the GDPR may impact companies and their potential exposure for cyber-related matters. Given the potential for larger fines and penalties, companies may want to increase their limits.

COMPLIANCE TIP

It is important to make sure that you have enough insurance coverage to properly defend against claims. Increasingly, $1 million in coverage is simply not enough to cover a proper defense. Insufficient limits may force an insured to settle a claim it would prefer to contest and may result in personal liability for the directors and officers.

Retention

Q 33.12.4   How do insureds determine the right retention?

Selecting the right retention is a complicated decision. Generally, an insured should select a retention that is above what it takes to resolve a typical cost of doing business claim, but below the point where satisfying the retention would have a significant negative impact on the insured's operations. Within that range, the insured must balance the premium cost of a policy with the lower retention amount against the premium cost of a policy with a higher retention amount.

One thing to keep in mind is that retentions rarely go down. Thus, moving to a higher retention will likely be a permanent choice.

Other Factors

Q 33.12.5   To what extent should an insured consider terms and conditions?

Perhaps the most important factors to consider when deciding which cyber liability policy to purchase are the terms and conditions of the policy itself. Terms and conditions in cyber liability policies are not standard, and different insurers have different philosophies about what type of claims they are willing to cover. An insured who saves a few dollars in premium by selecting an inferior policy may find they were "penny-wise but pound-foolish."

Q 33.12.6   ... claims handling?

Purchaser should never forget that they are purchasing cyber liability insurance to pay claims. Different insurers handle claims very differently. Before deciding to purchase a cyber liability policy, it is important to know the insurer's reputation for paying claims. Insureds may also find it helpful to know whether the insurer has its own experienced claims staff or whether it uses outside law firms for its claims.

Insureds with a global footprint may also want to consider whether their insurers have claims people in the relevant jurisdictions. Knowledge of local laws and customs may be very valuable in a claims situation.

Q 33.12.7   ... financial ratings?

The financial strength of an insurer is important. One way to deter-mine the financial strength of a company is to consider its rating from A.M. Best or a similar rating agency. Most brokers will only place poli-cies with an A-rated insurance carrier.

Q 33.12.8   ... longevity in the industry?

Some insurers try to time their entry and exit from particular areas of insurance to coincide with the hard and soft market cycle. While such insurers may be able to offer lower prices during "good times," it is typically better for an insured to work with an insurer that will remain in the market in both good and bad times. Insurers that are committed to a line of coverage typically understand that the rela-tionship between the insurer and insured is an important part of the coverage.

Negotiating Key Provisions of a Cyber Liability Insurance Policy

Overview

Q 33.13   Why do cyber liability insurance policies need to be negotiated?

Cyber liability policies are unlike many other types of insurance policies. There is no standard cyber liability insurance form. There is a lack of uniformity in terms and conditions, as well as in scope of coverage. Even the simplest cyber liability policy has an intimi-dating number of detailed definitions, exclusions, and conditions, with nuances of wording that may have very costly consequences. Narrow definitions and overly broad exclusions found in many off-the-shelf policies may mean the difference between a policy covering a multimillion-dollar loss or one that leaves insureds to pay the tab. As a result, comparing the premiums of cyber liability insurance is not informative. Instead, insureds must compare and contrast *each* cyber liability policy to ensure that it meets their risk transfer needs.

Fortunately, cyber liability insurance policy forms are not cast in stone. There is sufficient competition in the marketplace, and many cyber liability insurers are willing to consider suggestions and, in varying degrees, to tailor policies to meet an insured's needs by means of endorsements. Too few insureds avail themselves fully of this opportunity, and many discover shortfalls only after a claim arises.

**Real-Life Example of How Failure
to Negotiate May Limit Coverage**

The only service an insured company provided was moving goods from point A to point B. The E&O policy (which the company had purchased for several years) had an exclusion that said if the goods were damaged or lost or the shipment was delayed, there was no coverage. This exclusion essentially made the coverage worthless to the company.

Q 33.13.1   Who should negotiate the coverage?

Negotiating enhanced coverage is a formidable challenge for insureds. Cyber liability insurance policy negotiation requires the knowledge and experience of defense counsel, a claims expert, and a legal wordsmith. Here is why.

First, as stated above, a standard cyber liability insurance policy form does not exist. Cyber liability insurance policy forms vary significantly from one insurance company to the next. Some insurance companies offer, in addition to a general corporate form, different forms for financial institutions, healthcare organizations, mutual funds, and other specialized markets.

Second, the frequency of new policy forms is increasing. Each new policy has new language that may impact the coverage.

Third, the meaning of policy language frequently is unclear. The movement for plain-English contracts has not been widely embraced by cyber liability insurers.

> **Obtaining Broad Coverage Does Not Necessarily Cost More**
>
> Many insureds are surprised to learn that adding endorsements and making improvements to their coverage does not often increase their premium. Some insureds have added more than sixty enhancements to their policy without any increase in the premium.

Fourth, and perhaps most importantly, few buyers have a full appreciation of the many built-in pitfalls in standard policies. Until insureds have been through the complete cycle of working with an insurer—from negotiating policy terms to making a claim and receiving a "reservation of rights" letter to working through a coverage dispute—they cannot foresee many of the issues that an insurance company may raise to limit or deny coverage under a policy.

For all these reasons, it is unrealistic for insureds to expect a risk manager who reviews one cyber liability insurance policy per year to obtain top coverage. And, unless a broker specializes in cyber liability insurance and is an attorney, it is nearly impossible for him or her to stay on top of all of the market changes and the endorsements offered by each insurer. Insureds should engage a team of professionals. Otherwise, what they save now, they may pay for many times over in the future.

Q 33.13.2   What parts of the policy should be negotiated?

Broadly speaking, insureds should negotiate:

- coverage grants;
- definitions;
- exclusions;
- terms and conditions; and
- excess policies.

Negotiating Coverage Grants

Q 33.14   What should insureds know about negotiating coverage grants?

To ensure that it has strong cyber liability coverage, a purchaser should understand the coverage grants available along with what coverage it needs. There are many different coverage grants available, and they go by many different names in different policy forms—thus, it is not an easy task to figure this out. Some of the most common types of coverage grants are set forth in Figure 33-1 above.

In addition to the types of coverage available, the actual coverage grants should be carefully reviewed to ensure that the broadest coverage possible is obtained. The following are some examples of issues to consider when reviewing the coverage grants:

- Some policies only cover certain types of "data" and/or limit coverage based on when and where it exists.

- Many policies limit coverage to just electronic data. When possible, it is better to cover all types of data.

- Loss caused by insiders/employees should be covered. Some policies cover only loss caused by outsiders.

- Coverage should not require "updated" software protections. This may artificially limit coverage for many companies.

- Coverage should include state-sponsored attacks. Many policies will limit coverage by adding an exclusion or limiting definitions.

TIP: A company should be sure that its policy covers information managed by third parties, such as data-handling, -processing, and -storage services and cloud service providers. Often, companies assume that because they outsource these functions, they have no exposure and/or that their policies would respond if they are exposed. That is not always the case.

Negotiating Definitions

Q 33.15   What definitions should insureds negotiate?

Insureds often overlook the definitions in a cyber liability insurance policy. However, the definitions are what often determine the coverage. To illustrate this point, a few years ago, an insurer issued a D&O policy with no exclusions. Of course, this did not mean all risks were covered by the policy. Instead, the insurer narrowly defined terms such as "Claim" and "Loss" to exclude the risks it did not want to cover. Given that there are myriad definitions in each cyber liability insurance policy, and that each may impact coverage, insureds should carefully review and negotiate the definitions in light of the insureds' specific risk transfer needs. Definitions that insureds should focus on include:

- "application";
- "claim";
- "insured"; and
- "loss."

Q 33.15.1   What are the important considerations in negotiating the definition of "application"?

The definition of "application" is important because the application is the basis for coverage. If material information is omitted or misstated in the application, this may constitute application fraud, which could result in rescission of the policy. Consequently, it is in the insured's best interest to keep the definition as narrow as possible.

TIP: Directors and officers should take the time to review the application each year. The application is the basis of the insurance contract, and a careful review of the application may minimize the risk of rescission later.

Cyber liability policies often define the term "application" to include, in addition to the application form itself, any public document filed by the named insured with any federal, state, local, or foreign regulatory agency at any time. This definition is overly broad and may have a devastating effect on coverage. For example, an insurer should generally not be allowed to rely on a document filed with the Securities and Exchange Commission many years ago to deny coverage today.

One way to limit this risk is to narrow the definition of "application." By limiting the documents considered part of the application, an insured may reduce the chance that irrelevant and potentially stale information could affect its coverage.

Q 33.15.2 ... the definition of "claim"?

What constitutes a "claim" as defined by a cyber liability insurance policy is critical. It impacts the scope of coverage and triggers several obligations of the insurer and the insured. A claim is not limited to a lawsuit. It may include a written demand for monetary or other relief, a civil, criminal, or administrative proceeding or investigation, or even a regulatory action.

Although it is generally desirable to have a broad definition of claim, too broad a definition may be problematic. For example, some policy forms define "claim" to include both written and *oral* demands for monetary damages. The addition of an "oral demand" to the definition might seem like a desirable expansion of coverage. However, this addition may create coverage problems for the insureds. An insured who receives an oral demand might not recognize it as a claim and, thus, may not report it to the insurer in a timely manner: No timely notice, no coverage.

In addition, there is the problem of proof. Trying to establish what a disgruntled individual said to an officer of the company at a cocktail party three years earlier and trying to determine if it constituted a reportable demand for monetary damages could be a difficult task. To avoid potential coverage issues, it is generally better for insureds to ask their insurer to delete oral demands from the definition of "claim."

Q 33.15.3   ... the definition of "insured"?

The definition of "insured" may seem straightforward. However, the standard definition may omit key entities that the company intended to cover, so insureds may need to amend the definition to ensure that all appropriate entities have coverage.

For example, the typical definition of the term "insured" includes a named insured entity, its subsidiaries, and certain insured persons. The problem with this definition is that it clearly does not include a debtor in possession as an insured. When a company files for protection from its creditors under Chapter 11 of the Bankruptcy Code, the company becomes a debtor in possession. A debtor in possession is considered a separate legal entity from the company, despite the fact that many of the same directors and officers may still be involved in running the entity. Not including a debtor in possession in the definition of "insured" could leave a serious hole in the company's insurance protection. Fortunately, most insurers will, upon request, amend the definition of "insured" to include a debtor in possession.

Another potential shortcoming of the standard definition of "insured" is that many companies are part of a complicated structure that may include parent and subsidiary companies, sibling companies, unrelated companies that work closely together or even share resources or work, joint ventures, for-profit entities, and non-profit entities sponsored by a for-profit entity. A threshold question for a party purchasing cyber liability insurance is: What entities do we want to insure, and do they all fit under the definition of "insured"? Often, insureds desire to insure the collective risk of some mix of companies, some of which have relationships more complicated than parent-subsidiary. In such cases, it is critical that the company amend the definition of "insured" to include all entities that do not clearly fall under the standard definition.

Finally, it is important to determine the correct entity to list as the named insured or parent company. Coverage in a cyber liability policy typically flows down from the named insured, but not up the corporate chain. If the named insured is the parent company, the policy should cover all of the parent's subsidiaries. The reverse is not true. Sometimes companies name a subsidiary as the named insured for tax purposes, or because the subsidiary is where most of the business risk lies, only to find out later that, having done so, the parent company lacks coverage. Since the parent company is often named in a lawsuit regardless of whether it was ultimately responsible for the alleged action, it is generally not advisable to use a subsidiary as the named insured.

Q 33.15.4   ... the definition of "loss"?

The definition of "loss" is another important term in cyber liability insurance policies since there must be a loss for coverage to attach. Coverage of punitive damages may be an important reason for purchasing a cyber liability insurance policy, but the insurability of such damages varies between jurisdictions. To maximize the chances that punitive damages will be covered by the policy, the policy should have a "most favorable venue" provision that provides that the applicable law that *most* favors the insurability of punitive damages will apply when determining coverage.

Some jurisdictions may require a more specific most-favorable-venue provision that limits the potential venues to those that have some relation to the claim and/or the insurance contract. Such a provision may state that the most favorable law of any of the following jurisdictions will apply to determine the insurability of punitive damages:

(1)   the location of the named entity's headquarters or its principal place of business;

(2)   where the insurer is located;

(3)   where the alleged wrongful act took place;

(4)   where the claim is brought; or

(5)   any other jurisdiction that has a substantial relationship to the claim.

Negotiating Exclusions: Generally

Q 33.16   Which exclusions should insureds negotiate?

The exclusions found in most cyber liability insurance policies fall into one of five main categories:

(1) illegal/fraudulent conduct exclusions (for example, illegal profits, criminal acts, fraudulent or intentionally dishonest acts, and medical malpractice, if proven);

(2) other-insurance exclusions for claims covered by other types of policies exclusions (for example, claims for property damage, bodily injury, and workers' compensation);

(3) exclusions for claims that belong on previous or subsequent policies due to timing issues (for example, matters where the risk was noticed on another policy, the risk was known prior to the inception of the policy, or the litigation had commenced prior to the inception of the policy);

(4) insured-versus-insured exclusion for claims that are potentially collusive (for example, claims brought by or with the assistance of an insured);

(5) miscellaneous exclusions that are specific to cyber claims.

Also, in order to ensure that the acts of one insured person do not impact coverage for other, innocent insureds, a cyber liability insurance policy should contain an exclusion severability provision. An exclusion severability provision states that no wrongful act committed by any one insured shall be imputed to any other insured for purposes of determining the applicability of any of the exclusions.

Negotiating Exclusions: Illegal/Fraudulent Conduct Exclusion

Q 33.16.1   What are some important considerations when negotiating an illegal/fraudulent conduct exclusion?

Most cyber policies include exclusions for fraudulent and intentional illegal misconduct. How a policy determines whether a conduct exclusion applies, when that determination may be made, and who gets to make this determination are extremely important.

For example, must the determination of whether an insured committed fraud be made by a court, or can the insurer make the determination? Similarly, assuming a court must make the determination, must the court make the determination in the underlying action, or may the insurance company bring a new and separate action to determine the alleged fraud after the fact? An action against the insured by its insurance company, coming right behind a class action, is a most unappealing prospect for many insureds.

For this reason, many insureds prefer a "final, non-appealable adjudication" standard. This standard provides insureds with the maximum coverage possible and requires a final, non-appealable adjudication by a court in the underlying action to establish that the alleged wrongful conduct occurred. Without such a final non-appealable adjudication of wrongful conduct, the exclusion does not apply (that is, there is coverage available from the policy).

A less preferable alternative is an "in fact" determination. It is not altogether clear what constitutes an "in fact" determination or who gets to make that determination. However, it is certainly less than a final, non-appealable adjudication by a court and, therefore, less desirable from the perspective of providing the maximum coverage possible to the insureds. Of course, like many issues with cyber liability insurance coverage, providing the broadest coverage possible may make it possible for a "guilty" insured to dilute or exhaust the policy limit to the detriment of the other "innocent" insureds. As such, some insureds may prefer the "in fact" standard or some other hybrid of the "in fact" and final adjudication standards.

It is very important that the conduct exclusions apply only to intentional/fraudulent acts committed by the insureds. Intentional/fraudulent acts by others should be covered.

COMPLIANCE FACT

Typical illegal/fraudulent conduct exclusions exclude coverage for:

- intentional dishonest acts or omissions
- deliberate fraudulent acts or omissions
- deliberate criminal acts or omissions
- receipt of illegal profits
- receipt of illegal remuneration

Negotiating Exclusions: Other-Insurance Exclusions

Q 33.16.2   What are some important considerations when negotiating exclusions more properly covered by other insurance?

Cyber liability policies contain a number of exclusions designed to ensure that risks that are more properly covered by a different type of insurance policy are not covered by the cyber liability policy. For example, most cyber liability policies exclude the following types of claims:

- property damage and bodily injury claims, which may be covered by general liability insurance;

- workers' compensation claims, which may be covered by workers' compensation insurance;

- employment practices claims, which may be covered by employment practices liability insurance;

- losses related to the environment, which may be covered by environmental liability insurance; or

- ERISA claims, which may be covered by fiduciary liability insurance.

In order to guard against gaps in coverage between policies, it is important to negotiate each of these exclusions so that they are as narrow as possible. The following are some examples of how these exclusions need to be negotiated:

Property Damage/Bodily Injury Exclusion. Some policies exclude coverage for any claim "arising out of, based upon, or attributable to" property damage and bodily injury. This is too broad. Instead, the quoted language should be replaced with the word "for." This addresses the situation when there is an injury that is followed by a secondary lawsuit claiming a failure to supervise. A company's general liability policy might cover the direct liability associated with the injury, but it may not cover the subsequent lawsuit. With the change to "for," the company's cyber liability insurance policy could provide coverage.

TIP: At least one insurer has offered coverage for cyber-related property damage/bodily injury liability—for example, where a virus shuts down a computer system and that shut-down causes bodily injury. This type of coverage may be more important if the "standard" general liability policy adds exclusions for cyber-related claims, as is expected.

The property damage/bodily injury exclusion should also include a carve-back clause for mental anguish, emotional distress, and shock caused by a cyber event. Many plaintiffs will allege these types of damages after a breach.

Employment Practices Exclusion. Cyber liability policies often exclude coverage for employment practices claims. If a policy has such an exclusion, the insured needs to be sure that there is a carve-back clause for employment claims alleging privacy violations caused by a data breach.

ERISA Exclusion. As with the employment practices exclusion described above, a strong cyber liability policy will have a carve-back clause to the ERISA exclusion for claims alleging damages caused by a data breach of the insured's employee benefits program.

Negotiating Exclusions: Timing-Related Exclusions

Q 33.16.3   What are some important considerations when negotiating timing-related exclusions?

As discussed above, most cyber liability insurance policies are written on a claims-made basis, making timing critical to the determination of coverage (*see* Q 33.5, *supra*). To emphasize this point, most cyber liability policies will contain several timing exclusions. The three most common of these exclusions are:

(1)   the prior-notice exclusion;
(2)   the pending and prior litigation exclusion; and
(3)   the prior-acts exclusion.

In order to obtain maximum coverage, an insured should negotiate each of these exclusions.

Prior-notice exclusion. A typical prior-notice exclusion excludes any claim arising out of, based upon, or attributable to any facts or circumstances alleged or contained in any claim that was previously reported by the insured under a previous insurance policy. The risk with this exclusion is that an insurer may reject a reported claim. In such a situation, the insured may be left without coverage. As such, insureds should attempt to negotiate language that states that only those claims that are previously reported *and covered* by a previous insurance policy will be excluded by the new policy.

Pending and prior litigation exclusion. A typical pending and prior litigation exclusion excludes any pending or prior litigation and any new litigation that is based upon the same or essentially the same facts or circumstances as any pending or prior litigation. The intent of this exclusion is to ensure that the insurer is not tricked into insuring a "burning building." Insureds should consider asking the insurer to remove this exclusion or to limit the scope of the exclusion so that only litigation known to a select control group of insureds (for example, the CEO, CFO, and general counsel of the named insured) will be excluded from coverage.

Prior-acts exclusion. A typical prior-acts exclusion excludes coverage for any claims based upon wrongful acts that occurred prior to a certain date—often the inception date of the policy. Given the claims-made nature of the cyber liability insurance policy, a prior-acts exclusion has the potential to strip the cyber liability policy of all or most of its value, and insureds should avoid such an exclusion whenever possible. This is particularly important for cyber liability policies because cyber criminals and hackers may install spyware, viruses, and other malware long before a breach is discovered and the policy incepts.

Negotiating Exclusions: Insured-Versus-Insured Exclusions

Q 33.16.4   What are some important considerations when negotiating insured-versus-insured exclusions?

In the mid 1980s, many insurers added an "insured-versus-insured" exclusion to various types of management liability insurance policies to bar claims brought by or on behalf of one insured against another insured, the purpose of the exclusion being to avoid covering collusive, intercorporate disputes. For example, prior to the addition of the exclusion, a large financial institution filed a lawsuit against certain of its loan officers and then turned the loss over to its D&O insurer. By doing so, the insured essentially converted its D&O policy from a third-party liability coverage into a policy that could cover first-party business risk.

While there is clearly a need for an insured-versus-insured exclusion in the example above, many insured-versus-insured exclusions cast too broad a net and may severely impair much-needed coverage.

Many cyber liability insurers will agree to "carve back" certain claims for various reasons, including:

- failure to protect confidential information;

- failure to disclose a breach event in violation of law;

- the unintentional failure to comply with the insured's privacy policy; and

- violations of privacy statutes.

Often these carve-backs relate only to a specific coverage grant, so it is important to review each coverage grant separately.

Negotiating Exclusions: Miscellaneous Exclusions

Q 33.16.5   What kinds of miscellaneous exclusions might an insured negotiate, and what important factors should be considered when negotiating them?

The following are examples of some of the additional exclusions an insured may need to negotiate:

Mechanical/electronic failure exclusion. This exclusion needs to be limited so that if a cyber criminal causes the failure by means of a virus, spam attack, etc., the policy may respond.

Acts of war, invasion, and insurrection exclusion. Insureds should ensure that this exclusion does not exclude acts of "terrorism." Almost all cyber breaches could be considered acts of terrorism.

Laptop exclusion. Some cyber liability policies exclude coverage for portable electronic devices. The best option is to remove this exclusion. This may possible only be if the insured agrees to encrypt the data contained on the portable devices.

Patent, software, copyright infringement exclusion. Some cyber liability policies will cover infringement claims caused by non-management employees or outside third parties. Insureds should attempt to negotiate these carve-backs, if possible.

Negotiating Terms and Conditions

Q 33.17   Which terms and conditions should an insured negotiate?

Among the terms and conditions that should be negotiated are:

- the application severability provision;
- rescission;
- the forced settlement ("hammer") clause;
- the cancellation clause; and
- the notice and claim reporting provisions.

Q 33.17.1   What are some important considerations when negotiating the application severability provision?

Absent an "application severability provision," if any insured had knowledge of a fact that was misstated in the cyber liability insurance application (regardless of whether the insured knew the fact was misstated in the application), coverage under the policy could be voided for *all* insureds. A strong application severability provision ensures that the knowledge of an insured who knew of facts that were misrepresented in the application could not be imputed to any other insured for the purpose of determining whether coverage is available under the policy.

Q 33.17.2   ... when negotiating rescission?

Rescission—the act of completely voiding a policy due to a fraud or misrepresentation in the application for insurance—eliminates all coverage for all insureds back to the inception date of the policy.

Fortunately, rescinding a cyber liability insurance policy is not an easy task. Although the exact requirements vary by state, before an insurer can rescind a policy, the insurer must generally prove that there was a material misrepresentation in the application for insurance and that the insurer relied upon that misrepresentation when underwriting the risk. Since the insurer bears the burden of proof in establishing these elements, it will typically have to bring a successful lawsuit against its insured before it may rescind its policy. For many reasons, this is not something insurers want to do except in the most egregious of situations.

For this reason, among others, many insurers today will provide non-rescindable coverage upon request. However, insureds must be very careful here, as some non-rescindable endorsements may actually make it easier for insurers to deny coverage. For example, some endorsements make the policy fully non-rescindable, but then allow the insurer to determine whether there was a material misrepresentation in the application, or whether the insurer relied upon such a misrepresentation. This type of language shifts the burden of disproving the insurer's position to the insured. Thus, instead of having to go to court to prove that there was a material misrepresentation *and* reliance on that misrepresentation, the non-rescindable endorsement allows the insurer to simply deny coverage for the claim. To dispute the insurer's position, the insured must then bring the lawsuit and bear the burden of proving that it did not make a misrepresentation in the application and/or that the insurer did not rely on the alleged misrepresentation. For many insureds, such a provision would be less favorable and should be avoided. This is an area where a review by a cyber liability insurance expert may be extremely helpful.

Q 33.17.3   ... when negotiating the forced settlement ("hammer") clause?

A forced settlement clause, or "hammer" clause, provides that if the insurer agrees to fund a settlement within the policy limit but the insured rejects the settlement, the insurer's liability is capped at the amount of the rejected settlement plus any defense costs incurred up to that date. Insurers include this provision in their cyber liability policies to prevent insureds from fighting on principle with the insurer's money. By forcing a settlement, the insurer is essentially saying that if the insured wants to continue to fight, it should bear the risk of a less favorable resolution to the case.

While this may sound reasonable, there are many reasons why such a clause may be problematic. The following are some examples of how a hammer clause may be unfair:

Example 1: The insured is defending a claim where, if the case goes to trial, there is a 90% chance that the case would be resolved for $25,000 or less, but there is a 10% chance that the loss could be as much as $300,000. The plaintiff makes an offer to settle the claim for $250,000 (the amount of the policy's applicable retention). Using the hammer clause, the insurer "recommends" settlement to force the insured to accept the $250,000 settlement so that the claim could never reach the insurer's policy limit. Such a result is unfair since the insurer is forcing the insured to pay more than the claim is worth. To avoid this risk, the hammer clause must be limited so that the insurer may enforce the hammer only if the settlement exceeds the self-insured retention of the policy and/or the insurer is willing to fully fund the settlement.

Example 2: The plaintiff offers to settle a claim on the following terms: Company X pays $5 million and the insurer pays $1 million. Again, the insurer would have an incentive to "recommend" this settlement in order to limit its exposure. However, forcing the insured to accept this offer is unfair. To avoid this risk, the insurer should be required to fully fund any proposed settlement before it may use the hammer.

Example 3: The plaintiff offers to settle a claim with a nominal payment of $1,000, but the company must agree that it will no longer engage in a particular type of business practice. Clearly, enforcing the hammer clause without consideration of the value of discontinuing the business practice at issue is unfair. To ensure that an insurer cannot force this type of settlement, the hammer clause should be limited so that it may apply only if all damages are compensatory in nature.

Example 4: Finally, consider a situation where settling a lawsuit would require an admission of wrongdoing or would encourage other lawsuits. The cost of subsequent settlements could exceed the policy limit, and the policy might not provide coverage. To avoid these problems, insureds should request that the insurer remove the hammer clause from the policy. If an insurer will not delete the hammer clause, the clause should be limited so that it applies only if:

(1)   the settlement exceeds the self-insured retention;

(2)   the insurer is willing to fully fund the settlement, including the retention;

(3)   the settlement only involves compensatory damages (that is, there is no non-monetary relief required by the settlement); and

(4)   the settlement has no potential impact on other pending or expected cases against the insured.

Insureds should also insist that their insurer "soften the hammer" so that the insured would be liable only for a small percentage above any settlement recommended by the insurer (generally, insurers will agree to reduce the co-insurance from 50/50 to 90/10 or 80/20 upon request).

Q 33.17.4   ... when negotiating the cancellation clause?

The cancellation clause in a cyber liability insurance policy establishes when an insurer may cancel its policy. Many cyber liability insurance policies allow the insurer to cancel a policy for any reason or for no reason at all. Obviously, insureds would not want their cyber liability insurance policy canceled by an insurer that senses serious claims are coming (for example, when an insurer fears a data breach will be coming in the near future).

Many states have attempted to address this problem by requiring that all policies issued in their state include a "state amendatory endorsement," which limits how and when an insurer may cancel its policy. Unfortunately, few states have kept up with changing market conditions, and insurers are often willing to provide more protection against cancellation than a state requires in its mandatory endorsement. In fact, many of the mandatory state endorsements today actually reduce coverage for insureds rather than increase it. State laws on cancellation were intended to protect insureds by providing a minimum, not a maximum, amount of protection.

To be sure that a cyber liability insurance policy has the broadest possible protection against cancellation, insureds should negotiate their cyber liability insurance policies so that:

(1) the cyber liability insurance policy allows the insurer to cancel coverage only if the company fails to pay the premium when due; and

(2) if the cyber liability insurance policy has a state-required endorsement that limits when the insurer may cancel coverage, it must also have a state amendatory inconsistent endorsement, which states that, to the extent permitted by law, where there is an inconsistency between a state amendatory endorsement and any term or condition of the policy, the insurer shall apply the terms and conditions of either the amendatory endorsement or the policy that are more favorable to the insured.

Q 33.17.5   ... when negotiating the notice and claim reporting provisions?

Failure to give timely notice of a claim is a common reason insurers deny coverage for an otherwise covered matter. To avoid a denial of coverage, insureds should become very familiar with the reporting requirements of their cyber liability policies. The notice provisions in cyber liability policies can differ dramatically. The following are some of the many types of reporting requirements that exist:

Claims must be reported as soon as practicable within the policy period. This is the traditional "claims made and reported" language—and it is undesirable. The problem with this language is that the policy will only cover a claim made the day before the policy is about to expire if the insured reports that claim before the policy expires. This puts an unreasonable burden on the insured. This language also requires the insured to report a claim made early in the policy period as soon as practicable. This could leave an insured without coverage for a claim even if the claim was reported within the policy period. (For an illustrative example of the need to negotiate the notice provision, see the *Briggs Ave. LLC v. Insurance Corp. of Hannover* Case Study in chapter 32, which involved "as soon as practicable" language.)

> **TIP:** Even if a late-reported claim is ultimately accepted by an insurer, most insurers will not cover any expenses incurred prior to the date the notice was received. Thus, insureds are well served to notice claims as soon as they become aware of them.

Claims must be reported within thirty days. Some insureds require that a claim be reported within a set period of time (generally, within thirty to ninety days of when the claim was made). This language is also undesirable. Although it does soften the reporting requirement so that an insured could report a claim after the policy expiration date (a good thing), claims made early in a policy period could still be considered late if they were reported within the policy period.

Claims must be reported within the policy period, but a claim made in the last thirty days of the policy period may be reported for thirty days after the policy expires. This language softens the potentially harsh requirements in the previous provisions. It allows an insured to report a claim that comes within the last thirty days of the policy period for thirty days after the policy expires, relieving the unrealistic requirement that a claim made on the last day of the policy period be reported before the policy expires. It also allows an insured to report claims made early in the policy period at any time within the policy period, reducing the chances of a late notice.

Claims are accepted as long as the insurer is not prejudiced by the late notice. Some insurers now offer to cover a late-noticed claim unless the insurer was actually and materially prejudiced by the late notice. This is generally the best option for insureds when available.

In addition to the timing issues above, insureds should also seek to limit the insured persons whose knowledge will trigger the reporting requirements. Because the typical notice provision applies to all insureds and many of the insureds may not fully understand the cyber liability insurance reporting requirements, it is best to limit the reporting trigger to when the risk manager or general counsel of the named insured first learns of the claim.

For example, one insurer provides as follows:

> An Organization or an Insured shall, as a condition precedent to the obligations of the Insurer under this policy, give written notice to the Insurer of a Claim made against an Insured as soon as practicable after the Named Entity's Risk Manager or General Counsel (or equivalent position) first becomes aware of the Claim, but in all events no later than either:
>
> (1)   the end of the Policy Period or the Discovery Period (if applicable); or
>
> (2)   within 30 days after the end of the Policy Period or the Discovery Period (if applicable), as long as such Claim was first made against an Insured within the final 30 days of the Policy Period or the Discovery Period (if applicable).

Finally, insureds should insist on an email reporting option.

Negotiating Excess Policies

Q 33.18   How do excess policies typically work with the primary policy?

Most cyber liability insurance programs with more than $10 million in limit will require an excess "follow form" policy. Despite their name, few excess policies truly follow the terms and conditions of the primary insurance policy. Instead, most excess policies will add various terms and conditions that have the potential to significantly impact the overall protection provided by the cyber insurance program of insurance.

TIP: Many insurers use a D&O excess policy form as their excess form for their cyber liability placements. This may create unique coverage issues that should not be ignored. Insureds are well advised to review the excess policies to avoid unintended coverage gaps.

Notwithstanding the potential impact that these added terms and conditions may have, excess policies are often wholly neglected. Insureds fail to analyze or negotiate their excess policies for many reasons. Sometimes, they assume the excess policies are all the same and so just pick the cheapest one. Often, they simply run out of time to deal with the excess policies as the renewal date approaches.

This makes little sense because, once the limit of liability of the primary policy is exhausted, the excess policies will be very relevant to whether a claim will continue to be paid. In fact, in a large insurance program, the excess policies often constitute the vast majority of the limit of coverage.

Q 33.18.1   What are the potential consequences of failing to review and negotiate an excess policy?

The failure to review and negotiate an excess policy may result in a loss of coverage, particularly as it relates to excess policies' provisions addressing:

- attachment/exhaustion;
- arbitration; and
- appeals.

Q 33.18.2   What factors should be considered when negotiating an excess policy's attachment/exhaustion provision?

The point at which a policy will begin to provide coverage is referred to as the "attachment" or "exhaustion" point, and the provisions that determine attachment/exhaustion are perhaps the most important provisions in an excess policy. Some excess policies state that the excess insurer's liability for any covered loss will attach *only* after the *insurers* of the underlying policies have paid for loss equal to the full amount of the underlying limit. Such a provision could be interpreted to mean that payments by the insureds (or another source such as a Side A policy) to settle coverage disputes would not count toward the exhaustion of the underlying limit of liability.

Q 33.18.3   How can an insured negotiate an attachment/exhaustion provision to avoid an unfair result?

Strict attachment/exhaustion provisions have the potential to gut coverage. (See the *Qualcomm* Case Study in chapter 32, which illustrates this point.) To avoid this unfair result, insureds need to negotiate excess insurance policies so that they recognize payments *made by the insureds*, as well as any other source. An example of such a provision might provide that

> Underwriters shall be liable only after the insurers of each of the Underlying Policies *and/or the Insureds and/or any other source* have paid or have been held liable to pay the full amount of the Underlying Limit of Liability.

Insureds should be wary of variations of the above recommend language. For example, some insurers will offer a "shaving of limits" provision. Such a provision states that the excess insurer will attach once the underlying limit has been paid by the underlying insurers and/or the insureds, but that the excess insurer will receive the benefit of the underlying negotiations and will pay no greater a percentage of the excess limit than the lowest percentage paid by any underlying insurers. In other words, if the underlying insurer paid only 80% of its limit, the excess insurer would only have to pay 80% of its limit.

The problem with this solution is that there may be a reason to give a "discount" to an underlying insurer that does not exist with an excess insurer. For example, what if the reason for giving a discount to the underlying insurer is that the underlying policy had a different choice-of-law provision than the excess policy? In such a case, the reason to give a discount to the underlying insurer would not exist with the excess insurer. As such, it would be unfair for the excess insurer to benefit from the discount. Similarly, if the reason for the discount to the primary layer was due to a defense cost issue, an excess layer that is paying only liability should not receive the same discount.

Q 33.18.4   What factors should be considered when negotiating an excess policy's arbitration provision?

Some cyber liability insurance policies require disputes between the insured and the insurer to be resolved by arbitration (as opposed to litigation). Many insureds consider this a problem: Because litigation tends to be more insured friendly than arbitration, they would prefer to have the option to litigate coverage disputes.

This issue may be even more problematic in large insurance programs that require multiple insurers to build the total limit of coverage. Large insurance programs may have multiple and potentially inconsistent arbitration provisions. This type of inconsistency could force an insured to fight multiple battles on multiple fronts with potentially inconsistent results. Clearly, this is not what an insured wants from its insurance program. For example, in one program, the primary policy requires AAA arbitration and applies the laws of the State of Florida. The first excess policy requires UNCITRAL arbitration rules and applies the laws of Bermuda. A higher excess policy requires controversies to be resolved in London under the Arbitration Act of 1996. In addition to applying different laws to any given controversy, each of these arbitration provisions requires the dispute to be heard in different locations.

To avoid this result, an insured should attempt to remove all arbitration requirements from its policies. If this is not possible, an insured should seek to have all of the insurers agree to one arbitration method with only one choice-of-law provision to resolve any potential coverage disputes. Which law is chosen and which jurisdiction should be specified as the judicial "seat" of the arbitration are likewise matters of significant concern. Counsel experienced in such matters should be consulted.

Q 33.18.5   What factors should be considered when negotiating an excess policy's appeals provision?

Some cyber liability insurance policies allow an excess insurer to appeal an adverse judgment against an insured even if the insured has no desire to appeal. One reason an insurer may want to appeal a matter is that the insurer believes the jury awarded unreasonably high damages and that such damages might be reduced on appeal. By appealing the judgment, the insurer may be able to reduce its losses. The insured, on the other hand, may have no desire to appeal the jury award, especially if the insurer is fully covering the loss. Instead, the insured may prefer to leave the matter resolved and remove the distraction of the litigation.

Perhaps the most troubling aspect of an appeals provision is that most appeals provisions do not make the insurer responsible for any additional losses above the insurer's policy limit incurred as a result of the appeal. Thus, if instead of reducing the jury award on appeal, the case is remanded and the new jury returns an even higher award— one that exceeds the insurer's policy limit—the insured could potentially be required to pay for the increased award.

To avoid this result, an insured should negotiate to delete the appeals provision from its program.

> **TIP:** Taking the time to review and negotiate excess policies is essential. Insureds that fail to do so may discover that they have unfavorable provisions in their excess policies that may result in a loss of coverage in a claim situation. Since most excess insurers are willing to make the changes discussed above (and other significant changes) upon request *and for no additional premium,* insureds must take an active role in reviewing and negotiating their excess policies.

Claims

Reporting Claims

Q 33.19   When should an insured report a claim?

A claims-made-and-reported policy, by definition, requires that a claim be properly "noticed" during the policy period. A strict reading of this language means that:

(1)   a claim that arises a few days before a policy expires must still be reported before that policy expires for coverage to attach; and

(2)   a claim that occurs in the first few days of a policy may still be covered even if it is not reported until just before the policy expires.

The *Westrec Marina Management, Inc. v. Arrowood Indemnity Co.* Case Study in chapter 32 illustrates how insurers take this timing requirement very seriously.

TIP: An insured should be sure to provide notice to each of the excess insurers on the program. Failure to notice all of the excess insurers may result in a loss of coverage.

As previously discussed, some cyber liability insurance policies attempt to soften the strict timing requirements by allowing claims to be reported as soon as practicable, or as soon as practicable but in no event more than thirty days after the claim is made (*see* Q 33.17.5, *supra*). This type of language may create a "mini-tail" reporting period that allows a claim that occurs shortly *before* the policy expires to still be reported in a timely fashion *after* the policy expires. On the other hand, this type of language may exclude coverage on a claim that is not reported within the window set forth in the policy even if the policy has not yet expired. Nonetheless, given the obvious importance of ensuring a claim is reported in the appropriate time frame, it is vitally important that a company have a well-defined system in place for claims to be forwarded to the company's risk manager or general counsel and, ultimately, its insurer. Failure to provide clear direction to company managers may result in a delay in reporting and, in turn, a dispute or even a denial of coverage by the insurer.

TIP: Most management liability policies are written on a claims-made basis. To avoid late notice issues, insureds should notice all potentially relevant policies (D&O, EPLI, FI, Crime, CGL, etc.) at the same time.

Q 33.19.1   Are there instances in which an insured should consider *not* reporting a claim?

Generally, reporting a claim under a cyber liability insurance policy is not discretionary. Thus, even if a claim does not appear to have any merit or is unlikely to exceed the company's deductible or retention, the insured should still normally report it promptly. Nevertheless, some companies are concerned that reporting such claims may potentially result in higher premiums and/or less favorable coverage when the policy is renewed, and they will either not report or defer reporting the claim. However, the claims-made requirement of a cyber liability insurance policy does not afford a company the luxury of waiting to gauge the severity of a claim.

Q 33.19.2   What are the possible consequences of *not* reporting a claim?

Failure to promptly report a claim may result in an insurer denying coverage even if the claim later develops into a more substantive and insurable risk. This risk may be significant, as a claim that appears small or without merit may, nonetheless, result in large legal costs and/or liability. Hence, it is advisable to report all claims that are likely to fall within the ambit of coverage afforded by the cyber liability insurance policy and disregard any commercial consideration in connection with the claims reporting decision.

> **TIP:** The true test of an insurance program is how it responds to a claim. Starting with the decision of whether to put insurers on notice of a cyber liability claim or a circumstance and continuing through the structuring of a settlement agreement, insureds get better results when they take an active role in the claims process.

Q 33.20   What details should be included in the notice of claim?

Once it is clear that notice of a claim or circumstance should be sent, it is important to ensure that proper notice is given. For a claim, it is generally necessary to forward the written demand for relief to the insurer. When noticing circumstances, the cyber liability insurance policy may require a description of:

(1) the "wrongful act" or circumstance;

(2) the nature of the "wrongful act";

(3) the nature of the alleged or potential damage;

(4) the names of actual or potential claimants; and

(5) how the company first became aware of the claim or circumstance.

The policy will also state where the insured should send the notice. The insured should send all insurers (primary and excess) notice of any claim or potential claim even if the insured does not expect the claim to exceed the primary insurer's limit.

> **TIP:** Different insurers on the same cyber liability insurance program may have different notice requirements. To obtain coverage from all layers, it is important to notice each insurer and follow the reporting requirements of each excess insurance policy.

Defending Claims

Q 33.21   How are claims defended?

Most cyber liability policies are written on a "non-duty-to-defend" basis, allowing the insured (as opposed to the insurer) to manage and control the defense of the claim. This means that the insured may decide issues such as which defense counsel to retain and when and if it will settle the claim. Although a cyber liability insurer will still have a say in these important decisions (typically, such decisions are made with the consent of the insurer), a non-duty-to-defend policy is attractive to many cyber liability insureds given the types of claims that may be brought under a cyber liability policy.

Of course, some cyber liability insureds prefer a duty-to-defend policy. Typically, smaller companies or companies that do not have a legal department or other staff to manage a complex cyber liability claim will prefer such a policy.

Perhaps the best option, however, is a policy that allows the insured to choose whether it wants to run the defense for any particular claim. Many insurers today will allow the insured to choose whether any particular claim will be handled on a duty-to-defend or a non-duty-to-defend basis.

For further discussion of duty-to-defend and non-duty-to-defend coverage, see QQ 33.6–33.6.3, *supra*.

Post-Claim Issues

Reservation of Rights

Q 33.22   What happens after a claim is reported?

Generally speaking, the insurer will typically respond, shortly after an insured reports a claim, with a "reservation-of-rights" letter, discussing potential coverage issues raised by the nature of the claim. It is also possible that the insurer will issue a "denial-of-coverage" letter.

Q 33.22.1   What is a reservation-of-rights letter?

A reservation-of-rights letter, which an insurer will typically send shortly after an insured reports a claim, discusses potential coverage issues raised by the nature of the claim and explains why the claim may not be covered. Because an insurer is often deemed to have waived any issues that are not raised in a reservation-of-rights letter, many reservation-of-rights letters are extremely broad.

Although a reservation-of-rights letter is obviously for the insurer's benefit, it should not necessarily create an adverse relationship between the insurer and insured. It is the insurer's initial response, not its final decision on coverage. The reservation-of-rights letter may be useful to the insured because it provides an early indication of the insurer's position. It also allows the insured to take necessary steps to protect its potentially uninsured interests.

Denial of Coverage

Q 33.22.2   What is a denial-of-coverage letter?

If the claim reported by the insured appears to be outside the scope of coverage provided by the policy, or if the insured has not complied with the terms and conditions of the policy, the insurer may deny coverage and issue a denial-of-coverage letter. In many jurisdictions, a denial or disclaimer letter will effectively terminate the obligation of the insured to keep the insurer informed of claim developments. Regardless of whether a duty exists, however, it may be wise to continue to keep the insurer informed of case developments, as later developments may alter the insurer's coverage position. In addition, keeping the insurer apprised of developments may assist the insured if the coverage dispute is later litigated.

Duties and Obligations of Insureds

Q 33.23   What are an insured's obligations with respect to the insurer after a claim has been reported?

Most cyber liability insurance policies impose a duty to cooperate and to provide such information as the insurer may reasonably require. Assuming that the insurer does not deny coverage at the outset, it is incumbent upon the insured to keep the insurer informed of significant developments as they occur. Generally, this means that the insured must forward copies of pleadings, settlement demands, and significant court orders to the insurance company. The insured's defense counsel may also be required to provide periodic updates or case status reports to the insurer.

> **TIP:** Keeping the insurer informed can be helpful during settlement negotiations. Informed insurers tend to "buy in" to the defense strategy and are able to get authority to approve a settlement proposal more quickly.

Perhaps the most critical duty an insured has is to advise the insurer of any settlement negotiations at the time that they occur. Failure to keep the insurer advised of settlement talks will likely result in the insurer denying coverage even if the claim would have otherwise been covered. (For an illustrative example of the importance of this duty, see the *Vigilant Insurance Co. v. Bear Stearns Cos.* Case Study in chapter 32.)

Other duties of an insured include taking all reasonable steps to mitigate any damages.

Privileges and Protections

Q 33.24   Are communications related to a claim protected by the attorney-client privilege and work-product doctrine?

Not all communications between the insurer and the insured will be protected from discovery. In fact, the rules governing when a communication will be protected vary by jurisdiction; thus, an insured should always consult with legal counsel to determine the amount of protection afforded to a particular communication.

There may also be limits on the protection granted to communications between a director or officer and the company's in-house or outside counsel. Again, the amount of protection varies by jurisdiction, but communications between a director or officer and the corporate attorney may not be protected. This is of particular concern in cyber claims, as information provided to a non–law firm service provider may not qualify as privileged, may be discoverable, and may result in additional or more serious claims against the company.

Finally, issues concerning the attorney-client privilege and work-product doctrine sometimes arise when there are joint defense agreements. Since lawsuits often name multiple officers and directors and possibly other parties who are represented by more than one attorney, it is sometimes necessary to implement joint defense agreements so that the parties may present a united and cohesive front. Some jurisdictions recognize that communications between parties with a common legal purpose are protected. However, when the interests of the parties do not align legally, the protection may falter. Again, insureds should consult legal counsel on all matters pertaining to the attorney-client privilege and work-product doctrine.

TIP: Using a law firm to coordinate the response to a data breach may help protect the attorney-client privilege.

FIGURE 33-3

Common Mistakes in Claims Handling

Late notice.

Late notice is one of the easiest ways to deny coverage for a claim on a claims-made policy. Insureds should investigate each year before the renewal of the policy to determine if anyone knows of any claims or potential claims that may need to be reported to the insurers.

Failure to notice all layers and all policies.

Insureds must notify any claims or circumstances to all layers of the insurance program. Failure to notify any excess insurer may jeopardize the coverage for the entire tower above the missed insurer. Insureds should also confirm receipt of the notice by the insurers for the same reasons.

Failure to communicate.

Although a claim may put an insured at odds with an insurer, many insureds may benefit from working with an insurer as a business partner. Insurers may be a valuable source of knowledge and experience regarding a claim. For example, during the height of the stock option backdating claims, some insurers were sharing their experience about settlement ranges and terms with their insureds. This sharing of information allowed many insureds to resolve their claims more quickly and less expensively than they might have otherwise done.

FIGURE 33-4

Insureds' Checklist for Defending Cyber Liability Claims

❑   Promptly notice all claims to all insurers on your cyber liability program.

❑   Determine whether any other insurance policies might respond to the claim, and if so, notify those insurers as well.

❑   Once a claim is made, check to see if the consultants or law firms to defend the claim must be from a pre-selected list (panel counsel). Failure to use a panel counsel firm when required could result in a loss of coverage.

❑   Make sure all incurred costs are "reasonable and necessary to the defense of the claim." Take an active role in managing response and defense costs. As soon as possible, inform all insurers of the name of all consultants and law firms selected, as well as the hourly billing rates of the consultants and attorneys who will be responding to the claim.

❑   Insurers must approve the use of multiple firms to defend a claim. Absent a conflict, all insureds should use the same legal counsel.

❑   Determine whether any litigation management guidelines will apply. If so, share these with defense counsel promptly.

❑   Provide all bills to the insurers on a monthly basis and push for prompt audits of such bills—even before the retention is exhausted.

❑   Know that defense costs typically erode your limit, which means every dollar spent defending a claim reduces the amount available to pay a settlement or judgment.

❑   Use your insurer's experience on coverage matters to your advantage.

❑   Know that you need to obtain consent before settling or offering to settle claims.

Notes to Chapter 33

1.   Ponemon Inst. LLC, 2019 Cost of Data Breach Study: Global Analysis (July 2019).

2.   ADVISEN, INFORMATION SECURITY AND CYBER RISK MANAGEMENT: THE NINTH ANNUAL SURVEY ON THE CURRENT STATE OF AND TRENDS IN INFORMATION SECURITY AND CYBER RISK MANAGEMENT (Oct. 2019), https://cdn2.hubspot.net/hubfs/2558521/2019%20whitepapers/2019-zurich-information-security-and-cyber-risk-management.pdf (registration required).

3.   SYMANTEC, INTERNET SECURITY THREAT REPORT vol. 24 (Feb. 2019), https://www-west.symantec.com/content/dam/symantec/docs/reports/istr-24-2019-en.pdf.

4.   MCAFEE LABS THREATS REPORT 26 (Sept. 2016), www.mcafee.com/us/resources/reports/rp-quarterly-threats-sep-2016.pdf.

5.   MCAFEE LABS THREATS REPORT 26 (Sept. 2016), https://www.mcafee.com/enterprise/en-us/assets/reports/rp-quarterly-threats-aug-2019.pdf.

6.   APWG's Phishing Activity Trends Report, 3rd Quarter 2019, https://docs.apwg.org/reports/apwg_trends_report_q3_2019.pdf.

7.   *See* Apache Corp. v. Great Am. Ins. Co., 622 F. App'x 252 (5th Cir. 2016) (holding that the insurer was not liable for $7 million in company funds that were voluntarily transferred).

8.   NETDILIGENCE, 2019 CYBER CLAIMS STUDY 2019 report (2019), https://netdiligence.com/wp-content/uploads/2020/03/2019_NetD_Claims_Study_Report_1.2.pdf.

Appendix 33A

Glossary of Common Cyber Liability Insurance Terms

All-risk. A type of policy that provides protection against any claim that is not specifically excluded by the policy. The opposite type of coverage is a **named-peril** policy, which covers only those types of claims that are specifically listed in the policy.

Allocation. The split between covered and uncovered loss. Allocation usually occurs when there are covered and uncovered allegations in a claim or when there are allegations against covered and uncovered persons or entities.

Attachment/exhaustion. The attachment/exhaustion provision sets forth when an excess policy will provide coverage. Generally, this provision provides that the excess policy will only attach once the underlying policy limit is exhausted.

Bodily injury. A physical injury, sickness, disease, or death. Some policies will also include mental anguish or injury and other types of emotional distress, including mental tension, emotional distress, pain and suffering, or shock, whether or not resulting from injury to the body, sickness, disease, or death of any person.

Captive. An insurance company that is owned by a parent company and used to insure the parent's own risks.

Change-of-control provision. Generally details how certain events/ transactions will impact the insurance coverage. For example, the change of control provision might state that if the parent company is sold, the insurance will cease to provide going forward insurance coverage.

Claim. Generally defines the events that will trigger coverage under the cyber liability insurance policy. Most cyber liability insurance policies will define a "claim" broadly to include litigation, arbitration/mediation, and certain regulatory matters.

Claims-made. A type of policy that requires that a claim be made and reported during the policy period in order to be covered by the policy.

Coinsurance. Insurance that requires the insureds to retain some percentage of the risk of loss. For example, the cyber liability policy may provide that the insurer will pay 90% of a loss and that the insured shall pay the remaining 10%.

Communication. An electronic record or message created, generated, sent, communicated, received, or stored by electronic means that is capable of retention by the recipient at the time of receipt, including a telefacsimile transmission or email, and that was transmitted or purported to have been transmitted through a network.

Computer. A device or group of devices that by manipulation of electronic, magnetic, optical, or electromechanical impulses pursuant to a computer program can perform operations on data.

Computer system. Often defined as computer hardware, software, or components that are linked together through a network of two or more devices accessible through the Internet or internal network, or connected with data storage or other peripheral devices and are under ownership, operation, or control of, or leased by, an insured company. Some definitions will also include associated input and output devices, data storage devices, networking equipment and storage area network, or other electronic data backup facilities. Some definitions restrict "computer system" to devices that are linked together through a network of two or more devices accessible through the Internet or internal network, or connected with data storage or other peripheral devices (including wireless and mobile devices), provided that such hardware, software, components, devices, and internal networks are under ownership, operation or control of, or are leased by, an insured.

Conduct exclusions. In the cyber liability insurance context, the conduct exclusions remove coverage for certain wrongful acts committed by the insureds (for example, where the insured gains illegal profits or commits intentional misconduct or fraud).

Conduit injury. Injury sustained or allegedly sustained by a person because a system cannot be used, or is impaired, resulting directly from (1) a cyberattack into an insured's system, provided such cyberattack was then received into a third party's system; or (2) a natural person who has accessed a system without authorization, through an insured's system.

Confidential information. Any of the following in a company's or information holder's care, custody, or control, or for which a company or information holder is legally responsible:

1. Information from which an individual may be uniquely and reliably identified or contacted, including, without limitation, an individual's name, address, telephone number, Social Security number, account relationships, account numbers, account balances, account histories, and passwords;

2. Information concerning an individual that would be considered "nonpublic personal information" within the meaning of Title V of the Gramm-Leach-Bliley Act of 1999 (as amended) and its implementing regulations, or protected personal information under any similar federal, state, local, or foreign law;

3. Information concerning an individual that would be considered "protected health information" or "electronic protected health information" within the Health Insurance Portability and Accountability Act of 1996 (as amended) (HIPAA) or the Health Information Technology for Economic and Clinical Health Act (HITECH Act), and their implementing regulations, or protected health-related information under any similar federal, state, local, or foreign law;

4. Information used for authenticating customers for normal business transactions; or

5. Any third party's trade secrets, data, designs, interpretations, forecasts, formulas, methods, practices, processes, records, reports, or other item of information that is not available to the general public.

Consumer redress fund. A sum of money that the insured is legally obligated to deposit in a fund as equitable relief for the payment of consumer claims due to an adverse judgment or settlement of a regulatory proceeding. It typically does not include any sums paid that constitute taxes, fines, penalties, injunctions, or sanctions.

Content injury. Injury sustained or allegedly sustained by a person because of the actual or alleged infringement of:

1. a collective mark, service mark, or other trademarked name, slogan, symbol, or title;

2. a copyright;
3. the name of a product, service, or organization; or
4. the title of an artistic or literary work, resulting directly from cyber activities of an insured.

Continuity date. Generally the date on which the insureds first purchased cyber liability insurance from the insurer. Cyber liability policies typically exclude coverage for any claims or circumstances that could give rise to claims that were known to the insureds as of the continuity date.

Continuity of coverage. A continuation of the representations and warranties given by the insureds in the insurance application. Continuity of coverage is very important to insureds as it allows them to avoid making new representations and warranties at the renewal or when the insured changes insurers. This is a particularly important issue in a **claims-made** policy.

Crisis management expenses. Typically defined as the "reasonable and necessary" costs to retain: an independent attorney, an information security forensic investigator, and a public relations consultant. Some policies may also include limited advertising and public relations media and activities as well.

Cyberattack. Generally defined as the transmission of fraudulent or unauthorized data that is designed to modify, alter, damage, destroy, delete, record, or transmit information within a system without authorization, including data that is self-replicating or self-propagating and is designed to contaminate other computer programs or legitimate computer data, consume computer resources, or in some fashion usurp the normal operation of a system.

Data breach expenses. Includes reasonable and necessary expenses incurred by the insured or for which the insured becomes legally obligated to pay:

1. to retain third-party computer forensics services to determine the scope of a failure of network security;
2. to comply with privacy regulations, including but not limited to the consumer notification provisions of privacy regulations of the applicable jurisdiction that most favors coverage for such expenses;

3. with the insurer's prior written consent, to voluntarily notify individuals whose personal information has been wrongfully disclosed;
4. in retaining the services of a public relations firm, crisis management firm, or law firm for advertising or related communications solely for the purpose of protecting or restoring the insured's reputation as a result of a wrongful act;
5. to retain the services of a law firm solely to determine the insured's indemnification rights under a written agreement with an independent contractor with respect to a wrongful act expressly covered under an insuring agreement and actually or allegedly committed by such contractor; and
6. for credit monitoring services, but only if such disclosure of personal information could result in the opening of an unauthorized line of credit or other financial account.

Debtor in possession. A company that operates while under Chapter 11 bankruptcy protections.

Derivative suit. An action brought on behalf of the corporation by its shareholders against the corporation's directors and officers.

Diminishing-limits. A type of policy where defense costs incurred by the insureds reduce the limit of liability available to pay loss.

Discovery period. *See* **ERP**.

Disgorgement. A repayment of ill-gotten gains—money to which the insured did not have a right to in the first place. In the cyber liability insurance context, disgorgement most often arises in the context of the definition of "loss." Most cyber liability policies do not consider disgorgement to be a loss and, therefore, do not cover any disgorgement.

Duty-to-defend. A type of policy that requires the insurer to defend any covered lawsuit or claim brought against an insured.

Employee Retirement Income Security Act of 1974. *See* **ERISA**.

ERISA. Employee Retirement Income Security Act of 1974, the statutory scheme that regulates employee benefit plans.

ERP. Extended reporting period, an optional extension of coverage that allows insureds to report claims made during the ERP, provided that the wrongful act occurred prior to the expiration of the original policy period.

Extended reporting period. *See* **ERP**.

Final adjudication standard. Requires the insurer to cover allegations of fraud or illegal conduct against an insured unless and until there is a final, unappealable adjudication that determines that the insured committed the fraud or other illegal conduct alleged. *Compare* **Final determination standard**.

Final determination standard. Requires the insurer to cover allegations of fraud or illegal conduct against an insured unless and until there is a final determination by a court or other alternative dispute resolution proceeding that the insured committed the fraud or other illegal conduct alleged. The major difference between the final determination standard and the final adjudication standard is that with the final determination standard, the insurer would not be required to fund any appeals after a determination by a trial court that the insured committed the fraud or other illegal conduct.

First-party claim. Claim made by an insured for an insured's own losses. *See* **Claim**.

Forced settlement clause. Provides that if the insurer agrees to fund a settlement within the policy limit but the insured rejects the settlement, the insurer's liability is capped at the amount of the rejected settlement plus any defense costs incurred up to that date. Insurers include this provision in their cyber liability policies to prevent insureds from fighting on principle with the insurers' money. By forcing a settlement, the insurer is essentially saying that if the insured wants to continue to fight, it should bear the risk of a potentially less favorable resolution to the case. Also called a "**hammer clause**."

Fraudulent access or transmission. An act whereby a person has:

1. fraudulently accessed an insured's system without authorization;
2. exceeded authorized access; or
3. launched a cyberattack into an insured's system.

Hammer clause. *See* **Forced settlement clause**.

Informant. Any natural person providing information solely in return for monetary payment paid or promised by an insured.

Insured's computer system. A **computer system** (1) leased, owned, or operated by the insured; or (2) operated for the benefit of the insured by a third-party service provider under written contract with the insured.

Intellectual property law or right. Any:

1. certification mark, collective mark, copyright, patent, service mark, or trademark;
2. right to, or judicial or statutory law recognizing an interest in, any trade secret or confidential or proprietary information;
3. other right to, or judicial or statutory law recognizing an interest in, any expression, idea, likeness, name, slogan, style of doing business, symbol, title, trade dress, or other intellectual property; or
4. other judicial or statutory law concerning piracy, unfair competition, or other similar practices.

Internet. A group of connected networks that allow access to an insured's system through service providers using telephone service, digital subscriber lines, integrated service digital network lines, cable modem access, or similar transfer media.

Media. Objects on which data may be stored so that it may be read, retrieved, or processed by a computer. Often does not include paper.

Most-favorable-venue. In the cyber liability context, a clause that generally states that the parties should use the law of the venue most favorable to finding coverage to determine the insurability of punitive damages.

Named-peril. A type pf policy that covers only the hazards specifically named in the policy. Named-peril policies tend to be less expensive than **all-risk** policies, which cover all hazards unless the hazard is specifically excluded from coverage.

Network. Any and all services provided by or through the facilities of any electronic or computer communication system, including Fedwire, Clearing House Interbank Payment System (CHIPS), Society for Worldwide Interbank Financial Telecommunication (SWIFT) and similar automated interbank communication systems, automated teller machines, point-of-sale terminals, and other similar operating systems, and includes any shared networks, Internet access facilities, or other similar facilities for such systems, in which an insured participates, allowing the input, output, examination, or transfer of data or programs from one computer to an insured's computer.

Network security. Those activities performed by the insured, or by others on behalf of the insured, to protect against unauthorized access to, unauthorized use of, a denial-of-service attack by a third party directed against, or transmission of unauthorized, corrupting, or harmful software code to, the insured's computer system.

Occurrence coverage. Covers losses that were incurred during the effective dates of the policy regardless of when the claim for such losses is actually made.

Outsource provider. An entity not owned, operated, or controlled by an insured on which such insured depends to conduct its business.

Panel counsel. The list of pre-approved consultants, public relations firms, or law firms that some cyber liability insurance policies require be used.

PCI Data Security Standards. *See* **PCI-DSS.**

PCI-DSS. Payment Card Industry Data Security Standards, generally accepted and published payment card industry standards for data security.

PCI-DSS assessment. Any written demand received by an insured from a payment card association (such as MasterCard, Visa, American Express) or bank processing payment card transactions for a monetary assessment (including a contractual fine or penalty) in connection with an insured's noncompliance with **PCI-DSS** that resulted in a security failure or privacy event.

Pending and prior litigation exclusion. Eliminates coverage for any litigation or proceeding that relates to any litigation or proceeding pending on or prior to the inception of the policy (or some other designated date).

Personal information. Definitions vary significantly. Defined by some insurers as specific information such as an individual's name, Social Security number, medical or healthcare data, other protected health information, driver's license number, state identification number, credit card number, debit card number, address, telephone number, account number, account histories, or passwords. Defined by other insurers as any information:

1. from which an individual may be uniquely and reliably identified or contacted;
2. that would be considered nonpublic personal information, protected personal information, protected health information, or electronic protected health information; or
3. used for authenticating individuals for normal business transactions.

Most insurers exclude information that is lawfully made available to the general public for any reason, including but not limited to information from federal, state, or local government records.

Policy period. The period of time from the inception date of a policy until the expiration date of the policy or the cancellation of the policy, whichever comes first.

Prior acts exclusion. Excludes claims arising from wrongful acts occurring before the prior acts date. Prior acts exclusions are strongly disfavored in a **claims-made** policy, as they tend to significantly reduce the protection provided by the policy.

Privacy event. Any failure to protect confidential information (whether by "phishing," other social engineering technique or otherwise), including, without limitation, that which could result in an identity theft or other wrongful emulation of the identity of an individual or corporation.

Privacy notification expenses. The reasonable and necessary cost of notifying persons who may be directly affected by the potential or actual unauthorized access of a record, and (1) changing such person's account numbers, other identification numbers, and security codes; and (2) providing such persons (for a set period of time) with credit monitoring or other similar services that may help protect them against the fraudulent use of the record.

Privacy regulations. Includes the following statutes and regulations associated with the care, custody, control, or use of personally identifiable financial, medical, or other sensitive information:

1. Health Insurance Portability and Accountability Act of 1996 (as amended) (HIPAA) and Health Information Technology for Economic and Clinical Health Act (HITECH Act);
2. Gramm-Leach-Bliley Act of 1999;

3. California's Security Breach Notification Act (SB 1386) and Massachusetts' Standards for the Protection of Personal Information (201 C.M.R. 17.00);
4. Identity theft red flags under the Fair and Accurate Credit Transactions Act of 2003;
5. Section 5(a) of the Federal Trade Commission Act, 15 U.S.C. § 45(a), but solely for alleged violations of unfair or deceptive acts or practices in or affecting commerce; and
6. Other similar state, federal, and foreign identity theft and privacy protection legislation that requires commercial entities that collect personal information to post privacy policies, adopt specific privacy or security controls, or notify individuals in the event that personal information has potentially been compromised.

Quota share. A type of program that spreads loss among two or more insurers in preset percentages.

Related acts. Acts that are logically or causally connected by some common nucleus of facts (sometimes referred to as "interrelated wrongful acts"). Some policies may also define this term as a series of similar, related, or continuous acts.

Reputational injury. Injury sustained or allegedly sustained by a person because of an actual or alleged:

1. disparagement of such organization's products or services;
2. libel or slander of such natural person; or
3. violation of such person's rights of privacy or publicity, resulting directly from cyber activities of an insured.

Rescission. The act of completely voiding an insurance policy so that it is as if the policy had never been issued. Generally, the insurer returns any premium collected, and the insured returns to the position it would have been in if the insurance contract had never been bound. Rescission typically occurs only if there is a material misrepresentation in the application for insurance.

Reservation-of-rights letter. A letter from the insurer to the insured that sets forth all of the potential reasons why coverage may not apply to a particular claim.

Retention. The amount of risk retained by the insured before the insurance policy will begin to provide coverage. Similar to a deductible.

Retroactive date. Claims arising out of wrongful acts committed prior to the retroactive date are not covered by the cyber liability policy.

Reward expenses. The reasonable amount paid by an insured to an informant for information not otherwise available that leads to the arrest and conviction of persons responsible for a cyberattack, fraudulent access or transmission, or a threat.

Security breach notification law. Any federal, state, local or foreign statute or regulation that requires an entity collecting or storing confidential information, or any entity that has provided confidential information to an information holder, to provide notice of any actual or potential unauthorized access by others to such confidential information, including but not limited to, the statute known as California SB 1386 (California Civil Code § 1798.82 *et seq.*).

Security failure. A failure or violation of the security of a computer system that: (1) results in, facilitates, or fails to mitigate any: (a) unauthorized access or use; (b) denial-of-service attack; or (c) receipt, transmission, or behavior of a malicious code; or (2) results from the theft of a password or access code from an insured's premises, the computer system, or an officer, director, or employee of an insured by non-electronic means. A security failure generally does not include any of the foregoing that results, directly or indirectly, from any: (1) natural or man-made earth movement, flood, earthquake, seaquake, shock, explosion, tremor, seismic event, lightning, fire, smoke, wind, water, landslide, submarine landslide, avalanche, subsidence, sinkhole collapse, mud flow, rock fall, volcanic activity, including eruption and lava flow, tidal wave, hail, or act of God; or (2) satellite or other infrastructure failure.

Severability of exclusions. A provision that provides that the wrongful acts of one insured shall not be imputed to any other insured to determine the applicability of a given exclusion.

Severability of the application. Generally, all statements in the application for insurance are attributed to all insureds protected by the insurance contract. A provision that limits this general rule so that the statements in the application are not imputed to all insureds, but are instead deemed binding only on the particular person or persons who were responsible for making the statements.

Third-party claim. A claim that involves damage or harm to a party other than the insured or the insurer.

Website. The software, content, and other materials accessible via the Internet at a designated Uniform Resource Locator (URL) address.

34

Executive Compensation

Robert J. Friedman, Victoria H. Zerjav, Louis L. Joseph, Ariadna Alvarez, Nicole F. Martini, Kerry L. Halpern & Cory A. Thomas

This chapter is intended to assist corporate counsel by providing a roadmap through the many aspects of executive compensation. The chapter covers the basic elements of an executive compensation package and provides important information concerning the federal income tax and securities law rules that inform the executive compensation decisions and govern executive compensation awards.

Elements of Executive Compensation

Q 34.1 How do employers generally provide and document executive compensation arrangements?

Executive compensation may be provided pursuant to an employment agreement, a formal written plan, or on a discretionary or ad hoc basis.

Q 34.2   What types of compensation are usually provided by an employment agreement?

For publicly traded corporations, it is common for an employment agreement to provide one or more of the following compensation elements:

- Fixed cash compensation on an annual basis;

- Year-end cash bonus compensation based on various performance criteria, including individual, division, or company performance;

- Deferred compensation pursuant to the agreement or a related non-qualified plan, which may or may not include a rabbi trust;

- Restricted stock, stock options, or other stock awards, often with cashless exercise provisions that use built-up equity for the share purchase;

- Severance compensation under the agreement, or a related non-qualified severance compensation plan;

- Change-in-control compensation under the agreement or a related non-qualified plan, which becomes payable if the employer undergoes a change in control; and

- Other forms of employment-related benefits, including medical and life insurance, vacation or sick leave, or various forms of perquisites.

Q 34.2.1   What types of compensation are generally provided by a "plan"?

Employers generally provide one or more tax-qualified retirement plans for employees under Internal Revenue Code ("Code") section 401(a), such as a section 401(k) plan, defined benefit pension plan, profit sharing plan, employee stock ownership plan (ESOP), or cash balance pension. Qualified plan offerings may vary widely from company to company and from industry to industry. Welfare-type benefits, such as health, life, and disability coverages, are also generally provided through employer-sponsored plans.

Qualified retirement plans are subject to regulation by the IRS. Most retirement plans, as well as welfare plans, are also subject to the coverage of the Employee Retirement Income Security Act (ERISA), which is administered by the U.S. Department of Labor (DOL).

Some types of plans, such as unfunded "top-hat" plans providing benefits only to a select group of management or highly compensated employees, while subject to ERISA, are exempted from nearly all of the statute's substantive requirements.

Arrangements that do not defer the receipt of income to the termination of employment or beyond (and do not provide welfare-type benefits), even though formally documented as a "plan," are outside the scope of ERISA. Most equity-based incentive plans and short-term income deferral arrangements would fall within this category of plans.

Q 34.2.2   What types of compensation arrangements are not considered "plans"?

Under title I of ERISA, the U.S. Department of Labor (DOL) has issued regulations[1] providing that, if certain conditions and limitations are met, various kinds of compensation arrangements or programs will not be considered "plans" for purposes of ERISA.

For example, these DOL regulations exclude from ERISA coverage cash bonuses that are paid by the employer for work performed (unless the actual bonus payment is deferred until termination of employment), and various payroll practices, such as vacation and sick pay.

Q 34.2.3   What is severance pay?

A severance pay provision in an employment agreement or a severance pay plan typically provides for compensation to be paid to the executive in the event his or her employment is terminated by the company without cause. Severance may be paid in a lump sum, or in installments of a salary continuation nature. The amounts payable may vary based on the duration of the executive's employment, compensation level, and the period over which severance is to be paid.

Q 34.2.4   What is a change-in-control agreement or plan?

A change-in-control agreement or plan is quite different from a severance pay agreement or plan. Often, payments under a change-in-control agreement are triggered if, as part of a corporate transaction, there is a change in the corporation's controlling shareholders or a significant change in composition of the corporation's board of directors. A change in control may occur in a stock sale, asset sale, merger, private equity investment into the company, and many other forms of corporate transaction. A change-in-control agreement or plan might also be drafted to require a "double trigger" before the benefit is payable entailing both (1) a change in control and (2) a termination of employment, diminution in the executive's role or title, or other change in the executive's responsibilities following the change in control.

The receipt of compensation based upon a change in control may trigger Code section 280G, which prescribes special tax treatment for both the payor and recipient of "excess" parachute payments. Treasury Regulations under section 280G include several alternative definitions of a change in control based on changes in the ownership of the corporation's stock, a change in a majority of the board membership unapproved by the pre-change board, and sale of a substantial portion of a corporation's assets. The Securities and Exchange Commission (SEC) uses similar concepts for its own securities regulation and reporting requirements.

General Tax Rules

Q 34.3   What are the general rules that apply to taxation of executive compensation?

Individuals generally use the cash method of accounting for federal income tax purposes. This means that compensation paid becomes gross income and is subject to federal income tax when it is received by an executive. Even if it is not actually received in cash, income may be subject to taxation if the "constructive receipt" doctrine or the "economic benefit" doctrine becomes applicable. Constructive receipt of income occurs if the income is made available to the executive such that it could be drawn upon or received upon request.

Except in narrowly defined circumstances (*see* Q 34.7), the executive cannot postpone taxation of income by electively deferring its receipt, beyond when it would otherwise be paid. The economic benefit doctrine becomes applicable if an executive receives a non-cash economic benefit (such as funding of amounts payable in the future through a vehicle inaccessible to the employer's creditors) even though the cash is not currently available.[2]

Various Code sections also have been enacted to provide specialized income tax rules applicable to certain kinds of deferred income, such as Incentive Stock Options (ISOs), or to address and remedy certain perceived abuses in compensation timing or amount. Code section 280G, which provides special rules for "excess" golden parachute payments made to executives, is an example of a Code provision that may impose an extra penalty tax on an executive. These situations may also be addressed through Treasury regulations and IRS notices. Regulations sections 1.61-22 and 1.7872-15, which relate to the "economic benefit" regime and "loan" regime alternatives for an executive split-dollar life insurance benefit program, are examples of a regulatory approach.

Code section 409A, enacted into law by Congress in October 2004 and often referred to as the "anti-Enron provision," applies equally to public, private, and tax-exempt employers.[3] Code section 409A applies to non-qualified deferred compensation plans (including individual employment agreements) that defer the receipt of income from the year earned to a later year. When Code section 409A has not been complied with, the employee is subjected to income taxation before the compensation is actually paid to the employee and an additional 20% penalty tax on the compensation amount in question. If the violation arises during a tax audit of an earlier year, then interest on back taxes, and various other penalties, may become payable, subject to applicable Code provisions for the possible abatement of penalties.[4]

Q 34.3.1   What are gross-up covenants?

In some cases, compensation agreements and plans, such as change-in-control plans, phantom stock plans, and other stock-based or incentive compensation plans, provide for supplementary amounts to be paid by the employer to the executive to compensate for an extra income tax or tax penalty associated with payments from the plan. Payments under an incentive plan are sometimes intended to place the executive in the position he or she would have occupied had the compensation been eligible for capital gains treatment. In other situations, such as an excess parachute payment, the gross-up may be designed to cover the executive's 20% penalty tax.

COMPLIANCE FACT

Gross-up amounts are themselves subject to federal, state, and local income taxes, if any, as additional compensation paid to the executive. As a result, the amounts paid in a gross-up need to be increased to account for the extra income taxes that become payable from the executive's receipt of the grossed-up amount.[5]

Q 34.4   What is the general rule for the taxation of non-qualified deferred compensation?

An unsecured, unfunded promise by the employer to pay compensation in the future, which is entered into before the services are performed, should defer the receipt of the earned income until it is to be paid to the executive. Assuming that the requirements of Code section 409A are satisfied,[6] taxation of deferred compensation is postponed until payment is made to the executive even if the deferred compensation is earned and vested in an earlier year. The employer secures the benefit of the tax deduction on its corporate tax return at the same time that the executive receives and is subject to income tax on the payments received by the executive.

Q 34.4.1   Does a rabbi trust affect the treatment of a deferred compensation plan under the Code or ERISA?

Often a non-qualified deferred compensation plan is indirectly funded by what is called a rabbi trust. For income tax purposes, a rabbi trust is treated as a grantor trust (which means the employer owns the assets placed in the trust and the earnings on the trust investments are taxable to the employer). Since the employer's creditors may reach the trust's assets in the event of employer insolvency, thereby depriving the executive of the security of the trust's assets, this arrangement is considered by the IRS to be an unfunded promise to pay deferred compensation.

Q 34.4.2   How does Code section 83, concerning transfers of property as compensation for services, affect executive compensation?

Code section 83(a) provides detailed rules for the taxation of property, including employer stock, transferred in connection with the performance of services. This Code section requires inclusion in income of the fair market value of property (less any amount paid by the employee) transferred to an employee when such property becomes substantially vested (that is, is not subject to a substantial risk of forfeiture).

COMPLIANCE FACT

ERISA provides that a "top-hat" plan—that is, an unfunded non-qualified deferred compensation plan which covers only a select group of highly compensated or managerial personnel—is excluded from being subject to several aspects of ERISA that are applicable to pension plans. A top-hat plan will not be considered a funded plan for purposes of ERISA because it is indirectly funded with a rabbi trust.[7]

Q 34.4.3   How does Code section 422, concerning ISOs, affect executive compensation?

Under Code section 422, special federal income tax treatment applies to ISOs. If:

(a) no disposition of the shares is made by the employee within two years from the date of the granting of the ISO nor within one year after such shares are transferred to him or her by exercise of the ISO, and

(b) at all times from the date of the ISO grant and ending three months before the date of exercise, the option holder was an employee of either the granting corporation, a parent or subsidiary, or a corporation that assumes the stock option,[8]

then generally the employee will recognize a capital gain or loss from the sale or other disposition of the stock acquired pursuant to the exercise of the ISO.

Under Code section 421, when Code section 422(a) has been complied with, an ISO results in:

(a) no income to the employee on exercise of the option and purchase of the shares; and

(b) no business expense deduction for compensation paid by the employer corporation with respect to the shares transferred to the employee.

A disqualifying disposition of the shares by the employee (which occurs when the ISO holding period has not been complied with) results in ordinary income to the employee and a business expense deduction to the employer for the amounts involved.

Q 34.4.4   What is an incentive stock option (ISO)?

An ISO is defined in Code section 422 to mean an option to purchase stock that has been granted to an individual in connection with his or her employment but only if all of the following elements apply:

(a) the option is granted under a plan that is approved by the shareholders within twelve months before or after the plan is adopted and the plan sets forth the aggregate number of shares available;

(b) the option is granted to the employee within ten years after the plan is adopted, or the date it is approved by the shareholders, whichever is earlier;

(c) the option is not exercisable after ten years from the date the option is granted to the employee;

(d) the option price to be paid upon exercise is not less than the fair market value of the stock when the option was granted;

(e) the option is not transferable except by will or the laws of descent and is exercisable only by the employee during his or her lifetime; and

(f) the optionee, at the time of the option grant, does not own more than 10% of the total combined voting power of all stock of the corporation.

Code section 422(c) provides for a good-faith valuation, and fair market value must be determined without reference to any restrictions except those that by their terms will never lapse. Other special rules for disability, payment for stock purchased with stock options (that is, cashless exercise), etc., may also apply. Most important is the limitation specifying that options first exercisable in a single year may not cover shares worth more than $100,000 (determined as of the date of grant). Options will be treated as non-qualified stock options to the extent they exceed the $100,000 limit.

ISOs are not subject to regular income taxes when the option is granted to the employee when the option is exercised. Gains on the subsequent sale of the acquired shares are taxed at long-term capital gain tax rates if the holding period for "qualified" sales has been met—that is, two years from the date the option was granted and one year after the option exercise date. Notwithstanding this favorable tax treatment for regular income taxes, ISOs generate alternative minimum taxable income upon exercise, measured as the excess of the fair market value of the shares on the date of exercise over the option exercise price.[9] AMT treatment can thus subject the executive to tax prior to the sale of the underlying shares.

Q 34.4.5   What is the AMT?

The alternative minimum tax (AMT) is designed to reduce the ability of taxpayers to utilize certain tax benefits with the goal of assuring that all taxpayers pay at least a minimum amount of tax. The AMT takes certain defined items of gross income, deductions, tax credits, exclusions, allowances, and other items, less applicable exemption amounts, from which is derived the taxpayer's alternative minimum taxable income. A special AMT rate is applied to this income. The taxpayer's AMT liability is then compared to his or her regular income tax liability. If the AMT owed is less than the regular income tax liability for the tax year, no AMT is owed. If, however, the AMT exceeds the regular income tax calculation, then the applicable AMT amount is owed.

Q 34.4.6 How should an executive prepare for the AMT?

Executives should be conscious of the AMT requirements under the Code whenever they face a one-time compensation event. This can be especially important if ISOs are exercised triggering an AMT tax liability, which needs to be paid before the shares may be sold due to lock-up agreements, the twenty-four-month holding period required under Code section 422, or otherwise.

Q 34.4.7 What are the general tax rules for non-qualified stock options?

A non-qualified stock option, like an ISO, results in no income realized by the employee on the grant of the option assuming that the options do not have a readily ascertainable fair market value at that time, as defined in Treasury regulations section 1.83-7(a).[10] However, the exercise of the non-qualified stock option results in ordinary income equal to the fair market value of the shares purchased less the option exercise price. The employer has a corresponding income tax deduction in the same year the ordinary income is reported by the employee from his exercise of such non-qualified options.

Q 34.4.8 Are there adverse tax consequences from mispriced stock options?

In addition to all of the accounting, securities, and negative publicity issues raised by discounted and back-dated stock option awards, Code section 409A is also implicated when stock option awards are priced at below fair market value on the date of the grant. Unless discounted options are properly structured in advance to satisfy the requirements of Code section 409A, option holders may find themselves subject to income taxation, as well as the 20% penalty tax, as soon as they vest in their options, and on an ongoing, mark-to-market basis until the options are exercised.

Deferred Compensation

Q 34.5   What is deferred compensation?

Another mechanism for providing valuable compensation and benefits to corporate executives is through the use of deferred compensation. Deferred compensation refers to cash compensation that will be paid to the executive at some point in the future. There are different types of deferred compensation plans. For example, there are **qualified deferred compensation plans** (such as a traditional pension plan or a 401(k) plan) and **non-qualified deferred compensation plans**. There are many variations of non-qualified deferred compensation plans, and as a result non-qualified deferred compensation plans provide companies with greater flexibility for design purposes.

Non-Qualified Deferred Compensation Plans

Q 34.6   What are the general attributes of a non-qualified deferred compensation plan?

A non-qualified deferred compensation plan is not required to meet the qualified plan requirements under the Code. Accordingly, a non-qualified deferred compensation plan offers greater design flexibility than a qualified plan. In general, a non-qualified deferred compensation plan has no limits on the amount of compensation that can be deferred or the amount of benefit that can be paid, and is not subject to nondiscrimination requirements, vesting or coverage requirements. These relaxed rules allow employers to offer benefits under a non-qualified deferred compensation plan to an individual or to a limited group of executives. Some non-qualified deferred compensation plans are designed to provide additional retirement income to executives and others are designed to provide incentive compensation during employment or upon a change in control. A non-qualified deferred compensation plan will be subject to Code section 409A (and in the case of a state or local government or a tax-exempt entity, Code section 457 as well). Generally, a participant is not subject to taxation on any of the compensation deferred under the plan until receipt.[11] In such a situation, however, the company would not be entitled to a deduction for the compensation paid until the date of distribution.[12]

Q 34.6.1   What types of non-qualified deferred compensation plans are there?

Non-qualified retirement plans can provide benefits to executives in the form of additional retirement income in excess of amounts permitted to be accrued under or contributed to a qualified retirement plan. Non-qualified retirement plans include an "excess plan" and a "supplemental executive retirement plan" (SERP).

Excess plan. An "excess plan" is a plan that provides benefits to certain employees in excess of the Code section 415 limits, which limits the amount of annual contributions and benefits under qualified retirement plans).[13] An excess plan typically allows executives and highly compensated employees to defer money or to accrue benefits in excess of the amounts they accrue under the company's qualified plans. An unfunded excess plan is exempt from ERISA and is not required to be limited to a select group of management and highly compensated employees.

SERP. A SERP refers to a non-qualified retirement plan that provides a select group of management and highly compensated employees with additional retirement income. This plan is also sometimes referred to as a "top-hat" plan. A SERP, unlike an excess plan, can be designed to allow executives to defer money or accrue benefits in excess of the Code section 401(a)(17) compensation limits, the limitations on elective deferrals, to make up for limitations as a result of nondiscrimination testing, or to provide benefits that are not tied to a company qualified plan. Subject to Code section 409A,[14] a company has discretion to determine most of the plan terms and features.

Q 34.6.2   How does a non-qualified retirement plan work?

The following example demonstrates how: Assume that the chief executive officer of a company earns $750,000 annually and intends to defer 10% of her compensation into the company's 401(k) plan. Unfortunately, there are three problems with this scenario:

(1)   In 2017, the CEO could only defer $18,000 into the company's 401(k) plan plus an additional $6,000 as a catch-up contribution if over fifty years old;

(2) Under the Code, there is a $270,000 limit on compensation for determining benefits under qualified retirement plans; and

(3) Any amounts deferred may be further reduced as a correction method if the non-discrimination tests for the 401(k) plan failed.

However, if the company had an excess SERP, the CEO would be able to contribute the full 10% of her salary. The CEO's contributions would first be used to "max out" the 401(k) plan and then any spillover contributions due to Code or plan limits would be contributed to the excess plan. The same principles can apply with respect to defined benefit plans.

Q 34.6.3   Are there any requirements with respect to SERP?

A top-hat plan refers to an unfunded plan offered to a select group of management and highly compensated employees of the company. If structured correctly, a top-hat plan could provide for unlimited, tax-free deferral opportunities that would grow on a tax-free basis. Because a SERP provides retirement income to employees, it is a pension benefit plan covered by ERISA. ERISA subjects covered plans to reporting and disclosure, participation, vesting, benefit accrual and distribution, funding, and fiduciary responsibility requirements. An important exemption from ERISA applicable to non-qualified deferred compensation plans is the "top-hat" exemption.[15] Although a top-hat plan is subject to ERISA's reporting and disclosure requirements, the DOL has provided that such a plan could meet all of those requirements by filing a statement with the Secretary of Labor that includes the following information: the name and address of the employer; the employer's IRS identification number (EIN); a statement declaring that the employer maintains the plan or plans primarily for the purpose of providing deferred compensation for a select group of management or highly compensated employees; and a statement listing the number of such plans and the number of employees in each such plan.[16] Contributions into a top-hat plan may be contributed to a rabbi trust.[17]

Q 34.6.4   What is a select group of management and highly compensated employees?

The DOL has never formally answered the question of what constitutes a select group of management and highly compensated employees. Based on case law, it appears that a conservative estimate would be 5%–10% of the senior management and highest paid employees of the company. A greater number of participants could result in a challenge by the DOL and the loss of the three statutory exemptions.[18]

Q 34.6.5   May a deferred compensation plan be funded?

For tax reasons and to avoid many of ERISA's requirements, non-qualified deferred compensation plans are typically unfunded. However, a non-qualified deferred compensation plan may be funded. A funded non-qualified plan is one in which the employer maintains the plan by making contributions to a trust or by paying premiums into an annuity contract. The employee may or may not have to pay current income tax on the contributions depending on the employee's vested rights in the contributions. Funding a non-qualified deferred compensation plan may subject the plan to ERISA's various participation, vesting, funding, fiduciary responsibility, and plan termination insurance provisions.[19]

One way in which deferred compensation may be funded is through the use of life insurance products. Typically, the deferred amounts can be used to pay premiums on cash value life insurance. The cash value may then be available at retirement to supplement other income or, if the insured dies before retirement, the insured's designated beneficiary would receive the insurance policy's death benefit.[20]

If a non-qualified plan is unfunded, the plan merely involves the employer's present promise to pay amounts to the employee in the future. The employee is taxed only when those amounts are actually or constructively received by the employee or beneficiary.[21] One main concern with an unfunded plan from the executive's standpoint is that the payments are only conditioned on the company's promise to pay in the future. Often, particularly in the context of a change in control, executives may worry that the new company will not follow through on the promised benefits. Funding a rabbi trust is not considered funding for this purpose because creditors of the employer may reach the assets of the rabbi trust if the employer becomes insolvent. Moreover, for income tax purposes, the profits and losses earned by the trust before payout of the benefits to the executive are reported on the employer's federal tax return since the trust is treated as a grantor trust under Code section 671 due to the company creditor's access to the trust assets in an insolvency.[22]

Code section 409A(b) provides certain rules relating to funding and treats certain plans that would otherwise be treated as unfunded for purposes of ERISA as a funded arrangement for tax purposes. Code section 409A(b) applies to a trust where (i) assets are set aside or transferred to a trust outside the United States (unless substantially all of the services to which the non-qualified deferred compensation relates were performed in such jurisdiction); (ii) the trust is established or assets are transferred in connection with a change in the employer's financial health; or (iii) assets are transferred to a trust to provide non-qualified deferred compensation when the employer's defined benefit plan is "at risk."

Q 34.6.6   What is split-dollar insurance?

Split-dollar insurance is insurance in which the premiums for the policy on an employee are split between the insured employee and his or her employer. The typical form of split-dollar insurance provides that the employer pays the portion of the premium that relates to the yearly build-up in the cash value of the policy, while the employee pays the portion that relates to the insurance protection.

Q 34.6.7   How is split-dollar insurance taxed?

The way that split-dollar insurance is taxed changed in 2003. Currently, the taxation of split-dollar insurance depends on who owns the policy. If the employee owns the policy, the employer's premium payments are treated as loans to the executive. Thus, the executive is required to pay the employer a market-rate of interest on the loan (the "loan regime") or the executive will be taxed on the difference between market-rate interest and the actual interest. If the employer is the owner of the policy, the employer's premium payments are treated as providing a taxable economic benefit to the executive (the "economic benefit regime"), which includes both the executive's interest in the policy's cash value and current life insurance protection.[23] A split-dollar life insurance arrangement often provides deferred compensation because the employee has a legally binding right in one year to the payment of the cash value of the policy in a later year and, in such case, is subject to Code section 409A.[24] However, where a split-dollar life insurance arrangement only pays a death benefit or where the policy distributes the cash value within the short-term deferral period, the arrangement is exempt from Code section 409A.[25] In addition, the IRS has ruled that, if the "loan regime" applies to a split-dollar arrangement, Code section 409A does not apply to the split-dollar arrangement with an employee.

Taxation of Deferred Compensation Under Code Section 409A

Q 34.7   What rules does Code section 409A impose?

In response to actual and perceived abuses, Congress enacted sweeping changes to the taxation of benefits under non-qualified deferred compensation plans. The American Jobs Creation Act of 2004 added Code section 409A, which significantly impacted the design and operation of such plans. Code section 409A, which became effective January 1, 2005, affects all employers, whether public, private, or tax-exempt. Code section 409A imposes rules on the deferral elections, distributions, and funding with respect to deferred compensation earned or vested after December 31, 2004. Failure to comply with the requirements of Code section 409A may result in significant adverse tax consequences to the service provider.

After the enactment of Code section 409A, the IRS permitted employers and other plan sponsors to delay the amendment of the plan or arrangement until the issuance of final regulations, provided that they administer the plan or arrangement in good-faith compliance with the requirements of section 409A during the interim period. Final regulations were issued in April 2007 and all affected plans and arrangements had to be amended to conform to the requirements of Code section 409A by December 31, 2007. This deadline was later extended to December 31, 2008.

Q 34.7.1   What is a non-qualified deferred compensation plan for purposes of Code section 409A?

Generally, the term "non-qualified deferred compensation plan" means any plan or arrangement between a service provider and a service recipient that provides for the deferral of compensation by the service provider. It includes any agreement, method, or arrangement, including an agreement, method, or arrangement that applies to one person or individual. A plan may be adopted unilaterally by the service recipient or may be negotiated among or agreed to by the service recipient and one or more service providers or service providers' representatives.[26]

Q 34.7.2   What is a deferral of compensation?

In general, Code section 409A provides that a deferral of compensation has occurred if, during a taxable year, under the terms of the plan or arrangement and the relevant facts and circumstances, the "service provider" has a legally binding right in one year to compensation that is actually or constructively received in a later year.[27] A service provider does not have a legally binding right to compensation if that compensation can be unilaterally reduced or eliminated by the service recipient or other person after the services have been performed. The customary payroll practice in which a service provider is paid after the end of an employee's taxable year is not considered a deferral of compensation.

Q 34.7.3   Who is a "service provider"?

Code section 409A only applies to deferred compensation of a service provider who is a cash-basis taxpayer.[28] A service provider is a person who performs services for a service recipient. The term "service provider" includes:

(1) an individual, corporation, Subchapter S corporation, or partnership;

(2) a personal service corporation (as defined in Code section 269A(b)(1)), or a non-corporate entity that would be a personal service corporation if it were a corporation; or

(3) a qualified personal service corporation (as defined in Code section 448(d)(2)), or a non-corporate entity that would be a qualified personal service corporation if it were a corporation. A service provider may be either an employee of the service recipient or an independent contractor.[29]

Q 34.7.4 Who is a "service recipient"?

A service recipient is a person for whom services are performed and with respect to whom the legally binding right to compensation arises. The term "service recipient" includes the person who is the service recipient and all persons with whom such person would be considered a single employer under Code sections 414(b) (employees of controlled group of corporations) and 414(c) (employees of partnerships, proprietorships, etc., which are under common control).[30]

Q 34.7.5 Which non-qualified deferred compensation plans are subject to Code section 409A?

Code section 409A applies to all plans and arrangements that provide for the deferral of compensation, unless such plans and arrangements are specifically exempted.[31] Examples of the types of plans that are generally subject to the rules of section 409A are:

- unfunded, secured deferred compensation plans;

- severance;

- excess benefit plans;

- equity-based compensation arrangements, such as stock appreciation rights, restricted stock, phantom stock, and discounted options;

- supplemental executive retirement benefits (SERPs);

- plans that cover only one person, such as employment agreements and severance agreements; and

- non-qualified stock options having a below-market exercise price or deferral features, other than the right to exercise the option.

Section 409A Exemptions

Q 34.8   What types of plans and arrangements are generally exempt from the requirements of Code section 409A?

Certain deferred compensation plans and arrangements are specifically exempt from the requirements of Code section 409A.[32] These exemptions are:

- short-term deferrals;

- statutory stock options and employee stock purchase plans;

- certain non-statutory stock options;

- certain stock appreciation rights;

- restricted property and stock plans covered by Code section 83;

- qualified employer plans;

- welfare benefit plans and arrangements;

- certain foreign plans;

- certain severance payments;

- arrangements if both service provider and service receiver use the accrual method of accounting; and

- arrangements with independent contractors actively engaged in a trade or business.

Q 34.8.1   What are short-term deferrals?

One of the most important exemptions from Code section 409A is the short-term deferral. A common example is annual bonuses or other annual compensation amounts paid after the close of the tax year in which the services were performed. A short-term deferral occurs if compensation is actually or constructively received by the service provider by the later of:[33]

(1) the fifteenth day of the third month after the end of the service provider's first taxable year in which the amount is no longer subject to a substantial risk of forfeiture; or

(2) the fifteenth day of the third month after the end of the service recipient's first taxable year in which the amount is no longer subject to a substantial risk of forfeiture.

However, a payment not made within the two-and-a-half-month short-term deferral period may still qualify as a short-term deferral if, as a result of unforeseeable circumstances, it was administratively impractical to make the payment, or the payment would have jeopardized the solvency of the service recipient, and the payment is made as soon as is reasonably practicable.[34]

Q 34.8.2 What are statutory stock options and employee stock purchase plans?

Statutory stock options and employee stock purchase plans include plans that provide for the grant of an ISO, as described in Code section 422, and the grant of an option under an employee stock purchase plan described in Code section 423.

Q 34.8.3 What non-statutory stock options are exempt from the section 409A requirements?

A non-statutory stock option is exempt from Code section 409A only if:

(1) it is an option to purchase service recipient stock (which is generally stock of the entity for which the service recipient provides direct services on the date of grant, or any entity in a chain of entities in which each entity has the controlling interest in another entity in the chain, ending in the entity for which the service recipient provides direct services);

(2) the exercise price may never be less than the fair market value of the underlying stock on the date the option is granted;

(3) the receipt, transfer, or exercise of the option is subject to tax under Code section 83; and

(4) the option does not include any separate feature for the deferral of compensation, other than the deferral of the recognition of income until the exercise of the option.[35]

Q 34.8.4   What kinds of stock appreciation rights are exempt from the section 409A requirements?

The grant of stock appreciation rights is exempt from Code section 409A only if:

(1) it is a stock appreciation right with respect to service recipient stock (which is generally stock of the entity for which the service recipient provides direct services on the date of grant, or any entity in a chain of entities in which each entity has the controlling interest in another entity in the chain, ending in the entity for which the service recipient provides direct services);

(2) the compensation payable under the stock appreciation right does not exceed the difference between the fair market value of the stock on the date of the grant and the fair market value of the stock on the date of exercise;

(3) the stock appreciation right exercise price is not less than the fair market value of the underlying stock on the date of grant; and

(4) the stock appreciation right does not include any feature for the deferral of compensation other than the deferral of the recognition of income until the exercise of the stock appreciation right.[36]

Q 34.8.5   What are restricted property and stock plans covered by Code section 83?

Code section 409A does not apply to restricted property and stock plans covered by Code section 83 if (a) the restricted property is non-transferable and subject to a substantial risk of forfeiture and is therefore not currently includable in income under Code section 83 by the service provider, or (b) the restricted property is includable in income under Code section 83 solely because a valid election was made under Code section 83(b) by the service provider.[37]

Q 34.8.6 What are qualified employer plans?

Qualified employer plans include qualified retirement plans described in Code section 401(a), tax deferred annuities, simplified employee pension plans, SIMPLE plans, eligible deferred compensation plans described in Code section 457(b) and certain governmental excess benefit arrangements.

Q 34.8.7 What are welfare benefit plans and arrangements?

Welfare benefit plans and arrangements include bona fide vacation or sick leave, compensatory time, disability pay, or death benefit plans. It also includes certain health/medical savings and reimbursement arrangements.[38]

Q 34.8.8 What kinds of foreign plans are exempt from the Code section 409A requirements?

Foreign plans that are exempt from Code section 409A include certain nondiscriminatory plans sponsored by foreign entities that cover a wide range of employees, substantially all of whom are non-resident aliens.[39]

Q 34.8.9 What kinds of severance payments are exempt from Code section 409A requirements?

Separation payments made on account of a service provider's involuntary separation from service or participation in a "window program" are exempt from Code section 409A if:

(a) the amount is not more than two times the lesser of: (i) the service provider's annual compensation, or (ii) the maximum amount that can be taken into account under a qualified plan pursuant to Code section 401(a)(17) for such year ($280,000 for 2019); and

(b) the payment is made no later than December 31 of the second calendar year following the calendar year in which the separation occurs. Certain reimbursements of expenses are also permitted.[40]

A "window program" is a program established by the service recipient for a limited period of time (no more than a year) to provide separation pay to service providers who separate from service.

Q 34.8.10   What happens if the service provider uses the accrual method of accounting?

Arrangements between a service provider and a service recipient are exempt from Code section 409A if the service provider uses the accrual method of accounting for federal income tax purposes.[41]

Q 34.8.11   What if the service provider is actively engaged in the trade or business of providing substantial services?

Arrangements between a service provider and a service recipient are *not* deferred compensation if:[42]

(a) the service provider is actively engaged in the trade or business of providing substantial services, other than: (i) as an employee, or (ii) as a director of the corporation; and

(b) the service provider provides such services to two or more unrelated service recipients. There are special rules for determining whether the service provider and the service recipient are related.

COMPLIANCE FACT

If the service provider is an officer of, or performs management functions for, a service recipient, the service provider is considered related to the service recipient and therefore subject to the provisions of Code section 409A.

Q 34.8.12   Why is fair market value of stock important and how is it determined?

An accurate determination of fair market value of stock is necessary when determining if stock options, stock appreciation rights, and other equity-based compensation agreements are exempt from Code section 409A. Code section 409A has specific rules for determining fair market value. In general, if the stock is readily tradable on an established securities market, the fair market value of the stock may be determined with respect to actual transactions immediately before or after the grant or exercise, so long as the determination is made on a reasonable basis, consistently applied. In addition, an average price during a specified time period within thirty days before or after the grant or exercise, can be used, if the commitment to grant the stock right based on such valuation method is irrevocable before the beginning of the specified period, and the valuation method is consistently applied. In the case of stock that is not readily tradable on an established securities market, the value must be determined by the reasonable application of a reasonable valuation method. The final regulations under Code section 409A set forth several permissible valuation methods.[43]

Q 34.8.13   If a deferred compensation plan or arrangement is not exempt from Code section 409A, what restrictions are necessary to prevent immediate taxation to the service provider?

Amounts deferred under a non-qualified deferred compensation plan or arrangement that is not exempt from Code section 409A currently will be includable in a service provider's gross income unless: (a) the amounts are subject to a substantial risk of forfeiture, or (b) the plan or arrangement satisfies certain requirements.[44]

Q 34.8.14   What constitutes a "substantial risk of forfeiture"?

Compensation is subject to a substantial risk of forfeiture if the service provider's receipt of the compensation is conditioned upon (i) the performance of substantial future services by any person, or (ii) the occurrence of a condition related to the purpose of the compensation, and the possibility of forfeiture is substantial.[45] An amount will not be considered subject to a substantial risk of forfeiture beyond the time in which the service provider could have elected to receive the compensation. An amount is not subject to a substantial risk of forfeiture merely because the right to the amount is conditioned, directly or indirectly, upon the service performer refraining from performance of services for others (that is, a non-compete agreement).

A substantial risk of forfeiture will be disregarded if it is used to manipulate the timing of the inclusion of income or if it is illusory. It will also be disregarded if the enforcement of the forfeiture is not likely to occur. This is a possible problem if the service provider is a substantial shareholder or exercises control over the service recipient.

Q 34.8.15   If there is no substantial risk of forfeiture, what requirements must be satisfied?

If the plan does not provide that compensation deferred under the plan is subject to a "substantial risk of forfeiture," then, in order to avoid the compensation being included in the service provider's gross income under Code section 409A, the plan must impose restrictions on: (a) the time and form of distributions, and (b) the making of initial and subsequent deferral elections.[46]

Payment of Deferred Compensation

Q 34.8.16   Does Code section 409A restrict the time and form of payments of deferred compensation?

One of the most significant effects of Code section 409A has to do with the time and form of payments. One of the most common provisions of deferred compensation plans and agreements was to provide the service provider or the service recipient (sometimes both) with substantial discretion as to when and how deferred compensation would be paid. This discretion has been substantially restricted.[47]

Q 34.9   What are permitted "distribution events" under Code section 409A?

If a plan is subject to Code section 409A, compensation deferred under such plan may not be distributed earlier than the occurrence of one or more of the following events:

(1) the service provider's separation from service;

(2) the date on which the service provider becomes disabled;

(3) the service provider's death;

(4) a specified time (or pursuant to a fixed schedule) specified under the plan at the date the compensation is deferred;

(5) a change in the ownership or effective control of the service recipient corporation, or in the ownership of a substantial portion of the assets of the service recipient corporation; or

(6) the occurrence of an unforeseeable emergency.[48]

Q 34.9.1 When has a service provider separated from service?

Generally, an employee is deemed to have separated from service with the service recipient when such employee dies, retires, or otherwise has terminated employment with the service recipient.[49] An independent contractor is deemed to have separated from service with the service recipient upon the expiration of the contract (or, if more than one contract, all contracts) under which services are performed for the service recipient if the expiration constitutes a good-faith complete termination of the contractual relationship.[50]

Whether an employee has terminated his or her employment is based on whether the facts and circumstances indicate that the employee and the service recipient reasonably anticipate that no further services would be performed after a certain date or that the level of bona fide services the employee would perform after such date would permanently decrease to no more than 20% of the average level of bona fide services performed over the immediately preceding thirty-six-month period.[51] Facts and circumstances described in the preceding sentence include, but are not limited to, whether:

(1) the employee continues to be treated as an employee for other purposes;

(2) similarly situated service providers have been treated consistently; and

(3) the employee is permitted, and realistically available, to perform services for other service recipients in the same line of business.[52]

A service provider does not separate from service and service is treated as continuing intact while a service provider is on military, sick, or other bona fide leave of absence if the period of such leave does not exceed six months, or if longer, so long as the individual retains a right to reemployment with the service recipient under an applicable statute or by contract.[53] If the period of leave exceeds six months and the service provider does not retain a right to reemployment under an applicable statute or by contract, the employment relationship is deemed to terminate on the first date immediately following such six-month period.[54] Certain other limited situations exist where a longer period of absence may be substituted for the six-month period.[55]

Q 34.9.2   When is a service provider considered disabled?

A service provider is considered disabled if he or she meets one of the following requirements:

(1) The service provider is unable to engage in any substantial gainful activity by reason of any medically determinable physical or mental impairment that can be expected to result in death or that can be expected to last for a continuous period of not less than twelve months; or

(2) The service provider is, by reason of any medically determinable physical or mental impairment that can be expected to result in death or that can be expected to last for a continuous period of not less than twelve months, receiving income replacement benefits for a period of not less than three months under an accident and health plan covering employees of the service recipient.[56]

In addition to the two requirements above, a plan may provide that a service provider is deemed to be disabled if he or she is determined to be totally disabled by the Social Security Administration or the Railroad Retirement Board.[57] Additionally, a plan may provide that a service provider is deemed to be disabled if he or she is determined to be disabled in accordance with a disability insurance program sponsored by the service recipient, provided that the definition of whether an individual is disabled under such program meets the requirements set forth in (1) or (2) above.[58]

Q 34.9.3   What are the requirements for specified-time or fixed-schedule payments?

Amounts are payable at a specific time or pursuant to a fixed schedule if objectively determinable amounts are payable at a date or dates that are not discretionary and are objectively determinable at the time the amount is deferred.[59] For purposes of the preceding sentence, an amount is objectively determinable if it is either specifically identified (for example, $50) or if it may be determined at the time payment is due pursuant to an objective, nondiscretionary formula specified at the time the amount is deferred (for example, 50% of an account balance).[60] Amounts are not objectively determinable if the amount is based all or in part upon the occurrence of an event, including the consummation of a transaction by, or a payment of an amount to, a service recipient.[61]

Payment schedules with formula or other fixed limitations will not fail to be payable pursuant to a fixed schedule or payments when such payments are limited by objective, nondiscretionary formulas and when amounts are not under the effective control of a service provider and not subject to the discretion of the service recipient.[62]

After a specified time or fixed schedule has been established, any subsequent change in such time or schedule will constitute a change in the time and form of payment, subject to the subsequent deferral election requirements of Code section 409A.[63]

Q 34.9.4   What is a change-in-control event under Code section 409A?

The regulations under Code section 409A define what constitutes a change-in-control event. A change in control can be:

(1)   a change in ownership interests of the company;

(2)   a change in the effective control of the company; or

(3)   a change in the ownership of a substantial portion of the assets of the corporation.[64]

To qualify as a change-in-control event, the event described above must be objectively determinable and any requirement that any person certifies the occurrence of such event must be purely ministerial and cannot involve any discretion.[65]

To qualify as a change in ownership meeting the requirements of Code section 409A, the change will occur on the date that any one person, or group acquires more than 50% of the total fair market value or total voting power of the stock of the company.[66] For purposes of defining a change-in-control event in a plan, such plan may adopt a higher threshold than the 50% threshold set forth above, but may not adopt a lower threshold.[67]

A change in the effective control of the company occurs on: the date that any one person or group acquires (or has acquired during the twelve-month period ending on the date of the most recent acquisition by such person or persons) ownership of stock of the company possessing 30% or more of the total voting power of the stock of such company or the date a majority of members of the company's board of directors is replaced during any twelve-month period by directors whose appointment or election is not endorsed by a majority of the members of the company's board of directors before the date of the appointment or election.[68] For purposes of defining a change-in-control event in a plan, such plan may adopt a higher threshold than the 50% threshold set forth above, but may not adopt a lower threshold.[69] A change in the effective control of a company may also occur in a transaction where one of two corporations involved in a transaction has a change-in-control event that satisfies the definition of a change-in-control event under Code section 409A and a change in the effective control of a company may also occur when a person or group of persons acquires additional control of a company.[70]

Finally, a change in the ownership of a substantial portion of a company's assets occurs on the date that any one person or group acquires (or has acquired during the twelve-month period ending on the date of the most recent acquisition by such person or persons) assets from the company that have a total gross fair market value equal to or more than 40% of the total gross fair market value of all of the assets of the company immediately before such acquisition or acquisitions.[71]

Q 34.9.5   How is an "unforeseeable emergency" defined?

An "unforeseeable emergency" is a severe financial hardship to a service provider that results from an illness or accident of the service provider or his immediate family, a loss of a service provider's property due to casualties, or other similar extraordinary and unforeseeable circumstances arising as the result of events beyond a service provider's control.[72] Amounts that are payable as a result of an unforeseeable emergency must be limited to the amount necessary to satisfy such emergency, plus applicable taxes on such payment.[73] Service providers can retain discretion with respect to whether to apply for a distribution based on an unforeseeable emergency, and service recipients may also retain discretion with respect to whether to make a distribution available under a plan because of an unforeseeable emergency.[74]

Q 34.10   When can deferred compensation be paid?

To satisfy the requirements of Code section 409A, a plan or arrangement must specify when deferred compensation is to be paid. Deferred compensation may be paid upon the occurrence of a distribution event (as described above in Q 34.9), or at an objectively determinable time following the distribution event (for example, three months following the death of the service provider).[75] The plan or arrangement may provide for the payment upon the earlier or latest of more than one event.[76]

Compensation that is paid during the calendar year in which the event occurred or within the first pay period following the calendar year in which the event occurred is not considered to be deferred compensation and thus can be paid according to the normal pay schedule.[77]

In addition, amounts that are paid on or before the fifteenth day of the third month following the end of a service provider's taxable year (March 15 for calendar year taxpayers) is considered a "short-term" deferral and is also not considered to be deferred compensation within the meaning of Code section 409A.[78]

Q 34.10.1   When must payments to key employees of a public company be delayed?

A plan subject to Code section 409A must prohibit payments on account of separation from service to a "specified employee" prior to a date that is six months after the date of such employee's separation from service (or, if earlier, the date of death of the specified employee).[79] A specified employee for purposes of Code section 409A is generally defined to mean a key employee (as that term is defined under Code section 416(i)) of a publicly traded corporation.[80] Code section 416(i) provides that a key employee generally includes up to the fifty most highly compensated officers of his or her employer having annual compensation greater than $185,000 (note that this is an indexed amount applicable for 2020), 5% owners, and 1% owners having annual compensation from the employer greater than $150,000.[81]

Q 34.10.2   Under what conditions may a plan permit the acceleration of the time or schedule of any payments under the plan?

Code section 409A generally provides that no acceleration of the time or schedule of any payment may be allowed.[82] Certain exceptions to this non-acceleration rule exist under the Treasury regulations; some of the more common exceptions include exceptions for:

(1) payments pursuant to a domestic relations order, as defined in Code section 414(p)(1)(b);[83]

(2) payments made to avoid conflicts with certain ethics agreements or laws;[84]

(3) certain limited cash-out payments;[85]

(4) payments of FICA taxes on vested balances;[86]

(5) payments when a plan or arrangement fails to meet the requirements of Code section 409A;[87]

(6) payments made to avoid a non-allocation year under Code section 409(p);[88]

(7) payments for certain state, local, or foreign taxes;[89] and

(8)   payments made when there is a bona fide dispute as to a right of payment.[90]

An exception not noted above, but one of the most common exceptions, includes an acceleration of payments when a plan or arrangement is terminated.[91] Upon the termination of a plan or arrangement, if all like plans or arrangements are terminated, distributions are made between twelve and twenty-four months following the termination date of the plan or arrangement, and no similar-type plan or arrangement is adopted for five years following the date of termination, payments may be accelerated.[92] There are special rules if a plan or arrangement is terminated as a result of a change in control.[93] If the plan or arrangement is terminated within thirty days preceding or twelve months following a change-in-control event, distributions can be accelerated and payment made within twelve months of the date the plan sponsor irrevocably takes all actions necessary to terminate and liquidate the plan and all like plans or arrangements are terminated.[94]

Q 34.10.3   Under what circumstances can payments be delayed?

Generally, under Code section 409A, a delay of payments is not permitted; however, the Treasury regulations provide certain situations in which payments may be delayed.[95] Payments may be delayed if making the payment would jeopardize the service recipient's ability to continue as a going concern, provided that payment is to be made in the first taxable year in which the payment would no longer jeopardize the service recipient.[96]

In addition, payments may be delayed if the service recipient reasonably anticipates that making such a payment would cause the loss of a deduction under Code section 162(m)[97] or would violate federal securities or other applicable law.[98] Finally, the Commissioner of the IRS may also prescribe other situations in which payments may be delayed.[99]

Q 34.10.4   Does Code section 409A provide rules affecting initial and subsequent deferral elections?

Yes. Another significant effect of Code section 409A has to do with the timing and effective date of elections to defer compensation and subsequent changes to those elections.[100]

Q 34.10.5   When must an initial deferral election be made?

Generally, a plan must require initial deferral elections for the deferral of compensation to be made no later than the immediately preceding taxable year.[101] In the case of a person who first becomes eligible to participate in a plan, the election to defer compensation with respect to services to be performed subsequent to the election may be made within thirty days after the person becomes eligible to participate in the plan.[102]

Q 34.10.6   What are the special rules for an initial deferral election related to performance-based compensation?

An exception to the general rule is provided for performance-based compensation. If the services are performed over a "performance period" of at least twelve months, an initial deferral election may be made at any time up to six months prior to the end of the performance period, provided the service provider's right to compensation has not become both substantially certain to be paid and readily ascertainable.[103] Performance-based compensation is defined as compensation that is contingent on the satisfaction of pre-established organizational or individual performance goals.[104]

Q 34.10.7   What is the effect of changes to an existing election?

Code section 409A permits "subsequent elections" or subsequent changes in the time and form of a payment.[105] Subsequent elections are elections that are made after compensation has been deferred that changes either the time or form of distribution. A subsequent election must meet the following requirements:[106]

(a) The subsequent deferral election must not take effect until at least twelve months after the date on which the subsequent election is made;[107]

(b) If the subsequent election relates to a distribution payable upon (i) the service provider's separation from service, (ii) a specified time, or (iii) a change of control, then the first payment with respect to which such election is made must be deferred for a period of at least five years from the date the payment otherwise would have been made;[108] and

(c) If the subsequent election relates to a distribution that otherwise was to be paid at a specified time or pursuant to a fixed schedule, the election must be made at least twelve months before the date of the first scheduled payment.[109]

Compliance/Reporting Requirements

Q 34.11 What are the penalties for failure to comply with Code section 409A?

Failure to comply with the requirements of Code section 409A may result in substantial penalties for employees and other service providers who are parties to deferred compensation plans and arrangements. Service providers (generally, individuals) may be liable for:

(1) income taxes on all amounts deferred in the current and prior years;

(2) interest on the tax from the date the amount was first deferred or vested; and

(3) additional penalties equal to 20% of the deferred amounts included in the service provider's income.[110]

If, *at any time* during the taxable year, a non-qualified deferred compensation plan fails to meet the requirements of Code section 409A, or it is not operated in accordance with those requirements, all amounts deferred for the taxable year, and all preceding taxable years, are includable in gross income of the service provider for such taxable year, to the extent not subject to a substantial risk of forfeiture and not previously included in gross income.[111] Such amounts are also subject to interest and an additional income tax.[112] Interest is computed at the IRS underpayment rate, plus one percentage point.[113] The additional income tax is equal to 20% of the compensation required to be included in gross income.[114]

Q 34.11.1 What are the reporting requirements under Code section 409A?

Code section 409A requires that deferred compensation be reported to the IRS for the year deferred on the service provider's Form W-2 or Form 1099, even if the amounts are not currently includable in income by the service provider.[115] Also, any amounts required to be included in income under Code section 409A are subject to normal reporting and withholding requirements.[116]

Q 34.11.2 When did Code section 409A become effective?

Code section 409A is effective for amounts deferred or amounts that became vested and non-forfeitable in tax years beginning after December 31, 2004.[117] Compensation deferred under a plan or arrangement during tax years beginning prior to January 1, 2005, and earnings thereon, are "grandfathered" and not subject to the new rules unless the plan or arrangement is "materially modified" after October 3, 2004.[118] An amount is considered deferred prior to January 1, 2005, if, before that date, the service provider has a legally binding right to receive the amount and the amount is earned and vested.[119]

Q 34.11.3 What is a "material modification" of a plan?

A plan is "materially modified" if a benefit or right existing on October 3, 2004, is enhanced or a new benefit or right is added.[120] Amending a plan to conform to the requirements of Code section 409A is not considered a material modification; however, amending a plan to add a provision permitted by Code section 409A, such as permitting distributions upon a change in control, if the provision was not previously in the plan, is considered a material modification.[121]

Q 34.11.4   How can Code section 409A "failures" be corrected?

If a deferred compensation plan is subject to Code section 409A, the plan document must comply with Code section 409A, and the plan must be operated in accordance with Code section 409A. Failure of the plan document to contain the necessary provisions is referred to as a "document failure." Failure of the plan to be operated in accordance with the requirements of Code section 409A is referred to as an "operational failure." The IRS has established procedures by which taxpayers may correct certain unintentional document and operational failures, thereby obtaining relief from part or all of the additional taxes imposed for violating the provisions of Code section 409A.[122]

With respect to operational failures, the IRS provided guidance in Notice 2007-100,[123] which was clarified and expanded by Notice 2008-113.[124] Under Notice 2008-113, only the following operational failures could be corrected:

(a) failure to defer an amount or the incorrect payment of an amount payable in a subsequent taxable year;

(b) the incorrect payment of an amount that is payable in the same taxable year or the incorrect payment to a specified employee;

(c) excess deferrals of compensation in the same taxable year; and

(d) the correction of the exercise price of a stock right otherwise excluded from the definition of non-qualified deferred compensation.[125]

Some corrections are not available to "insiders" (officers, directors, or 10%-or-more owners). To qualify for relief, the service provider is required to repay the service recipient any amounts erroneously paid or made available to the service provider.[126]

With respect to document failures, the IRS issued Notice 2010-6 to encourage employers to review their non-qualified deferred compensation plan documents and correct those provisions that were not in compliance with Code section 409A.[127] Only certain failures described in the notice can be corrected, and they can be corrected only if they are inadvertent or unintentional.[128] Generally, Notice 2010-6 does not provide any relief for document failures related to linked plans or stock rights, or with document provisions that provide a service provider with the discretion to accelerate a payment under the document.[129]

Shortly after IRS Notice 2010-6 was issued, the IRS issued Notice 2010-80, expanding the types of plans eligible for relief and the available correction methods for operational failures.[130] Notice 2010-80 also provides relief for information that service recipients had to provide service providers with respect to certain document failures.[131]

Generally, a taxpayer seeking relief under the IRS procedures has the burden of demonstrating that it is eligible for the relief and that the requirements for the relief have been met.[132] Relief is not available if a federal income tax return for the service recipient or service provider is under examination with respect to a non-qualified deferred compensation issue for any taxable year in which a failure exists.[133] Relief is also not available for intentional failures or if the failure is directly or indirectly related to participation in a listed transaction under Treasury regulations section 1.6011-4(b)(2).[134]

Correction procedures usually require that (a) the service recipient provide the service provider with certain information prior to the W-2 filing date and (b) certain information be provided on the service recipient's and service provider's tax returns for the correction year.[135]

Offshore Non-Qualified Deferred Compensation Plans

Q 34.12   Are there any special rules that apply to offshore non-qualified deferred compensation plans?

Yes. The Emergency Economic Stabilization Act of 2008[136] added Code section 457A. Section 457A is intended to limit the payout of nonqualified deferred compensation by entities that are indifferent to the timing of a tax deduction for the compensation expense.[137] This section imposes significant restrictions on the ability of offshore entities to defer income payable to a service provider beyond twelve months following the year in which compensation is earned. Code section 457A applies to agreements or arrangements that defer income and that:

(1) provide for amounts payable to a service provider;

(2) are "non-qualified deferred compensation plans";

(3) are maintained by a "non-qualified entity"; and

(4) do not include a "substantial risk of forfeiture."

For purposes of Code section 457A, a "service provider" includes any individual or entity that performs services for a service recipient in exchange for compensation or other taxable benefits.

Q 34.12.1   What is a "non-qualified deferred compensation plan" under Code section 457?

Under Code section 457, a non-qualified deferred compensation plan is defined with reference to the broad definition in Code section 409A, as described earlier in this chapter, and includes certain guaranteed payments under partnership arrangements and certain equity appreciation plans. A plan will be a non-qualified deferred compensation plan if it is sponsored (in whole or in part) by a non-qualified entity (as defined below) as of the last day of such non-qualified entity's taxable year.

Non-qualified stock options granted at fair market value do not constitute non-qualified deferred compensation plans for purposes of Code section 457A.

Q 34.12.2   What is a "non-qualified entity"?

A non-qualified entity includes:

(1) any foreign corporation unless substantially all its income is

  (a) connected to a U.S. trade or business, or

  (b) is subject to a comprehensive foreign income tax scheme; and

(2) any partnership unless substantially all of its income is allocated to persons other than

  (a) foreign persons with respect to whom such income is not subject to a comprehensive foreign income tax, and

  (b) organizations that are exempt from tax under title 26 of the U.S. Code.

Q 34.12.3   What is a substantial risk of forfeiture?

A service provider's rights are subject to "substantial risk of forfeiture" only if they are conditioned upon the future performance of substantial services by the service provider. A non-compete arrangement is not conditioned on the performance of services. Also, an arrangement under which vesting occurs upon attaining certain performance goals is not a substantial risk of forfeiture. A substantial risk of forfeiture will be treated as ended if the service provider dies or becomes disabled. Code section 457A also defines service provider with reference to the broad definition in Code section 409A, which includes both individuals and corporate entities.

Q 34.12.4   What rules does Code section 457A impose?

Code section 457A prohibits certain entities that are indifferent as to when they may take a tax deduction for compensation, including many offshore organizations, from paying compensation more than twelve months following the year in which compensation is earned— that is, it permits the deferral of income only for twelve months following the tax year in which it was earned.

Code section 457A provides that, if the compensation cannot be determined and paid out within this time period, the compensation becomes includable in the service provider's income at the time that the compensation becomes determinable and, at such time, is subject to a premium interest charge computed back to the year in which the compensation was earned, plus a 20% federal penalty tax (in addition to any other applicable taxes such as ordinary income tax, capital gains tax, or tax pursuant to Code section 409A).

Q 34.12.5   Are there any exceptions to the requirements of Code section 457A?

Yes. Compensation paid within the twelve months following the year in which compensation is no longer subject to a substantial risk of forfeiture is exempt from Code section 457A (although it may still be subject to Code section 409A). Additionally, to the extent compensation remains subject to a substantial risk of forfeiture, it is exempt from Code section 457A and is earned when such risk of forfeiture has ended, at which point it becomes taxable. Additionally, there is an exception for single assets directly held by investment funds which are not actively managed by the fund or a related person.

There also is an exception for independent contractors. The independent contractor is not a service provider if the independent contractor satisfies the following rules: it is actively engaged in the trade or business of providing services; and it provides significant services to two or more service recipients to which the independent contractor is not related and that are not related to each other.

Golden Parachute Payments

Q 34.13   What are golden parachute payments?

Many executive compensation agreements provide that the executive will receive significant additional compensation payments, particularly in the event the executive loses his or her job in connection with a change in control of the employer. Such payments are referred to as "golden parachute payments" and may include a package consisting of payments of cash bonuses, vesting of stock rights and other benefits. If the value of the payments exceeds a certain amount, the payments that constitute "excess parachute payments" (as described below) are not deductible by the corporation,[138] and the executive is subject to a 20% excise tax.[139]

Q 34.13.1   What types of payments are considered parachute payments?

The rules for golden parachute payments are set forth in Code section 280G and the related Treasury regulations. An executive does not have to terminate employment for the rules to apply. Basically, a payment to (or for the benefit of) an executive is a parachute payment if:

(a)   the executive is a "disqualified individual";

(b)   the payment is "in the nature of compensation";

(c)   the payment is contingent on a change in the ownership or effective control of the corporation (or a change in the ownership of a substantial portion of the assets of the corporation); and

    (d) the aggregate present value of all such payments equals or exceeds three times the executive's "base amount."[140]

Q 34.13.2   What types of payments are exempt?

Code section 280G and the accompanying regulations provide that certain payments are exempt from the golden parachute rules:

    (a) payments to an executive made by a small business corporation (generally an S corporation);

    (b) payments to an executive made by corporations that are not publicly traded before the change in control if the payment was approved by shareholders in control of at least 75% of the outstanding shares prior to the change (as determined under specified rules);[141]

    (c) payments to an executive made from tax-qualified retirement plans and arrangements; and

    (d) payments to an executive that constitute reasonable compensation for services rendered before, on, or after the date of the change in control. The taxpayer has the burden of proof to establish by clear and convincing evidence that the payment is reasonable compensation.[142]

Q 34.13.3   What are "excess parachute payments"?

Parachute payments are considered excess parachute payments to the extent the present value of the aggregate amount of the parachute payments to the executive equals or exceeds the executive's base amount.[143]

Q 34.13.4   What is an executive's "base amount"?

An executive's "base amount" is the executive's average annual compensation includible in gross income for services performed for the corporation during the five years preceding the year in which a change in ownership or control occurs.[144] Practitioners frequently look to Box 1 on Form W-2 for the applicable year to determine the gross income. Special rules apply for determining the base amount when the individual has performed services for less than five years preceding the year of the change in ownership or control.

Q 34.13.5   Which executives are "disqualified individuals"?

An executive is a "disqualified individual" if he or she is an individual who is an employee, independent contractor, or other person specified in the regulations who performs personal services for the corporation and who is an officer, shareholder, or highly compensated individual of the corporation. Personal service corporations and similar entities are generally treated as individuals for this purpose.

In general, for purposes of determining who is a disqualified individual:[145]

(a) an officer includes an administrative executive who is in regular and continued service to the corporation; however, no more than the lesser of (i) fifty employees, or (ii) the greater of (A) three employees or (B) 10% of the employees of the corporation, can be officers;[146]

(b) a shareholder is defined as an individual who owns more than 1% of the value of all outstanding stock of the corporation;[147] and

(c) a highly compensated individual is defined as an employee (or former employee) who is among the highest paid 1% of employees of the corporation (or an affiliated corporation) or, if less, the employee is among the 250 highest paid employees of the corporation (or member of its affiliated group).[148]

Q 34.13.6   What are "payments in the nature of compensation"?

In general, payments in the nature of compensation include all payments that arise out of an executive's employment relationship and are related to his or her performance of services. Such payments include wages, salary, bonuses, severance pay, fringe benefits, stock options, and other equity-based awards, and other similar payments. Many practitioners treat profits interest awards to be "payments in the nature of compensation" for purposes of Code section 280G. The payments may be made by the acquired or acquiring corporation.[149]

Q 34.13.7 What payments are considered "contingent on a change in ownership or control"?

In general, a payment is contingent on a change in ownership or control if the payment would not have been made to the executive "but for" (a) the change in ownership or control of the corporation or the ownership of its assets, or (b) an event that is closely associated with or materially related to a change in such ownership or control.[150]

There is a rebuttable presumption that any payments made to an executive pursuant to an agreement entered into or amended within one year of a change in ownership or control, is a payment that is considered contingent on a change in ownership or control. For measurement of time purposes, as a technical matter, this includes the twelve months before and the twelve months after the change in ownership or control.

Q 34.13.8 Is there a minimum "threshold" for change-in-control payments to be considered excess parachute payments?

If the aggregate present value of the compensation payments to an executive as a result of a change in ownership or control does not equal or exceed three times his or her base amount, the payments are not considered parachute payments and therefore, there is no "excess" parachute payment.[151]

Q 34.13.9 How are excess parachute payments taxed?

Excess parachute payments are fully taxable to the executive and are subject to Federal Insurance Contributions Act (FICA) and Federal Unemployment Tax Act (FUTA) taxes. Code section 4999 provides that an executive who receives excess parachute payments will also be liable for a 20% excise tax on the amount of the excess parachute payment. The employer is required to deduct and withhold the excise tax, as well as income and employment taxes, from payments made to the executive. Excess parachute payments are not, however, deductible by the corporation.

Equity and Equity-Based Compensation

Q 34.14 What are the advantages of equity-based compensation?

Companies have a broad range of options in compensating their employees. Offering equity-based compensation to executives accomplishes two main goals:

(1) The recipients of equity compensation will be interested in creating value to the company and increasing the value of the company's stock; and

(2) The nature of offering equity compensation to executives lends itself as a retention tool because of vesting periods and the time needed to create value in the equity compensation.

Types of Equity Awards

Q 34.14.1 What are the different types of equity compensation plans?

Any company has the ability to grant equity awards to its employees, officers, directors, and consultants. Equity awards can take the form of stock options, stock awards, and performance awards. An award of stock options can be either a grant of qualified stock options (called ISOs) or non-qualified stock options. Stock awards typically consist of grants of restricted stock, restricted stock units (RSUs), stock appreciation rights, or performance units/performance shares. Performance awards or performance units are awards that historically have been granted to certain executives in order to comply with Code section 162(m), but the use is becoming more widespread as performance-based compensation is considered a positive governance practice applauded by institutional shareholders.

Q 34.14.2 Do equity awards have to be issued pursuant to a plan?

Equity awards are typically granted pursuant to a plan. In certain cases, such plans must be approved by shareholders, as discussed later in this chapter. Occasionally, equity awards are granted outside of a plan, although these grants are awarded in conjunction with another form of agreement, such as an employment agreement. A commonly used form of equity plan is called an "omnibus" plan, which provides the company with discretion to grant all the different types of equity awards, rather than have a separate plan for each type of equity award.

Q 34.14.3   What are the main differences between granting an ISO and a non-qualified stock option?

The main difference between an ISO and a non-qualified stock option is how the company and the recipient of the option are taxed.

Q 34.14.4   What are the rules with respect to ISOs?

Unlike non-qualified stock options, Code section 422 provides the other requirements for an option to qualify as an ISO (*see* Q 34.4.4).

Q 34.14.5   What are the rules with respect to non-qualified options?

Unlike ISOs, there are only a few important rules to remember when dealing with grants of non-qualified options. First, all options that are granted at a discount to the fair market value of the stock on the date of grant (except for options granted pursuant to a qualified employee stock purchase plan under Code section 423) will subject the option to Code section 409A. Second, if a discounted option is granted whereby the option price is far less than the fair market value of the company stock on the date of grant (typically, at least 50% or less than the fair market value of the company stock on the date of grant), the award of options actually may be considered a grant of the company stock, which would cause different taxation to the recipient.

Q 34.14.6   What are restricted stock and restricted stock units?

A grant of restricted stock provides the recipient with shares of stock of the company (that is, stock is actually delivered to the recipient, whether in paper or book entry form) that are subject to a substantial risk of forfeiture, until such time as the recipient vests in the stock. Vesting conditions for restricted stock usually fall into one of two categories: time-based vesting and performance vesting (based on subjective and/or objective individual and/or corporate goals). A combination of these conditions can also be used as a vesting condition. A recipient of restricted stock commonly enjoys all of the rights of any other stockholder, even prior to vesting, such as the right to vote the shares and the right to receive dividends and distributions. A grant of restricted stock typically will provide the recipient with a choice in taxation (*see* Q 34.8.5) and will not be subject to Code section 409A.[152]

Restricted stock units are phantom stock units that track the actual stock price but are not represented by actual shares of stock. The units represent a promise by the employer to pay the shares at some future date. The units are normally subject to the same vesting requirements as restricted stock. RSUs do not have voting rights or dividend rights.

Q 34.14.7 What is a stock appreciation right (SAR) and how do SARs work?

A SAR is an award that provides the recipient with the ability to recognize gain based on the appreciation in value of a set number of shares of company stock over a set period of time. Like a stock option, the valuation of a stock appreciation right operates in that the employee benefits from any increases in stock price above the price set in the award, except that the employee will not be required to pay an exercise price to exercise them. The recipient just receives the net amount of the increase in the stock price in either cash or shares of company stock, depending on the plan terms. SARs are sometimes granted in tandem with stock options (either ISOs or NSOs) to help finance the purchase of the options and/or pay tax if any is due upon exercise of the options (sometimes referred to as "tandem options").

SARs are granted at a set price, and generally have a vesting period and an expiration date. Once a SAR vests, the recipient can exercise it at any time prior to its expiration. The value of SARs does not reflect stock dividends or stock splits. Generally, SARs must be granted with a grant price equal to the fair market value of the company stock on the date of grant, or the SAR will be subject to Code section 409A.[153]

Q 34.14.8 What is a restricted stock unit, and what is phantom stock?

A grant of restricted stock units, or RSUs, is a promise to pay stock in the future, whether upon vesting or at a later date. Sometimes this type of award is also called "phantom stock," which typically is the company's promise to pay a bonus (likely cash) in the form of the equivalent of the value of company shares. Unlike SARs, RSUs and phantom stock can reflect dividends, typically through a mechanism called dividend equivalent units, which can be paid out immediately to the recipient or converted into additional RSUs and phantom stock shares that are paid out on vesting (or delivery of the shares, if applicable). Settlement of RSUs (that is, delivery of underlying stock) and phantom stock payments are usually made at a fixed, predetermined date (whether it is vesting or a later date). RSUs and phantom stock are, therefore, subject to Code section 409A, although such awards could be short-term deferrals under Code section 409A, depending on the terms of the awards.[154]

Q 34.14.9 What are performance units and performance shares?

Performance unit/performance share plans are offered by a large percentage of publicly traded companies. These plans are designed to pay awards if the corporation meets predetermined, long-term performance objectives (for example, return on equity). At the beginning of the performance period, the employer establishes goals designed to measure the degree of success during the performance period, typically three to five years.

The corporation's compensation committee approves the goals proposed by senior management and decides the manner in which payouts are to be calculated. These goals may be financial or operational in nature. One or more measures are often used.

Generally, an executive receives a grant of such units or "stock" at no cost. Normally, no stock is granted or transferred until the end of the performance period. The executive then earns the right to receive the monetary value of some or all of the units or stock at the end of the performance period. Normally, these plans provide for minimum, target, and maximum levels of performance and the payout amounts at each level.

At the end of the performance period, performance is assessed and awards paid. The value to be received depends upon the company's long-term performance. For example, an executive may be granted 5,000 units that will pay $1,000 each if certain target goals are achieved. If performance is above the targets, the employee may receive additional units that pay out at the same rate ($1,000 each) or at a higher payout per unit ($1,250 each). Performance units are typically paid in cash, but may be paid in a combination of cash and stock.

Q 34.14.10   Can a company reissue stock options if the price goes down?

Until December 1998, a company was able to cancel underwater options (options that have a negative value because the current stock price is lower than the exercise price) and replace them with new options without much consequence. However, under Interpretation No. 44, Accounting for Certain Transactions Involving Stock Compensation, which was adopted by the Financial Accounting Standards Board (FASB) on March 31, 2000, and made retroactively effective to December 15, 1998, a repricing of an underwater option resulted in the exercise price being treated as variable for the remaining life of the option.

For this purpose, the variable accounting treatment meant that the difference between the revised exercise price and the value of the underlying stock when the repriced option was exercised, forfeited or expired unexercised had to be recognized as a compensation expense for financial accounting purposes. In addition, as the company's stock price increased, a periodic charge to earnings was required to be reported. The variable accounting treatment under Interpretation No. 44 discouraged option repricings and led employers to use alternatives to compensate executives, such as cashing out the options.

FASB changed the accounting treatment of option repricings when it issued Statement No. 123 (revised 2004), *Share-Based Payment* (FAS 123(R)), effective for most public companies for reporting periods that start after June 15, 2005, and for non-public companies for fiscal years beginning after December 15, 2005. FAS 123(R) applies the fair value method of accounting to option repricing. This means that the fair value of the option immediately before the repricing is compared to the fair value of the option immediately after the repricing and if the fair value of the option after the repricing is higher, the company must recognize the incremental value of the repriced option over the remaining service period. Accordingly, the total compensation charge related to the repricing will be fixed at the time of the repricing. In September 2009, FAS 123(R) was recodified as FASB ASC Topic 718.

Q 34.14.11   What are the concerns about back-dated stock options?

Back-dating options refers to the practice that some companies have used to manipulate the dates of option grants. The manipulation typically occurs in one of three ways:

(1) The grant date is set to a time when the stock was selling at a historical low point;

(2) The grant date is set to a time right before a news release that is expected to have a positive effect on the market price of the stock; and

(3) The grant date is set to a time right after the release of negative news that has a negative effect on the market price of the stock.[155]

Back-dated stock options can create significant problems for the company and the recipient of a back-dated stock option. The SEC has come down very hard on senior executives of companies who have back-dated options, with penalties being levied against the responsible parties reaching into the millions of dollars. Additionally, back-dated option recipients will be subject to Code section 409A and the penalties thereunder and may lose the special tax treatment for ISOs. Finally, in most cases, audited and unaudited financial statements will have to be restated to reflect the correct accounting for the back-dated options.

Financial Accounting for Equity and Equity-Based Compensation

Q 34.15 What are the general rules about accounting for options?

Accounting for options is now governed by ASC Topic 718 (formerly FAS 123(R)). Under ASC Topic 718, companies are required to show the fair value of their stock option awards on their income statements. The fair value is typically determined by using an option-pricing model, such as Black-Scholes or Monte Carlo simulation, to determine the value of the stock options. The valuation of fair value must, at a minimum, take into account:

(1) the exercise price of the option;

(2) the expected term of the option;

(3) the current price of the underlying shares;

(4) the expected volatility of the price of the underlying shares for the expected term of the option;

(5) the expected dividends on the underlying shares; and

(6) the risk-free interest rate.

With respect to options with a graded vesting schedule, ASC Topic 718 allows companies to account for the award on a straight-line basis over the service period covered by the entire award. With respect to performance-based awards, ASC Topic 718 makes them equivalent to other forms of equity compensation as long as they do not vest based on increases in a company's stock price. Performance-based awards based on length of service or general financial goals can be "trued up" at the end of the vesting period. This means that the company only expenses the shares that actually vest. A company whose performance awards vest based on the company stock price must show the cost of all awards as an expense.

Q 34.15.1   How are SARs and phantom stock accounted for?

The company must record a compensation charge on its income statement as the employee's interest in the award increases. So from the time the grant is made until the award is paid out, the company records the value of the percentage of the promised shares or increase in the value of the shares, prorated over the term of the award. In each year, the value is adjusted to reflect the additional pro rata share of the award the employee has earned, plus or minus any adjustments to value arising from the rise or fall in share price.

Unlike accounting for variable award stock options, where a charge is amortized only over a vesting period, with phantom stock and SARs, the charge builds up during the vesting period, then after vesting, all additional stock price increases are taken as they occur when the vesting is triggered by a performance event, such as a profit target. In this case, the company must estimate the expected amount earned based on progress towards the target. The accounting treatment is more complicated if the vesting occurs gradually. Each tranche of vested awards is treated as a separate award. Appreciation is allocated to each award pro rata to time over which it is earned.

The accounting treatment is different if the SARs or phantom stock awards are settled in shares. In this case, the company must use a formula to estimate the present value of the award at grant, making adjustments for expected forfeitures.

Q 34.15.2   How are RSUs and performance units and performance shares accounted for?

The cost of restricted stock, RSUs and performance shares/performance units is based on the fair market value of the underlying stock on the grant date. The fair market value of the stock on the grant date for public companies is typically either the closing price on the grant date or the average of the high and low price on that date.

Dividends or dividend equivalents (if any) paid during the vesting or performance period are not recognized additional compensation costs unless both (i) the underlying awards are later forfeited, and (ii) the dividends are not repaid. The cost for a dividend-paying company that grants non-dividend-paying awards is reduced by the present value of estimated foregone dividends during the vesting period; however, this is not a common practice.

Equity awards with market conditions (such as total shareholder return (TSR)), performance shares or units are valued for accounting purposes on a Monte Carlo simulation model. This model has the ability to run multiple situations simultaneously. When valuing a TSR performance share or unit, the Monte Carlo runs similarities of future stock prices for both the target company and the comparator group companies to determine the fair value of the award.

Securities Law Issues

Q 34.16 What kinds of obligations and limits do the securities laws place upon companies and executives?

Federal securities laws affecting executive compensation and corporate governance hugely impact companies and their executives. Specifically, the following securities laws govern obligations and limitations on companies and their executives: the Securities Act of 1933, the Securities Exchange Act of 1934, the Sarbanes-Oxley Act of 2002,[156] the Dodd-Frank Wall Street Reform and Consumer Protection Act of 2010,[157] and the Jumpstart Our Business Startups Act of 2012.[158] The SEC also issues rules and regulations pursuant to these statutes. These laws:

- impose disclosure obligations on companies in periodic reports and proxy statements;

- require the registration of company securities offered or sold in connection with executive compensation plans and arrangements;

- require the disclosure of certain executives' and owners' exercise of public company securities' options;

- require the disclosure of certain benefit plans and shareholder approval of certain benefit plans;

- restrict the ability of company insiders to profit from trading of company securities;

- limit the ability of certain executives to resell company securities received under compensation arrangements;

- impose certain trading blackouts when other company employees are not permitted to sell securities in a Code section 401(k) or other company-sponsored individual retirement account plan;

- require resolutions for public company proxy statements;

- impose "clawbacks" of incentive compensation from executives, in certain situations; and

- require disclosure of public company pay-ratio between executives and employees.

Proxy Disclosure Rules

Q 34.16.1 What is the current landscape for company disclosure obligations with respect to executive compensation?

The SEC issues the rules governing the disclosure of the compensation of executives and directors of public companies, based on the acts mentioned above. Federal securities laws require clear and succinct disclosure about compensation paid to CEOs, CFOs, and other executives of publicly listed companies. Specifically, in 2009, the SEC adopted additional amendments to the executive officer and director compensation disclosure rules, which had seen a major update in 2006. Most of these rules affect disclosure of proxy statements and annual reports filed under the Securities Exchange Act of 1934 and registration statements filed under the Securities Act of 1933. Amendments in 2006 required that information be presented in plain English, and amendments in 2009 required succinct reporting of stock options, stock awards, and performance awards grant values.

Companies must disclose material information required to understand the company's compensation structure for "named executive officers" in the compensation discussion and analysis in the annual proxy statement (or referred to by reference in the annual Form 10-K). Namely, those elements of compensation policies that are "material" to investors must be disclosed, including how levels of compensation are reached and why compensation decisions were reached.

Additionally, companies are required to provide a detailed overview of the company's executive pay practices in the summary compensation table and additional tabular disclosure, in the annual proxy statement (or referred to by reference in the annual Form 10-K). The summary compensation table must include the total compensation paid to the company's named executive officers for the previous three fiscal years and must be followed with additional tabular disclosure with detailed information breaking down compensation components in the previous completed fiscal year. These tables will include, among other things, information about grants of stock options and stock appreciation rights; long-term incentive plan awards; pension plans; and benefits in employment contracts, including deferred amounts and perquisites.

The pay ratio disclosure rules also require that companies disclose the median annual total compensation of all company employees excluding the CEO, and the total annual compensation of the CEO, plus the ratio of the two to highlight the discrepancy between the two.

Companies are now also required to include a resolution in their proxy statements every one, two, or three years asking shareholders to approve, in a nonbinding vote, the compensation of their named executive officers, disclosed per the requirements explained above ("say-on-pay"). A separate resolution is also required every six years to determine whether the say-on-pay vote should take place every one, two, or three years (the "say-on-frequency" vote).

Companies going through a merger or other corporate transaction are required to solicit shareholder approval of "golden parachute" compensation payable to its named executive officers through a separate nonbinding vote at the same meeting that the shareholders are asked to approve the transaction that triggers "golden parachute" payments (the "say-on-golden parachute" vote) unless such golden parachute compensation has been approved as part of a say-on-pay vote. Any proxy statement soliciting say-on-golden parachute votes must include clear and simple disclosure of the golden parachute arrangements and amounts.

Q 34.16.2   Are there special disclosure rules for varying issuers?

Smaller reporting companies, foreign issuers, and emerging growth companies are subject to less stringent disclosure rules and obligations than those summarized here.

Q 34.16.3   What is included in the compensation discussion and analysis?

Under the proxy disclosure rules, the company must include a compensation discussion and analysis (CD&A), which is a narrative overview of the company's compensation objectives and policies for named executive officers. The CD&A must be presented without resorting to boilerplate disclosure. The CD&A must discuss the material elements of the compensation awarded to, earned by, or paid to the named executive officers. The discussion must be designed to answer and provide material information concerning the following questions:[159]

- What are the compensation program's objectives?

- What is the compensation program designed to reward?

- What is each element of compensation?

- Why does the company choose to pay each element?

- How is each element determined (amount and, where applicable, the formula)?

- How do each element and the company's decisions regarding that element fit into the company's overall compensation objectives and affect decisions regarding other elements?

- Whether the company has considered the most recent shareholder advisory vote regarding say-on-pay, in determining their compensation policies and decisions and, if so, how such consideration has affected compensation decisions and policies.

Other required disclosures will vary based on facts and circumstances, but the SEC has identified the following list of potential material information which, among other items, may need to be discussed in the CD&A, if applicable to the company:[160]

- Policies for allocating between long-term and currently paid-out compensation;

- Policies for allocating between cash and non-cash compensation, and among different forms of non-cash compensation;

- For long-term compensation, the basis for allocating compensation to each different form of award;

- How the determination is made as to when awards are granted, including awards of equity-based compensation such as options;

- What specific items of corporate performance are taken into account in setting compensation policies and making compensation decisions;

- How specific elements of compensation are structured and implemented to reflect these items of the company's performance and the executive's individual performance;

- How specific forms of compensation are structured and implemented to reflect the named executive officer's individual performance and/or individual contribution to these items of the company's performance, describing the elements of individual performance and/or contribution that are taken into account;

- Policies and decisions regarding the adjustment or recovery of awards or payments if performance measures are restated or adjusted in a manner that would reduce the award or payment;

- The factors considered in decisions to increase or decrease compensation materially;

- How compensation or amounts realizable from prior compensation are considered in setting other elements of compensation (for example, how gains from prior option or stock awards are considered in setting retirement benefits);

- With respect to any contract, agreement, plan, or arrangement, whether written on unwritten, that provides for payments at, following, or in connection with, any termination or change in control, the basis for selecting particular events as triggering payment;

- The impact of accounting and tax treatments of a particular form of compensation;

- The company's stock ownership guidelines and any policies regarding hedging the economic risk of such ownership;

- Whether the company engaged in any benchmarking of total compensation or any material element of compensation, identifying the benchmark and, if applicable, its components (including component companies); and

- The role of executive officers in the compensation process.

Q 34.16.4   What period does the CD&A cover?

The CD&A must cover compensation for the last fiscal year, but the company may also be required to discuss post-termination compensation arrangements, ongoing compensation arrangements, and policies that the company will apply on a going-forward basis. The company should also address actions that were taken after the last fiscal year's end to the extent such actions will assist shareholders in understanding compensation of the named executive officers for the last fiscal year, and, in some situations, the SEC has indicated it may be necessary to discuss prior years in order to give context to the disclosure provided.[161]

Q 34.16.5   What must be included in the summary compensation table and the additional tabular disclosures?[162]

The summary compensation table must include, for each of the named executive officers, for the three preceding fiscal years:

- name and principal position;

- base salary (cash and non-cash);

- bonus earned (cash and non-cash);

- aggregate grant date fair value of stock awards;

- aggregate grant date fair value of options;

- dollar value of earnings for services performed under non-equity incentive plans;

- change in pension value and non-qualified deferred compensation earnings;

- all other compensation, including perquisites, gross-ups, amounts paid for resignation, retirement, severance, change in control, company contributions to vested and unvested defined contribution plans, company-paid insurance premiums, and the dollar value of any dividends not otherwise reported; and

- the total of the above.

Additional tabular disclosure requires disclosure, for the previous fiscal year, for each named executive officer, of:

- grants of plan-based awards; including grant date, estimated future payouts under non-equity incentive plan awards (based on the threshold, target, and maximum level of performance), estimated future payouts under equity incentive plan awards (based on the threshold, target, and maximum level of performance), all other stock awards, all other option awards, exercise or base price of option awards, and grant date fair value of stock and option awards;

- outstanding equity awards at fiscal year-end, including, for option awards, the number of securities underlying unexercised options for exercisable, unexercisable, and unearned options, option exercise price, option expiration date, and for stock awards, unvested shares or units, value of unvested shares or units, unearned shares or units, and the value of unearned shares or units;

- option exercises and stock vested during the last fiscal year, including, for option awards, shares acquired on exercise and value realized on exercise, and for stock awards, shares acquired on vesting and value realized on vesting;

- pension benefits, including the years of credited service, present value of accumulated benefit, and payments during the last fiscal year;

- non-qualified deferred compensation, including the executive's contribution in the previous fiscal year, the company's contribution in the previous fiscal year, the aggregate earnings (or losses) in the previous fiscal year, aggregate withdrawals and distributions, and the aggregate balance at fiscal year-end; and

- director compensation, including the fees earned or paid in cash, stock and option awards, non-equity incentive plan compensation, change in pension and non-qualified deferred compensation earnings, and all other compensation.

Q 34.16.6   What disclosure is required as a result of "say-on-golden parachute"?

The company must disclose named executive officers' golden parachute arrangements in the proxy statement for shareholder approval of a merger, sale of assets or similar transactions, and in annual proxy statements when a company seeks to rely on the exception for a separate merger proxy shareholder vote by including the golden parachute disclosure in the annual proxy statement soliciting the say-on-pay vote.

Say-on-golden parachute requires tabular disclosure of golden parachute compensation, including cash severance payments, value of accelerated or exercised equity awards, pension and non-qualified deferred compensation enhancements, perquisites and personal benefits, tax reimbursements, and any other additional compensation. To clarify, the table requires the disclosure of the value of any compensation, whether present, deferred or contingent, based on any acquisition, merger, or sale, or other disposition of all or substantially all company assets.

Q 34.16.7   Are narratives required with respect to the tabular disclosures?

Yes. Narrative disclosures that supplement the tabular disclosures are required of any material factors necessary to an understanding of the information disclosed therein. In addition, narrative disclosure is required for each contract, agreement, plan, or arrangement that provides for a payment at, following, or in connection with any termination or change in control or change in an executive's responsibilities. Such disclosure must quantify the amount of such payments and benefits.[163]

Q 34.16.8   Which executives are named executive officers?

A company's executive compensation disclosure must cover the "named executive officers" (NEOs), which include:

- each individual who served as the Principal Executive Officer (PEO) during the last fiscal year;

- each individual who served as the Principal Financial Officer (PFO) during the last fiscal year;

- the three other highest paid executive officers employed as of fiscal year end; and

- up to two additional executives who would have been among the top three highest paid if they had been employed by the company as of fiscal year end.

Notwithstanding the general rule above, no disclosure is required with respect to an executive other than the PEO or PFO if salary and bonuses paid to such individual did not exceed $100,000.[164] In addition, it is possible that one of the three other highest paid executive officers should not be included as a NEO if his/her compensation relates to overseas assignments that is attributable predominantly to those assignments.[165] Further, NEOs of smaller reporting companies and emerging growth companies are limited to each individual PEO and the two other highest paid executive officers employed as of fiscal year-end, with up to two additional executives who would have been among the top two highest paid if they had been employed by the company as of fiscal year-end.[166]

Q 34.16.9   What if performance targets/goals contain sensitive information?

Award targets that contain confidential commercial or business information such as specific quantitative or qualitative performance-related factors are not required to be disclosed in the CD&A. The company is not required to formally seek confidential treatment of omitted information, but omitted information will be subject to the same standards as information a company requests be treated as confidential. The company must also disclose how difficult it will be for the executive and/or how likely it will be for the company to achieve the undisclosed target.[167]

Q 34.16.10   What disclosures are required for director compensation?

Under the proxy disclosure rules, the company must include a director compensation table in its disclosure that sets forth the total compensation, inclusive of fees earned or paid in cash, stock awards, option awards, non-equity incentive plan compensation, change in pension value and nonqualified deferred compensation earnings, and all other compensation, paid to or earned by each non-employee director during the most recent fiscal year. The director compensation table is similar to the summary compensation table. If a NEO is also a director and his or her compensation for service as a director is fully reflected in the summary compensation table, then no disclosure is required for such individual in the director compensation table.[168]

Q 34.16.11   Are narratives required with respect to the tabular disclosures?

Yes. Narrative disclosures that supplement the tabular disclosures are required of any material factors necessary to an understanding of the information disclosed therein. In addition, narrative disclosure is required for each contract, agreement, plan, or arrangement that provides for a payment at, following, or in connection with any termination or change in control or change in an executive's responsibilities. Such disclosure must quantify the amount of such payments and benefits.[169]

Q 34.16.12   What is a perquisite or personal benefit?

Perquisites are a non-cash vehicle to compensating and incentivizing executives. An item is *not* a perquisite or personal benefit if it is integrally and directly related to the performance of the executive's duties. The SEC views the "integrally and directly related" requirement as being a narrow one, and it may extend, among other things, to office space at a company business location, a reserved parking space that is closer to business facilities but not otherwise preferential, or additional clerical or secretarial services devoted to company matters, and does not extend it to items that facilitate job performance, such as use of company-provided aircraft, yachts or other watercraft, commuter transportation services, additional clerical or secretarial services devoted to personal matters, or investment management services.[170]

Otherwise, an item is a perquisite or personal benefit if it confers a direct or indirect benefit that has a personal aspect, without regard to whether it may be provided for some business reason or for the convenience of the company, unless it is generally available on a non-discriminatory basis to all employees. Common executive perquisites include transportation benefits, welfare benefits, relocation benefits, tax gross-ups, and post-employment perquisites.

Q 34.16.13   Must perquisites and personal benefits be disclosed?

Under the proxy disclosure rules, the perquisites and personal benefits paid or made available to the NEOs must be identified narratively in a footnote and included in the "All Other Compensation" column of the summary compensation table if, for any one of the NEOs in the aggregate, they exceed $10,000. If any single perquisite has a value exceeding the greater of $25,000 or 10% of total perquisites, its value also must be separately disclosed in a footnote. Perquisites are required to be valued on the basis of the aggregate incremental cost to the company and its subsidiaries of providing the perquisite.[171]

Q 34.16.14   What disclosures are required for grants of stock options and stock appreciation rights?

The summary compensation table must include the aggregate fair value of an award (determined as of the date of grant), attributable to service during the fiscal year (in a manner similar to ASC Topic 718), of options, stock appreciation rights, and similar equity instruments that have option-like features.

The grants of plan-based awards table must include the fair value as of the date of grant, as determined under ASC Topic 718, of options, stock appreciation rights and other stock-based awards, and the number of options granted in the last fiscal year. The table must show the full grant date fair value on a grant-by-grant basis, and the aggregate fair value of the award (determined as of the date of grant) just as in the summary compensation table. The company also must disclose each instance in special columns if any of the following situations occurred in which: (a) the grant date differs from the date on which the compensation committee takes action or is deemed to take action to grant an award (the company must disclose the date of the actual committee or board action); (b) a stock option exercise price is less than closing market price on grant date (the company must explain the methodology for determining the exercise price in a footnote or a textual narrative and must show the closing market price in a special column in the table); and (c) a non-equity incentive plan award is denominated in units or other rights (the company must disclose the units or other rights awarded).

Companies must also disclose all outstanding options, stock appreciation rights, and similar equity instruments that have option-like features and unvested stock awards held by the named executive officers as of the most recent fiscal year-end on the outstanding equity awards at fiscal year-end table.[172]

In the CDA, the company must discuss the aspects of its option grant program, plan, or practice relating to the timing and pricing of option grants. With respect to timing, the discussion should include:

(1)   how its option grant program or practice is coordinated with the release of material non-public information;

(2)   how its option grant program or practice with respect to executives fits with its program or practice with respect to grants to employees more generally;

(3)   the role of the compensation committee in approving and administering such program or practice, including the information taken into account by the compensation committee in determining whether and in what amount to make the grants and whether the compensation committee delegated any aspect of the actual administration of such program or practice to any other person;

(4) the role of executives in the company's program or practice of option timing;

(5) whether the company sets the grant date of option grants to new executives in coordination with the release of material non-public information; and

(6) whether the company plans to time, or has timed, its release of material non-public information for the purpose of affecting the value of executive compensation.[173]

With respect to option pricing, the discussion should address whether the option grant program or practice allows the company to set the exercise price based on the stock's price on a date other than the actual grant date and whether such program or practice allows the company to grant options with an exercise price based upon average prices (or lowest prices) of the company's stock in a period preceding, surrounding, or following the grant date.[174]

Other Disclosure Rules for Executives and Directors

Q 34.16.15 Are there other SEC-required disclosure rules that relate to executives and directors?

At the time that the SEC issued the proxy disclosure rules in 2006, the SEC issued revised disclosure rules in the areas of related-person transactions, director independence, and certain other corporate governance matters. Additionally, the Dodd-Frank Act directed the SEC to establish several new rules that relate to executives and directors. Those rules, briefly described, are as follows:

- The company must disclose employee compensation policies and practices if the risks arising from them "are reasonably likely to have a material adverse effect" on the company.[175] Such disclosure is not required if the company determines the practices are not reasonably likely to have a material adverse effect on the company.

- The company must disclose for each director and any nominee for director the particular experience, qualifications, attributes, or skills that led the board to conclude that the person should serve as a director for the company.[176] The company must disclose whether, and if so, how a nominating committee or the board considers diversity in identifying nominees for director.[177]

- The company must describe the board leadership structure and provide a statement as to why the company believes it is the appropriate structure for it given the specific characteristics or circumstances of the company, including whether one person serves as both chairman of the board and the PEO or whether those offices are filled by separate individuals, and if one person holds both positions, whether there is a lead independent director and what role the lead independent director plays in leading the board.[178]

- The company must include at least once every three years a non-binding say-on-pay proposal in its proxy statement regarding the compensation of executives.[179] The company must also include at least once every six years, a non-binding say-when-on-pay proposal in its proxy statement to determine whether the say-on-pay vote will occur every one, two, or three years.[180] The company is required to disclose in its compensation discussion and analysis whether, and if so how, it considered the results of the most recent say-on-pay vote.[181]

- Beginning with the company's first annual report, annual proxy statement, or information statement filed for fiscal years beginning on 2017, the company will need to disclose (1) the median of the annual total compensation of all employees other than the PEO, (2) the annual total compensation of the PEO, and (3) the ratio of these amounts.[182]

- The company must provide a narrative description of any termination or severance provisions or agreements applicable to any one of the NEOs, such as in the NEO's employment agreement or incentive award agreements.[183]

- The company must provide a stock ownership table that lists, as of "the most recent practicable date," the number and percentage of shares beneficially owned by (i) each director and director nominee; (ii) each NEO; (iii) the directors and executive officers as a group (which includes all executive officers, not just NEOs); and (iv) each stockholder holding more than 5% of the class of shares (typically obtained from publicly available SEC filings such as Schedule 13D, Schedule 13G, Form 3, Form 4, and Form 5).[184]

- For fiscal years beginning on or after July 1, 2019,[185] the company must describe, in its proxy or information statement for the election of directors, any practices or policies it has adopted regarding the ability of its employees, including officers or directors, to purchase securities or other financial instruments or engage in transactions that hedge or offset any decrease in the market value of company equity granted as compensation or held directly or indirectly by the employee or director.[186] If the company does not have any such practices or policies, the company must disclose that fact or state that hedging transactions are generally permitted.[187]

- Although not an SEC-required disclosure, the Nasdaq Stock Market requires, effective August 1, 2016, that its listed companies disclose on their websites and/or in their proxy or information statements, compensation paid by third parties to directors or nominees for directors.[188]

Q 34.16.16   What are the disclosure requirements regarding related-party transactions?

The company must disclose information regarding any transaction since the beginning of the company's last fiscal year, or any currently proposed transaction, in which the company was or is to be a participant, involving an amount in excess of $120,000, and in which a related person had or will have a direct or indirect material interest. In connection with related-party transactions, the company must provide:

- the name of the related person and the basis on which such person is a related person;

- the related person's interest in the transaction with the company;

- the approximate dollar amount involved in each transaction;

- the approximate dollar value of the amount of the related person's interest in the transaction, computed without regard to the amount of profit or loss;

- in the case of indebtedness, the largest amount of principal outstanding for the period reported, the amount of principal and interest paid during the period reported and the rate of interest payable on the indebtedness; and

- any other information that is material to investors.[189]

Companies are also required to disclose their policies and procedures for approving related-party transactions. Such disclosure includes:

- the types of transactions covered by such policies and procedures;

- the standards applied pursuant to such policies and procedures;

- the persons or groups of persons who are in charge of applying such policies and procedures; and

- whether such policies and procedures are in writing and, if not, how such policies and procedures are evidenced.[190]

In addition, the company must disclose any transaction required to be disclosed under the rules that was not required to be reviewed under the company's related-party transaction policies and procedures or where such policies and procedures were not followed.[191]

Q 34.16.17   What are the disclosure requirements regarding other corporate governance matters?

Companies also are required to disclose as part of their corporate governance-related disclosure the following:

- their processes and procedures for the consideration and determination of executive and director compensation, including the scope of authority of the compensation committee;

- whether the compensation committee has a charter;

- the role of the executive officers in determining the amount or form of executive and director compensation;

- the role of compensation consultants in determining or recommending the amount or form of executive and director compensation, and if any compensation consultant's work raised any conflict of interest, disclosure of the nature of the conflict and how the conflict is being addressed;

- each person who served as a member of the compensation committee (or participated in executive compensation deliberations if there is no compensation committee) and an indication of who was an officer or employee of the company during the fiscal year and each person who was formerly an officer of the company; or

- whether an executive officer of the company (i) served as a member of the compensation committee (or equivalent) of another entity, one of whose executive officers served on the compensation committee of the company or as a director of the company, or (ii) served as a director of another entity, one of whose executive officers served on the compensation committee (or equivalent) of the company.[192]

A company must state the total number of meetings of the board of directors (including both regularly scheduled and special meetings) that were held during the last fiscal year, and must note each incumbent director that attended fewer than 75% of the aggregate of total board of director meetings and board committee meetings for committees on which the director served.[193] The company must also state whether or not it has standing audit, nominating, and compensation committees of the board of directors, or committees performing similar functions, and if so, identify each committee member, state the number of committee meetings held by each such committee in the last fiscal year, and describe the functions of each such committee.[194]

The company must state whether the board of directors provides a process for security holders to send communications to the board of directors and, if no process exists, state the basis for the view of the board that it is appropriate to not have such a process.[195]

In addition, a company must file or furnish a Form 8-K upon the occurrence of certain triggering events. The Form 8-K disclosures may include information relating to executive pay and benefits.[196]

Q 34.16.18 Are company disclosures required to include a Compensation Committee Report?

Under the SEC's disclosure rules, the Compensation Committee Report (CCR) is part of the company's corporate governance disclosure. The CCR must be furnished once during the fiscal year and must be included or incorporated by reference through a company's proxy statement into the company's Form 10-K. The CCR is required to state whether the compensation committee reviewed and discussed the CDA with management and whether, based on the review and discussions, the compensation committee recommended to the board that the CDA be included in the annual report, proxy statement, or information statement.[197]

Q 34.16.19 Do the CEO and CFO certifications apply to the CDA and the CCR?

Under the SEC's rules, the CDA is "filed" for security law purposes and, therefore, the CEO and CFO certifications apply to the CDA. The CCR is "furnished" for security law purposes and, therefore, the CEO and CFO certifications do not apply to the CCR.[198]

Treatment of NQDC Plans As Securities

Q 34.17 For purposes of registration requirements under the Securities Act of 1933, what is a "security"?

The basic definition of "security" includes any note, stock, treasury stock, bond, debenture, participation in a profit-sharing arrangement or investment contract. Under this definition, in the context of executive compensation, shares of stock offered in connection with a benefits plan and options to purchase stock are "securities." Participation interests in employee benefit plans, including plans that do not involve any purchase of employer stock, may be considered securities under certain circumstances.[199]

Q 34.17.1 Is an interest in a non-qualified deferred compensation plan treated as a "security" under federal securities law?

The SEC's current position with respect to the treatment of non-qualified deferred compensation (NQDC) plans was established in 1991. Prior to such time, the SEC took "no-action" ruling positions on NQDC plans where the interests in the plans were not registered under the Securities Act of 1933. In 1991, in the SEC's "Current Issues and Rulemaking Projects," the SEC provided its current view on NQDC plans. In the report, the SEC stated that it would no longer grant requests for no-action. The determination of whether the participant's interest in a NQDC plan is a security is to be made by the company and to the extent that such interests are securities, registration would be required unless the interests would qualify for an exemption.

The interests in a NQDC plan are not generally treated as securities that are subject to registration under the provisions of the Securities Exchange Act of 1934 and the Investment Company Act of 1940. However, consistent with its 1991 position, in an excerpt from the 2000 Current Issues and Rulemaking Projects Outline, the SEC stated that due to the increase in NQDC plans, they are not willing to "disregard the argument that the debt owing to plan participants is analogous to investment notes, which typically are viewed as debt securities." Whether a NQDC plan arrangement involves securities is determined by an analysis of all the facts and circumstances.[200]

Q 34.17.2 When might a participant's interest in a NQDC plan be treated as a "security" under federal securities law?

The definition of "security" under the Securities Act of 1933 includes, among other things, investment contracts. The issue with respect to NQDC plans is whether such plan is an investment contract. The U.S. Supreme Court established the test for determining whether an investment contract is a security in *SEC v. W.J. Howey Co.*[201] Under the *Howey* case, a financial interest will be an investment contract if

(1) there is an investment of money,

(2) in a common enterprise,

(3) with an expectation of profits,

(4) principally derived from the efforts of others.

The SEC held that interests in an employee benefit plan are considered securities by the SEC if the plan is both voluntary and contributory, because the action on the part of the participant under such plan would be sufficient to meet the test under *Howey*.[202]

Arguably, NQDC plans fail to meet the test for an investment contract established in *Howey* because

(1) the participants are deferring compensation for tax savings purposes, rather than making an investment,

(2) there is no expectation of profit in the investment sense,

(3) there is no investment in a common enterprise because each participant has a separate account, and

(4) there is no profit derived from the effort of others (other than possibly the company's continued solvency).

Q 34.17.3   Does the Securities Act of 1933 require registration of sales of stock in connection with employee stock plans?

In general, the Securities Act of 1933 requires the registration of the offer or sale of stock in connection with employee stock plans, including stock option plans and other stock rights plans that are settled in stock. Registration must be effective by the earliest date on which an option or other stock right may be exercised.[203] However, one or more exemptions from registration may be available, as discussed below.

Q 34.17.4   Does the Securities Exchange Act of 1934 require registration of sales of stock in connection with employee stock plans?

The registration requirement under section 12(g) of the Securities Exchange Act of 1934 might be triggered if the company has more than $10 million in assets and has a class of stock held by 2,000 or more record holders or by 500 or more record holders that are non-accredited investors (as defined in Rule 501(a) of the Securities Act of

1933).[204] The SEC has granted relief from this requirement for companies that have granted options to more than 500 employees if certain requirements are met.[205]

Exemptions from Registration Requirements

Q 34.18 Are there any exemptions from the registration requirements of the Securities Act of 1933 that apply to interests in a NQDC plan or the stock sold to a participant in connection with an employee stock plan?

There are four exemptions from registration that may apply to the interests in a NQDC plan or an employee stock plan:

Securities Act Rule 701 provides an exemption to private companies for securities issued pursuant to certain compensatory benefit plans and contracts. For purposes of Rule 701, "securities" includes interests in a NQDC plan or an employee stock plan. A "compensatory benefit plan" is any purchase, savings, option, bonus, stock appreciation, profit sharing, thrift, incentive, deferred compensation, pension, or similar plan. No filing with the SEC is required to apply the Rule 701 exemption.

Section 4(a)(2) of the Securities Act of 1933 provides an exemption that may apply to certain top-hat NQDC plans. Section 4(a)(2) transactions do not involve a public offering and are made to a sophisticated group that has a relationship to the company, which alleviates the need for the safeguards of the Securities Act of 1933.

Regulation D provides three different exemptions, each of which depends on not exceeding maximum dollar limits. The three exemptions are summarized as follows:

- Rule 504: an exemption for sales up to $5 million within a twelve-month period by a private company.[206] This exemption is not available to any issuer that would be disqualified under the disqualification provision set forth in Rule 506(d).[207]

- Rule 506: provides both a safe harbor exemption and a non–safe harbor exemption. Rule 506(b) provides a safe harbor exemption for an unlimited amount of sales to no more than thirty-five non-accredited purchasers and to an unlimited number of accredited investors, provided that neither general solicitation nor advertising are used to market the securities and appropriate disclosure is provided. In addition, the non-accredited investor, either alone or with a purchaser representative, must be "sophisticated," meaning they must have sufficient knowledge and experience in financial and business matters to make them capable of evaluating the merits and risks of the prospective investment. Rule 506(c) permits broad solicitation and advertising, provided that the investors are all accredited investors and reasonable steps are taken to verify that the investors are all accredited investors (such as reviewing Forms W-2, tax returns, bank and brokerage statements, credit reports, and the like).

Section 3(a)(11) is the "intrastate offering exemption." Section 3(a)(11)'s exemption is available if the offer or sale of securities involves residents of a single state by a company that is incorporated in the same state and conducts substantial business activity in the state. A safe harbor for meeting the exemption is available pursuant to Rule 147.

Q 34.18.1   What form should be used to register interests in NQDC plans and the stock sold pursuant to employee stock plans?

Employers that have previously registered stock under the Securities Act of 1933 typically use Form S-8 to register interests in NQDC plans and the stock to be sold in connection with an employee stock plan. The employer company must have filed all required reports due under the Securities Exchange Act of 1934 during the past twelve months. The Form S-8 may be used only if the participants are employees, non-employee directors, general partners, trustees (when the issuer is a business trust), consultants or advisers (provided the consultant or advisor is a natural person that provides bona fide services to the issuer that are not in connection with the offer or sale of securities in a capital-raising transaction and do not directly or indirectly promote or maintain a market for the issuer's securities), and the offer and sale is made pursuant to an employee benefit plan. Under certain circumstances, Form S-8 may also be used if participants include insurance agents or former employees (including executors, administrators, or beneficiaries of the estates of deceased employees, guardians or members of a committee for incompetent former employees, or similar persons authorized by law to administer the estate or assets of former employees). However, Form S-8 is not available for securities to be issued to entities.

Disclosure and Reporting Requirements

Q 34.18.2   If a NQDC plan or employee stock plan is registered, what disclosures must be made to plan participants?

The company must provide participants with a prospectus or documents constituting a prospectus that meets the requirements of section 10 of the Securities Act of 1933. The company is not required to file the prospectus with the SEC if Form S-8 is used.

Rule 428 under the Securities Act of 1933 provides requirements applicable to Form S-8 prospectuses, including timing for delivery of the prospectus, the persons who should receive the prospectus, and the documents to be delivered with the prospectus.

Q 34.18.3   If a NQDC plan or employee stock plan is not registered, are there any disclosure requirements?

If a private company is relying on a Rule 701 exemption, the company must give all participants a copy of the benefit plan or contract, as well as certain other information if the amount of securities sold exceeds $10 million in any twelve-month period, such as a copy of the plan's summary plan description (if subject to ERISA) or a summary of the material terms of the plan (if not subject to ERISA), risk factors associated with the investment, and financial statements required under Regulation A, Form 1-A.[208]

If the company is relying on the exemption under Rule 506(b) of Regulation D, the company must give all non-accredited investors the information set forth in Rule 502(b).[209]

Q 34.18.4   Do the anti-fraud provisions of federal securities law apply to disclosures in connection with NQDC plans and employee stock plans?

Yes. The company must avoid a misstatement or omission of material information.[210]

Q 34.18.5   Are there other disclosures to the SEC required in connection with NQDC plans and employee stock plans?

Companies are required to file certain reports and exhibits when establishing or amending an employee benefit plan that is deemed to be a "material contract." The term "material contract" is defined under Item 601 of Regulation S-K. Generally, plans, agreements, and arrangements for the benefit of executives and/or directors will be "material contracts" unless they are available to all employees generally and provide for a uniform method of the allocation of benefits that does not favor management participants.[211]

Form 8-K must be filed by the company within four business days of the adoption or amendment of a "material contract."[212] In addition, benefit plans that are deemed to be "material contracts" must be filed as exhibits to a company's Forms 10-K and 10-Q, and other periodic reports under the Securities Exchange Act of 1934, and to registration statements under the Securities Act of 1933.[213]

Shareholder Approval

Q 34.18.6   What plans must be approved by shareholders pursuant to stock exchange requirements?

Unless exempted, equity compensation plans must be approved by shareholders under the rules of the New York Stock Exchange and the Nasdaq Stock Market. In general, equity compensation plans are those that provide for the issuance or delivery of equity securities to directors, officers, employees, or other service providers. Shareholder approval is also required when a material amendment is made to such plans, including, but not limited to, a material increase in the number of shares to be issued under the plan (to the extent such increase is not attributed solely to a reorganization, stock split, merger or similar transaction) and a material increase in the class of participants eligible to participate in the plan. Plans involving phantom stock or that merely track stock performance and are settled in cash only are not subject to shareholder approval requirements.[214]

Q 34.18.7   What plans are exempt from the shareholder approval requirements of the stock markets?

Generally, the following plans or arrangements are not subject to shareholder approval:[215]

- Plans available to shareholders generally, such as dividend reinvestment plans.

- Tax-qualified plans that meet the requirements of Code section 401(a) or 423.

- Certain excess plans for key employees that allow for benefits in excess of the limits under Code section 402(g).

- Grants to a person not previously an employee or director of the company, or following a bona fide period of non-employment, as an inducement material to the individual's entering into employment with the company, provided such issuances are approved by either the issuer's independent compensation committee or a majority of the issuer's independent directors. Promptly following an issuance of any employment inducement grant, a company must disclose in a press release the material terms of the grant, including the recipient(s) of the grant and the number of shares involved.

Proxy Advisory Firms

Q 34.18.8   What is the role of proxy advisory firms in the approval of equity-based compensation plans or programs?

Proxy advisory firms, including Institutional Shareholder Services (ISS), provide analysis and recommendations that affect the votes of the shareholders of publicly traded companies. In recent years, proxy advisory firms have placed greater scrutiny on equity-based compensation programs and have developed very detailed criteria for evaluating these plans and determining whether the proxy advisory firm will recommend a vote in favor or against an equity-based compensation plan.

Q 34.18.9 How does ISS determine whether it will recommend that shareholders vote for or against an equity–based compensation plan?

ISS publishes annually the Equity Compensation Plan Scorecard (the "Scorecard"), describing multiple positive and negative factors on which equity-based compensation programs for employees and related proposals are evaluated by ISS. The Scorecard was most recently updated on December 6, 2019.[216] The equity compensation proposals evaluated under the Scorecard include proposals to approve a stock option plan, approve a restricted stock plan, approve an omnibus stock plan, and approve a stock appreciation rights plan (stock-settled). Certain amendments to these plans may also be evaluated under the Scorecard.

The factors considered by the Scorecard are grouped into three pillars: Plan Cost Pillar, Plan Features Pillar, and Grant Practices Pillar. ISS established a score for each factor on the Scorecard. Not all factors are weighed equally.

Generally, in order to receive a favorable recommendation from ISS, the plan must score at least 53 points (55 points for the S&P 500 model) out of a possible 100 points on the Scorecard. However, there are certain "overriding factors" (discussed below) that could cause ISS to issue a recommendation to vote against the approval of a plan, even when the plan reached or exceeded the required score.

Q 34.18.10 What are the scoring factors considered by ISS when evaluating an equity compensation plan?[217]

Plan Cost Pillar. The scoring factors in this pillar evaluate the estimated cost associated with the transfer of equity from shareholders to employees. This cost is evaluated taking into account the company's industry and peer companies (Shareholder Value Transfer).

Plan Features Pillar. The scoring factors in this pillar evaluate whether the plan's design includes certain negative factors such as whether:

- the plan does not include specific disclosure of the treatment of awards on a change in control;

- the plan grants broad discretionary vesting authority;

- the plan's provisions allow liberal share recycling;

- awards are not subject to a one-year minimum vesting;

- dividends are paid prior to vesting of the underlying award.

Grant Practices Pillar. The scoring factors in this pillar evaluate the company's practices when granting awards under the equity compensation plans, such as:

- the company's three-year average burn rate relative to its industry and index peers;

- the estimated duration of the plan;

- the provisions of any grants issued to the CEO (including the vesting schedule, the proportion of the CEO's awards and whether they are subject to performance conditions);

- the inclusion of clawback provisions in the plan;

- the inclusion of post-exercise/post-vesting shareholder requirements.

Q 34.18.11   What are the overriding factors considered by ISS?

Certain egregious plan features will cause ISS to issue a negative recommendation, regardless of the plan's overall score. These include: a liberal change in control definition that does not include a full double trigger; a plan provision allowing repricing or a cash buyout of underwater options or SARs without shareholder approval; using the plan as a vehicle for problematic pay practices or a pay-for-performance misalignment; if the plan is deemed to be excessively dilutive to the shareholders' holdings; if the plan contains an evergreen feature; and any other feature or practice deemed detrimental to shareholder interests (such as tax gross-ups).

Q 34.18.12 Are the equity compensation plans evaluated and scored equally regardless of company size or special circumstances?

No. The Scorecard attributes different maximum pillar scores, depending on whether the entity falls within the S&P 500, Russell 3000, or Non–Russell 3000. It also considers special cases within these categories, such as companies that have recently had their IPO, were spun off or emerged from bankruptcy.[218]

Limiting Resales of Stock

Q 34.18.13 Under what circumstances and conditions can a plan participant resell public company securities purchased or otherwise received through an employee benefit plan?

The rules for resales of stock received under an employee benefit plan depend upon whether the stock is registered or unregistered and whether the participant is an affiliate or a non-affiliate.[219] Resales of registered stock are permitted without restriction.

If the participant is a non-affiliate and has held the unregistered stock for at least one year, resales of the unregistered stock are permitted under Rule 144 without complying with the provisions of Rule 144 (*see* Q 34.18.15) other than the manner of sale requirements in 144(f).

If the participant is an affiliate, resales of the unregistered stock are permitted if the participant satisfies the conditions of Rule 144, except the one-year holding period requirement does not apply.

Q 34.18.14 Who is an affiliate for purposes of resales?

Rule 144(a)(1) provides that an affiliate is a person that directly, or indirectly through one or more intermediaries, controls, or is controlled by, or is under common control with, the employer company. An affiliate includes an executive officer, a director or large shareholder, in a relationship of control with the issuer.

Q 34.18.15   What are the conditions that must be met under Rule 144?

Rule 144 imposes the following conditions:

- There must be adequate current information about the issuing company publicly available before the sale can be made. This condition will be satisfied if the employer is subject to the reporting requirements of section 13 of the Securities Exchange Act of 1934 and has filed all reports required under section 13 for the twelve months preceding the sale of the stock.

- The participant has held the stock for at least one year.

- The amount of stock sold by the participant during any three-month period does not exceed the greater of 1% of the outstanding shares or the average weekly reported volume of trading in the stock for the four calendar weeks preceding the participant's notice of sale that is filed with the SEC.

- A Rule 144 sale must be effected in a broker's transaction or directly with a market maker.

- Notices must be filed with the SEC and the national exchange on which the employer stock is traded.

Blackout Periods

Q 34.18.16   Does Sarbanes-Oxley prohibit trading by executives of a company stock during pension blackout periods?

Yes. Section 306(a) of the Sarbanes-Oxley Act of 2002 prohibits directors and executive officers from trading company stock and derivative securities during any blackout period when at least 50% of the company's 401(k) plan participants are blacked out from buying or selling company stock in their plan accounts. The prohibition applies only to stock acquired by the director or officer in connection with his or her service for the company. The SEC issued Regulation BTR to provide rules governing the section 306(a) prohibition.

Q 34.18.17   Does Regulation BTR provide any exemptions to the trading prohibition?

Yes. Regulation BTR provides a number of exemptions. The exempt transactions include:

- acquisitions under dividend reinvestment plans;

- purchases or sales in connection with tax-qualified plans (other than a transaction involving a discretionary transaction under the section 16 rules);

- grants or awards under an option or other stock rights plan that provides a formula or that occur automatically;

- acquisitions or dispositions pursuant to a gift transaction or a post-death transfer; and

- acquisitions or dispositions pursuant to a domestic relations order.

Q 34.18.18   Is there a notice requirement relating to the trading prohibition?

The company must give the directors and officers and the SEC notice that a blackout period is going to occur. The notice is timely only if it is given no later than five business days after the company receives notice of the blackout period from the plan administrator. If the company does not receive such notice, the company's notice must be given at least fifteen days before the first day of the blackout period. The company also must file a Form 8-K.[220]

Q 34.18.19   What remedies apply to a violation of the trading prohibition?

The violation is subject to an SEC enforcement action. In addition, the company, or a shareholder on behalf of the company, may bring an action to recover any profit made by the director or executive officer as a result of a prohibited transaction.[221]

Q 34.18.20 Does Sarbanes-Oxley impose any other restrictions impacting executive compensation?

Under Sarbanes-Oxley, a company's chief executive officer and chief financial officer must forfeit bonuses and other incentive compensation if the company is required to prepare an accounting restatement due to material noncompliance or misconduct relating to financial reporting requirements. In addition, the law allows the SEC to freeze certain payments to directors and executives during an investigation of the company for securities law violations. Sarbanes-Oxley also prohibits loans by the company directly or indirectly to executives and directors.[222]

Notes to Chapter 34

1. 29 C.F.R. § 2510.3-2.
2. *See, e.g.*, Treas. Reg. § 1.61-2(d) and Rev. Rul. 79-24, 1979-1 C.B. 60.
3. Additional Code sections and Treasury regulations apply to tax-exempt entities, which goes beyond the scope of this chapter.
4. After the enactment of Code section 409A, the IRS permitted employers and other plan sponsors to delay amendment of a plan or arrangement until the issuance of final regulations, provided they administered the plan or arrangement in good-faith compliance with the requirements of section 409A during the interim period. Final regulations were issued in April 2007 and all affected plans and arrangements had to be amended to conform to the requirements of section 409A by December 31, 2007.
5. Treas. Reg. § 1.61-2(d); Safe Harbor Water Power Corp. v. United States, 303 F.2d 928 (Ct. Cl. 1962); Rev. Rul. 74-75, 1974-1 C.B. 19, as modified in Rev. Rul. 86-14, 1986-1 C.B. 304; Rev. Rul. 68-507, 1968-2 C.B. 485; Old Colony Tr. Co. v. Comm'r, 279 U.S. 716 (1929).
6. *See* Q 34.7.
7. *See* Q 34.6.1.
8. A section 424(a) transaction is a corporate merger, consolidation, acquisition of property or stock, separation, reorganization, or liquidation if an ISO is assumed or a substitution for an old option occurs with a new option that is issued and certain aggregate value tests are met when tested before and after the transaction occurs.
9. I.R.C. § 83(a).
10. *Id.*
11. Non-qualified deferred compensation accrued or earned under a non-qualified deferred compensation plan sponsored by a tax-exempt entity and governed by Code § 457(f), is taxable at the time of vesting.
12. I.R.C. §§ 61, 162, 402(b), 451.
13. ERISA § 3(36).
14. *See* Q 34.7.
15. Unfunded excess plans, payroll practices, and certain bonus plans are also exempt from certain ERISA requirements. ERISA §§ 4(b)(1), (2), and (5); 29 C.F.R. §§ 2510.3-1(b), 2510.3-2(c).
16. 29 U.S.C. §§ 1051(2), 1081(a)(3), 1101(a)(1); in providing statutory exemptions, the statute uses phrase "unfunded" and a "select group of managerial or highly compensated employees." U.S. Dep't of Labor, Advisory Opinion 90-14A (May 8, 1990), is instructive in its content, even though it was informally withdrawn by the DOL and may not be relied upon.
17. *See* Q 34.4.1.

18. *See* 29 U.S.C. §§ 1051(2), 1081(a)(3), 1101(a)(1); *see also* Demery v. Extebank Deferred Compensation Plan (B), 216 F.3d 283 (2d Cir. 2000) (where 15% was allowed for an exempt plan where all participants were in management *and* were highly compensated); Foley v. Am. Elec. Power, 425 F. Supp. 2d 863 (S.D. Ohio 2006); *see also* Cramer v. Appalachian Reg'l Healthcare, Inc., 2012 WL 5332471, at *2 (E.D. Ky. Oct. 29, 2012). *But see* Carrabba v. Randalls Food Mkts., 252 F.3d 721 (5th Cir. 2001) (holding that a group of "all" management could not, by definition, be viewed as a "select" group).

19. ERISA § 301(a)(3); *see In re* IT Grp., Inc., 305 B.R. 402 (Bankr. D. Del. 2004), *aff'd*, 448 F.3d 661 (3d Cir. 2006).

20. Whether a non-qualified deferred compensation plan is considered "funded" for purposes of ERISA depends in large part on whether the assets of the insurance policy have been placed beyond the reach of the employer's general creditors.

21. Treas. Reg. § 1.451-2(a); Ross v. Comm'r, 169 F.2d 483 (1st Cir. 1948).

22. *See* I.R.C. § 671; Treas. Reg. § 1.671-1, -2.

23. Treas. Reg. §§ 1.61-22, 1.7872-15.

24. I.R.S. Notice 2007-34.

25. Treas. Reg. § 1.409A-1(a)(5); *see also* Q 34.8.1.

26. *Id.* § 1.409A-1(a)(1).

27. *Id.* § 1.409A-1(b)(1).

28. Treas. Reg. § 1.409A-1(f)(1).

29. *Id.* § 1.409A-1(f).

30. *Id.* § 1.409A-1(h)(3).

31. *Id.* § 1.409A-1(a)(1).

32. *Id.* § 1.409A-1(a).

33. *Id.* § 1.409A-1(b)(4).

34. *Id.* § 1.409A-1(b)(4)(ii).

35. *Id.* §§ 1.409A-1(b)(5)(i)(A), 1.409A-1(b)(5)(iii)(E).

36. *Id.* §§ 1.409A-1(b)(5)(i)(B), 1.409A-1(b)(5)(iii)(E).

37. *Id.* § 1.409A-1(b)(6).

38. *Id.* § 1.409A-1(a)(5).

39. *Id.* § 1.409A-1(a)(3).

40. *Id.* § 1.409A-1(b)(9).

41. *Id.* § 1.409A-1(f)(1).

42. *Id.* § 1.409A-1(f)(2).

43. *Id.* § 1.409A-1(b)(5)(iv)(B).

44. I.R.C. § 409A(a)(1)(A).

45. Treas. Reg. § 1.409A-1(d).

46. I.R.C. § 409A(a)(1)(A)(i)(I).

47. *Id.* § 409A(a)(2).

48. I.R.C. § 409A(a)(2)(A); Treas. Reg. § 1.409A-3(a).

49. Treas. Reg. § 1.409A-1(h)(1).

50. *Id.* § 1.409A-1(h)(2).

51. *Id.* § 1.409A-1(h)(1)(ii).
52. *Id.*
53. *Id.* § 1.409A-1(h)(1)(i).
54. *Id.*
55. *Id.*
56. *Id.* § 1.409A-3(i)(4)(i).
57. *Id.* § 1.409A-3(i)(4)(iii).
58. *Id.*
59. *Id.* § 1.409A-3(i)(1)(i).
60. *Id.*
61. *Id.*
62. *Id.* § 1.409A-3(ii)(A)–(B).
63. *See* I.R.C. § 409A(a)(4)(c); Treas. Reg. § 1.409A-2(b)(1).
64. Treas. Reg. § 1.409A-3(i)(5).
65. *Id.*
66. *Id.* § 1.409A-3(i)(5)(v).
67. *Id.*
68. *Id.* § 1.409A-3(i)(5)(vi)(A).
69. *Id.*
70. *Id.* § 1.409A-3(i)(5)(vi)(B)–(C).
71. *Id.* § 1.409A-3(i)(5)(vii)(A).
72. *Id.* § 1.409A-3(i)(3)(i).
73. *Id.* § 1.409A-3(i)(3)(ii).
74. *Id.* § 1.409A-3(i)(3)(iii).
75. *See* I.R.C. § 409A(a)(2).
76. Treas. Reg. § 1.409A-3(d).
77. *Id.* § 1.409A-1(b)(3).
78. *Id.* § 1.409A-1(b)(4).
79. *Id.* § 1.409A-1(c)(3)(v).
80. *Id.* § 1.409A-1(i)(1).
81. I.R.C. § 416(i)(1).
82. Treas. Reg. § 1.409A-3(j)(1).
83. *Id.* § 1.409A-3(j)(4)(ii).
84. *Id.* § 1.409A-3(j)(4)(iii).
85. *Id.* § 1.409A-3(j)(4)(v).
86. *Id.* § 1.409A-3(j)(4)(vi).
87. *Id.* § 1.409A-3(j)(4)(vii).
88. *Id.* § 1.409A-3(j)(4)(x).
89. *Id.* § 1.409A-3(j)(4)(xi).
90. *Id.* § 1.409A-3(j)(4)(xiv).
91. *Id.* § 1.409A-3(j)(4)(ix).
92. *Id.* § 1.409A-3(j)(4)(ix)(C).
93. *Id.* § 1.409A-3(j)(4)(ix)(B).
94. *Id.*

95. *See id.* § 1.409A-2(b)(7).

96. *Id.* § 1.409A-3(d).

97. *Id.* § 1.409A-2(b)(7)(i).

98. *Id.* § 1.409A-2(b)(7)(ii).

99. *Id.* § 1.409A-2(b)(7)(iii).

100. *See id.* § 1.409A-2(a).

101. *Id.*

102. *Id.* § 1.409A-2(a)(5).

103. *Id.* § 1.409A-2(a)(8).

104. *Id.*

105. *Id.* § 1.409A-2(b).

106. *Id.* § 1.409A-2(b)(1).

107. *Id.* § 1.409A-2(b)(1)(i).

108. *Id.* § 1.409A-2(b)(1)(ii).

109. *Id.* § 1.409A-2(b)(1)(iii).

110. I.R.C. § 409A(a)(1)(B).

111. Further Guidance on the Application of Section 409A to Nonqualified Deferred Compensation Plans, 73 Fed. Reg. 74,380, 74,381 (Dec. 8, 2008).

112. I.R.C. § 409A(a)(1)(B).

113. *Id.* § 409A(a)(1)(B)(I).

114. *Id.* § 409A(a)(1)(B)(II).

115. I.R.S. Notice 2008-115 (Dec. 29, 2008), as modified by I.R.S. Notice 2010-6 (Jan. 9, 2010).

116. *Id.*

117. Treas. Reg. § 1.409A-6(a)(1)(i).

118. *Id.*

119. *Id.*

120. *Id.* § 1.409A-6(a)(4)(i).

121. *Id.*

122. *See, e.g.*, I.R.S. Notice 2008-113 (Dec. 22, 2008); I.R.S. Notice 2010-6.

123. I.R.S. Notice 2007-100 (Dec. 26, 2007).

124. I.R.S. Notice 2008-113 (Dec. 22, 2008).

125. *Id.*

126. *Id.*

127. I.R.S. Notice 2010-6.

128. *Id.*

129. *Id.*

130. I.R.S. Notice 2010-80 (Nov. 30, 2010).

131. *Id.*

132. *See* I.R.S. Notice 2010-6, as modified by I.R.S. Notice 2010-80.

133. *Id.*

134. *Id.*

135. *Id.*

136. The Emergency Economic Stabilization Act of 2008 is Division A of Pub. L. No. 110-343, 122 Stat. 3765.

137. Code section 457A, however, can also affect offshore investment funds and multinational employers with operations in multiple countries.

138. I.R.C. § 280G(a).

139. *Id.* § 4999(a).

140. *Id.* § 280G(b)(2)(B).

141. Treas. Reg. § 1.280G-1; Q&A-7.

142. I.R.C. § 280G(b)(5); Treas. Reg. § 1.280G-1, Q&A-5.

143. I.R.C. § 280G(b)(1); Treas. Reg. § 1.280G-1, Q&A-3.

144. I.R.C. § 280G(b)(3); Treas. Reg. § 1.280G-1, Q&A-34.

145. I.R.C. § 280G(c); Treas. Reg. § 1.280G-1, Q&A-15.

146. Treas. Reg. § 1.280G-1, Q&A-18.

147. Treas. Reg. § 1.280G-1, Q&A-17.

148. Treas. Reg. § 1.280G-1, Q&A-19.

149. Treas. Reg. § 1.280G-1, Q&A-11(a).

150. *Id.* § 1.280G-1, Q&A-22.

151. I.R.C. § 280G(b)(2)(A); Treas. Reg. § 1.280G-1, Q&A-30.

152. *See id.* § 83(a), (b); I.R.S. Notice 2005-1, 2005-1 C.B. 274.

153. *See generally* I.R.S. Notice 2005-1, 2005-1 C.B. 274.

154. *Id.*

155. *See, e.g.,* Testimony Concerning Optional Backdating, Before the U.S. Senate Committee on Banking, Housing and Urban Affairs (Sept. 6, 2006) (statement of Christopher Cox, Chairman, U.S. Securities and Exchange Commission).

156. Sarbanes-Oxley Act of 2002 (SOX), Pub. L. No. 107-204, 116 Stat. 745.

157. Dodd-Frank Wall Street Reform and Consumer Protection Act of 2010 (Dodd-Frank), Pub. L. No. 111-203, 124 Stat. 1376.

158. Jumpstart Our Business Startups Act of 2012 (JOBS Act), Pub. L. No. 112-106, 126 Stat. 306.

159. Regulation S-K, Item 402(b)(1)(i)–(vii).

160. *Id.,* Item 402(b)(2).

161. *Id.,* Item 402(b)(2), instruction 2.

162. *Id.,* Item 402(b).

163. *Id.,* Item 402(j).

164. *Id.,* Item 402(a)(3), instruction 1.

165. *Id.,* Item 402(a)(3), instruction 1.

166. *Id.,* Item 402(m)(2).

167. *Id.,* Item 402(b), instruction 4.

168. *Id.,* Item 402(k).

169. *Id.,* Item 402(j).

170. Exchange Act Release No. 53,185 (Jan. 27, 2006).

171. Regulation S-K, Item 402(c)(2)(ix), instruction 4.

172. *Id.,* Item 402(f).

173. Executive Compensation and Related Person Disclosure, Exchange Act Release Nos. 33-8732A, 34-54302A, 71 Fed. Reg. 53,158, 53,163–64 (Nov. 7, 2006).

174. *Id.*

175. Regulation S-K Item 402(s).

176. *Id.*, Item 401(e).

177. *Id.*, Item 407(c)(2)(vi).

178. *Id.*, Item 407(h).

179. Securities Exchange Act of 1934 § 14A(a)(1).

180. *Id.* at 14A(a)(2).

181. Regulation S-K, Item 402(b)(1)(vii).

182. *Id.*, Item 402(u).

183. *Id.*, Item 402(j).

184. *Id.*, Item 403.

185. For companies that qualify as a smaller reporting company or emerging growth company, this requirement applies for fiscal years beginning on or after July 1, 2020.

186. Regulation S-K, Item 407(i).

187. *Id.*

188. Nasdaq Stock Market Rule 5250(b)(3).

189. Regulation S-K, Item 404(a).

190. *Id.*, Item 404(b)(1).

191. *Id.*, Item 404(b)(2).

192. *Id.*, Item 407(e)(2)–(4).

193. *Id.*, Item 407(b)(1).

194. *Id.*, Item 407(b)(3).

195. *Id.*, Item 407(f).

196. *See* Form 8-K, Item 5.02(e).

197. Regulation S-K, Item 407(e)(5).

198. Securities Act Release No. 8732A § II.B.3, Exchange Act Release No. 54,302A (Aug. 29, 2006).

199. Securities Act of 1933 § 2(a)(1).

200. Current Issues and Rulemaking Projects Outline (Nov. 14, 2000), § VIII.A.12.

201. SEC v. W.J. Howey Co., 328 U.S. 293 (1946).

202. Securities Act Release Nos. 6188 (Feb. 1, 1980) and 6281 (Jan. 15, 1981).

203. 17 U.S.C. § 77a *et seq.*

204. 15 U.S.C. § 78l(g)(1)(A).

205. 17 C.F.R. § 240.12h-1.

206. On October 26, 2016, the SEC adopted amendments to Rule 504 that became effective on January 20, 2017. The amendments to Rule 504 increased the permissible amount offered and sold from $1 million to $5 million. As a result of the increase under Rule 504, the SEC also repealed Rule 505 effective May 22, 2017.

207. 17 C.F.R. § 230.504(b)(3).

208. 17 C.F.R. § 230.701(e).

209. 17 C.F.R. § 230.502(b).

210. *See, e.g.*, 15 U.S.C. §§ 77k, 77l(a)(2), 77q(a).

211. 17 C.F.R. § 229.601(b)(10)(iii)(C)(4).

212. Instruction B(1) to Form 8-K.

213. 17 C.F.R. § 229.601(a) (providing a table of required exhibits for various forms under the Securities Act of 1933 and the Exchange Act of 1934).

214. NYSE Listed Company Manual § 303A.08; NASD Rule 4350(i).

215. *Id.*

216. ISS, UNITED STATES EQUITY COMPENSATION PLANS: FREQUENTLY ASKED QUESTIONS (Dec. 6, 2019), https://www.issgovernance.com/file/policy/active/americas/US-Equity-Compensation-Plans-FAQ.pdf.

217. *Id.*

218. *Id.*

219. Securities Act of 1933, Rule 144, 17 C.F.R. § 230.144.

220. Rule 104 of Regulation BTR, 17 C.F.R. § 245.104.

221. Sarbanes-Oxley Act of 2002 § 306(a)(2).

222. *Id.* § 402.

35

Institutions of Higher Education

Paul G. Lannon, Jr. & Nathan A. Adams IV[*]

Colleges, universities, and other institutions of higher education[1] operate within special environments regulated by federal, state, and local laws. These regulations govern a broad range of activities, including admissions, financial aid, discrimination, sponsored research, intellectual property, campus safety, and privacy, to name just a few. Consequently, the compliance concerns are vast and constantly changing. Instead of attempting the Sisyphean task of cataloguing each one, this chapter highlights and addresses in depth the more prominent federal compliance obligations.

[*]   The authors wish to acknowledge Ieuan G. Mahony, Maximillian J. Bodoin, and Katrina Chapman for their contributions to this chapter.

Overview

Compliance Programs

Q 35.1   Is it necessary for an institution to have a compliance program?

Yes. The sheer number of regulations governing the activities of higher education, as well as the gravity of violating many of those regulations, necessitates a comprehensive and well-maintained compliance program. Moreover, depending on the activity, a particular statute may mandate a specific compliance program. For example, if an institution has been awarded a government contract of $5 million or more and the contract has a performance period of 120 days or longer, then the Federal Acquisition Regulation (FAR)[2] requires a compliance and ethics program in connection with that contract.[3] Likewise, if an institution offers a preferred lender list in connection with a student's choice for financial aid, then the Higher Education Act (HEA) requires that institution to develop a code of conduct for its financial aid personnel to comply with.[4]

More generally, institutions are responsible for ensuring that their faculty and staff comply with their mounting legal requirements, many of which are referenced and discussed in this chapter. Creating an effective compliance program serves as a sword, prompting education and training about an institution's particular requirements.[5] If implemented properly, the compliance program may also operate as a shield, helping to protect an institution from enhanced enforcement and fines. As explained in chapter 2, the Federal Sentencing Guidelines permit corporate entities, including institutions of higher education, to use implementation of a compliance program as a mitigating factor for fines if an employee engages in wrongdoing or violates a compliance obligation in his work on behalf of the institution.[6]

TIP: An institution's compliance efforts should identify and address legal and ethical risks related to identifying, investigating, and reporting wrongdoing.

This responsibility of institutions to ensure their faculty and staff understand and comply with mounting legal requirements was crystallized through the highly publicized Penn State scandal involving former assistant football coach Jerry Sandusky. The Penn State situation also brought home the fact that perceived ethical failures have the potential to seriously harm an institution in numerous ways. Formal compliance with a legal requirement may not suffice in the court of public opinion, even where legal or regulatory violations are not charged.

Sandusky was convicted on forty-five counts of child sex abuse–related charges, all occurring while he was employed at Penn State. Sandusky was alleged to have used his position at the university to help him target the children. Penn State drew harsh criticism and attention because officials allegedly received reports or knew about the sex abuse and failed to take appropriate action. In connection with this scandal, various university officials were charged with having been told of the abuse, yet failing to report it to authorities, in violation of state laws requiring reporting of suspected child abuse.[7] Federal authorities also launched an investigation of Penn State related to the alleged cover-up as well as Clery Act violations.[8] The scandal led to the firing of Penn State's president and its once-revered head football coach.[9] Moreover, Penn State faces numerous civil liability claims by the alleged victims[10] and has reached confidential settlements with some of them.[11]

This case has many lessons and brings home the immense consequences associated with potential legal and ethical failures. Among the most significant are:

(1) the importance of establishing and maintaining a process for reporting and investigating potential violations that is perceived by all employees and staff as both independent and impartial;

(2) understanding that a true commitment to ethical behavior (doing the right thing) is more important than trying to "keep a lid on" potential scandals; and

(3) that the perception of a cover-up of wrongdoing usually does more to damage an institution's reputation and pocketbook than the underlying wrongdoing alone.

All of these lessons make it crucial for an institution to design, implement, and maintain a compliance and ethics program that demonstrates a real commitment to both legal compliance and ethical behavior.

Q 35.1.1   What should a compliance program for a higher education institution entail?

An institution's compliance program should aim to prevent and detect criminal conduct and promote an organizational culture and "tone from the top" that encourages ethical conduct and a commitment to compliance with the law.[12] Ideally, the program should encompass the several basic components set forth within the Federal Sentencing Guidelines and discussed in chapter 2. These components include:

(1) high-level company personnel who exercise effective oversight and have direct reporting authority to the governing body or appropriate subgroup (e.g., Audit Committee);

(2) written policies and procedures;

(3) training and education;

(4)   effective lines of communication;

(5)   standards enforced through well-publicized disciplinary guidelines;

(6)   internal compliance auditing and monitoring;

(7)   response to detected offenses and corrective action plans; and

(8)   periodic risk assessments.

Q 35.1.2   Who should be involved in the implementation of a compliance program at institutions of higher education?

An effective compliance program requires a comprehensive approach with strategic participation from the institution's governing board, president, and compliance officer and committee, as well as the specific operational units within the institution.[13] A breakdown of the types of responsibilities and potential designation of responsibilities is set forth below.[14]

Governing Board. The governing board should be responsible for setting the "tone from the top" and establishing a culture of compliance that recognizes compliance as an institutional value that is the responsibility of every employee. This may be accomplished through broad expressions of support for the institution's compliance efforts and "doing what is right," allocating sufficient resources to develop and address compliance concerns, and authorizing swift corrective action when negative compliance incidents occur. Ultimately, the governing board should have oversight responsibility for the compliance program.[15]

President/Office of the President. The office of the president should assist in efforts to cultivate a culture of compliance by reinforcing the tone from the top as one that places a high value on institutional compliance. The office should serve as the spokesperson for the institution, capitalizing on opportunities to deliver its message of compliance. It should be kept apprised of the institution's compliance activities and have oversight responsibility in connection with training, monitoring, and auditing.[16]

Compliance Officer and/or Compliance Committee. The compliance officer and committee serve as the backbone of the compliance program. They have intimate knowledge of the legal and regulatory requirements and compliance activities of the institution. They should meet regularly to review compliance activities and make recommendations for improvements. In addition, they should have the authority to receive, review, and investigate issues and reported violations. They should have direct reporting access to the governing board to enable swift action if necessary. They also should keep the governing board and office of the president apprised of compliance activities and potential breaches.[17]

Operations Units. The various divisions, departments, and other operations units within an institution are closest to the regulatory and legal issues faced by the institution. The issues are embedded in their daily operations, and as such, the employees within these operational units often have the best insight into heightened compliance concerns that they encounter on a daily basis. It is also more likely that they have a hands-on understanding of which training and monitoring methods will work best with their units. Operations units should share this knowledge with the compliance officer to help shape a strategic plan for compliance objectives and training methods. The units should be involved in the training as well. In addition, the operations units should be involved in implementing corrective actions based on investigations of compliance concerns. The units should have a clear understanding of their reporting obligations.[18]

COMPLIANCE FACT

Compliance is not one-size-fits-all.

When organizing a compliance program at a higher educational institution, there is no one-size-fits-all model to follow. The key to an effective compliance program is ensuring that controls are in place to prevent and detect wrongdoing, based on the particular risks facing the institution, setting clear expectations and lines of reporting any wrongdoing, and instilling an organizational culture that encourages ethical conduct.

Risk Assessment

Q 35.2   What are the greatest areas of risk for institutions?

The level of risk faced by an institution varies greatly based on the institution and its activities. To determine which areas generate the greatest risks, each institution should conduct a risk assessment of its activities. A risk assessment looks at the institution's level of activity within a specified area as well as the likely impact of that activity. This usually entails evaluating factors such as regulatory and legal requirements, audit results, recent litigation or settlements, compliance complaints, employee claims, industry enforcement trends, and the existence and sufficiency of internal controls in place, such as policies, training, and auditing.[19]

Many of the more salient risk areas are referenced within this chapter and include:

- diversity in admissions,
- disability,
- student assistance/federal student aid,
- campus security,
- privacy/security of student records and information,
- data security,
- Title IX—gender equality and prevention of discrimination and harassment,
- copyright protection,
- ownership of intellectual property,
- government-sponsored research, and
- false claims.

Diversity in Admissions

Q 35.3   May academic institutions take race and gender into account when making admissions decisions?

Academic institutions may take race into account when making admissions decisions, but only after undertaking a searching inquiry into compliance with, as applicable, the Equal Protection Clause[20] or Title VI.[21] Race-based admissions decisions are presumptively unconstitutional[22] and, therefore, must satisfy strict scrutiny or, in other words, must further a "compelling governmental interest" in the "least restrictive" or most "narrowly tailored" manner.[23] Even private institutions must meet these standards if they participate in federal financial aid programs, because Title VI applies to all programs in a college that receives federal financial assistance.[24]

The standard for gender-based admissions policies is at least that of intermediate scrutiny. The Equal Protection Clause applies to public universities and requires affected institutions to demonstrate an "exceedingly persuasive justification" to take gender into account.[25] For this, the institutions must show at least that the "discriminatory means employed" are substantially related to important governmental objectives.[26] In addition, Title IX[27] applies to public undergraduate institutions and public and private institutions of vocational, professional, and graduate education, except certain religious educational institutions.[28] Some federal courts have granted female students greater protection under Title IX than under the Equal Protection Clause by applying strict scrutiny to evaluate academic policies.[29] Some states have also adopted statutes that prohibit sex discrimination at educational institutions.[30]

Q 35.3.1   When do institutions have a compelling interest to consider race in admissions?

An institution may have a compelling interest in attaining a diverse student body.[31] An institution may consider race and gender critical to this, but efforts to achieve racial balancing have been struck down. The concept of diversity is broader than quotas or balancing tests.[32] Diversity is understood to comprise a wide variety of demographic factors, such as religion, income, and national origin. Diversity also encompasses unusual travel abroad, intellectual achievement, leadership qualities, community service, overcoming personal adversity or special needs, language fluency, employment and military experience, and extraordinary awards and honors.[33] The pedagogical justification must correspond to the level of diversity sought, and that level must be identified prospectively. The challenge for institutions is to articulate the level of diversity sought as a recognizable threshold so that it is clear when an institution's objective has been met, although not as a percentage of a particular group merely due to race or ethnic origin, but consonant with academic objectives.[34]

The institution must clearly articulate the pedagogical justification for why achieving diversity (including racial and gender diversity) is at the heart of the institution's educational mission.[35] Justifications for race-sensitive policies approved by the courts include:

- promoting cross-racial understanding;

- helping to break down racial stereotypes;

- enabling students to better understand persons of different races;

- achieving a "critical mass" of students;

- preparing students to function as professionals in a multi-cultural workforce and pluralistic society;

- cultivating the next set of leaders, including the effective participation by members of all racial groups in civic life;

- increasing the diversity of perspective in classroom discussion;

- producing new knowledge stemming from diverse outlooks;

- enabling frequent, comfortable, and normal inter-group interaction; and

- avoiding racial isolation.[36]

A periodic study will ordinarily be essential to determine the level of diversity attained at the institution, the extent to which diversity-conscious admissions decisions are achieving the institution's pedagogical objectives, and the continued need for the diversity-conscious policies. As an example of periodic study, academic institutions have examined diversity on university-wide, degree program, department, and classroom bases to determine the extent of under-enrollment of minority and female students.[37]

Q 35.3.2   When is an institution's implementation of a race-conscious admissions policy narrowly tailored?

A race-conscious admissions policy is narrowly tailored consistent with the strict scrutiny standard when:

(1) race is merely a "plus" factor in admissions, not a quota;[38]

(2) applicants are not isolated by race in pools or otherwise;[39]

(3) applicants are given a highly individualized, holistic review;[40]

(4) race-neutral alternatives to increase diversity are considered;[41] and

(5) the race-conscious policy has a limited duration and depends for renewal on periodic review of the program.[42]

Impermissible pooling of minority applicants occurs when minorities are considered separately from non-minorities.[43] Mechanical and predetermined bonus points linked to race or ethnicity are the antithesis of individualized review.[44] Additionally, a system is not holistic if it is not "flexible enough to consider all pertinent elements of diversity in light of the particular qualifications of each applicant, and to place them on the same footing for consideration, although not necessarily according them the same weight."[45]

An academic institution need not exhaust every conceivable race-neutral alternative to race-conscious admissions policies. In fact, a university may supplement a race-neutral alternative with a race-sensitive plan,[46] but does require a careful inquiry into whether a university could achieve sufficient diversity without using racial classifications.[47] Alternatives include, for example, increasing the pool of minority applicants through community outreach efforts (e.g., adopt-a- minority high school programs) and scholarship programs (e.g., first-in-family scholarships).[48] Sunset provisions contingent upon evaluation of the importance of a race-sensitive admissions policy in light of the pedagogical reasons for the program and the success of the program are also required to implement a narrowly tailored constitutional policy.[49]

Q 35.3.3   In what circumstances may the consideration of gender in admissions be constitutional?

The U.S. Supreme Court has not yet ruled on when gender-based admissions policies are constitutional, but it has held that a "gender-based classification favoring one sex can be justified if it intentionally and directly assists members of the sex that is disproportionately burdened."[50] The justification must be genuine, not hypothesized or invented post hoc in response to litigation.[51] Some cases suggest that the state must demonstrate an "exceedingly persuasive justification" for a gender-based classification.[52] An asserted need for "gender diversity" that is no more than "a front for . . . gender balancing" is insufficient.[53]

In addition, the justification for a gender-sensitive policy should not rely on "archaic and stereotypic notions" about the sexes or have as its purpose to "exclude or 'protect' members of one gender because they are presumed to suffer from an inherent handicap or to be innately inferior. . . ."[54] An admissions system that awards automatic points on the basis of gender without any individualized assessment may be no less objectionable than one that does so on the basis of race.[55] In fact, it is likely that in gender-based admissions cases a court will consider many of the same factors weighed in race-based admissions cases.[56] An undergraduate gender-based admissions policy at a public institution may also be subject to a claim under Title IX.[57]

Q 35.3.4   Are all gender-based admissions policies subject to Title IX's ban on sex-based discrimination?

Title IX provides that "[n]o person in the United States shall, on the basis of sex, be excluded from participation in, be denied the benefits of, or be subjected to discrimination under any education program or activity."[58] However, Title IX's ban on sex-based discrimination is not absolute. Several exceptions apply. With regard to admissions to educational institutions, "Title IX applies only to institutions of vocational education, professional education, and graduate higher education, and to public institutions of undergraduate higher education."[59] Consequently, Title IX permits *private* colleges to deny admission to its *undergraduate* programs on the basis of sex. A similar express exception applies to social fraternities and sororities: Title IX does not apply to the membership practices of "a social fraternity or social sorority which is exempt from taxation under section 501(a) of title 26, the active membership of which consists primarily of students in attendance at an institution of higher education."[60]

Title IX and sex discrimination are discussed in further detail below (*see* Q 35.19 *et seq.*).

Q 35.4   What are the consequences of a noncompliant admissions policy?

Institutions that fail to ensure that their race- or gender-sensitive admissions policies comply with the Equal Protection Clause risk private enforcement efforts by accrediting agencies or individuals and advocacy groups opposed to affirmative action in admissions. State and federal departments of education and state and federal civil rights commissions may also investigate colleges and universities. Successful actions brought under 42 U.S.C. § 1983 entitle plaintiffs to attorney fees and costs.

Disability

Q 35.5   What obligations regarding disability should an institution be aware of?

Title II and Title III of the Americans with Disabilities Act (ADA)[61] and section 504 of the Rehabilitation Act of 1973 (the "Rehabilitation Act")[62] impose similar requirements[63] and apply to public and private institutions.[64] Title II of the ADA prevents a disabled person, as defined by the statute, who is "otherwise qualified" for the benefit in question from being excluded from the benefit on the basis of a disability.[65] Title III and the Rehabilitation Act also require that institutions reasonably accommodate a disabled person who is otherwise qualified academically, as long as the institution is a private entity that owns, leases, or operates a place of public accommodation (for ADA purposes) and receives federal funding (for Rehabilitation Act purposes).

The institution would not be required to make an accommodation that would "fundamentally alter the nature of the public accommodation."[66]

In 2008, Congress amended the ADA and Rehabilitation Act in a manner likely to expand their applicability to the admissions, employment, and other practices of postsecondary institutions.[67] The ADA Amendments Act of 2008 (ADAAA)[68] stated that the definition of disability must be "construed in favor of broad coverage of individuals under this Act, to the maximum extent permitted by the terms of this Act."[69] The ADAAA includes a non-exhaustive list of major life activities subject to impairment, which is likely to expand available legal protection to include the following activities:[70]

caring for oneself	walking	learning
performing manual tasks	standing	reading
seeing	lifting	concentrating
hearing	bending	thinking
eating	speaking	communicating
sleeping	breathing	working

The ADAAA also covers individuals with episodic impairments such as epilepsy and asthma.[71]

Altogether, these changes appear to have expanded the class of protected individuals.[72] To illustrate, before the ADAAA, "learning" was identified as a major life activity that could be substantially limited, but the Department of Justice issued guidance indicating that the degree of limitation posed should be evaluated in relation to "most people."[73] As a result, lower courts held that plaintiffs with learning disabilities seeking extra time to take the medical bar exam and a separate testing room were not protected because they showed a history of significant scholastic achievement as compared to most people.[74] This led some to conclude that a plaintiff's status as a graduate student itself negated class membership on the basis of a learning disability. The congressional record relating to the ADAAA[75] lends support to the view that Congress meant to reject these holdings in favor of *Bartlett v. New York State Board of Law* Examiners,[76] where the court held that a university must take an individualized look at the method and manner in which the plaintiff achieved academic success to decide whether in select ways the student may in fact be disabled.[77]

Q 35.5.1   How should institutions respond to the ADAAA?

The ADAAA reaffirms the principle that disabled students may not compel institutions "to eliminate academic requirements essential to the instruction being pursued by a student." Essential academic requirements may include both academic and technical requirements, "with technical requirements embracing all 'nonacademic admissions criteria that are essential to participation in the program in question.'"[78] Although universities do not need to lower these standards, the burden is upon them to demonstrate that they considered alternative means (including their feasibility, cost, and effect) and came to a rationally justifiable conclusion that the alternatives would either lower academic standards or require substantial program alteration.[79]

Select legislative reports confirm that colleges should be willing "to make modifications in order to enable students with disabilities to meet . . . academic requirements."[80] Modifications may include changes in the length of time permitted for the completion of degree requirements, substitution of specific courses required for the completion of degree requirements, and adaptation of the manner in which specific courses are conducted.[81] An institution is financially responsible for auxiliary aids and services unless it can demonstrate that the cost is an undue burden.[82] Higher education institutions must have appropriate policies and procedures proffering accommodations and give the utmost care to record keeping.

In the wake of tragedies like the April 2007 massacre at Virginia Tech (*see* Q 35.9.4), applicants and students with known psychiatric disabilities create especially acute challenges. Although institutions need not admit or continue to serve students who present a direct threat to self, others, or property—such students are "not otherwise qualified"—institutions must still take care to engage in individualized and objective assessment, sound evidence of probable and proximate injury, and consideration of reasonable mitigating policies, practices, or procedures.[83]

Student Assistance/Federal Student Aid

Institutional Eligibility

Q 35.6   What are the eligibility requirements for an institution to participate in federal student aid (FSA) programs?

The U.S. Department of Education (DOE) must certify the eligibility of all institutions participating in FSA programs under Title IV of HEA. Institutional eligibility requirements can be found at 34 C.F.R. § 600 *et seq.* and in the second volume of the *Federal Student Aid* Handbook.[84]

The DOE recognizes three types of eligible institutions:

(i)   institutions of higher education,

(ii) proprietary institutions of higher education, and

(iii) postsecondary vocational institutions.

Institutions of higher education and postsecondary vocational institutions may be public or private, but they must be non-profit. By contrast, a proprietary institution of higher education must be private and for-profit.

To be eligible, an institution must:

(a)   have state authorization to provide a postsecondary education program in that state;

(b)   have accreditation by a nationally recognized accrediting agency or have met the alternative requirements, if applicable; and

(c)   admit as regular students only individuals with a high school diploma or its recognized equivalent, or individuals beyond the age of compulsory school attendance in the state where the institution is located.

Proprietary and postsecondary vocational institutions must also comply with the "two-year rule," which requires institutions to demonstrate that they have been legally authorized to provide (and have been continuously providing) the same postsecondary instruction for which they now seek FSA for at least two consecutive years (with allowances for changes to program length and subject matter made because of new technology or requirements of other federal agencies).

Program Eligibility

Q 35.7   What are the requirements for an academic program to be eligible for FSA?

At institutions of higher education, programs eligible for FSA must:

(a) lead to an associate's, bachelor's, graduate, or professional degree,

(b) be at least a two-academic-year program that is acceptable for full credit toward a bachelor's degree, or

(c) be at least a one-academic-year training program that leads to a degree, certificate, or other recognized educational credential and that prepares a student for gainful employment in a recognized occupation.[85]

For proprietary and vocational institutions, there are three types of programs eligible for FSA. Each program must provide training for gainful employment in a recognized occupation and meet at least one of the following criteria:

(1) require at least a fifteen-week (instructional time) undergraduate program of 600 clock hours, sixteen semester or trimester hours, or twenty-four quarter hours;

(2) require at least a ten-week (instructional time) program of 300 clock hours, eight semester or trimester hours, or twelve quarter hours; or

(3) require at least a ten-week (instructional time) undergraduate program of 300 to 599 clock hours.[86]

Within a type-1 program, institutions may accept students without an associate's degree or the equivalent. A type-2 program is for graduate or professional students and may accept only students with an associate's degree or the equivalent. A type-3 program, known as a short-term program, is limited to the Federal Family Educational Loan

(FFEL) program and the Federal Direct Loan (DL) program[87] financial aid and must admit as regular students some persons who have not yet completed an associate's degree or the equivalent. Short-term programs must also satisfy the following additional requirements:

(a) have verified completion and placement rates of at least 70%;

(b) not be more than 50% longer than the minimum training period required by state or federal agencies, if any, for the occupation for which the program of instruction is intended; and

(c) have operated for at least one year.[88]

Specific FSA programs will have further eligibility requirements.

Participation Requirements

Q 35.8 What requirements must an institution comply with in order to participate in FSA programs?

To participate in FSA programs, an institution must have a current Program Participation Agreement (PPA),[89] signed by the institution's president or chief executive officer and by an authorized representative of the Secretary of Education. By signing the PPA, an institution certifies that it will comply with the program statutes, regulations, and policies governing the FSA programs. Failure to meet the terms of a PPA could result in suspension or termination from FSA programs. Failure to meet the terms of a PPA has also triggered False Claims Act liability.[90] An institution seeking FSA must comply with certain statutory obligations, including compliance with the Campus Security Act (also known as the Clery Act, discussed below); certain federal civil rights and anti-discrimination laws, including Title VI of the Civil Rights Act of 1964,[91] and its implementing regulation,[92] which prohibit discrimination on the basis of race, color, or national origin;[93] specific preferred lender arrangement disclosures to students borrowing under the FFEL program[94] as required by the Secretary of Education;[95] and a written copyright protection plan designed to educate students and staff about the proper use of copyrighted materials, prevent the unauthorized distribution or use of copyrighted materials, and provide notice to students that the unauthorized distribution of copyrighted materials, including peer-to-peer file sharing, is unlawful and may subject them to civil or criminal penalties.[96]

The HEA sets forth many additional specific obligations for institution participation in Title IV programs, including requirements related to:

- incentive compensation and employment compensation for recruitment activities;

- preferred lender lists;

- an institution code of conduct;

- private education loan disclosures;[97]

- institutional and financial assistance information for students;[98]

- exit counseling for borrowers; and

- private lenders' relationships and activities with institutions and students.

Incentive Compensation

Q 35.8.1   What limitations are there on the compensation of student recruiters?

Title IV of the HEA strictly prohibits compensating student recruiters, admissions officers, and financial aid administrators based on their success in securing enrollments or financial aid.[99] The purpose of this compensation restriction is to diminish the financial incentives for enrolling unqualified students. This restriction only applies to Title IV programs. Thus, it does not apply, for example, to the recruitment of foreign students residing in foreign countries who are not eligible to receive federal student assistance.

Q 35.8.2   What types of compensation plans are permitted for student recruiters under Title IV?

Prior to July 2011, the DOE expressly recognized twelve safe harbors, which described specific payment arrangements that did not violate the incentive compensation prohibition.[100] Initially, in the DOE's view, these safe harbors were acceptable because they reflected situations that did not pose a significant risk of fraudulent or unscrupulous procurement of federal funding. For example, it was permissible to have a compensation plan that increased a recruiter's compensation as long as the increase was not based "solely" on signing up new students or assisting them in obtaining financial aid. The DOE grew skeptical, however, concluding that many institutions were merely paying lip service to the regulations and were still improperly compensating recruiters based on the number of students recruited.[101]

In July 2011, the DOE explicitly eliminated the safe harbor provisions. The new regulations now prohibit:

- any merit-based adjustment to employee compensation based in any part, directly or indirectly, upon success in securing enrollments or the award of financial aid;[102] and

- any profit-sharing payments to any person or entity engaged in student recruitment or admission activity or in making decisions regarding the award of Title IV HEA program funds.[103]

It is now clear that the only compensation plans permitted for student recruiters or admissions personnel are those plans where compensation is in no way connected to the person's success in securing student enrollments or financial aid.

Preferred Lender Lists

Q 35.8.3   What requirements and limitations are there on institutions providing students with a list of preferred lenders?

Institutions may provide students with a list of preferred or recommended lenders, but only if the list:

(a) does not limit a borrower's choice of lenders,

(b) contains no fewer than three lenders unaffiliated with each other, and

(c) does not include lenders that offer the institution any financial or other benefits in exchange for inclusion on the list.[104]

An institution choosing to offer a preferred lender list must:

(i)   disclose the method and criteria for selecting the lenders;

(ii)   provide comparative information to prospective borrowers about interest rates and other benefits offered by the lenders;

(iii)   include a prominent statement that students are not required to use any of the listed lenders;

(iv)   not assign a first-time borrower's loan to a particular lender; and

(v)   not delay the certification of loans for borrowers who choose to use a lender not on the preferred list.

The institution must update the preferred lender list at least annually.[105]

The method and criteria used to select preferred lenders must include payment of origination or other fees for borrowers, competitive terms of conditions, including interest rates, and high-quality servicing and benefits beyond the standard terms. If the institution endorses private loans, the list must include at least two lenders that are not affiliates of one another. For each lender, the list must disclose affiliates and describe the affiliation.[106] The institution must include a statement indicating on its website and in any publications, mailings, or electronic messages distributed to prospective or current students or their families discussing financial aid opportunities that the institution may not deny or impede a borrower's loan certification if he or she chooses a lender not on the preferred lender list.[107]

State laws may add further limitations, particularly regarding consumer protection and truth in lending.

Code of Conduct

Q 35.8.4   What are an institution's obligations regarding a code of conduct?

An institution participating in Title IV programs must develop, publish, and comply with a code of conduct for its financial aid personnel.[108] The code must be published on the institution's website and annually to those who have FSA responsibilities. At a minimum, the code of conduct must contain provisions prohibiting:

- conflicts of interest;

- revenue sharing arrangements;

- the solicitation or acceptance of gifts, receipt of fees, payments, or other financial benefits for consulting services by anyone in the institution with responsibilities for student loans, assistance with call centers, or staffing;

- the acceptance of funds to be used for private loans in exchange for providing concessions to a private lender; and

- the acceptance of anything of value except reimbursement for reasonable expenses by an employee with responsibilities for financial assistance that sits on a lender's advisory board or commission.

Student Loan Information Notification and Disclosure

Q 35.8.5 What are an institution's disclosure and notification obligations regarding student loan information?

When an institution is lending Title IV funds, it must notify the borrower, in easy-to-understand terms, what the borrower's rights and responsibilities are, and what the consequences of default are, including the disclosure of the default to consumer credit agencies.[109] The borrower must receive this information when the loan is first approved. Thereafter, the institution must make several additional disclosures, either in written or electronic form, before disbursing the loan.[110] Among the required disclosures are:

- a prominent statement that the loan must be repaid;

- the principal amount of the loan;

- charges associated with the loan;

- the interest rate;

- information regarding the payment of interest while the borrower is in school, if applicable;

- repayment information including the types of repayment plans available and an estimate of the borrower's monthly payment, consolidation, or refinancing options;

- information on deferral, forbearance, and loan forgiveness options; and

- information on the consequences of default.[111]

Not less than thirty days or more than 150 days before the borrower's first loan payment is due, institutional lenders must disclose, among other things:

- the name of the lender or loan servicer, and the payment address;

- the date repayment begins and a repayment schedule;

- an estimate of the balance owed;

- interest rate information;

- fees associated with repayment;

- the borrower's prepayment rights;

- repayment options, and benefits;

- consolidation and refinancing options; and

- additional resources for the borrower to receive advice on loan repayment.[112]

During the repayment term, institutional lenders must provide each borrower with a bill for each payment. The bill must detail:

- the original principal;

- the current balance;

- the interest rate;

- the total amount paid in interest;

- the aggregate amount paid on the loan;

- a description of any fees charged to the borrower during the preceding payment period;

- the next payment due date;

- the lender's or servicer's address and toll-free phone number; and

- a reminder that the borrower has the option of changing repayment plans.[113]

If a borrower notifies the institution about a difficulty making loan payments on time, the institution must provide information on available repayment plans, the requirements for a forbearance, and other options available to avoid default.[114] For borrowers that are sixty days or more delinquent, institutional lenders must disclose the date on which the loan will default, the minimum payment the borrower must make to avoid default, options available to avoid default, discharge options, and additional resources where the borrower may receive assistance.[115]

Institutions should also review applicable state lending laws.

Counseling for Borrowers

Q 35.8.6   What obligations does an institution have regarding financial counseling for students?

Institutions must provide entrance and exit counseling to a student borrower.[116] The counseling can be done in person, online, or through documents that the borrower acknowledges having received and reviewed.[117] The counseling must address the loan's effect on the student's eligibility for other federal financial assistance, the ability to pay interest on some loans while in school, descriptions of loan forgiveness plans and forbearance requirements, and debt management techniques.[118]

Private Lenders

Q 35.8.7   What requirements and limitations are there on the activities of private lenders?

The Private Student Loan Transparency and Improvement Act (Title X of the HEA), which amends the Truth in Lending Act (TILA), making it applicable to all private student loans, prohibits a private student loan lender from offering gifts to an institution or its employees or agents in exchange for any advantage in providing private loans to the institution's students. A private lender may not use an institution's name, logo, mascot, or any other representation of the institution to market its loans. An institution's financial aid personnel may not receive anything of value for serving on an advisory board for a lender, aside from reimbursement for reasonable expenses. Private lenders may not penalize borrowers for prepayment of their loans.[119] Furthermore, any private lender that has a preferred lender arrangement with an institution must provide an annual report to that institution, including a copy of the disclosures required to be made when a loan is approved[120] for each type of private loan the lender plans to offer to a student at the institution.[121]

Penalties

Q 35.8.8   What are the penalties for violating Title IV student aid regulations?

The regulations concerning an institution's PPA with the DOE specifically require the institution to agree that it is liable for all "improperly spent or unspent funds received under Title IV . . . programs . . . and . . . [r]efunds that the institution . . . may be required to make."[122] Title IV expressly authorizes the DOE to impose civil fines of up to $25,000 for each violation of the statute or regulations.[123] A separate violation can occur each time Title IV financial aid is disbursed improperly. In the case of students recruited under illegal incentive-based compensation schemes, the DOE has taken the position that a separate violation occurs each time one of those students obtains federal financial aid. In contrast, the DOE will count "the total of violations caused by a repeated mechanical systemic unintentional error as a single violation," unless there was prior notice of the problem and the servicer failed to correct it.[124] The DOE can also order "corrective actions," which may include payment to the DOE of any Title IV funds "improperly received, withheld, disbursed, or caused to be disbursed."[125] The monetary penalties, consequently, can be enormous.

Compromise is built into the system. The DOE is expressly authorized to "compromise" any civil penalty proposed by the OIG.[126] The DOE is also required to weigh the appropriateness of the penalty against the size of the institution and the gravity of the violation.[127] Penalties are appealable.[128]

Violations may also lead to suspension or termination from Title IV programs.[129] The suspension may not exceed sixty days unless a longer suspension is agreed to, or the DOE begins a limitation or termination proceeding against the institution.[130] A termination ends an institution's participation in a Title IV program.[131] Termination is typically reserved for situations where an institution has consistently violated Title IV and the implementing regulations, and attempts to remedy the situation have failed.[132]

Short of terminating an institution, the DOE may limit participation in Title IV programs.[133] Limitations can be applied to:

(1) the number or percentage of students enrolled in an institution who may receive Title IV funds;

(2) the percentage of an institution's total receipts from tuition and fees derived from Title IV program funds;

(3) the requirements for a surety, in a specified amount; and

(4) other conditions that the DOE deems reasonable and appropriate.[134]

Campus Safety and Security

Q 35.9   What liability does an institution have for violence on campus?

The general rule is that an institution has no duty to control the conduct of a third person so as to prevent that person from causing physical harm to another.[135] However, exceptions to this rule prevail when an institution voluntarily assumes the duty through the conduct of its representatives[136] or by contract.[137] A duty can also be imposed where there is a special relationship between the institution and a third person such as exists between:

- employee and employer;[138]
- landlord and tenant;[139]
- business and invitee;[140] and
- in a minority of jurisdictions, college and student.[141]

With respect to colleges and their students, special relationships are recognized in very limited circumstances, typically involving custodial care, actual knowledge of intent to commit suicide or self-harm,[142] or reasonably foreseeable criminal activity.[143]

When there exists a legal duty of care between an academic institution and an injured third person, the next inquiry under negligence law is to determine the standard of care due under the relevant circumstances. In making that determination, the institutions should consider the custom and practice within the academic community and expert testimony. If that standard was breached, the next question is whether there is a direct causal connection between the breach of duty and damages to another.

Foreseeability is a factor in determining both duty and proximate cause.[144] Harm is foreseeable when there is knowledge of a specific threat.[145] Foreseeability can also arise from like-kind threats or general threats within the same scope as the injury.[146] Lastly, foreseeability can be imputed when an institution is not actually aware of a risk but reasonably should have been.[147]

Q 35.9.1   What are the requirements of the Clery Act?

The Jeanne Clery Disclosure of Campus Security Policy and Campus Crime Statistics Act (the "Clery Act")[148] (originally known as the "Crime Awareness and Campus Security Act") requires institutions participating in FSA programs to:

(1) publish an annual security report detailing certain crimes committed on campus and at affiliated locations for the previous three calendar years,[149]

(2) publish campus safety policies,[150]

(3)   compile and disclose campus crime statistics,[151]

(4)   report to the campus community crimes that represent a threat to students and/or employees "in a manner that is timely and will aid in the prevention of similar crimes,"[152] and

(5)   maintain and disclose daily crime log information.[153]

(6)   offer primary prevention and awareness programs to all new students and employees to promote awareness of sex offenses;

(7)   comply with specified standards for investigation and conduct of student discipline proceedings in cases of domestic violence, dating violence, sexual assault, and stalking; and

(8)   explain to victims their options regarding law enforcement and judicial safeguards.[154]

The annual security report must describe campus policies concerning the following subjects:

(i)   procedures and facilities for students and others to report criminal activity or other emergencies occurring on campus and policies concerning the institution's response to such reports;

(ii)   policies concerning security and access to campus facilities and security considerations used in the maintenance of campus facilities;

(iii) policies concerning the enforcement authority of campus law enforcement units and their relationship with state and local police agencies;

(iv)   policies relating to the monitoring and recording through local police agencies of criminal activity at off-campus student organizations that are recognized by the institution;

(v)   policies regarding the possession, use, and sale of alcoholic beverages, enforcement of under-age drinking laws, and the possession, use, and sale of illegal drugs; and

(vi)   policies regarding sexual assault and procedures to follow when a sex offense occurs.[155]

Q 35.9.2   What requirements has the Violence Against Women Reauthorization Act imposed on colleges and universities?

The Violence Against Women Reauthorization Act (VAWA), signed into law March 7, 2013, imposes obligations for reporting, student discipline, and prevention of crime on campus. At a minimum, VAWA amends the Clery Act by requiring that institutions:

(1)   add domestic violence, dating violence, and stalking to the categories of criminal offense reported;

(2)   add national origin and gender identity to the hate crime categories reported;

(3)   withhold victims' names with respect to the "timely reports" of criminal activity;

(4)   explain to victims their rights and options as they relate to law enforcement and judicial safeguards;

(5)   follow specified standards for investigation and conduct of student disciplinary proceedings in sex offense cases; and

(6)   offer and maintain primary prevention and awareness programs that promote awareness of sex offenses to new students and employees.

Authorization for VAWA funding and programming expired in February 2019. Competing bills to reauthorize VAWA are presently pending in Congress.

Q 35.9.3   What are the repercussions for failing to comply with the Clery Act?

The Clery Act does not create a private right of action, nor is it supposed to establish a standard of care,[156] but it may certainly be influencing the non-statutory standard of care by requiring policies that themselves create a threshold standard of care. In addition, the DOE is authorized to impose civil fines of up to $25,000 per violation on an educational institution that has "substantially misrepresented" the nature of the crimes required to be reported.[157] It may also limit, suspend, or terminate the institution's participation in federal financial aid programs.[158]

Q 35.9.4 What are some best practices for preventing and responding to campus violence?

In the wake of incidents such as the April 2007 massacre at Virginia Tech, where a senior at that school killed thirty-two people in two separate shooting attacks, and the February 2008 shooting at Northern Illinois University, where six people were killed, states and universities have investigated and issued multiple reports establishing best practices for preventing and responding to campus violence.[159] Due to the Clery Act and for other reasons, most schools have complied with the most rudimentary of these national standards by adopting an all-hazards emergency response plan (ERP), implementing an emergency mass notification and communications system, and providing on-campus mental health services for students.[160] The policy for use of the mass notification system should indicate the kinds of events that would initiate the use of the system, who is authorized to launch the system, the parties that should be notified, and what information should be provided.[161] Redundant means of mass communication are also important.[162]

A slightly smaller percentage of colleges have put in place a multi-disciplinary "threat assessment team" (TAT), begun training personnel regarding privacy and information sharing laws and policies such as FERPA and HIPAA, agreed to a memorandum of understanding or a mutual aid agreement with community partners such as law enforcement agencies and mental health providers, and begun to train students, faculty, and staff about mass notification systems and their roles and responsibilities in an emergency.[163] The TAT should meet weekly and include members from campus police, residential life, counseling services, faculty, and the graduate and undergraduate school deans.[164]

Additional recommended steps for preventing and responding to campus violence include:

- ☐ Repair/replace exterior doors.[165]

- ☐ Conduct an inquiry of school applicants (especially graduate students) about unusual academic histories, criminal records, and disciplinary actions.

- ☐ Include public safety as part of the school orientation process.

❑ Conduct annual vulnerability assessments of the campus and regular reviews of the ERP.

❑ Educate faculty, staff, and students about recognizing and responding to signs of mental illness and potential threats.

❑ Adopt a policy outlining how and to whom faculty and staff should refer students who may be threatening.

❑ Have multiple reporting systems to enable the reporting of threatening behavior anonymously and conveniently.

❑ Have an interoperable communication system with all area responders.

❑ Ensure that all responder agencies are trained in the National Incident Management System (NIMS) and the Incident Command System (ICS).

❑ Install CCTV cameras and electronic access control systems.

❑ Provide "active shooter response training" to campus police.

❑ Provide on-campus or off-campus, by agreement, specialized mental health services (e.g., substance abuse, eating disorders, suicide).

❑ Submit potentially violent writings, drawings, and other forms of expression for forensic behavioral review.

❑ Ensure adequate campus safety staffing levels.

❑ Provide lethal weapons to campus police, training in the use of personal and specialized firearms, and the means to gain forcible entry to locked spaces.

❑ Drill emergency preparedness.

❑ Establish a trained behavioral health trauma response team.

❑ Develop plans to stand-up a joint information center with a public information officer.

❑ Plan for victim services in the aftermath of a tragic event including short- and long-term counseling for first responders, students, staff, and their families.[166]

Q 35.9.5   What is the role of legal counsel in improving campus security?

Legal counsel should be consulted in the drafting of campus security documents. Legal counsel will be particularly helpful in interpreting the recent changes to the Clery Act, given the ambiguity of the changes and the absence of regulatory guidance from the DOE. In addition, counsel should either be on a school's threat assessment team or be readily available to the TAT. As one campus violence report explained:

> Attorneys can play an integral role in threat assessment and violence prevention and should be involved early in the process of dealing with more severe and credible threats. These professionals are familiar with privacy and confidentiality issues. They can also facilitate obtaining judicial injunctions and Temporary Restraining Orders, and assist in preparing legal documents to handle potentially dangerous persons or situations.[167]

Privacy of Student Education Records/Information—FERPA

Q 35.10   What is FERPA?

The Family Educational Rights and Privacy Act (FERPA) is a federal law designed to protect the privacy of student education records.[168] FERPA first came into effect on November 19, 1974, and has gone through several amendments.[169] FERPA applies to all secondary and postsecondary schools that receive funds from any program administered by the DOE, whether public or private, including funding from federal financial aid programs.[170] FERPA's protections cover elementary school, high school, and postsecondary records. In elementary and high school, the privacy rights created by FERPA mostly flow to parents; however, once a student turns eighteen and enrolls in an institution of higher education, all of the FERPA rights transfer to the student.[171] FERPA does not protect records that only contain information about an individual generated after the student has left the college or university.[172] Accordingly, alumni and fund-raising records generally fall outside FERPA.[173] On the other hand, information that was part of the individual's education record while at the institution is still protected by FERPA after graduation, as are any records produced after graduation that directly pertain to an individual's previous attendance at the institution.[174]

Privacy Rights

Q 35.10.1   What are the privacy rights students have under FERPA?

FERPA confers three privacy rights upon parents/students:

(1)   The right to inspect and review their own individual education records.[175]

(2)   The right to request that the college amend any information in the education record that the student believes is inaccurate, misleading, or otherwise in violation of the student's privacy rights.[176] The college then must follow further FERPA regulations to determine whether the record needs amendment. That process is discussed further below.

(3)   The right to consent before an institution may disclose personally identifiable information in the student's education records.[177] The consent must specify the records to be disclosed, state the purpose of the disclosure, and identify the party or parties who will receive the disclosure.[178] The right to nondisclosure without consent is subject to several exceptions, discussed in detail below.[179]

Q 35.10.2   Who enforces FERPA?

The DOE's Family Policy Compliance Office (FPCO) enforces FERPA.[180] The Secretary of the DOE designates the FPCO to investigate, process, and review complaints and FERPA violations, as well as to provide technical assistance to ensure FERPA compliance.[181] The FPCO may require a college to submit reports, information on policies and procedures, annual notifications, training materials, or other information needed to carry out its enforcement responsibilities.[182]

Q 35.10.3   Can a student bring a lawsuit against an institution for FERPA violations?

No. In *Gonzaga University v. Doe*, the Supreme Court determined that FERPA creates no private right of action.[183] The *Gonzaga* decision means that students may not sue colleges or universities in state or federal court for purported FERPA violations.[184] Instead, individuals must file a written complaint with the FPCO to assert any alleged violations.[185]

FERPA Investigations

Q 35.10.4   What is the process for FERPA investigations by the FPCO?

The FPCO enforces FERPA by investigating complaints that a college violated an individual's protected rights.[186] However, the FPCO may also decide to investigate a college's FERPA compliance on its own initiative even when no complaint is pending.[187] It may also decide to continue with an investigation if a complaint is filed but later withdrawn.[188] If a complaint is filed, it must contain specific allegations that give a reasonable basis to believe a FERPA violation occurred.[189] When such a complaint is received, the FPCO reviews the complaint, any information the college submits on its behalf, and other relevant information.[190] It may also permit the parties to submit further written or oral arguments and information pertaining to the alleged violation.[191] After the investigation, the FPCO will give the individual who filed the complaint, if any, and the college or university a written notice of its decision and the reasons why it came to the determination.[192]

The FPCO may not find that an institution violated FERPA based on a "single instance" of releasing a protected record without student consent.[193] The institution must have a "policy or practice" of allowing the release of protected student records before the FPCO will take enforcement measures.[194]

FERPA Violations

Q 35.11   What are the consequences of a FERPA violation?

If the FPCO determines that a FERPA violation exists, the FPCO will send the institution a list of conditions to meet within a certain time frame.[195] If the institution complies, the complaint is resolved. If the institution does not comply, the FPCO may take any of the following actions:

(1)   withhold further payments under any applicable federal program;

(2)   issue a complaint to compel compliance through a cease-and-desist order; or

(3)   terminate the institution's eligibility to receive federal funding.[196]

"Education Records"

Q 35.12   How does an institution determine what constitutes "education records" covered by FERPA?

Understanding what documents are protected by FERPA is essential to ensuring compliance with the regulations.[197] FERPA broadly defines "education records" as those records that are: (1) directly related to a student, and (2) maintained by an educational agency or institution or by a party acting for the agency or institution.[198] Protected information can be recorded in "any way including, but not limited to, handwriting, print, computer media, video or audio tape, microfilm, and microfiche."[199]

Subject to the exceptions discussed below, FERPA protects all "personally identifiable information" in the student record.[200] Personally identifiable information is anything that makes a student's identity "easily traceable," including the name of the student's parents, the family address, a "personal identifier" (such as the student's Social Security number or student number), "indirect identifiers" (such as date of birth, place of birth, mother's maiden name), information "linked or linkable to a specific student" that would allow someone to identify the student with "reasonable certainty," or information from a student record when disclosed to someone believed by the institution to know the student's identity.[201]

Q 35.12.1   What information is excluded from the definition of "education records"?

FERPA explicitly excludes several categories of documents from the education record.[202] The following categories of records are not FERPA-protected and may be disclosed without student consent:

(1) Records that are kept in the sole possession of the maker, used only "as a personal memory aid," and are not accessible or revealed to any other person, except someone serving as a temporary substitute for the person that made the record.[203] That includes the personal notes kept by a teacher that are not accessible to anyone else at the university or college.

(2) Records of the institution's campus safety department kept in the course of its duties to protect the security and safety of the campus community.[204] The records must be created by a law enforcement unit, for a law enforcement purpose, and maintained by the law enforcement unit.[205] Records created as part of college or university disciplinary actions against a student are still protected as part of the student's education record and are not part of this exception.[206] In addition, records created by a law enforcement unit for a law enforcement purpose but maintained by another office in the university or college are still considered part of a student's education record and protected by FERPA.[207]

(3) The employment records of a student who is employed by the college or university, as long as those records are made and maintained in the regular course of business, relate exclusively to the student's status as an employee of the school, and are not available for any other purpose.[208] Employment records of a student who is employed by the college or university as a result of the student's status as a student are still considered education records and are not part of this exception.[209]

(4) Student medical and mental health records that are

    (i) made or maintained by a physician, psychiatrist, psychologist, or other recognized medical professional;

    (ii) made, maintained, or used only in connection with treatment of the student; and

    (iii) disclosed only to those who are providing the treatment. Treatment does not include remedial educational activities that may be part of a program at the college or university.[210]

(5) Records created or received by an institution after an individual no longer attends the institution are not part of the education record; however, records that directly relate to the individual's earlier attendance at the institution remain protected.[211]

(6) Grades on peer-graded papers before they are collected and recorded by a teacher are not protected.[212]

Student Access to Records

Q 35.13　When must an institution allow students to view their education records?

Under FERPA, students must be given the opportunity to inspect and review their education records.[213] An institution must comply within a reasonable period of time, not to exceed forty-five days after receipt of the student's request.[214] In addition, FERPA requires institutions to respond to a student's reasonable requests for explanation or interpretation of the contents of the record.[215] If the student cannot exercise the right to inspect and review the records, the institution must either provide the student with a copy of the records requested or identify another means that allows the student to review them.[216] An institution may charge a fee for copying student records, as long as the fee does not effectively prevent students from exercising the right to review their education records.[217] FERPA does not allow the school to charge for searching for or obtaining the records, only to copy them.[218] The regulations bar institutions from destroying any education records that a student has requested an opportunity to view.[219] Finally, an institution is not required to give a student access to medical treatment records, but a student may request that the institution provide the record to a physician or other appropriate professional of the student's choice.[220]

Q 35.13.1   Are there any limits on students' rights to access their education records?

There are some limits on the inspection rights FERPA gives to students. First, if an education record details information about more than one student, a student may only inspect and review the information specific to that particular student.[221] An institution may refuse to allow a student to inspect and review financial records, including the financial documents relating to the student's parents.[222] A student is excluded from viewing confidential letters of recommendation in the file, as long as the student signed a waiver of the right to inspect the letters and they are related to the student's admission, application for employment, or receipt of an honor.[223] The names of the individuals who provided letters of recommendation must still be provided upon request to a student who waived the right to inspect them, and the institution may only use those letters for their intended purpose.[224] A student can revoke a waiver of the right to view confidential letters of recommendation, but the revocation only covers subsequent letters; the student still cannot inspect any letters sent before the waiver was revoked.[225]

Q 35.13.2   Can students amend their education records after inspecting them?

Once a student inspects the contents of an education record, FERPA confers on the student the right to request the amendment of any information in the record that the student finds inaccurate, misleading, or otherwise in violation of the student's privacy rights.[226] If the institution determines that the student is correct, the institution must amend the record and notify the student in writing of the change.[227] On the other hand, if the school determines that the information in the education record is not inaccurate, misleading, or otherwise in violation of the student's privacy rights, it must tell the student of the right to place a statement in the file commenting on the contested information and/or noting disagreement with the school's decision.[228]

The amendment right is interpreted to apply only to things like typographical errors and is not means for a student to challenge decisions made by teachers, such as the criteria a teacher used to determine the final grade in a class.[229]

Exceptions to Student Consent

Q 35.14   When is student consent not required for disclosure?

There are several situations where FERPA breaks from the general rule that student consent is needed before disclosing personally identifiable information in education records, including:

- when the information is not deemed to harm privacy interests (such as directory information);

- when the student is a dependent for federal tax purposes;

- when disclosure is to certain outside institutions for educational purposes;

- when disclosure is between schools; and

- when there is a court order or subpoena.[230]

Similarly, FERPA allows protected information to be disclosed in certain situations of health or safety emergency. Each situation where consent is not required for disclosure is discussed below.

Q 35.14.1   What is disclosable "directory information"?

"Directory information" means information in a student record that would not cause harm to a student or violate privacy rights if disclosed.[231] Directory information in a student record includes, but is not limited to:

- name, address, telephone number;

- student ID number, if it cannot be used to gain access to education records, except in conjunction with one or more factors that authenticate the user's identity;

- email address;

- photograph;

- date and place of birth;

- major field of study;

- grade level;

- enrollment status;

- attendance data;

- participation in officially recognized school activities and sports;

- height and weight of members of athletic teams;

- degrees received;

- most recent educational institution attended; and

- honors and awards received.

Directory information does not include a student's Social Security number.[232]

The general requirement that information in a student record may not be disclosed without consent does not apply to "directory information."[233] Institutions must give public notice to enrolled students of the type of personally identifiable information designated as directory information before that information may be disclosed.[234] Students must also receive public notice of the right to refuse to let the institution designate any or all of that information as directory information and the time period within which the student must notify the school in writing that the information may not be disclosed without consent.[235]

In 2011, FERPA was amended to clarify the regulations governing directory information. The amendments provide that a student's decision to opt out of disclosure of directory information does not allow a student to refuse to wear or display an identity card that includes directory information. Institutions may enforce policies that require students to use or wear student identity cards. The 2011 amendments also permit an institution to develop a limited directory information policy that permits disclosure only to specific parties or for specific purposes, or both.[236] This change was intended to address concerns raised by school officials who, alarmed about the increase in identity theft, expressed a need to protect the privacy of students' directory information.[237]

Adopting a limited directory information policy is optional. If an educational institution decides to adopt such a policy it must limit its directory information disclosures to those specified in the public notice.[238]

An institution does not have to give former students public notice and the opportunity to refuse consent unless the former student refused consent while still in attendance.[239]

Q 35.14.2   When can parents view education records without the student's consent?

Institutions may choose to disclose education records without student consent to parents who still claim the student as a "dependent" for federal tax purposes as defined in section 152 of the Internal Revenue Code.[240] If a student is under twenty-one years old, institutions do not need to obtain consent to disclose education records to the student's parents relating to a violation of drug or alcohol rules.[241]

Q 35.14.3   Does FERPA allow a student's former high school to send records to a university or college?

FERPA allows a student's former high school to transfer records to the postsecondary institution where the student is enrolled, upon the institution's request.[242] The student's former high school must make a reasonable attempt to notify the student at the student's last known address before transferring records to the college or university, unless the former school's annual FERPA notice provides that it forwards education records to other schools where the student seeks or intends to enroll upon the new school's request or unless the transfer is initiated by the student.[243] Upon request by the student, the former school must also give the student a copy of the record it disclosed. If these conditions are met, an institution may receive any information in the education record of a student's former school, as long as the record is forwarded because of the student's enrollment at the college or university.[244]

Q 35.14.4   What types of outside institutions can access student education records?

Institutions can sometimes disclose education records to outside institutions without first obtaining student consent.[245] The following types of organizations qualify to receive education records without student consent:

(1) A contractor, consultant, volunteer, or other party that provides outsourced institutional services or functions that would normally be performed by college or university employees.[246] The college or university may disclose personally identifiable information to such a party only for the function that party provides to the institution, and only on the condition that the third party will not disclose the information to any other party without the student's prior consent.[247] The use and maintenance of the education records must remain under the college's or university's direct control.[248] The third party may only use the protected information for the purpose designated by the college or university when it disclosed the record.[249]

(2) Information may be disclosed to another school, school system, or institution of postsecondary education where a student seeks or intends to enroll, or where the student is already enrolled. The disclosure must be related to the student's enrollment or transfer.[250]

(3) Student records may be disclosed to government agencies, including the Comptroller General of the United States, the Attorney General of the United States, the Secretary of the DOE, or state and local educational authorities.[251] The disclosure to these agencies may only be in connection with an audit or evaluation of federal or state education programs, or the enforcement of federal legal requirements relating to education programs.[252] Information collected must be protected so that the students are not personally identified by anyone other than the officials or agencies that received the records, unless the student gives written consent for the disclosure or the collection of the personally identifiable information is specifically authorized by federal law.[253]

(4) An institution may disclose information to an outside institution in connection with a student's application for financial aid.[254] The disclosure must be necessary to determine aid eligibility, amount, conditions of the aid, or aid terms and conditions.[255]

(5) Disclosure may be made to state and local officials specifically authorized to receive information relating to reporting or disclosure under the regulations of the juvenile justice system and the system's ability to service the student who is the subject of the record.[256] The officials and authorities that receive the records must certify in writing to the institution that the information will not be disclosed to any other party, except as provided under state law, without the written consent of the student.[257]

(6) An institution may also disclose information to organizations conducting studies for, or on behalf of, educational agencies or institutions to develop, validate, or administer predictive tests, administer student aid programs, or improve instruction.[258] The institution must enter into with the organization a written contract that specifies the purpose, scope, and duration of the study and the information to be disclosed; requires the organization to use personally identifiable information only to meet the study's purposes; requires the study to be conducted in a manner that does not permit personal identification of parents or students by anyone other than representatives of the organization with legitimate interests in the study; and specifies that the information must be returned or destroyed when no longer needed for the study.[259] The institution does not have to initiate the study or agree with or endorse its results.[260]

(7) Disclosure may be made to accrediting organizations for the purposes of an institution's accreditation.[261]

(8) Lastly, an institution may disclose student records to an agency case worker or other representative of a state or local child welfare agency or tribal organization, who has the right to access a student's case plan, as determined by the local, state,

or tribal organization, when the organization is legally responsible for the care and protection of the student.[262]

Q 35.14.5 Can college and university officials share information in the education record with each other?

FERPA allows protected information in student records to be shared without student consent with college officials, including teachers, who the institution determines have a "legitimate educational interest" in the student record.[263] The institution must publish a description of the criteria it uses to determine who is a "school official" and what is considered a "legitimate educational interest."[264]

Q 35.14.6 What if there is a court order or subpoena for information in a student's education record?

Institutions may disclose education records without consent to comply with a judicial order or lawful subpoena.[265] Before disclosing the information, the institution must make a reasonable effort to notify the student about the order or subpoena to give the student an opportunity to seek protective action.[266] Prior notice to the student is not required if disclosure is made in compliance with a federal grand jury subpoena or any other subpoena issued for a law enforcement purpose where the court orders that the contents of the subpoena or information obtained in response to it must not be disclosed, or if information is requested in regard to an act of domestic or international terrorism as defined by federal law.[267]

Q 35.14.7 What happens to protected records when there is a legal action between the student and the educational institution?

If a student initiates legal action against an educational institution, the institution may disclose relevant information in the education record to the court, without the student's consent, for the purpose of defending itself.[268] Should the institution initiate legal action against a student, the institution may also disclose, without the student's consent, information in the student's record that is relevant to prosecuting its claims.[269]

Q 35.14.8   What is the health or safety emergency exception?

FERPA allows records to be disclosed without a student's consent "in connection with an emergency, [to] appropriate persons if the knowledge of such information is necessary to protect the health or safety of the student or other persons."[270] The ability to release information in case of a health or safety emergency is subject to the regulations adopted by the DOE.[271] The DOE will not substitute its judgment for that of the college or university if the information available to school officials at the time of the release creates a rational basis for the determination a health or safety emergency exists.[272] The institution must keep a record in the student file of reasons for invoking the health or safety emergency exception and list the parties that received the information.[273]

Over the years, the DOE adopted regulations strictly construing the emergency exception.[274] FERPA's 2009 amendments removed the strict construction requirement in an attempt to provide "greater flexibility and deference" to administrators who seek to invoke the emergency exception to effectively protect the health or safety of an individual or the greater campus community.[275] Accordingly, FERPA now states that colleges may take into account "the totality of the circumstances" surrounding a threat to the health or safety of a student or others.[276]

FERPA requires the college or university to determine that there is an "articulable and significant threat" before information may be disclosed under the emergency exception.[277] The "articulable" threat does not mean that the threat must be verbal, but that the school must be able to articulate the nature of the threat when it makes its disclosure record.[278] The DOE explains that a significant threat may be "a threat of substantial bodily harm, to any person," including threats of "a terrorist attack, a natural disaster, a campus shooting, or the outbreak of an epidemic such as e-coli."[279] It can also be "a situation in which a student gives sufficient, cumulative warning signs that lead [the institution] to believe the student may harm himself or others at any moment."[280] The emergency exception is not intended to apply to the mere threat of an emergency (such as emergency preparedness activities), unless there is a determination that the emergency is imminent.[281]

Q 35.14.9   To whom may institutions disclose information in case of a health or safety emergency?

The health or safety emergency exception gives institutions the ability to disclose a student education record without consent to "appropriate" parties if that information is necessary to protect the health or safety of the student or others.[282] The individuals who receive the disclosure do not have to be the parties responsible for protecting the student or the community.[283] Instead, disclosure may be made to any party who will be able to help the college gather necessary information to address the threat.[284]

The DOE affirms that the following parties may receive information under the emergency exception:[285]

(1) Current or prior peers of the student or mental health professionals who can provide the institution with information to assist in protecting against the threat.

(2) A potential victim and the parents of a potential victim as "other individuals" whose health or safety needs to be protected.

(3) Other institutions that the student previously attended. The other institution may rely on the current institution's determination that an emergency exists to also disclose personally identifiable information from the student's former education records to the student's current institution to help address the threat.

(4) Law enforcement officials the institution determines can be helpful to provide appropriate protection from the threat.

(5) The student's parents or legal guardians.

The institution must make its own determination about which officials may disclose student records to appropriate parties, like the student's parents, whose knowledge of the record is necessary to protect the health or safety of the student or others.[286] The DOE recommends that institutions create a policy identifying the officials who will access and disclose information under the emergency exception.[287] Institutions are encouraged to create a "threat assessment program" that includes creating a "threat assessment team" made up of individuals with a wide degree of expertise, including law enforcement.[288]

Outsourcing Records

Q 35.15   When does FERPA allow outsourcing of information in student education records?

The 2009 FERPA amendments provide that information in the student records may be outsourced without student consent to contractors, consultants, volunteers, and other outside service providers an institution uses as "school officials" to perform institutional services and functions.[289] Information may only be outsourced when it is the type of service that would normally be performed by institution employees.[290] The DOE made the change to its regulations to support its policy that FERPA does not require institutions to provide all institutional services and functions "on an in-house basis."[291] Institutions may outsource information for such activities as fundraising, debt collection, enrollment and degree verification, transcript distribution, and information technology services.[292] Information in student records may not be outsourced for the purpose of a service that the institution would not otherwise provide; for instance, it may not be outsourced to outside parties for marketing purposes.[293]

Q 35.15.1   What steps must be taken to comply with FERPA when student education records are outsourced?

Institutions must ensure that they comply with FERPA requirements before choosing to outsource information in the student record. Outsourced information must stay under the direct control of the disclosing school.[294] For purposes of FERPA, "direct control" means retaining control over the outside institution's maintenance and use of information from student records; it does not affect the outside institution's status as an independent contractor.[295] The institution may outsource information to the outside institution only on the condition that the outside institution will not re-disclose it to any other party.[296] The outside institution may only use the protected information for the purpose designated by the college or university when it disclosed the record.[297]

Enforcement

Q 35.16   What guidance does the DOE provide for protecting access to student records within an institution?

The FERPA amendments, effective January 8, 2009, sought to specify the steps an institution must take to enforce the requirement that only college officials with a "legitimate educational interest" may view information in the education record.[298] The amendments were made because parents and students expressed concern that college officials have unrestricted access to students' education records, particularly when they are maintained electronically.[299] Institutions also reported confusion about proper methods to safeguard student records with electronic record-keeping.[300] The final regulations responded to the issue by requiring colleges to use "reasonable methods" to ensure that teachers and other institution officials only have access to the records in which they have a legitimate educational interest.[301] The "reasonable methods" requirement applies whether an institution chooses physical, technological, or administrative controls to restrict access to education records.[302]

The preamble to the latest FERPA revision defines "risk of unauthorized access" as the likelihood that records may be targeted for compromise and cause resulting harm.[303] Methods to protect records are "reasonable" if they reduce the risk those particular records will be targeted.[304] The greater the potential harm from unauthorized access, the greater the protection required.[305] High-risk records, like Social Security numbers or information that could be used to steal a student's identity, should receive greater protection than medium- or low-risk records, such as those that simply contain directory information.[306] The DOE provides that "reasonableness depends ultimately on ... the usual and customary good business practices of similarly situated institutions," which means institutions must undertake "ongoing review and modification of methods and procedures as standards and technologies change."[307]

Institutions that already use "role-based security features" that grant access to electronic records based on an institution official's professional responsibilities should be in compliance with the "reasonable methods" requirement.[308] Institutions that do not currently implement those security features should use the DOE's recent guidance to ensure they are in compliance with the new regulations.[309] An institution does not have to use physical or technological access controls; it can also use an effective administrative policy that restricts access to student records to only those officials with a legitimate educational interest.[310] If a student complains an unauthorized official gained access to the student's records, the burden is on the institution to prove the official in question had a legitimate educational interest in the record.[311]

Record-Keeping Requirements

Q 35.17 What records does FERPA require an institution to keep after it discloses information in a student education record?

When an institution discloses personally identifiable information in a student record, it must make a separate record documenting the disclosure.[312] The record of disclosure must be maintained in the file with the student's education records and kept for as long as the student records are maintained.[313] Disclosure records must identify the parties who requested or received personally identifiable information from the education record and the legitimate interest the parties had in obtaining the information.[314] For example, if the record is disclosed as part of a health or safety emergency, then the institution must record the threat to health or safety that formed the basis for the disclosure and the parties who received the information.[315]

A record of disclosure does not have to be made if the disclosure was made to the student or parent of a dependent student, a college official with legitimate educational interests, a party with written consent from the student to receive the information, a party seeking directory information, or to comply with a judicial order or lawfully obtained subpoena.[316]

Q 35.17.1   What should the institution include in its annual FERPA notice?

Institutions are required to file an annual notice that provides students with notice of their FERPA rights.[317] The notice must include information about the right to

(1) inspect and review education records;

(2) seek to have records the student believes to be inaccurate, misleading, or otherwise in violation of the student's privacy rights amended;

(3) consent to disclosures of personally identifiable information, except to the extent that FERPA authorizes disclosure without consent; and

(4) file a complaint with the FPCO within the DOE if the student believes that the institution violated any of the student's privacy rights.[318]

The notice must include the procedure for exercising the right to inspect and review records and for requesting record amendment.[319] If the institution seeks to routinely disclose information in a student record to other institution officials with a "legitimate educational interest" without student consent, the notice must also indicate the criteria the institution uses to determine who is a "school official" and what creates a "legitimate educational interest."[320]

The institution may provide the notice by any means "reasonably likely" to inform students of their rights, including students with disabilities.[321] A useful model notification of rights under FERPA is available on the FPCO website at www2.ed.gov/policy/gen/guid/fpco/ferpa/ps-officials.html.

Security/Privacy of Student Medical Records—HIPAA

Q 35.18   How are student health/medical records protected by institutions?

The Health Insurance Portability and Accountability Act of 1996 (HIPAA) is another major federal statutory scheme that seeks to protect the privacy of records.[322] HIPAA applies exclusively to information contained in health records.[323] An institution that provides healthcare to students "in the normal course of business" is considered a healthcare provider under HIPAA.[324] If the institution conducts electronic transactions covered by HIPAA, then it is a "covered entity" subject to "HIPAA Administrative Simplification Rules for Transactions and Code Sets and Identifiers."[325] For a detailed rendition of HIPAA, as well as its consequences if violated, refer to chapter 27, HIPAA Security and Privacy.

Q 35.18.1   How does FERPA interact with HIPAA?

Even when an educational institution is a covered entity under HIPAA, it is not required to comply with HIPAA if the only health records the institution maintains are "education records" or "treatment records" as defined by FERPA.[326] FERPA defines "education records" as records that are "directly related" to a student and "maintained" by the school.[327] "Treatment records" are those made about a student eighteen years or older, attending an institution of higher education, by a physician, psychiatrist, psychologist, or other recognized professional or para-professional acting in that capacity, used only in connection with providing treatment to a student, and not available to anyone other than those providing the treatment, except that a student may request the records also be reviewed by another medical professional.[328] Student treatment records are excluded from the protected education record; however, the moment that an institution discloses treatment records for any purpose other than treatment, they are subject to all FERPA requirements, including student rights to consent to disclosure and to inspect the records.[329] To disclose treatment records for any purpose, an institution must obtain student consent or meet one of the exceptions to student consent, as discussed in the FERPA section above (*see* Q 35.14 *et* seq.).[330]

Most of the medical records created by an institution will be subject to FERPA's regulations, not to HIPAA.[331] The HIPAA Privacy Rule "specifically excludes" records protected by FERPA.[332] However, if an institution also provides healthcare to individuals who are not students, those records must still comply with the HIPAA Privacy Rule.[333] An institution that operates a clinic open to staff or the public must comply with FERPA with respect to health records of student patients and the HIPAA Privacy Rule for the health records of non-student patients.[334] Patient records created by a hospital affiliated with a university are subject to HIPAA rules because hospitals provide services "without regard to the person's status as a student" and do not provide services to students on behalf of the university.[335] If a university-affiliated hospital runs the student health clinic on behalf of the university, those records are subject to FERPA, not HIPAA.[336]

Q 35.18.2 When are student records protected under HIPAA?

When a student's treatment records are disclosed to a third-party healthcare provider for the purpose of providing treatment to the student, or when the student requests the records be reviewed by another medical professional, the records become subject to the HIPAA Privacy Rule if the third-party healthcare provider is a HIPAA-covered entity.[337] Accordingly, the third-party provider must follow the HIPAA regulations to protect all "individually identifiable health information" related to the individual's past, present, or future physical or mental health, information related to its provision or healthcare, and the past, present, or future payment for the provision of healthcare to the individual.[338] Detailed information about compliance with requirements of the HIPAA Privacy Rule is available on the Department of Health and Human Services website, at www.hhs.gov/ocr/privacy/hipaa/under-standing/summary/index.html, as well as in chapter 27, HIPAA Security and Privacy.

Title IX and Sex Discrimination

Covered Institutions; Prohibited Behavior

Q 35.19   What is Title IX?

Title IX of the Education Amendments of 1972 provides the following:

> No person in the United States shall, on the basis of sex, be excluded from participation in, be denied the benefits of, or be subjected to discrimination under any education program or activity receiving Federal financial assistance.[339]

Common sources of federal financial assistance include student loans and awards, work-study programs, and research grants.

The Title IX prohibition on sex discrimination applies to all aspects of an institution's education programs or activities, including admissions, course work, employment, athletics, and other extracurricular activities. Title IX prohibits staff-on-student and student-on-student sexual harassment when officials with actual knowledge act with deliberate indifference to the discrimination.[340] Prohibited conduct also includes discrimination based on a student's actual or potential parental, family, marital status, or pregnancy and childbirth status.[341] Some argue that Title IX also prohibits discrimination and harassment against transgender students.[342]

Exemptions from Title IX coverage include, but are not limited to, the following: private institution admissions; public graduate program admissions; religious organizations with contrary religious tenets; military service and merchant marine academies; and membership in tax-exempt social fraternities or sororities.[343] Institutions are also prohibited from retaliating against any person who exercises Title IX rights.[344]

Q 35.19.1   Does Title IX apply to employees?

Yes. Title IX also prohibits employment discrimination based on sex, although there is presently a split among the federal circuits as to whether plaintiffs can pursue civil claims for employment discrimination under Title IX when Title VII of the Civil Rights Act of 1964 covers the same workplace conduct.[345] Title IX does not have the same procedural requirements as other federal employment discrimination statutes, nor does it contain any cap on monetary damages that may be recovered, but courts addressing Title IX employment discrimination claims will generally apply the same evidentiary standards applied in Title VII sex discrimination cases.[346]

Enforcement and Penalties

Q 35.19.2   What are the penalties for noncompliance with Title IX?

The DOE's Office for Civil Rights (OCR) is charged with administrative enforcement of Title IX. An institution will be held liable under Title IX if OCR finds that the institution knew or should have known about sex discrimination but failed to act promptly to eliminate the discrimination, address its effects, and prevent its recurrence. OCR may suspend or terminate federal funding to a noncompliant institution or may refer the matter to the U.S. Department of Justice for litigation.[347] Administrative complaints must be filed with OCR within 180 days of the alleged act of discrimination, although OCR may extend the filing deadline at its discretion.[348] Individuals can bring suit under Title IX and recover monetary damages and injunctive relief.[349] To recover monetary damages, a plaintiff must prove that the institution had actual knowledge of sex discrimination or was deliberately indifferent to it.[350] Reasonable attorney fees may be awarded to the prevailing party in the court's discretion under 42 U.S.C. § 1988(b).

Obligations of Covered Institutions; Compliance

Q 35.20   How is an institution obligated to respond to claims of sexual harassment among students?

Title IX requires covered educational institutions to "adopt and publish grievance procedures providing for prompt and equitable resolution" of student complaints alleging a Title IX violation.[351] In September 2017, OCR withdrew its April 4, 2011 "Dear Colleague" letter and its April 29, 2014 Questions and Answers on Title IX and Sexual Violence, which imposed specific mandates governing the procedures educational institutions were required to follow in investigating, adjudicating and resolving disciplinary matters involving sexual misconduct, including sexual harassment and sexual violence, among students. OCR has replaced this rescinded guidance with a new Q&A on Campus Sexual Misconduct, which explains OCR's current expectations of schools, and affirmed the Revised Sexual Harassment Guidance, issued in 2001 and the additional guidance in the "Dear Colleague" letter on Sexual Harassment, issued on January 25, 2006.[352]

In May 2020, the U.S. Department of Education released new Title IX regulations, which became effective on August 14, 2020.[353] The regulations require colleges to provide live hearings. The rules include a narrower definition of sexual harassment, written and substantive advance notice to the responding party of the alleged misconduct, a presumption that the accused is innocent preceding the decision-making process, strict equality of access to evidence, cross-examination between the parties, a right to an advisor, and permitting a clear and convincing evidence standard. As of the time of this writing, the Biden Administration has announced plans again to modify these regulations.[354]

Interpreting the statutory requirement for prompt and equitable resolution of sex discrimination complaints, OCR asserts in the September 2017 Q&A on Campus Sexual Misconduct that an institution that knows or reasonably should know of possible sexual harassment against students must take "steps to understand what occurred and to respond appropriately."

To fulfill this obligation, OCR requires covered institutions to incorporate the following policies and procedures when conducting disciplinary proceedings that involve sexual misconduct:

- reasonably prompt and equitable time frames for investigation and grievance resolution;

- an equitable investigation, based on sufficient evidence to reach a fair, impartial determination of claims;

- no "gag orders" or restricting the ability of either party to discuss the investigation;

- written notice to the responding party of the allegations once the school decides to open an investigation that may lead to disciplinary action with sufficient details and time to prepare a response *before* any initial interview;

- a written report at the conclusion of the investigation summarizing all relevant exculpatory and inculpatory evidence;

- a preponderance-of-the-evidence standard or a clear and convincing evidence standard should be used to determine responsibility as to each allegation of misconduct;

- equal opportunity to present relevant witnesses and evidence, cross-examine witnesses and evidence, or submit questions to be asked of parties and witnesses;

- equal and timely access to any information used at the proceeding during the informal and formal disciplinary meetings and hearings;

- equal access to documents and materials provided by the parties prior to the proceeding;

- equal access to administrators overseeing the disciplinary process;

- equal treatment in whether attorneys may participate and how they may participate in the proceedings;

- equal opportunity to respond to the report in writing in advance of the decision of responsibility;

- appellate rights solely by the responding party or by both parties, if any appellate rights are provided;

- discipline in proportion to the violation; and training of those acting as the investigator.

Additional obligations imposed by the Clery Act include:

- simultaneous written notice to both parties of the results of the proceeding and procedures to appeal, including notice of any initial, interim, or final decision, any sanctions imposed, and the rationale for the result and the sanctions;

- notice to victims of their rights and options with respect to law enforcement and judicial safeguards;

- provision of primary prevention and awareness programs;

- annual training of officials conducting disciplinary hearings involving sexual misconduct;

- notice about confidentiality for victims;

- equal rights and opportunities for parties to disciplinary proceedings involving sexual misconduct; and

- notice of sanctions or protective measures that may result from a disciplinary proceeding involving sexual misconduct.

How Title IX requirements interact with the requirements of the Clery Act as recently amended by VAWA is discussed above (*see* Q 35.9 *et seq.*).

Q 35.20.1   How can institutions minimize the risk of sexual discrimination and harassment on campus?

Each institution covered by Title IX is required to designate at least one employee as a Title IX coordinator.[355] The risk of sex discrimination and harassment on campus can be significantly reduced by integrated training and awareness programs led by the Title IX coordinator. The Title IX coordinator oversees compliance efforts, development and implementation of agreements procedures, and the investigative resolution of Title IX complaints. The name and contact information of the Title IX coordinator should be published to students and employees. The duties of the Title IX coordinator may be allocated to designated deputies, as appropriate.

Furthermore, institutions must have written policies and procedures for reporting Title IX violations and conducting prompt and equitable investigations of those complaints. Institutions must also take reasonable and timely corrective measures. Those employees participating in Title IX investigations or disciplinary proceedings must be trained appropriately. Sexual harassment and discrimination awareness programs for students and employees became mandatory March 2014 pursuant to VAWA and should have a demonstrable effect on reducing sex discrimination and harassment on campus.

Athletics Programs

Q 35.21   What does Title IX require of athletics programs?

Title IX requires athletics programs to show that they are achieving parity in three key areas:

1. *Financial Assistance.* All financial assistance based on athletic ability should be available on a substantially proportional basis to the number of male and female participants in the institution's athletic program.[356]

2. *Equal Treatment.* Male and female athletes should receive equivalent treatment, benefits, and opportunities, such as: provision of equipment and supplies; scheduling of games and practice times; travel and per diem allowance; opportunities for coaching and academic tutoring; assignment and compensation of coaches and tutors; provisions of locker rooms, practice and competitive facilities, medical and training facilities, and housing and dining facilities; and publicity, recruitment, and support services.[357]

3. *Equal Participation.* The athletic interests and abilities of male and female students must be equally effectively accommodated.[358]

Q 35.21.1   How does an athletics program demonstrate compliance with Title IX's "financial assistance" component?

Institutions that provide athletic scholarships are required to provide reasonable opportunities for the awards to members of each sex in proportion to the participation rate of each sex in intercollegiate athletics.[359] In order to demonstrate compliance, the institution must show the total amount of financial assistance awarded to men and women to be substantially proportionate to their participation rates in athletic programs.[360] For example, if 65% of an institution's intercollegiate athletes are male, the total amount of aid going to male athletes should be approximately 65% of the financial aid dollars the institution awards.

Disparities in awarding financial assistance may be justified by legitimate, nondiscriminatory (gender-neutral) factors.[361] For example, at some institutions the higher costs of tuition for out-of-state residents may cause an uneven distribution between scholarship aid to men's and women's programs as long as the programs are not the result of limitations on the availability of out-of-state scholarships to either men or women.[362]

Q 35.21.2   ... the "equal treatment" component?

Equal athletic benefits and opportunities require "equal treatment" and "effective accommodation." For equal treatment, there must be equivalence in the availability, quality and kinds of other athletic benefits and opportunities provided male and female athletes.[363] Toward this end, the EEOC examines a "laundry list" of factors for equal treatment, including:

- provision of equipment and supplies (e.g., quality, suitability, amount, maintenance, replacement, and availability);

- scheduling of games and practice times (e.g., pre-season and post-season number, length, and time of day);

- travel and per diem allowances (e.g., mode of transport, housing furnished, length of stay, per diem amount, and dining arrangements);

- provision of housing and dining facilities and services (including laundry facilities, parking space, and maid service);

- provision of medical and training (including conditioning and weight training) facilities and services (e.g., medical personnel, insurance coverage, and athletic trainers);

- provision of locker room, practice and competitive facilities (e.g., quality, availability, exclusivity of use, and maintenance);

- opportunities to receive coaching and academic tutoring (e.g., quality, availability, and funding for full-time and part-time coaches, tutors and grad assistants);

- assignment and compensation of coaches and tutors (e.g., training, experience, professional standing, contract terms, working conditions and compensation); and

- publicity and promotion (including availability and quality of sports information personnel and quantity and quality of publications).

Under this equivalency standard, if a comparison of program components indicates that benefits, opportunities, or treatment are not equivalent in quality, availability, or kind, the institution may still be in compliance with the law if the differences are shown to be the result of nondiscriminatory factors.[364]

Q 35.21.3   ... the "equal participation" component?

The equal participation component, also referred to as effective accommodation, requires that the selection of sports and levels of competition effectively accommodate the interests and abilities of members of both sexes.[365] Toward this end, an institution must demonstrate "equity in athletic opportunity," or the opportunity for individuals of each sex to participate in sports, and "equity in levels of competition," or the opportunity for athletes of each sex to have competitive team schedules that equally reflect their abilities.

There are three safe harbors for institutions to demonstrate equity in athletic opportunity, the first of which is widely considered the safest:

1. The number of participation opportunities for male and female athletes is substantially proportionate to their respective enrollments; or

2. The institution has a history and continuing practice of expanding participation opportunities responsive to the developing interests and abilities of the underrepresented sex; or

3. The institution is fully and effectively accommodating the interests and abilities of the underrepresented sex.[366]

For substantial proportionality, there is a debate about which athletes count and what deviance from exact proportionality is permitted.[367] For the program expansion test, debate concerns how long the record of expansion must extend and whether a record of merely eliminating male teams is sufficient.[368] For the third test, OCR asks:

- Is there unmet interest in a particular sport?
- Is there sufficient ability to sustain a team in the sport?
- Is there a reasonable expectation of competition for the team?

For this test, institutions commonly turn to surveys, but their sufficiency is debated. OCR looks for multiple nondiscriminatory methods of assessment.

Q 35.21.4   How can an institution show "equity in levels of competition"?

Evidence of equity in levels of competition requires evidence that athletes of each sex have competitive team schedules that equally reflect their abilities. There are two safe harbors:

1. whether the competitive schedules for men's and women's teams, on a program-wide basis, afford proportionally similar numbers of male and female athletes equivalently advanced competitive opportunities; or

2. whether the institution can demonstrate a history and continuing practice of upgrading the competitive opportunities available to the historically disadvantaged sex as warranted by developing abilities among the athletes of that sex.

Intellectual Property and Copyright Protection

Copyright Basics

Q 35.22   What does the Copyright Act protect?

The Copyright Act protects "original works of authorship fixed in any tangible medium of expression."[369] The act identifies categories of original works of authorship, which include, among other things, books, sound recordings, movies, plays, choreographic works, photographs, sculptural works, websites, and architectural works.[370]

Q 35.22.1   How is a copyright created?

Creating a copyright is relatively simple. All that is needed is an "original" work of authorship that is fixed in a tangible medium of expression.[371] Very little originality is required for something to be considered an "original" work. Authors are not obligated to produce a new or novel work, but the work should display "at least some minimal degree of creativity."[372] As low as the bar for originality is, facts themselves do not constitute originality. Copyright law protects the *expression* of facts and ideas in an underlying work, and not the facts or ideas themselves. For example, while a professor's particular depiction of the Battle of Waterloo may be protectable under copyright law, the fact that it took place is not protectable. The bar for having a work "fixed in a tangible medium of expression" is also low and extends to creations accessible via computer memory and not simply tangible, physical embodiments of works.[373]

COMPLIANCE FACT

No Formalities Required

A copyright is created the instant an original work of authorship is "fixed" under the Copyright Act. U.S. law no longer requires authors to register a copyright or provide notice to create a copyright. Although registration and notice have been removed as prerequisites, there is still value to registering a copyright and providing notice. Registration is required in the United States if the copyright owner wishes to sue a potential infringer.[374] In addition, if an author registers a work within three months of its publication or an infringement, then the author may also be entitled to seek reasonable attorney fees and statutory damages.[375] Statutory damages range from a minimum of $750 up to $30,000, and as high as $150,000 for willful infringement.[376]

Q 35.22.2   What benefits does a copyright holder enjoy?

The Copyright Act extends certain exclusive rights to copyright holders, including:

- the right to copy the copyrighted work;

- the right to distribute the copyrighted work;

- the right to perform the copyrighted work;

- the right to display the copyrighted work;

- the right to create derivatives of the copyrighted work (such as making adaptations of, or modifications to, the copyrighted work); and

- the right to make digital audio transmissions (in the case of sound recordings).[377]

Authors of copyrighted works have the ability to grant rights, or transfer ownership, in portions or all of the exclusive rights listed above to other parties.[378] For example, the author of a novel could grant or transfer all of her rights in the novel to a film producer, so that the latter could make a movie based on it. The exclusive rights, however, may be diminished through statutory exceptions[379] that allow the protected work to be used without the owner's approval.

The Work-for-Hire Doctrine

Q 35.23   Who owns the copyright in faculty-produced work?

The answer depends on the circumstances in which the work was produced. Generally, a copyright is owned by the author of the protected work. The Copyright Act, however, recognizes situations in which another entity owns the copyright. One such situation is "work made for hire," which is defined as

(1)   "a work prepared by an employee within the scope of his or her employment," *or*

(2)   a "work specially ordered or commissioned for use. . . ."[380]

Thus, when employees prepare protectable work within the scope of their employment, the employer typically owns the copyright.[381]

Institutions may be able to secure ownership in applicable copyrights if the work was specially ordered or commissioned by the institution. An example of this would be a new website that a university engaged an outside vendor to develop. However, only certain works specially ordered or commissioned by an institution are owned by the institution, including:

- a contribution to a collective work;

- a part of a motion picture or other audiovisual work;

- a translation, supplementary work, compilation, instructional text;

- a test, as well as answer material for a test; or

- an atlas.[382]

Moreover, simply commissioning a work that falls within the above categories is *not* sufficient; the parties must expressly agree *in writing* that the work shall be considered a "work made for hire."[383] Institutions should consider these requirements when engaging an independent contractor to prepare a foreword to a book or a documentary about the institution. An institution should also consider including contract provisions in any agreement it enters into with an independent contractor whereby the latter assigns all of its right, title, and interest in and to the commissioned work, including all associated intellectual property rights. In doing so, the institution may capture more than it would otherwise receive under the work-for-hire doctrine.

The Academic Exception

Q 35.23.1   Are there any exceptions to the work-for-hire doctrine?

The application of the work-for-hire doctrine in the academic setting may not be as straightforward. Some courts traditionally recognized a so-called academic exception, under which academic writing was presumed not to be a work made for hire.[384] The exception was based on the assumption that the "work" created by the professor was not rendered "within the scope" of the professor's employment because higher education institutions did not supervise their faculty in the preparation of academic books and articles. It was further assumed that the institutions were poorly equipped to exploit the works.[385] Accordingly, under this rule, if a professor chose to reduce the lectures to writing, the professor, and not the institution employing the professor, would own the copyright in the lectures.[386]

The continued strength of the academic exception, however, is questionable in light of amendments to the Copyright Act.[387] Commentators, moreover, have pointed out weaknesses in the reasoning underlying the exception.[388] More importantly, the academic exception is based on the assumption that the work falls "outside" the instructor's duties, as the instructor is hired to instruct—not to create—academic works. Where an instructor is hired specifically to create an online course, the basis for the exception disappears, and the copyright would most likely belong to the institution.

TIP: Sample contract language for commissioned work

The list of categories of work falling under "work specially ordered or commissioned" is fairly restrictive. For example, computer software usually falls outside of the work-for-hire doctrine. In addition to relying on statutory protections, institutions should consider securing their rights in copyrighted material contractually. An institution might consider using the following template contract language to obtain an assignment of commissioned work:

> VENDOR hereby irrevocably assigns and transfers to INSTITUTION all of VENDOR's right, title, and interest in and to the WORK PRODUCT, including all associated intellectual property rights. For the avoidance of doubt, this assignment includes (but is not limited to) the exclusive right to enforce, sue upon, obtain relief, and recover damages for infringement of the Work Product.

> **TIP:**
>
> ***Faculty contracts:*** An institution should be cognizant of any pro-
> vision in its policies or in a faculty member's employment agree-
> ment that effectively undermines the copyright interests that the
> institution may otherwise enjoy and establishes copyright owner-
> ship with the faculty member.
>
> ***Student work:*** Students are neither employees of an institution
> nor independent contractors; consequently, institutions likely do
> not have a copyright claim to student works unless the student
> is also an employee and the work falls within the work-for-hire
> doctrine.

Q 35.23.2   Can a faculty member use copyrighted materials without permission from the copyright owner?

Yes. In addition to the fair-use doctrine discussed below, the following exceptions exist that permit a faculty member to use copyrighted materials without permission from the owner.

The face-to-face teaching exemption. The Copyright Act allows
faculty and students to perform or display copyrighted work without
the permission of the copyright holder if the performance or display
is done "in the course of face-to-face teaching activities of a nonprofit
educational institution."[389] Moreover, the particular performance or display must be done in a classroom or similar place devoted to instruction.[390] If the previous requirements are met, teachers and students
can play television programs, movies or sound recordings, perform
plays, or read novels, provided, however, that the particular copy of
the motion picture or other audiovisual work was not unlawfully made
or the person responsible for the display or performance knew or had
reason to believe that the copy was not lawfully made. The face-to-
face teaching exemption *only* addresses performance and displaying
of copyright work and does not include things like copying, distributing, and making derivative works. Moreover, institutions should
note that the exemption is limited to the classroom and other similar

places and would not cover, for example, school performances, graduation ceremonies, or other general school events.

The TEACH Act. Recognizing that the face-to-face teaching exemption fails to address the advent of technologies that bring faculty and students together without the need for a physical presence, Congress introduced the Technology, Education and Copyright Harmonization Act of 2001 (the "TEACH Act"). While the face-to-face teaching exemption is limited to classrooms and similar settings, the TEACH Act provides for the performance and display of certain works on websites and in distance education settings without obtaining permission from the copyright holder.[391] Moreover, unlike the broad exemption afforded under the face-to-face teaching exemption, the TEACH Act has specific limitations on what materials may be used, the manner in which they may be used, and the technological restrictions that must be in place to protect the utilized materials from improper access.[392]

The Fair-Use Doctrine

Q 35.24   What is "fair use," and does it apply to institutions of higher education?

The fair-use doctrine allows a copyrighted work to be used, in certain circumstances, without permission from the copyright owner.[393] The Copyright Act states that "fair use of a copyrighted work . . . for purposes such as criticism, comment, news reporting, teaching . . . is not an infringement of copyright."[394] Four factors are used when determining whether a particular use of copyrighted material is a "fair use" under the Copyright Act, including:

(1) The purpose and character of the use, including whether such use is of a commercial nature or is for nonprofit educational purposes;

(2) The nature of the copyright work (Where is the copyrighted work on a spectrum of fact to fantasy?);

(3) The amount and substantiality of the portion used in relation to the copyrighted work as a whole; and

(4) The effect of the use upon the potential market for or value of the copyrighted work.

Fair use is an affirmative defense to a claim of copyright infringement and a fact-intensive investigation that is conducted in a legal proceeding. The above factors must be considered as a whole and cannot be evaluated in isolation. Although each factor appears straightforward in the Copyright Act itself, a large body of case law has developed a variety of nuances that must be examined. Ultimately, there is no bright- line test.

Copyright Policy

Q 35.25   Should an institution implement a copyright policy?

Yes. Implementing an institution-wide copyright policy may provide certain protections that institutions would not otherwise be entitled to enjoy. For example, under the Copyright Act, courts shall

> remit statutory damages in any case where an infringer believed and had reasonable grounds for believing that his or her use of the copyrighted work was a fair use under section 107, if the infringer was . . . an employee or agent of a nonprofit educational institution, library, or archives acting within the scope of his or her employment who infringed by reproducing the work in copies or phonorecords . . . .[395]

Given the potential reduction in exposure that a nonprofit educational institution may enjoy under section 504 of the Copyright Act, institutions should take steps to ensure that their faculty are familiar with the fair-use doctrine, which can be achieved by introducing a copyright policy.

COMPLIANCE FACT

Agreement on Guidelines for Classroom Copying in Not-for-Profit Educational Institutions

During debate over the 1976 Copyright Act, guidelines were included in the House of Representatives Report on the pending

---

bill.[396] Backed by content holders and industry supporters, the guidelines were advertised as intending to help educators better understand the fair-use provisions relating to copying protected work for educational use. It should be emphasized, however, that the guidelines are not legally binding. Moreover, while they appear to provide some certainty for the fair-use doctrine, critics point out the guidelines are very rigid and much more restrictive than what is available under the fair-use doctrine.

Liability for Copyright Infringement

Q 35.26   What exposure does an institution face if found liable for copyright infringement?

A party defending against claims of copyright infringement faces a number of possible penalties, including the actual damages suffered by the copyright owner, as well as profits made by the infringer as a result of the infringing activity.[397] Instead of actual damages, a copyright holder may seek statutory damages, which gives courts the flexibility to award from $750 to $30,000 per infringed work.[398] Moreover, if a court concludes that the infringement was committed willfully, the ceiling of the statutory damage award is raised to $150,000.[399] In addition to monetary relief, an injured party can request an injunction, through which a party asks the court to order another party to act, or refrain from acting, in a particular manner.

TIP: Fair use is a *defense* to an allegation of copyright infringement. Institutions should consider other options before simply relying on the fair-use defense, such as:

*   whether the institution has a statutory right to use the copyrighted materials, such as those rights afforded by the face- to-face teaching exemption or the TEACH Act;

- whether the institution should seek express permission from the copyright holder to use the protected material, which may be difficult if the copyright holder cannot be found or demands compensation;

- whether a license for the material is available through copyright brokers;[400] or

- whether there are grounds for asserting that the institution has an implied right to use the protected work, which may be the case if the surrounding circumstances suggest that the copyright owner gave the institution permission to use the protected material.

Q 35.26.1   Can an institution be liable for copyright infringement based on the acts of its students or faculty?

As a general proposition, an institution can be held liable for the acts of its students or faculty under a theory of indirect liability. (As discussed elsewhere in this chapter, there are steps that an educational institution can take to reduce the potential liability for copyright infringement based on the actions of its students or faculty.) Indirect liability comprises two separate theories: contributory infringement and vicarious liability. Contributory infringement rests on the premise that a third party, such as a university, can be liable for the actions of the copyright infringer if the university (1) knew or should have known of the infringing activity, and (2) provided a material contribution in the form of assistance or inducement to the alleged infringement. Vicarious liability can be found where a party has (a) the right and ability to control another party, and (b) receives a direct financial benefit from allowing the infringement to occur. Consider a student using the computer networks provided by his university to illegally share music files with other students as an example of potential contributory infringement. Institutions could also be held vicariously liable for the actions of its faculty, unless protected under the Digital Millennium Copyright Act (discussed below).

In addition to contributory infringement and vicarious liability, institutions present an attractive target due to joint and several liability. Under joint and several liability, a plaintiff can seek to recover the full damage amount from multiple defendants, regardless of each defendant's relative responsibility. The case of a copyright holder suing a student and his college for copyright infringement presents a good example. The copyright holder is awarded a $1 million judgment, and the court finds that the student is 98% responsible for the infringement and the college is 2% responsible. Under joint and several liability, the copyright holder could seek to enforce the judgment against the college alone, requiring it to pay the total amount. The college's recourse would then be to sue its own student to recover $980,000. The theory behind joint and several liability is that defendants are better able to allocate damages among themselves. It protects the injured party against the possibility that one of the defendants is unable to pay the allocated portion of liability. Unless the student is independently wealthy, it is safe to assume that a plaintiff will be focusing on the institution to collect when joint and several liability applies.

Q 35.26.2   Can an institution limit its exposure from students who use the institution's computer network to commit copyright infringement?

Although institutions that provide Internet access to their students face exposure for transmitting copyrighted material through an institution's networks, this exposure can be mitigated through affirmative steps. In 1999, Congress enacted the Digital Millennium Copyright Act (DMCA)[401] to establish a safe harbor from copyright infringement for Internet service providers (ISPs). Institutions, if acting as ISPs, can qualify for the safe harbor protections afforded under the DMCA and avoid contributory infringement for copyright infringement committed by their students.[402]

Provided that all of the DMCA's requirements are met, an institution acting as an ISP may be granted immunity from suit for the following four types of activities:

(1) **Transitory digital network communications.**[403] The transitory safe harbor addresses situations in which students are

using a university's network to illegally share copyrighted material. The DMCA provides a safe harbor for the automatic transmission of material through the ISP's network if the transmission was initiated by someone other than the service provider; the transmission, storage, routing, or provision of connections is provided through an automatic technical process without selection of material by the service provider; the service provider does not select recipients or modify the content; the material is stored for no longer than is necessary; and the material is not generally accessible to others besides the intended recipient.[404]

(2) **System caching.**[405] System caching is the process through which data and information can be accessed by a computer faster by saving a copy of the data locally instead of requiring the requesting party to go back to the original source of the data.

(3) **Information residing on systems or networks at the direction of users.**[406] This safe harbor protects against infringement resulting from the posting of copyrighted material on a network controlled by an institution. To qualify for this safe harbor, the institution must

   (a) have no actual knowledge that the material is infringing;

   (b) not be aware of facts or circumstances from which infringing activity is apparent;

   (c) take action expeditiously to remove the material;

   (d) not receive a financial benefit directly attributable to the infringing activity in cases in which the university has the right to control the activity;

   (e) designate an agent to receive notifications of claimed infringement;

   (f) make certain information about the designated agent available on its website;

   (g) provide certain information to the Copyright Office; and

(h) comply with the requisite notice and take-down procedures after receiving a proper notification from the copyright holder (or a party acting on the authority of the copyright holder) that the material is infringing copyrighted work.[407]

(4) **Information location tools.**[408] The DMCA also provides a safe harbor for ISPs for referring or linking users to online locations containing infringing material through hypertext links or other information location tools, provided, of course, the ISP complies with the necessary requirements.

To qualify for any of the safe harbors, an ISP or host must also adopt, implement, and inform users of its policy that provides for the termination of user access to the ISP's system or network where the user is a repeat infringer.[409] Such a policy may include features that would allow an institution to monitor user activity and note repeated complaints about a particular user's actions. The policies should be published and publicized so that students are aware of the monitoring that is taking place and understand the consequences of infringement.

Q 35.26.3   Does the DMCA address copyright infringement by faculty and graduate students?

The DMCA contains provisions stating that, under certain circumstances, faculty members and graduate students employed by an institution that acts as an ISP will not be deemed employees of that institution for purposes of liability and their knowledge or awareness of their infringing activities will not be attributed to the institution.[410] To qualify for this status, the following conditions must be met:

- The faculty member's or graduate student's infringing activities must not involve the provision of online access to instructional materials that are or were required or recommended within the proceeding three-year period by that faculty member or graduate student;

- The institution has not, within the preceding three-year period, received more than two notifications under the DMCA that the faculty member or graduate student was infringing; and

- The institution provides all of its system and network users with informational materials that accurately describe and promote compliance with U.S. copyright laws.

TIP: Compliance with the DMCA

The DMCA is a valuable resource for protecting against certain liability threatening institutions due to the growing popularity of computer networking and file sharing. Protection under the DMCA, however, is not automatic, and coming into compliance to enjoy the benefits of the safe harbor is not easy. An institution wishing to meet the requirements of the DMCA should seek legal counsel.

Export Controls

Q 35.27 Why should U.S. institutions of higher education be concerned with export controls?

One does not intuitively connect universities with the highly technical and complex system of U.S. export controls. The word "export" in its common usage might lead some to believe that concerns about export controls arise only when they are shipping something abroad. Generally, the U.S. export controls regime is shaped by economic, national security, and foreign policy interests, and places restrictions on the shipping of defense items or dual-use items (items that have both commercial and military applications) and on most types of dealings with sanctioned persons and destinations under U.S. embargoes.[411] The controls do not stop at the actual hardware, but encompass information necessary for the design, production, development, or use of the controlled item.

Universities are in the business of expanding knowledge through teaching and research and—with the unlikely exception of test equipment and the more likely reality of traveling abroad with a personal laptop—rarely ship anything abroad. But as institutions that share and transfer knowledge, universities have come into the sights of U.S. export enforcement personnel and are struggling to square the nightmarish restrictions of export controls when it comes to teaching and sharing information and knowledge in an open academic environment.

Export controls present unique challenges to an institution of higher education because they require balancing concerns about national security and U.S. economic vitality with traditional concepts of unrestricted academic freedom and publication and dissemination of research findings and results. University researchers and administrators need to be aware that these laws may apply to research, whether sponsored or not. However, it also is important to understand the extent to which the regulations do not affect normal university activities.[412]

For a more detailed overview of export control issues, see chapter 19.

Federally Sponsored Research

Q 35.28   What specific requirements pertaining to research sponsored by a federal grant or contract should institutions be aware of?

Conducting research with federal dollars comes with hefty federal obligations. Most of these obligations are set forth within the grant or contract funding documents itself. However, the Office of Management and Budget (OMB) issued the Uniform Administrative Requirements, Cost Principles, and Audit Requirements for Federal Awards, which is guidance that encompasses numerous additional demands on recipient institutions.[413]

In addition, specific regulations from the agency administering the funding often require various internal control and reporting obligations.[414] Other federal statutory and regulatory obligations exist that impose compliance obligations on recipients of federal funds, such as the civil False Claims Act (FCA).

Among the obligations that present the greatest concerns to many institutions are:

- time and effort reporting;
- summer salary calculations and reporting;
- cost transfers; and
- cost sharing.

Additionally, institutions should be aware of issues related to federally funded human-subject research, research supported by "stimulus" money, and patentable inventions created with the help of federal funds.

Accounting and Reporting Effort and Costs

Q 35.28.1   What are an institution's obligations regarding time and effort reporting?

Many grant agreements support faculty time and effort on research projects. Often the salaries charged to a sponsored project are set initially on the basis of an estimate before the work is performed. The institution must then submit some form of "after-the-fact" confirmation, affirming the distributed costs represent actual costs, unless some other satisfactory alternative method is reached with the federal agency. If a faculty member's time deviates "substantially" from the estimates provided, then the federal granting agency's prior approval is required. "Substantially" has been recognized as a faculty member's effort reduced by 25% or work not performed for a period of three or more months.[415] It is not necessary to report short fluctuations in a faculty member's workload as long as the distribution of time is reasonable over the longer term (such as an academic period).

These requirements have proven problematic for many institutions when faculty and principal investigators report greater progress made than they actually achieved. This "over-reporting" may violate the terms of the grant, as well as the civil FCA, because it may be viewed as a knowing submission of a false claim for payment with federal dollars. The implications of the civil FCA in this area are discussed in detail below.

Q 35.28.2   ... summer salary calculations and reporting?

The accounting of summer salaries for faculty working on sponsored research is an aspect of effort reporting that poses significant challenges to institutions. Stipends must be included as a part of the faculty member's total salary: The faculty member's base rate of pay received from the institution must be equal to or more than the rate paid under the grant or contract.[416] For example, where a faculty member is paid a base salary of $90,000 for working a nine-month school year, that faculty member has a $10,000-per-month base salary rate. If she conducts research pursuant to a federal grant during the remaining three summer months, then her allowable compensation may not exceed her base salary rate of $10,000 per month.[417] She cannot be compensated more than $10,000 per month or $30,000 for working the months of June, July, and August.

In addition, an institution must be careful to ensure that the base rate encompasses the compensation for all the work that the faculty member does during the summer months. In instances where a faculty member conducts the sponsored research 70% of her time during the summer months and during the remaining 30% she continues to engage in other institutional or administrative activities, such as proposal writing, then the institution may not charge 100% of an individual's salary to a federally sponsored research project. Only the percentage of the faculty member's time that is allocated to the research may be charged to the research grant. In the example provided, it would be up to 70%, or $7,000 per month.

Q 35.28.3   ... cost transfers?

Cost transfers refer to the moving of a transaction cost from one sponsored project to another. The cost accounting standards for higher educational institutions require cost transfers to be reasonable, allocable, and allowable under the sponsored research agreement.[418] Many grant agreements prohibit the moving of one transaction from one sponsored project to another, except in specified circumstances. Some institutions have encountered problems with this requirement due to shortages in grant funding that may exist. An improper cost transfer may violate the terms of the grant agreement as well as implicate the civil FCA, as described in detail below.

Q 35.28.4   ... cost sharing?

Cost sharing is most often represented as an institution's financial contribution toward a sponsored project. The uniform administrative requirements for institutions of higher education set the threshold standard for what may be allocated as a cost-share expense.[419] The cost must:

(a)   be verifiable from the recipient's records,

(b)   not be included as contributions from any federal award,

(c)   be necessary and reasonable for the objectives of the project or program,

(d)   be an allowable cost under the terms of the grant itself,

(e)   not be paid by the federal government under another award, except when authorized by statute,

(f)   be provided for in an approved budget when required by the federal awarding agency, and

(g)   not be unrecovered indirect costs unless prior approval is received from the awarding agency.

Human-Subject Research

Q 35.28.5   ... human-subject research?

The Department of Health and Human Services requires numerous basic protections in connection with human-subject research.[420] An institution of higher education's institutional review board (IRB) must comply with standards relating to:

- membership;[421]

- written procedures;[422]

- written assurances;[423]

- IRB review;[424]

- maintenance of records for a minimum three-year period;[425] and

- early research termination.[426]

In addition, the IRB is required to have specific procedures for protection of:

- pregnant women involved in research;[427]
- human fetuses and neonates involved in research;[428] and
- prisoners involved in biomedical and behavioral research.[429]

Patentable Inventions

Q 35.28.6   ... patentable inventions created with federal money?

The Bayh-Dole Act,[430] also known as the University and Small Business Patent Procedures Act, sets forth guidelines that provide protection and ownership rights of inventions created by institutions with the help of federal funds. The act is important because it reversed a long-standing presumption of title and permits an institution to elect to pursue ownership of an invention ahead of the government. The act applies to all inventions conceived or first actually reduced to practice in the performance of a federal grant, contract, or cooperative agreement. This is true even if the federal government is not the sole source of funding for either the conception or the reduction to practice.[431] The act does not apply to federal grants that are primarily for the training of students and post-doctoral scientists. It sets forth various requirements in connection with the protection of intellectual property rights.[432] Some of the more salient requirements fall into three broad categories related to disclosure, title requirements, and reporting.

Relating to disclosure, the act requires an institution to disclose its invention to the funding agency within a reasonable time after it is disclosed internally to the institution.[433] Procedures must be in place to ensure that inventions are promptly identified and timely disclosed.[434] This includes a written agreement with faculty and technical staff requiring disclosure and assignment of inventions.[435] The act also requires the designation of a point of contact for communications on matters relating to patent rights.[436]

Relating to the retention of title, the act provides that an institution must adhere to a specific decision timeline in connection with expressing its intent to retain title in an invention.[437] It also requires an institution to execute and promptly deliver to the agency all instruments necessary to establish or confirm government rights in inventions that the institution elects to retain and then to convey title to the agency when requested so that the government may obtain patent protection throughout the world.[438]

Finally, the Bayh-Dole Act requires the submission of periodic reports regarding the utilization of the invention in accordance with the funding agency's request.[439]

False Claims Act Considerations

Q 35.29   How does False Claims Act liability affect institutions?

Civil False Claims Act liability is one of the most significant risks of inaccurate certifications, reporting, and other submissions. Institutions that receive or administer federal funding may subject themselves to liability under the civil FCA[440] if they make inaccurate certifications or reports that are paid with federal dollars; use "false statements" or certifications that are material to a false claim; conspire to violate the act; and fail to disclose and return overpayments or other obligations owed to the government. (For a more detailed analysis of the FCA and the risks and liabilities it can cause, see chapter 12.) This act creates liability for the "knowing" submission of false or fraudulent claims to the U.S. government. "Knowing" can include both actual knowledge and "reckless disregard" or "deliberate ignorance" of compliance obligations. Violators can be required to pay treble damages plus civil penalties between $5,500 and $11,500[441] for each false claim submitted. The FCA also permits private citizens with information about the submission of false claims to file a civil false claims action on behalf of, and in the name of, the United States. These actions are referred to as qui tam (or "whistleblower") lawsuits, and the person who brings them is permitted by statute to share in any recovery that is obtained for the government. Another potential consequence of violating the FCA is the possibility of being suspended, debarred, or excluded from future participation in government-funded programs.[442]

In addition to the federal False Claims Act, many states have their own similar statutes.

Since the inception of the FCA, the government has—as have whistleblowers—aggressively pursued FCA cases against government contractors, healthcare providers, and pharmaceutical manufacturers, while institutions of higher education initially were not "on enforcement's radar." However, since the mid-1990s, institutions increasingly have become targets of FCA enforcement. The uptick in activity is best seen in the areas of improper medical billing, certifications regarding adherence to state and federal laws, and federally sponsored research. Few claims have made their way to trial or verdict. Instead, as discussed below and similar to civil FCA activity in other industries, institutions have entered into settlement agreements to resolve the allegations. Many of these settlements are entered into without the institutions admitting liability and with the promise to develop their compliance programs.

Q 35.29.1   How does improper medical billing expose institutions to False Claims Act liability?

Teaching hospitals and universities have been targeted for allegations related to improperly billing medical services to a federally funded program, such as Medicaid or Medicare. Liability may attach when the institution submits a false claim for payment or reimbursement for medical services provided. This may occur when services are "knowingly" or "recklessly" billed inaccurately, often causing the federal agency to pay more than the institution was to receive. Some of the more prominent settlements are set forth below.

Q 35.29.2   How do certification requirements regarding adherence to federal and state laws expose institutions to False Claims Act liability?

Civil FCA liability has begun to gain greater traction within the higher-education community related to certifications made in connection with the receipt of government funding. In particular, in 2006, the Ninth Circuit confirmed that an institution could face FCA liability when it falsely certifies compliance with a statute or regulation that is a condition to government payment.[443] Ultimately, the court will entertain claims of liability as long as a certified statement is know-ingly false when made and that statement is a condition to payment by the government.[444] "Knowingly" includes claims or certifications that are made in "reckless disregard" of their accuracy. Therefore, certifi-cations that are made without confirmation regarding their accuracy could potentially lead to significant liability. Below are a few exam-ples of cases where significant settlements were reached in the face of alleged false certification of adherence to federal and state laws.

 CASE STUDIES: *FCA Settlements Involving Institutions and Medical Billing*

The Clinical Practices of The University of Pennsylvania (Dec. 1995).[445] A $30 million settlement of allegations that the insti-tution submitted false Medicare bills for services performed by hospital residents when they were allegedly performed by faculty teaching physicians. The government claimed, among other things, that attending physicians may receive Medicare reimbursement only if they are personally involved in the care of Medicare ben-eficiaries being treated by residents. The settlement also resolves allegations of billing errors, as well as coding errors regarding the level of services provided by attending physicians.

The University of Texas Health Science Center at San Antonio (June 1998).[446] A $17.2 million settlement of allegations that the center submitted false claims for reimbursement to several fed-erally funded healthcare insurance programs. A component of the university allegedly submitted claims to Medicare, Medicaid, and other federal programs between January 1990 and December 1995 without possessing sufficient documentary evidence to sup-port those claims.

The University of California (Feb. 2001).[447] A $22.5 million settle-ment of allegations that physicians at teaching hospitals at UCLA and four other campuses overbilled the government in filing Medi-care claims. The payment was to compensate for overcharges for physician services at the medical centers between 1994 and 1998.

New Jersey University Hospital (June 2009).[448] A $2 million settlement of allegations that the hospital submitted duplicate claims for payment under Medicaid when it submitted claims for outpatient physician services that physicians working in the hospital's outpatient centers also billed.

Robert Wood Johnson University Hospital (Hamilton) (Mar. 2010).[449] A $6.35 million settlement of allegations that the hospital fraudulently inflated its charges, in the form of supplemental outlier payments, to Medicare patients in order to obtain larger Medicare reimbursements.

University of Texas Southwestern Health Systems (UTSW) (Sept. 2011).[450] A $1.4 million settlement of allegations that UTSW and Parkland Health and Hospital System violated the civil FCA and Texas Medicaid Fraud Prevention Act by causing "up-coded" claims to be submitted to Medicare and Medicaid for teaching physician–related items and services between 2004 and 2007.

Columbia University (Oct. 2011).[451] A $955,000 settlement of allegations that Dr. Erik Golubaff, Columbia University, and the New York Presbyterian Hospital fraudulently caused Medicare to be overbilled for urological procedures and tests that were medically unnecessary. This settlement alleged that from 2003 to 2009, in addition to Dr. Golubaff conducting medically unnecessary procedures and tests, he billed for them in a way to generate improper and excessive reimbursements and billed Medicare for more procedures than he was physically able to perform.

Temple University (May 2012).[452] A $1,088,574 settlement of allegations resolving Temple's voluntary disclosure that Dr. Joseph Kubacki, formerly the Chairman of Temple's Ophthalmology Department, and Temple University improperly billed the United States for medical services provided by residents as though they had been performed by attending physicians.

Baylor University Medical Center (Nov. 2012).[453] A $907,355 settlement with Baylor Health Care System and Health Texas Provider Network related to allegations that Baylor submitted improper claims to Medicare from 2006 through May 2010. The government alleged that Baylor either inaccurately billed or double-billed Medicare for several procedures affiliated with radiation treatment plans.

Duke University Health System (Mar. 2014).[454] A $1 million settlement of allegations that Duke, a nonprofit corporation that runs three hospitals, violated the federal and North Carolina False Claims Acts by making false claims related to the alleged improper (1) billing of the government for services provided by medical trainees and physician assistants (PAs) during surgeries, and (2) increasing of billing by unbundling claims when the unbundling was not appropriate.

Q 35.29.3   How has federally sponsored research exposed institutions to False Claims Act liability?

FCA liability within the context of federally sponsored research is largely attributed to inaccurate reporting of costs and effort expended by faculty members and principal investigators. The government's theory has been that the institution inaccurately represented to the government the status of the faculty's effort and cost expended and, therefore, improperly received funding based on these false submissions. In several instances, the institutions reached settlements with the government to resolve these allegations. Some of the more prominent case studies of FCA settlements related to federally sponsored research funding are set forth below.

Q 35.29.4   Are public institutions immune from claims under the False Claims Act?

Public institutions are not immune from claims brought by the federal government; however, they may be immune from suits by private citizens unless state law authorizes the claim. The Eleventh Amendment prohibits suits in federal courts against public institutions of higher education and other state government entities by a state's own citizens or citizens of another state or foreign country.[455] However, the Eleventh Amendment does not bar the United States itself from bringing suit against a state in federal court.[456] Therefore, a public institution is not immune from suit when the federal government itself intervenes in a private suit brought under the FCA.

 CASE STUDIES: *FCA Settlements Involving Institutions and Certifications of Adherence to Federal/State Laws*

Alta Colleges, Inc. (Apr. 2009). A $7 million settlement of allegations that Alta made false representations to receive federal financial student aid. In particular, it was alleged that it misrepresented that it met Texas state licensing requirements related to: (a) state job-placement reporting and (b) program compliance with professional license requirements. The government alleged that Alta obtained the requisite state licensing by misrepresenting to the state licensing agency that it complied with these requirements.[457]

University of Phoenix (Dec. 2009).[458] A $78.5 million settlement of a long-running FCA qui tam suit that alleged the institution unlawfully rewarded recruiters for enrolling students. This suit came after a 2006 Ninth Circuit decision that held that an institution could be liable when it falsely certifies compliance with any statute or regulation that is a condition of government funding.

Rush University Medical Center (Mar. 2010).[459] A $1.5 million settlement of allegations that Rush violated the FCA by entering into impermissible financial arrangements with physicians in the form of rent concessions on medical office space leased to those physicians. The government took the position that to submit bills to Medicare and Medicaid for services referred by the physicians with whom Rush had impermissible financial relationships constituted false claims under the civil FCA. According to the government, the Stark Law prohibited Rush from billing Medicare and Medicaid for those services, and Rush improperly certified in its cost reports that the services were provided consistent with applicable law.

Fort Valley State University (a/k/a University Systems of Georgia) (Jan. 2010).[460] A $500,000 settlement of allegations that, from June 1, 2001, to April 30, 2007, the university's senior administrators and personnel falsely certified compliance with the specific requirements of a $2.5 million National Science Foundation cooperative agreement.

 CASE STUDIES: *FCA Settlements Involving Institutions and Federally Sponsored Research*

University of Minnesota (Nov. 1998).[461] A $32 million settlement, $4.7 million of which went to resolve inflated billings related to federal grants, of allegations that the university illegally profited by selling an unlicensed drug, failed to report to the National Institutes of Health income from selling the drug, improperly tested the drug on patients without their informed consent, and inflated billings on twenty-nine federal grants. The university also allegedly charged salaries and supplies to federal grants for employees who did not work on the grant and for supplies that were not used toward the research funded with the grant.

Northwestern University (Feb. 2003).[462] A $5.5 million settlement of allegations that the university violated the FCA related to federally sponsored medical research grants. The university allegedly overstated the percentage of its researchers' work effort that it was able to devote to the grant and failed to comply with the grant's requirement that a specified percentage of the researchers' effort be devoted to the grant.

Johns Hopkins University (Feb. 2004).[463] A $2.6 million settlement of allegations that the university overstated its principal investigator's effort on federal projects—the work amounted to more than 100% of the individual's time.

Harvard University (July 2004).[464] A $3.3 million settlement of allegations that the university overcharged federal grants by seeking reimbursements for the salaries of researchers who did not work on the grant or who did not meet citizenship requirements, and for equipment and supplies not used on the grant projects.

Florida International University (Feb. 2005).[465] An $11.5 million settlement of allegations that the university improperly billed researchers' salaries, travel, and administrative expenses during a seven- to ten-year period.

University of Alabama at Birmingham (Apr. 2005).[466] A $3.39 million settlement of allegations that the university and two related entities overstated the percentage of work effort that the researchers were able to devote to the grant. It was also alleged that Medicare was improperly billed for clinical research trials that were also billed to the sponsor of research grants.

St. Louis University (July 2008).[467] A $1 million settlement of allegations that the university engaged in a scheme to defraud the government by overstating the time certain faculty members were spending on grants received from the Centers for Disease Control and Prevention. The university allegedly failed to comply with federal requirements to maintain a system that accurately tracked hours worked on by federal grants.

Yale University (Dec. 2008).[468] A $7.6 million settlement for allegations to resolve two types of claims related to the FCA and related common law requirements in the management of more than 6,000 federally funded research grants. The first allegation concerned some improper cost transfers. Researchers were allegedly motivated to carry out these transfers when the federal grant was near its expiration date, and the remaining funding had to be expended or returned to the government. The second allegation concerned researchers submitting time and effort reports for summer salaries paid from federal grants. They allegedly falsely charged 100% of their summer effort to federal grants when, in fact, they expended significant effort on other unrelated work.

Weill Medical College of Cornell (Mar. 2009).[469] A $2.6 million settlement of allegations of false statements made to the National Institutes of Health and the Department of Defense in connection with Weill's federal grant applications. An investigator allegedly failed to disclose the full extent of her various active research projects, depriving the government of its ability to assess the investigator's ability to perform the projects in the grant application. Weill allegedly knew, or should have known, that this investigator failed to fully disclose her active research projects in the grant applications, because the totality of her research commitments exceeded 100% of her available time.

Morehouse College (Aug. 2011).[470] A $1.2 million civil settlement related to allegations of improper use of grant funds awarded by NASA and the NSF, which were intended to encourage participation by students in the science, technology, engineering, and mathematics fields of study. That investigation allegedly revealed that a former employee at Morehouse responsible for administering the grants had expended some funds for personal travel expenses and equipment and services that were not permitted under the terms of the grant.

However, when the federal government does not intervene and the suit is brought by a qui tam plaintiff, the institution's jurisdiction may dictate its immunity exposure under the FCA. The Fifth Circuit and D.C. Circuit have made it clear that an FCA suit against a public institution will be barred under the Eleventh Amendment when the federal government has not actively intervened in the action.[471] However, the Fourth Circuit and Eighth Circuit have held that, since a qui tam suit against a state is essentially a suit by and for the United States, then the Eleventh Amendment does not preclude a qui tam suit in federal court.[472] Until the Supreme Court or Congress weighs in definitively, it is important for public institutions to be aware of the perils of the FCA and to be just as vigilant as private institutions to ensure the accuracy and reliability of their accounting and reporting.

COMPLIANCE FACT

Despite the Eleventh Amendment's immunity protections, public institutions of higher education remain exposed to FCA liability. Even though some jurisdictions are more lenient than others in their view of who is permitted to bring suit, the various FCA settlements against public universities demonstrate that a public institution's exposure to FCA liability is real and should be taken seriously.

Q 35.30   How can an institution limit its exposure to False Claims Act liability?

Establishing a compliance program that has checks in place for accuracy in reporting and adherence to accounting and tracking standards will help to limit an institution's exposure to the FCA. For example, the program should set forth affirmative policies and procedures related to the accounting and tracking of bills submitted related to work performed and costs expended. The institution also should educate and train its faculty and staff on the procedures and periodically audit submissions being made to federal agencies. Moreover, the institution should develop a confidential means for faculty and staff to bring potentially inappropriate billing and reporting practices to the institution's attention to be addressed before they create a foundation for FCA allegations.

When an institution has an effective compliance program in place, it may argue more convincingly that it did not knowingly submit false claims, but rather that any such claims either were innocent mistakes or were the independent and unauthorized acts of faculty or staff.[473]

Notes to Chapter 35

1. For ease of reference, colleges, universities, and higher-education institutions are referred to herein as "institutions."

2. The FAR is codified in 48 C.F.R. pts. 1–53. *See* chapter 15, Government Contractors (discussing compliance programs and the FAR).

3. The compliance and ethics program is required to: (1) have a written code of business ethics and conduct; (2) have the code available to all employees involved in performance of the contract; (3) encourage "due diligence" to prevent and detect improper conduct; (4) promote an organizational culture that encourages ethical conduct and a commitment to compliance with the law; (5) promote the timely disclosure, in writing, to the agency Office of the Inspector General (OIG), with a copy to the contracting officer, whenever the contractor has credible evidence of a violation of federal criminal laws or a violation of the civil False Claims Act (31 U.S.C. § 3729 *et seq.*); and (6) promote the full cooperation in government audits, investigations, or corrective actions relating to contract fraud and corruption.

4. Higher Education Act of 1965, Pub. L. No. 89-329, 79 Stat. 1219 (codified at 20 U.S.C. § 1001 *et seq.*), *amended by* Higher Education Opportunity Act, Pub. L. No. 110-315, 122 Stat. 3078 (Aug. 14, 2008). References hereinafter to "HEA" and sections thereof are to the Higher Education Act of 1965 as amended. *See* HEA §§ 153(c)(3), 487(a)(25), 487(e).

5. This was recognized in 2005 when draft compliance guidance was submitted by the Office of Inspector General (OIG) for recipients of Public Health Service (PHS) research awards. The draft guidance elaborated on the fundamental principles of a compliance program for colleges, universities, and other recipients of PHS awards for biomedical and behavioral research. The proposed guidance emphasized written policies, review at regular intervals, and broad promulgation. *See* 70 Fed. Reg. 71,312 (Nov. 28, 2005).

6. U.S. SENTENCING GUIDELINES MANUAL § 8C2.5(f); *see also* Nathan A. Adams IV, *Academic Compliance Programs: A Federal Model with Separation of Powers*, 41 J.C. & U.L. 1 (2015).

7. *See* Press Release, Pa. Attorney Gen., Child Sex Charges Filed Against Jerry Sandusky, Two Top Penn State University Officials Charged with Perjury & Failure to Report Suspected Child Abuse (Nov. 5, 2011).

8. *See* Press Release, U.S. Dep't of Educ., U.S. Department of Education to Investigate Penn State's Handling of Sexual Misconduct Allegations (Nov. 9, 2011), www.ed.gov/news/press-releases/us-department-education-investigate-penn-states-handling-sexual-misconduct-alleg.

9.   *See* Penn State Live, Report of the Board of Trustees [for Penn State University] Concerning Nov. 9 Decisions (Mar. 12, 2012), http://live.psu.edu/story/58341#rss49.

10.   *See* Kris Maher, *Penn State Faces Years in Court*, WALL ST. J., June 25, 2012, at A3, http://online.wsj.com/article/SB10001424052702304870304577486532081723146.html (noting that at least one alleged victim filed suit against Penn State University alleging that the university failed to protect him from Sandusky); *see also* Kevin Johnson, *After Sandusky Verdict, Focus Now Shifts to Penn State*, USA TODAY (June 24, 2012), www.usatoday.com/news/nation/story/2012-06-23/sandusky-penn-state-abuse-scandal/55782164/1.

11.   *See* Morganne Mallon, *Penn State Board of Trustees Vote to Settle Lawsuit with Person Abused by Jerry Sandusky*, DAILY COLLEGIAN (Apr. 9, 2015), www.collegian.psu.edu/news/campus/article_6ef93ec6-ded7-11e4-998a-e36930ab25c3.html; *see also* Ross Levitt & Lauren Russell, *Lawyer: Penn State Victim Reaches First Settlement in Jerry Sandusky Victim Suits*, CNN (Aug. 17, 2013), www.cnn.com/2013/08/17/justice/penn-state-sandusky-victim-settlement/.

12.   U.S. SENTENCING GUIDELINES MANUAL § 8B2.1(a).

13.   *See, e.g.*, Thomas A. Butcher, Compliance: A Practical Protocol of the Entire Campus and Beyond, at 10–11 (Seminar Material for NACUA 48th Annual Conference, June 22–25, 2008).

14.   *See id.* at 7–10; Adams, *supra* note 6, at 17.

15.   Butcher, *supra* note 13, at 7; Adams, *supra* note 6, at 17–18.

16.   Butcher, *supra* note 13, at 10; Adams, *supra* note 6, at 17–18.

17.   Adams, *supra* note 6, at 18–19.

18.   *Id.* at 22–23.

19.   *See* Kwamina Williford & Daniel Small, *Establishing an Effective Compliance Program: An Overview to Protecting Your Organization*, ASS'N OF CORP. COUNSEL (Jan. 15, 2013), www.acc.com/legalresources/quickcounsel/eaecp.cfm#ra; *see also* Robert F. Roach et al., Risk Management in Higher Education: A Guide to Building an Effective Compliance and Risk Management Program & Counsel's Role, NACUA Virtual Seminar Presentation (Dec. 10, 2010).

20.   U.S. CONST. amend. XIV ("No state shall . . . deny to any person within its jurisdiction the equal protection of the laws."); Fisher v. Univ. of Tex. at Austin, 133 S. Ct. 2411, 2417 (5th Cir. 2013) ("It is . . . irrelevant that a system of racial preferences in admissions may seem benign. Any racial classification must meet strict scrutiny . . . .").

21.   Title VI states, "No person in the United States shall, on the ground of race, color, or national origin, be excluded from participation in, be denied the benefits of, or be subjected to discrimination under any program or activity receiving federal financial assistance." 42 U.S.C. § 2000d.

22.   Fullilove v. Klutznick, 448 U.S. 448, 537 (1980); Adarand Constr., Inc. v. Peña, 515 U.S. 200, 223 (1995).

23.   Grutter v. Bollinger, 539 U.S. 306, 326 (2003); Gratz v. Bollinger, 539 U.S. 244, 270 (2003).

24. *Grutter*, 539 U.S. at 343; *Gratz*, 539 U.S. at 247; Students for Fair Admissions, Inc. v. President and Fellows of Harvard College, 980 F. 3d 157, 185 (1st Cir. 2020) (applying Title VI).

25. *See* United States v. Virginia (*VMI*), 518 U.S. 515, 524 (1996) (citing Miss. Univ. for Women v. Hogan, 458 U.S. 718, 724 (1982)).

26. *VMI*, 518 U.S. at 533; *Hogan*, 458 U.S. at 724; Craig v. Boren, 429 U.S. 190, 197 (1976).

27. Title IX states, in pertinent part, "No person in the United States shall, on the basis of sex, be excluded from participation in, be denied the benefits of, or be subjected to discrimination under any education programs or activity receiving Federal financial assistance. . . ." 20 U.S.C. § 1681(a).

28. 20 U.S.C. § 1681(a)(1), (3).

29. *See* Klinger v. Dep't of Corr., 107 F.3d 609, 614 (8th Cir. 1997); Jeldness v. Pearce, 30 F.3d 1220, 1227 (9th Cir. 1994); Cannon v. Univ. of Chi., 648 F.2d 1104, 1106 (7th Cir.), *cert. denied*, 454 U.S. 1128 (1981), *and* 460 U.S. 1013 (1983); Johnson v. Bd. of Regents of Univ. Sys. of Ga., 106 F. Supp. 2d 1362, 1367 (S.D. Ga. 2000), *aff'd on other grounds*, 263 F.3d 1234 (11th Cir. 2001).

30. *See, e.g.*, CAL. EDUC. CODE § 6625 (West 2002); COLO. REV. STAT. § 22-7-403 (2005); D.C. CODE § 2-1402.41 (2001); ME. REV. STAT. ANN. tit. 5, § 4602(1) (2001); MINN. STAT. §§ 363A.03, 363A.13, 363A.23 (2001); MONT. CODE ANN. § 49-2-307 (2006); 24 PA. STAT. ANN. § 5004 (West 2001); S.D. CODIFIED LAWS § 20-13-22 (2002).

31. *Grutter*, 539 U.S. at 328.

32. Parents Involved in Cmty. Sch. v. Seattle Dist., 551 U.S. 701, 722–23 (2007) (citing *Grutter*, 539 U.S. at 330).

33. *See Grutter*, 539 U.S. at 338.

34. *See* Fisher v. Univ. of Tex. at Austin, 133 S. Ct. 2411, 2421 (2013).

35. *Grutter*, 539 U.S. at 338.

36. *See generally id.* at 319–20, 330–33; *Students for Fair Admissions, Inc.*, 980 F. 3d at 186.

37. *See* Fisher v. Univ. of Tex., 645 F. Supp. 2d 587, 593–94 (W.D. Tex. 2009), *aff'd*, 631 F.3d 213 (5th Cir. 2011), *vacated and remanded*, 758 F.3d 274 (5th Cir. 2014), *aff'd*, 136 S. Ct. 2198 (2016).

38. *Grutter*, 539 U.S. at 334.

39. *Cf. Gratz*, 539 U.S. at 254–56.

40. *Grutter*, 539 U.S. at 337; *Fisher*, 133 S. Ct. at 2419–20.

41. *Grutter*, 539 U.S. at 339.

42. *Id.* at 342.

43. *Gratz*, 539 U.S. at 254–56.

44. *Id.* at 274.

45. *Grutter*, 539 U.S. at 337.

46. Fisher v. Univ. of Tex., 758 F.3d 633, 657 (5th Cir. 2014), *aff'd*, 136 S. Ct. 2198 (2016).

47. *See Fisher*, 133 S. Ct. at 2420.

48. *Grutter*, 539 U.S. at 339; *Fisher*, 758 F.3d at 647–48; *cf. Parents Involved*, 551 U.S. at 734.

49. *Grutter*, 539 U.S. at 342.

50. *Hogan*, 458 U.S. at 728 (citing Schlesinger v. Ballard, 419 U.S. 498 (1975)).

51. *VMI*, 518 U.S. at 533.

52. *Id.* at 531.

53. *Johnson*, 106 F. Supp. 2d at 1375–76 & n.10 ("The desire to 'help out' men who are not earning baccalaureate degrees in the same numbers as women . . . is far from persuasive.").

54. *Hogan*, 458 U.S. at 725; *accord VMI*, 518 U.S. at 533.

55. *See Johnson*, 106 F. Supp. 2d at 1371.

56. *See* Debra Franzese, Comment, *The Gender Curve: An Analysis of Colleges' Use of Affirmative Action Policies to Benefit Male Applicants*, 56 AM. U. L. REV. 719, 739–48 (2007).

57. 20 U.S.C. § 1681(a).

58. *Id.*

59. *See* 20 U.S.C. § 1681(a)(1).

60. *Id.* § 1681(a)(6).

61. Under Title II of the ADA, "no qualified individual with a disability shall, by reason of such disability, be excluded from participation in or be denied the benefits of the services, programs, or activities of a public entity, or be subjected to discrimination by any such entity." 42 U.S.C. § 12132. Under Title III of the ADA, "[n]o individual shall be discriminated against on the basis of disability in the full and equal enjoyment of the goods, services, facilities, privileges, advantages, or accommodations of any place of public accommodation." 42 U.S.C. § 12182(a).

62. Section 504 of the Rehabilitation Act of 1973 provides, "No otherwise qualified individual with a disability . . . shall solely by reason of her or his disability, be excluded from the participation in, be denied the benefits of, or be subjected to discrimination under any program or activity receiving Federal financial assistance . . . ." 29 U.S.C. § 794(a). "Program or activity" includes a college, university, or other postsecondary institution or a public system of higher education. 29 U.S.C. § 794(b)(2)(A).

63. *See* Manickavasagar v. Va. Commonwealth Univ. Sch. of Med., 667 F. Supp. 2d 635, 643 (E.D. Va. 2009) (citing Baird *ex rel.* Baird v. Rose, 192 F.3d 462, 468 (4th Cir. 1999)); Mershon v. St. Louis Univ., 442 F.3d 1069, 1076 n.4 (8th Cir. 2006); Betts v. Rector & Visitors of Univ. of Va., 145 F. App'x 7, 10 (4th Cir. 2005); Ernest v. Univ. of Phx., 2009 WL 4282006, at *3 (S.D. Cal. Nov. 25, 2009).

64. Title II of the ADA applies to public postsecondary institutions. 42 U.S.C. § 12132. Title III of the ADA applies to private places of public accommodation to include an undergraduate or postgraduate private school, but excludes religious organizations or entities controlled by religious organizations. 42 U.S.C. §§ 12181(7)(J), 12182, 12187. Title III authorizes only a suit for injunctive relief. *See* Kahn v. N.Y. Univ. Med. Ctr., 328 F. App'x 758, 759 (2d Cir. 2009). The ADA does not have a federal funding requirement. *See Mershon*, 442 F.3d at 1076 n.4. In

contrast, the Rehabilitation Act applies only to public or private postsecondary institutions receiving federal financial assistance. 29 U.S.C. § 794(a), (b)(2)(A). Some courts require that the federal dollars fund the particular program at issue in the plaintiff's claim. *See* Datto v. Harrison, 2009 WL 3104988, at *2 (E.D. Pa. Sept. 28, 2009).

65. *Manickavasagar*, 667 F. Supp. 2d at 643–44 (citing *Betts*, 145 F. App'x at 10); *accord* Brettler v. Purdue Univ., 408 F. Supp. 2d 640, 662 (N.D. Ind. 2006) (to establish claim under Title II of ADA, plaintiff must prove: (1) that he is a qualified individual, (2) with disability, (3) that he was excluded from participation in or denied benefits of services, programs, or activities of public entity, or was otherwise discriminated against by any such entity, (4) by reason of his disability).

66. *Mershon*, 442 F.3d at 1076 (citing Amir v. St. Louis Univ., 184 F.3d 1017, 1027 (8th Cir. 1999) (as discussed above, the ADA does not require federal funding, but the Rehabilitation Act does; and Title III may be alleged against a public institution without the federal funding requirement)); *accord Manickavasagar*, 442 F. Supp. 2d at 644 (citing Baucom v. Potter, 225 F. Supp. 2d 585, 591 (D. Md. 2002)).

67. Many courts are declining to apply the ADA to events occurring before its effective date. *See* Herzog v. Loyola Coll. in Md., Inc., 2009 WL 3271246, at n.3 (D. Md. Oct. 9, 2009).

68. ADA Amendments Act of 2008, Pub. L. No. 110-325, § 2, 122 Stat. 3553.

69. *Id.* § 4.

70. *Id.*

71. *Id.* § 2(a)(4)–(5).

72. *See* Jenkins v. Nat'l Bd. of Med. Exam'rs, 2009 WL 331638 (6th Cir. Feb. 11, 2009).

73. *See* 28 C.F.R. pt. 36, app. B (2008); *see also* Wong v. Regents of Univ. of Cal., 379 F.3d 1097, 1109 (9th Cir. 2004).

74. *See* Price v. Nat'l Bd. of Med. Exam'rs, 966 F. Supp. 419 (S.D. W. Va. 1997); *accord* Wong v. Regents of Univ. of Cal., 379 F.3d 1097 (9th Cir. 2004); Steere v. George Wash. Univ. Sch. of Med. & Health Sci., 439 F. Supp. 2d 17 (D.D.C. 2006); Dixson v. Univ. of Cincinnati, 2005 WL 2709628 (S.D. Ohio Oct. 21, 2005).

75. *See* 154 CONG. REC. H8290-91 (daily ed. Sept. 17, 2008); Singh v. George Wash. Univ. Sch. of Med. & Health Sci., 597 F. Supp. 2d 89 (D.D.C. 2009).

76. Bartlett v. N.Y. State Bd. of Law Exam'rs, 156 F.3d 321 (2d Cir. 1998), *cert. granted and vacated*, 527 U.S. 1031 (1999), *remanded*, 226 F.3d 69 (2d Cir. 2000).

77. *See* 226 F.3d at 82. In *Bartlett*, plaintiff, a Ph.D. who had also completed her law degree, claimed that she had dyslexia and repeatedly applied to take the New York State Bar exam, requesting that she be given unlimited or extended time, permission to tape-record her essays, and permission to circle her test answers in the booklet rather than on the testing sheet. Each time, the board denied the request, finding that she did not have a legal disability.

78. Tips v. Regents of Tex. Tech Univ., 921 F. Supp. 1515, 1518 (N.D. Tex. 1996).

79. *See* Wynne v. Tufts Univ. Sch. of Med., 932 F.2d 19 (1st Cir. 1991).

80. Statement of the Managers to Accompany S. 3406.

81.   *See* Wendy F. Hensel, *Rights Resurgence: The Impact of the ADA Amendments Act on Schools and Universities*, 25 GA. ST. U. L. REV. 641, 680 (2009) (citing H.R. REP. NO. 110-730, pt. 1, at 11 (2008)).

82.   *See* United States v. Bd. of Trs. for Univ. of Ala., 908 F.2d 740 (11th Cir. 1990).

83.   *See* Karin McAnaney, *Finding the Proper Balance: Protecting Suicidal Students without Harming Universities*, 94 VA. L. REV. 197, 223 (2008) (citing Letter from Michal Gallagher, Team Leader, Office for Civil Rights, U.S. Dep't of Educ., to Dr. Jean Scott, President, Marietta Coll. 3 (Mar. 18, 2005)).

84.   *See* 2009–2010 Federal Student Aid Handbook (U.S. Dep't of Educ. 2009), vol. 2, ch. 1, "Institutional Eligibility," at 2-1. The entire 909-page handbook, comprising an index, the Application and Verification Guide, and six numbered volumes, can be downloaded from the DOE's Information for Financial Aid Professionals (IFAP) website. *See* http://ifap.ed.gov/fsahandbook/attachments/0910FSA HandbookIndex.pdf.

85.   34 C.F.R. § 668.8(c)(1)–(3).

86.   *Id.* § 668.8(d).

87.   *See id.* § 685.402.

88.   *Id.* § 668.8(e)(1).

89.   *See id.* § 668.14.

90.   *See* Hendow v. Univ. of Phx., 461 F.3d 1166, 1176–77 (9th Cir. 2006) (holding that an institution can be liable under the False Claims Act when it falsely certifies compliance with a statute or regulation that is a condition of government funding received in connection with an institution's program participation agreement).

91.   42 U.S.C. § 2000d *et seq.*

92.   34 C.F.R. pt. 100.

93.   Title IX of the HEA, 20 U.S.C. § 1681 *et seq.*, which prohibits gender discrimination in any academic program or activity receiving federal financial assistance, and section 504 of the Rehabilitation Act of 1973, 29 U.S.C. § 794, and its implementing regulation, 34 C.F.R. pt. 104, which prohibits discrimination on the basis of disability.

94.   *See* 34 C.F.R. § 682.401.

95.   *See* HEA § 152(a)(1)(A).

96.   *See id.* § 485(a)(1)(P).

97.   *See id.* § 152(a)(1)(B).

98.   *See id.* § 485.

99.   34 C.F.R. § 668.14(b)(22)(i); 20 U.S.C. § 1094(a)(20) (stating that an institution "will not provide any commission, bonus, or other incentive payment based directly or indirectly on success in securing enrollments or financial aid to any persons or entities engaged in any student recruiting or admission activities or in making decisions regarding the award of student financial assistance, except this paragraph shall not apply to the recruitment of foreign students residing in foreign countries who are not eligible to receive Federal student assistance").

100. Those safe harbors permitted exceptions to the rule based on fixed salaries being adjusted based on a multitude of criteria, non–Title IV course work, employer contracts, profit sharing, program completions, pre-enrollment clerical staff, certain managers and supervisors, token gifts, profit distribution, Internet support, third-party restricted and unrestricted activities. 34 C.F.R. § 668.14(b)(22)(ii)(A)–(L) (2001).

101. *See* 75 Fed. Reg. 66,872, 66,873 (Oct. 29, 2010) (noting that the DOE has been repeatedly advised by institutional employees that facts other than the number of students recruited are not truly considered when compensation decisions are made, and that they are identified only to create the appearance of compliance with the HEA). This skepticism is shared by whistleblowers. *See, e.g.,* United States v. Educ. Mgmt. Corp. (EDMC), 2:07 CV-00461 (W.D. Pa. 2007) (where two whistleblowers filed an $11 billion suit against EDMC alleging that its compensation plan that mirrored the regulations' pre-2011 safe harbor provisions was merely a front for its practice of allowing incentive compensation based solely on the number of students recruited). In an unprecedented move, in August 2011, the Civil Division of the DOJ intervened in the *EDMC* case, acknowledging its view that this EDMC claim was worth pursuing. In May 2012, the *EMDC* court refused to dismiss the complaint.

102. *See* 34 C.F.R. § 668.12(a)(22)(ii)(A).
103. *See id.* § 668.12(a)(22)(ii)(B).
104. *See id.* § 682.212(h).
105. *Id.*
106. *See* HEA § 487(h).
107. *See id.* § 153(c)(3).
108. *See id.* §§ 493(a)(25), 493(e).
109. *Id.* § 433(c).
110. *Id.* § 433(a).
111. *Id.*
112. *Id.* § 433(b).
113. *Id.* § 433(e)(1).
114. *Id.* § 433(e)(2).
115. *Id.* § 433(e)(3).
116. *Id.* § 485(b)(1).
117. *Id.*
118. *Id.*
119. *See* TILA § 140(a)–(e).
120. *See id.* § 128(e).
121. *See id.* § 128(e)(5), (11).
122. *See* 34 C.F.R. § 668.14(b)(25).
123. *See* 20 U.S.C. § 1094(c)(3)(B); 34 C.F.R. § 668.84(a).
124. 34 C.F.R. § 668.92(a)(5)(i).
125. *Id.* § 668.95(b).

126. *See* 20 U.S.C. § 1094(c)(3)(b)(ii).

127. *See id.; see also* 34 C.F.R. § 668.92.

128. *See* 34 C.F.R. §§ 668.90, 668.91, 668.98.

129. *See id.* § 668.85.

130. *See id.* § 668.85(a)(3).

131. *See id.* § 668.94.

132. *See* Yorktowne Bus. Inst., 1993 WL 591773, at *1 (Dep't of Educ. Office of Hearings & Appeals July 1, 1993).

133. *See* 34 C.F.R. § 668.86.

134. See *id.* § 668.93.

135. RESTATEMENT (SECOND) OF TORTS § 315 (1965).

136. Nova Se. Univ., Inc. v. Gross, 758 So. 2d 86 (Fla. 2000) (since university had control over graduate student's conduct by requiring her to do mandatory internship and by assigning her to specific location, it assumed correlative duty of acting reasonably in making that assignment); *see also* Mullins v. Pine Manor Coll., 449 N.E.2d 331 (Mass. 1983) (college undertook a duty to provide students in dormitories with protection from criminal acts of third parties, in this case rape).

137. *See, e.g.*, Duarte v. State, 151 Cal. Rptr. 727 (Ct. App. 4th Dist. 1979) (claim stated for breach of warranty of habitability in residence contract when state university student was raped and murdered in her residence hall); Cutler v. Bd. of Regents of Fla., 459 So. 2d 413 (Fla. 1st Dist. Ct. App. 1984) (allowing plaintiff to amend complaint to attach her rental contract with the university to attempt to state a claim for breach of warranty of habitability).

138. *Id.* § 314A.

139. *See* Cutler v. Bd. of Regents of Fla., 459 So. 2d 413 (Fla. 1st Dist. Ct. App. 1984) (college had a duty to student as tenant in her dormitory as a landlord to protect her from assault and rape); Nero v. Kan. State Univ., 861 P.2d 768 (Kan. 1993) (providing housing to students conferred upon the university all the rights and responsibilities that any landlord would have); Miller v. New York, 467 N.E.2d 493 (N.Y. 1984) (college liable for rape of student by a third party for failing to lock outer door to dormitory).

140. *See* Furek v. Univ. of Del., 594 A.2d 506 (Del. 1991) (college students are invitees, and universities owe them a duty to "regulate and supervise" student activities that are foreseeable and within the university's control).

141. Most courts have rejected the university-college student relationship alone as a basis for liability. *See* Bradshaw v. Rawlings, 612 F.2d 135 (3d Cir. 1979), *cert. denied*, 446 U.S. 909 (1980); Beach v. Univ. of Utah, 726 P.2d 413 (Utah 1986); Booker v. Lehigh Univ., 800 F. Supp. 234 (E.D. Pa. 1992), *aff'd*, 995 F.2d 215 (3d Cir. 1993); Campbell v. Bd. of Trs. of Wabash Coll., 495 N.E.2d 227 (Ind. Ct. App. 1986); Crow v. State of California, 271 Cal. Rptr. 349 (Ct. App. 1990); Hartman v. Bethany Coll., 778 F. Supp. 286 (N.D. W. Va. 1991); Leonardi v. Bradley, 625 N.E.2d 431 (Ill. App. Ct. 1993), *appeal denied*, 633 N.E.2d 6 (Ill. 1994); Millard v. Osborne,

611 A.2d 715 (Pa. Super. Ct.), *appeal denied*, 615 A.2d 656 (Pa. 1992); Murrell v. Mt. St. Clare Coll., 2001 WL 1678766 (S.D. Iowa 2001); Rothbard v. Colgate Univ., 235 A.D.2d 675 (N.Y. App. Div. 1997); Tanja H. v. Regents of Univ. of Cal., 278 Cal. Rptr. 918 (Ct. App. 1991). But there are exceptional circumstances when the court finds a special relationship between college and student. *See* Schieszler v. Ferrum Coll., 236 F. Supp. 2d 602 (W.D. Va. 2002) (college had special relationship with student who hanged self where, inter alia, college officials were aware that student had emotional problems and indicated intent to commit suicide); Shin v. Mass. Inst. of Tech., 19 Mass. L. Rptr. 570, 2005 WL 1869101 (Super. Ct. 2005) (university had special relationship with student who committed suicide because university was well aware of student's suicidal ideation). The trend appears to be toward an expansion of this type of liability especially in the area of suicidal ideation.

142. *See, e.g.*, Nguyen v. Mass. Inst. of Tech., 479 Mass. 436 (2018) (recognizing limited exception for actual knowledge of student's intent to commit suicide).

143. *See, e.g.,* Mullins v. Pine Manor Coll., 389 Mass. 47, 51–52 (1983) (imposing duty of physical security against foreseeable criminal activity, including trespassers).

144. *See, e.g.*, McCain v. Fla. Power Corp., 593 So. 2d 500, 502 (Fla. 1992) ("The duty element of negligence focuses on whether the defendant's conduct foreseeably created a broader 'zone of risk' that poses a general threat of harm to others. . . . The proximate causation element, on the other hand, is concerned with whether and to what extent the defendant's conduct foreseeably and substantially caused the specific injury that actually occurred. In other words, the former is a minimal threshold *legal* requirement for opening the courthouse doors, whereas the latter is part of the much more specific *factual* requirement that must be proved to win the case once the courthouse doors are open. As is obvious, a defendant might be under a legal duty of care to a specific plaintiff, but still not be liable for negligence because proximate causation cannot be proven.") (emphasis in original).

145. *See, e.g.*, Jesik v. Maricopa Cty. Cmty. Coll. Dist., 611 P.2d 547 (Ariz. 1980) (reversing summary judgment against community college when student was shot by third party whom he reported twice to security guard as threatening him); Peterson v. S.F. Cmty. Coll., 685 P.2d 1193 (1984) (college had a duty to prevent attempted rape on a stairway in the college's parking lot where prior attacks happened); Schieszler v. Ferrum Coll., 236 F. Supp. 2d 602 (W.D. Va. 2002) (college liable when student committed suicide after campus police aware of student's prior attempt merely asked him to sign a statement promising not to harm self); Tarasoff v. Cal. Bd. of Regents, 551 P.2d 334 (Cal. 1976) (college liable when treating psychotherapist failed to warn a third party whom a student patient had threatened).

146. *See, e.g.*, Duarte v. State, 151 Cal. Rptr. 727 (Ct. App. 4th Dist. 1979) (liability arose from rape and murder of student in dorm because university had knowledge of a chronic pattern of violent assaults, rapes, and attacks on female

members of the university community); Mullins v. Pine Manor Coll., 449 N.E.2d 331 (Mass. 1983) (women's college liable to student who was raped on campus by intruder who took her from her dormitory where director of student affairs had warned students during freshman orientation of dangers inherent in being housed at a women's college near metropolitan area short distance from bus and train lines to Boston).

147. *See* Collins v. Sch. Bd. of Broward Cnty., 471 So. 2d 560 (Fla. 4th Dist. Ct. App. 1985) (school liable for sexual assault of student in shop class when teacher left room; had teacher been at desk he would have seen the assault).

148. 20 U.S.C. § 1092.

149. *Id.* § 1092(f)(1); 34 C.F.R. § 668.46(b).

150. 20 U.S.C. § 1092(f)(1), (8)(B).

151. *Id.* § 1092(f)(1)(F); 34 C.F.R. § 668.46(c).

152. 20 U.S.C. § 1092(f)(3); 34 C.F.R. § 668.46(e); Havlik v. Johnson & Wales Univ., 509 F.3d 25, 28 (1st Cir. 2007).

153. 20 U.S.C. § 1092(f)(4)(A), (B); 34 C.F.R. § 668.46(f). Campus law enforcement records are excluded from coverage under the Family Educational Rights and Privacy Act of 1974 (FERPA), 20 U.S.C. § 1232g.

154. Violence Against Women Reauthorization Act, Pub. L. No. 113-4, tit. III, 127 Stat. 54, 89–92 (2013).

155. 20 U.S.C. § 1092(f)(1), (8); 34 C.F.R. § 668.46(b).

156. 20 U.S.C. § 1092(14)(A). In addition, evidence regarding compliance or noncompliance with the Clery Act is not admissible except with respect to an action to enforce it. *Id.* § 1092(14)(B).

157. *Id.* §§ 1092(13), 1094(c)(3)(B).

158. *Id.* § 1094(c)(3)(A).

159. *See, e.g.*, APPLIED RISK MANAGEMENT, REPORT TO MASSACHUSETTS DEPARTMENT OF HIGHER EDUCATION, CAMPUS VIOLENCE PREVENTION AND RESPONSE: BEST PRACTICES FOR MASSACHUSETTS HIGHER EDUCATION 45 (June 2008), www.arm-security.com/pdf/ ARM_MA_Colleges_Campus_Violence_Prevention_And_Response.pdf [hereinafter CAMPUS VIOLENCE]; MASS SHOOTINGS AT VIRGINIA TECH APRIL 16, 2007: REPORT OF THE VIRGINIA TECH REVIEW PANEL (Aug. 2007), www.vtreviewpanel.org/report/index. html [hereinafter VTRP REPORT]; STATE OF ILLINOIS CAMPUS SECURITY TASK FORCE REPORT TO THE GOVERNOR (Apr. 15, 2008), www.ready.illinois.gov/pdf/CSTF_Report_ PartI.pdf [hereinafter CAMPUS SECURITY].

160. *See* CAMPUS VIOLENCE, *supra* note 159, at ii, 13–14.

161. *Id.* at 39.

162. *Id.*

163. *Id.* at 14–16.

164. *Id.* at ii, 44–45.

165. *Id.* at iii, 33–34. Replace doors that can be chained one to another to prevent access and escape. *Id.* at 33.

166. *Id.* at i–vi, 31–46; VTRP REPORT, *supra* note 159, at 146. *See generally* CAMPUS SECURITY, *supra* note 159, at Prevention and Mental Health Committee Findings & Recommendations (unpaginated).

167. CAMPUS VIOLENCE, *supra* note 159, at 45.

168. *Family Educational Rights and Privacy Act (FERPA)*, U.S. DEP'T OF EDUC. (June 26, 2015), www2.ed.gov/policy/gen/guid/fpco/ferpa/index.html.

169. Legislative History of Major FERPA Provisions (June 2002), www2. ed.gov/policy/gen/guid/fpco/pdf/ferpaleghistory.pdf; Family Educational Rights and Privacy Act (codified at 20 U.S.C. § 1232g); 34 C.F.R. pt. 99.

170. Family Educational Rights and Privacy Act (FERPA), Final Rule, 34 C.F.R. pt. 99, Section-by-Section Analysis (Dec. 2008) [hereinafter FERPA Section-by-Section Analysis], www2.ed.gov/policy/gen/guid/fpco/pdf/ht12-17-08-att.pdf; U.S. Dep't of Educ., Office of Commc'ns & Outreach, Guide to U.S. Dep't of Educ. Programs Fiscal Year 2011, at 66–80 (2009), www2.ed.gov/programs/gtep/gtep2011. pdf.

171. 34 C.F.R. § 99.5.

172. *Id.* § 99.3.

173. FERPA Section-by-Section Analysis, *supra* note 170, at 3.

174. Steven J. McDonald, *The Fundamentals of Fundamental FERPA, in* NEW FERPA REGULATIONS: COMPLIANCE FOR COLLEGES AND UNIVERSITIES, at 54–55 (NNACUA, Virtual Seminar Handouts, Jan. 29, 2009); FERPA Section-by-Section Analysis, *supra* note 170, at 3.

175. 20 U.S.C. § 1232g(a)(1)(A).

176. *Id.* § 1232g(a)(2); 34 C.F.R. §§ 99.20–.22.

177. 20 U.S.C. § 1232g(b)(2)(A); 34 C.F.R. §§ 99.30–.31.

178. 34 C.F.R. § 99.30(b)(1)–(3).

179. *Id.* § 99.31.

180. *Id.* § 99.60.

181. *Id.* § 99.60(b)(1)–(2).

182. *Id.* § 99.62.

183. Gonzaga Univ. v. Doe, 536 U.S. 273, 286 n.5 (2002).

184. *Id.*

185. 34 C.F.R. § 99.63.

186. *Id.* § 99.64(b).

187. *Id.*

188. *Id.*

189. *Id.* § 99.64(a).

190. *Id.* § 99.66(a).

191. *Id.*

192. *Id.* § 99.66(b).

193. E. Theuman, *Validity, Construction, and Application of Family Educational Rights and Privacy Act of 1974 (FERPA)*, 112 A.L.R. FED. 1, § 12[c] (1993) (citing 20 U.S.C. § 1232(a), (b), (e); Commonwealth v. Buccella, 751 N.E.2d 373 (Mass. 2001)).

194. Gonzaga Univ. v. Doe, 536 U.S. 273, 288 (2002) (citing 20 U.S.C. § 1232g(b)(1)–(2)) (noting the FERPA prohibits funding an educational institution with a policy or practice of permitting the release of education records).

195. 34 C.F.R. § 99.66(c).

196. 20 U.S.C. § 1232g(b)(2), (f); 34 C.F.R. § 99.67.

197. *See* Owasso Indep. Sch. Dist. v. Falvo, 534 U.S. 426, 431, 434 (2002) (finding that the determination of whether there is a FERPA violation turns on the definition of what is considered part of a student record).

198. 20 U.S.C. § 1232g(a)(4); 34 C.F.R. § 99.3.

199. 34 C.F.R. § 99.3.

200. 20 U.S.C. § 1232g(b)(1).

201. 34 C.F.R. § 99.3.

202. 20 U.S.C. § 1232g(a)(4)(B)(i)–(iv).

203. 34 C.F.R. § 99.3.

204. *Id.* §§ 99.3, 99.8.

205. *Id.* § 99.8.

206. *Id.* § 99.8(b)(2)(ii).

207. *Id.* § 99.8(b)(2)(i).

208. *Id.* § 99.3.

209. *Id.*

210. *Id.*

211. *Id.*

212. *Id.*

213. *Id.* § 99.10(a).

214. *Id.* § 99.10(b).

215. *Id.* § 99.10(c).

216. *Id.* § 99.10(d)(1)–(2).

217. *Id.* § 99.11(a).

218. *Id.* § 99.11(a)–(b).

219. *Id.* § 99.10(e).

220. *Id.* §§ 99.3, 99.10(f).

221. *Id.* § 99.12(a).

222. *Id.* § 99.12(b)(1).

223. *Id.* § 99.12(b)(3).

224. *Id.* § 99.12(c)(2)(i).

225. *Id.* § 99.12(c)(3)(i)–(ii).

226. 20 U.S.C. § 1232g(a)(2); 34 C.F.R. §§ 99.20–.22.

227. 34 C.F.R. § 99.21(b)(1).

228. *Id.* § 99.21(b)(2).

229. Steven J. McDonald, *The Fundamentals of FERPA, in* NEW FERPA REGULATIONS: COMPLIANCE FOR COLLEGES AND UNIVERSITIES, at 67 (NACUA, Virtual Seminar Handouts, Jan. 29, 2009) (citing Adatsi v. Mathur, 934 F.2d 910 (7th Cir. 1991); and Tarka v. Cunningham, 741 F. Supp. 1281, 1282 (W.D. Tex.), *aff'd,* 917 F.2d 890 (5th Cir. 1990)).

230. 34 C.F.R. § 99.31.
231. *Id.* § 99.3.
232. *Id.*
233. 20 U.S.C. § 1232g(b)(1).
234. 34 C.F.R. § 99.37(a)(1).
235. *Id.* § 99.37(a)(2)–(3).
236. *See id.* § 99.37(d).
237. 76 Fed. Reg. 75,604, 75,631 (Dec. 2, 2011).
238. *See id.*
239. 34 C.F.R. § 99.37(b).
240. *Id.* § 99.31(a)(8).
241. *Id.* § 99.31(a)(15).
242. 20 U.S.C. § 1232g(b)(1)(B); 34 C.F.R. § 99.34(b).
243. 20 U.S.C. § 1232g(b)(1)(B); 34 C.F.R. § 99.34(a)(1).
244. 34 C.F.R. § 99.31(a)(2).
245. *Id.* § 99.31.
246. *Id.* § 99.31(a)(1)(i)(B)(1).
247. *Id.* § 99.33(a)(1).
248. *Id.* § 99.31(a)(1)(i)(B)(2).
249. *Id.* § 99.33(a)(2).
250. *Id.*
251. *Id.* § 99.31(a)(3).
252. *Id.* § 99.35(a)(1).
253. *Id.* § 99.35(a)(2).
254. *Id.* § 99.31(a)(4).
255. *Id.* § 99.31(a)(4)(A)–(D).
256. *Id.* § 99.31(a)(5).
257. *Id.* § 99.38(b).
258. *Id.* § 99.31(a)(6)(i).
259. *Id.* § 99.31(a)(6)(ii)(A)–(C).
260. *Id.* § 99.31(a)(6)(iv).
261. *Id.* § 99.31(a)(7).
262. 20 U.S.C. § 1232(6)(2)(B) (incorporating amendments made by the Uninterrupted Scholars Act of Jan. 2013).
263. 20 U.S.C. § 1232g(a)(7)(B)(h)(1)–(2); 34 C.F.R. § 99.31(a).
264. 34 C.F.R. § 99.7(a)(3)(iii).
265. *Id.* § 99.31(a)(9)(i).
266. *Id.* § 99.31(a)(9)(ii).
267. *Id.* § 99.31(a)(9)(ii)(A)–(C).
268. *Id.* § 99.31(a)(9)(iii)(B).
269. *Id.* § 99.31(a)(9)(iii)(A).
270. 20 U.S.C. § 1232g(b)(1)(I).
271. *Id.*
272. 34 C.F.R. § 99.36(c).

273. *Id.* § 99.32(a)(5)(i)–(ii).
274. FERPA Section-by-Section Analysis, *supra* note 170, at 13.
275. *Id.*
276. 34 C.F.R. § 99.36(c).
277. *Id.*
278. Family Educational Rights and Privacy, Final Regulations, 73 Fed. Reg. 74,838 (Dec. 9, 2008) (to be codified at 34 C.F.R. pt. 99).
279. *Id.*
280. *Id.*
281. *Id.*
282. 20 U.S.C. § 1232g(b)(1)(I).
283. 73 Fed. Reg. 74,838 (Dec. 9, 2008).
284. *Id.*
285. *Id.*
286. *Id.*
287. *Id.*
288. *Id.*
289. FERPA Section-by-Section Analysis, *supra* note 170, at 5.
290. 34 C.F.R. § 99.31(a)(1)(i)(B)(1).
291. FERPA Section-by-Section Analysis, *supra* note 170, at 5.
292. *Id.*
293. *Id.*
294. *Id.*; 34 C.F.R. § 99.31(a)(1)(i)(B)(2).
295. FERPA Section-by-Section Analysis, *supra* note 170, at 6.
296. 34 C.F.R. § 99.33(a)(1).
297. *Id.* § 99.33(a)(2).
298. FERPA Section-by-Section Analysis, *supra* note 170, at 6.
299. *Id.*
300. *Id.*
301. *Id.*; 34 C.F.R. § 99.31(a)(1)(ii).
302. FERPA Section-by-Section Analysis, *supra* note 170, at 6.
303. *Id.*
304. *Id.*
305. *Id.*
306. *Id.*
307. *Id.*
308. *Id.*
309. *Id.*
310. 34 C.F.R. § 99.31(a)(1)(ii).
311. FERPA Section-by-Section Analysis, *supra* note 170, at 6.
312. 34 C.F.R. § 99.32(a)(1).
313. *Id.* § 99.32(a)(2).
314. *Id.* § 99.32(a)(3)(i)–(ii).
315. *Id.* § 99.32(a)(5)(i)–(ii).

316. *Id.* § 99.32(b)(d)(1)–(5).

317. *Id.* § 99.7(a)(1).

318. *Id.* § 99.7(a)(2)(i)–(iv).

319. *Id.* § 99.7(a)(3)(i)–(ii).

320. *Id.* § 99.7(a)(3)(iii).

321. *Id.* § 99.7(b).

322. *Health Information Privacy*, U.S. DEP'T OF HEALTH & HUMAN SERVS., www. hhs.gov/ocr/privacy/index.html.

323. *Id.*

324. U.S. DEP'T OF HEALTH & HUMAN SERVS. & U.S. DEP'T OF EDUC., JOINT GUIDANCE ON THE APPLICATION OF THE FAMILY EDUCATIONAL RIGHTS AND PRIVACY ACT (FERPA) AND THE HEALTH INSURANCE PORTABILITY AND ACCOUNTABILITY ACT OF 1996 (HIPAA) TO STUDENT HEALTH RECORDS 3 (Nov. 2008) [hereinafter JOINT GUIDANCE], www2.ed.gov/ policy/gen/guid/fpco/doc/ferpa-hipaa-guidance.pdf.

325. *Id.*

326. *Id.*; 45 C.F.R. § 160.103(2)(i)–(ii).

327. JOINT GUIDANCE, *supra* note 324, at 6; 34 C.F.R. § 99.3.

328. JOINT GUIDANCE, *supra* note 324, at 6–7; 34 C.F.R. § 99.3.

329. JOINT GUIDANCE, *supra* note 324, at 7; 34 C.F.R. § 99.30.

330. JOINT GUIDANCE, *supra* note 324, at 7; 34 C.F.R. §§ 99.30, 99.31(a).

331. JOINT GUIDANCE, *supra* note 324, at 3, 7.

332. *Id.* at 8.

333. *Id.* at 7.

334. *Id.*

335. *Id.* at 9.

336. *Id.*

337. *Id.* at 8.

338. *Health Information Privacy: Summary of the HIPAA Privacy Rule*, U.S. DEP'T OF HEALTH & HUMAN SERVS., www.hhs.gov/ocr/privacy/hipaa/understanding/sum mary/index.html.

339. *See* 20 U.S.C. § 1681(a).

340. Davis v. Monroe Cty. Bd. of Educ., 526 U.S. 629, 648 (1999).

341. *See* 34 C.F.R. § 106.40.

342. *See* Letter from U.S. Dep't of Justice Civil Rights Div. & U.S. Dep't of Educ. Office for Civil Rights, to Asaf Orr re Conclusion of Investigation in DOJ Case No. DJ169-12C-79, OCR Case No. 09-12-1020 (July 24, 2013), www.nclrights.org/wp-content/uploads/2013/09/Arcadia_Notification_Letter_07.24.2013.pdf (concerning OCR investigation of school district's refusal to let a transgendered boy use the boys' restroom).

343. 20 U.S.C. § 1681.

344. *See* Jackson v. Birmingham Bd. of Educ., 544 U.S. 167 (2005).

345. *Compare* Lakoski v. James, 66 F.3d 751 (5th Cir. 1996) (holding that Title VII provides the exclusive remedy for sex-based employment discrimination in federally funded institutions) and Waid v. Merrill Area Pub. Schs., 91 F.3d 857

(7th Cir. 1996) (holding that Title VII preempted plaintiff's claims for equitable relief under Title IX), abrogated on other grounds by Fitzgerald v. Barnstable Sch. Comm., 555 U.S. 246 (2009), *with* Doe v. Mercy Catholic Med. Ctr., 850 F.3d 545 (3rd Cir. 2017) (holding that medical residents had a private right of action to bring claims under Title IX for sex-based discrimination in employment) and Lipsett v. Univ. of P.R., 864 F.2d 881 (1st Cir. 1988) (holding that a medical resident, who was both an employee and a student within a university's residency program, could bring a private cause of action under Title IX against the university for sexual harassment perpetuated by other medical resident).

346. *See id.*

347. *See* Gebser v. Lago Vista Indep. Sch. Dist., 524 U.S. 274 (1998) (enforcing the requirement to establish prompt and equitable grievance procedures).

348. 34 C.F.R. §§ 100.7, 100.71.

349. *See* Franklin v. Gwinnett Cty. Sch., 503 U.S. 60 (1992); Cannon v. Univ. of Chi., 441 U.S. 667 (1979).

350. *See* Davis v. Monroe Cty. Bd. of Educ., 526 U.S. 629 (1999).

351. *See* 34 C.F.R. § 106.8(b).

352. *Q&A on Campus Sexual Misconduct* (Sept. 2017), https://www2.ed.gov/about/offices/list/ocr/docs/qa-title-ix-201709.pdf; *Revised Sexual Harassment Guidance: Harassment of Students by School Employees, Other Students or Third Parties* (Jan. 19, 2001), https://www2.ed.gov/about/offices/list/ocr/docs/shguide.html; *Dear Colleague Letter* (Jan. 25, 2006), https://www2.ed.gov/about/offices/list/ocr/letters/sexhar-2006.html.

353. 85 Fed. Reg. 30026 (May 19, 2020).

354. Press Release, Dep't of Ed., Department of Education's Office for Civil Rights Launches Comprehensive Review of Title IX Regulations to Fulfill President Biden's Executive Order Guaranteeing and Educational Environment Free from Sex Discrimination (Apr. 6, 2021), https://www.ed.gov/news/press-releases/department-educations-office-civil-rights-launches-comprehensive-review-title-ix-regulations-fulfill-president-bidens-executive-order-guaranteeing-educational-environment-free-sex-discrimination.

355. *Id.* § 106.8(a).

356. *Id.* § 106.37(c).

357. *Id.* § 106.41(c)(2)–(10).

358. *Id.* § 106.41(c)(1).

359. *Id.* § 106.41.

360. Policy Interpretation, 44 Fed. Reg. 239 (Dec. 11, 1979).

361. *Id.*

362. *Id.*

363. 34 C.F.R. § 106.41(c)(2)–(10).

364. Policy Interpretation, 44 Fed. Reg. 239.

365. 34 C.F.R. § 106.41(c)(1).

366. Policy Interpretation, 44 Fed. Reg. 239.

367. *See* Biediger v. Quinnipiac Univ., 691 F.3d 85 (2d Cir. 2012) (3.62% disparity violates Title IX); Equity in Athletics, Inc. v. Dep't of Educ., 639 F.3d 91 (4th Cir. 2011), *cert. denied*, 132 S. Ct. 1004 (2012) (1%–2% disparity is not significant).

368. Mansourian v. Regents of Univ. of Cal., 602 F.3d 957 (9th Cir. 2010) (denying institution summary judgment on grounds that the record demonstrated a history of program expansion that lasted from 1996 to 2000).

369. 17 U.S.C. § 102.

370. *See id.*

371. *See id.*

372. Feist Publ'ns, Inc. v. Rural Tel. Serv. Co., 499 U.S. 340, 345 (1991).

373. *See* Midway Mfg. Co. v. Artic Int'l, Inc., 547 F. Supp. 999 (N.D. Ill. 1982).

374. 17 U.S.C. § 411.

375. *Id.* §§ 504–05.

376. *Id.* § 504(c).

377. *Id.* § 106.

378. *Id.* § 201.

379. *See* Q 35.24.

380. 17 U.S.C. § 101.

381. The Supreme Court identified certain factors that characterize what constitutes the "employer-employee" relationship for purposes of determining whether an individual should be considered an "employee" for purposes of a work made for hire. *See* Cmty. for Creative Non-Violence v. Reid, 490 U.S. 730 (1989). Although the Court did not provide an exhaustive list, most of the factors characterize a regular, salaried employment relationship. *See id.*

382. 17 U.S.C. § 101.

383. *Id.*

384. *See* Hayes v. Sony Corp. of Am., 847 F.2d 412, 416 (7th Cir. 1988); *see also* Dreyfuss, *The Creative Employee and the Copyright Act of 1976*, 54 U. Chi. L. Rev. 590, 597–98 (1987).

385. *Hayes*, 847 F.2d at 416. For example, in rejecting a publisher's contention that a professor was an employee, and his work a "work for hire," a California court held that:

> [t]his contention calls for some understanding of the purpose for which a university hires a professor and what rights it may reasonably expect to retain after the services have been rendered. A university's obligation to its students is to make the subject matter covered by a course available for study by various methods, including classroom presentation. It is not obligated to present the subject by means of any particular expression. As far as the teacher is concerned, neither the record in this case nor any custom known to us suggests that the university can prescribe his way of expressing the ideas he puts before his students. Yet expression is what this lawsuit is all about. No reason has been suggested *why a university would want to retain the*

ownership in a professor's expression. Such retention would be useless except possible for making a little profit from a publication and for making it difficult for the teacher to give the same lectures, should he change jobs.

Williams v. Weisser, 273 Cal. App. 2d 726 (1969) (emphasis added). *See generally* 5 EDUCATION Law § 14.01[2][a][r] (James A. Rapp, ed., Matthew Bender 1999).

386. *See* 1 M.B. NIMMER & D. NIMMER, NIMMER ON COPYRIGHT § 5.03[B][1][b], at 5-32 (Matthew Bender 1999).

387. *Hayes*, 847 F.2d at 416; Weinstein v. Univ. of Ill., 811 F.2d 1091, 1093–94 (7th Cir. 1987) ("the statute [17 U.S.C. § 201(b)] is general enough to make every academic article a 'work for hire' and therefore vest exclusive control in universities rather than scholars").

388. *See, e.g.,* Todd Simon, *Faculty Writings: Are They "Works for Hire" Under the 1976 Copyright Act?,* 9 J.C. & U.L. 485, 495–99 (1982).

389. 17 U.S.C. § 110(1).

390. *See id.*

391. *See id.* § 110(2).

392. *See id.*

393. *Id.* § 107.

394. *Id.*

395. *Id.* § 504(2).

396. H.R. REP. NO. 94-1476, at 65–74 (1976).

397. *See* 17 U.S.C. § 504(b).

398. 17 U.S.C. § 504(c). As stated above, the statutory damages are calculated on a "per work" basis. For example, if a defendant made one million copies of the same novel, then a successful plaintiff could receive up to $30,000 (assuming the infringement was not willful) in statutory damages as only one copyrighted work was involved.

399. *Id.* § 504(c). Copyright violations are also considered federal crimes when the infringement is done willfully with intent to profit. The penalties vary with prison sentences of up to ten years in some instances. *See* 18 U.S.C. § 2319.

400. Several companies have compiled large portfolios of copyrighted material through negotiations with authors, which can then be licensed by other end users. For example, the Copyright Clearance Center handles text-based works. *See* www.copyright.com. The benefit to this model is that end users do not need to track down individual authors, and authors do not need to negotiate separate agreements with each end user.

401. Digital Millennium Copyright Act (DMCA), Pub. L. No. 105-304, 112 Stat. 2860 (1998).

402. Although the DMCA can shield a university from contributory liability, it does not protect against vicarious liability—the safe harbor does not extend to *employees* of the university.

403. 17 U.S.C. § 512(a).

404. *See id.* Although section 512(a) (like the other safe harbors) provides a list of requirements for the transitory safe harbor, it should be noted that the DMCA contains obligations *in addition* to those listed for each safe harbor.

405. 17 U.S.C. § 512(b).

406. *Id.* § 512(c).

407. *See id.*

408. *Id.* § 512(d).

409. *Id.* § 512(i)(1)(A).

410. *Id.* § 512(e).

411. For a general and more detailed overview of U.S. export controls, see chapter 19. Three principal agencies regulate exports from the United States: the U.S. Department of State Directorate of Defense Trade Controls (DDTC) administers export control of defense exports under the International Traffic in Arms Regulations (ITAR); the U.S. Department of Commerce Bureau of Industry and Security (BIS) administers export control of so-called dual-use technology exports under the Export Administration Regulations (EAR); and the U.S. Department of the Treasury Office of Foreign Assets Control (OFAC) administers exports to embargoed countries and designated entities under OFAC regulations.

412. *See* Council on Governmental Relations, Export Controls and Universities— Information and Case Studies (Jan. 2, 2004), https://www.cogr.edu/sites/default/files/COGR_Brochure_-_Export_Controls_and_Universities_-_Information_and_Case_Studies.pdf.

413. *See* Uniform Administrative Requirements, Cost Principles, and Audit Requirements for Federal Awards, 78 Fed. Reg. 78,590 (Dec. 13, 2013) [hereinafter Super Circular] (to be codified at 2 C.F.R. § 200.430), www.federalregister.gov/articles/2013/12/26/2013-30465/uniform-administrative-requirements-cost-principles-and-audit-requirements-for-federal-awards. In December 2013, this Super Circular superseded and streamlined the requirements of seven previously issued circulars, three of which were significant to higher education institutions. They were (1) OMB Circular A-21: Cost Principles for Educational Institutions, (2) OMB Circular A-110: Uniform Administrative Requirements for Grants and Agreements with Institutions of Higher Education, Hospitals, and Other Non-Profit Organizations; and (3) OMB Circular A-133: Audits of States, Local Governments, and Non-Profit Organizations. Copies of the OMB circulars that are superseded by this guidance may be found on OMB's website. *See Circulars*, OFFICE OF MGMT. & BUDGET, www.whitehouse.gov/omb/circulars_default/.

414. *See, e.g.*, Department of Defense Grant and Agreement Regulations, 32 C.F.R. § 21.100 *et seq.*

415. *See* Super Circular, 2 C.F.R. § 200.308.

416. *See id.* § 200.430.

417. Council on Government Relations, Policies and Practices: Compensation, Effort Commitments and Certification, at 23 (Mar. 1, 2007).

418. *See* Super Circular, 2 C.F.R. § 200.400 *et seq.*

419. *See id.* § 200.306.

420. *See* 45 C.F.R. § 46.

421. *See id.* § 46.107 (noting that the review board must have five members, with varying backgrounds to promote complete and adequate review of research activities commonly conducted by the institution).

422. *See id.* § 46.108.

423. *See id.* § 46.103.

424. *See id.* §§ 46.109, 46.501.

425. *See id.* § 46.115.

426. *See id.* § 46.123.

427. *Id.* § 46.201.

428. *Id.*

429. *See id.* § 46.301.

430. Bayh-Dole Act, 35 U.S.C. §§ 200–12.

431. *See* 37 C.F.R. § 401.1.

432. *Id.*

433. 35 U.S.C. § 202(c)(1); 37 C.F.R. § 401.14(c)(1).

434. *See* 37 C.F.R. § 401.5(h).

435. *See id.* § 401.14(f)(2).

436. *See id.* § 401.5(b) (referencing section 401.14, Standard Patent Rights Clauses).

437. *See* 35 U.S.C. § 202(c); 37 C.F.R. § 401.14(c).

438. *See* 37 C.F.R. § 401.14(f)(1).

439. *See* 35 U.S.C. § 202(c)(5); *id.* § 205 (agency has discretion to withhold); 37 C.F.R. § 401.8; *id.* § 401.14(h); *id.* § 401.13(c).

440. False Claims Act (FCA), 31 U.S.C. § 3729 *et seq.*

441. *See* 31 U.S.C. § 3729(a)(1) (statutory penalty range of $5,000 to $10,000 per claim, "as adjusted by the Federal Civil Penalties Inflation Adjustment Act of 1990"); 28 C.F.R. § 85.3(a)(9) (increasing the penalties for False Claims Act violations to a range of $5,500 to $11,500, effective Sept. 29, 1999).

442. In practice, the FCA is enforced against institutions through civil actions. However, criminal penalties do exist. The government may seek criminal penalties for basically the same behavior that forms the basis of a civil False Claims Act action. *See* 18 U.S.C. § 287. As in civil actions, the government is required to demonstrate that the violation was "knowing." Unlike civil actions, however, the government is required to prove the allegation beyond a reasonable doubt, rather than to the lesser civil standard of "preponderance of the evidence." Violations are punishable by up to five years in prison and fines of up to $500,000 for organizations and $250,000 for individuals. *See* 18 U.S.C. §§ 287, 3559, 3571. The government might instead seek an "alternative fine" of twice the gain or loss that resulted from the conduct, which may be above the applicable statutory maximums. *See* 18 U.S.C. § 3571.

443. *See* Hendow v. Univ. of Phx., 461 F.3d 1166, 1176–77 (9th Cir. 2006); *see also* U.S. *ex rel.* Main v. Oakland City Univ., 426 F.3d 914 (7th Cir. 2005).

444. *See id.*

445. *See Medicare Fraud Case Settled for $30 Million*, HEALTHCARE FIN. MGMT., Feb. 1, 1996.

446. *See* Press Release No. 98-278, U.S. Dep't of Justice, Health Center in San Antonio Will Pay US $17.2 Million to Settle False Claims Act Case (June 12, 1998), www.justice.gov/opa/pr/1998/June/278.html.

447. *See* Kenneth R. Weiss, *UC to Pay $22.5 Million in Medicare Investigation*, L.A. TIMES, Feb. 3, 2001, http://articles.latimes.com/2001/feb/03/local/me-20621.

448. *See* Press Release No. 09-566, U.S. Dep't of Justice, New Jersey University Hospital to Pay Additional $2 Million to Resolve Fraud Claims That Facility Double Billed Medicaid (June 9, 2009), www.justice.gov/opa/pr/2009/June/09-civ-566.html.

449. *See* Press Release No. 10-293, U.S. Dep't of Justice, New Jersey Hospital to Pay $6.35 Million to Resolve Allegations of Inflating Charges to Obtain Higher Medicare Reimbursement (Mar. 19, 2010), www.justice.gov/opa/pr/2010/March/10-civ-293.html (noting the settlement and explaining that, "[i]n addition to its standard payment system, Medicare provides supplemental reimbursement, called 'outlier payments,' to hospitals and other health care providers in cases where the cost of care is unusually high. Congress enacted the supplemental outlier payments system to ensure that hospitals have the incentive to treat inpatients whose care requires unusually high costs.").

450. *See* Press Release, U.S. Dep't of Justice, U.S. Attorney James T. Jacks, N. Dist. of Tex., UTSW and Parkland Resolve Allegations of Improper Physician Supervision of Surgical Residents (Sept. 1, 2011), www.justice.gov/usao/txn/PressRel11/utsw_parkland_residents_settle_pr.html.

451. *See* Press Release No. 11-299, U.S. Dep't of Justice, U.S. Attorney Preet Bharara, S.D.N.Y., Manhattan U.S. Attorney Recovers $995,000 in Damages in Health Care Fraud Lawsuit Against Columbia University and New York Presbyterian Hospital (Oct. 6, 2011), www.justice.gov/usao/nys/pressreleases/October11/trusteesofcolumbiaunivnypresbyterianhospitalanddrgoluboffsettlementpr.pdf.

452. *See* Press Release, U.S. Attorney's Office, E. Dist. of Pa., United States Settled with Temple University and Dr. Joseph Kubacki over Improper Billing (May 15, 2012), www.justice.gov/archive/usao/pae/News/2012/May/temple,kubacki_release.htm.

453. *See* Press Release No. 12-1413, U.S. Dep't of Justice, Baylor University Medical Center to Pay More Than $900,000 for False Medicare Claims for Radiation Oncology Services (Nov. 12, 2012), www.justice.gov/opa/pr/2012/November/12-civ-1413.html.

454. *See* Press Release, U.S. Attorney's Office for the E. Dist. of N.C., Duke University Health System, Inc. Agrees to Pay $1 Million for Alleged False Claims Submitted to Federal Health Care Programs (Mar. 21, 2014), www.justice.gov/usao/nce/press/2014/2014-mar-21.html.

455. *See, e.g.*, Seminole Tribe of Fla. v. Florida, 517 U.S. 44 (1996) (prohibits suits in federal courts against state governments by its citizens); ERWIN CHEMERINSKY, FEDERAL JURISDICTION 394 (Aspen 4th ed. 2003) (prohibits suits in federal courts against state governments by citizens of another state or by a citizen of a foreign country).

456. *See* U.S. *ex rel.* Long v. SCS Bus. & Tech. Inst., Inc., 173 F.3d 870, 882 (D.C. Cir. 1999) (citing West Virginia v. United States, 479 U.S. 305, 311 (1987)).

457. *See* Press Release No. 09-367, U.S. Dep't of Justice, Alta Colleges to Pay $7 Million to Resolve False Claims Act Allegations (Apr. 29, 2009), www.justice. gov/opa/pr/2009/April/09-civ-367.html.

458. *See* Kate Moser, *Qui Tam Suit Against University Nets $78.5 Million Settlement,* RECORDER (CALLAW), Dec. 15, 2009, www.law.com/jsp/article.jsp?id= 1202436337644&Qui_Tam_Suit_Against_University_Nets_Million_Settlement#; *Hendow,* 461 F.3d at 1176–77.

459. *See* Press Release No. 10-240, U.S. Dep't of Justice, Chicago Hospital to Pay More Than $1.5 Million to Resolve Medicare False Claims Act Allegations (Mar. 9, 2010), www.justice.gov/opa/pr/2010/March/10-civ-240.html.

460. *See* Press Release, U.S. Attorney's Office, M.D. Ga., Board of Regents for the University System of Georgia Agrees to Pay the United States of America $500,000 to Resolve Allegations of Violations of the False Claims Act at Fort Valley State University (Jan. 10, 2010), www.justice.gov/usao/gam/press_releases/2010/ 01_11_2010.html.

461. *See* Press Release No. 98-549, U.S. Dep't of Justice, University of Minnesota Pays $32 Million to Settle Allegations of Selling an Unlicensed Drug and Mishandling NIH Grant Funds (Nov. 17, 1998), www.justice.gov/opa/pr/1998/ November/549civ.htm.

462. *See* Press Release No. 03-076, U.S. Dep't of Justice, Northwestern University Will Pay $5.5 Million to Resolve False Claims Act and Common Law Allegations (Feb. 6, 2003), www.justice.gov/opa/pr/2003/February/03_civ_076.htm.

463. *See* Jeffrey Brainard, *Johns Hopkins Settles Charges of Overbilling,* CHRON. HIGHER EDUC. (Mar. 12, 2004), http://chronicle.com/article/Johns-Hopkins-Settles-Charges/35473.

464. *See* Jeffrey Brainard, *Accounting for Researchers' Time: Recent Legal Settlements Are Highlighting a Longstanding Conflict Between Universities and the Federal Government,* CHRON. HIGHER EDUC., July 16, 2004, at A20.

465. *See Florida International U. Agrees to $11.5-Million Settlement with Government over Grants Accounting,* CHRON. HIGHER EDUC., Feb. 15, 2005.

466. *See* Press Release No. 05-194, U.S. Dep't of Justice, University of Alabama-Birmingham Will Pay U.S. $3.39 Million to Resolve False Billing Allegations (Apr. 14, 2005), www.justice.gov/opa/pr/2005/April/05_civ_194.htm.

467. *See* Press Release, Dep't of Justice, U.S. Attorney's Office, N.D. Ga., St. Louis University Agrees to Pay $1 Million to Settle Federal False Claims Act Allegations (July 8, 2008), www.justice.gov/usao/gan/press/2008/07-08-08.pdf.

468. *See* Press Release, U.S. Attorney's Office, D. Conn., Yale University to Pay $7.6 Million to Resolve False Claims Act and Common Law Allegations (Dec. 23, 2008), www.justice.gov/usao/ct/Press2008/20081223-1.html.

469. *See* Press Release No. 09-051, U.S. Attorney's Office, S.D.N.Y., Weill Medical College of Cornell University to Pay over $2.6 Million to Settle Federal Civil Fraud Charges (Mar. 6, 2009), www.justice.gov/usao/nys/pressreleases/ March09/weillmedicalcollegesettlementpr.pdf.

470. *See* Press Release, U.S. Attorney's Office, N.D. Ga., Morehouse Settles Misuse of Funds Case (Aug. 4, 2011), www.justice.gov/usao/gan/press/2011/08-04-11.html; *see also* NASA OFFICE OF INSPECTOR GEN., SEMIANNUAL REPORT APRIL 1, 2011–SEPTEMBER 30, 2011, at 20 (Oct. 31, 2011), http://oig.nasa.gov/SAR/sar0911.pdf.

471. *See* U.S. *ex rel.* Foulds v. Tex. Tech Univ., 171 F.3d 279, 294 (5th Cir. 1999) (reasoning that the decision by the United States to maintain a passive role compels us to conclude that the private citizen, not the United States, has "commenced or prosecuted" the suit); U.S. *ex rel.* Long v. SCS Bus. & Tech. Inst., Inc., 173 F.3d 870, 882–84 (D.C. Cir. 1999) (holding that "a state is not a person who may be held liable [by a citizen] under [the] False Claims Act" and explaining that a qui tam relator was a "real party in interest" against the state because the federal government did not intervene).

472. *See* U.S. *ex rel.* Berge v. United States, 104 F.3d 1453, 1458–59 (4th Cir. 1997) ("[S]tates have no Eleventh Amendment immunity against the United States ab initio. Therefore, there is no reason Congress would have displaced it in the False Claims Act."); U.S. *ex rel.* Rodgers v. Arkansas, 154 F.3d 865, 868 (8th Cir. 1998); U.S. *ex rel.* Milam v. Univ. of Tex. M.D. Anderson Cancer Ctr., 961 F.2d 46, 50 (4th Cir. 1992).

473. *See* chapter 12, The False Claims Act.

36

Labor and Employment Law

Kenneth A. Jenero

An extensive and complicated labyrinth of federal, state, and local laws governs the relationship between companies and their employees. The task of maintaining a program for compliance with these myriad requirements falls upon management at all levels, typically with the human resources department taking the lead in coordinating the compliance efforts. A detailed prescription for a compliance program focused on labor and employment requirements could fill many volumes. Rather than attempt to offer such a prescription here, which is not possible given the scope of this book, this chapter provides an overview[1] that is intended to enable compliance officers to identify those principal areas of labor and employment law compliance on which they should focus.

The substantive discussion in this chapter is limited exclusively to federal labor and employment law requirements. A discussion of the many requirements imposed by state and local governments—even at a relatively superficial "issue spotting" level—would far exceed the confines of this book. However, managers charged with compliance responsibility must be mindful of the fact that state and even local governments (particularly large cities) have become increasingly active and aggressive in adopting and enforcing their own laws for regulating the workplace. While many state and local labor and employment laws are patterned on federal laws, they often expand upon the federal regulatory scheme.[2] This means that companies must be careful to explore and understand the labor and employment law nuances of all of the jurisdictions in which they operate.

Employment Eligibility and Verification

Q 36.1   What are an employer's obligations regarding documentation of an employee's legal authorization to work in the United States?

The Immigration Reform and Control Act of 1986 (IRCA),[3] which prohibits the employment of individuals who are not legally authorized to work in the United States, requires employers to verify each new employee's identity and work authorization by completing an Employment Eligibility Verification Form I-9 for the employee.

Eligibility Verification Form I-9

Q 36.1.1   What are the Form I-9 requirements?

All employers are subject to the I-9 requirement. A separate Form I-9 must be completed for each employee hired for employment in the United States. This includes citizens and non-citizens. Section I of the form, Employee Information and Attestation, must be completed no later than the employee's first day of employment. Section II of the form, Employer or Authorized Representative Review and Verification, must be completed within three business days of the employee's first day of employment.

The U.S. Citizenship and Immigration Service (USCIS) released a revised version of Form I-9, Employment Eligibility Verification, on October 21, 2019. Instructions for how to download the Form I-9 are available on the USCIS's Form I-9 page.[4]

Form I-9 requires the employee to submit and attest to certain specified information establishing his or her identity and authorization to work. The I-9 Form includes Lists of Acceptable Documents that an employee may submit. The law prohibits employers from specifying which documents employees may submit from these lists. Employers should ensure that they are familiar with employment eligibility verification documentation requirements, including which documents are "acceptable I-9 documents" under current regulations. Employers are responsible for physically examining the documents submitted by the employee and certifying that:

(1) they have done so;

(2) the documents appear to be genuine and to relate to the employee; and

(3) to the best of their knowledge, the employee is authorized to work in the United States.

Q 36.1.2   What are the consequences of failing to comply?

The U.S. Department of Labor (DOL) and other agencies make a review of I-9 forms a routine part of any audit or investigation they conduct. Employers who fail to comply with the I-9 requirements or who knowingly employ illegal workers are subject to fines and, in some circumstances, criminal prosecution.

TIP: Most employers find that, to be prepared for a review of I-9 forms in an audit or investigation by the DOL or other agency, it is administratively simpler to retain I-9 forms in separate files that are designated for that purpose—usually alphabetically by employee name. It is easier to collect requested I-9 forms from such files than it is to pull them from each individual's personnel file.

Credit Reports and Background Checks

Q 36.1.3   What federal laws governing employment background checks must an employer comply with?

The Fair Credit Reporting Act (FCRA)[5] applies whenever an employer uses, for any employment-related purpose, certain credit bureau reports and background checks furnished by individuals or entities in the business of providing such reports and checks. (Note that state laws may impose more stringent requirements on employment background checks.) The FCRA's definition of the types of reports and checks that trigger its requirements is broad, encompassing not only true credit reports, but also reports on such matters as driving records, criminal records, work histories, interviews with personal acquaintances, personal characteristics, modes of living, and general reputation.

Q 36.1.4   What does the FCRA require?

Whenever the FCRA is triggered, the employer must make certain written disclosures to the affected applicant or employee and secure the applicant's or employee's written consent prior to obtaining and using FCRA-covered information about that individual. The consent must be set forth on a stand-alone document separate from the employment application. Additional disclosures are required if the covered information is a factor in an adverse employment decision— for example, a refusal to hire, denial of a promotion, or disciplinary action. This includes notice prior to taking the adverse action and after a final decision is made.

Q 36.1.5   What are the consequences of failing to comply?

Violations of the FCRA subject the employer to civil penalties, including nominal damages (if no actual damages exist), actual damages (including emotional distress), and punitive damages, plus attorneys' fees and costs, where there is "willful noncompliance" with the act.

Employment Discrimination — Statutory Framework

Q 36.2   What federal laws govern employment discrimination?

The broadest nondiscrimination statute is Title VII of the Civil Rights Act of 1964,[6] which prohibits discrimination on the basis of race, color, religion, sex, pregnancy, and national origin. The following are the other major federal statutes prohibiting employment discrimination:

- Age Discrimination in Employment Act;
- Americans with Disabilities Act;
- Genetic Information Nondiscrimination Act;
- Immigration Reform and Control Act; and
- Equal Pay Act.

Q 36.3   What types of discrimination are prohibited?

A variety of federal statutes prohibit discrimination against job applicants and employees based on:

- race;
- color;
- religion;
- sex;
- pregnancy;
- national origin;
- citizenship and immigration status;
- genetic information;
- age (if at least 40 years old);
- disability;
- retaliation; and
- "association" with a person in a protected class.

Title VII: "Disparate Treatment" Discrimination

Q 36.4   What is "disparate treatment" discrimination?

Title VII requires that job applicants and employees not be treated differently because of their protected characteristics—namely, race, color, religion, sex, pregnancy, and national origin. This is referred to as "disparate treatment" discrimination. For example, an employee may not be given a lower-paying job, different benefits, or harder assignments because she is Hispanic. Title VII prohibits employers from acting on stereotypes and assumptions—rather than facts—about an applicant's or employee's abilities, traits, or performance. "Majority" employees and employees perceived to be minorities also are protected. For example, employers cannot discriminate against white male employees because of their race or gender, and employers may be committing national origin discrimination if they disadvantage employees thought to be Hispanic (even though they are not Hispanic in fact).

Title VII: "Disparate Impact" Discrimination

Q 36.4.1   What is "disparate impact" discrimination?

Title VII prohibits discrimination arising from neutral policies or practices that have a disproportionately adverse effect on minority employees and are not reasonably related to the necessities of the business. This is referred to as "disparate impact" discrimination. An employer likely would commit disparate impact discrimination against minority employees by requiring a high school diploma for minimum-skill, entry-level manual-labor jobs, because a high school diploma is not actually required to perform such jobs and, statistically, minority employees have a lower high school graduation rate. Another example of disparate impact discrimination would be imposing an English-only language requirement on housekeeping employees, whose duties do not require English-language proficiency.

Title VII: "Association" Discrimination

Q 36.4.2   What is "association" discrimination?

Title VII prohibits discrimination against an applicant or employee because he or she is married or related to, or associates with, a person or persons in a protected class. This is referred to as "association discrimination." For example, an employer cannot lawfully refuse to hire an otherwise-qualified job applicant because she is a white woman dating or married to a black man.

Title VII: Religious Discrimination and Accommodation of Religious Beliefs

Q 36.4.3   How must an employer protect an employee's rights regarding religion?

Title VII's prohibition against religious discrimination means that employers must allow employees to practice their own religious beliefs and cannot endorse, promote, or require specific religious practices or beliefs against an employee's wishes. In addition, employers must ensure that employees are not harassed because of their religious beliefs.

Beyond prohibiting religious discrimination, Title VII requires employers to make requested reasonable accommodations to the religious practices of employees, so long as the accommodation does not impose an "undue hardship" on the employer's business. Such accommodations might include time off for religious observances. An accommodation might create an "undue hardship" for an employer if it would require the employer to bear unreasonable expenses, diminish the efficiency of performance of other jobs, cause co-workers to carry the accommodated employee's share of potentially hazardous or burdensome work, or if less disruptive or burdensome accommodations would achieve the same result.

Title VII: Pregnancy Discrimination

Q 36.4.4   What are the rules regarding a pregnant employee?

Discrimination based on pregnancy or pregnancy-related conditions is a prohibited form of sex discrimination under amendments to Title VII enacted by the Pregnancy Discrimination Act (PDA).[7] An employer cannot refuse to hire and cannot fire, transfer, reduce benefits to, or otherwise take adverse action against a woman because she is pregnant, thought to be pregnant, planning to become pregnant, has given birth to a child, or is suffering from pregnancy-related conditions. It also is unlawful to subject a female to harassment because of pregnancy, childbirth or related medical conditions.

Women who are pregnant or affected by pregnancy-related conditions must be treated in the same manner as other applicants or employees with similar limitations. An employer must respond to the temporary incapacities of pregnant employees in the same manner that it would respond to the temporary incapacities of male employees. For example, if the employer would modify the job duties, transfer the worker to a different job, or offer unpaid leave to a temporarily incapacitated male employee, those same opportunities must be extended to a pregnant employee. In addressing pregnant employees' need for leaves and returns to work during and after the pregnancy, employers must follow their customary procedures for requiring medical documentation and must hold jobs open for pregnant employees who are on leave if the jobs would be held for male employees who are on leave.

Employers cannot restrict pregnancy benefits to pregnant employees who are married. In addition, pregnant employees must be allowed to work, or return to work, as long as they are able to perform their jobs.

Title VII: National Origin Discrimination

Q 36.4.5   What are indications of discrimination based on national origin?

Title VII's prohibition against national origin discrimination means that employers cannot treat employees or applicants differently because they are, or are thought to be, of a particular national origin or ancestry (such as Italian-American) or because they "look foreign," have an accent, or are not fluent in English (unless the absence of an accent or English-language fluency is a legitimate job requirement). Requiring only job applicants who "look foreign" or "sound foreign" to verify their eligibility to work in the United States would be a form of national origin discrimination.

Q 36.4.6   Can an employer insist that English be spoken in the workplace?

Title VII prohibits employers from imposing requirements that only English be spoken in the workplace, absent a legitimate business reason for the rule. Even when there is a legitimate reason for such a rule, the requirement to speak "English only" cannot extend to breaks, meal periods, or other conversations unrelated to work activities.

IRCA: Citizenship and Immigration Status Discrimination

Q 36.5   What are an employer's obligations regarding discrimination based on citizenship or immigration status?

The IRCA prohibits employers from engaging in certain immigration-related unfair employment practices. Employers generally may not discriminate against individuals with respect to hiring or firing because they are or are not U.S. citizens, or because of their immigration status, provided that they are legally authorized to work in the United States. The law also prohibits immigration-related document abuse, which includes situations in which an employer:

(1) requests more documents than are required to verify employment authorization and identity;

(2) requests documents different from those required to verify employment authorization and identity;

(3) rejects documents that reasonably appear to be genuine and related to the employee; or

(4) requires certain documents over others based on an employee's citizenship or immigration status.

The IRCA also includes an anti-retaliation provision that makes it unlawful for employers to intimidate, threaten, coerce, or retaliate against a person who:

(1) files a charge alleging an immigration-related unfair employment practice;

(2) participates in an investigation or prosecution of a discrimination complaint;

(3) contests action that may constitute discrimination;

(4) asserts his or her rights under anti-discrimination laws; or

(5) asserts another person's right under anti-discrimination laws.

ADEA: Age Discrimination

Q 36.6   What are an employer's obligations regarding discrimination based on age?

The Age Discrimination in Employment Act (ADEA)[8] protects persons who are at least forty years old against age discrimination. An employer may not refuse to hire or discharge someone based on his or her age or on the suspicion that age makes the individual unfit for the job. In addition, most mandatory retirements based on age are illegal, although retirement eligibility programs in which age is a factor can be legal under certain circumstances.

ADA: Disability Discrimination

Q 36.7   How is a disability protected in the workplace?

The Americans with Disabilities Act (ADA)[9] prohibits employment discrimination against a "qualified individual with a disability." The ADA makes it illegal to refuse to hire or to discharge someone merely because he or she has a disability, has a record or history of a disability, or is regarded as having a disability. Employers must determine whether the disability prevents the individual from performing the essential functions of the job that he or she holds or is seeking. Employers also must determine whether there are any reasonable accommodations that would enable the disabled individual to perform the essential functions of the job.

Q 36.7.1   What is the ADA's definition of "disability"?

The ADA's definition of "disability" is very broad, encompassing applicants and employees who:

- have a physical or mental impairment that substantially limits one or more major life activities (for example, caring for oneself, performing manual tasks, seeing, hearing, eating, lifting, bending, speaking, breathing, learning, reading, concentrating, thinking, communicating, and working); or

- have a record or history of such physical or mental impairment; or

- are regarded (accurately or inaccurately) as having such an impairment.

In addition to readily detectable impairments such as deafness, blindness, or paraplegia, the ADA protects persons suffering from less obvious impairments such as long-term diseases (for example, AIDS, emphysema, cancer) and mental illnesses (for example, major depression).

Q 36.7.2   What qualifies a person as entitled to protection under the ADA?

To be protected by the ADA, an applicant or employee must be a "qualified individual with a disability." This means that the person must (1) have the required education, experience, and skills for the job, and (2) be able to perform the essential functions of the job with or without reasonable accommodations for the disability.

Q 36.7.3   What are the "essential functions" of a position?

The "essential functions" are the fundamental duties of the job. The inquiry into whether a particular function is essential initially focuses on whether the employer actually requires employees to perform the functions that the employer asserts are essential. If the individual who holds the position is actually required to perform the function, the inquiry then centers around whether removing the function would fundamentally alter the position.

The following factors are relevant to the determination of whether a function is "essential":

- whether the position exists to perform a particular function;

- the number of other employees available to perform the function or among whom performance of the function can be distributed;

- the degree of expertise or skill required to perform the function;

- the terms of written job descriptions prepared by the employer before advertising or interviewing applicants for the job;

- the employer's judgment as to what functions are essential;

- the terms of applicable collective bargaining agreements;

- the work experience of past employees in the job or of current employees in similar jobs;

- the time spent performing the particular function; and

- the consequences of failing to require the employee to perform the function.

Q 36.7.4 What are an employer's "reasonable accommodation" obligations under the ADA?

The ADA requires employers to provide "reasonable accommodations" to qualified applicants or employees with known disabilities to enable the applicants to apply for jobs and the employees to perform the essential functions of their jobs, *unless* the accommodations would pose an undue hardship on the employer. In general, an accommodation is any change in the work environment or in the way things customarily are done that enables an individual with a disability to enjoy equal employment opportunities. Such accommodations may involve:

(1) modifications to equipment, working conditions, or schedules;

(2) altering when and/or how an essential function is performed;

(3) restructuring a job by reallocating or redistributing non-essential job functions;

(4) providing unpaid leaves of absence; or

(5) providing supportive devices to assist persons with hearing, vision, or speech limitations.

For individuals with mental disabilities, different supervisory methods may be required in some circumstances. Reassignment to a vacant position also is a potential reasonable accommodation when accommodation within the individual's current position would pose an undue hardship.

The ADA does not require employers to eliminate or alter essential functions of a job as a form of reasonable accommodation. Employers are not required to provide personal use items such as glasses or hearing aids. In addition, employers are not required to adopt an applicant's or employee's preferred accommodation if equally effective but less expensive or less disruptive alternatives are available.

COMPLIANCE FACT

To avoid liability, employers should be sure to consider reassigning a disabled employee to a vacant position for which he or she is otherwise qualified, before terminating an employee who is unable to perform the essential functions of his or her current position with or without reasonable accommodations.

Q 36.7.5   What is considered an "undue hardship" regarding an employer's provision of reasonable accommodations?

What constitutes an "undue hardship" may vary from one employer to the next. There is no bright-line rule. It requires an analysis of the particular employer involved, the particular accommodation requested, and its impact on the employer's operations. The question is whether the action would require "significant difficulty or expense" when considered in light of the following factors:

(1)   the accommodation's nature and cost;

(2)   the overall financial resources of the employer as a whole;

(3)   the overall size, structure and function of the employer's workforce;

(4)   the number, type, and location of the employer's facilities; and

(5)   the geographic separateness and administrative and fiscal relationship of the facility in question to the overall employer.

Q 36.7.6   What kind of standards can employers maintain for disabled employees?

The ADA permits employers to select the best qualified applicants for employment or promotion—that is, employers may make decisions based on reasons unrelated to the existence or consequences of a disability. Further, the ADA does not require that employers lower production or behavior standards for persons with disabilities, nor does it require employment of persons who are direct threats to the health or safety of themselves or co-workers. The ADA allows employers to prohibit the use of alcohol at the workplace and to hold illegal drug users and alcoholics to the same standards of performance and behavior as other employees.

Q 36.7.7   How does the ADA affect an employer's use of medical inquiries and medical examinations?

Employers cannot ask about the existence, nature, or severity of any disability before extending an offer of employment. However, employers can tell applicants about the specific duties of the job, ask how the applicant would perform specific tasks, and ask if the applicant can perform the essential functions of the job being sought.

Employers cannot require medical examinations or tests searching for information about physical or mental disabilities before a job offer is extended. They may, however, condition a job offer on the satisfactory completion of a *post-offer* medical examination if it is required of all employees entering the same job classification. If an individual is not hired because a post-offer medical examination reveals a disability, the reasons for not hiring the individual must be job-related and consistent with business necessity. In general, this means that the disability prevents the employee from performing the essential functions of the position at issue. The employer also must be able to show that no reasonable accommodation was available that would enable the individual to perform the essential functions or that the accommodation would impose an undue hardship.

A post-offer medical examination may disqualify an individual if the employer can demonstrate that he or she would pose a "direct threat" in the workplace (that is, a significant risk of substantial harm to the health or safety of the individual or others) that cannot be eliminated or reduced below the direct threat level through reasonable accommodation. However, a post-offer medical examination may not disqualify an individual with a disability who is currently able to perform the essential functions of the position because of speculation that the disability may present a risk of future injury.

After a person starts work, a medical examination or inquiry of an employee must be job-related and consistent with business necessity. Employers may conduct employee medical examinations where:

(1)   there is evidence of a job performance or safety problem;

(2)   the examination is required by other federal laws;

(3)   the examination is needed to determine the employee's current fitness to perform a particular job; or

(4)   the examination is voluntary and is conducted as part of an employee health and wellness program.

Tests for illegal use of drugs are not medical examinations under the ADA and are not subject to the restrictions of such examinations. However, it typically is recommended that drug tests also be administered in the *post-offer* context because they may reveal other disability-related information about the individual that would be unlawful to request at the pre-offer stage.

Q 36.7.8   How does ADA protection extend to an employee's family?

The ADA protects applicants and employees from discrimination because they are married or related to, or associated with, an individual with a disability. For example, an employer cannot refuse to hire an otherwise qualified job applicant because the applicant has a severely disabled minor child who might impose a financial burden on the group medical plan if the child were enrolled.

Q 36.7.9   What are the ADA's confidentiality requirements?

The ADA requires that employers keep employee medical information (including, but not limited to, information from medical examinations and inquiries) in confidential files separate from the regular personnel files. Access to these confidential files must be restricted to persons with a legitimate need to have access to them. This means that medical information may be disclosed only to:

(1)   supervisors and managers who need to know the information for purposes of assessing restrictions on the employee's work or duties and requested accommodations;

(2) first aid and safety personnel, as appropriate, if the disability requires medical treatment; and

(3) government officials investigating compliance with the ADA, upon request.

GINA: Genetic Information Discrimination

Q 36.8 What are the rules governing an employer's collection or use of genetic information and discrimination based on genetic information?

The Genetic Information Nondiscrimination Act of 2008 (GINA)[10] prohibits discrimination based on genetic information in health insurance and employment. With limited exceptions, GINA prohibits employers, employment agencies, and unions from acquiring or using individual or family member genetic information when making decisions regarding hiring, termination, compensation, terms or conditions of employment, or privileges of employment. "Genetic information" means information about genetic tests of an individual or his or her family members, and the manifestation of any disease or disorder in such family members. Employers may only acquire employees' genetic information with the employees' knowing and voluntary written consent, except for limited purposes such as in connection with a company-sponsored voluntary health and wellness program or to comply with the certification provisions of the Family and Medical Leave Act or similar state laws.

EPA: Gender-Based Pay Discrimination

Q 36.9 What are the rules governing pay differences between men and women?

While all of the discrimination prohibitions discussed above apply to discrimination in pay, the Equal Pay Act (EPA)[11] specifically prohibits discriminatory pay practices based on gender and imposes specific guidelines for assessing pay differences between men and women. Under the EPA, male and female employees working in the same establishment must be paid equally if they are performing "equal work"—that is, work that requires equal skill, effort, and responsibility and that is performed under similar working conditions. Because job *content* and not job *titles* is the critical focus under the EPA, these requirements apply even if the men and women have different job titles. The EPA also prohibits gender-based pay differences between persons who now hold and once held the same job. For example, a woman cannot be replaced in a job by a higher-paid male employee unless the pay differential is warranted by some factor other than sex.

Q 36.9.1   What kinds of pay differences are allowed?

The EPA permits male-female pay differentials if they are based on seniority, merit, quality or quantity of production, or other factors unrelated to sex.

COMPLIANCE FACT

The EPA prohibits an employee's pay from being lowered to correct a gender-based pay differential. To correct the problem, the wages of the lower-paid employee must be *increased*.

Workplace Harassment

Q 36.10   What types of harassment are prohibited?

Harassment based on any of the characteristics protected by the equal employment laws discussed above (race, color, religion, sex, pregnancy, national origin, age, or disability) is a prohibited form of discrimination. In addition, a harassing or hostile work environment directed at a particular individual or group because of that individual's or group's protected characteristic is unlawful, even if the content of the harassment or hostility is not tied to the protected characteristic. For example, if a supervisor intentionally singles out women or Black employees for harsher treatment relative to other employees (such as in the form of more onerous work assignments, yelling, and belittling comments), that conduct is discriminatory even though the supervisor is not making sexual or racist comments.

Sexual harassment is the most common type of harassment claim. Sexual harassment may occur between individuals of different genders or individuals of the same gender, regardless of the positions of the individuals within the organization. In addition to "hostile environment" harassment, "quid pro quo" harassment is prohibited. Quid pro quo harassment occurs when there are demands for sexual favors or for submission to sexually related conduct as a condition of employment, or when employment-related actions are based on submission to or rejection of such demands.

In addition to sexual harassment, claims of racial and religious harassment are a growing area of liability for employers. Employers should have an active commitment to keeping their workplaces free of verbal, physical, visual, or electronic content based on sex, race, religion, and other legally protected characteristics.

COMPLIANCE FACT

An employer may be held liable for harassing conduct of managers, employees, contractors, vendors, customers, or anyone else who is present in the workplace. Regardless of the source of the harassing conduct, the employer has a duty to take appropriate steps to address it.

Q 36.10.1   What kinds of conduct constitute harassment?

Among the types of conduct that can give rise to claims for unlawful harassment are unwelcome and offensive:

- comments,
- depictions,
- touching,
- gestures,
- jokes, or
- other verbal or physical behavior based on an individual's protected characteristic.

In general, the harassing conduct must be "severe" and "pervasive" to be actionable.

TIP: The determination of what satisfies the "severe" and "perva-sive" threshold requirement is highly fact-specific, and employers should not assume that an isolated or seemingly trivial incident of harassment can be safely ignored. A "zero-tolerance" policy toward harassment based on legally protected characteristics is the most prudent course.

Retaliation

Q 36.11   How does federal law protect employees from retaliation?

Retaliation is a form of prohibited discrimination under the federal anti-discrimination laws discussed above. Employers may not retaliate in any manner against employees who oppose or complain about sus-pected discrimination, or who participate in investigations or other proceedings dealing with discrimination claims, regardless of whether the opposition, complaint, or participation is inside the employer's operations (e.g., to a supervisor or member of the human resources staff) or external (e.g., with the EEOC or a court). For example, an employee cannot be discharged or moved to a less desirable job because that employee opposed what he or she reasonably believed to be sexual harassment, complained to a supervisor that minorities are mistreated at the company, or asserted that older workers were disproportionately selected for layoff.

Retaliation claims often are made in conjunction with underlying claims of discrimination and they often are more difficult to defend than the underlying claim. Employers must proceed carefully in dealing with individuals who oppose, complain about, or otherwise support processes relating to alleged discriminatory acts. A finding of discrimination on the underlying claims is not necessary for an employee to succeed on a related retaliation claim.

Employment Discrimination—General Compliance Issues

Prohibited Actions

Q 36.12 What types of employment-related actions are subject to the discrimination prohibitions?

The prohibitions on discrimination in employment extend to both applicants and employees and to all aspects of the employment relationship. Discrimination is prohibited in recruiting, testing, hiring, wages and benefits, promotions, application of policies, use of employer facilities, participation in employer-sponsored events, training, discipline, working conditions, leaves of absence, layoffs, terminations, and all other aspects of the employment relationship.

Affirmative Accommodation

Q 36.13 What affirmative accommodation obligations are imposed by employment discrimination laws?

Most employment discrimination laws are prohibitive in nature—that is, they specify what employers may *not* do rather than affirmative steps that the employers must take. The two principal exceptions to this general approach are the affirmative duty to make requested accommodations to religious practices and the duty to accommodate disabled applicants and employees.

In both instances, the employer need only make "reasonable" accommodations that do not impose an "undue hardship" on the employer's business. As noted above (*see* QQ 36.7.4 and 36.7.5), what actions are "reasonable" and what constitutes "undue hardship" are highly fact-specific determinations that should be made only with the assistance of personnel or counsel who are experienced in these matters. These determinations should not be left to lower-level, front-line managers. A coordinated, consistent approach must be adopted.

The failure to make accommodations that are reasonable and do not create an undue hardship can constitute a violation of Title VII (for religious accommodations) or the ADA (for disability accommodations) with the same consequences as intentional acts of discrimination.

Written Policies, Training, and Enforcement

Q 36.14   What written statements and policies should be adopted to help assure nondiscrimination compliance?

Employer recruiting materials, advertisements, applications, and related documents should state that the employer is an equal employment opportunity (EEO) employer and should, where appropriate, note the protected characteristics on the basis of which discrimination is be prohibited. Similar statements should be included in employee handbooks, policy manuals, postings, and other employment-related written materials. Postings for job openings and promotion opportunities also should contain such statements.

All of the above types of materials should, where appropriate, invite disabled individuals to make their needs for reasonable accommodations known if the accommodations are necessary to permit the individual to complete the application process or to perform the essential functions of the job.

Q 36.14.1   What are the basic components of an effective EEO policy?

Employers should adopt a comprehensive policy against unlawful discrimination, harassment, and retaliation in the workplace. At a minimum, the policy should do the following:

- The policy should include a statement of the employer's commitment to maintaining a work environment that is free of all forms of unlawful discrimination, harassment, and retaliation, as well as the prohibition of such conduct at all levels of the organization. The harassment section of the policy should not be limited to sexual harassment; it should also address harassment on the basis of race, color, religion, national origin, age, disability, and other legally protected characteristics.

- The policy should include a specific definition of unlawful sexual harassment (including same-sex sexual harassment) and a non-exclusive list of the types of behavior that are prohibited (for example, physical assaults of a sexual nature or other intentional physical conduct; unwanted sexual advances, propositions, or sexual comments; subjecting an employee to adverse employment conditions because of his or her rejection of sexual advances, propositions, or comments; and displays of pornographic sexual pictures, posters, calendars, books, graffiti, or objects).

- The policy should include a complaint procedure that identifies multiple individuals with whom employees may lodge complaints of discrimination, harassment, and retaliation, and enables them to bypass direct supervisors who may be the objects of the complaint.

- The policy should include procedures for promptly and thoroughly investigating discrimination, harassment, and retaliation complaints, and for taking appropriate remedial action if the complaints are substantiated. The policy should make clear that individuals who violate the EEO policy will be subject to disciplinary action, up to and including termination.

- The policy should address confidentiality issues. Specifically, the policy should make clear that while an alleged victim's confidentiality will be considered, the need for a thorough investigation and proper remediation of unlawful conduct does not permit a guarantee of absolute confidentiality.

- The policy should make clear that it prohibits retaliation against any employee who files an internal or external complaint of unlawful discrimination, harassment, or retaliation, or who participates in any related investigation or legal proceeding.

The EEO policy should be reduced to writing and disseminated to all employees. Every employee should be required to sign a document stating that he or she received the policy. This document should be retained in the employee's personnel file. Employers also should post the EEO policy in conspicuous places where employees are likely to read it. In addition, employers should periodically remind their employees of the policy through other means, such as communications from high-ranking corporate officials, internal newsletters, and departmental staff meetings.

Q 36.14.2   What other steps should employers take to ensure compliance with the nondiscrimination laws?

Employers should conduct training programs on discrimination, harassment, and retaliation issues for all employees. The training programs should review the various components of the employer's EEO policy and provide concrete examples of what is and is not considered unlawful discrimination, harassment, and retaliation. Separate training programs should be conducted for supervisors, managers, and corporate executives, emphasizing their particular obligations to:

(1)   observe the terms of the policy;

(2)   ensure that the employees under their supervision are aware of, and comply with, the policy;

(3)   ensure that complaints of discrimination, harassment, and retaliation are promptly and thoroughly investigated; and

(4)   implement appropriate remedial action, after consulting with responsible human resources professionals, when prohibited conduct occurs.

It also is imperative that employers enforce their EEO policy, including the prohibitions against discrimination, harassment, and retaliation. Responsibility for overseeing enforcement of the policy should be assigned to a relatively high-ranking corporate official. Supervisors, managers, and executives should be held accountable for complying with and enforcing the policy. Their performance should be evaluated, in part, on their fulfillment of these responsibilities. In addition, designated corporate officials should be responsible for periodically monitoring the employer's compliance efforts, including the effectiveness of the complaint and investigation procedures. The EEOC and the courts have made it clear that it is not enough for employers to have an EEO policy. They must take affirmative steps to ensure that the policy is enforced and that the employees, in fact, are reasonably protected from all forms of unlawful workplace discrimination, harassment, and retaliation.

It is equally important that employers fully document all of their compliance efforts. This includes the implementation and communication of the policy, all complaints lodged under the policy, all related investigatory efforts, and all related remedial actions taken by the employer. Employers bear the burden of proving that they have exercised reasonable care to prevent and correct unlawful workplace behavior. There is no defense available to the employer if it cannot prove its elements to the satisfaction of a judge or jury. Documentation is always the best way to do that.

Notice Requirements

Q 36.15   What notice requirements are imposed by employment discrimination laws?

Title VII, the ADEA, the ADA, the PDA, IRCA, GINA, and the EPA all require that employers display certain posters informing employees of their rights to be free from discrimination and other prohibited conduct, and how to contact the Equal Employment Opportunity Commission or other designated government enforcement agency to file complaints of unlawful conduct. The failure to meet the notice-posting requirement could result in an extension or tolling of the statute of limitations establishing the time period in which employees are required to file such complaints.

Wage-and-Hour Issues

Fair Labor Standards Act

Q 36.16   What minimum wage and overtime requirements apply generally to employees?

The Fair Labor Standards Act (FLSA)[12] requires that employers pay a specified minimum wage and overtime pay for hours in excess of forty per work week to employees who are not otherwise "exempt" from the requirements. Overtime must be paid at the rate of one and one-half times the employee's "regular" hourly rate. In computing the "regular" hourly rate, most forms of pay beyond the employee's straight hourly rate (for example, most types of bonuses, shift differentials, premiums, and other cash payments) must be considered.

Although the minimum wage requirement is specified in terms of an hourly rate, the FLSA does not require that non-exempt employees subject to the minimum wage and overtime requirements be paid only on an hourly basis. Certain types of salary and piece rate pay plans are acceptable if, when reduced to an hourly rate, they provide pay that is at or above the specified minimum rate.

Employees generally cannot waive their rights to minimum or overtime wages.

COMPLIANCE FACT

The current federal minimum wage is $7.25. It has not been raised since 2009. Many states have laws that provide much higher minimum wages for employees, which must be followed. They are not preempted by the federal law.

Q 36.16.1　Which employees and employers are subject to the minimum wage and overtime requirements?

All employees who are engaged in interstate commerce and are not otherwise subject to an exemption—by virtue of either the type of industry in which they work or the type of job they perform—are subject to the FLSA's minimum wage and overtime requirements.

Although the FLSA has a complex exemption scheme, most employers engaged in interstate commerce are subject to its requirements for some or all of their employees.

FLSA Exemptions

Q 36.16.2　Who is exempt from the minimum wage and overtime requirements?

Lines of business in which there are full or partial exemptions from FLSA requirements include transportation, bulk oil distribution, domestic service, forestry, and agriculture. Employers operating in these industries should carefully determine the extent to which they may be exempt from FLSA requirements before assuming that any exemption applies.

The most common exemptions, which apply to both the minimum wage and overtime requirements, extend to "white collar" workers such as executives, administrators, and professionals. Specific rules apply in determining whether an exemption applies. The exemption determination must be carefully made by personnel who are experienced and knowledgeable in such matters. Exemptions are construed narrowly by the DOL and the courts.

TIP: The misapplication and overuse of minimum wage and overtime exemptions is the most common source of claims, investigations, backpay liability, and other penalties and losses under the FLSA. Employers should use great care in making exempt/non-exempt classifications under the FLSA.

Q 36.16.3 What are the rules for application of the standard "white collar" exemptions?

Two sets of requirements must be met for an employee to qualify for one of the "white collar" exemptions. First, the employee must perform duties that qualify under the rules for the exemption. Second, the employee must be paid on a "salary basis," as discussed more fully below.

To qualify as an exempt "executive," the employee's primary duty must be the management and supervision of two or more full-time equivalent employees in a discrete, recognized unit of the business.

An exempt "administrative" employee is one whose primary duty involves (1) non-manual work that is directly related to the management or general business operations of the employer or the employer's customers, and (2) the exercise of discretion and independent judgment with respect to matters of significance.

To qualify as an exempt "professional," the employee's primary duty must:

(1)   require the use of advanced knowledge in a field of science or learning customarily acquired through a prolonged course of specialized education and instruction;

(2)   be primarily intellectual in character; and

(3)   require the consistent exercise of discretion and judgment.

As discussed below, there also is an exemption for certain highly paid computer professionals.

Neither job titles nor written job descriptions should be relied upon in making exemption determinations. While those items may be helpful, the most important determinant of whether an employee is exempt under one of the "white collar" exemptions is what the employee actually spends his or her work time doing. The employee's day-to-day duties must be carefully examined.

TIP: One of the most common mistakes employers make in the area of wage-and-hour law is treating all salaried employees as exempt, without regard to whether they meet the applicable duties test.

Q 36.16.4   What is required to establish that the employee is paid on a "salary basis" for purposes of the standard white collar exemptions?

In addition to meeting the specified duties requirements, an employee must be paid on a "salary basis" to qualify for one of the white collar exemptions. The U.S. Department of Labor issued a final rule defining and delimiting the exemptions for executive, administrative, professional, outside sales and computer employees, effective January 1, 2020.[13] The final rule increased the minimum requirement for payment on a "salary basis"—from $455 per week (the equivalent of $23,660 per year) to $684 per week (the equivalent of $35,568 per year), exclusive of board, lodging or other facilities.

In order to satisfy the "salary basis" test, the employee's salary may not be subject to any deductions or variations, except in very limited circumstances permitted under the FLSA regulations. For example, the salary may not be subject to deductions or variations based on the quality or quantity of the employee's work, partial day absences, absences occasioned by the employer (e.g., absences caused by an employer shutting down operations for a day due to low demand for its goods or services), or absences for jury or witness duty.

If an exempt employee works any portion of a workday, he or she generally must be paid the full salary attributable to that workday. Similarly, if the employee works any time during the week, he or she generally must be paid the predetermined salary for the entire week unless one of the limited exceptions for making deductions for full-day absences applies. In general, deductions can be made for full-day absences only when (1) the absence is initiated by the employee for personal reasons other than sickness or disability, or (2) the absence is due to sickness or disability and the related deduction is made in accordance with the terms of *bona fide* sickness or disability leave policy (for example, the deduction is for a full-day absence prior to the employee's becoming eligible for paid leave under the sickness or disability policy or after the employee has exhausted all of the paid leave to which he or she is entitled under the policy).

Employers who pay their employees a salary, but do not strictly comply with the technical rules governing payment on a "salary basis," will lose the benefit of the white collar exemption. Employers also will lose the exemption if they have an "actual practice" of making improper deductions from an otherwise exempt employee's salary. Factors to consider when determining whether an employer has an "actual practice" of making improper deductions include, but are not limited to:

- the number of improper deductions, particularly as compared to the number of employee incidents warranting deductions;

- the time period during which the employer made the improper deductions;

- the number and geographic location of both the employees whose salary was improperly reduced and the employees reporting to the responsible manager; and

- whether the employer has a clearly communicated policy permitting or prohibiting improper deductions.

There is an often-overlooked provision embedded in the 2004 revisions to the DOL's regulations defining the tests for the white collar exemptions that shields employers from the potentially harsh consequences of improper deductions from the salaries of exempt employees under the FLSA. According to the DOL's "safe harbor" regulations, if an employer (1) has a clearly communicated policy prohibiting improper deductions, including a related complaint procedure, (2) promptly reimburses employees for improper deductions, and (3) makes a good- faith commitment to comply in the future, the employer will not lose the exemption unless the employer willfully violates the policy by continuing to make improper deductions after receiving an employee complaint.[14]

TIP: Employers should carefully examine their policies and practices pertaining to exempt employees' pay and deductions to ensure that the salary basis pay requirements are being satisfied.

Q 36.16.5   What are the rules applicable to "highly compensated" white collar employees?

The FLSA regulations contain a special provision for "highly compensated" employees. The final rule, effective January 1, 2020, increased the minimum salary threshold for a highly compensated employee from total annual compensation of $100,000 to total annual compensation of $107,442. Total annual compensation may include commissions, nondiscretionary bonuses, and other nondiscretionary compensation earned by the employee. It does not include board, lodging or other facilities, or payments for medical insurance, payments for life insurance, contributions to retirement plans, or the cost of other fringe benefits.

Under the final rule, to qualify for exemption as a highly compensated employee, the following requirements must be met:

(1) The employee must earn total annual compensation of $107,432 or more, which includes at least $684 per week paid on a salary or fee basis;

(2) The employee's primary duty must include performing office or non-manual work; and

(3) The employee must customarily and regularly perform at least one of the exempt duties or responsibilities of an exempt executive, administrative or professional employee.

For example, an employee may qualify as an exempt highly compensated executive if the employee customarily and regularly directs the work of two or more other employees, even though the employee does not meet all of the other requirements in the standard test for exemption as an executive. "Customarily and regularly" means greater than occasional but may be less than constant. It includes work normally and recurrently performed every workweek, but does not include isolated or one-time tasks.

Q 36.16.6   Who qualifies for the "computer-related professionals" exemption?

The FLSA provides a narrow exemption for certain computer-related professionals. The exemption applies only to computer systems analysts, computer programmers, software engineers, and other highly skilled workers in the computer field who have extensive expertise and involvement with software-related functions. Employees who deal principally with computer hardware or who merely use computers in performing other functions do not qualify for the exemption.

To qualify for the exemption, a computer-related professional must be engaged in:

(1) the application of systems analysis techniques and procedures, including consulting with users to determine hardware, software, or system design specifications;

(2) designing, developing, documenting, analyzing, creating, testing, or modifying computer systems or programs, including

prototypes based on and related to user or system design specifications;

(3) designing, documenting, testing, creating, or modifying computer programs related to machine operating systems; or

(4) any combination of the above duties that requires the same level of skills.

Employees who meet the duties requirements must either be paid on a salary or fee basis (as described above) at a rate of not less than $684 per week (effective January 1, 2020), or be paid an hourly rate of at least $27.63.

Q 36.16.7   Can "compensatory time off" be provided in lieu of overtime pay?

Except in one limited circumstance, private-sector employers may not use "compensatory time" or "time off" as a substitute for overtime pay. Under rulings of the DOL's Wage and Hour Administrator, the sole exception is when (1) time off is granted during *the same pay period* in which the overtime was worked, and (2) the time off is granted at the rate of one and one-half hours for each hour of overtime worked.

Thus, if an employee works forty-five hours in the first week of a two-week pay period, the employee could be given 7.5 hours of compensatory time in the second week of that same pay period (reducing the employee's hours of work in the second week to 32.5) in lieu of overtime pay for the five hours of overtime in the first week. If the overtime were worked in the second week of the pay period, compensatory time in the following week would not be an acceptable substitute for overtime pay because that following week is in a different pay period than the one in which the overtime was worked.

Working Hours

Q 36.16.8   What are compensable hours of work?

The FLSA imposes numerous technical requirements for determining what are "hours of work" for purposes of the minimum wage and overtime requirements. In general, all time during which the employee (1) is performing any services for the employer, (2) is engaged to wait to perform services and is not otherwise free to use the time predominantly for his or her own benefit, or (3) is required by the employer to engage in work-related activities (for example, to attend a mandatory training class), is compensable work time. Time worked at home also is compensable.

Employees cannot be required or permitted to work "off the clock" or to under-report their time. Such practices violate the FLSA even when they are taken in direct contravention of employer policies that expressly prohibit them. According to the DOL, the employer's recourse is to take appropriate disciplinary action against the offending employee. It cannot refuse to pay the employee for all of the time that he or she actually worked, including the time that was worked off-the-clock or that was under-reported.

A variety of technical rules apply to travel time, training time, on-call time, sleeping time (for jobs where extended presence on the employer's premises is required), waiting time, and other activities. Employers should examine their employees' work and time-keeping practices carefully to ensure that all compensable time is properly captured on time records.

Other FLSA Requirements

Q 36.16.9   What other requirements does the FLSA impose on employers?

The FLSA contains child labor provisions that severely limit the jobs, tasks, days, and hours that legally can be worked by employees younger than eighteen years of age.

Like most employment-related statutes, the FLSA also prohibits employer retaliation against employees who oppose, complain about, or participate in investigations of suspected minimum wage, overtime, or other FLSA violations. Such activity is protected whether it is within the employer's operations or external (for example, with the DOL).

Compliance Steps

Q 36.16.10   What steps should employers take to ensure compliance with the FLSA?

Employers should ensure that they pay the required hourly rates for non-exempt employees and the required minimum salaries for exempt employees. In addition, employers should adopt policies dealing with the appropriate exempt/non-exempt classification of employees, overtime pay, recognition and recording of work time, and other requirements based on a full examination of the FLSA's requirements.

To help avoid wage-and-hour liability, employers should consider adopting and enforcing policies for non-exempt employees that:

- prohibit the employees from working any overtime without the prior authorization of their supervisor;

- prohibit the employees from beginning work before or after their scheduled starting time, or continuing to work after their scheduled quitting time, without the prior authorization of their supervisor;

- prohibit the employees from "clocking in" more than five minutes prior to their scheduled starting time or "clocking out" more than five minutes after their scheduled quitting time;

- require the employees to "clock out" at the beginning of their meal period and "clock in" immediately upon returning to work following their meal period;

- prohibit the employees from working through all or any part of their meal period; and

- inform employees that violations of any of the foregoing policies will subject them to appropriate disciplinary action.

As noted above, if an employee violates one of these policies, the employer's only recourse, according to the DOL, is to issue appropriate disciplinary action, such as a warning, suspension, or discharge. Even though the employee worked the additional time (for example, prior to clocking in or during his or meal period) without the required authorization and in violation of the employer's written policy, he or she still must be paid for the time worked. However, the existence of the policy and issuance of discipline against offending employees should serve to deter violations and promote compliance with the policies.

The FLSA also requires employers to keep accurate records of hours worked by non-exempt employees. Appropriate time-charging and record-keeping policies and practices should be implemented to satisfy these requirements.

In addition, employers should note that many states and some localities have laws that require the payment of minimum and overtime wages higher than those specified by the FLSA. Employers must comply with those stricter laws; the FLSA establishes a floor, not a ceiling, on such wages.

Q 36.16.11 What notice requirements are imposed by the FLSA?

Employers must post notices prescribed by the DOL to inform employees of the applicable minimum wage, overtime requirements, and other rights and obligations under the FLSA.

Benefits[15]

ERISA

Q 36.17 What types of benefit programs are subject to federal regulation?

The Employee Retirement Income Security Act (ERISA)[16] regulates both pension plans and certain welfare benefit plans, such as group health and disability insurance plans. Any benefit plan that is funded by either payments to a trust fund or set-aside account, or to a third-party benefits provider or administrator, should be examined to determine if it is covered by ERISA.

Q 36.17.1   What does ERISA generally require?

ERISA requires employers to provide various disclosures and notices to employees, comply with their pension and benefit plans as announced to the employees, manage their plans in a responsible manner, and not discriminate with respect to pension plan eligibility and benefits. ERISA also sets minimum standards to ensure that employee benefit plans are established and maintained in a fair and financially sound manner.

One of the most important requirements for employers is ERISA's imposition of fiduciary obligations on employer plan sponsors. This means that employers who manage and control plan funds must act for the exclusive benefit of the participants and beneficiaries, administer the plans in a prudent manner, and avoid conflicts of interest. It also requires employers to fund the plans and benefits in accordance with both the law and the plans' terms.

Q 36.17.2   What are the reporting requirements associated with employee benefit plans?

Employers with ERISA-covered plans must file a variety of reports with, and make various disclosures to, various federal agencies—primarily the IRS and the DOL's Pension and Welfare Benefits Administration. Numerous reporting and disclosure requirements also apply with respect to participants and beneficiaries of ERISA plans.

Q 36.17.3   What is multiemployer withdrawal liability?

The Multiemployer Pension Plan Amendments Act of 1990 (MPPAA) amended ERISA to provide for the imposition of multiemployer withdrawal liability when an employer who was making contributions to an underfunded multiemployer defined benefit pension has a complete or partial withdrawal from the plan. The MPPAA was enacted to protect multiemployer pension plans (such a jointly administered union-management plans) and their participants from employers terminating their participation in less than fully funded plans, leaving the remaining contributing employers with the obligation to fund the participants' vested benefits.

A plan is underfunded when the actuarial value of the vested benefits—the promised future benefits accrued by participants—exceeds the value of the plan's assets. Withdrawal liability represents an employer's share of the *entire* plan's unfunded vested benefits (UVBs), not just those of the withdrawing employer. An individual employer's share of the plan's total UVBs is equivalent to the ratio between the employer's contributions to the plan and the total contribution made to the plan by all participating employers for the same period. As a result, employers often are shocked by the amount of withdrawal liability they are assessed. They also often are surprised that other trades or businesses under "common control" with the withdrawing employer (e.g., parents, subsidiaries, and brother-sister affiliates) may be jointly and severally liable for the assessed liability.

Withdrawal liability generally is triggered in one of two ways. A complete withdrawal occurs when an employer permanently ceases to have an obligation to contribute to the plan or permanently ceases all covered operations under the plan. This can occur as a result of the sale of the assets of the business, or where an employer goes out of business, negotiates out of its collective bargaining obligation to contribute to the plan, or terminates its collective bargaining agreement altogether. A partial withdrawal occurs when an employer has a decline of 70% or more in its contribution base units over a three-year period or has a partial cessation of its obligation to contribute to the plan.

This is a very complicated area of the law with many nuances and special provisions that are well beyond the scope of this chapter. However, employers should be aware of the MPPAA's provisions, and consult with experienced counsel, when entering into collective bargaining relationships, negotiating collective bargaining agreements, developing union exit strategies, buying or selling businesses that are contributing to a multiemployer pension plan, or contemplating other actions that may create or trigger withdrawal liability.

COBRA

Q 36.18 What statute governs the continuation of employee medical insurance?

The Consolidated Omnibus Budget Reconciliation Act (COBRA)[17] requires that an employer who sponsors a group health insurance plan provide covered employees and their dependents with the option of continuing their medical insurance (at the employee's own expense) after specified "qualifying events" that would otherwise cause a loss of coverage. A qualified employee or dependent may elect continuation coverage for up to eighteen months in most cases, but longer in some circumstances such as a loss of coverage due to disability or divorce.

Q 36.18.1 What are "qualifying events" under COBRA?

The COBRA right to continue health insurance coverage is triggered by the occurrence of any of the following "qualifying events":

- termination of the covered employee's employment, except for discharge for gross misconduct;

- reduction in the covered employee's work hours that results in a loss of medical insurance coverage;

- divorce or legal separation of the covered employee causing loss of coverage for a non-employee spouse or dependents; and

- death of the covered employee.

Q 36.18.2 What are the notice requirements under COBRA?

COBRA imposes a variety of disclosure and notice requirements on employers. The most important of these requirements is that following the occurrence of a "qualifying event," the employer must issue to the affected employee and dependents a detailed written notice that describes COBRA's health insurance coverage continuation rights and the procedures and the deadlines for exercising those rights.

HIPAA

Q 36.19   What are the HIPAA requirements?

The Health Insurance Portability and Accountability Act (HIPAA)[18] imposes various requirements on employer-sponsored health insurance plans and healthcare providers. HIPAA provides for improved portability of health insurance coverage when employees change employers, sets limits on "preexisting condition" exclusions from group medical coverage, and prohibits discrimination against employees in enrollment based on health-related factors or because they have made health insurance claims.

HIPAA also regulates the use and disclosure of "protected health information" (PHI) by "covered entities," including health plans, healthcare clearinghouses, and healthcare providers. Under the HIPAA privacy rule, PHI can only be disclosed and used in specific circumstances, and even then only as minimally necessary. HIPAA requires covered entities to develop policies concerning the collection, handling, disclosure, use, and safeguarding of PHI and to provide training to employees who will administer the policies.

Normally, an employer will only deal with covered entities, not actually be one. However, if an employer has any kind of health clinic operations available to employees, provides a self-insured health plan for employees, or acts as an intermediary between its employees and healthcare providers, it will find itself handling the kind of health information that is protected by the HIPAA privacy rule.

Family and Medical Leave

The Family and Medical Leave Act

Q 36.20   What are an employer's obligations regarding family and medical leave?

The Family and Medical Leave Act (FMLA)[19] requires employers to provide up to twelve weeks of unpaid leave annually to eligible employees who need time off work for certain qualifying reasons. The employer must continue the employee's medical benefits during FMLA leave and must reinstate the employee to his or her job (or a substantially equivalent one) upon completion of the leave. The FMLA also requires that various notices be posted, that various disclosures be given to employees, and that employers keep records of employee use of FMLA leave.

Eligibility

Q 36.20.1   Who qualifies for FMLA leave?

FMLA leave is available to individuals working for employers of fifty or more employees who have been employed for at least twelve months and worked at least 1,250 hours during the previous twelve months. The employee's twelve months of employment with the employer need not be consecutive months. Generally speaking, all "compensable hours of work" within the meaning of the FLSA are counted toward the 1,250-hour requirement under the FMLA. To be eligible for FMLA leave, the employee must be employed at a work site at which the employer employs at least fifty or more employees within a seventy-five-mile radius.

Q 36.20.2   When is FMLA leave available?

FMLA leave is available for any one or more of the following reasons:

- an employee's serious health condition that causes him or her to miss to work;

- a serious health condition afflicting the employee's spouse, child, or parent;

- the birth or care of a newborn child;

- the placement with the employee of a child for adoption or foster care; and

- certain "qualifying exigencies" related to military service of the employee or a family member.

FMLA leave also is available for certain qualifying circumstances requiring care of a family member injured in military service or suffering from a condition aggravated by military service. As noted in Q 36.20.13 below, eligible employees may take up to twenty-six weeks of servicemember leave during a single twelve-month period. Leave taken for other FMLA-qualifying reasons during the applicable twelve-month period will reduce the amount of servicemember leave available to the employee.

The FMLA regards a "spouse" as a legal or common law spouse and not a "domestic partner" or "significant other." A "parent" for FMLA purposes is a biological parent and anyone in loco parentis when the employee was a minor. "Parent" does not include parents-in-law.

"Serious Health Condition"

Q 36.20.3 What qualifies as a "serious health condition" under the FMLA?

The FMLA defines a "serious health condition" as an illness, injury, impairment, or physical or mental condition that involves in-patient care or continuing treatment by a healthcare provider. "Inpatient care" means an overnight stay in a hospital, hospice, or residential medical care facility. A serious health condition involving "continuing treatment by a healthcare provider" includes any one or more of the following:

- a period of incapacity (that is, an inability to work, attend school, or perform other regular daily activities) of more than three consecutive full calendar days, and any subsequent treatment or period of incapacity relating to the same condition that meets certain requirements set forth in the DOL's FMLA regulations;[20]

- any period of incapacity due to pregnancy or for prenatal care;

- any period of incapacity or treatment for such incapacity due to a chronic serious health condition;

- a period of incapacity which is permanent or long term due to a condition for which treatment may not be effective (for example, Alzheimer's disease, a severe stroke, or the terminal stages of a disease); and

- any period of absence to receive multiple treatments by a healthcare provider for certain procedures or conditions, including restorative surgery after an accident or other injury, and conditions that would likely result in a period of incapacity of more than three consecutive days in the absence of medical intervention or treatment (for example, cancer, severe arthritis, or kidney disease).

Q 36.20.4   Does "serious health condition" include ADA-covered disabilities or work-related injuries?

Conditions that qualify as disabilities under the ADA, as well as work-related injuries covered by state workers' compensation laws, will be covered by the FMLA if they meet the FMLA's definition of a "serious health condition." However, the FMLA may cover conditions that do not rise to the level of an ADA-protected disability. For example, the medical condition may be a short-term condition from which the employee will fully recover. Such a condition likely will be covered by the FMLA, but not the ADA.

TIP: One of the most common FMLA mistakes employers make is not treating work-related injuries as "serious health conditions." Employers should be sure to satisfy the requirements of the FMLA with respect to qualifying work-related injuries to ensure that the employee's time off is counted against his or her FMLA leave entitlement.

Parental Leaves

Q 36.20.5   Is a leave for the birth or adoption of a child permitted only for the mother?

No. The FMLA requires that parental leave be given to both female *and* male employees who request it in connection with the birth or adoption of a child. Thus, a new father may take leave to care for a newborn baby even though his non-employee wife is also at home with the baby. If both parents are employed by the same employer, their total FMLA leave time for a birth or adoption is limited to twelve weeks. For their own serious health conditions, however, they each are entitled to twelve weeks.

Application and Notice Requirements

Q 36.20.6   How does an employee request FMLA leave?

Employees must comply with their employer's usual and customary requirements for requesting leave and provide enough information for their employer to reasonably determine whether the FMLA may apply to the leave request. When an employee seeks leave for an FMLA-qualifying reason for the first time, the employee need not expressly assert FMLA rights or even mention the FMLA. However, if an employee later requests additional leave for the same qualifying condition, the employee must specifically reference either the qualifying reason for the leave or the need for FMLA leave.

Q 36.20.7   Are there restrictions on how FMLA leave time may be taken?

An employee may use his or her twelve-week allotment of FMLA leave either in a single block or, in some instances, intermittently. If the leave is necessitated by a serious health condition of the employee or a family member, the employee is entitled to take the leave intermittently, subject to the requirement that the employee schedule any planned treatments so as not to unduly disrupt the employer's operations. If the leave is sought in connection with the birth or adoption of a child, it may be taken intermittently only with the employer's consent.

An employee who is entitled to intermittent leave may use the leave in increments as small as one hour or may request a reduced leave schedule (such as working only half-days or working only three days per week). The total hours and days used are aggregated and counted against the twelve-week entitlement. For example, if an employee normally scheduled to work five days per week must take FMLA leave for two days every week to get treatment for a serious health condition, the employee could continue on such intermittent FMLA leave for up to thirty weeks.

Q 36.20.8   What notice and medical documentation are required for FMLA leave?

An employee generally must request leave at least thirty days in advance when the need for leave is foreseeable. If such notice is not possible, the employee must give notice as soon as possible and practicable under the circumstances.

Covered employers must post a notice explaining rights and responsibilities under the FMLA. They also must include information about the FMLA in their employee handbooks or provide information to new employees upon hire.

When an employee requests FMLA leave or the employer acquires knowledge that leave may be for an FMLA-qualifying reason, the employer must provide the employee with notice concerning his or her eligibility for FMLA leave and his or her rights and responsibilities under the FMLA. The employer also must notify the employee whether leave is designated as FMLA leave and the amount of leave that will be deducted from the employee's FMLA entitlement.

An employer may require an employee requesting FMLA leave for a serious health condition of the employee or a family member to provide medical certification supporting the need for leave. An employer also may require second or third medical opinions (at the employer's expense), periodic re-certifications of a serious health condition, and reports during the leave about the employee's status and intent to return to work.

The FMLA regulations set forth specific requirements regarding the contents of the required notices and the time limits within which employers must respond to leave requests under the FMLA, provide employees with the required notices, and seek medical certifications and re-certifications. Employer must be careful to comply with all of the applicable requirements. The failure to do so could prevent the employer from being able to count the leave against the employee's FMLA leave entitlement and expose the employer to an FMLA interference claim.

Pay and Benefits During Leave

Q 36.20.9   What are the requirements pertaining to pay during FMLA leave?

FMLA leave is unpaid. There is no requirement to provide any wages or salary for the employee's time while on FMLA leave.

Employees may choose to use accrued paid leave during FMLA leave that is taken for a reason that qualifies under the employer's applicable paid leave program. In addition, and subject to certain exceptions, an employer may require that an employee who qualifies for FMLA leave use accrued paid leave during the FMLA period and count that paid leave time against the twelve-week FMLA leave allotment.

Q 36.20.10   What are the requirements pertaining to benefits during FMLA leave?

Group medical insurance coverage must be continued during an employee's FMLA leave on the same terms and conditions as before the commencement of the leave. If the employer normally pays all premiums for the coverage, those premium payments must be made during the FMLA leave. If a portion of the premiums is normally deducted from the employee's pay, the employee can be required to pay that same amount during the leave.

Returning from Leave

Q 36.20.11   What are an employer's obligations to an employee returning from FMLA leave?

An employee returning to work within the maximum FMLA leave period must be reinstated to the same job he or she held before the leave or to a substantially equivalent job. A job is "substantially equivalent" if it involves similar duties and responsibilities on the same shift and has equivalent pay and benefits. The employee is entitled to be returned to the same or a substantially equivalent position even if the employee was replaced during his or her leave or the position has been restructured to accommodate the employee's absence.

The reinstatement requirement does not apply if the employee otherwise would have been terminated for reasons unrelated to the FMLA leave (for example, a reduction in force that would have eliminated the employee's job). The FMLA regulations specifically provide that an employee has no greater right to reinstatement or other benefits and conditions of employment than if the employee had been continuously employed during the FMLA leave period.

Certain individuals who qualify as a "key employee" as defined under the FMLA are not entitled to reinstatement if they are informed of their "key employee" status before their FMLA leave commences.

An employee's use of FMLA leave cannot result in the loss of any employment benefits that were earned before the leave, nor can FMLA leave be counted against an employee under a "no-fault" attendance program.

Qualifying Exigency Leave

Q 36.20.12   What is "qualifying exigency" leave?

The FMLA permits employees to take leave to attend to certain qualifying exigencies arising out of the fact that the employee's spouse, son, daughter, or parent is on covered active duty or has been notified of an impending call or order to active duty in the U.S. Armed Forces. For purposes of qualifying exigency leave, "covered active duty" generally means duty during the service member's deployment to a foreign country. "Qualifying exigencies" include, but are not limited to, the following events arising out of the service member's serving, or being called or ordered to, active duty:

(1)   attending certain military events;

(2)   arranging for alternative childcare;

(3)   addressing certain financial or legal arrangements;

(4)   attending certain counseling sessions; and

(5)   attending post-deployment reintegration briefings.

Leave for a qualifying exigency may be taken on an extended, intermittent, or reduced-hours basis.

Military Caregiver Leave

Q 36.20.13   What leave rights does an employee caring for a sick or injured service member have?

The FMLA permits eligible employees who are the spouse, son, daughter, parent, or next of kin of a covered servicemember to take up to twenty-six weeks of leave to care for the servicemember during a single twelve-month period. The "single twelve-month period" begins on the first day the eligible employee takes servicemember FMLA leave and ends twelve months after that date. A "covered servicemember" is:

- a member of the U.S. Armed Forces (including a member of the National Guard of the United States or the reserves) who is undergoing medical treatment, recuperation or therapy, or is otherwise on the temporary disabled retired list, for a serious injury or illness that was incurred in the line of duty on active duty and renders the servicemember medically unable to perform his or her duties; or

- a veteran who is undergoing medical treatment, recuperation, or therapy for a serious illness or injury (as defined above), and who was a member of the U.S. Armed Forces at any time during the five-year period preceding the date on which the veteran undergoes the medical treatment, recuperation or therapy.

Servicemember FMLA leave may be taken on an extended, intermittent, or reduced-hours basis when medically necessary. An individual who takes servicemember FMLA leave is limited to an aggregate total of twenty-six weeks of leave during a single twelve-month period for all types of FMLA leave. In other words, leave taken for other FMLA-qualifying reasons during the same twelve-month period in which the employee takes servicemember FMLA leave will reduce the amount of servicemember FMLA leave available to the employee.

Compliance Steps

Q 36.20.14   What steps should employers take to ensure compliance with leave-related legal requirements?

Employers should adopt written policies that set forth employee FMLA rights, the employer's procedures for implementing FMLA requirements, the use of medical certifications and recertifications, employee's rights and obligations while on leave, and conditions on reinstatement. Persons responsible for implementing the employer's FMLA leave policy must be trained to recognize non-typical leave situations (such as sporadic absences due to a chronic health condition) and to know what type of information is sufficient to trigger an FMLA leave.

The FMLA requires that employers display certain posters informing employees of their FMLA rights and how to file claims if they believe their FMLA rights have been denied or violated.

A compliance program also should ensure that employers do not treat employees differently because they have sought or used FMLA leave. Retaliation against employees who oppose or complain of suspected FMLA violations, or who participate in investigations of FMLA violations, is prohibited. This is true regardless of whether the complaint or participation is inside the employer's operations or external (for example, with the DOL).

Employers also must be aware of leave-related legal obligations imposed by the ADA. For example, the EEOC takes the position that an employer violates the ADA if it automatically terminates an employee upon the expiration of his or her FMLA leave entitlement. An employer may be required to provide the employee with additional unpaid leave as a form of reasonable accommodation if the employee's underlying medical condition rises to the level of an ADA-protected disability. The EEOC would require an employer to provide additional leave subject to its showing that continuing the leave would impose an undue hardship. Most courts, however, would only require an employer to provide additional leave for a relatively short and definite time period, after which the employees will be able to return to work and perform the essential functions of his or her position. Indefinite or open-ended leave generally is not required.

Before terminating an employee who is unable to return to work at the expiration of his or her maximum FMLA leave (or such longer period of time permitted under the employer's policy), the employer should explore the facts of the particular case, including:

(1)   the nature and extent of the employee's ongoing functional limitations;

(2)   how long those limitations are expected to last;

(3)   the nature and extent of any planned treatment or therapy; and

(4)   the length of time the treatment or therapy is expected to continue.

This information will enable the employer to make an informed and individualized decision regarding whether providing additional leave would be required as a form of reasonable accommodation.

Military Leave

Uniformed Services Employment and Reemployment Rights Act

Q 36.21   What statute governs military leave?

The Uniformed Services Employment and Reemployment Rights Act (USERRA)[21] requires an employer to give employees unpaid leave to serve in the U.S. Army, U.S. Navy, U.S. Marine Corps, U.S. Air Force, U.S. Coast Guard, Public Health Service, Air or Army National Guard of the United States, or the reserves, and to reinstate employees to work upon return from such leave. These requirements apply regardless of whether the employee's military service is voluntary or compulsory. USERRA also prohibits employer discrimination against job applicants or employees based on their military service.

Notice Requirements

Q 36.21.1   What notice requirements does USERRA impose?

Employers must post notices informing employees of their rights under USERRA.

Employees must give reasonable notice of their need for military leave. In addition, various notice periods are prescribed for employees to give notice to their employers that they are released from military service and ready to return. The length of the "return to work" notice depends on the length of the leave.

Pay and Benefits During Leave

Q 36.21.2   How must pay and benefits be handled for employees on military leave?

USERRA does not require that an employee be paid while on military leave. However, it does require that the employee be given the same benefits (if any) as are provided to employees on other types of leaves. USERRA provides employees on military leave the right to continue their group medical insurance for a maximum period equal to the lesser of: (1) the twenty-four-month period beginning on the date on which the person's military absence begins, or (2) the day after the date on which the person fails to apply for or return to a position of employment. Employees on military leave also have the option of electing to continue their group medical insurance under COBRA (discussed above).

Returning from Leave

Q 36.21.3   What requirements apply to reinstatement of employees returning from military leave?

USERRA requires that an employee returning from military service be reinstated to the position that he or she would have held if the military duty had not occurred, for up to five years after the military leave began. If the employee has been on leave for more than ninety days, the employer may return the employee to a different position for which he or she is qualified if the position has the same seniority, status, and pay as the position the employee would have held had there been no leave. An employer is relieved of the reinstatement obligation only in very limited circumstances (for example, if the employee would have been released in a reduction in force that occurred during the leave).

Reinstated employees may not be discharged except for "cause" for certain periods of time (up to a maximum of one year) after their return, depending on the length of their military service.

Plant Shutdowns and Mass Layoffs

Worker Adjustment Retraining and Notification Act

Q 36.22   What are an employer's obligations with respect to plant closings and layoffs?

The Worker Adjustment Retraining and Notification Act (WARN)[22] requires that covered employers give affected employees sixty days' written notice of a "plant closing" or "mass layoff" at a single site of employment, or sixty days' pay in lieu of notice. In general, employers are covered by WARN if they have 100 or more employees, not counting employees who have worked less than six months in the last twelve months or employees who work an average of less than twenty hours a week.

Q 36.22.1   What events trigger WARN requirements?

A plant closing or a mass layoff triggers WARN's notice requirements. A "plant closing" is either the closure of the entire site of employment or the cessation of discrete operations resulting in a loss of employment for at least fifty employees. A "mass layoff" occurs if 500 employees are released from a single site or if one-third of the employees at the site—but at least fifty employees—are released.

The fifty-employee minimum that triggers the notice requirement can be met by the aggregation of discrete employment losses over any ninety-day period for related reasons. Thus, an employer making phased reductions in force must, at the time of each employment loss action, look back ninety days and ahead ninety days to determine if the fifty-employee threshold has been or will be met. If the threshold is or will be satisfied, then the sixty-day notice or pay-in-lieu of notice must be given to the affected employees.

Q 36.22.2   What notices must be given if a WARN trigger event occurs?

The sixty-day notice must be given to affected employees, any union that represents the employees, and certain state and local government agencies (for example, dislocated worker units). The notice must be in writing; its required content varies to some extent for each of the required recipients of the notice.

Q 36.22.3   When must the notices be given?

WARN notice must be given a minimum of sixty days prior to the employment loss for each affected employee. The sixty-day period is measured on an employee-by-employee basis, such that each individual employee must receive at least sixty days' notice of the date of his or her employment loss. Exceptions to the sixty-day requirement apply in limited situations involving a "faltering company," "unforeseen business circumstances," or a "natural disaster."

Polygraphs

Employee Polygraph Protection Act

Q 36.23   When may polygraphs be used for employment-related purposes?

The Employee Polygraph Protection Act (EPPA)[23] generally prohibits employer use of polygraphs (defined broadly to include a wide array of electro-mechanical devices used to detect lying) with job applicants and employees. Polygraphs may be used only in very limited circumstances, such as certain instances of suspected employee theft. As a practical matter, there is almost no use of polygraphs by private sector employers due to the tight restrictions that EPPA imposes.

Q 36.23.1   What limitations apply to the use of polygraphs?

In the limited situations where a polygraph may be used, EPPA requires that prior to the polygraph examination the employer provide extensive and specific disclosures to the person to be tested about the reasons for and nature and content of the examination. In addition, there are extensive qualification requirements for the polygraph examiner and detailed procedural prescriptions for the examination.

The EPPA also prohibits employers from threatening employees or applicants with the use of a polygraph, regardless of whether a polygraph examination is ever actually administered.

Union and Other Protected Concerted Activity Under the National Labor Relations Act

Q 36.24   What employee activity is protected under the NLRA?

The National Labor Relations Act, as amended by the Taft-Hartley Act (NLRA),[24] guarantees non-supervisory employees the right to organize and participate in a union, to bargain collectively with the employer about terms and conditions of employment, and to engage in other group activities for mutual aid and protection. The broad term that encompasses this protected conduct is "concerted activity." Employees also have the right to refrain from joining or supporting a union or engaging in other concerted activity. The NLRA's protections apply to union and non-union employees alike.

Under the NLRA, an employee's conduct is "concerted" when it involves union organizing efforts, collective bargaining, or other union-related activities. Other conduct related to terms and conditions of employment is considered "concerted" when the employee:

(1) acts with or on the authority of other employees and not solely by and on behalf of himself or herself;

(2) seeks to initiate, induce, or prepare for group action; or

(3) brings truly group complaints to the attention of management.

An employee's concerted activity is protected by the NLRA as long as it relates to terms and conditions of employment and is not exercised in a way that is patently and substantially disloyal, malicious, opprobrious or disruptive to workplace discipline. The NLRB has interpreted the employees' statutory right to engage in concerted activity as protecting (1) employees' discussion of, comments on, complaints about, and efforts to change their wages, benefits, and working conditions, and (2) employees' expression of concerns about how they are treated, employee discipline and discharge issues, and other matters relating to their terms and conditions of employment. The NLRA covers protected activities undertaken through any medium, including in-person communications and electronic communications through email and various social media platforms.

Subject to a variety of arcane and fact-specific limitations, the employer generally must permit non-supervisory employees to engage (or refrain from engaging) in concerted activity. The NLRA prohibits employer discrimination based on union (or anti-union) affiliations and activities, as well as interference with employees' exercise of their rights to engage in other concerted activity. Disciplining or discharging an employee for engaging in concerted activity is an unfair labor practice and subjects the employer to a make-whole remedy, including compensating the employee for lost wages and benefits and reinstating the employee to his or her former position.

Q 36.24.1   What legal obligations apply when employees try to join or form a union?

The process by which employees may establish a union is highly regulated through a large body of both substantive and procedural legal regulations formulated and administered primarily by the National Labor Relations Board (NLRB). While an employer has the right to communicate its views on unionization, that right is not unfettered and must be exercised with careful attention to the applicable legal requirements.

Q 36.24.2   What are the compliance implications of employees unionizing?

If employees form a union that is properly certified by the NLRB or lawfully recognized by the employer following a showing that a majority of the employees in the bargaining unit support the union, then the employer must deal with the union as the employees' exclusive representative. The employer must bargain with the union in good faith concerning all terms and conditions of employment affecting the employees. Employers may not change any terms or conditions of employment without reaching agreement with the union or impasse. Direct dealing with individual employees regarding terms and conditions of employment is strictly limited.

Q 36.24.3   What are the compliance implications of a collective bargaining agreement?

The duty to bargain does not require the parties to reach agreement as long as they bargain in good faith. However, once a union is in place, the employer and the union typically are able to negotiate a collective bargaining agreement that memorializes the terms and conditions of employment to which the parties have agreed for the union-represented employees. Such agreements typically specify the wages, hours, and other working conditions of the employees in considerable detail. The employer must abide by the terms of the agreement for its duration and generally cannot force the union to engage in mid-term bargaining about terms and conditions of employment contained in the agreement. To the surprise of many employers, the NLRA also requires employers to maintain most of the terms and conditions of employment contained in an expired collective bargaining until the parties reach agreement on a successor contract or bargain to impasse (at which point the employer unilaterally may implement the terms of its last offer to the union, subject to further bargaining). The failure to abide by these contractual and statutory requirements can result in findings of a breach of contract by an arbitrator and/or findings of unfair labor practices by the NLRB.

Occupational Safety and Health

Coverage, Standards, and Enforcement

Q 36.25   What federal law governs workplace safety and health?

The Occupational Safety and Health Act (the "Act")[25] promotes workplace safety and health through the development and enforcement of safety standards. The Act is enforced primarily through workplace inspections. Employers who violate the law are subject to potentially substantial citations and penalties. The Act also creates a variety of record-keeping, reporting and notice obligations for employers.

Q 36.25.1 Which employers are covered by the Act?

In general, the Act's coverage extends to all employers and their employees in the United States, the District of Columbia, Puerto Rico, and all other territories under the jurisdiction of the federal government. As defined by the Act, an employer is any "person engaged in a business affecting commerce who has employees, but does not include the United States or any State or political subdivision of a State." Therefore, the Act applies to employers and employees in such varied fields as manufacturing, construction, longshoring, agriculture, law and medicine, charity and disaster relief, and private education.

Q 36.25.2 What are OSHA standards?

In carrying out its duties, the Occupational Safety and Health Administration (OSHA) is responsible for promulgating legally enforceable standards. OSHA standards may require conditions, or the adoption or use of one or more practices, means, methods, or processes reasonably necessary and appropriate to protect workers on the job. It is the responsibility of employers to become familiar with standards applicable to their establishments and to ensure that employees have and use personal protective equipment when required for safety. Employees must comply with all rules and regulations that are applicable to their own actions and conduct.

OSHA standards fall into four major categories: general industry, maritime, construction, and agriculture. Where OSHA has not promulgated specific standards, employers are responsible for following the Act's general duty clause. The general duty clause states that each employer "shall furnish . . . a place of employment which is free from recognized hazards that are causing or are likely to cause death or serious physical harm to his employees."

Q 36.25.3   Are employers subject to workplace inspections under the Act?

To enforce its standards, OSHA is authorized to conduct workplace inspections. Every establishment covered by the Act is subject to inspection by OSHA compliance safety and health officers. Under the Act, upon presenting appropriate credentials to the owner, operator or agent in charge, an OSHA compliance officer is authorized to:

- Enter without delay and at reasonable times any factory, plant, establishment, construction site or other areas, workplace, or environment where work is performed by an employee of an employer; and

- inspect and investigate during regular working hours, and at other reasonable times, and within reasonable limits and in a reasonable manner, any such place of employment and all pertinent conditions, structures, machines, apparatus, devices, equipment and materials therein, and to question privately any such employer, owner, operator, agent or employee.

Inspections generally are conducted without advance notice. There are, however, special circumstances under which OSHA may give notice to the employer, but even then, such a notice typically will be less than twenty-four hours. These special circumstances include:

- imminent danger situations that require correction as soon as possible;

- inspections that must take place after regular business hours or that require special preparation;

- cases where notice is required to ensure that the employer and employee representative or other personnel will be present; and

- situations in which the OSHA area director determines that advance notice would produce a more thorough or effective inspection.

Employers receiving advance notice of an inspection must inform their employees' union representative or arrange for OSHA to do so. If an employer refuses to admit an OSHA compliance officer, or if an employer attempts to interfere with the inspection, the Act permits appropriate legal action.

Based on a Supreme Court ruling, OSHA may not conduct warrantless inspections without an employer's consent. It may, however, inspect after acquiring a judicially authorized search warrant based upon administrative probable cause or upon evidence of a violation.

OSHA has established the following system of workplace inspection priorities based on the severity of the situation:

- imminent-danger situations in which there is a reasonable certainty that a danger exists that can be expected to cause death or serious physical harm immediately or before the danger can be eliminated through normal enforcement procedures;

- catastrophes and fatal accidents resulting in hospitalization of three or more employees;

- employee complaints of alleged violations of standards or of unsafe or unhealthful working conditions;

- programmed or planned inspections aimed at specific high-hazard industries, occupations or health situations; and

- follow-up inspections designed to determine whether previously cited violations have been corrected.

Q 36.25.4   What penalties is an employer subject to for violating the Act?

If violations of the Act are found, OSHA will determine what citations, if any, will be issued, and what penalties, if any, will be proposed. Citations inform the employer and employees of the regulations and standards alleged to have been violated and of the proposed length of time set for their abatement. The employer will receive citations and notices of proposed penalties by certified mail. The employer must post a copy of each citation at or near the place a violation occurred, for three days or until the violation is abated, whichever is longer.

The penalties that may be imposed depend on the nature and severity of the underlying violation. OSHA prescribes several types of violations for which employers may be cited and penalized:

- Other-than-serious violation: A violation that has a direct relationship to job safety and health, but probably would not cause death or serious physical harm. In determining the amount of the penalty, if any, OSHA considers the employer's good faith (that is, demonstrated efforts to comply with the Act), its history of previous violations, and the size of its business.

- Serious violation: A violation where there is substantial probability that death or serious physical harm could result and that the employer knew, or should have known, of the hazard. There is a mandatory penalty for such violations, which may be adjusted downward based on the employer's good faith, its history of previous violations, the gravity of the alleged violation, and the size of the business.

- Willful violation: A violation that the employer knowingly commits or commits with plain indifference to the law. The employer either knows that what he or she is doing constitutes a violation, or is aware that a hazardous condition existed and made no reasonable effort to eliminate it. There is a mandatory minimum penalty for each willful violation, which may be adjusted downward depending on the size of the business and the employer's history of previous violations. Usually, no credit is given for good faith. If an employer is convicted of a willful violation of a standard that has resulted in the death of an employee, the offense is punishable by a court-imposed fine, imprisonment, or both.

- Repeated violation: A violation of a regulation, rule, or order, found upon re-inspection, that is substantially similar to a prior violation. Significant penalties may be imposed for each such violation. To be the basis of a repeated violation citation, the original citation must be final. A citation under contest may not serve as the basis for a subsequent repeated violation citation.

- Failure to abate prior violation: Failure to abate a prior violation may result in a civil penalty for each day the violation continues beyond the prescribed abatement date.

- De minimis violation: De minimis violations are violations of standards that have no direct or immediate relationship to safety or health. Whenever de minimis conditions are found during an inspection, they are documented in the same way as any other violation, but are not included in the citation.

Additional violations for which citations and proposed penalties may be issued include:

- falsifying records, reports or applications;

- violations of posting requirements; and

- assaulting a compliance officer, or otherwise resisting, opposing, intimidating, or interfering with a compliance officer while he or she is engaged in the performance of his or her duties.

Q 36.25.5   Does the Act protect employees against retaliation?

Employees have a right to seek safety and health on the job without fear of punishment. That right is spelled out in section 11(c) of the Act,[26] which prohibits employers from punishing or discriminating against employees for exercising rights such as:

- complaining to an employer, union, OSHA or any other government agency about job safety and health hazards;

- filing safety or health grievances;

- participating on a workplace safety and health committee or in union activities concerning job safety and health; or

- participating in OSHA inspections, conferences, hearings, or other OSHA-related activities.

OSHA investigates complaints alleging a violation of the Act's anti-retaliation provision. If an employee has been illegally punished for exercising safety and health rights, OSHA asks the employer to restore that worker's job earning and benefits. If necessary, and if it can prove discrimination, OSHA takes the employer to court. In such cases, the worker does not pay any legal fees.

Q 36.25.6   Does OSHA create any record-keeping, reporting, or notice obligations for employers?

Covered employers with more than ten employees must maintain records of occupational injuries and illnesses as they occur. The purposes of keeping records are to permit survey material to be compiled, to help define high hazard industries, and to inform employees of the status of their employer's safety and health record. OSHA record-keeping is not required for certain low-risk industries, such as retail trades and some service operations.

Record-keeping forms are maintained on a calendar year basis. They are not sent to OSHA or any other agency. They must be maintained for five years at the establishment and must be available for inspection by representatives of OSHA and other designated agencies. Many specific OSHA standards have additional record-keeping and reporting requirements.

All employers (including those exempt from the record-keeping requirements) must comply with the applicable OSHA standards, display the OSHA poster, and report to OSHA within eight hours any accident that results in one or more fatalities or the hospitalization of three or more employees. Employers are responsible for keeping employees informed about OSHA and about the various safety and health matters with which they are involved. OSHA requires that each employer post certain materials at a prominent location in the workplace and provide employees with certain relevant information. These notice obligations include:

- posting a "Job Safety and Health Protection" workplace poster (OSHA 2203 or state equivalent) informing employees of their rights and responsibilities under the Act;

- making copies of the Act and relevant OSHA rules and regulations available to employees, upon request;

- posting summaries of petitions for variances from standards or record-keeping procedures;

- posting copies of all OSHA citations for violations of standards; and

- posting the summary page of the "Log and Summary of Occupational Injuries and Illnesses" (OSHA No. 200).

All employees have the right to examine any records kept by their employers regarding their exposure to hazardous materials or the results of medical surveillance. Occasionally, OSHA standards or related research activities will require an employer to measure and record employee exposure to potentially harmful substances. Employees have the right (in person or through their authorized representative) to be present during the measuring process and examine records of the results. Under these substance-specific requirements, each employee or former employee has the right to see his or her examination records and must be told by the employer if his or her exposure has exceeded the levels set by applicable standards. The employee also must be told what corrective measures are being taken.

In addition to having access to records, employees in manufacturing facilities must be provided information about all the hazardous chemicals in their work areas. Employers are to provide this information by means of labels on containers, material safety data sheets, and training programs.

Compliance Steps

Q 36.25.7   What steps should employers take to ensure compliance with the Act?

Employers should develop appropriate policies and procedures to identify and ensure compliance with all applicable OSHA rules and regulations, to respond effectively to OSHA workplace investigations, to protect employees' rights under the Act, and to comply with the applicable record-keeping, reporting, and notice requirements. The following is a list of employer responsibilities under the Act, which should be addressed in corresponding employer policies and procedures. Employers must:

- meet their "general duty" responsibility to provide a workplace free from recognized hazards that are causing or are likely to cause death or serious physical harm to employees, and comply with standards, rules, and regulations issued under the Act;

- be familiar with mandatory OSHA standards and make copies available to employees for review upon request;

- inform all employees about the Act and applicable OSHA standards;

- examine workplace conditions to make sure they conform to applicable standards;

- identify and reduce or eliminate workplace safety and health hazards;

- make sure employees have and use safe tools and equipment (including appropriate personal protective equipment) and that such equipment is properly maintained;

- use color codes, posters, labels, or signs when needed to warn employees of potential hazards;

- establish or update operating procedures and communicate them so that employees follow safety and health requirements;

- provide training required by OSHA standards (for example, hazard communication, lead, etc.);

- report to the nearest OSHA office within eight hours any fatal accident or one that results in the hospitalization of three or more employees;

- keep OSHA-required records of work-related injuries and illnesses, and post a copy of the totals from the last page of OSHA No. 200;

- post, at a prominent location within the workplace, the OSHA poster (OSHA 2203) informing employees of their rights and responsibilities;

- provide employees, former employees and their representatives access to the Log and Summary of Occupational Injuries and Illnesses (OSHA 200) at a reasonable time and in a reasonable manner;

- provide employees and their authorized representatives with access to employee medical records and exposure records;

- cooperate with the OSHA compliance officer by furnishing names of authorized employee representatives who may be asked to accompany the compliance officer during an inspection;

- not discriminate against employees who properly exercise their rights under the Act;

- post OSHA citations at or near the worksite involved; and

- abate cited violations within the prescribed period.

Government Contracting

Q 36.26   What laws govern employment issues with government contractors?

The Rehabilitation Act of 1973,[27] the Vietnam Veterans Readjustment Assistance Act,[28] and a variety of other laws apply to employers that contract with the federal government, whether as a prime contractor or subcontractor. These laws prohibit discrimination against applicants or employees based on race, color, sex, national origin, religion, disability, and Vietnam-era or special disabled veteran status.

In addition, Executive Order 11246 requires covered employers to engage in a self-analysis to identify any "under-utilization" of women or minorities in the workforce—that is, a statistical workforce analysis to determine whether fewer women and minorities exist in a job group than would be reasonably expected in light of the availability of qualified workers in the job market.

Affirmative Action Plans

Q 36.26.1   How must employers comply with requirements regarding identifying under-utilization of women or minorities?

Executive Order 11246 requires each covered federal contractor to develop and implement a detailed affirmative action plan (AAP)—a set of specific and results-oriented procedures to identify and remedy any under-utilization or to preserve the existing situation if there is no under-utilization. The AAP must include goals, timetables, and plans for ensuring the diversity of the workforce and must address the employer's efforts to hire, promote, and fairly compensate women, minorities, Vietnam-era veterans, and disabled persons. Employers must create and retain certain documents concerning implementation of the AAP and may periodically be audited by the DOL's Office of Federal Contract Compliance Programs to assess their efforts.

There are numerous highly technical requirements that apply to AAPs and the related legal requirements. Employers doing business with the federal government should develop a good understanding of those requirements to ensure compliance.

Wages and Benefits

Q 36.26.2   What types of prevailing wage requirements might apply?

The Service Contract Act of 1965,[29] Davis-Bacon Act,[30] Walsh-Healey Public Contracts Act,[31] and a variety of other statutes require employers who contract with the federal government to pay certain specified "prevailing" wages and benefits to their employees. These requirements are usually referred to in the employer's contract with the government, but in some instances they may apply even if the contract fails to contain any such reference. Federal contractors should assess their contracts to determine if they implicate such prevailing wage requirements and should ensure that the applicable requirements are being satisfied.

Other Executive Orders

Q 36.26.3   What other Executive Orders apply to federal contractors?

Executive Order 13496 requires federal contractors and subcontractors to notify employees of their rights under the National Labor Relations Act. The notice requirements apply to contracts entered into on and after June 21, 2010. The requirements do not apply to:

(1)   contracts under $100,000;

(2)   subcontracts below $10,000;

(3) government contracts for work performed exclusively outside the territorial United States; or

(4) collective bargaining agreements.

The Executive Order requires that the contractor post a notice in conspicuous places in its plant and offices where employees engage in activities relating to the performance of the contract, including all places where notices to employees customarily are posted. The required poster is available from the DOL's Office of Labor-Management Standards (OLMS). Electronic posting cannot be substituted for physical posting. However, if notices are posted electronically, contractors must include a link to the OLMS's website. The contractor also must include the notice provision in every purchase order and subcontract.

The required notice:

(1) lists the employees' rights under the NLRA to form, join, and support a union and to bargain collectively with their employer,

(2) provides examples of unlawful employer and union conduct that interferes with those rights, and

(3) indicates how employees can contact the NLRB with questions or to file complaints.

Contractors who do not comply with the Executive Order may have their contract cancelled, terminated or suspended, in whole or in part, and may be declared ineligible for further government contracts.

Federal contractors are subject to a host of other Executive Orders, which are prone to change from one Administration to another. One example is Executive Order 13495, "Nondisplacement of Qualified Workers Under Service Contracts," which required federal government service contractors to provide qualified workers on a federal service contract, who would otherwise lose their jobs as a result of completion or expiration of a contract, with the right of first refusal for employment with the successor contractor. Successor contractors generally were precluded from hiring any new employees under the contract until this right of first refusal had been provided. EO 13495, which originally was issued by President Clinton, has been rescinded and then replaced several times, depending on the President's political persuasions. After being reinstated by President Obama in 2009, President Trump rescinded EO 13495 on October 31, 2019. It is likely that it will be reinstated by President Biden.

Federal contractors and subcontractors must closely track and comply with all applicable Executive Orders as part of their compliance program.

Notes to Chapter 36

1.   The fact that only an overview is provided should not, however, be viewed as minimizing the importance of compliance in this area. There is probably no area of legal compliance that arises more frequently in the day-to-day operation of a business than labor and employment compliance. For most businesses, employment-related actions (and inaction) are one of their most frequent sources of legal claims. Whether these claims take the form of a lawsuit, an administrative charge, or a governmental investigation, they have high potential to create significant costs, sizeable liabilities, and bad publicity, which can seriously damage an employer's public image. It is only because of the sheer breadth of labor and employment regulation that a fuller discussion is not possible here.

2.   For example, many state statutes and local ordinances extend nondiscrimination laws to characteristics such as sexual orientation, marital status, or personal appearance that are not expressly protected by federal statutes. Likewise, many state minimum wage statutes and local "living wage" or "prevailing wage" ordinances guarantee higher minimum wages or more generous overtime pay requirements than federal law provides. Paid leave is another area where state and local governments have led the way.

3.   8 U.S.C. § 1324a *et seq.*

4.   https://www.uscis.gov/i-9.

5.   15 U.S.C. § 1681 *et seq.*

6.   42 U.S.C. § 2000e *et seq.*

7.   *Id.* § 2000e(k) *et seq.*

8.   29 U.S.C. § 621 *et seq.*

9.   42 U.S.C. § 12111 *et seq.*

10.   *Id.* § 2000ff *et seq.*

11.   29 U.S.C. § 206 *et seq.*

12.   *Id.* § 201 *et seq.*

13.   Final Rule, Defining and Delimiting the Exemptions for Executive, Administrative, Professional, Outside Sales and Computer Employees, 84 Fed. Reg. 51230 – 51308 (Sept. 27, 2019).

14.   *See* Wage & Hour Div., U.S. Dep't of Labor, Fact Sheet No. 17G: Salary Basis Requirement and the Part 541 Exemptions Under the Fair Labor Standards Act (FLSA) (rev. July 2008), www.dol.gov/whd/overtime/fs17g_salary.pdf (noting safe harbor).

15.   Given the breadth and depth of the compliance issues that the Patient Protection and Affordable Care Act creates for employers, those issues are addressed separately in chapter 28 of this book.

16.   29 U.S.C. § 1001 *et seq.*

17.   26 U.S.C. §§ 106(b), 162(k), 4980B; 29 U.S.C. §§ 1161–67; 42 U.S.C. §§ 300bb-1 to 300bb-8.

18.   Pub. L. No. 104-191, 110 Stat. 1936 (Aug. 21, 1986); 42 U.S.C. § 1320d *et seq.* See chapter 27 for more detailed coverage of HIPAA compliance issues.

19.   29 U.S.C. § 2601 *et seq.*

20.   *Id.* § 825.100 *et seq.*

21.   38 U.S.C. § 4301 *et seq.*

22.   29 U.S.C. § 2101 *et seq.*

23.   *Id.* § 2001 *et seq.*

24.   *Id.* § 141 *et seq.*

25.   *Id.* § 651 *et seq.*

26.   *Id.* § 660(c).

27.   *Id.* § 791 *et seq.*

28.   38 U.S.C. § 4212 *et seq.*

29.   41 U.S.C. § 351 *et seq.*

30.   40 U.S.C. § 3141 *et seq.*

31.   41 U.S.C. § 35 *et seq.*

37

Anti–Human Trafficking

William N. Shepherd, Barbara A. Martinez &
Jeff Schacknow

Human Trafficking is the exploitation of people for compelled labor, services, or commercial sex. It is modern-day slavery. Slavery is an abomination that has plagued societies for generations. But executives, general counsel, and compliance officials may rightly ask: "What does human trafficking or slavery have to do with my company?" The answer is simple: If your business is part of an international supply chain, the service or hospitality industry, or the financial services industry, your U.S.-based company may very well be exposed to both criminal and civil liability for violations of anti-trafficking laws. Furthermore, your company may be required to comply with relatively new and wide-ranging federal and state anti–human trafficking regulations.

In addition to enforcing criminal violations of anti-trafficking laws, the federal government and a growing number of state governments are trying to impact human trafficking, even when it occurs on the other side of the world, by focusing their efforts on the "consumer" side of slave labor. Failed efforts to stop trafficking at the enslavement side of the problem are being replaced by regulations forcing U.S. companies to dig deep into their own supply chain and certify to the federal government that their producers do not violate anti–human trafficking laws. Likewise, state enforcement is growing in this area, with California leading the charge into the business community space with public notification requirements. Increased regulation in this area, together with activists seeking to uncover potentially misleading statements made to consumers, is likely coming in the future.

While beyond the scope of this chapter's coverage of the U.S. laws and regulatory regime, the United Kingdom Modern Slavery Act of 2015 places significant supply chain burdens on companies doing business in the U.K. The U.K. is not alone. In 2018, Australia enacted the Modern Slavery Act, and nations throughout the region are meeting to discuss business and government approaches to fighting slavery.

This chapter first looks at the principal anti-trafficking laws as well as regulations and then considers the responsibilities of individual companies in eliminating human trafficking from their supply chains and in managing their enforcement risks.

Overview of Anti-Trafficking Laws

Q 37.1   The Trafficking Victims Protection Act and Reauthorization Acts

Congress enacted the Trafficking Victims Protection Act (TVPA) in 2000. The TVPA was the first comprehensive legislation to penalize human trafficking in the United States.[1] The TVPA criminalized a list of offenses constituting or facilitating human trafficking. Two of the statutes enacted in 2000—18 U.S.C. §§ 1589 (Forced Labor) and 1591 (Sex Trafficking)—form the basis of almost every federal criminal human trafficking violation today.

Since 2000, the TVPA (including the Forced Labor and Sex Trafficking statutes) has been amended and expanded on multiple occasions by subsequent Trafficking Victims Protection Reauthorization Acts (TVPRAs). In 2003, Congress added a civil cause of action, which allowed trafficking victims to sue their traffickers for money damages in federal court.[2] In 2008, the TVPRA's reauthorization greatly expanded the scope of who could face civil liability for human trafficking.[3] Today, the TVPRA's enumerated violations range from recruiting a person into a trafficking offense to withholding passports or immigration documents in furtherance of Fraud in Foreign Labor Contracting.[4] Notably, alleged trafficking victims have begun using the 2008 reauthorization of TVPRA to bring civil claims against major hotel brands, arguing the extreme position that these global brands knew or should have known about individual instances of trafficking that may have occurred at local hotel locations.

Criminal Exposure

Q 37.2   Who is subject to prosecution under the TVPRA?

In addition to traffickers directly involved in the exploitation of victims, whoever benefits, financially or by receiving anything of value, from a "venture" engaged in human trafficking or forced labor may be prosecuted if they knew or recklessly disregarded the criminal activity.[5] A "venture" means any group of two or more individuals associated in fact, whether or not a legal entity.[6] The case law demonstrates, however, that the participation must be the criminal venture itself, not an ancillary act or as an unknowing cog in a much broader criminal wheel.[7]

Q 37.3   Does the TVPRA apply to human trafficking that occurs overseas?

The TVPRA provides for additional jurisdiction in certain human trafficking offenses. Title 18, United States Code, section 1596 provides that U.S. courts have extra-territorial jurisdiction over any involuntary servitude, forced labor, labor trafficking, and sex trafficking offense if:

(1)   the alleged offender is a national of the U.S. or an alien lawfully admitted for permanent residence in the U.S.; or

(2)   an alleged offender is present in the United States, irrespective of the nationality of the alleged offender.

     CASE STUDY: *United States v. Baston*

In *United States v. Baston*, the U.S. Court of Appeals for the Eleventh Circuit upheld a conviction in a sex trafficking case using the extraterritorial jurisdiction provision of the TVPRA. Baston trafficked seven women in the Middle East, Australia, and the

---

United States. Six victims testified at trial that they had been trafficked for sex beginning in 2011 in Miami and various other cities. The United States relied on the TVPA's extraterritorial provision for those offenses that occurred overseas. The court held that section 1596(a)(2) is a valid exercise of Congress's authority under Article 1 of the Constitution and that the TVPA provided a basis for conviction of the overseas conduct.[8] This is a similar analysis for how courts would interpret jurisdiction for the Foreign Corrupt Practices Act.

Penalties

Q 37.4   What are the criminal penalties for human trafficking under the TVPA?

Criminal violations for involuntary servitude, forced labor, or labor trafficking carry a statutory maximum penalty of twenty years' imprisonment. If death results or if the violation includes kidnapping, an attempt to kidnap, aggravated sexual abuse, or an attempt to kill, the defendant shall be imprisoned for any term of years or life.[9]

Sex trafficking by force, fraud, or coercion, or of a minor under the age of fourteen carries a mandatory minimum term of fifteen years' imprisonment and a maximum of life imprisonment. Sex trafficking of a minor who is at least fourteen years old that does not involve force, fraud, or coercion carries a mandatory minimum term of ten years' imprisonment.[10]

Enforcement

Q 37.5   Who handles the criminal investigations and prosecutions involving human trafficking?

The Department of Justice (DOJ) emphasizes and aggressively prosecutes human trafficking cases. DOJ created a specialized Human Trafficking Unit (HTU) within its Civil Rights Division in 2007 to lead the anti-trafficking prosecution effort. HTU handles and oversees human trafficking cases involving adults and forced labor. They collaborate with DOJ's Child Exploitation and Obscenity Section, which focuses on child exploitation cases including sex trafficking of minors.[11]

Additionally, the U.S. Attorneys' Offices nationwide prosecute human trafficking cases. Every federal district in the country has an Assistant United States Attorney who is designated as the Human Trafficking Coordinator. The coordinators are tasked with handling human trafficking prosecutions and working closely with a federal anti-trafficking task force in their area. Typically, Homeland Security Investigations, the Federal Bureau of Investigation, the Department of Labor, and the Department of State, and state and local law enforcement entities are included in the federal task forces. These task forces also often include agency representatives, non-governmental organizations, faith-based organizations, representatives from the private sector, and community members to combat human trafficking.

In 2018, DOJ brought 230 human trafficking prosecutions (213 sex and 17 labor prosecutions), charged 386 defendants (361 sex and 25 labor trafficking cases), and secured criminal convictions against 526 traffickers.[12]

Q 37.6   Are victims of human trafficking eligible for immigration status?

Victims of human trafficking may seek a T visa, which is a form of immigration benefit that is available to victims of trafficking. The maximum number of T visas issued is 5,000 annually. In 2018, 1,279 T visas were issued and 551 were denied. Congress created this status in 2000 as part of the TVPA.

Civil Liability

Q 37.7   Who is subject to civil liability under the TVPRA?

The 2008 reauthorization of TVPRA extended the range of civil liability to include anyone who knew or should have known of the trafficking and financially benefited from it.[13] For years, cases were brought under this amended section of TVPRA against those that were arguably working with the traffickers but who were not directly involved in the operation.[14] These cases had mixed results.

Then, in 2019, a wave of new lawsuits were filed against global hotel brands, along with local hotel operators, alleging that, under the 2008 amendment to TVPRA, these hotel companies failed to take sufficient steps to prevent trafficking at local hotels. These cases hit a crescendo when counsel for the plaintiffs moved for them all to be consolidated as part of a single multi-district litigation, similar to how the current nationwide opioid litigation is being handled. In early 2020, the Judicial Panel on Multidistrict Litigation issued an order denying the plaintiffs' request.[15] The Panel's decision was based, in part, on the variation in facts alleged between the different plaintiffs cases,[16] but, during oral arguments, left the door open for the possibility of renewed multi-district litigation efforts against each hotel brand, individually.

With the multi-district litigation effort denied, litigation continues in the underlying cases. Importantly, there has been disparate legal treatment from the various court systems around the country. For example, the Southern District of Ohio has given a novel, broad reading to the statute and has allowed several cases to survive initial motions to dismiss brought by the hotel brands.[17] A more straightforward approach by the Northern District of Georgia has resulted in the dismissal of several TVPRA lawsuits as vague regarding their allegations of how the hotel-brand defendants could be liable.[18] While a motion to dismiss from individual hotel operators may not succeed against a well-pled complaint, the corporate franchisors, being removed from the actual hotel operation, are much differently situated. As the Northern District of Georgia has ruled, these corporates franchisors could not reasonably be profiting financially as a part of a sex trafficking venture, as the language of the TVPRA requires. Other courts still wrestle with the varied facts and nuanced legal theories. As of the time of this publication, several motions to dismiss remain pending in similar suits filed across the country.

Regulatory Overview

Q 37.8   What are the principal sources of regulation for U.S. businesses with regard to anti–human trafficking?

U.S. businesses face proactive due diligence regulations imposed by the federal government and more passive market-force-minded regulations imposed by the state of California and the UK government for those U.S. businesses doing significant business in the UK. The federal regulations are prescriptive and demand U.S. businesses that fall under the regulatory regime take specific due diligence steps and make specific representations, which carry criminal penalties if falsified. The California and UK regimes on their face are more about mandatory public notice of company practices, with the goal that the marketplace will demand trafficking-free supply chains and consumers will gravitate towards those companies that implement high standards. While that is the plain language of both the California and UK laws, the enforcement authorities have developed guidance that show they often demand more than what is specifically required. We go through each below.

On the federal side, Executive Order 13627, "Strengthening Protections Against Trafficking in Persons in Federal Contracts," signed by President Obama on September 25, 2012,[19] imposes requirements on certain entities. The executive order adopts a zero-tolerance policy regarding "trafficking" in persons and pushes the global enforcement burden squarely onto the shoulders of companies and their executives.

On January 29, 2015, the Federal Acquisition Regulation (FAR) Council published a final rule implementing Executive Order 13627 and Title XVII of the National Defense Authorization Act, and on the same date, the Department of Defense published a final rule to augment the Defense Federal Acquisition Regulation Supplement (DFARS). These rules continue the policy of placing the burden of enforcement on companies.

As of May 2020, Executive Order 13627 remains in force and effect. Furthermore, President Trump and his administration continue to support an anti–human trafficking focus.[20] In December 2018, the U.S.

government amended the rule issued in 2015 by the FAR to further define "recruitment fees."[21] The amended rule, which applies to all federal contractors and their subcontractors, became effective on January 22, 2019, and is entitled, "Federal Acquisition Regulation: Combating Trafficking in Persons-Definition of 'Recruitment Fees.'" It provides that "[r]ecruitment fees means fees of any type, including charges, costs, assessments, or other financial obligations, that are associated with the recruiting process, regardless of the time, manner, or location of imposition or collection of the fee."[22] The 2019 Department of State's Trafficking in Persons Report (TIP) Report stated, "While this definition applies only in the context of public procurement by the U.S. government, it represents a model for global efforts to define the types of fees and costs that should no longer be borne by recruited workers to reduce the risk of exploitation and human trafficking."

Executive Order 13627

Covered Businesses and Activities

Q 37.9   What U.S. businesses are subject to the anti-trafficking regulations of Executive Order 13627?

All government contractors identified in Executive Order 13627 are subject to anti–human trafficking supply chain regulations. Companies subject to the executive order include public and private entities wherever located that carry out business operations in the United States and have annual global receipts exceeding $100 million. There are additional requirements, which are explained below, for those companies that sell or contract for goods or services outside of the United States valued at $500,000 or more.

Q 37.9.1   What does the executive order consider to be "trafficking in persons"?

The executive order covers a wide range of unlawful trafficking-related activities such as:

- the use of forced or coerced labor to perform any part of the work required by a government contract;

- the recruitment, harboring, transportation, provision, or obtaining of a person for labor or services through the use of force, fraud, or coercion for the purpose of subjection to involuntary servitude, peonage, debt bondage or slavery; or

- the procurement of a "commercial sex act"—which means an act in which anything of value is given in return for sex—or a sex act that is induced by force, fraud, or coercion or in which the person induced to perform such an act has not attained eighteen years of age.

General Obligations

Q 37.9.2   What are the principal obligations imposed by the executive order?

The executive order imposes proactive requirements on U.S. companies that do business with the federal government. It forces contractors to investigate their supply chain and certify to the government that their supply chain is free of the taint of human trafficking.

The executive order imposes enhanced obligations for federal contractors and subcontractors to act affirmatively to prevent trafficking and forced labor, including a formal compliance program and annual certifications of compliance. More specifically, the order requires companies working for the U.S. government to comply with a series of basic conduct mandates. Those include prohibitions against misleading or fraudulent recruitment practices during the recruitment of employees; charging employees recruitment fees; and destroying, confiscating, or otherwise denying access to employee identification documents (passport, driver's license, etc.). It also requires contractors and subcontractors to pay return transportation costs for employees traveling to take expatriate jobs, permit full audits and inspections, and to notify the Inspector General of the pertinent agency of any noncompliance.

For those companies that sell or contract for goods or services outside of the United States—valued at $500,000 or more—each must maintain a compliance plan during the term of the contract, which includes:

- an awareness program for employees regarding human trafficking;

- a process for reporting potential violations;

- a recruitment and wage plan that ensures that wages meet applicable host country legal requirements or explains any variance;

- a housing plan that ensures that the housing meets host country housing and safety standards or explains any variance; and

- procedures to prevent subcontractors from engaging in trafficking in persons, and to monitor, detect, and terminate any subcontractors or subcontractor employees that have engaged in such activities.

Disclosures

Q 37.9.3 What disclosures does the executive order require covered businesses to make?

The executive order does not explicitly require disclosures. However, ten categories of disclosures are referenced in H.R. 898, a congressional bill related to reauthorization of the TVPA of 2000. These categories should provide guidance for potential future required compliance effort disclosures:

(1) Maintain a policy to identify and eliminate risks of human trafficking in supply chains, and disclose the text of the policy or a description of its substantive elements;

(2) Maintain a policy prohibiting the use of the company's products, facilities, or services to facilitate human trafficking;

(3) Verify product supply chains to evaluate and address risks for human trafficking and disclose the following:

    (a) the greatest risks and measures to eliminate those risks;

    (b) whether the verification was conducted by a third party; and

    (c) whether the verification process included consulting independent sources, and if so, disclose the independent source's certification or written comments;

(4) Conduct audits of suppliers to evaluate compliance with the company's standards for eliminating human trafficking in supply chains, and disclose whether the verification was not an independent, unannounced audit;

(5) Assess suppliers' supply chain management and procurement systems to verify if suppliers have appropriate procedures to identify risks of human trafficking within suppliers' own supply chains;

(6) Require suppliers in the supply chain to certify compliance with human trafficking laws in the country or countries in which the supplier does business;

(7) Maintain internal accountability standards, supply chain and procurement systems, and procedures for employees or contractors who fail to meet company standards regarding human trafficking, and disclose such standards and systems;

(8) Provide employees who directly manage supply chains with training regarding human trafficking and mitigating risks within the supply chain;

(9) Ensure suppliers' recruitment practices comply with the company's standards for eliminating exploitive labor practices that contribute to human trafficking by conducting audits of labor recruiters and then disclosing the results of the audit; and

(10) Ensure remediation is provided to any identified victims within supply chains.[23]

Q 37.9.4 What are the possible consequences of noncompliance with the executive order?

Civil sanctions or criminal actions for false statements to the government can result if a business's certifications that their supply chain is free of human trafficking are knowingly false. False certifications might also lead to allegations of violations of the civil False Claims Act.

Final FAR and DFARS Rules

Q 37.10 What recent regulatory changes will impact business compliance in the future?

On January 29, 2015, the Federal Acquisition Regulation Council published a final rule in the *Federal Register*[24] that attempts to implement the Executive Order and Title XVII of the National Defense Authorization Act (NDAA). This final rule continues the policy that contractors and subcontractors must act affirmatively against human trafficking. This final FAR rule became effective on March 2, 2015.[25] In addition, on January 29, 2015, the Department of Defense published a final rule to augment the Defense Federal Acquisition Regulation Supplement.[26]

The final FAR rule implements and expands upon core anti-trafficking policies as provided in the executive order and Title XVII of NDAA. For all federal contracts, the rule prohibits:

- destroying, confiscating, concealing, or denying access to an employee's identification documents;

- using fraudulent or misleading practices during employee recruitment;

- charging recruitment fees[27] from employees, or arranging housing failing to meet host country's standards;

- failing to provide written employment contracts or recruitment agreements in the employee's native language prior to the employee leaving his or her country of origin; and

- failing to provide return transportation or the cost of return transportation at the end of the employment contract.[28]

Under the final FAR rule, contractors are required to notify the agency inspector general, the agency official responsible for suspension and debarment actions, and, if appropriate, law enforcement officials, if contractors become aware of "credible" violations. Furthermore, the final rule requires the contractor to include, in the Federal Awardee Performance and Integrity Information System, any substantiated allegations in an administrative proceeding for violations of the executive order or the Trafficking Victims Protection Act.[29]

In addition, the rule implements additional requirements for contracts where the portion of the contract performed outside the United States exceeds $500,000. For contracts of this size, it requires that contractors establish and publish, at their workplace and on their website, a compliance plan appropriate to the size of the contract and nature and scope of activities performed.[30] Contractors are required to include the following in their compliance plans:

- an awareness program informing employees about the U.S. government's zero-tolerance human trafficking policy, the contractor's prohibited trafficking-related activities and actions that will be taken against violating employees;

- a process for employees to report activities inconsistent with the zero-tolerance policy of the government;

- a recruitment and wage plan permitting only the use of recruitment companies with trained employees, prohibiting the charging of recruitment fees to the employee and ensuring wages meet applicable legal requirements of the host country or explanations of variances;

- a housing plan (if housing is arranged or provided) ensuring compliance with host-country legal requirements; and

- procedures to prevent agents and subcontractors from engaging in trafficking, and to monitor, detect, and terminate any agents or subcontractors that have engaged in such activities.[31]

In addition to compliance plans, prior to receipt of an award and on an annual basis thereafter, federal contractors would have to certify implementation of the compliance plan and certify that neither the contractor nor agents or subcontractors have engaged in trafficking or that appropriate remedial measures have been taken if abuse has been found.[32]

On December 8, 2016, the Office of Federal Procurement Policy's Office of Management and Budget published a notice and request for comments entitled "Anti-Trafficking Risk Management Best Practices & Mitigation Considerations Guidance," which references a draft memorandum that lays out a developed set of best practices and mitigation considerations, which should be considered in developing compliance plans.[33]

California Transparency in Supply Chains Act

Covered Businesses

Q 37.11　What U.S. businesses are subject to regulations under the California Act?

All "California businesses"—whether headquartered in California or not—that meet certain definitions are subject to anti–human trafficking supply chain regulations under the California Act. The California Act requires any company that is a retail seller or manufacturer, does business in California, and has annual worldwide gross receipts that exceed $100 million to disclose its efforts to eradicate slavery and human trafficking from the company's direct supply chain for tangible goods offered for sale.[34] A "retail seller" means a business entity with retail trade as its principal business activity code, as reported on the entity's tax return. A "manufacturer" means a business entity with manufacturing as its principal business activity code, as reported on the entity's tax return. A company is deemed to be "doing business in California" if:

(1)　it is organized or commercially domiciled in California;

(2)　sales in California for the applicable tax year exceed the lesser of $500,000 or 25% of the company's total sales;

(3)　the real property and the tangible personal property of the company in California exceed the lesser of $50,000 or 25% of the company's total real property and tangible property; or

(4)　the amount paid in California by the company for compensation exceeds the lesser of $50,000 or 25% of the total compensation paid by the company.[35]

General Obligations

Q 37.11.1   What are the principal obligations imposed by the California Act?

A "California business" that falls under the California Act is mandated to have a public statement on its website that outlines the company's efforts to ensure its products are free of the influence of human trafficking.

If a business falls under the California Act, it must disclose its compliance efforts, if any, in five separate categories:

(1) Verify product supply chains to evaluate and address risks of human trafficking and slavery, and disclose if the verification was not conducted by a third party;

(2) Audit suppliers to evaluate their compliance with company standards for human trafficking and slavery in supply chains, and disclose if said audits were not independent and unannounced;

(3) Require direct suppliers to certify that materials used in the product comply with the laws regarding human trafficking and slavery of the country or countries in which they are doing business;

(4) Maintain internal accountability standards and procedures for employees or contractors failing to meet company standards regarding human trafficking and slavery; and

(5) Train company employees and managers who have direct responsibility for supply chain management on human trafficking and slavery, particularly on how to mitigate such risks within supply chains.[36]

The five categories of disclosures mandated by the California Act must be posted on a company's website with a conspicuous link from the homepage.[37] In the event that a company does not maintain a website, a written disclosure must be provided to a consumer within thirty days of a written request.[38]

A resource guide designed to assist companies in addressing these five required disclosure categories was issued by former California Attorney General Kamala Harris. "[I]ntended to help covered companies by offering recommendations about model disclosures and best practices for developing such disclosures,"[39] *The California Transparency in Supply Chains Act: A Resource Guide* "discusses how a company can provide disclosures that comply with the law, as well as enhance consumers' understanding of its anti-trafficking and anti-slavery efforts."[40] The resource guide provides the statutory language, distills the key requirements, and provides model and "less informative" disclosures.[41]

Legislative History

Q 37.12   How did the California Act come about?

The California Act was introduced by State Senator Darrell Steinberg on February 27, 2009, in an effort to fill a perceived legislative void in the fight against human trafficking.[42] While laws criminalizing human trafficking existed, California lawmakers found little effort focused on the marketplace where goods and products they perceived to be tainted by human trafficking flowed freely.[43]

As originally introduced, the bill required companies subject to the act to disclose "*a policy* setting forth its efforts to comply with federal and state law regarding the eradication of slavery and human trafficking from its supply chain."[44] To that end, the original bill established the Commission to Combat Slavery and Human Trafficking (the "Commission") designed to assist companies subject to the act with developing policies to eradicate slavery and human trafficking.[45] However, subsequent amendments to the bill indicate lawmakers thought merely requiring companies to establish policies did not adequately further the goal of eradicating human trafficking within supply chains. An early amendment to the bill replaced the requirement to disclose *a policy* with the requirement that companies disclose their *efforts* to eradicate slavery and human trafficking in their supply chains.[46]

Opponents of the bill highlighted the lack of guidance as to what constitutes compliance.[47] The Commission may have provided such guidance, but an early amendment eliminated the Commission due to an inability to determine the associated cost.[48] As mentioned above, California's Office of the Attorney General remedied this deficiency by publishing in April 2015 a resource guide for company compliance.[49] Other opponents argued the bill essentially requires companies to enforce federal and state law and subjects them to ridicule for failure to enforce such laws, which they are powerless to do.[50]

Lawmakers responded to the concern that the California Act required companies to do more than merely disclose any efforts, including none, to eradicate human trafficking within supply chains with an amendment to the bill. On June 30, 2010, California Senate Bill 657 was amended to require companies to "disclose to what extent, *if any*, that the retail seller or manufacturer does each of the following [five mandates]."[51] The additional language "if any" was intended to clarify that the act does not require companies to do anything other than disclose any efforts, including none, to eradicate human trafficking in their supply chains.[52]

In September 2010, then–California Governor Arnold Schwarzenegger signed into law California Senate Bill 657, the California Transparency in Supply Chains Act of 2010, which became effective on January 1, 2012.

Q 37.12.1   How is the way the California Act intends to combat human trafficking different from measures that only criminalize human trafficking?

The California Act is intended to empower consumers with information regarding companies' efforts to eradicate human trafficking in their supply chains.[53] The theory is that market forces will spur companies to take steps to ensure suppliers comply with applicable anti–human trafficking laws. If Company *A*'s disclosures reveal extensive measures to eradicate human trafficking in its supply chain and Company *B*'s disclosures reveal it takes no action, presumably consumers would be more likely to buy Company *A*'s products. If Company *B* wants to remain competitive in the market, the legislators hope it will increase efforts to eradicate human trafficking in its supply chain and its disclosures will reflect those significant steps.

A related theory is that by requiring only the largest retailers and manufacturers to disclose their efforts to eradicate human trafficking in their supply chains, companies in a position to have the most impact will have increased leverage with their suppliers.[54] If a supplier does not comply with human trafficking laws or resists a company's efforts to eradicate human trafficking in the supply chain, companies may refuse to do business with that supplier. Thus, California lawmakers intended the California Act to empower consumers and companies alike to use their economic leverage to prevent human trafficking within supply chains.[55]

Enforcement and Other Initiatives

Q 37.13   To date, how has the California Act been enforced?

The California Act empowers the state's attorney general to bring injunctive relief actions against companies to enforce compliance with its requirements.[56] The California Act directs the California Franchise Tax Board to provide the state's attorney general with a list of companies required to disclose based on tax returns filed for taxable years beginning on or after January 1, 2011.[57] The initial list was given to the attorney general on November 30, 2012, and a new list will be submitted each year on November 30.[58] The list for the 2014 tax year of potentially covered companies produced by the Franchise Tax Board indicated approximately 1,700 companies likely subject to the act.[59]

Even though the California Act gives the attorney general enforcement authority, it includes no provision for funding enforcement measures. The attorney general received the initial list of companies required to comply with the act on November 30, 2012, but to date we have not identified any lawsuits filed by the attorney general to enforce the act. Other enforcement measures may have been taken, but the attorney general's office will not release information regarding alternative enforcement until the actions become public.

Q 37.13.1   Does the private plaintiff trial bar have an ability to bring suit to enforce the California Act?

Arguably, yes. California's Unfair Competition Law provides an additional avenue for the attorney general, as well as private litigants, to enforce the act.[60] California's Unfair Competition Law prohibits unfair or fraudulent conduct related to virtually any business activity.[61] Remedies include injunctive relief and restitution.[62] To date, the attorney general has not sought to enforce the California Act under California's Unfair Competition Law in court.[63] However, the trial bar has shown interest through information requests and the filing of a handful of lawsuits.

One indication of potential interest by the trial bar is that initial requests for companies subject to the requirement as listed by the California Franchise Tax Board were requested by NGO groups, law students, and plaintiff trial firms. The list of companies was not disclosed as a public record because the attorney general views the information as private tax information exempt from disclosure since one of the triggering events is based on sales as recorded in the tax rolls. While the list of companies has not been disclosed, the interest in the list from the trial bar may be a clear harbinger of things to come.

As anticipated, during late 2015, plaintiffs filed lawsuits in California connected with the California Act. Two notable class action lawsuits were filed in federal district courts in California. The first, *Sud v. Costco Wholesale Corp.*,[64] alleged that Costco sold, contrary to the disclosures on its website, farmed prawns that were fed fishmeal sourced by the use of slave labor in Thailand. This lawsuit alleged violations of the California Unfair Competition Law, False Advertising Law, and the Consumer Legal Remedies Act. The second case, *Barber v. Nestlé USA Inc.*,[65] alleged violations of the same California laws in connection with fish caught by slaves and sold in Fancy Feast cat food. After the district court dismissed the case, plaintiff filed a notice of appeal with the Ninth Circuit. In 2018, the Ninth Circuit affirmed the dismissal (and affirmed dismissals in similar cases). Neither lawsuit accused the companies of violating the California Act, yet both invoke the California Act in the complaints. Several similar lawsuits have been filed to date.[66] These lawsuits could potentially be an indication of future litigation aimed at publicly shaming companies.[67]

Responding to increasing pressure from consumers and media outlets, some companies, notably Nestlé in 2015, investigated their supply chains. Nestlé contracted with Verité to investigate its supply chain connected to seafood originating in Thailand. The investigation revealed substantial human trafficking abuses and Nestlé publicly admitted such in November 2015.[68]

Compliance Programs

Federal Guidelines for Businesses

Q 37.14 Are there any federal anti–human trafficking guidelines for companies to follow?

The Executive Order provides that by September 25, 2013, member agencies of the President's Interagency Task Force to Monitor and Combat Trafficking in Persons (PITF) shall identify industries and sectors at particular risk for human trafficking violations and notify agencies of such identified industries and sectors. Thereafter, agencies shall consult with the Office of Federal Procurement Policy of the Office of Management and Budget to adopt and publish guidance, safeguards, and compliance assistance to eradicate human trafficking and forced labor in federal contracts. The PITF held meetings on January 5, 2016,[69] and October 24, 2016, and most recently issued a 2019 report[70] outlining its progress.

While the PITF has not yet published any guidelines, there is another area of federal regulation that may be instructive. The 2008 Farm Bill[71] established the Consultative Group to Eliminate the Use of Child Labor and Forced Labor in Imported Agriculture Products. In April 2011, the Consultative Group published guidelines for use by companies wanting to eliminate child and forced labor from their supply chains.[72] Until agency guidelines are implemented, the U.S. Department of Agriculture (USDA) guidelines are instructive for companies wanting to take proactive steps now. The USDA guidelines are beneficial to companies irrespective of which law applies to them. Moreover, companies not subject to the Executive Order or the California Act are well advised to use the USDA guidelines as a resource to create a culture of "corporate social responsibility" compliance.

Corporate Social Responsibility

Q 37.15   What is the role of "corporate social responsibility" in anti–human trafficking compliance?

The trend toward "corporate social responsibility" (CSR) policies that promote good corporate citizenship has greatly accelerated over the past several years.[73] For example, in 2004 Harvard University's Kennedy School of Government launched the "Corporate Social Responsibility Initiative," based on:

> the underlying premise that while governments ultimately bear the responsibility for ensuring public welfare, there is a need to construct a new understanding of the roles, responsibilities and boundaries of the private sector, especially major corporations, and to explore new types of partnership, and new governance and business models for creating public value.[74]

In recent years a number of large companies have joined the "Ethical Trade Initiative" (ETI), which has established corporate codes of practice implementing human rights, ethical labor practices, and environmental protection standards.[75] Some companies also have agreed to implement the CSR principles of the United Nations Global Compact, which promotes ten universally accepted principles in the areas of human rights, labor, environment and anti-corruption.[76] In response to real concerns about labor exploitation in the developing world, many companies have felt compelled to develop CSR policies and procedures to police their supply chains to ensure they are not making or selling products that are tainted by human trafficking, slavery, and child labor.

Government regulators have followed the trend toward CSR compliance. Notably, the California Act, signed in September 2010, predates the federal efforts. Both have their roots in the criminal laws that saw an uptick in domestic human trafficking rescues in the United States, but that also often saw dissatisfying efforts in the prosecution of their captors. This was coupled with global media attention on the working conditions in developing countries and a series of tragedies associated with factory fires and other tragedies that raised awareness of the issues of human trafficking and forced labor. Cases that had traditionally focused on the slave trade in prostitution were moving their focus to the issues of human trafficking and forced labor.

As President Obama ended his first term, he took hold of this issue and increased the federal government's oversight and regulations in this area. On September 25, 2012, he spoke at the Clinton Global Initiative and announced that his administration was going to do more to focus on helping the "20 million human trafficking victims around the world," and signed Executive Order 13627, designed to strengthen compliance with the TVPA among companies that contract and subcontract with the federal government. "As one of the largest purchasers of goods and services in the world, the U.S. government will lead by example. . . . American tax dollars must never be used to support the trafficking of human beings. We will have zero tolerance, we mean what we say, and we will enforce it."

While these government efforts attempt to fill a void in current anti-trafficking laws, they also add to the growing pressure on companies to develop risk management and compliance policies that advance responsible corporate citizenship. Additional pressure to further develop compliance and monitoring programs has been placed on businesses with the finalizing of the FAR and DFARS rules in January 2015.

President Trump has reiterated the federal government's commitment to rooting out human trafficking. At a White House summit on January 31, 2020, commemorating the 20th anniversary of the Trafficking Victims Protection Act, Trump touted his administration's efforts, including "allocating" increased funds towards DOJ trafficking prosecutions and legislation strengthening the Department of Homeland Security's "Blue Campaign" to increase public awareness of the issue.

Q 37.16   Why is it important for companies to develop risk management and compliance policies with regard to human trafficking?

Executive Order 13627, the California Act, and the final FAR and DFARS rules add to the growing pressure on companies to develop risk management and compliance policies that advance new paradigms of responsible corporate citizenship. Many large companies likely fall under the purview of these mandates, even if the activities that such companies perform in California or the United States are relatively small. Furthermore, some companies may not even be aware the disclosure requirements apply to them. Accordingly, companies should take steps now to create a culture of CSR compliance to ensure their procedures are accurate and reflect well on their corporate reputations. Not only do the mandates require specific actions, but the media and the public at large seem unlikely to absolve organizations that have made little effort to investigate their risks in this area.

The mandates require disclosure, but inaccurate disclosures will be a separate and distinct problem in their own right, one that could bring civil liability along with government action. This international supply chain due diligence needs to be coordinated with other legal and regulatory compliance obligations so that companies can maximize efficiencies from existing compliance and internal investigation efforts associated with other anti-corruption statutes such as the Foreign Corrupt Practices Act. Companies must be proactive in developing appropriate CSR compliance measures to avoid injunctions or civil actions, stay competitive, and ensure their public image is not tarnished by irresponsible corporate citizenship.

Q 37.17   Are there additional risks and considerations for publicly traded companies in the context of investor relations?

The growing focus on Socially Responsible Investing (SRI) and investing focused on Environment, Social and Governance (ESG) issues has begun to have an impact on public companies responding to investor concerns. The Sustainable Investment Institute reports a growing number of shareholder questions and increased focus on human rights. Impact investors are searching for investment vehicles that meet their social goals and investment houses work to develop strategies for those investors. The efficacy of these strategies will be tested in the years ahead as companies move on and off these platforms, but clearly this a growing area for ESG impact investors and companies will face tests from those seeking these types of financial products.

Q 37.18   How can companies be proactive in eliminating human trafficking from their supply chains and managing their enforcement risks in this area?

In general, companies are advised to:

* set standards regarding human trafficking;

* analyze their CSR compliance obligations;

* perform risk assessments; and

* implement monitoring for violations, including third-party review and verification.

Q 37.18.1   How should a company set standards regarding human trafficking?

Companies are advised to set standards regarding human trafficking that meet or exceed the more stringent of national laws and International Labour Organization (ILO) standards.[77] Standards should be articulated through means such as codes of conduct, labor/human rights policies, and collective bargaining agreements.[78] Further, companies should set additional standards relevant to their particular operations.[79] These standards should be communicated to suppliers, workers, producers, and other relevant stakeholders in the areas of sourcing.[80] Companies should also establish protocols for workers and stakeholders to report violations of company standards.[81] Moreover, companies should notify victims and affected stakeholders of any complaints received and the resolution of such complaints.[82]

Q 37.18.2   … analyze its CSR compliance obligations?

The analysis of a company's CSR compliance obligations should begin with a review of the company's current suppliers. After organizing supplier information by country, the company can rank-order its suppliers according to their location in "at risk" countries, on the assumption that suppliers located in those nations will require additional compliance oversight. A leading authority relied on by enforcement authorities on country-specific corruption is Transparency International, a nongovernmental organization that monitors and publicizes corporate and political corruption in international development. Each year, Transparency International releases a Corruption Perceptions Index (CPI), which sets forth a comparative ranking of corruption worldwide. The CPI ranks 182 nations on the prevalence of corruption within each country, based upon surveys of business people. These surveys and assessments include questions related to the bribery of public officials, kickbacks in public procurement, embezzlement of public funds, and the effectiveness of public sector anti-corruption efforts. Countries and territories are assessed scores on a scale of 0 (highly corrupt) to 10 (very clean).

Q 37.18.3   ... perform risk assessment?

The USDA guidelines, discussed above, advise companies to engage in supply chain mapping, beginning with the producer, to identify areas most at risk for human trafficking.[83] Risk assessments should include:

- gathering information on prevalence of human trafficking in areas where the product is sourced;

- consulting with local stakeholders about social, economic, and cultural factors relevant to human trafficking, as well as labor recruitment practices, gaps in government policies, and access to judicial systems; and

- examining the impact of the company's pricing and procurement policies on human trafficking risks.[84]

Risk assessment should be updated periodically as companies gain experience implementing new efforts to eradicate human trafficking within supply chains.[85]

Q 37.18.4   ... implement monitoring for violations, including third-party review and verification?

Companies should implement a continuous monitoring system.[86] Auditors, whether internal staff or an outside organization, should be familiar with local languages and practices and have the appropriate skills and knowledge to evaluate and respond to human trafficking situations.[87]

If violations occur, companies should remediate by working with suppliers to implement corrective measures, provide positive incentives such as preferred supplier lists or price premiums, and negative incentives where appropriate such as termination, suspension or reduction in contracts.[88] Remediation should also include resources for victims' services.[89]

Finally, companies should seek independent third-party review of their programs.[90] The guidelines suggest a combination of independent third-party monitoring and independent third-party verification.[91] The former should include unannounced and announced visits to suppliers to determine compliance with human trafficking standards.[92] Monitors should visit a representative sample of supplier worksites on a continuous basis with particular focus on times of higher risk for human trafficking.[93] Monitors should provide companies with a report of their findings and include recommendations for remediation where suppliers did not implement the company's standards.[94]

Unlike monitoring, verification does not require evaluating suppliers.[95] Rather, verifiers evaluate the company's implementation of its program to determine compliance with the program and with the company's human trafficking standards.[96] Verification should be conducted at least annually by certification bodies complying with relevant ISO or IEC standards.[97] Verifiers should have knowledge and skills relevant to human trafficking standards.[98] Verifiers should test a company's audit data to determine whether data systems are reliable and should witness the company's monitoring activities.[99] Verifiers should provide companies with a report identifying weaknesses in the companies' programs and requiring remediation to address weaknesses.[100] Finally, verifiers should provide the public with a list of companies under review, approved, suspended, or withdrawn.[101]

Notes to Chapter 37

1. *See* Victims of Trafficking and Violence Protection Act of 2000, Pub. L. No. 106-386 § 102(a), 114 Stat. 1464, 1467 (2000).

2. 18 U.S.C. § 1595; *See also* Trafficking Victims Protection Reauthorization Act of 2003, Pub. L. No. 108-193, § 4(a)(4)(A), 117 Stat. 2875, 2878 (2003).

3. *See* William Wilberforce Trafficking Victims Protection Reauthorization Act of 2008, Pub. L. No. 110-457, 122 Stat. § 5067, Title II, § 221(2)(2008), 117 Stat. 2875, 2878 (2003), *amended by* Justice for Victims of Trafficking Act of 2015, Pub. L. No. 114-22, 129 Stat. 247, title I, § 120 (2015).

4. *See* 18 U.S.C. §§ 1589-1597.

5. 18 U.S.C. §§ 1589(b) and 1591(a)(2).

6. 18 U.S.C. §§ 1591(e)(5) and 1593A.

7. In *United States v. Afyare*, a criminal case brought under the TVPA, the Sixth Circuit affirmed the District Court's holding that "mere membership in the gang or association of two or more [d]efendants [i]s insufficient to prove a venture under Section 1591(a)(2) and to be a [a] participant in the venture, the [prosecution] ha[s] to prove that the [d]efendant committed an 'overt act' to advance the sex trafficking activities charged." 632 F. App'x 272, 283 (6th Cir. 2016) (quoting United States v. Afyare, 2013 WL 2643408) (M.D. Tenn. June 12, 2013) (alterations in original). To illustrate its reasoning, the *Afyare* court posed the hypothetical in which a defendant:

> joins a soccer team with some sex traffickers, who sponsor the team financially (i.e., pay for travel accommodations, uniforms and equipment, training, etc.) using the money they generate from sex trafficking activities. And assume that the sex traffickers do not conceal the source of this money from the rest of the team, such that our defendant knows (or recklessly disregards clear knowledge) that his teammate-sex-trafficker-sponsors are engaged in sex trafficking.

Id. at 286. The Sixth Circuit found these hypothetical facts would **not** mean the defendant "participated" in a venture:

> We agree with the district court and find that § 1591(a)(2) targets those who participate in sex trafficking; it does not target soccer players who turn a blind eye to the source of their financial sponsorship. As a result, in this example, we would require the prosecution to prove that the defendant actually participated in a sex-trafficking venture. We would find it irrelevant that he played on a soccer team with sex traffickers (or frequented a restaurant with them or carpooled with them) and would exclude that evidence as irrelevant.

Id. (emphasis added); *see also* Geiss v. Weinstein Co. Holdings LLC, 383 F. Supp. 3d 156, 169 (S.D.N.Y. 2019) ("The participation giving rise to the benefit must be participation in a sex-trafficking venture, not participation in other activities engaged in by the sex traffickers that do not further the sex-trafficking aspect of their venture.") (emphasis in original).

8. *See* United States v. Baston, 818 F.3d 651 (11th Cir. 2016).

9. 18 U.S.C. §§ 1584(a), 1589(d), 1590(a).

10. 18 U.S.C. § 1591(b).

11. *See* Attorney General's Annual Report to Congress on U.S. Government Activities to Combat Trafficking in Persons FY 2018, at 22.

12. *Id.* at 27.

13. 18 U.S.C. § 1595.

14. *See, e.g.,* Geiss v. Weinstein Co. Holdings LLC, 383 F. Supp. 3d 156, 169 (S.D.N.Y. 2019) ("The participation giving rise to the benefit must be participation in a sex trafficking venture, not participation in other activities engaged in by the sex traffickers that do not further the sex-trafficking aspect of their venture.") (emphasis in original).

15. *See In re* Hotel Indus. Sex Trafficking Litig., No. MDL 2928, 2020 WL 581882, at *2 (U.S. Jud. Pan. Mult. Lit. Feb. 5, 2020).

16. *Id.*

17. *See, e.g.,* M.A. v. Wyndham Hotels & Resorts, Inc., 425 F. Supp. 3d 959, 971-72 (S.D. Ohio 2019); H.H. v. G6 Hosp., LLC, No. 2:19-CV-755, 2019 WL 6682152, at *6 (S.D. Ohio Dec. 6, 2019).

18. Jane Doe 1 v. Red Roof Inns, Inc., 1:19-CV-03840-WMR, 2020 WL 1872335 (N.D. Ga. Apr. 13, 2020); Jane Doe 2 v. Red Roof Inns, Inc., 1:19-CV-03841-WMR, 2020 WL 1872337 (N.D. Ga. Apr. 13, 2020); Jane Doe 3 v. Red Roof Inns, Inc., 1:19-CV-03843-WMR, 2020 WL 1872333 (N.D. Ga. Apr. 13, 2020); Jane Doe 4 v. Red Roof Inns, Inc., 1:19-CV-03845-WMR, 2020 WL 1872336 (N.D. Ga. Apr. 13, 2020) (each noting the absence of any well-pled allegation that the hotel franchisor defendants "ever dealt with" the plaintiffs or their alleged traffickers).

19. Exec. Order No. 13,627, 77 Fed. Reg. 60,029 (Oct. 2, 2012) (signed Sept. 25, 2012).

20. *See* Exec. Order on Combating Human Trafficking and Online Child Exploitation in the United States (Jan. 31, 2020); *see also* Exec. Order No. 13,773, Enforcing Federal Law with Respect to Transnational Criminal Organizations and Preventing International Trafficking, 82 Fed. Reg. 10,691 (Feb. 9, 2017), www.white house.gov/the-press-office/2017/02/09/presidential-executive-order-enforcing-federal-law-respect-transnational ("Sec. 2. Policy. It shall be the policy of the executive branch to: (a) strengthen enforcement of Federal law in order to thwart transnational criminal organizations and subsidiary organizations, including criminal gangs, cartels, racketeering organizations, and other groups engaged in illicit activities that present a threat to public safety and national security and that are related to, for example: (i) the illegal smuggling and trafficking of humans. . . .");

Elizabeth Dias, *Trump Signs Bill Amid Momentum to Crack Down on Trafficking*, N.Y. TIMES (Apr. 11, 2018), https://www.nytimes.com/2018/04/11/us/backpage-sex-trafficking.html. Notably, on April 11, 2018, U.S. President Donald Trump signed into law the Allow States and Victims to Fight Online Sex Trafficking Act (FOSTA), in response to public concerns about websites like Backpage.com and others allowing users to advertise sex-trafficking services. The law amends several federal laws, including the Communications Decency Act (CDA). Section 230 of the CDA provides that "[n]o provider or user of an interactive computer service shall be treated as the publisher or speaker of any information provided by another information content provider." It is only because of CDA section 230 that social media and user content sites are able to survive, for the simple reason that without the CDA, such social media sites would be viewed as publishers and, therefore, liable for all the potentially false, defamatory or illegal content posted by millions of users. FOSTA makes a dent in the CDA, and every website operator should be aware of it. FOSTA adds a clause to the CDA that clarifies that the CDA has no effect on civil suits or state criminal cases related to federal sex-trafficking crimes. It also amends the Mann Act, which prohibits interstate prostitution, by adding a section prohibiting using a website to "promote or facilitate the prostitution of another person." Further, it amends the federal criminal code to impose fines and possible jail sentences for anyone who "owns, manages, or operates an interactive computer service [ ], or conspires or attempts to do so to promote or facilitate the prostitution of another person." Violations of the law are punishable by up to ten years in prison (or up to twenty-five years if aggravating circumstances are present).

21.   FAC 2019-01, FAR Case 2015-017.

22.   83 FR 65466-02.

23.   H.R. 898, 113th Cong. § 109 (2013).

24.   80 Fed. Reg. 4967.

25.   *Id.*; *see* 48 C.F.R. § 52.222-50.

26.   80 Fed. Reg. at 4999. This final DFARS rule would, in certain instances, add the requirements of: (1) posting a hotline poster regarding human trafficking and whistleblowing when work is performed either in the United States or outside and, if a substantial portion of the employees do not speak English then the posters must be provided in the language spoken by a substantial part of the workforce; (2) adding a new representation that hiring practices address Combating Trafficking in Persons and are complying with requirements; and (3) integrating an employee bill of rights. *See id.* at 4999–5001.

27.   Effective January 22, 2019, "recruitment fees" means fees "of any type, including charges, costs, assessments, or other financial obligations, that are associated with the recruiting process, regardless of the time, manner, or location of imposition or collection of the fee." 83 Fed. Reg. 65,466 (Dec. 20, 2018); FAR 52.222-50. These recruitment fees include, but are not limited to, fees for the following when associated with the recruiting process:

(i) Soliciting, identifying, considering, interviewing, referring, retaining, transferring, selecting, training, providing orientation to, skills testing, recommending, or placing employees or potential employees; (ii) Advertising; (iii) Obtaining permanent or temporary labor certification, including any associated fees; (iv) Processing applications and petitions; (v) Acquiring visas, including any associated fees; (vi) Acquiring photographs and identity or immigration documents, such as passports, including any associated fees; (vii) Accessing the job opportunity, including required medical examinations and immunizations; background, reference, and security clearance checks and examinations; and additional certifications; (viii) An employer's recruiters, agents or attorneys, or other notary or legal fees; (ix) Language interpretation or translation, arranging for or accompanying on travel, or providing other advice to employees or potential employees; (x) Government-mandated fees, such as border crossing fees, levies, or worker welfare funds; (xi) Transportation and subsistence costs . . . ; (xii) Security deposits, bonds, and insurance; and (xiii) Equipment charges.

Id.

28.   80 Fed. Reg. at 4967, 4987, 4990.

29.   *Id.* at 4984–86.

30.   *Id.* at 4967, 4985.

31.   *Id.* at 4991.

32.   *Id.* at 4983 (the compliance plan and certification requirements do not apply to a contract for "commercially available off-the-shelf items").

33.   81 Fed. Reg. 88,707 ("The Office of Federal Procurement Policy (OFPP) in the Office of Management and Budget (OMB) is seeking comment on a draft memorandum that it has developed in coordination with the Office to Monitor and Combat Trafficking in Persons in the Department of State (DOS) and the Department of Labor (DOL), as Co-Chairs of the Procurement and Supply Chains Committee of the Senior Policy Operating Group of the President's Interagency Task Force to Monitor and Combat Trafficking in Persons (the 'SPOG Committee'), to address anti-trafficking risk management best practices and mitigation considerations. This guidance is designed to help an agency determine if a contractor is taking adequate steps to meet its anti-trafficking responsibilities under the Federal Acquisition Regulation (FAR)."). In connection with this, the OMB, Department of Labor, and Department of State released a draft memorandum for public comment. Draft for Public Comment, Anti-Trafficking Risk Management Best Practices & Mitigation Considerations (Dec. 7, 2016), https://obamawhitehouse.archives. gov/sites/default/files/omb/memoranda/2017/draft-anti_trafficking_0.pdf. This draft memorandum lays out a developed set of best practices and mitigation considerations to help contracting officers determine if a contractor is taking steps to meet anti-human trafficking requirements under the FAR. These best practices provided internal steps including: appoint an accountable official; develop a code

of conduct and policies around trafficking; train workers; implement whistleblower protections; develop a compliance plan. It also provided external steps including: understand the supply chain; engage with subcontractors; validate protections; perform compliance reviews; develop targeted corrective action plans. If a trafficking violation has been reported, the draft memorandum provides potential mitigating factors including whether the contractor: took remedial steps on its own (such as to provide reparation to victims) or abated a violation when directed to do so by the contracting officer; became aware of the violation because of an effective monitoring program and/or whistleblower program; had risk mitigation tools in place at the time an incident arose; notified to the U.S. government immediately of any violations; cooperated with investigations; took logically sequenced and managed steps to increase its understanding of the supply chain; is a new entrant to the federal marketplace or an experienced federal contractor. *Id.*

34. CAL. CIV. CODE § 1714.43(a)(1).

35. *See* CAL. REV. & TAX. CODE § 23101(b).

36. CAL. CIV. CODE § 1714.43(c).

37. *Id.* § 1714.43(b).

38. *Id.*

39. Press Release, State of Cal. Dep't of Justice Office of Attorney Gen., Attorney General Kamala D. Harris Issues Guide for Companies to Comply with the California Transparency in Supply Chains Act (Apr. 13, 2015), https://oag.ca.gov/news/press-releases/attorney-general-kamala-d-harris-issues-guide-companies-comply-california.

40. THE CALIFORNIA TRANSPARENCY IN SUPPLY CHAINS ACT: A RESOURCE GUIDE, at i (2015) [hereinafter RESOURCE GUIDE], https://oag.ca.gov/sites/all/files/agweb/pdfs/sb657/resource-guide.pdf.

41. *Id.* The United Kingdom enacted the Modern Slavery Act 2015, c. 30 (Eng.), to combat human trafficking. The Modern Slavery Act contains a transparency in supply chains provision similar to the California Act. Section 54 of the Slavery Act requires certain commercial organizations to prepare and publish a statement setting out the steps that the organization has taken during the financial year to ensure that slavery and human trafficking are not taking place in: (a) any of its supply chains; and (b) any part of its own business (an "anti-slavery statement"). The Slavery Act is relevant to all companies with a turnover, or group turnover (that is, the total turnover of a company and its subsidiaries), of 36 million or more that are either incorporated in the United Kingdom or carry on a business in the United Kingdom. Companies with subsidiaries in the United Kingdom will need to analyze whether the Slavery Act applies to them. *See id.* § 54; *see also* Home Sec'y, U.K., Transparency in Supply Chains Etc.: A Practical Guide, https://assets.publishing.service.gov.uk/government/uploads/system/uploads/attachment_data/file/649906/Transparency_in_Supply_Chains_A_Practical_Guide_2017.pdf. On January 1, 2019, Australia's Modern Slavery Act 2018 became effective, bringing a statutory reporting requirement to larger companies operating in

Australia. Modern Slavery Act 2018, No. 153, 2018, https://www.legislation.gov.au/Details/C2018A00153. Australia now requires businesses above a certain size (consolidated revenue of A$100 million) to report annually on the risks of modern slavery in their supply chains, the action they have taken to assess and address those risks, and the effectiveness of their response. Smaller businesses are able to report voluntarily. The report must be approved by the board of directors and signed by a director, and will be publicly available. The first reporting year will be July 2019 to June 2020, with the reports due by December 31, 2020. *See also* Fiona David & Reginald Ramos, *The Bali Process: Responding to the Challenges of Modern Slavery*, AUSTRALIAN INST. OF INT'L AFFAIRS (Mar. 25, 2016), www.internationalaffairs. org.au/australianoutlook/the-bali-process-responding-to-the-challenges-of-modern-slavery/.

42. Assemb. Comm. on Judiciary, Analysis of S.B. 657 (Reg. Sess. 2009–2010).
43. *Id.*
44. S.B. 657 (Cal. Feb. 27, 2009).
45. *Id.* § 8305(a)–(b).
46. S.B. 657 (Cal. 2009), as amended June 23, 2010 (emphasis added).
47. Assemb. Comm. on Judiciary, Analysis of S.B. 657 (Reg. Sess. 2009–2010).
48. S.B. 657 (Cal. 2009), as amended June 1, 2009; *see also* Sen. Appropriations Comm., Analysis of S.B. 657 (Reg. Sess. 2009–2010).
49. RESOURCE GUIDE, *supra* note 40.
50. *See supra* note 47.
51. S.B. 657 (Reg. Sess. 2009–2010) as amended June 30, 2010.
52. *See supra* note 47.
53. *Id.*
54. *Id.*
55. *Id.*
56. CAL. CIV. CODE § 1714.43(d).
57. CAL. REV. & TAX. CODE § 19547.5(1).
58. *Id.* § 19547.5(2).
59. RESOURCE GUIDE, *supra* note 40, at 3.
60. *See* STROOCK & STROOCK & LAVAN LLP, 2017 ANNUAL OVERVIEW OF CALIFORNIA'S UNFAIR COMPETITION LAW AND CONSUMER LEGAL REMEDIES ACT 21 (Mar. 2017).
61. *Id.* at 1.
62. CAL. BUS. & PROF. CODE § 17535 (2012).
63. John Pickles & Shengjun Zhu, Capturing the Gains, The California Transparency in Supply Chains Act, at 7 (Working Paper No. 15) (Feb. 2013), www.capturingthegains.org/pdf/ctg-wp-2013-15.pdf.
64. Sud v. Costco Wholesale Corp., No. 3:15-cv-03783 (N.D. Cal. filed Aug. 19, 2015) (motion to dismiss granted). The Ninth Circuit affirmed the district court's dismissal on July 20, 2018. Case No. 17-15307, 731 F. App'x 719 (9th Cir. July 20, 2018).
65. Barber v. Nestlé USA, Inc., 154 F. Supp. 3d 954 (C.D. Cal. 2015), *aff'd*, No. 16-55041, 730 F. App'x 464 (9th Cir. July 10, 2018) (affirming dismissal).

66. *See, e.g.*, McCoy v. Nestlé USA, Inc., 173 F. Supp. 3d 954 (N.D. Cal. 2016), *aff'd*, No. 16-15794, 730 F. App'x 462 (9th Cir. July 10, 2018) (affirming dismissal); Dana v. Hershey Co., 180 F. Supp. 3d 652 (N.D. Cal. 2016), *aff'd*, No. 16-15789, 730 F. App'x 460 (9th Cir. July 10, 2018) (affirming dismissal); Hodsdon v. Mars, Inc., 162 F. Supp. 3d 1016 (N.D. Cal. 2016), *aff'd*, 891 F.3d 857 (9th Cir. 2018); Wirth v. Mars Inc., No. SA CV 15-1470-DOC (KESx), 2016 WL 471234 (C.D. Cal. Feb. 5, 2016), *aff'd*, No. 16-55280, 730 F. App'x 468 (9th Cir. July 10, 2018) (affirming dismissal). None of these lawsuits attempt to hold the company liable for violating the California Act, yet they invoke it in the complaints. In some of the cases noted above, the defendant companies were able to obtain dismissal of the lawsuits, in part, because they were in compliance with the California Act. In general, courts have ruled that companies are protected by the "safe harbor doctrine," if the California Legislature has permitted certain conduct or considered a situation and concluded no action should lie. Because the act states who must disclose, what they must disclose, and how it must be disclosed, courts have held that compliance under the California Act is a defense to cases brought under the California Unfair Competition Law, False Advertising Law and the Consumer Legal Remedies Act seeking to require more robust anti–human trafficking disclosures and actions.

67. *Id.*

68. Verité, A Verité Assessment of Recruitment Practices and Migrant Labor Conditions in Nestlé's Thai Shrimp Supply Chain: An Examination of Forced Labor and Other Human Rights Risks Endemic to the Thai Seafood Sector, www.verite.org/sites/default/files/images/NestleReport-ThaiShrimp_prepared-by-Verite.pdf; *see Nestlé Admits to Forced Labour in Its Seafood Supply Chain in Thailand*, GUARDIAN, Nov. 24, 2015, www.theguardian.com/global-development/2015/nov/24/nestle-admits-forced-labour-in-seafood-supply-chain.

69. *See* John Kerry, U.S. Sec'y of State, Remarks at the Annual Meeting of the President's Interagency Task Force to Monitor and Combat Trafficking in Persons (PITF) (Oct. 24, 2016), https://2009-2017.state.gov/secretary/remarks/2016/10/263476.htm.

70. *See* https://www.state.gov/wp-content/uploads/2019/10/2019-PITF-Report-Web.pdf.

71. Food, Conservation, and Energy Act of 2008, Pub. L. No. 110-234, 122 Stat. 923.

72. *See* Consultative Group to Eliminate the Use of Child Labor and Forced Labor in Imported Agricultural Products Request for Comment on Guidelines for Eliminating Child and Forced Labor in Agricultural Supply Chains, 76 Fed. Reg. 20,305, 20,305–309 (Apr. 12, 2011) [hereinafter Consultative Group Request for Guidelines], www.gpo.gov/fdsys/pkg/FR-2011-04-12/pdf/2011-8587.pdf.

73. The issues have become even more pertinent in light of the worldwide Covid-19 pandemic. Vulnerable persons may feel increased pressure from companies to work in dangerous conditions for reduced pay. *See* ADDRESSING THE RISK OF

MODERN SLAVERY DURING THE PANDEMIC, https://www.jdsupra.com/legalnews/addressing-the-risk-of-modern-slavery-10359/?origin=CEG&utm_source=CEG&utm_medium=email&utm_campaign=CustomEmailDigest&utm_term=jds-article&utm_content=article-link. This will likely only increase as these companies' bottom lines take a hit with reduced consumption/demand from the pandemic. *Id.* A comprehensive commitment to corporate social responsibility will prevent unforeseen, world-altering events from wreaking havoc on supply chains.

74.   JANE NELSON, LEADERSHIP, ACCOUNTABILITY, AND PARTNERSHIP: CRITICAL TRENDS AND ISSUES IN CORPORATE SOCIAL RESPONSIBILITY, REPORT OF THE CSR LAUNCH EVENT (2004).

75.   *See* ETHICAL TRADING INITIATIVE, THE ETI BASE CODE, https://www.ethical trade.org/sites/default/files/shared_resources/ETI%20Base%20Code%20%28 English%29.pdf.

76.   *Our Mission*, UNITED NATIONS GLOBAL COMPACT, www.unglobalcompact. org/what-is-gc/mission; *The Ten Principles of the UN Global Compact*, UNITED NATIONS GLOBAL COMPACT, www.unglobalcompact.org/what-is-gc/mission/principles.

77.   Consultative Group Request for Guidelines, 76 Fed. Reg. at 20,307.

78.   *Id.*

79.   *Id.* at 20,308.

80.   *Id.*

81.   *Id.*

82.   *Id.*

83.   *Id.*

84.   *Id.*

85.   *Id.*

86.   *Id.*

87.   *Id.*

88.   *Id.*

89.   *Id.*

90.   *Id.* at 20,308–09.

91.   *Id.* at 20,309.

92.   *Id.*

93.   *Id.*

94.   *Id.*

95.   *Id.*

96.   *Id.*

97.   *Id.*

98.   *Id.*

99.   *Id.*

100.   *Id.*

101.   *Id.*

Index

(References are to questions unless otherwise indicated.)

A

B

C

D

E

F

G

H

I

J

M

Q

procedures
    complaints. *See subhead:* complaints
    defendant's learning that action is pending, 12.13.3
    intervention by government, 12.13.2
  retaliation against whistleblower, prohibition of
    contracting partners, whistleblower working for or associated
      with, 12.23.1
    current employee as whistleblower, 12.23
    statute of limitations, 12.23.2
  service of complaint, 12.13
  settlement, negotiation of, 12.22
  whistleblower/relator
    generally, 12.10
    limitations on, 12.11, 12.12
    parties who can be, 12.11, 12.12

R

RCRA. *See* Resource Conservation and Recovery Act (RCRA)
Records management program
  applicable law, retention periods set by, 5.8
  backup systems, relation to, 5.11.1
  benefits of, 5.1
  blockchain technology, 5.6.3
  business rules, 5.1.1
  components of, 5.1.1
  designing program, 5.1.4
  disaster recovery plans, relation to, 5.11.1
  discovery. *See* Electronic discovery
  duplicate records, treatment of, 5.6.5
  electronically stored information (ESI)
    blockchain technology, 5.6.3
    discovery. *See* Electronic discovery
    European Commission standards, 5.6.2
    generally, 5.6
    geographic location of, 5.1.3

S

T

Toxic Substances Control Act (TSCA) (*cont'd*)
    polychlorinated biphenyls (PCBs), regulation of
        disposal requirements, 21.16.2
        generally, 21.16
        marking requirements for materials containing PCBs, 21.16.2
        permissible uses of PCBs, 21.16.1
        record-keeping requirements, 21.16.2
        storage requirements, 21.16.2
        waste manifests, 21.16.2
    pre-manufacture notice (PMN) requirements, 21.13.2
    purpose of, 21.13
    reporting requirements, 21.13.3
Trade Agreements Act
    government contractors, compliance issues for
        requirements, 15.17.5
        threshold, 15.17.2
Trade secrets, protection of
    compliance program, as risk area to address in, 2.5.1
Training and education
    anti-money laundering compliance programs, 29.20.13
    attorney training related to SEC Rule 205 and Sarbanes-Oxley Act
      requirements, 30.29, 30.29.1
    employees requiring, 2.8.1, 2.8.2
    export compliance programs, 19.8.4
    generally, 2.8
    government contractor compliance programs
        generally, 15.3.3
        parties who should participate in training, 15.3.4
    managed care organizations (MCOs) compliance programs, 25.6.3
    Medicare Part D compliance programs, 24.16.3
    periodic training and communication, requirement for, 2.8.3
    records management program, 5.9.1, 7.3
Travel rules of House and Senate. *See* Gift and travel rules of House
  and Senate
Truth in Negotiations Act (TINA) provisions
    civil penalties, 15.7.14
    "cost or pricing data"
        generally, 15.7.11, 15.10.11
        submission of, 15.7.12

V

W